Oracle Performance Tuning

Oracle Performance Tuning
Second Edition

Mark Gurry and Peter Corrigan

O'REILLY™

Cambridge · Köln · Paris · Sebastopol · Tokyo

Oracle Performance Tuning, Second Edition
by Mark Gurry and Peter Corrigan

Copyright © 1996 and 1993 O'Reilly & Associates, Inc. All rights reserved.
Printed in the United States of America.

Editor: Deborah Russell

Production Editor: John Files

Printing History:

October 1993:	First Edition.
December 1993:	Minor Corrections.
June 1994:	Minor Corrections.
November 1996:	Second Edition.

This book is printed on acid-free paper with 85% recycled content, 15% post-consumer waste.
O'Reilly & Associates is committed to using paper with the highest recycled content available
consistent with high quality.

ISBN: 1-56592-237-9   [8/97]

Table of Contents

Preface

Although many things have changed since we wrote the first edition of this book three years ago, some things have not. For example, the Oracle relational database management system (RDBMS) is still the most popular database management system in use today. Organizations ranging from government agencies to small businesses, from large financial institutions to universities, use Oracle to make sense of their data. Running on computers as diverse as mainframes, minicomputers, workstations, PCs, and Macintoshes, Oracle provides virtually identical functions across machine boundaries.

Oracle offers tremendous power and flexibility, but at some cost. It is a large and complex data-processing environment, including dozens of software components, hundreds of statements, commands, and utilities, and about 50 volumes of documentation. Although in theory Oracle could be administered by a single user, in practice its administration and use are most commonly shared by many people performing a number of specific design, administrative, and programming roles.

With this multiplicity of functions and users comes the potential for diffusion—and confusion—when things go wrong. Because Oracle is a thoroughly tested and well-functioning system, what goes wrong isn't basic operation, but performance. With any large piece of software operating in the real world, the number of users increases as time goes on and organizational needs grow. More and more data needs to be managed. More complex queries need to be processed. More reports need to be produced. Groups within the organization need new capabilities. As new operating system releases and networking features are added to the environment, programmers develop more demanding applications. The load on the system grows, and performance suffers. And people in the organization start to ask questions:

"I've been waiting 30 minutes for a response to my query—what's going on?"

"My system administrator says our system is I/O-bound—what can I do?"

"Our application ran fine in testing, but the response is terrible now that we're in production—help!"

"Our backups take too long—how can we speed them up?"

"Our database is fully normalized, but response time is bad—why?"

How do you respond to these questions? Some organizations buy more powerful and expensive computers. Some hire expert consultants. Although you may eventually find that adding computing power is necessary, there is a lot you can do to increase the performance of the system you already have. That's why we wrote this book: to share what we've learned—sometimes at great expense to our patience and hairlines—during our nearly 20 years of tuning Oracle systems. Every Oracle manager, designer, programmer, database administrator, and system administrator has a bottom drawer crammed full of helpful tips, tricks, traps, articles, and email messages that help them run their Oracle systems more efficiently. What we've tried to do in this book is to collect the contents of these bottom drawers and organize them into a comprehensive collection of performance tuning suggestions for Oracle.

This book is the result of our own experiences with a number of different Oracle systems. We've used at least ten different platforms at a dozen different sites—ranging from government to manufacturing to finance, and from mainframe to minicomputer to personal computers and workstations. The book reflects our own experiences, and those of many other Oracle users and administrators throughout the world. In this book, we pull together our real-life experiences in the hope that we can save you the headaches we've all suffered while trying to get a little better response, to use a little less memory, and to get that report out a little bit faster.

This book is aimed especially at people who use Oracle, of course. But what it has to say about database performance and tuning has meaning beyond the confines of an Oracle system. Sites running any large database system—Informix, Sybase, Progress, Ingres, even nonrelational systems using a hierarchical or network model—share common performance problems and can benefit from the tune-ups we suggest in this book. We try to answer general questions that go beyond the specifics of the Oracle products:

- How important is tuning—what does it buy you?

- How can you tune at each stage of the system development life cycle?

- How can you coordinate your tuning efforts with those of other people at your site so there are no weak links in the great tuning extravaganza? Will too many cooks spoil the broth?

- How can you use your site's own unique configuration of memory, disk, CPU, and networking connections to best advantage?

- How can you examine and understand your site's own workload, turnaround requirements, and response times?

- How can you be proactive—not reactive—so you can nip tuning problems in the bud, or keep them from occurring in the first place?

This book takes a thorough look at database performance problems, but it does not attempt to teach you how to use the Oracle products and features it describes. We assume in this book that you are familiar with SQL and the other Oracle tools, statements, and concepts we mention. We are not attempting to teach you how to use any of these Oracle products, but to tune them so they work more efficiently in your own particular environment. (Remember, you have 50 volumes of documentation!) Rather than a coordinated tutorial, this book is a collection of tips and tricks in many different areas. Start with the sections of most concern to you, and use them in conjunction with Oracle's own product and performance manuals.

This book cannot cover all the details of tuning specific operating systems. Oracle runs on so many hardware and software platforms that we can't address all of the machine- and operating system-specific performance issues that may arise. You'll have to look carefully at your own system and system documentation for help in this area.

As we've mentioned, in most Oracle shops, responsibility for system operation and use is distributed among a number of types of administrators and users. Depending on who you are and what your responsibilities are, you may be more interested in some parts of the book than in others. Most readers will read Part I, the parts of the book pertaining to their own job roles, and a number of the appendixes. However, don't forget that your role overlaps others, and that the tuning and performance decisions that others make will affect your own ability to improve system efficiency. Reading, or at least skimming, the other sections of this book should help you to coordinate your job with others in your organization.

This book is divided into seven parts.

Part I, *Overview*

Chapters 1 and 2 introduce performance and tuning issues, and describe overall system tuning operations and common performance problems with different phases of development and different system resources (memory, disk, CPU, network).

Part II, *Tuning for Managers and Planners*

Chapters 3 and 4 describe how the equipment and configuration decisions you make during the planning stage will affect system performance for years to come. These chapters focus on management checkpoints that affect performance, the standards you need to establish for Oracle database and application design and development, and the decisions you'll need to make about response times and workload at your site.

Part III, *Tuning for Designers and Analysts*

Chapter 5 describes how to design for performance without sacrificing functionality. If you don't design for performance, the chances that your application will perform successfully are slim, regardless of the tuning magic of the database administrators (DBAs), programmers, and system administrators at your site. The tuning advice in this chapter focuses on normalizing and denormalizing your database and defining indexes.

Part IV, *Tuning for Programmers*

Chapters 6 through 8 describe how to get the best performance out of your programs. The tuning advice in these chapters focuses on SQL, PL/SQL, and locking strategies.

Part V, *Tuning for Database Administrators*

Chapters 9 through 14 describe how to structure, monitor, and tune your database so it uses memory and disk efficiently. These chapters show you how to tune a new database, how to monitor and tune an existing one to remedy performance problems, and how to use a variety of Oracle diagnostic and tuning tools. Several chapters in this part are new in this second edition— those describing parallel server, parallel query, and backup and recovery.

Part VI, *Tuning for System Administrators*

Chapters 15 through 18 describe how to tune long-running jobs so they don't degrade overall system performance, how to tune in a client-server environment, how to perform capacity planning, and how to do certain kinds of system-specific tuning.

Part VII, *Appendixes*

Appendixes A through G contain summary material. Appendix A is a summary of the features in recent Oracle releases, particularly those that have an impact on performance. Appendix B lists the common questions we hear about performance, their answers, and references to sections of the book where you can learn more. Appendix C contains a summary of how you can tune the Oracle Financials product. Appendix D describes the Oracle Performance Pack. Appendix E summarizes tuning suggestions for Oracle Forms. Appendix F provides two case studies that demonstrate common tuning issues. Appendix G a list of Oracle's dynamic performance tables, is provided on the companion disk.

Conventions Used in This Book

The following typographic conventions are used in this book:

Italic	is used in term definitions and for filenames, directory names, and command names. It is also used to highlight comments in command examples.
Bold	is used in examples for emphasis, to show the feature being described in the section containing the example.
`Constant Width`	is used in examples to show the SQL, PL/SQL, or SQL*DBA input that you enter, it is also used to show the output from commands or programs.
`Constant Bold`	is used in examples to show prompts displayed by SQL*DBA and other products.
`Constant italic`	is used in examples to show variables for which a context-specific substitution should be made. The variable *`filename`*, for example, would be replaced by some actual filename.
. . .	stands for text in an example of code or output that has been omitted for clarity or to save space.

Which Oracle Release?

In general, the suggestions in this book apply to Oracle systems running on all platforms, from mainframes to PCs, from VSE to VMS to UNIX to DOS. In a few cases, our comments apply to one particular hardware platform or operating system. In these cases, we'll clearly note this limitation.

Most Oracle shops are now running Oracle7. But some are running Version 6 or even Version 5. Although we mainly share our experiences with the various releases of Oracle7 and look ahead to Oracle8, most of the tips and tricks described in this book are of equal use whatever version you are running. (Appendix A summarizes the major features of the various releases.) For instances where a tuning suggestion is applicable only to one specific version, we'll note that in the text.

About the Disk

You will find a high-density PC disk included with this book. This disk is a companion to the book; it includes the full versions of the many scripts shown, in part or in full, in the printed book. The following text files are on the disk:

disk.id
> Disk version identifier.

readme.txt
> Text describing the structure and contents of the disk.

chapnn
> Directories for various chapters of the book. The scripts printed in the book reference the filenames in these directories.

appg
> Directory containing *appg.txt,* a listing of the Oracle dynamic performance tables.

mgextras
> Directory containing additional tuning scripts developed by Mark Gurry.

Comments and Questions

A note about the advice in this book: we try to give you the benefit of our experience tuning many databases, and we've tried to standardize our experiences as best we can. The fact is, though, standard advice isn't always enough for nonstandard situations. In very large and complex organizations—and there are many Oracle sites that run 25 hours a day (or so it seems), servicing 25,000 or more online users—you'll find that there is no substitute for your experience and your ability to be flexible and adaptive. With such applications, you'll need to experiment, compromise, take risks, and take precautions; in short, you'll need to cope with whatever is thrown at you! We'd appreciate it if you'd share your experiences with us so we can include advice in future editions of this book that may help others take advantage of what you've learned.

We have tested and verified all of the information in this book to the best of our ability, but you may find that features have changed slightly (or even that we have made mistakes!). Please let us know about any errors you find, as well as your suggestions for future editions, by contacting the publisher:

O'Reilly & Associates
101 Morris Street
Sebastopol, CA 95472
1-800-998-9938 (in the U.S. or Canada)
1-707-829-0515 (international or local)
1-707-829-0104 (FAX)

You can also send us messages electronically. See the backmatter in the book for information about all of O'Reilly & Associates' online services.

Acknowledgments

We owe a debt to many people who have helped us get to this point. We both started our computing careers back in the days when computer resources were expensive and hard to find. Code had to run efficiently—or it wouldn't run at all. As hardware prices have come down, too many people have forgotten the art of tuning. We are grateful, though, that we learned the early discipline of coding right from the start with performance in mind.

The First Edition

The idea for the first edition of this book first came to us when Mark was asked by a customer to determine whether it would be feasible to use client-server computing at a large site in Australia where client machines were located as much as 2000 miles away from the server. The team had eight days to bring response times down from as much as 22 seconds to under 2.5 seconds. Making this deadline required a lot of tuning research and a little magic. After the dust had settled, Mark started working with Peter and with Shane Hocking (a Telecom Oracle DBA and senior technical support) on the idea of a book on performance tuning. In a series of meetings at the RedSox Hamburger shop in Melbourne, we discussed our respective bottom drawers of performance tips over burgers and fries. After some time, Shane decided to withdraw from the project, but with the help of some experts like Andrew McPherson (an Oracle DBA and senior technical support) and Stuart Worthington (an Oracle consultant currently specializing in Oracle Financials administration and tuning in Germany), we continued to meet, to argue over contents and structure, and to scribble ideas. We are grateful to Andrew for suggesting that we structure the book into parts aimed at the different types of Oracle users. Our goal was to have a book in time for the Asian Pacific

Oracle User Group Conference to raise money for our user group, and with a good many long nights we had one.

That early book draft changed almost beyond recognition in that first year. Bill Johnson (the marketing director of MARKADD and a former newspaper editor and author), and Chris Jones and John Darragh (and John's staff) from Oracle Australia helped us a great deal by covering our draft with red ink and good ideas. People started to ask for the book in Australia and elsewhere, and we found ourselves spending far too much time printing copies and waiting in line at the Australian Post. We decided to take the next step and see if we could find an international publisher who would be interested in the book.

We had long admired O'Reilly & Associates and the Nutshell guides. *System Performance Tuning* by Mike Loukides was a particular favorite. We took a chance and sent the book off to Tim O'Reilly. To our surprise, Tim himself called one day to say he might be interested. (Being ORA fans, having Tim on the phone to us was like having Queen Elizabeth call a royalist!) Tim recommended that we contact acquisitions editor Deborah Russell in the Cambridge office because she had an interest in database books. We sent email back and forth, arguing about possible new material and restructurings, and we were delighted to finally get the go-ahead. Working with Debby, who was so clearly a professional editor, has been terrific. We have been very happy with the editorial guidance (i.e., her insisting again and again that we needed to write clearly and explain completely), as well as the speed with which our sometimes rough text was transformed into readable prose as our little book mushroomed to almost three times its original size. We were all determined to have a book in print in time for the International Oracle User's Group (IOUG) conference in the Autumn of 1993, and doing so took many nights and weekends on all our parts.

Writing, editing, and producing this book was a feat made possible by advances in computing and connectivity. We wrote the book in Richmond, Australia on our separate personal computers (Peter on a PC, Mark on a Mac), then sent our Microsoft Word files to Debby in Cambridge, Massachusetts—some on Mac disks and others via email. Because of the 14-hour time difference, we communicated throughout the hectic cycle of editing and rewriting almost exclusively by email (with a little help from Federal Express, FAX machines, and occasional phone calls at odd hours). The three of us wrote and rewrote these files until that final moment when the book was converted to O'Reilly's own FrameMaker format for final production. Along with our other acknowledgments, a hearty thank-you goes to the Internet for making possible almost instantaneous communication across continents, time zones, and hardware platforms.

We have so many other people to thank. In addition to Shane Hocking, Andrew McPherson, Chris Jones, John Darragh, and Stuart Worthington for their early contributions (and a special thanks to Stuart for writing Appendix C), we would like to thank those who reviewed the revised version of the book on a very tight schedule; they come from all over the world, from the United States to Australia to Germany; this is appropriate since Oracle is very much an international product. Thanks to Martin Picard, president of Patrol Software and former Director of Networking Products at Oracle; Ian McGregor from the Stanford Linear Accelerator Center; Bob Fees, a senior information technology management consultant; Lurline Archay, director of Park Lane in Australia, president of the Australia and New Zealand Oracle user group, and IOUG vice-president; analyst/programmers Frank Magliozzi, Colin Trevaskis, and Ross Young; Paul Kendall, project leader of ECPLAN, a large Telecom Oracle application; and Joyce Chan, an analyst/designer who formerly worked for Oracle in Canada. Thanks to Michael Corey who reviewed the book and contributed the Foreword for the first edition. We are very grateful for these review comments and have made every effort to integrate them into the book. Thanks as well to all of the people we've worked with, too many to be named, at Oracle sites through the years and around the world. Many of your suggestions, warnings, tips, and caveats have made their way into this book.

Please note that, although a number of people who work for Oracle read this manuscript and made suggestions for improvements, they did so in an informal way. Their help is not to be construed as an official endorsement of this book by Oracle Corporation.

A big thank-you to all of the people at O'Reilly & Associates who brought this book into being. In addition to thanking Debby Russell, who made it all happen, we're grateful to Leslie Chalmers, who managed the production, and Lar Kaufman, Mike Sierra, Clairemarie Fisher O'Leary, and Stephen Spainhour, who formatted the final text under a very tight deadline; to Gigi Estabrook, who worked against the clock to get the text out for technical review; to Edie Freedman and Jennifer Niederst who designed the cover and the internal format; to Chris Reilley and Michelle Willey who created the figures; and to Ellie Cutler who helped with the index.

A final thank you to our wives, Mary Corrigan and Juliana Gurry, for all their support during the writing of this first edition.

The Second Edition

When we finished the first edition of this book back in 1993, we were sure that there was nothing more to say about Oracle performance tuning. We'd written the book on it. But time and technology march on. After a year or so, we started noticing more and more Oracle features worthy of mention, and we kept writing our own scripts to monitor and improve the systems we worked on. Around the middle of 1994, we said to each other, "It's time to think about doing this again." So we did. In this new edition, we looked carefully at every bit of the old book: many chapters have changed beyond recognition; some chapters have been dropped; new ones have been added, reflecting changes in or additions to Oracle technology. The result is many hundreds of pages of additional text and an accompanying disk.

We couldn't have written this second edition without a lot of help and encouragement. Special thanks to three very helpful people from Oracle U.S.: Gary Hallmark, whose knowledge of Oracle is legion; Anjo Kolk for his special help with parallel server; and Ken Morse for his great work on the Oracle Performance Pack and for his review of the material in the book. Another very special thank-you to Stuart Worthington who once again took responsibility for preparing Appendix C.

Again, thanks to the good people at O'Reilly & Associates: Debby Russell, our editor; John Files, the production manager for the project; Nancy Kotary and Nicole Gipson-Arigo, who helped a great deal with production work of all kinds; Edie Freedman and Nancy Priest, who designed the cover and interior format respectively; Chris Reilley, who prepared the figures; Barbara Willette, the copyeditor; Danny Marcus, the proofreader; and Seth Maislin, the indexer.

Personal thanks to Mark's wife Juliana and to Peter's wife Mary and son Matthew for putting up with us during this long period of extra work. As with the first edition, they spent many months listening to us say, "We're almost finished." Finally, once again, we are!

I

Overview

Part I introduces the process of performance tuning in the Oracle system: what does your organization get out of tuning, who takes responsibility for tuning, when do they tune, and when do they stop tuning? It takes a look at the tools Oracle provides to help in the tuning process and at the special tuning requirements for the latest versions of the Oracle RDBMS. It also looks at the most common sources of performance problems in Oracle.

1

Introduction to Oracle Performance Tuning

The past few years have seen many significant advances in technology that, in theory, can significantly improve the performance of your Oracle Relational Database Management System (RDBMS). These technologies include Redundant Arrays of Inexpensive Disks (RAID), Symmetric Multiprocessing (SMP), and Massively Parallel Processing (MPP). Despite these advances, and to some extent because of them, performance remains key to your application's success. It's an issue that you need to deal with on an ongoing basis, through all the stages of your system's life cycle: from planning to design to programming to testing to production. Your responsibility for performance never stops. Even after a system is in production, you'll need to keep monitoring, tuning, and improving it as time and circumstances change.

Performance tuning was a simpler process in the old days of a mainframe computer, a centralized database, and batch jobs. But technology is continually changing, and requirements for tuning must change along with it. Several major developments in computing have had a dramatic impact on performance issues for Oracle products:

Downsizing

In recent years, organizations have felt increasing pressure to downsize or rightsize their hardware configurations. Inevitably, though, when an organization makes the decision to save hardware dollars by replacing its mainframe with a system costing one-tenth as much, the organization doesn't downsize its throughput needs and response time expectations. Its users, who are accustomed to mainframe response times, continue to expect the same performance from the downsized system. If anything, an organization expects more, not less, when it moves to a new system. It's not impossible to get

3

equivalent or better responsiveness when you move from a mainframe to a smaller system, but it's going to take some work. Performance tuning is vital.

Client-server and distributed databases

New technologies demand new types of tuning. With client-server (which we'll discuss later in this chapter and in detail in Chapter 16, *Tuning in the Client-Server Environment*), and distributed databases, your user processes may now communicate with the RDBMS over a network instead of within a single processor. As your system grows to encompass new platforms, new operating systems, and new network models, you'll find that you'll need to know more about the overall computing environment to get decent performance out of your system.

Parallel server

In a parallel server environment (which we'll discuss in Chapter 12, *Tuning Parallel Server*), there are multiple instances, usually running on different machines. All may access a single database on shared disks. In such environments, you may suddenly have cross-instance locking problems to contend with. However, if you can use the architecture to your advantage and avoid the locking problems, a parallel server will present you with improved scalability and recoverability.

Multithreaded server

With the multithreaded server and other transaction processors, users share a number of server processes. In such environments, you'll sometimes confront situations in which one user encounters poor performance and suddenly other users pile up behind the hopeless user as in a Fifth Avenue traffic jam. If multithreaded servers are used effectively, however, a machine that ordinarily would have enough memory to service a few hundred users can comfortably process several thousand users.

Graphical user interfaces (GUIs)

GUIs have added a new dimension to databases and database access, but the new graphical interfaces require special kinds of tuning to avoid dragging down the performance of a system. GUI front ends are no longer the exception; they are now the rule. Users no longer accept systems that use character-based screens. They've been spoiled by Windows-based applications for several years now, and their expectations are much higher than they used to be. Because GUIs make systems more usable and more friendly, GUIs may also open doors to more users in your system.

Large binary objects (BLOBs)

Objects such as graphical data and Web access have been part of some rapid advances in many applications. Oracle handles the storing of BLOBs and also provides a Web interface for them. Tuning of BLOBs and Web access are an important part of your overall performance strategy; if you're not dealing with them now, you will be in the future.

An increase in users and processes

As time goes on, more users, administrators, and managers within your organization become familiar with the Oracle RDBMS and its associated products. Managers find that they can get quick results from the system, so they make more queries. The organization grows and diversifies, so more data is added to the database. As users, data, and capabilities grow, you'll need to tune your system so that it absorbs the increased load and continues to give you the performance you need.

Data warehouses are now using Oracle databases more and more to fulfill their requirements. Databases of 800 gigabytes or more are no longer a dream; they are a reality. Data warehousing allows organizations to make critical decisions based on the core information stored within the central repository—timely and accurate information that is critical in making correct corporate-wide decisions. From a tuning perspective, how can you manage a huge database and provide the response times that management expects to assist in decision making?

Fortunately, Oracle is a highly tunable system that provides many automatic tools for monitoring operations and diagnosing slowdowns and bottlenecks. Although tuning is a time-consuming and demanding process, you'll find that Oracle gives you the necessary tools and support for this task. The Oracle Performance Pack, which is part of Oracle Enterprise Manager, is an excellent example of a tool that significantly aids in tuning. You'll also find that the time, money, and energy you spend tuning your system pays you back by saving your organization money and making your users happy. By tuning your system in the right way, you'll often find that you can turn a slow and nearly unusable system into a usable one—and a usable system into a real powerhouse.

Why Tuning?

What does your organization get out of performance tuning? Tuning benefits the bottom line and also the people in your organization and your customer base.

Financial Benefits of Tuning

Tuning saves your organization money in several different ways:

- If you thoroughly tune the system you have, you can often avoid buying additional equipment.

- You can downsize your configuration and reap huge savings. By tuning this downsized system, you can often get the same performance or even better performance than you got from your larger, more expensive configuration.

- If you have less, and cheaper, hardware, you'll also pay less for maintenance and both hardware and software upgrades.

- Saving on computing equipment and support frees up money that can be spent on other resources (e.g., market research or advertising) or lets you cut your product costs. In these ways, tuning can potentially give your organization a market advantage over your competitors.

- A high-performance, well-tuned system produces faster response times and better throughput within your own organization. This makes your users more productive. You may discover that half the number of staff can achieve the same level of throughput after your system is tuned.

"Downsizing" and "rightsizing" are the buzzwords you hear in database circles, as you do everywhere in the computing world today. Downsizing means spending less on computing hardware to achieve the same, or even better, results. This trend is made possible because of the emergence of client-server and transaction processors, such as Oracle's multithreaded server. With such technologies, you can get increased computing resources per dollar at the low end of the market (PCs and LANs, in particular).

The old unitary model, in which one mainframe or large minicomputer serves all of your computing needs, is still viable in many organizations. However, even in such organizations, the users are demanding GUI frontends, and you must use a client-server architecture to service such frontends. Many other organizations are also finding that they can save a large amount of money by adopting a client-server model. The reality is that many small, powerful computers can offer more processing power per buck than a single larger computer.

With a client-server model, Oracle runs across several computers, rather than running on a single, considerably more expensive mainframe computer. One computer (the server) coordinates access to the Oracle database, and the other computer (the client) serves the application programs and users. There are usually many clients in the configuration. Client-server computing, in contrast to traditional unitary computing, shares the computing load across machine boundaries, with each machine performing specialized functions. There are many viable types of client-server configurations. Some sites use a minicomputer as the server, and they provide all of their staff with PCs or workstations. Others use PCs exclusively. (Chapter 16 discusses the general issues of client-server configurations.)

Multithreaded servers, in which many users share a number of server processes, present another new model. We recently worked at a site that used a transaction processor similar to a traditional multithreaded server. Forty-eight hundred concurrent users used the transaction processor to perform heavy numbers of inserts and updates. The users were running an impressive-looking GUI frontend and were doing some of the screen validation using reference data stored in 60 local distributed databases that had data propagated to them via Oracle snapshot logs. The server, which had under 500 megabytes of memory and four processors, replaced a mainframe that cost more than 40 times as much as the server. That server would have supported fewer than one-sixth of the required number of users if the application had been developed in a unitary fashion (because of a 2-gigabyte upper limit on memory).

The cost savings that you can achieve by going to a client-server, distributed database, or multithreaded server configuration can be significant. Many sites such as the one mentioned previously use a combination of the three. The initial purchase, the hardware upgrades, and the annual maintenance are all factors. We have consulted for organizations that were spending tens, or even hundreds, of millions of dollars unnecessarily on supporting a mainframe or huge minicomputer configuration. A lot of this expense is in ongoing upgrades and support.

Moving to a new architecture is not a one-sided or trivial decision. The decision will impose new demands on everyone in your organization. With the new architecture, it is vitally important that your Oracle system be tuned to achieve performance that rivals mainframe performance. Client-server in particular introduces new tuning issues. For example, in a client-server environment, passing packets of data over a network (rather than within a single mainframe computer) slows down processing considerably. To make performance as good as it can be, you'll need to minimize network traffic by performing as much work as possible at either end of the network link and reducing necessary data transfers.

Human Benefits of Tuning

In addition to the financial benefits of performance tuning, there are human benefits to consider. Nothing can be more frustrating for an employee who is trying to be productive than having to wait for computing resources or finding response time painfully slow. You can dramatically improve response time by tuning your Oracle system.

Some organizations we've worked at have instituted tuning service agreements between the computing staff and the users. These agreements specify, among other things, what acceptable response time is within the organization. How do you define "acceptable"? Each organization needs to make its own assessment. In general, "acceptable" is what a user requires to get the day's work through the computer system or to provide adequate response times to customers. Some organizations include tuning agreements in their contracts for system development and maintenance. A client need not accept a system until response times are below or equal to those specified by the agreement. Once the system is in production, that organization may suffer payment penalties if response times exceed expectations. (For a discussion of assessing response times and tuning agreements, see Chapter 3, *Planning and Managing the Tuning Process*.)

In addition to increasing the productivity and morale of your own users, a well-tuned system benefits your organization's customers. If your Oracle system does online transaction processing or otherwise serves customers who expect speedy, real-time responses to queries, poor response time can cause a lot of unhappiness and lose business. A customer who telephones to inquire about the activity in his or her bank account expects a quick response and does not expect to hear an excuse about the slowness of the account inquiry screen.

One insurance site where we worked had 100 phone operators handling phone inquiries and making insurance sales. Management was concerned about the time taken for the operators to answer the calls and, more important, the number of callers who hung up because of the frustration of waiting in the phone queue. They decided to pay their operators a 20% bonus if they could reduce the number of clients hanging up to half the current level (often as many as 50% of the calls). After careful investigation, the organization discovered that most of the time taken to answer phone inquiries resulted from poor application response times, not operator slowness. Now that the system has been tuned, the operators are receiving their 20% bonus, and management is ecstatic because business has been booming ever since.

Who Tunes?

Tuning is not the sole responsibility of the system administrator or any single individual. It's a broad activity that has an impact on many different types of people in your organization. As was mentioned in the Preface, we have organized this book in separate parts aimed at distinct types of readers, each of whom performs a specific role in your system. Although there is a considerable amount of overlap in the topics and, in some organizations, in the roles, this presentation focuses attention on the particular activities that are most likely to be of concern to particular types of people.

The system planner/manager

>   This person oversees the entire tuning process, from planning to production and ongoing monitoring. This person is the one who will usually have to carry the blame if the application is not performing. The section that follows, called "Planning the System," contains an overview of the decisions made

during the planning process that have an impact on performance. Chapter 3 describes this process in greater detail.

The designer/analyst

This person or group designs the architecture and data model, as well as the overall application, for performance. The section below, called "Designing and Analyzing the Application," contains an overview of the decisions made during the design process that have an impact on performance. Part III describes this process in detail.

The programmer

This person or group develops the application and tunes all program code for performance. Testing is an often neglected part of this process. Programmers need to be aware that the quality assurance (QA) staff is supposed to work on functionality testing, not testing lazy programmers' untuned code. The section called "Developing the Application" contains an overview of the decisions made during the development process that have an impact on performance, and the section called "Testing and Assuring Quality in the System" describes the testing of the application and the database. Part IV describes this process in detail.

The database administrator (DBA)

This person is usually involved in the design of the database and takes responsibility for tuning the database for performance as well as ongoing database tuning once the system is in production. The section called "Monitoring Performance During Production" describes the type of monitoring the DBA performs. Part V describes DBA functions in detail.

The system administrator

In addition to the overall operating system maintenance performed by the system administrator, this person monitors Oracle performance by juggling the system resources needed by both Oracle applications and the other systems within the organization. With the emergence of RAID technology, logical volume management, and raw devices, the system administrator must have a better understanding of the Oracle database components and must work more closely with the DBA than ever before. The section called "Monitoring Performance During Production" describes the type of monitoring the system administrator performs. Part VI describes the system administrator functions that are relevant to Oracle performance tuning.

When Do You Tune?

Too many people think of tuning as an add-on, as tinkering that you do when the engine starts faltering and people start complaining. Wrong! Performance is a design goal, something you build into the system from the beginning, not something you fiddle with only when things go wrong and time is short. But performance is also something you never finish and forget about. It's something to be concerned about through the entire life cycle of your Oracle system.

In this section, we talk about increasing performance during various stages of system development (shown in Figure 1-1): planning, analyzing, and designing the data model and programs; developing the application; testing and "QA"-ing the application; and monitoring the system after it goes into production.

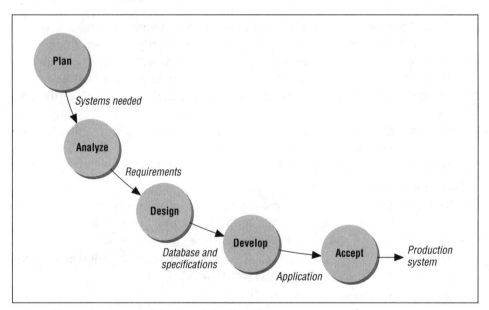

Figure 1-1. Stages of system design and development

Planning the System

If you make bad performance decisions during the first stage of the system development cycle, you'll regret them forever. Here is a brief list of what needs to be done before you even start designing your Oracle database and developing your programs. Although many of these activities and decisions are typically performed by management, they affect all of the people in an organization, and everybody should have an opportunity to share information and opinions during this stage. Obviously, certain activities (for example, looking at hardware/software resources and choices) should be coordinated with the system administrator.

1. Describe all the systems and applications that your organization needs. Performance will be far better down the road if you can think globally during this phase. Make sure that you define all your applications in an integrated way

so that all of the data required by different applications are stored in a single, coordinated data model. You have many ways of implementing the data model into your database. The simplest way, the single-database model, means you won't need to exchange data between applications. The problem with this approach, however, is often scalability. Other options include distributed database, having separate databases for each application or for each geographic location, or having a single database with separate schemas. These options can overcome the scalability problem by providing multiple machines, each of which runs a separate parallel server instance.

2. Select your organization's architecture. As you investigate different products that you might incorporate into your configuration, be sure to assess their performance implications, not just the functions they offer. Do your homework by asking people at other sites how their performance has been affected—for better or worse—by the products you're considering. Leave "bleeding edge" technology to the research laboratories, but make sure that your applications have all the features that your clients need. Remember that GUIs are now proven technology and a necessity for almost every application that is going to move into production.

Here are some of the questions to ask during this stage:

Hardware/software resources

- Should we use a client-server, distributed database, transaction processor, or unitary model? All are now workable options.

- Is there a need to replicate our data?

- What should the line speeds be?

- Where should we put the physical hardware?

- What size and speed do we need from our hardware?

- Will we be able to upgrade whatever we buy to suit our future needs?

- What are the overnight batch windows, (e.g., 8:00 p.m. to 7:00 a.m.)?

- Should we be striping or mirroring our database files?

- Should we be using the Oracle parallel query option to reduce batch processing run-times by making better use of parallel processing and striping?

Database resources

- What are the Oracle database requirements (memory, etc.)?

- What are the backup and recovery expectations?

- What is the likely transaction mix? Mainly transactions? Mainly reporting?
- Is the database a data warehouse that is used for decision support access?

User resources

- What is the expected number of online and other users during the day and overnight?
- What are the user resource requirements (GUI workstations, etc.)?
- Are there any ad hoc inquiry users?
- Are there any long-running reports or updates that must run during peak online usage times?

3. Be sure to project for future growth in your hardware/software selection. The number of users may dramatically increase, for example, depending on your own organizational needs and budgets. Chapter 17, *Capacity Planning*, describes in detail how you can examine your system requirements and plan for the future. Typically, the system administrator will conduct the capacity-planning study, but you'll need to track results closely.

4. Plan for scheduling delays. You may need to wait a long time for equipment to be delivered. Try to project your hardware/software configuration needs as much as 18 to 24 months in advance. Place your orders at least three to six months in advance to avoid problems with vendors' long lead times.

5. Set standards for system design and development. Chapter 4, *Defining System Standards*, describes software selection, version control, and other areas you'll need to be concerned about.

6. Determine what acceptable response times will be for the system. Chapter 3 describes how to establish and monitor response times for your site.

Designing and Analyzing the Application

The design stage is crucial to ensuring good performance later on. All the tuning wisdom of your site's programmers, DBAs, and system administrators can't make up for the slowdowns that will result from bad design and architecture decisions during this analysis/design stage.

Here is a brief list of the tuning activities you'll have to perform during this stage:

1. Design the data model for performance. Sound design is a combination of doing it by the book and using your head. Doing it by the book means doing a classic relational analysis of the data: what are the entities, relationships, and attributes of the data? The goal of relational database design is to normalize the data as best you can. But on top of that classic database design, you'll need to apply a good dose of common sense. Where should you denor-

malize the data? Where should you introduce redundancy in the data to increase performance? There are a lot of real-world decisions that only you can make regarding what design is best for your data and for what your users are actually going to be doing with the data.

2. Design your programs for performance. Make sure to design your programs in a modular way that permits later change and tuning. For example, if several programs need to perform a common function, such as updating account details, design your application so that the update code exists as a small, separate module that each program can call as needed. Adding logic to this update program, or tinkering with it to increase performance, need be done only once, with all the calling programs reaping the benefits.

   Modularization produces other benefits. Small programs typically require less memory than large ones, so your overall memory requirements are reduced. Modularization also simplifies maintenance, because any changes to the module are made only once, rather than separately for each program that includes the code.

3. Make use of constraints, packages, procedures, functions, and triggers. They provide excellent performance improvements, particularly in a client-server environment, in which their use will significantly cut down on packet transfer rates.

4. Decide when to use indexes on tables. Learning to design indexes effectively should be a priority for any designer. Retrieval of data using indexes is usually much faster than retrieval by scanning tables from start to finish. Typically, an indexed retrieval takes no more than a few physical reads from disk to retrieve the necessary rows from the table, whereas an unindexed retrieval may take several thousand reads. The problem is compounded when tables are being accessed as a group, or joined, without being able to use indexes. Chapter 5, *Designing for Performance*, gives you pointers for when to use indexes and when you'll do better not to use them. Because developers sometimes find later on that indexes can improve the performance of their programs, you'll have to coordinate index design with your development staff.

5. Become familiar with the Oracle parallel query option (described in Chapter 13, *Tuning Parallel Query*). The feature offers substantial run-time improvements for long-running batch jobs. Using it will make your jobs run much faster than they would with conventional indexes, because a single task will be able to use multiple processors to process data simultaneously.

6. When you design your data model, accommodate your interfaces. Because GUI interfaces are an essential part of most Oracle systems, you'll usually be stuck with using a client-server environment. GUI products offer a new dimension in user friendliness and quality of presentation, but they also present

design problems. During the design stage, you need to figure out how the GUIs will address the data in your Oracle database and how you can balance your processing across the client and the server to place as little impact on the network as possible.

7. Be aware of the harmful effect that ad hoc and long-running report users can have on your online transaction processing (OLTP) users. You might want to consider the alternative of presenting data to the ad hoc reporting user in the form of a spreadsheet that can be transferred down to a local server nightly (if the data from last night are current enough). Another alternative is to build redundant reporting tables to avoid ad hoc users having to continually process hundreds of millions of rows for a result that could be returned in a small fraction of the time from a denormalized table. You'll have to consider a trade-off here: Does the convenience of ad hoc users' being able to get timely responses justify the additional cost of maintaining redundant tables?

For details about design trade-offs, see Chapter 5, *Designing for Performance*, and Chapter 9, *Tuning a New Database*.

Developing the Application

During the development stage, you'll create the actual tables, indexes, and programs that the application needs. Here's what you'll have to do during this stage:

1. Choose the optimizer you will use. The Oracle optimizer is a part of your system that examines each SQL statement and chooses the optimal execution plan, or retrieval path, for the statement. The execution plan is the sequence of physical steps the RDMBS must perform to do the database retrieval you've requested. You have a choice between the traditional rule-based optimizer and the more intelligent new cost-based optimizer. Chapter 6, *Tuning SQL*, describes how the optimizers work and explains how you can complement or override their efforts to achieve better performance. We strongly recommend that any new application be developed and tuned for the cost-based optimizer. The cost-based optimizer did have many early teething problems, but it has now matured into a solid and reliable product. One advantage of using the cost-based optimizer is that better decisions are made by the parallel query option and the Oracle distributed database option. Its use will also produce better recommendations by Oracle Expert, which we describe in Appendix D, *Oracle Performance Pack*. The most important advantage of the

cost-based optimizer is that less experienced coders can achieve tuned code in a much shorter time than they would using the rule-based optimizer.

2. Tune your SQL statements. There are many ways of accomplishing the same results with alternative statements. With the help of the Oracle optimizer and your own knowledge of your system, you can get the best possible performance out of your statements. Your developers must be familiar with the EXPLAIN PLAN and TKPROF utilities and use them extensively when they develop their code.

3. Decide which locking strategy is best for your application. You have a choice of table locking or row locking. Become familiar with foreign key constraint locking considerations. Chapter 8, *Selecting a Locking Strategy*, describes the issues.

Testing and Assuring Quality in the System

During this stage, you test the system before it is moved into production. In addition to performing functional testing on all individual program modules, make sure that all of the modules work well together and that performance is acceptable for both individual modules and the system as a whole. Here is a brief list of the tuning activities you'll have to perform during this stage:

1. Make sure the volume of data you are using for testing is large enough. If you have too little data in the database, performance problems often won't surface. (They'll wait until production!)

2. Make sure you run on the same type of configuration that will be used for production. If production users will be running client-server, make sure your testing staff does too.

3. Make sure to test on a configuration that runs at the same speed as, or more slowly than, the one that will be delivered to production users. Although it sounds obvious, many testers forget to take the speed differential into account and may test on a faster configuration. Response times that are adequate on the test system may be too slow when you finally go to production. If you're able to test the database on a configuration that's slower than the production configuration, all the better. Then, when you move to production and a faster system, you'll have a little extra performance up your sleeve!

4. Make sure you aren't sharing the machine with production users. The QA staff will be testing new versions of programs. If QA and production are sharing a machine, you may find that faulty programs cause performance problems that affect the response times of the production users.

5. Inform your DBA of what you learn about performance problems. Be aware of the response time requirements set down in your performance service

agreement, and list all of the programs that exceed the desired response times. Although your job may not ordinarily involve performance testing, you'll learn a lot while you test for functionality. During QA, the DBA has a final chance to fine-tune the database to provide better performance. It's much harder to do a redesign once the system is in production. If you can give good information to the DBA during this stage, he or she will be able to use your input to tune the database for performance before production begins.

Monitoring Performance During Production

Tuning is a job that's never done. Throughout the life of your Oracle system, you'll need to keep monitoring performance, considering the needs of your system's users, and tinkering with the tools that let you tune the system effectively.

Ideally, the database and programs that are delivered for production are already well-oiled machines that are raring to go. When production users start using the database in a serious way, they'll hardly be starting from scratch. But, inevitably, using a database in a production environment adds new stresses and strains that can't always be detected during testing. And as time goes on, and more users and more data is added to the configuration, increasing demands are placed on the database.

Throughout the life of the Oracle system, the DBA and the system administrator, in conjunction with the project manager, share responsibility for monitoring the system and the data, trying to make sure that Oracle makes effective use of all of the system's resources: memory, disk I/O, CPU, and the network. Chapter 2, *What Causes Performance Problems?*, outlines performance issues for each of these resources.

Special monitoring responsibilities of the DBA include:

1. Be proactive in tracking performance problems. You can't just wait for complaints and react to them. Many users don't report response problems at all. Other users report problems at the slightest opportunity and may tend to overreact to them. You'll have to figure out, in conjunction with your project manager, what's really going on in your system. See the section "Managing the Problem of Response Time" in Chapter 3 for a discussion of assessing complaints about response time.

2. Be sure to monitor all Oracle performance screens and exercise all tools on a regular basis. Chapter 10, *Diagnostic and Tuning Tools*, describes the tools you can use to identify bottlenecks and optimize performance in your system. The Oracle Performance Pack, described in Appendix D, provides sophisticated and useful tuning capabilities.

3. From time to time, run procedures against the production database, just as users would. Record response times at discrete intervals throughout the day using the same forms that production users most commonly use. (See Chapter 3 for details.)

Special monitoring responsibilities of the system administrator include:

1. Make sure the speed of the hardware and the network are acceptable for the amount and type of processing that is going on.

2. Apply all system fixes and operating system improvements to ensure that users will be able to use the latest releases from Oracle and other vendors.

3. Monitor performance by checking on free memory, paging and swapping activity, and CPU, disk, and network activity.

4. Coordinate all Oracle tuning with overall operating system tuning. The system administrator is usually also responsible for administering office automation, system software, and other resources in the system. Make sure that these applications coexist with Oracle and do not negatively affect Oracle RDBMS performance (and vice versa).

5. If RAID technology (striping and mirroring), logical volume management, and/or raw devices are being used, the system administrator must be totally aware of the implications of applying the technology to different parts of the database. For example, using striping with parity (the RAID option) on redo logs can considerably slow down the writing to your redo logs by having to continually calculate and then write to the parity disk. (See Chapter 9 for details.)

The DBA and the system administrator need to coordinate all tuning and monitoring activities. Together, they will decide whether there is a need to reorganize the database, provide contiguous space on disk for new files, and perform various other tuning tasks.

A Look at Recent Versions

When Oracle7 was introduced, users found that the new version offered tremendous improvements in performance. Oracle7.3 offers better performance, as well as many tools that allow you to further tune your system. With the introduction of the Oracle Performance Pack (particularly the Oracle Expert and Oracle Trace tools), Oracle7.3 extends the ability of the DBA to tune the database for performance, and Oracle8 offers even better performance than Oracle7.3.

In most cases, you will simply be able to transfer your entire application from Oracle7.0 to Oracle7.1, Oracle7.2, Oracle7.3, and Oracle8 without difficulty and reap the benefits. However, in some cases, you will have to rework your database and applications to take advantage of the new features.

The most remarkable improvements in Oracle7.1, 7.2, 7.3, and Oracle8 performance are at sites where programmers have not known how to optimize their programs for performance. This is because the cost-based optimizer that is available in the later versions is a much more refined and reliable product than the earlier Oracle7 releases.

When combined with SQL*Net Version 2, Oracle7.0 greatly improves performance in client-server environments by substantially reducing the number of packets that needed to be transferred across the network. Oracle7.1, 7.2, 7.3, and Oracle8 further refine and reduce the number of packets transferred, to provide even better performance.

Here are summaries of the major new Oracle7.1, Oracle7.2, Oracle7.3, and Oracle8 features that have an impact on performance. For more information about these and other features, see Appendix A, *Summary of New Features*.

Oracle7.1 Performance Features

The following are the major performance features available in Oracle7.1:

- Read-only tablespaces avoid ongoing backups and ease maintenance.

- The parallel query option improves the performance of bulk operations that require full table scans, such as the grouping of data and index creation. It can also help in data loading. Parallel query uses multiple CPUs to perform a single task.

- The COMPATIBLE parameter allows full table scans to bypass the buffer cache (if the parameter is set to 7.1.5 or higher).

- PL/SQL improvements include being able to include functions in the WHERE clause and being able to process statements in parallel using the parallel query option.

- The CACHE clause can be included in the CREATE TABLE and ALTER TABLE statements to allow the tables data to be cached into the buffer cache in the System Global Area (SGA).

- New performance tables include:

V$COMPATIBILITY	V$COMPATSEG
V$CONTROLFILE	V$DATAFILE
V$LOCK	V$NLS_VALID_VALUES
V$OPTION	V$PQ_SESSTAT
V$PQ_SLAVE	V$PQ_SYSSTAT
V$PWFILW_USERS	

Oracle7.2 Performance Features

The following are the major performance features available in Oracle7.2:

- Sorting can bypass the buffer cache by setting the SORT_DIRECT_WRITES= parameter to TRUE. SORT_WRITE_BUFFERS indicates the number of buffers a user will have to service the direct writes, and SORT_WRITE_BUFFER_SIZE is the size of each buffer.

- Tables and indexes can be created, avoiding the redo logs by using the UNRE-COVERABLE clause.

- Hash clusters can be created using SQL expressions to assist with reducing collisions. Hash clusters perform a calculation on the key field to create an address within a table, thus avoiding the need to store an index.

- Hash joins are provided in Oracle7.2.2 and later to provide performance improvements to SQL statements that perform a join. The hash join is an alternative to nested loops and sort merges. Hash joins are particularly effective for decision support databases. There are three new INIT.ORA parameters, HASH_JOIN_ENABLED, HASH_AREA_SIZE, and HASH_MULTIBLOCK_IO_COUNT, and a new hint, USE_HASH.

- The V$SESSION, V$SESSTAT, and V$SQLAREA tables have had indexes added to them to considerably speed up queries against them. For a full list of all of the indexes on the V$ tables, select from the V$INDEXED_FIXED_COLUMN table.

- The parallel server feature provides many performance enhancements:

  — All inserts for the same parallel cache management (PCM) lock are batched to avoid contention issues with free list groups.

  — Indexes support free list groups.

  — Two new commands (ALTER TABLE *tname* DISABLE TABLE LOCK and ALTER TABLE *tname* ENABLE TABLE LOCK) allow you to disable all locking on a particular table to avoid lock contention.

  — Multiple lock processes can run in parallel to release locks after an instance recovery.

  — When a block is written to disk, the lock is released as soon as the block is written. Previous versions had to wait for the entire batch of blocks before the lock got released.

  — Multiple accesses can be made to a block before it is pinged to disk to satisfy a request from another instance. Previously, only one access was allowed.

— New tuning information is made available on pings per data file, and on the library and dictionary caches. A column has also been added to the V$BH table to allow you to view all blocks covered by a single PCM lock.

- You can now turn on SQL_TRACE for your own or somebody else's session using the DBMS_SYSTEM.SET_SQL_TRACE_IN_SESSION procedure. (Refer to Chapter 10 for details.)

- The following performance tables have been enhanced (see Appendix G, *Dynamic Performance Tables*):

V$LATCHHOLDER   V$OPEN_CURSOR
V$FIXED_TABLE   V$SESSION
V$SQLAREA

- Additional performance tables have been added:

V$BACKUP_STATE
V$BH
V$CACHE
V$CACHE_LOCK
V$PING
V$DB_PIPES
V$EVENT_NAME
V$FALSE_PING
V$FIXED_VIEW_DEFINITION
V$INDEXED_FIXED_COLUMN, V$INSTANCE
V$LOCK_ACTIVITY
V$LOCK_ELEMENT
V$LOCK_WITH_COLLISIONS
V$OBJECT_DEPENDENCY
V$PWFILE_USERS
V$SQL
V$SQLTEXT
V$SQLTEXT_WITH_NEWLINES
FILEXT$

Oracle7.3 Performance Features

The following are the major performance features available in Oracle7.3:

- Several INIT.ORA parameters (HASH_AREA_SIZE, HASH_JOIN_ENABLED, and HASH_MULTIBLOCK_IO_COUNT) can have their values dynamically adjusted without shutting down and restarting the database via the ALTER SYSTEM/SESSION SET *parameter name* = *value*. (Many more parameters will be able to be dynamically adjusted as you upgrade to future Oracle7.3 and Oracle8 releases.)

- The ALTER INDEX *indexname* REBUILD; statement allows you to rebuild your index from an existing index without having to access the table.

- The EXPORT utility has a new option, DIRECT, which allows you to bypass the buffer cache when performing an export.

- Setting MAXEXTENTS UNLIMITED provides an unlimited number of extents for database objects.

- The ALTER TABLSPACE *tablespace* COALESCE statement allows you to coalesce the alignment of free space into larger chunks to assist with performance. It also allows you to coalesce at times of the day when it will have a limited effect on your database performance.

- A facility has been reduced to deallocate unused space from a table, index, or cluster. Unfortunately, only space that has never been used is removed. Space that had been used but had rows deleted cannot be freed up. Use the statement ALTER TABLE tablename DEALLOCATE UNUSED [KEEP INTEGER].

- There is a new temporary tablespace type that boosts sort performance. Use the CREATE TABLESPACE tablespace TEMPORARY statement to select this type.

- A big concern with the cost-based optimizer prior to Oracle7.3 was that it was unaware of data skewness. For example, a column WORK_STATUS might indicate the status of work being performed by your company. Assume that you have 50,000,000 rows that have a value of 'DONE' and 100 rows that have a value of 'NEW'. With the cost-based optimizer, a WHERE work_status = 'NEW' statement will result in a full table scan because the optimizer assumes an even spread of data. However, if you apply a histogram using the ANALYZE TABLE or the stored procedures ANALYZE_OBJECT, ANALYZE_ SCHEMA, or ANALYZE_DATABASE (all stored in the DBMS_UTILITY package), the index on work_status will be used, despite the fact that the column has only two distinct values.

- You can now perform updates, deletes, and inserts on views that join tables, as long as the join does not contain a DISTINCT, AGGREGATION, GROUP BY, START WITH, CONNECT BY, UNION ALL, MINUS, or INTERSECT clause.

- PL/SQL package bodies are significantly smaller than they were in previous versions. Package specifications containing a large number of parameters are also smaller.

- You can now overcome latch contention for the least-recently-used (LRU) chain in the buffer cache by setting the DB_BLOCK_LRU_LATCHES parameter. Setting the parameter allows multiple latches to service the LRU, eliminating much of the latch contention.

- Parallel server has been further enhanced by the following changes:

  Fine-grained locking allows you to significantly reduce the number of database blocks handled by a single parallel cache management (PCM) lock. This was a performance concern with previous versions of the parallel server because all dirty blocks under the one PCM lock had to be written to disk simultaneously if any of the blocks were required by another instance. Note, however, that fine-grained locking is not available on all platforms.

  Oracle now uses instance information to assist with load balancing across instances. This information is particularly useful when you are using parallel query on a parallel server instance.

  A GUI tool is now available to let you view multithreaded server usage across multiple parallel server instances. See the MTS_LISTENER_ADDRESS parameter.

- There is now a built-in transaction trace facility that will assist with pinpointing performance bottlenecks. The tables V$TRANSACTION, V$ROLLSTAT, and V$LOCKED_OBJECT all contain transaction information.

- EXPLAIN PLAN places several new columns in the PLAN_TABLE to assist with tuning the parallel query option and for use by the optimizer. The columns are:

  OTHER_TAG
  SERIAL
  SERIAL_FROM_REMOTE
  PARALLEL_COMBINED_WITH_PARENT
  PARALLEL_COMBINED_WITH_CHILDPARALLEL_TO_SERIAL
  PARALLEL_TO_PARALLEL
  PARALLEL_FROM_SERIAL
  COST
  CARDINALITY
  BYTES

- A new tool, Oracle Trace. provides detailed tuning information for the client, network, and server components of a client-server application. Tuning details are traced by default for Oracle7.3 and later databases and for SQL*Net 2.3 and later. You can also place calls into your application code to allow Oracle Trace to closely monitor all components of your application.

- Antijoin logic has been added to allow significantly faster response times for the NOT IN clause. You must use the cost-based optimizer to benefit from this logic. Set the INIT.ORA parameter, ALWAYS_ANTI_JOIN. You can use the hints MERGE_AJ for sort merge antijoins, and HASH_AJ for hash antijoins.

- The following dictionary views are now available:

ALL_HISTOGRAMS	DBA_HISTOGRAMS
USER_HISTOGRAMS	DBA_FREE_SPACE_COALESCED
DBA_UPDATEABLE_COLUMNS	ALL_UPDATEABLE_COLUMNS
DEFCALL	REPCAT$_REPOBJECT

- The following performance tables have either been changed or added:

V$CACHE_LOCK	V$SQL
V$SQLAREA	V$LATCH
V$LATCHNAME	V$LIBRARYCACHE
V$LOCKED_OBJECT	V$ROLLSTAT
V$SESSTAT	V$SORT_SEGMENT
V$SYSSTAT	V$TRANSACTION
V$RECOVERY_STATUS	V$RECOVERY_FILE_STATUS

- Bitmap indexes save storage and improve performance for columns that have a low cardinality.

- Triggers are now compiled.

- Partitioned views allow tables and indexes to be broken into many tables and indexes. Doing so speeds up the administration time considerably without losing any performance advantages on query access. For example, a table may contain five years' worth of information and be 7.5 gigabytes in size. The table can be broken into five single financial year tables, each table having a CHECK CONSTRAINT on it specifying the date range. A UNION ALL view can be placed over the tables to allow the table to appear as one to the users.

Oracle8 Performance Improvements

The following are the major performance features available in Oracle8:

- Partitions are introduced as an extension of the Oracle7.3 partitioned views. The difference is that they need to have intelligence in the application code to know the table from which to perform inserts, updates, and deletes. The partitions provide excellent performance improvements for very large databases.

- Multithreaded server can now support more than 10,000 users. The threads improve performance by reducing context switching and providing better prioritization.

- Parallel server has significantly improved inter-instance communication and more extensive load sharing.

- Many more INIT.ORA parameters can now be changed dynamically using the commands ALTER SYSTEM/SESSION SET *parameter name = value*.

- You can now perform parallel inserts, updates, and deletes.

- You can save considerable storage and improve access times using the new INDEX ONLY TABLEs.

- LOB columns (BLOB, CLOB, NCLOB, and BFILE) can be as large as 4 gigabytes. You can specify the BLOB and CLOB columns in a separate tablespace from the rest of the table. BFILE columns are stored in a file external to the database.

How Much Tuning Is Enough?

A perfectly tuned system is a movable target. When do you know that you've tuned enough? In our years at the front, we've found that most sites tune too little but that some actually do tune too much.

Some sites are downright paranoid about performance monitoring. They instruct their DBAs and system administrators to stare into monitor screens all day, waiting for poor response to occur—kind of like air traffic controllers waiting to avert a disaster. Complete vigilance is unrealistic. Some perverse law states that poor response times occur only at the moment that the unwitting DBA takes a short break. Most organizations are far better off implementing a way to report performance exceptions automatically. Oracle has many tools that will assist you, including Oracle Trace, Oracle Expert, and the large number of V$ tables, many of which can be used to raise events to trigger action if performance becomes unsatisfactory.

Some DBAs are always tinkering with INIT.ORA parameters and other system settings. You can certainly make major performance improvements by doing this; we explain in Chapter 9 the settings that we recommend. Be sure not to make too many changes at once, however, or you won't know which changes actually cause improvements in performance. There also comes a point when the system is in balance and it's better not to fiddle around with these settings, trying to achieve infinitesimally small performance improvements. It's the law of diminishing returns. At some point, your time is better spent elsewhere.

Another problem with changing parameters is that sometimes improving performance in one area of the system may degrade performance in another. For example, adding an index to a table may improve performance for certain programs but may actually hurt the performance of others. You'll have to be careful and sensitive about making changes once your system is in production. For best results, always monitor performance in the QA environment before you make a change in the production system. The ideal situation is to have a copy of your production database to test your changes before applying them against the production database. Unfortunately, many sites don't have the luxury of being able to afford the production copy.

The cost-based optimizer provides many benefits, such as allowing developers to write tuned code very quickly. Many of the Oracle products also rely on the cost-based optimizer to make the best possible performance decision. The problem with the optimizer, however, is that your code may perform one way in your development and test environments and perform differently in production. This is because the behavior of the optimizer relies on statistics such as the numbers of rows and data distribution stored on each table and index. It is important that you have a mechanism to test the effect of your changes on the production database before changes are moved into production. As we've mentioned, either use a production database copy to test the new code or establish a standard dictating that you hand all critical statements to your DBA, who can obtain the EXPLAIN PLAN execution statistics from the production database.

Another way to balance your tuning efforts is to make sure that tuning remains a team effort. If a developer tests every possible SQL statement alternative before completing a program, the program will never get written. If the system administrator spends many hours a day tuning the Oracle system, that effort will be at the expense of other important work, such as backing up and recovering files, installing new hardware and software, and so on. You'll need to work together at your own site to find the right balance for your own system and staff. If you have a tuning service agreement (described in detail in Chapter 3), the requirements of that agreement are the bottom line for how much tuning you must do. You must tune until you reach the agreed-upon response times. Beyond that, monitor on an ongoing basis to make sure the response times are maintained. Any other tuning is a matter of debate and agreement among the people in your own organization.

2

What Causes Performance Problems?

There are many reasons for poor performance in an Oracle system, ranging from a poor choice of architecture to inappropriate database design to specific programming problems to human factors. This chapter briefly outlines the areas in which things can go wrong. Subsequent chapters describe performance problems in much more detail and describe how you can tune the different aspects of the system for better performance.

Problems with Design and Development

After tuning quite a few Oracle sites, we have observed a pattern in which performance problems slow down processing. Figure 2-1 shows our observations of (a) where the problems occur and (b) how hard, comparatively, it is to fix them.

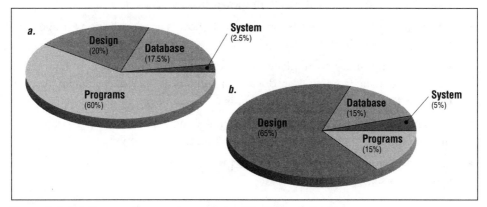

Figure 2-1. (a) Causes of poor response times; (b) effort required

Design

The best way to fix performance in your system is to keep performance problems from occurring in the first place. Obviously, this isn't always possible—or even likely. (Why else would you have bought this book?) As Figure 2-1 shows, though, fixing problems that result from poor design of your data model and programs isn't as simple as resetting a parameter or running a diagnostic. The only way to contend with poor design is to reorganize and recode.

Do your best to make your design as sound as it can be the first time around. However skilled your programmers may be, if they are writing programs against improperly tuned database tables, their chances of producing code that results in adequate response time is minimal. Similarly, however skilled the DBA's monitoring and tuning of the database, if programmers have coded programs that pay no attention to performance, the overall chances of good performance are bleak.

Design problems are typically caused by analysts and designers who have not:

- Considered performance when selecting an architecture. For example, if you are using the client-server architecture, you must reduce the number of packets you are transferring across the network by using packages, procedures, constraints, functions, and triggers.

- Considered performance when setting up the data model.

- Designed programs that are appropriate for a relational database.

- Designed programs that are appropriate for the hardware configuration being used.

- Received the necessary training to design for performance.

- Separated long-running report users from online users.

- Allowed for ad hoc user access in the design (despite the fact that it is required on the first day the system moves into production).

- Performed adequate analysis on data volumes, data distribution, usage, and transaction peaks and troughs.

- Put a purging strategy in place. Without such a strategy, when conversion occurs and data from the production system is replaced, you may be burdened with huge amounts of data that is no longer needed.

- Become familiar with the design features Oracle provides to assist performance (e.g., the parallel query option and partitioned views).

- Learned about the types of locking problems that can potentially bring a system to a standstill.

Programs

Program problems are typically caused by programmers whose SQL statements do not perform well enough to provide your users with the necessary response times. The main causes of SQL performance problems are:

- Inappropriate use of indexes through not coding correctly.

- Using the incorrect optimizer.

- Not being aware of the cost-based optimizer behavior in the production database. This optimizer can make different decisions in production from those made in development.

Database

Database problems are typically caused by DBAs who have not:

- Used the machine's resources effectively.

- Worked closely enough with the systems administrator when database files have had RAID technology applied to them.

- Structured the database to spread disk I/O appropriately (including choice of tablespaces, placement of data files, correct sizing of tables and indexes, etc.) through operating system striping, Oracle striping, or the placement of data files on to appropriate disks to avoid disk bottlenecks.

- Set INIT.ORA parameters to avoid contention for redo logs and other objects.

- Set up the database to use the most appropriate optimizer. If the cost-based optimizer is being used, all tables and indexes must be analyzed adequately.

- Made effective use of memory.

- Been proactive and made the application development team aware of poorly performing SQL and locking and contention problems.

As a consequence, any of the following might occur:

- Excessive disk I/O or unbalanced disk I/O.

- Disk I/O that is badly balanced across disks.

- A database that is fragmented and contains many chained and migrated rows.

- A database that is not effectively indexed.

- Database contention and locking problems.

Systems

Systems problems occur as a result of:

- Other (non-Oracle) systems adversely affecting Oracle.

- An untuned operating system.

- Using RAID technology inappropriately on Oracle database files, for example, using striping with parity (RAID5) on redo logs.

- A machine size or configuration that is inadequate to support Oracle.

Problems with System Resources

To get the best performance out of your system, you must be aware of how the four basic components of your machine environment interact and affect system performance:

Memory
> Memory bottlenecks occur when there isn't enough memory to accommodate the needs of the site. When this happens, excessive *paging* (moving portions of processes to disk) and *swapping* (transferring whole processors from memory to disk to free memory) occur.

Disk I/O and controllers
> Disk and controller bottlenecks occur when one or more disks or a disk controller exceeds its recommended I/O rate.

CPU
> CPU bottlenecks occur when either the operating system or the user programs are making too many demands on the CPU. This is often caused by excessive paging and swapping. There might also be an inadequate number of CPUs on your machine.

Network
> Network bottlenecks occur when the amount of traffic on the network is too great or when network collisions occur. Network bottlenecks are of particular concern when you are running a client-server or distributed database environment.

Remember that memory, disk I/O, CPU, and network problems don't exist in a vacuum. Each of these problems affects the other resources as well. At the same time, an improvement in one resource may cause better performance of the others. For example:

- If your organization buys more memory, the CPU may need to spend less time handling paging and swapping operations that occur because memory is scarce. This helps to avoid CPU bottlenecks as well.

- If you have a disk I/O bottleneck, you might be able to use memory to store more data, thus avoiding having to read the data from disk a second time.

- If you have a network traffic problem in a client-server environment, you might be able to improve things by using more memory, disk I/O, and CPU on either the client or the server side to avoid having to transfer data across the network.

Remember that in tuning your resources, the goal is to use all resources as fully as possible without running them dry. Some people seem to believe that a site is performing well when memory is plentiful, CPU and disk I/O are close to zero, and network traffic is low. This sounds a lot like a site that has overspent on hardware (or perhaps your users have decided not to use the system). Your system is meant to be fully utilized.

What constitutes an ideally tuned system? It's a matter of debate. We say that you should tune in such a way that:

- As close as possible to 100% of your memory is used.

- Your disk load is spread evenly across devices, and all of your disks are operating marginally within their recommended maximum I/O rates.

- As close as possible to 100% of your CPU is used during peak periods, with no user programs waiting for the CPU.

- If you have multiple CPUs, each CPU is sharing the load evenly.

- Network traffic is only marginally below the maximum recommended, with no collisions.

- An insignificant amount of paging and swapping is going on.

- User throughput and response times meet the standards established for your organization (see the discussion in Chapter 3, *Planning and Managing the Tuning Process*).

The key is to get all of these resources to work together. In Figure 2-2, we show an untuned system. In such a system, one component degrades before all the others. In this particular case, when you attempt to achieve more throughput, you are stopped by a memory bottleneck (that is, all of the memory has been used, and paging and swapping have become excessive, as we will describe in later sections). In this example, if you add more memory, the CPU will be the next item to cause a performance bottleneck, followed by disk I/O and the network.

In a perfectly tuned system, on the other hand, all factors degrade simultaneously. As illustrated in Figure 2-3, up until the point at which performance finally starts to degrade, all system resources are in balance, and throughput is optional. Note, though, that if the throughput required at your site is substantially less than the

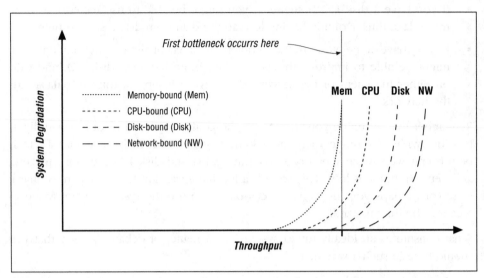

Figure 2-2. An untuned system

point at which your components begin to degrade (even after allowing for planned expansion to your application), this may indicate that you have bought more hardware than you really need.

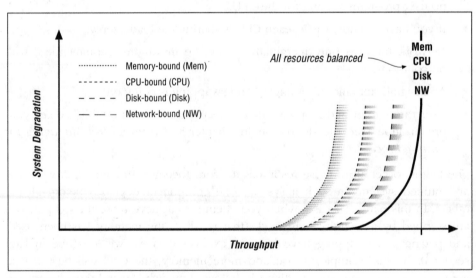

Figure 2-3. A perfectly tuned system

Memory Problems and Tuning

In general, the more memory that is available to your system, your applications, and the individual data structures within the applications, the faster your programs will run. How much memory is enough memory? A good rule of thumb is to use as much as possible but never to let the free memory in your system drop below 5%. If free memory drops below 5%, you run the risk that when the next user logs on, your system will not have enough memory to service that user.

If there isn't enough memory to handle the demands upon it, the operating system will react by paging and may eventually resort to swapping entire processes from memory to disk to free up memory. Then, the next time a swapped process is needed, the system will have to copy the entire memory image for that process from disk back into memory. The worst situation we have encountered was one site that had its System Global Area (SGA) swapped out of memory. Because disk access is so much slower than memory access (sometimes tens or even hundreds of thousands of times slower), performance suffers whenever the system needs to go to the disk in this way.

Paging and swapping affect the CPU as well. When demands are placed on the operating system to provide memory for additional processes, CPU performance also suffers. The bulk of the machine's CPU is consumed by paging and swapping activities. Instead of servicing user requests, memory and CPU are occupied with shuffling data back and forth.

It's also possible to leave too much memory free. Although conserving memory is an admirable performance goal, remember that it's not efficient to have memory sitting unused on your computer instead of using it to store data. If you have more than 10% free memory during peak usage times, then you're not using memory effectively.

Don't assume that you need to buy more memory just because your memory usage is close to 100%. There are many ways to reduce demands on memory by proper tuning and careful management. One important way is to control the number of users and processes in the system.

Every user who logs on to an Oracle system uses memory. User patterns vary a lot. Some users might limit themselves to running Pro*C, which needs about 1 megabyte of memory. Others may log on four times each, with each login requiring 5 megabytes of memory. The amount of memory used depends upon a number of variables:

- The program the user is running.
- The product or language in which the program is written.

- Various Oracle and operating system parameters.
- The operating system that is being used.
- The number of users logged on.
- The number of times each user is logged on.
- The types of operations each user is performing.

At some sites we've worked at, we've found users logged on to a machine as many as six times. Each user who runs SQL*Forms uses as much as 5 megabytes of memory. If you get into a situation in which each user is actually using 30 megabytes (because of being logged on six times) and forcing your system to be short of memory, no amount of tuning will result in good performance. Usually, your system administrator is responsible for specifying who can log on to the system and how many times.

Even when a user isn't doing any work on the system, memory may be used. For example, some users log on, look at one or two screens, and then stay logged on the rest of the day. Others remain logged on when they go to lunch. Logged-on users are still using memory, even though no active work is being performed. Such users can affect the response times of other users if memory is scarce and paging and swapping become excessive. Sophisticated operating systems are able to identify dormant processes, such as those in which a user may not have performed any activity for 15 minutes (although this function requires CPU usage, which may also be a scarce resource). In other systems, you can write your own scripts to do the same thing. If you can manage it, try to set up a policy that forces users to log off the system under such circumstances. This policy will improve performance *and* security.

Several parameters in your site's INIT.ORA file can be reset to improve memory performance. Some parameters (e.g., SORT_AREA_SIZE, SORT_DIRECT_WRITES, SORT_WRITE_BUFFERS, and SORT_WRITE_BUFFER_SIZE), which the DBA can reset to allow Oracle to sort a larger amount in memory, are allocated once in the INIT.ORA file, but the resources are applied to each user session. The system-wide parameter DB_BLOCK_BUFFERS sets the size of the buffer cache, and the SHARED_POOL_SIZE is used to size the area that contains Oracle's dictionary information in memory as well as shared SQL and PL/SQL code. There is only a single buffer cache and shared pool area which are shared among all users. (For a complete discussion of memory tuning parameters, see Chapter 9, *Tuning a New Database*, and Chapter 11, *Monitoring and Tuning an Existing Database*.) Remember that these parameters will not tell the whole story; you'll also need to consider factors such as the number of times a user can log on, the non-Oracle software on your machine, and other such factors.

The time required to access data that is in your computer's memory is much faster than the time required to access it from disk. Oracle provides a number of ways to store both user data and its own data dictionary data in memory (e.g., the users who are allowed to use the system, the table definitions, the access rights users have on the various tables). Figure 2-4 shows how Oracle structures different components in memory and who at your site typically takes responsibility for tuning these components.

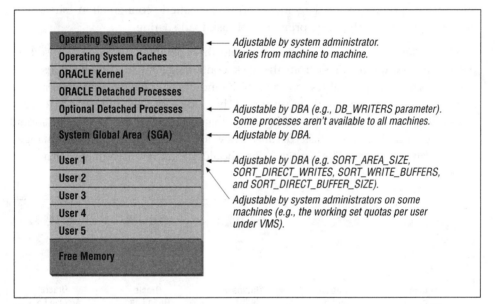

Figure 2-4. Tuning of memory components

Disk I/O Problems and Tuning

With Oracle, as with any large database system, there is a lot of disk activity. Physical memory is never large enough to handle all of a system's program and data needs, so data must be brought in from disk as needed. Access to even the fastest disk is orders of magnitude slower than memory access (even with such recent performance-boosting disk technologies as RAID). With the enormous amounts of data stored and processed by the typical RDBMS, disk I/O can become a major performance problem. As we mentioned in the previous section, memory problems can also affect disk activity when memory limitations cause excessive paging and swapping.

The way in which you organize data on disk can have a major impact on your overall disk performance. Most Oracle systems have a number of disks that share the system's data load. Try to spread the disk workload as evenly as possible across drives to reduce the likelihood of performance problems occurring from disk overloading. You should also consider operating system striping and mirroring for your database files as well as Oracle striping for your data files. Oracle is written to take advantage of new technologies in all database processing, and certain Oracle features, such as the parallel query option, rely on them being in place.

There are a number of specific ways you can reduce performance problems that arise from poor disk management. The simplified configuration shown in Figure 2-5 illustrates the basic principles of disk load sharing.

As shown here, it normally pays to separate the operating system disk (used for paging and swapping files) from the disk containing Oracle database files. It is also advisable to put tables on one disk and their indexes on another disk, because these are accessed in unison. (The index locates the *rowid* address, which is then read from the table using that address.) The redo logs should usually be on their own disk because they are written to as data is changed (which can be often). The archive logs should be on a different disk from the others.

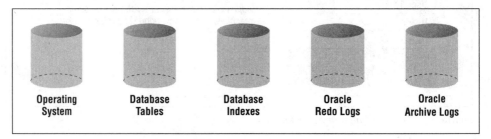

| Operating System | Database Tables | Database Indexes | Oracle Redo Logs | Oracle Archive Logs |

Figure 2-5. A typical disk configuration

When tables, indexes, and rollback segments are created, they are assigned an initial storage allocation. If that allocation is exceeded, Oracle must assign additional extents in a process called dynamic extension. Access to data is most efficient if extents are contiguous. When a table's extents are discontiguous (potentially scattered all around the disk), access is much slower because the system needs to scan these discontiguous areas. This problem of disk fragmentation, illustrated in Figure 2-6, is a common cause of disk bottlenecks. In this example, data from the ACCOUNTS table is spread across the database. The disadvantage of storing data in this way is the excessive head movement required to retrieve groups of ACCOUNTS data. If tables and indexes are sized correctly so that one contiguous area on disk (extent) contains all of the data, the time required to retrieve data is considerably less.

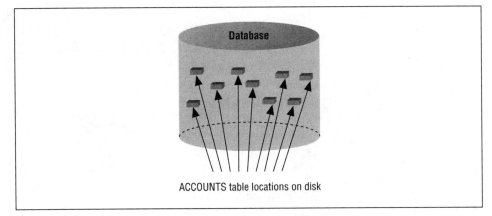

ACCOUNTS table locations on disk

Figure 2-6. Database fragmentation

Disk chaining and migration, illustrated in Figure 2-7, is another possible cause of disk problems. When a row in a table is updated and the amount of free space available in the current data block is not large enough to store the row data, Oracle has to migrate the row to another block; hence the term *migration*. The single row is spread across several discontiguous locations on disk, with the first block storing the address to which the row has been moved. All index access to the row now goes first to the original block to get the row's new address and then proceeds to the second block, causing an extra physical read. This situation can be avoided by correctly sizing the table, as we describe later in this book.

With chaining, a physical row can't physically fit into one physical block. This problem is prevalent in tables that contain the LONG or LONG RAW datatype, where graphical data may be stored in a table. You must be careful to set the DB_BLOCK_SIZE large enough to overcome this problem. Oracle8 assists with the problem by having a special LONG tablespace type.

The goal of tuning an Oracle program is to reduce the number of times that the program needs to access the database on disk. There are a number of ways to reduce database accesses. One important way is indexing, discussed in Chapter 5, *Designing for Performance*. Severe disk problems can occur either because indexes were specified incorrectly during system design or because the indexes were mistakenly dropped.

Several INIT.ORA parameters can be reset to improve disk I/O performance. Two particularly important ones are LOG_CHECKPOINT_INTERVAL, which specifies how often dirty blocks are written from the buffer cache to the database, and LOG_BUFFER, which controls the size and frequency of the writes for all changes made to your data from the log buffer in memory to the redo logs on disk. For a complete discussion of disk I/O tuning parameters, see Chapters 9 and 11.

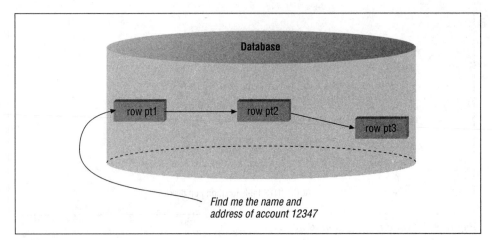

Figure 2-7. Disk chaining

CPU Problems and Tuning

The CPU controls the activities of the other resources in your system, and it executes user processes. While all computer hardware costs have dropped in recent years, CPU continues to be more expensive than memory and disk. Although there are occasional situations in which a CPU is genuinely not fast enough to cope with the workload at a site, these situations are rare. With symmetric multiprocessors (SMPs) and massively parallel processors (MPPs) becoming more and more popular and inexpensive, a new question is: "How many CPUs do we need?" Before buying an expensive new CPU or purchasing additional CPUs for your SMP and MPP machine, make sure that your CPU problems are not being caused by any of the following:

- Untuned applications.

- Users being logged on multiple times.

- Long-running batch jobs running during prime production hours.

- Other types of memory or disk I/O bottlenecks.

- Having undersized or oversized memory allocations for Oracle memory structures (particularly the buffer cache sized by setting the DB_BLOCK_BUFFERS parameter and the shared pool area sized by the SHARED_POOL_SIZE parameter). If the buffer cache or shared pool is set too small, the CPU will continually be shuffling items into and out of memory in panic mode.

CPU problems frequently occur when too many processes are trying to use the CPUs at the same time. We've talked about the stresses paging and swapping put on your system. In the worst case, paging and swapping turn into *thrashing*, a dire situation in which the whole CPU is dedicated to simply moving processes from memory to disk and back again. To avoid this worst case, don't let your system run out of memory! Be particularly careful with your per-user memory settings, including SORT_AREA_RETAINED_SIZE, SORT_AREA_SIZE, SORT_WRITE_ BUFFERS, and SORT_WRITE_BUFFER_SIZE.

Because the CPU services the operating system and user programs, usually correcting the disk and memory bottlenecks in your system will also help to alleviate CPU bottlenecks. Memory bottlenecks have a more severe effect on CPU than do disk I/O bottlenecks. Excessive paging and swapping, if they occur, make continual demands on CPU, whereas disk I/O demands CPU only after data is returned from disk—a slower process than returning data from memory. Although your system administrator can often transfer the more damaging memory bottleneck to disk, and thus ease the pressure on the CPU, this is usually a temporary measure. You may eventually need more memory.

The major way in which you can keep CPU problems from occurring is to avoid running long jobs during times of peak usage in online transaction processing systems. Although sites need to decide on standards that make sense for them, our own personal bias is to either move long jobs to a different machine (using a backup database) or move summary data to a local PC to allow a user to perform his or her required analyses without affecting the online user response times. The other alternative is to run the reports during off-peak hours. We define long-running jobs in a very strict way: Anything that takes longer than 3 minutes to run! (See the discussion of managing such jobs in the section "Managing the Problem of Long-Running Jobs" in Chapter 3 and of tuning such jobs in Chapter 15, *Tuning Long-Running Jobs.*)

On some computers, you can tune CPU use by assigning priorities to some of the processes in your system. If priority setting is available on your machine, you have two alternatives. You can try setting the priorities of long-running jobs lower than those of the interactive processes to make sure that they don't interfere with the processes being run by online users. Alternatively, you can set the priorities of certain long-running jobs higher than those of the interactive processes at certain times of day, so that they run as quickly as possible and then get out of the way.

Remember, work being performed by the long-running jobs may also be performed by the Oracle detached processes DBWR (database writer) and LGWR (log writer). Be sure you never change the priorities of these processes or any other Oracle process.

Many long-running jobs tend to be I/O-bound rather than CPU-bound, so although they do consume a large amount of CPU, they consume even more I/O. This problem is especially serious if the long-running jobs need to access the same disks accessed by the interactive users. To improve performance, avoid having users run long-running jobs on the same system that is used for online transaction processing during times of prime online usage.

Network Problems and Tuning

Network bottlenecks occur when the amount of data that needs to be transferred across the network exceeds the network capacity. In client-server configurations particularly, data distributed on different machines must often be transferred over the network. By tuning your programs to reduce the need for database access, and by carefully distributing data on your machines and disks, you can often greatly reduce the volume of data that needs to be sent.

Here are some suggestions that might help. For detailed information, see Chapter 16, *Tuning in the Client-Server Environment.*

- If you are running client-server, try to keep all long-running jobs at the database server end if possible.

- If you are propagating data across databases, send only what is needed. Figuring out the exact data requirements may take longer in the short term but could help network traffic significantly in the long term.

- Before transferring data, including reports, across the network, make sure you use any data compression utilities available in your operating system (e.g., *compress* for UNIX).

- If the users at your site frequently download report files to their personal computers for use with their packages, consider producing nightly extract files and placing them on file servers to reduce network traffic.

- Use packages, procedures, triggers, functions, and constraints to have as much work done at the server end as possible.

II

Tuning for Managers and Planners

Part II describes what managers, planners, and project leaders of Oracle systems need to know about tuning: what response times are acceptable in your system, how can you manage the workload to produce better response times, do you need a larger computer? It outlines the critical management checkpoints that affect performance in your system, and it describes briefly the design and development standards that you need to formulate during the planning stage.

3

Planning and Managing the Tuning Process

Chapter 1, *Introduction to Oracle Performance Tuning*, and Chapter 2, *What Causes Performance Problems?*, introduced the Oracle tuning process and explained why tuning is so necessary in the Oracle environment. This chapter focuses on the questions you'll need to ask, and the decisions you'll need to make, about system performance and tuning from a planning and management point of view:

- What response times are acceptable in your system?

- How can you manage the workload at your system to produce better response times?

- Can your system perform effectively with the system resources you have, or do you need a larger machine, more memory, or other resources?

- What are the crucial management checkpoints for tuning at your site?

Chapter 4, *Defining System Standards*, discusses another management function: the standards that need to be set for system design and development to improve the chances that a system will perform well. The rest of this book describes the specific choice of database design approaches, the use of SQL and related statements in programs, and the selection of appropriate diagnostic and tuning tools.

Managing the Problem of Response Time

In most systems, the bottom line for performance is response time. Users don't care whether the system slows down because of a problem with memory, disk, CPU, networking, or a workload that's too large for the available system resources. The net effect is the same: users can't get their queries and reports run as fast as they need to.

Face the facts. Users will never thank you for making response time fast. Users will always want faster response times, even when performance is already blazing. Particularly when a site has downsized from a mainframe to a smaller machine or from a large minicomputer running a unitary architecture to a client-server environment, users will continue to expect mainframe response times and are likely to be disappointed, at least until tuning brings the speed up.

You may not be able to please all of the users all of the time, but there are some very important things you can do to minimize complaints and maximize user satisfaction.

- Formulate a policy for how to deal with response time problems. To whom do users complain? Who investigates and acts on the reported problems?

- Assess the truth of the situation. Managers often say to us, "My production users keep complaining that response times are poor. The support staff denies the claim. How can I figure out the truth of what's going on?"

- Act swiftly to improve response times if the complaints are, in fact, warranted. Our experience tells us that most times they are, so never ignore them.

Planning for Complaints About Response Time

Here are some suggestions for formulating a policy to handle response time complaints and reporting:

- Make sure users know who handles complaints. When response time problems occur, users must know how to report the details to the appropriate person or group. If correct reporting channels are not in place, users probably won't try to figure out how to report their concerns. Instead, they'll complain to their co-workers, and this informal discussion may be very damaging to the credibility of the system and its administrators. It's helpful to set up a chain of communication for all response time complaints, just so that all the people who need to know about the problem are, in fact, notified. Here's a typical chain:

  — Production users report the problem to a production support team.

  — The production support team then reports the problem to the development team, the DBA, or the system administrator.

— The development team reports the problem to the DBA with a recommended solution.

— The DBA and system administrator report the problem to each other or to the development team with recommended solutions, where applicable.

- Make sure the DBA and the system administrator are geared up to respond quickly to response time problems. Ideally, they should be proactive with performance problems; they should be aware of the problems and should work on fixing them even before the users raise a complaint. Oracle provides many tools to assist in this work, such as the Oracle Performance Pack (see Appendix D, *Oracle Performance Pack*) and various other tools documented in Chapter 10, *Diagnostic and Tuning Tools*.

- Check what else is going on in the system. Be sure to find out about the user's CPU usage and disk I/O, as well as internal locking information from the Oracle monitor screens. Here's what you should record:

— User's name

— User's phone number

— User's login ID

— Machine user is logged on to

— Where user is located

— Application user is running

— Program (and version of the program) user is running

— Date and time the problem occurred

— Description of what was being done with any key field values being entered

— Response time (total, or amount up to the present, if the function is still running)

— Any additional information that you think might be useful in solving the response time problem (e.g., screen dumps)

Remember to take complaints about response time seriously even when those complaints come from people on your own staff. Complaints about response time are legitimate, even if they come from developers, DBAs, system administrators, or QA staff. Any user of a computer system can experience poor response times, and any user's productivity can be damaged when he or she can't get the throughput needed on a certain day.

Investigating Complaints About Response Time

How do you decide whether your users' complaints about response times warrant making changes? The problem is that you usually have a maze of conflicting information. Your staff may provide you with a lot of information about how well individual SQL statements perform against the database and how long it takes the network to process a particular request. That doesn't necessarily tell you what the individual user is experiencing.

Here are some suggested steps to follow:

- Make sure the problem really is one of response time. Sometimes, another problem may actually cause the slowness in response. We've known users whose terminals were unplugged and others who, not knowing how to activate a response from an application, waited for a response that the application had not yet received. When users are trained in how to use the system, they must also receive training in how to detect poor response time and what to do to be sure the problem really is at the system end. That's why collecting all of the information we listed in the previous section is a good idea.

- Check the complaint against the standard and against other users' experiences. Sometimes, although users complain about response times, those times may not be too far off the mark; for example, the standard may be 2.5 seconds, and the response comes back in 2.6 seconds. (Our observations at sites tell us that this is the exception, not the norm, however.) When a user reports a response problem, it's good practice to check the response times of other users who are running the same function.

- To investigate particular complaints, run procedures against the production database, just as users would. Record response times at different times throughout the day. Try to use the same forms that production users most commonly use. (It's a good idea to do this monitoring on a regular basis, even when you aren't investigating complaints.)

SQL*Forms and SQL*Menu provide a function that allows you to automate this process by recording the keystrokes a user would type to a typical database query. Typically, you record the time of day just before running the recorded procedure, then run various forms using the recorded keystrokes, and then record the time of day once again after exiting the procedure.

Oracle7.2 and later versions provide a mechanism to call a procedure (see the DBMS_APPLICATION_INFO package) from within your programs to record the module that you are running, the action within the module, and any client information that you wish to store. You can then obtain information from the VSQL, VSQLAREA, and V$SESSION performance tables in the database to view the performance of any action being performed within any module. This mechanism works regardless of whether you are using SQL*Forms or GUI frontends.

You will need to query the V$ tables regularly and raise an event when the response times exceed a certain level. If you are proactive in watching out for response time problems, it is also useful to gather information on an ongoing basis to determine trends in performance that might be deteriorating over time. Figure 3-1 is an example of the kind of report that many sites produce daily to track performance problems. Statistics are gathered for each major transaction in the system. When the response time exceeds the acceptable (as it did at 10:30, 11:00, and 11:30 in the example), it is best to have an automated means of gathering more information to assist in tuning.

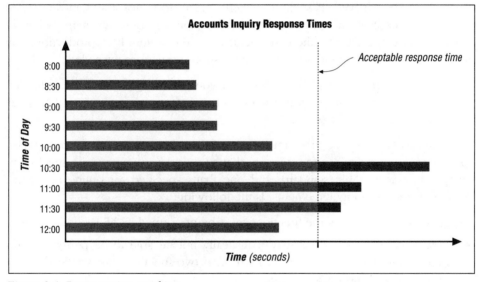

Figure 3-1. Response time tracking

The problem with the method described here is that it does not take into account network delays in GUI frontend client-server environments. Oracle Trace, which is available in Oracle7.3 and later, gives you the ability to break up overall client-server response times into client response time, network response time, and database server response time for each transaction or even for action within the transaction.*

---

* Oracle Trace is part of the Oracle Performance Pack, which is an extra-cost option that you can purchase with Oracle Enterprise Manager. If you have serious performance concerns at your site, it is well worth purchasing this program. See Appendix D for details on how to use Oracle Trace, and other performance tools.

Considering a Tuning Service Agreement

How do you define "acceptable response time"? Acceptability is a somewhat amorphous concept. What's acceptable to one user may be totally unacceptable to another. It's a good idea to establish a standard for acceptable response time—a standard that makes sense for your organization and the work your users need to perform. Then you'll have a yardstick you can use to measure actual system operations and to resolve user complaints about performance. You and your users won't continually be arguing about whether system performance is good or bad.

More and more organizations are adopting the notion of tuning service agreements. These agreements, made between the computing staff and their clients, provide an effective way to ensure that optimal response times are achieved and continue to be achieved. If such agreements are in force for a system developed for a client, the client may not accept a system until response times are below or equal to those specified by the agreement. Once the system is in production, you may be subject to payment penalties if the response times are exceeded.

Tuning agreements are a good idea within your own organization as well. You also have a responsibility to your own developers to provide a system that offers them decent response times.

Expectations for response times must be realistic. Sub-half-second response times, for example, are ridiculous for a system that supports many users on a small minicomputer. A reasonable standard, and one that's specified for online interactive queries by many tuning agreements, is the following:

- Ninety-five percent of the functions must be performed in 2.5 seconds or less.

- Certain complex functions may realistically not be able to be performed this quickly. But there should be no more than two functions per application that exceed 2.5-second response time.

- No response time may exceed 10 seconds. (If it does, it should be run in batch.)

In addition to specifying acceptable response times, service agreements should also specify up-time for a system and should include a plan for disaster recovery.

It is important that you benchmark your application throughout its development life cycle to ensure that the expected response times are realistic. A price/performance ratio will emerge from the benchmark; for example, response times of 2.0 seconds could be achieved, but the cost savings may be considerable if the performance expectation is not quite as tight and you could use a smaller, less expensive machine to achieve 2.5-second response times.

Brilliant performance may be able to be provided at a prohibitive cost. Consider the trade-offs before finalizing any agreement on response times. This issue may lead to adjustments to the response time expectations, as agreed to by the relevant parties. Another issue that may force a renegotiation of response times is a determination that the workload is inconsistent with the expected workload as currently specified.

Tuning service agreements do more than just protect system users. They also place more pressure on the designer and the DBA to design for performance and on the development team to code for performance. (The sidebar presents a skeleton for a tuning service agreement.)

Managing the Problem of Long-Running Jobs

Sometimes organizations pay a lot of attention to tuning interactive jobs and not nearly enough to tuning or scheduling long-running jobs. Carefully pruning your response time from 3 seconds down to 2.5 seconds for your interactive jobs won't make much difference if the long-running jobs hog the system for many minutes or even hours. We recently worked at a bank that had the overnight jobs run for so long during end of month processing that they crept into prime online usage times. The tellers were not impressed, nor were the people standing in line waiting to get served.

Every organization has a set of reporting or accounting functions that take a long time to run, some for many hours. Too often, sites try to run long-running jobs at the same time that interactive users are demanding speedy responses to their queries. The long-running jobs can get a stranglehold on system resources, making the system unworkable and many hundreds of users very unhappy. Often, there is no reason to run long-running jobs during times of peak usage in the system. A little common sense in scheduling such jobs will help your overall performance a lot.

Although it's true that all the tuning in the world won't make these long-running, resource-intensive jobs complete in seconds, or even minutes, it is nevertheless possible to improve their performance quite a bit. Remember, improving interactive performance by reducing a query's response time from 4 seconds to 2 seconds (a 50% performance improvement) yields a savings of 2 seconds. But improving a 10-hour-long batch job by the same 50% yields a saving of 5 hours!

Just as you impose required response times on interactive jobs, consider imposing similar standards on batch jobs. These jobs might be moved to overnight or otherwise nonpeak processing, particularly on single-processor machines. If it is

Tuning Service Agreement

This agreement is between the following entities:

- The software development group
- The hardware vendor
- The facilities management group
- The client

All parties must agree in principle to the response times listed in this agreement.

A. Inclusions and Exclusions

A.1 The tuning service agreement includes the following:

- Response times required for online users
- Batch reporting run times such as statement printing
- Batch update run times
- Overnight jobs having to run within the overnight time window 8:00 p.m. to 6:00 a.m.

A.2 The tuning service agreement excludes the following:

- The required "uptime" of the machine. This factor may affect the achievable response times, however, if workload increases to cover the lost time. The uptime is part of an operational service level agreement that will be agreed to by the client and the facilities management group

  The tuning service agreement will be based on having current workload expectations remain consistent. The workload information includes the number of concurrent users at all sites, the types of programs that the users will be using, and the mix of usage between background (batch) jobs (such as reporting) and online query and update users. Include an appendix listing details on expected workload levels.

B. Requirements

The overriding requirements of the tuning service agreement are as follows:

B.1 Achieving necessary throughput to keep the company operating

- Response times must be adequate to allow the client to process the required workload on the computer system to fulfill the client's business objectives in a timely and professional manner. If adequate response time is not provided, there may simply not be enough hours in the day to get the workload through. (Most sites add a clause in this part of the tuning service agreement that specifies that the users must get the workload through within specified working hours, for example, 8:00 a.m. to 7:00 p.m.) This requirement is mandatory.

B.2 User Satisfaction

- The application users must receive response times with which they are comfortable and happy. Poor response times can cause frustration and stress, particularly when the system is being used to service the general public in real time. Some workers get paid bonuses for achieving levels of throughput, which will be jeopardized by poor performance; this adds to the stress.

- This requirement is highly desirable. One factor that may affect it is a workload that is higher than expected. This requirement must be achieved with the client receiving and being comfortable with any explanation given regarding response times that exceed those expected. Exceptions to the required response times must be very infrequent.

C. Regular Response Time Reporting

- A method must be established to automatically report all response times that do not fall within the required times, and the action that will be taken that will remedy the problem must be well documented and agreed to. Users often remain silent when response times fall beyond those expected, and others complain when response times are within the agreement. Oracle Trace is the preferred tool, with reports being produced daily on major transaction response times at selected intervals during the day.

D. Response Time Requirements

Two possible response time requirements that have been obtained from the way other sites operate are the following:

D.1 Scenario 1

- 95% of online queries will respond within 2.5 seconds.
- No online query will ever exceed 8 seconds.
- 95% of online updates visible to the user will respond within 2.5 seconds.
- No online update visible to the user will ever exceed 8 seconds.
- Online reporting must complete within 3 minutes if run during core hours.
- Otherwise, overnight reporting in total must be completed outside core hours.

- Any other business requirements (e.g., quarterly statements) must complete within *n* hours (state the number in the agreement).

D.2 Scenario 2

- All echoes of characters will respond within 0.*nn* of a second (state the number in the agreement). (Echo is the amount of time it takes to go from one character to the next when entering data.)

- Moving from field to field will take no longer than 0.1 second.

- Moving from menu option to menu option will take no longer than 1 second.

- Calling up and displaying a form will take no longer than 1 second.

- A transaction inquiry will take no longer than 2.5 seconds; list any exceptions (e.g., searching on all surnames that have "%DER%" in them).

- A transaction commit will take no longer than 2 seconds; list any exceptions (e.g., high-speed data entry mode may require a faster response time, whereas applying many contributions may accept a slower response time).

- A LIST OF VALUES display will take no longer than 2.5 seconds; list any exceptions.

- Online reporting will take no longer than 3 minutes; be careful to place long-running reports into the overnight batch queue or on to a separate machine.

- Batch jobs (printing, etc.) are listed with their required response times; the jobs may be itemized as required.

possible to have these jobs run on machines other than those used for heavy transaction processing, that will also improve performance. Consider downloading reporting data to databases or into spreadsheets on local servers overnight.

You can also impose tuning agreements on long-running jobs, just as you do on interactive jobs. The specifics of the tuning agreement for long-running jobs will have to be worked out within your organization; sites differ greatly in what they need to produce. A general rule of thumb that many sites follow is to run, during off-peak hours, any job that takes more than 3 minutes. As we mention in Chapter 2, we take a stricter approach than this; the cutoff that we recommend is 45 seconds. In other words, if you are running in an OLTP system, any job that takes more than 45 seconds should be run on a different machine (against a backup database) or moved to off-peak hours. For complete information about keeping long-running jobs from affecting your system's performance, see Chapter 15, *Tuning Long-Running Jobs*.

Managing the Workload in Your System

To speak of "tuning users" has a nasty, computer-centric sound to it. But, in fact, your human users may be able to cooperate in ways that will have an enormous effect on system performance without hindering their own productivity at all. To tune your system effectively, you need to understand the people behind the system. How many people are using the system? What are they doing? What are their expectations? What are their priorities? In short, what is the expected workload?

In most Oracle systems, the workload isn't constant from one week or day or hour to the next. For example, over the course of a single day, you'll typically find that peak interactive usage occurs for about 6 hours a day, between 9:30 a.m. and 12:00 p.m. and between 1:30 p.m. and 5:00 p.m. Over the course of a year, you're likely to find that the height of system activity occurs just before the end of a financial year, as users are finalizing the year's accounts and developing budgets for the next financial year. Over the course of your system's lifetime, you'll probably find that the workload grows gradually, but significantly, as the number of users logging on to the system increases. This steady increase is known as workload creep. Don't let it creep up on you, catching you without adequate resources to operate effectively.

Although you may not have the power to change your users' daily or yearly activities to even out performance, you can at least be aware of these peaks and valleys in system use, and you can use this information to improve overall system performance. Be sure to ask your users what they really need; maybe their requirements are flexible and you can shift scheduling to improve overall performance in the system:

- Does a particular report need to be run immediately, or is tomorrow morning soon enough?

- Will the jobs that are scheduled for overnight processing actually be completed overnight or might they continue into the next day?

- For batch jobs, when do they need to run? On one particular night of the week or any night? Once every two weeks? Quarterly? Annually? Make sure you know the schedules for these batch jobs well in advance, so that you can factor them into the overall schedule while keeping performance high.

- For sets of reports, do they need to be run in any particular order?

The most difficult kind of system to administer and plan for is one in which users request many resource-intensive, ad hoc reports in an unpredictable fashion. Unfortunately for your ability to sleep at night, as PC-based reporting tools gain popularity and the number of PC users increases, this unpredictable use of the system is likely to grow significantly. If you plan carefully, though, you'll be able to accommodate such users without adversely affecting your other users and your overall system performance.

Once you have a handle on what the workload tends to be in your system, remember to plan for unanticipated emergencies. If an unexpectedly large workload appears one day, you don't want to plunge the entire organization into chaos.

At some sites, staggered hours help system performance a good deal. For example, some people in the organization may begin work at 7:00 a.m. and go home at 3:00 p.m. Others may come in at 3:00 p.m. and leave at 11:00 p.m. Other organizations may offer flextime in which employees can arrive and leave within a 3-hour spread. Whenever work is staggered in this way, you'll notice better performance, even when you don't explicitly change any of your procedures. When you tune specifically to take advantage of this scheduling, you'll get even better results.

You'll have to be particularly careful about scheduling long-running jobs when your organization is an international one. For example, when it is 4:00 p.m. in San Francisco, it's 9:00 a.m. the next day in Melbourne, Australia. Such an international spread can be advantageous in distributing the workload in systems that offer 24-hour online help systems, for example. Oracle's worldwide support centers are an excellent example of the way global computing is heading, with support set up on the U.S. West Coast, on the U.S. East Coast, and in Australia. But in such staggered environments, it may also be hard to know when to run long-running, resource-intensive batch jobs and backups. Such jobs have the potential for severely disrupting online response time.

If you stay flexible and creative, you'll find a way to make workload scheduling work to the advantage of system performance. Consider the case in which users from Boston and New York share a computer system. When it's 6:00 p.m in Boston, it's also 6:00 p.m. in New York. When online users go home, the long-running overnight reports begin running. Because comparatively few users are logged on at this time, there is no serious impact on interactive user response times. Now suppose that users from Los Angeles join the system. When it is 6:00 p.m. in Boston and New York, it's only 3:00 p.m. in Los Angeles, prime working time. Continuing to run overnight reports at this time would have a serious impact on the new users' response times. The obvious move is to adjust the overnight processing so that reports are run after most of the Los Angeles users have logged off, a 3-hour difference. (Although this seems to be a very obvious adjustment, we're constantly amazed at how resistant people are to changing their schedules and procedures; we've had to fight this battle many times!)

Remember that normal system administration is a part of the mix of jobs at your site. At one site we visited, users complained that their response time was poor in the morning but fine in the afternoon. None of the application's long-running jobs were being run during the day. But the system administrator ran a backup job first thing every morning, and this job had a serious impact on application performance. When we recommended that the backup be run late at night or earlier in the morning, we were told that the computing staff was not allowed to work outside normal business hours. Not a very enlightened policy: This decision cost the company productivity, throughput, and ultimately revenue. At another site we were asked to tune, we discovered that the DBA would analyze all of the tables and indexes in his 15-gigabyte database when he arrived for work at 9:00 a.m.

Making the Decision to Buy More Equipment

As we mentioned in Chapter 1, by tuning your system effectively, you can often avoid the need to buy a larger computer or more memory or disk resources. Before you spend any money on equipment, ask these questions—of yourself and your computing staff:

Q: *Has your application been completely tuned in single-user mode? Is every response time within the standard specified in your service agreement?*

A: There can be no exceptions to the rule. Do not proceed past this point until your application is totally tuned!

Q: *What is your average amount of memory per user, the expected disk I/Os per user, and the average CPU MIPS per user in the current configuration?*

A: You must know what you are using now before you can assess statistics for any new equipment or applications you'll be considering.

Q: *What is the expected growth rate in users at your site?*

A: You'll usually need to plan for growth; but in some organizations, the number of users will actually be expected to drop over time. Make sure you have correct projections for your own organization.

Q: *What resources are causing the most performance problems in your system? Is the machine short of memory? Is it experiencing CPU wait times? Is it I/O bound? Is it experiencing network bottlenecks?*

A: Make sure you get solid answers from your DBA and system administrator.

Chapter 2 introduced the specific memory, disk, CPU, and network bottlenecks that may occur and suggested some basic ways to deal with them. Later chapters provide much more detail on how you can tune these resources to best advantage.

If you've tuned your system as effectively as you can and you're still experiencing major problems in resource availability and response time, you'll probably have to face the decision to buy more equipment. You may need a new computer, or you may need to upgrade only certain components (e.g., more memory, more processors, additional disks). Don't just blindly add to the configuration you already have. This is an opportunity to ask whether it's time to consider moving to a client-server configuration or whether it might be possible to downsize in some other way.

Here are some suggestions for gathering the information you need to make a solid decision about what equipment you need:

- Ask other organizations that may be running the equipment you're considering about their experiences. Do this for hardware but also for software, including software packages developed by Oracle. Be sure to focus your questions on the performance of the products they're running.

- Do a capacity planning study for your site. In this study, you perform benchmarks on your site's current use of memory, disk, CPU MIPS, and the network and calculate what additional equipment is needed to produce acceptable performance. You'll usually ask your system administrator to perform this study, as described in Chapter 17, *Capacity Planning.*

- Shop around for the best equipment and prices. Before you buy anything, ask your vendors to let you run some sample programs on the type of computer you're planning to buy or to add memory or disk on a trial basis to see how well it meets your performance needs. Most vendors will go along with this plan.

- Make sure that whatever equipment you buy can be readily upgraded so that you'll be able to cope with more users, additional applications, or new functions within existing applications. One of the big advantages of a client-server architecture is that you can add power to the client side without disrupting overall processing.

Remember that because Oracle products are so portable, most applications can be developed on a small computer and later ported to your larger production machine.

Management Checkpoints

Figure 3-2 shows the key checkpoints you'll need to be aware of as a manager or system planner. The section "When Do You Tune?" in Chapter 1 introduces each of these major processes and their effect on performance.

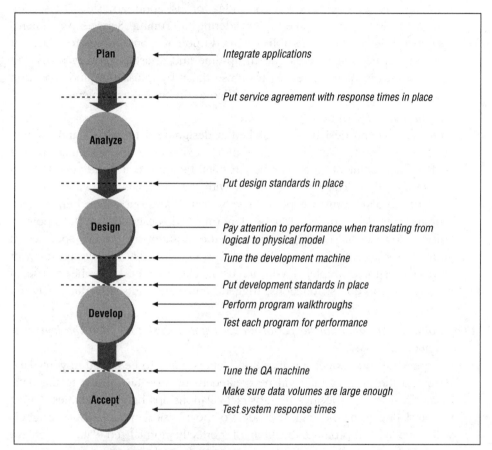

Figure 3-2. Tuning checkpoints for managers and planners

Checkpoint 1: Integrate applications

Your data model, applications, RDBMS, hardware, and other software aren't all stand-alone entities. Each affects the other. If you develop an application without considering its impact on other hardware and software in your system, or vice versa, you're very likely to end up having performance problems. Figure out ahead of time, not afterward, how your systems will communicate. An important point to consider here is how to transfer data between applications. If you don't carefully plan ahead of time for how applications will exchange data, data transfer might impose a huge burden on your computer resources.

Checkpoint 2: Put a tuning service agreement in place

A tuning service agreement is a good idea for just about any site. The section earlier in this chapter called "Considering a Tuning Service Agreement" describes briefly how to establish agreed-upon response times for different types of functions as well as system up-time and disaster recovery plans. Put a mechanism in place to record response times by transaction and report on whether they are exceeding those specified in the tuning agreement.

Checkpoint 3: Put design standards in place

Most analysts and designers are skilled at designing data models and normalizing data. But few of them have much experience in designing from a performance point of view. For best results, be sure to include your DBA in the design effort. The DBA can work with the designers to review the data model from a performance point of view, can figure out where performance requirements demand that data be denormalized (described in Checkpoint 4 below), and can help designers to meet the requirements you've specified at your site for acceptable response times. It is essential that you design for your architecture; for example, if you are using client-server, make heavy use of packages, procedures, functions, triggers, and constraints to reduce network traffic.

Checkpoint 4: Pay attention to performance when translating from the logical to the physical model

The physical data model specifies how data is going to be stored in your database and the indexes that will be created to provide fast access to the data. The logical model specifies the abstract relationships between entities. Often, in translating from the logical model to the physical model, your designers will have to compromise the goal of perfectly normalized data to achieve good performance. If you don't pay attention to performance at this stage, the costs to repair performance problems later on will be huge, as we show in Chapter 2. Regardless of how talented your programmers, DBAs, and system administrators may be, they will be fighting a losing battle in their efforts to make an inadequate physical data model perform well.

NOTE   Although CASE tools can often be very helpful, they sometimes do not take real-world constraints and requirements into account. If you follow CASE guidelines to the letter, you're likely to end up with beautifully normalized data that may slow your system to a crawl. Many CASE tools don't even offer options for translating logical to physical models in a way that provides for performance.

One of the things CASE methods often don't address is denormalization, which we mention briefly above. Denormalization is the process of storing redundant data to lessen the number of database reads necessary to retrieve that data. Although the goal in any relational database system is normalization to the fullest extent possible, sometimes denormalization is needed to make programs meet the response time goals established for them. In Chapter 5, *Designing for Performance*, we describe some situations in which you'll need to denormalize your data to achieve better performance.

Make sure that your physical data model is reviewed by the DBA to ensure that it provides the best performance possible for your system.

Checkpoint 5: Tune the development machine

Good performance isn't a privilege of production users alone. Don't forget that your programmers may be laboring under tight deadlines; they'll never meet these deadlines if they're waiting half the day for the system to respond.

Checkpoint 6: Put development standards in place

Performance is a programming goal, too. Include performance in your programming standards. Optimize each SQL statement so that you get the best possible response time out of it. It is essential that your coders be aware of which optimizer they are to use and are handed a list of all tables, their indexes, constraints, and triggers. Code all programs carefully and neatly so that it's easier to read through program code during tuning.

Checkpoint 7: Perform program walk-throughs

Perform a program walk-through before any programming begins at your site. Make sure all technical specifications are reviewed from a performance, as well as a functional, perspective. For each program, limit the walk-through to a 1-hour session, which should be attended by the designer, one or more of your programmers, and the DBA. If the walk-through uncovers any inadequacies in performance, make sure these are remedied before programming begins. This will keep your developer from having to make major changes after the code has been completed and will result in better overall performance.

Checkpoint 8: Test each program for performance

Make sure your programmers test each of their programs for performance before they release them for testing in the quality assurance environment. Let them know that it isn't professional to send untuned programs to QA and expect the testers to find response time problems. Make sure your programmers are using the Oracle tools designed to diagnose performance problems and improve performance. (See the discussion of EXPLAIN PLAN, TKPROF, and other tools in Chapter 10.)

Checkpoint 9: Tune the quality assurance machine

Your QA machine must be tuned so that it does realistic performance testing of all programs. The ideal situation is to have a quantity of data that is similar to your production database. If you are using the cost-based optimizer, it may behave differently in production from the way it behaves in QA because of the different statistics gathered on the tables and indexes.

The QA environment is your last chance to test programs for functionality and performance before moving them into production. If all your QA response times are poor, it will be difficult to gauge how effectively a program will perform in production. Poor response times caused by an inefficiently tuned machine will also increase the time it takes to test programs. Make sure the environment you use for testing is consistent with the production environment (e.g., client-server, parallel server, RAID, archivelog mode, etc.), and make sure you are testing on a configuration that runs at the same speed as, or slower than, the production machine.

Checkpoint 10: Make sure test data volumes are large enough

If QA data volumes are not large enough, programs will perform well in testing but may perform abysmally in the production environment. As was mentioned earlier, the cost-based optimizer may act totally differently if the data volumes and data distribution are significantly different. Make sure that your QA data volumes are as similar as they can be to those that will be used in production.

Checkpoint 11: Test response times

You must reject any program that doesn't meet the response time standards specified in your site's tuning service agreement. The DBA should work with the QA staff to investigate the reasons for the poor response time. Once they have a hypothesis, report the information to the programmer who will be fixing the offending program.

Performance Hints for Managers

Here is a summary list of key performance hints that will help you to plan and manage your Oracle system to get the best performance out of it. We've touched on some of the more important of these in this chapter and in earlier chapters.

- If possible, make sure your development staff consists of people who have worked on highly tuned Oracle applications in the past. There is no substitute for experience.

- Identify and correct potential problems early in the development life cycle. If poor decisions are made during analysis and design, fixing the problem later on will take a lot longer and cost a lot more money. We show this relationship in Figure 3-3.

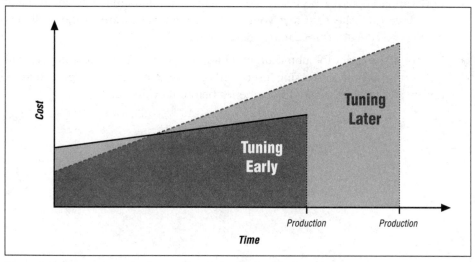

Figure 3-3. Comparison: tuning earlier versus later

- Make sure you have solid standards (for software selection, version control, modular programming, system libraries, shared packages, procedures, functions, and other such topics) in place at all stages of the development life cycle.

- Put in place a tuning service agreement that includes strict response time requirements. If you are buying a canned package, make sure that package also meets your standards for response time. You must have a method of extracting daily response times from your DBAs to enforce the accountability against the tuning service agreement.

- Do not allow developers and quality assurers to work on the same machine as production users.

- Remember that, like one bad apple in the barrel, one Oracle program, or even one SQL statement, that performs very poorly has the potential to degrade the performance of all of the functions in the system. Worse still, if you put an untuned application on a machine that was previously running tuned applications, the untuned application will degrade the performance of all of the applications on the machine.

- Make sure that programs are developed and maintained in a modular fashion. This will decrease development time and memory requirements, and it will make the application easier to maintain.

- Make sure to log inactive users off the system after a specified period of time. Also, monitor those users who repeatedly log on two or three times, making sure there is a genuine need for their behavior.

- Code applications to best suit the particular configuration you are running. For example, make sure that your staff members are aware of the additional coding considerations for tuning client-servers.

- Do not allow users to submit untuned ad hoc queries that will compete with online transaction processing users on your system. Set up a procedure to review and tune all such ad hoc queries before they are run.

4

Defining System Standards

As part of planning and managing your Oracle system, you and the other members of your project team need to establish rigorous system standards for design, programming, and testing. This book does not dictate any particular set of standards, nor does it describe standards in any detail. There are a number of good reference books on design, programming, and testing methodologies. To these general recommendations, you'll have to add and customize areas of particular concern to your own organization.

In this chapter, we remind you that performance—the performance of your final application and even the performance of your project development team—depends largely on how carefully you have set standards for design, programming, and testing and on how rigorously you have enforced those standards.

Selecting a Common Design Methodology

There are many methodologies you can choose from to design and develop your system. Your selection ranges from crude in-house products to complex CASE tools, like Oracle*CASE, as well as many third-party products. The choice is up to you. You will have to take into account such factors as your application's complexity, your budget, your development schedule, your project team's experience, and even the style and communication channels of your organization.

Whatever you select, select it early. We can't stress too emphatically the importance of having a standard methodology in place from the beginning of a project. Organizations that decide, in the middle of a project, to adopt even the most powerful CASE tool find that it's very hard, and disruptive in terms of both time and budget, to switch horses in midstream.

Selecting Your Software

At the very start of the project, you also need to choose the set of development tools you'll be using. There are a large number of Oracle and third-party tools. Here, too, your choice depends on a myriad of considerations, including hardware configuration, in-house staff experience, the availability of supplementary consultants with certain credentials, geography, project deadlines, and budget.

There are a number of software decisions you need to make. The most important decisions involve the choices of an online interface and a report interface. Examples of online interfaces from which you're likely to choose are:

- SQL*Forms
- SQL*Plus
- Third-party GUIs such as SQL Windows, Power Builder, and Visual Basic
- Pro*C, Pro*C++, Pro*COBOL, or one of the other Pro* languages
- Oracle Call Interface (OCI)

Examples of report interfaces from which you're likely to choose are:

- SQL*Reportwriter
- SQL*Plus
- SQL*Report
- SQR

- Pro*C, Pro*C++, Pro*COBOL, or one of the other Pro* languages
- Oracle Call Interface (OCI)

You'll also typically use a spreadsheet package such as Lotus 1-2-3 or Excel that can communicate with your database.

Make sure to select readily available, easy-to-learn tools, and make sure all of your developers are actually using them. Although in theory it might seem like a good idea to let individual programmers code in whatever language they're most productive in, this *laissez-faire* attitude can wreak havoc on your project. At one organization where we worked, a high-powered consultant was allowed to code in Assembler, and he worked miracles by generating a huge amount of code in a short amount of time. Unfortunately, the miracle worker couldn't follow through. He departed for Cuba, leaving a half-finished debugging nightmare behind.

Remember, too, that the choices you make have financial consequences. At another organization, we saw a superb system that was developed on time and met all user requirements. Unfortunately, this system called for the use of a GUI that necessitated a minimum 90-megahertz Pentium with 16 megabytes of memory on every user desk. There went the development budget!

Selecting Your Hardware

In this modern age of technology, we are confronted with an enormous number of choices when selecting our hardware. Every vendor will categorically assure you that its hardware or RAID technology is the fastest, cheapest, and most reliable around. But not all vendors can be right. We are not going to debate what is the best hardware for your site, but will simply summarize some of the choices you will need to investigate and the questions you will need to ask to make this important decision.

Hardware Type

We're not experts in current-day computer hardware; when confronted with the responsibility of selecting hardware for a project, we always ask the following questions of the site:

Current hardware preferences
   What is the current computer(s) being used? Does the site have an affiliation with that hardware vendor? Can a special deal be struck on a machine trade-in and/or trade-up?

Current hardware expertise

What are the site's hardware strengths? Often the right technical people can make up for a seemingly inferior hardware selection. Do not be fooled by that old saying "We can always retrain our own people." Exploiting your current knowledge base is much easier than training and/or replacing people.

Strategic Oracle platforms

One of the drawbacks of Oracle's commitment to port its software to all hardware platforms is the fact that it cannot do this all at once. Obviously, the more popular ports are always first. This can mean that a less used hardware port could be as much as 6 to 12 months behind the latest Oracle release. This becomes very annoying when you hear those famous words: "Fixed in the next release."

Common Oracle platforms

Another valuable thing to look for when you select a hardware platform is strength in numbers. Why face all the hardships of breaking new ground and reporting each new problem? Wouldn't it be a lot nicer to know someone else has been there first and that a patch is ready and waiting for you? The more popular hardware platforms also seem to be better tested during the quality assurance (QA) phases because of the higher number of beta sites involved in the QA exercises for those platforms.

Application budget

An obvious issue to consider when choosing your hardware platform is your budget restrictions. This does not simply mean how much the hardware costs up front, but also its ongoing maintenance and its upgrade/expansion options. It is not unusual for an application to quickly exceed its initial hardware requirements. This can be as a result of poor capacity planning and simple changes in application scope. Whatever the reason, discovering that your initial hardware purchase has already "maxed out" and that you need to trade up to the next hardware level can be very embarrassing

Application lifetime

Another important issue to consider when selecting your hardware path is the expected lifespan and growth rate of the application. An application with a rapid growth in the user base or an expected data volume blowout needs to have an acceptable hardware upgrade path. Conversely, applications with a fixed user base and a readily determinable lifespan allow you to be more frugal about your hardware choices; you need only purchase hardware that meets today's requirements.

Hardware Configuration

Once the hardware platform has been decided, sites need to immediately begin hardware configuration planning. This should not be done after the hardware has been chosen but as part of the hardware decision process. For example, if you intend to use a RAID, this should be taken into account when choosing your hardware. Each platform offers its own variant of each hardware configuration, and some will be better suited to your application needs than others.

The following list details some of the more common configurations available for consideration:

RAID

> RAID technology has grown in leaps and bounds over the last few years and is becoming increasingly popular with Oracle applications. RAID offers a number of configuration levels, each providing an increasing level of redundancy at an equally increasing cost. Configurations can vary from low-level hardware implementations to more complicated volume manager software packages. You need to offset the cost of RAID against the level of safety. Note that the cost is not always in real dollars but can be at the expense of application performance.

Disk mirroring

> Disk mirroring is a very popular mode of application protection, but it is rather disk-intensive. Every database disk needs to be duplicated. Disk mirroring is also a very important hardware configuration parameter that needs to be considered when selecting your hardware platform. Budget aside, you need to be sure that your computer has sufficient disk mounts, disk control capacity, disk power suppliers, and so on.

Disk striping

> Disk striping is almost always coupled with mirrored disks to give all the protection and performance improvements of striped, mirrored technology with none of the RAID overhead. Hardware vendors all seem to provide their own style of disk striping. Some vendors insist on an odd number of disks within the stripe; others enforce restrictions on the size of the physical stripe. These parameters will influence your application's performance and ultimately your hardware decision. A disk striping configuration returns high performance at a high cost, in both dollars and hardware. Once again, you need to be sure that your hardware has sufficient capacity to cope with extra disk requirements.

Raw devices

Many UNIX sites favor operating their disks as raw devices. The use of raw devices means that Oracle can perform I/O directly to the disk rather than through the operating system disk cache. This can lead to dramatic I/O performance improvements but is generally regarded as harder to administer. Not all hardware vendors offer raw devices, and not all hardware vendors require their use. You will need to compile a concise set of possible application requirements before deciding on your hardware vendor.

Other

Many other technology choices need to be considered before you can proceed with your hardware selection, including:

- SMP (symmetric multiprocessing) and/or MMP (massively parallel processing)
- Parallel server
- Client-server (fat or thin)

We'll discuss these technologies later in the book.

Setting Up Screen and Report Templates

An important way of ensuring the continuity of system development is to make sure that templates (skeletons) of all screen styles and reporting modes are stored in default libraries. Ensure a senior staff member develops these skeletons after consulting with representatives of the user base that will be using the screens and reports.

Here are some of the key elements to consider in developing skeletons:

Module name

Include the module name in the header at the top of any screen or report, as shown in Figure 4-1. The program name allows modules to be identified easily—for example, when users need to communicate over the telephone. Also include the program version identifier when possible.

Program description

Include a program description in the header at the top of any screen or report. The description should identify as precisely as possible the function of the program that produces the screen or report. By setting up this description to be modifiable by users (stored in the database), you can allow individual users to customize their screens.

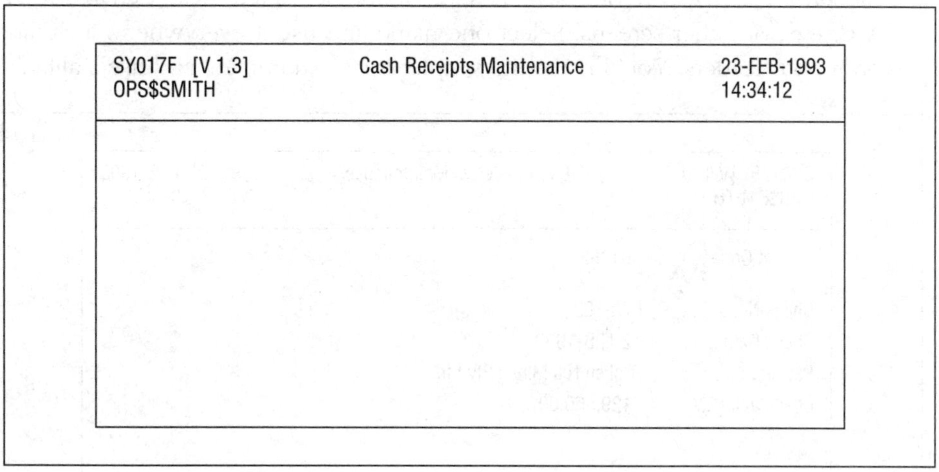

```
SY017F  [V 1.3]         Cash Receipts Maintenance        23-FEB-1993
OPS$SMITH                                                14:34:12
```

Figure 4-1. Sample screen header

Usercode

Include the database usercode in the header at the top of any screen or report. Including the usercode enables problems to be tracked and fixed more easily, and allows reports to be distributed to users.

Screen layout

Define common conventions for all screens displayed by the application(s) so that each screen has a common look and feel, as shown in Figure 4-2. This area of standards has grown in importance with the introduction of GUI development tools. Choices that you will need to make about the screen layout include:

- What colors can be used?

- What is the largest canvas I can design?

- When should I use model windows?

- What GUI tools are available? Examples include buttons, toolbars, scrollbars, checkboxes, radio groups, and list items.

- Should fields be left- or right-justified?

- How should numeric field displays be formatted?

- How should date displays be formatted?

- Should field prompts be left- or right-justified? Should they be followed by a colon?

Field naming

Establish strict guidelines for the naming of all fields. Fields must have consistent names from one module to the next. For example, a field that's called

ACCOUNT_CODE on one screen should not be called ACC_CODE, ACCT, A/C, etc., on other screens. Select one name and use it everywhere, including on report headers. You'll make life simpler for programmers and users alike.

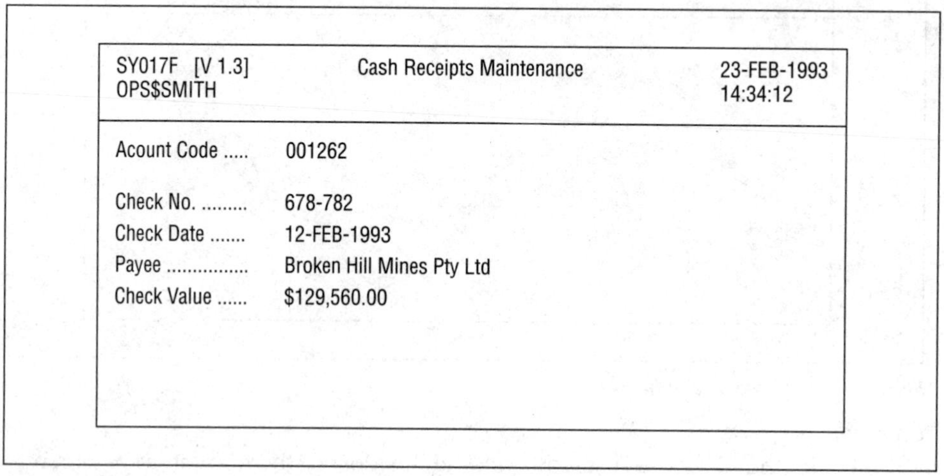

```
 SYO17F  [V 1.3]        Cash Receipts Maintenance          23-FEB-1993
 OPS$SMITH                                                 14:34:12

 Acount Code .....   001262

 Check No. .........  678-782
 Check Date .......  12-FEB-1993
 Payee ...............  Broken Hill Mines Pty Ltd
 Check Value ......  $129,560.00
```

Figure 4-2. Sample screen skeleton

Pop-up position

Anchor your layered pop-up windows at a common screen location, as shown in Figure 4-3. Windows at specific levels should all look the same from one module to the next.

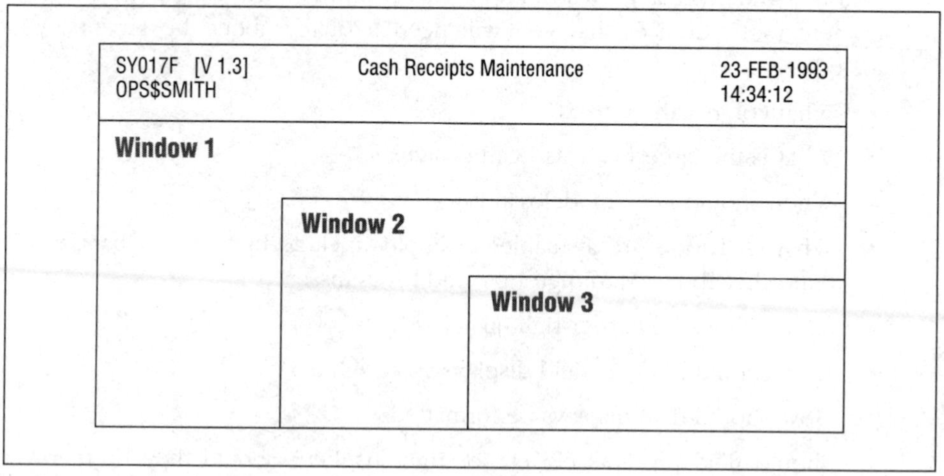

```
 SYO17F  [V 1.3]        Cash Receipts Maintenance          23-FEB-1993
 OPS$SMITH                                                 14:34:12

 Window 1

          Window 2

                    Window 3
```

Figure 4-3. Pop-up windows

Using Modular Programming Techniques

During this early standardization phase, make sure that all developers know how important it is to use modular programming techniques. Don't let them develop large, complex programs, even if these modules are going to perform miracles. It's in the interest of an efficient application to break all tasks down to their lowest manageable units. In addition to making programs easier to develop and test, the modular approach also allows applications to share software modules and build generic system libraries.

GUI applications are a good example of why modular programming is so important, as we show in Figure 4-4 and Figure 4-5. Rather than develop enormous, unmaintainable programs, we can build smaller, manageable windows and can link them to form complex user operations. This modular approach is completely invisible to the end user but enormously simplifies development. It also allows modules to be shared more easily and facilitates recursive functionality.

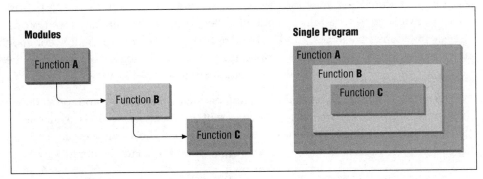

Figure 4-4. Modular versus single program

In addition to increasing the performance of application developers, modularization also increases run-time performance. As each function is exited, it releases individual module resources, so overall overhead is significantly reduced. In contrast, a program that contains all system functions has only two choices: release all of its resources at exit time, or release none of them.

Defining System Libraries

During the design phase, and continuing into the start of programming, a senior staff member, typically a senior analyst/programmer, needs to take responsibility for the defining and coding of the standard system libraries. These libraries are

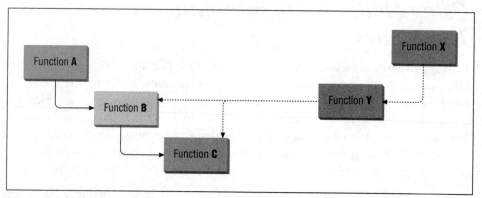

Figure 4-5: Modular programming

invaluable in speeding up the coding process, controlling application function-ality, and performing system-wide maintenance.

The introduction of Oracle7 has meant the coming of age of Oracle *system libraries*. We are finally able to move beyond the handful of local SQL*Forms and PL/SQL procedures and functions to which we were restricted in the past. Now we have available to us a fully integrated code-sharing environment. Stored proce-dures, functions, packages, and table triggers enable us to share common functionality across the entire application. Stored database objects can be accessed from any Oracle-compliant development tool.

Be sure to document all common stored packages, functions, and procedures, and make sure your entire programming staff is aware of what is available to them. If they don't know what has already been coded, how can they take advan-tage of them? There is nothing worse than developing sharable libraries only to find out that everyone has written their own.

Common system libraries are not just limited to stored database objects. Applica-tions (especially GUI applications) should exploit all system code-sharing possibilities for libraries. Application users should be involved in the initial GUI presentation drafts. Then a core development team should be deployed to design and implement skeletons. These skeletons can then be used for the remainder of the build phase to provide a common look and feel for the application.

Develop GUI skeletons at least for the following:

- Window headers and footers
- Standard item properties
- Common, sharable toolbars
- Visual attributes

- Application menus
- Standardized, consistent help interface

Enforcing Program Version Control

Because Oracle runs on so many platforms, no one version-control utility can handle all developer needs. As a consequence, developers frequently argue about which utility is best to use. For most platforms, there are several viable possibilities for version control. For example, UNIX provides SCCS and RCS, VMS supports CMS, and a number of proprietary utilities are available for MS-DOS. The important thing is that you select *one* version control system and stick with it.

Make sure that you are using a version-control utility that has won the trust of the people in your organization and that you enforce its use. We can't overemphasize how important it is to use version control, particularly when you are migrating your programs. We've seen many days and weeks of back-breaking development quickly disappear when an incorrect program migration erased all evidence of the correct version!

Many GUI development tools, SQL*Forms included, present a particular version control problem. Even a single, unimportant change within an application module—for example, changing the field sequencing within a block—can result in several hundred lines of altered code for the version control utility. Although not a single line of code has actually been changed (they have simply been resequenced), you'll have to wade through a maddening amount of output.

Establishing Documentation Standards

Everybody complains about documentation—writing it and using it. But don't underestimate its importance. The standardization phase is the time to draw up a documentation methodology and establish a uniform style of presentation for all documentation of programs, screens, reports, etc. Now is also the time to select the products you'll be using for word processing and other documentation tasks. Make sure that everybody on the project team knows what is expected of them in terms of documenting whatever design or code they are responsible for, what products they are to use, and where the documentation is to be stored. You should also consider hiring professional technical writers to assist in this task.

These are the documentation areas you'll need to standardize:

- Program specifications: how to present them
- Program functionality: how to present it
- Unit testing: plans and results

- Module testing: plans and results

- System testing: plans and results

- User modifications: what's allowed and how to report them

- Bugs: how to report them

- Migration: what the plans are

- Version control: what type and how to enforce it

Establishing Database Environment Standards

It's important that you select and create database environment standards during the early stages of application development. By database environment standards, we mean how the database is going to be structured, both internally and externally. You'll need to address and resolve (if possible) these issues before any program development commences:

Database SID

> The first thing we need to do during this stage is to create a new database instance. What is the SID going to be called? We have worked with a wide variety of database SID naming standards. They have ranged from Norse gods to the Seven Dwarfs. As silly as this may sound, at least some standard was in place, and we knew what was expected.

Disk layout

> Which disks are allocated to database files? How many disks do we have, and how can they be best used? In allocating database disks, an increasingly common problem is the misuse of volume managers. Logical disk volumes are spread across several physical disk partitions. This may add a little interest to the system administrator's day but can result in disaster for the DBA. We always insist that each logical disk be mapped one-to-one to a physical disk (unless RAID or striping is being used).

> If your platform is constrained to a maximum partition size that is smaller than the addressable disk size, try to show some common sense when naming the mount points. For example, a 4-gigabyte disk may need to be partitioned into two 2-gigabyte volumes. It gives an unsuspecting DBA a fighting chance of laying out his or her database in a recoverable manner. For example:

> /u20_A   *(Partition A of Disk u20)*
> /u20_B   *(Partition B of Disk u20)*

Database data file layout

After deciding on a SID identifier and disk-naming standard, you need to create a default database. How is the database to be structured? What do you called each datafile? Where do you place the datafiles?

As an initial database setup, we always insist on five default tablespaces. They are:

SYSTEM	/.../.../SID/SID_system01.dbf
RBS	/.../.../SID/SID_rbs01.dbf
TEMP	/.../.../SID/SID_temp01.dbf
TOOLS	/.../.../SID/SID_tools01.dbf
USERS	/.../.../SID/SID_users01.dbf

These tablespaces have an agreed-upon size, naming convention and disk allocation. The number (01) is included in the data file name to distinguish several data files for the one tablespace. Once this is completed, you can then add application tablespaces.

Large rollback segment

Preallocating rollback segments encourages developers to use them appropriately. Adopting one or more large rollback segments enables developers to use this rollback segment in their larger updating routines, as shown below:

```
SET TRANSACTION USE ROLLBACK SEGMENT rbs_large;
```

Tablespace structure

An application's tablespace structure should be designed for flexibility, simplicity, and I/O balance. Establish a minimum tablespace division of data and indexes. This allows for I/O spreading, recovery flexibility, and use of future technology (i.e., Oracle8 has introduced "index only" tablespaces). We like to always enforce a minimum tablespace division based on table and index, by application module.

GL_DATA	/.../.../SID/SID_gl_data01.dbf
GL_INDEX	/.../.../SID/SID_gl_index01.dbf
AP_DATA	/.../.../SID/SID_ap_data01.dbf
AP_INDEX	/.../.../SID/SID_ap_index01.dbf

Object-naming standards

You need to select and document naming standards before you create tables, indexes, packages, triggers, etc. This may seem to be a simple task, but sadly it's often overlooked. Naming standards need to include acceptable terminology and abbreviations. For example:

Description	-> Desc
Number	-> No
Supplier Number	-> Supp_No

It is always a good idea to get the users involved at this early stage to ensure that they use the correct terminology. Object-naming standards usually come down to personal preference. As long as they are agreed upon, documented, and enforced, their actual makeup is not important. Our preference is to prefix all objects with an application abbreviation and suffix them with their object type; we also like to avoid long, cumbersome table and column names. Just because you *can* use up to 30 characters does not mean that you *must!*

Table	-> GL_Wkly_Trans
Index	-> GL_Wkly_Trans_PK, GL_Wkly_Trans_U1
Trigger	-> GL_Wkly_Trans_T1
View	-> GL_Wkly_Trans_V
Sequence	-> GL_Wkly_Trans_Seq

Object structure

It's important to settle on a consistent object structure definition. This helps in performance, troubleshooting, and future maintenance. In particular, investigate INITIAL and NEXT extent sizes, as well as step-ups and ranges for PCTFREE and PCTUSED, PCTINCREASE, MINEXTENTS and MAXEXTENTS, and FREELISTS.

Security Standards

Every site needs to design, document, implement and enforce database security standards. Establish these standards at the beginning of a project, not at the end. The structure and enforcement can influence a number of key application design decisions. Some of the more common Oracle-specific security issues are listed below:

Usercode

How are the Oracle usercodes to be set up? Are all users going to use a single generic application user? Does every user have his or her own password, or will operating system OPS$ password validation be used? Are remote client-server connections allowed and, if so, how will they be tracked?

Resource profiles

Will your application resources be controlled by database-level resource profiles? These profiles act as resource governors, preventing run-away and/or rogue processes and terminating idle database connections. They can prove very handy during the development and QA cycle of your application. Setting these profiles down to very low thresholds, we are able to immediately identify potentially poor SQL and/or long-running processes that may need to be readdressed.

Access roles

Developers need to decide on role-naming standards, access levels, and default privileges. Application object ownership can also influence and be determined by your particular implementation of roles. For example, table SELECT privileges may be controlled via roles, whereas accessing those tables within local objects (views, packages, procedures, functions, triggers, and packages) isn't possible via roles. The DBA needs to grant explicit SELECT privileges to the usercode in question.

Archive mode

Is the production database going to operate in archive mode? Should the development and QA database also be placed in archive mode to simulate production conditions? Whether databases are in or out of archive mode has a direct influence on application backup strategies. This, in turn, influences the batch-processing window(s) and how we design our own long-running jobs.

Performance Standards

The final area that we like to standardize before proceeding with an application's development is performance guidelines and good programming practices. This may sound complicated, but it's actually quite simple. Assemble your best technical people in a room for a few hours and pick their brains about their past experiences. Compile a quick list of do's and don'ts. Couple these with the best programming practices, and you'll end up with a substantial and very valuable book of technical programming standards recommendations. Remember that what is obvious to you might need to be spelled out for the less-experienced members of your team. Formalizing your organization's experience in a single document will pay for itself many times over.

The following list covers some of the more productive performance standards. For further information on this information, consult the relevant sections of this book.

Expected response times

It is always a good practice to negotiate an agreed-upon goal for response time. This gives the developers an understanding of what is expected while enlightening the users on what is possible. Normally we aim to meet response times of the following magnitude:

On-line processing:	Less than 2.5 seconds for 95% of transactions.
	Less than 10 seconds for 100% of transactions.
Reporting:	Less than 3 minutes for 95% of background reports.
Overnight reporting:	All reports finished before start of business next day.

Explicit cursors

Always encourage your programmers to use explicit cursors. Explicit cursors are defined within the DECLARE section of the PL/SQL block and require a little more programming effort than implicit cursors. Implicit cursors perform a second database fetch for every cursor execution. This second fetch is unnecessary and can be avoided. The associated resource overheads are minimal, but they do exist. The use of explicit cursors is especially important for client-server applications.

Exploiting the trigger WHEN clause

Programmers and DBAs need to be aware of the potential overhead associated with database triggers. Triggers are held within the database in an uncompiled state (until Oracle7.3) and need to be parsed and compiled on every execution. This overhead is often unnecessary. Exploiting the WHEN portion of a trigger definition can prevent much unnecessary processing. The WHEN clause is stored in compiled form as part of the database trigger header and is executed before the trigger body. This means that a well-constructed WHEN clause can mean the difference between an unnecessary execution of the trigger and no execution at all.

Favoring procedures, functions, and packages over triggers

Replace large triggers with stored procedures, functions, or packages. The modified trigger simply performs a call to the stored object that contains the code. This helps to cut down on repeated, unnecessary PL/SQL parsing of the trigger text.

Thin and/or fat clients

Plan carefully before you begin your client-server application. Developers need to be aware of the traps and pitfalls that are associated with client-server technology and tutored on how to avoid them. In addition, programmers need to know whether the destination client-server environment is meant to be *fat* or *thin* and how this will influence the structure and execution of their code.

Build the database schema first

Every application should go through a logical design phase. The logical design is then transposed into a physical database design. (The physical design involves tables, indexes, constraints, etc.) The physical schema needs to be in place before programming begins. Although the schema will not be final at this point, a significant portion of it will be stable. DBAs who believe that they can add indexes, primary keys, constraints, and referential integrity just before the launch date are in for a rude awakening!

Exploit SQL hints

Developers need to be educated on how to exploit SQL hints for better statement performance. This area includes how to debug, tune, and benchmark SQL statements.

Pin large database objects into the SGA

Large stored procedures and packages should be pinned into the SGA at database startup. This moves the overheads associated with object parsing and compiling from the calling program to the startup procedure. It will generate noticeable application performance improvements.

Regular code walkthroughs

With the evolution of relational database technology and SQL-based data interfaces, less and less emphasis is being placed on the structure, consistency, and maintainability of our code. Initial program coding is only the first phase of a program's life cycle. Be sure that your code adheres to application standards, is well documented, and is easily maintainable. Regular code walkthroughs help to achieve this goal, especially for the newer members of your team.

INIT.ORA parameters

We are amazed at the number of applications that are battling the evils associated with default database installations. A few minutes spent tuning a handful of INIT.ORA parameters can outperform months and months of programmer tuning. DBAs must be just as diligent with the development and QA database environments as they are with the production. Protecting programmers from performance problems will make their own jobs a lot easier.

III

Tuning for Designers and Analysts

Part III describes what Oracle system designers and analysts need to know about tuning: how can you best design your data model for performance, how far should data normalization go and when can you improve performance by denormalizing data, what is the special role of indexes in improving database design?

5

Designing for Performance

Your design is the foundation of your application. As with any construction, if your foundation is weak, your construction is doomed to failure. This chapter helps you put a design in place that will provide your users with ongoing acceptable response times. Chapter 12, *Tuning Parallel Server*, Chapter 13, *Tuning Parallel Query*, Chapter 14, *Tuning Database Backup and Recovery*, Chapter 15, *Tuning Long-Running Jobs*, and Chapter 16, *Tuning in the Client-Server Environment* all provide additional design information. We recommend that you read these other chapters to complement the information provided in this chapter.

Common Design Problems

Before we discuss how to put an effective design in place, let's reflect on the most common design problems that occur at sites that experience performance problems. Here are some examples of potential problems:

- Translating a logical data model directly to a physical data model. It is very rare for a fully normalized data model to provide adequate performance. If too much code is produced against a normalized model with no thought given to performance, the time needed to undo the code can be considerable.

- Having an inadequate knowledge of how to produce a tuned data model. Some sites don't have the necessary skills to tune the design. This chapter helps to overcome this problem.

- Having a design that will have both online users and long-running batch jobs concurrently accessing the same tables and indexes and within the same database. There is not a database product in the world today that can provide acceptable response times when batch jobs thrash disks and flood memory that online users are sharing.

- Designing programs in a "storybook" fashion, rather than a modular fashion. The storybook approach produces large programs that often contain logic that is repeated across several other programs.

- Incorrect, inadequate, or overuse of indexes.

- A lack of review from a performance perspective. Many project leaders are single-minded about meeting a deadline and have no concern for performance. They develop the application with the attitude that they'll simply add a few indexes after the application is placed into production. Many of these applications fail because, although they've met a deadline, they are unworkable for the end users. The amount of rework to make the system perform often means that the time taken to achieve a workable system is considerably longer than it would be if the application had been checked for performance all through the development life cycle.

- Inadequate analysis of data volumes, data distribution, and transaction peaks and troughs. To be able to produce the required response times, you must have a thorough understanding of how your programs will be used and the amount of work that the programs will be required to perform.

- Producing reports on a totally normalized database. A large number of sites have problems getting their overnight reporting requirements through within their allocated time window. The reports scan many millions of rows and run for many hours to produce a report that could have been produced in a few seconds had a denormalized running total table been maintained in the database.

- Not envisaging the ad hoc requirements of your database. Many development teams promise ad hoc access to the production database without putting any thought into the effect that such access may have on online user response times.

- Inappropriate use of programming products. A common example is the situation in which client-server forms have been developed with no use of stored packages, procedures, functions, and triggers. The amount of network traffic ends up destroying all reasonable response times.

- Not designing to suit your configuration or architecture. A typical example is the situation in which a site uses an option such as parallel server without a thorough understanding of the need to design the application to avoid damaging locking across instances.

- Not allowing for increased system usage. The application design must be tuned to allow for the table's sizes and the number of users that the application will have, not what it has on the first day of going into production.

- Making use of "bleeding edge" technology. Leave the use of unproven products and technologies to the research areas, rather than using your production users as test cases.

Choosing an Architecture

Oracle offers the following major architectural choices:

- Unitary architecture
- Client-server architecture
- Parallel server architecture
- Distributed database architecture
- Multithreaded server architecture

Each architectural option has its own performance implications, which you need to consider before using. Selecting an inappropriate architecture can reduce your chance of providing adequate response times to your users. Don't be a pioneer. Use a tried and true architecture.

We strongly recommend that you take advantage of such industry advances as operating system striping, mirroring, and multiprocessor architecture. They help to improve the performance of all of the architecture options we've mentioned. You should also have a thorough understanding of Oracle's parallel query option, documented in Chapter 13, *Tuning Parallel Query*.

Unitary

The unitary architecture runs your application on a single computer. The computer can use multiple processors and disk performance enhancing facilities such as RAID technology. Many unitary systems have a maximum number of processors and memory, which you must become familiar with. You will often find that the maximum number of processors that can be used effectively is far fewer than the maximum that can be installed. If scalability is a factor, be careful that you don't find yourself running out of resources.

On a unitary system, the Oracle code is stored once, the application code is stored once, and there is a single database. The unitary solution is the easiest to administer. It is also still the most widely used architecture and has a tried and true performance record. However, the unitary architecture has the disadvantage of not providing the GUI interface that most new applications are demanding. The unitary option is usually not the most cost-effective option. If you have a plan to develop using unitary architecture, there is no guarantee that the application will run well if it's later transferred to client-server. (This is because the transfer of packets in the unitary environment is not a factor.)

Client-Server

With a client-server architecture, the users are on a separate machine from the one on which the database instance resides. The architecture involves processor-to-processor communication through a network, which is the weakest performance link. Client-server architecture is usually the most cost-effective type of architecture, and cheaper upgrade paths are available if you need to scale upward. It gives you the freedom to choose client machines from many vendors. You can also configure client machines to best suit the function being performed. Using client-server architecture can also help you to overcome CPU and memory bottlenecks. However, it might not help with disk I/O bottlenecks.

The biggest disadvantage of using client-server is that it requires additional knowledge of how to code to avoid excessive network traffic. Network traffic that is too high may cause severe degradation in response time. To achieve acceptable performance, you will need to take advantage of stored packages, procedures, functions, database triggers, and constraints. Other problems with client-server architecture include the amount of effort required to distribute Oracle and application code and the skills required that your staff will need to support the different operating systems.

For detailed information about this architecture, see Chapter 16, *Tuning in the Client-Server Environment.*

Parallel Server

With the parallel server architecture, there are multiple instances accessing a single database. Although the instances may reside on a single computer, they usually reside on different computers. Both machines are cabled to the shared disks. Parallel server applications are suited to CPU-intensive applications, not disk I/O-intensive applications. They are also suited to applications that are query-intensive. Applications that run well with this architecture are those that allow the users on one instance to access one set of tables, while another instance accesses a separate set of tables. For example, you may have all of your Oracle Financials users on one instance on machine A and the personnel application users accessing the personnel tables through the other instance.

With parallel server, the biggest performance concern is cross-instance locking. Cross-instance locking can cause continual writing of blocks to disk as one instance requests a row that is in the group of blocks that the other instance has modified. The row might not be the same row that the other instance has changed. Do not use parallel server without benchmarking your applications. If used incorrectly, it can cause abysmal response times. If used correctly, however, it can provide excellent performance as well as a degree of recoverability. If one machine is lost, the instance can be started on the second machine and thus keep the database running.

For detailed information about this architecture, see Chapter 12.

Distributed Database

The distributed database architecture can be very cost-effective. A distributed database can overcome memory, I/O, and CPU bottlenecks by splitting the load across machines that are strategically located at distributed locations. They can also provide excellent scalability. The disadvantage of such an architecture is the administration overhead to maintain the Oracle and application code and the local databases. Transferring reference data can also be a concern, although snapshot logs function well for reference data.

The biggest performance concern with this architecture is the amount of data that must be passed between the various databases and the locking problems. If the site accesses and updates 99.5% of its local data and 0.5% of the distributed data, it can be made to work well. If you update and access more than 10% of your data in other locations, it can cause terrible locking and performance problems. It is common to have a combination of client-server and distributed database architectures with a GUI frontend being used against a local database.

For detailed information about this architecture, see Chapter 12.

Multithreaded Server

In the multithreaded server architecture, many users share a number of server processes. In Oracle terms, you may have 2,000 users logged on to an Oracle database. (In fact, the Oracle database may have only 100 users (server processes) logged on, but each server process is servicing 20 end users.) The biggest advantage of using the multithreaded server is its scalability. It allows 2,000 or more users to fit onto a machine that would usually have memory to service only 300 users. However, it can't help applications that are CPU- or disk I/O-bound. From a performance perspective, you must benchmark the number of users that one server process can handle. The earlier versions of the multithreaded server allowed very few processes per server, which made the product unusable. The later releases of the product show significant improvements.

If you use the multithreaded server, be aware that any performance degradation in your database creates a traffic jam situation. If one user is seeing poor performance, all of the users using the same server as that user have to wait for the user to complete the transaction. In other words, all of your transactions tend to perform only as well as your worst-running transaction.

Tuning Your Data Model

The most fundamental part of tuning your Oracle system is to make sure at the outset that your data model is well structured and normalized. If your tables and columns are not initially structured in a way that enforces simplicity and efficiency, your applications are doomed to failure. The most powerful hardware, the most sophisticated software, and the most highly tuned data access and programs won't succeed in manipulating your database in an acceptable amount of time.

In nonrelational databases—those based on hierarchical or network models—structures and programs are designed and implemented as a unit. The relational data model is different. Designing according to a relational model is both simpler and more powerful than designing according to one of the older models. With a relational design, you can design the database as a completely separate step from the design of the procedures that access these structures. The physical design of the database can be completed and verified before any procedural design begins.

There are four important rules to follow in designing your database and making sure your design goals become reality:

- Develop a sound and thorough database design, as well as a comprehensive overall system design, before you allow any coding to begin.

- Monitor carefully how well your logical data model (e.g., the abstract definition of the data your system needs and how the data is to be structured into tables) can be translated to a physical data model (e.g., the actual tables and their arrangement in the data files).

- Test, test, test! Throughout detailed design and coding, keep testing to be sure that your design is a sound one, and make adjustments for performance as needed.

- Make sure that you coordinate your efforts with others at your site. Because the DBA is so often aware of database performance issues, he or she can lend expertise to the design effort. And because programmers have experience in coding around bad design decisions, they too can provide input to the overall design.

Although the goal of any relational database system is a fully normalized database, performance is sometimes at odds with the abstractions of normalization. This chapter describes situations in which you'll get much better performance out of your system by denormalizing certain tables in your database.

Indexes are an important part of the design effort, as we discuss later in this chapter. Too often, designers don't take the time to index. The section in Chapter 6, *Tuning SQL*, called "Using Indexes to Improve Performance" supplements our discussion here by describing how indexes affect the performance of your SQL statements.

Database Definitions: A Quick Review

We assume, in this book, that you know at least the basics about relational databases and how data is structured and handled in such a system. There are many excellent books on relational design, including, of course, the classic works of E.F. Codd and C.J. Date. We do think it might be helpful to include some brief definitions of the terms that underlie any discussion of database design:

Entity
> An entity is any person, place, or thing in your system. For example, an entity might be an employee, a location of a branch office, or an invoice in a financial system. You define these entities in the form of tables.

Table
> A table is the basic unit of data storage in the database. A table is a uniquely named, two-dimensional array made up of columns and rows. A table may represent a single entity in your system (e.g., bank accounts), or it may represent a relationship between two entities in your system (e.g., the relationship between a bank account and the prevailing interest rate). In formal relational database language, a table is called a *relation*.

Column
> A column is one attribute of an entity (e.g., name, interest rate, or homeroom number). A column has a unique name within a table. Columns within a table are nondecomposable, that is, they can't be broken down further. Columns are arranged in an arbitrary order; that is, their order is not significant. Typically, the number of columns in a table remains constant over time.

Row

A row is a unique entry within a table (e.g., one student, one order, or one bank account). A row contains the actual data describing the student, order, or account. A row is equivalent to a *record*. Because row data often change over time, rows, unlike columns, are dynamic. Rows within a table are also arranged in an arbitrary order; their order is not significant.

Primary Key

A primary key is a column (or a group of columns) within a table that can be used to uniquely identify a row in that table. The choice of primary keys is a very important design decision. Meaningful primary keys simplify the relationships between tables and increase the performance of your applications.

Every table must have a primary key. All of the other columns in the table depend on the primary key. If a primary key consists of more than one column, it is known as a *composite*, or *concatenated*, key. It is not always easy to identify a primary key in a file. According to Third Normal Form (see the definition below), a key must satisfy these three rules to qualify as a primary key:

- The primary key must uniquely identify each row in the table. For example, a student identification number uniquely identifies each row in the student table because each student has a unique ID.

- If a primary key consists of more than one column, each column of the concatenated primary key is required to uniquely identify each row. For example, a primary key might be a homeroom number. Because a particular school has several buildings, with duplicate room numbers, you must know the building number as well as the room number. The composite primary key is the combination of these two numbers.

- Each row can be uniquely identified by only one primary key. If the student ID is the primary key, only the student ID identifies the student. There must be no other unique ID in the rows of the student table.

Foreign key

A foreign key is a column (or, for a composite key, a group of columns) in one table that corresponds to a primary key in another table. Foreign keys are used to show relationships between tables. For example, each row in a student table contains information about one student. One column in the student table is the student's homeroom (HMRM_NO). A second table, the homeroom table, contains one row for each homeroom in a school. HMRM_NO is the primary key in the homeroom table. In the STUDENT table, the corresponding HMRM_NO column is the foreign key.

Association

An association is a relationship between entities. Several different types of relationships may exist, as shown in Figure 5-1. The three basic types are:

- *One-to-one (1:1).* For example, an employee can have one, but only one, spouse defined in the employee table.

- *One-to-many (1:M).* For example, an employee can have many children defined in the children table.

- *Many-to-many (M:M).* For example, a company can produce many parts. A part can be produced by many companies. Companies and parts are in a many-to-many relationship.

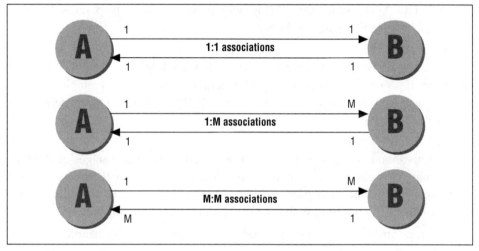

Figure 5-1. Types of associations

Attribute

An attribute is a characteristic or a quality of an entity or an association. For example, an attribute of a employee ID might be that it is in the range 1–100. An attribute of a student might be the student name.

Prime table

A prime table is a core application table around which an application revolves (e.g., EMP in a personnel system, LOAN_MASTER in a credit union system).

Dependent table

A dependent table is a table that cannot exist on its own. It has a composite (multicolumn) primary key, at least part of which is the primary key of a prime table. For example, the PURCHASE_ORDER table has a purchase order as its key. The dependent table, PO_LINE_ITEMS, has PO/ITEM_NUM as its key and cannot contain records that do not have a corresponding prime table record.

Associative table

An associative table is a table that links two tables together (e.g., parts and suppliers). The PARTS table is a prime table; the SUPPLIERS table is a prime table, and the PARTS/SUPPLIERS table links which parts are available from a single supplier or which supplier a part can be purchased from.

History table

A history table usually contains a date column (and possibly a time column) as part of a composite primary key. A history table for a supplier might be SUPPLIER/DATE/PART/QTY. This would simply list all parts sold by a supplier since the company began.

Recursive table

A recursive table is a table that has a foreign key that actually references other rows from the same table. For example, suppose every employee has a manager who is also an employee. The MGR_CODE is a foreign key to the same EMP table.

Normalization

Normalization is a term that is heard often during the early stages of database design. It is the process of breaking down all items to their lowest level, making sure that each piece of data can be uniquely identified and is not duplicated. There are three basic principles of data normalization:

- A normalized table does not contain any redundant information.

- A normalized table does not contain any repeating columns.

- A normalized database contains only the tables necessary to define the data.

Normalization is the ideal in any relational system, although as we discuss later in this chapter, it is necessary in certain circumstances to violate some of the principles of normalization to increase performance.

First Normal Form (1NF)

Putting data in First Normal Form means arranging data in separate tables in which the data in each table is similar and each table has a primary key. Each attribute can be represented by an individual value. 1NF tables cannot have any attribute with multiple values; in other words, repeating groups are not allowed. Figure 5-2 illustrates First Normal Form.

SUP#	POSTCODE	CITY	PART#	QUANTITY
GM	2000	Melbourne	P100	300
GM	2000	Melbourne	P200	200
GM	2000	Melbourne	P300	400
GM	2000	Melbourne	P400	200
GM	2000	Melbourne	P500	100
GM	2000	Melbourne	P600	100
FORD	1000	Sydney	P100	300
FORD	1000	Sydney	P200	400
TOYO	1000	Sydney	P200	200
TOYO	2000	Melbourne	P200	200
CHEV	2000	Melbourne	P400	300
CHEV	2000	Melbourne	P500	400

Figure 5-2. First Normal Form

Second Normal Form (2NF)

> Putting data in Second Normal Form means removing data that depend on only part of the key. Each row of a table must be uniquely identified by key value(s) within the row. In a table, every 2NF non-key attribute must be fully dependent on the primary key. Figure 5-3 illustrates Second Normal Form.

Third Normal Form (3NF)

> Putting data in Third Normal Form means eliminating everything in tables that does not depend on a primary key. Each row attribute must be identified only by the key value(s); that is, every non-key column is solely dependent on the primary key. Figure 5-4 illustrates Third Normal Form.

Fourth Normal Form (4NF)

> This form is identical to 3NF, but some non-key attributes have multivalued dependencies, independent of other attributes. For example, consider the example in Figure 5-5; MVD is a multivalued dependency.

Normalizing a Database

Normalizing a database is a straightforward, but rather detail-oriented, process. A detailed discussion of normalization is beyond the scope of this book. However, because normalization is basic to designing a high-performance system, we've included some summary information here on the normalization steps, just as a

SUP#	POSTCODE	CITY
GM	2000	Melbourne
FORD	1000	Sydney
TOYO	1000	Sydney
CHEV	2000	Melbourne
HYUN	3000	Perth

SUP#	PART#	QUANTITY
GM	P100	300
GM	P200	200
GM	P300	400
GM	P400	200
GM	P500	100
GM	P600	100
FORD	P100	300
FORD	P200	400
TOYO	P200	200
TOYO	P200	200
CHEV	P400	300
CHEV	P500	400

Figure 5-3. Second Normal Form

SUP#	CITY
GM	Melbourne
FORD	Sydney
TOYO	Sydney
CHEV	Melbourne
HYUN	Perth

CITY	POSTCODE
Perth	3000
Melbourne	2000
Sydney	1000

Figure 5-4. Third Normal Form

reminder. Refer to more detailed references on relational design for complete information.

- Identify all of the entities that make up your system, and organize them into tables.

- Identify all of the relationships between the entities in your system. Add to your tables as necessary, or create new tables that express these relationships.

- Identify all of the attributes of the entities in your system. Add to your tables as necessary, or create new tables that express these attributes.

Within each of these steps, there are several substeps, described in the sections that follow.

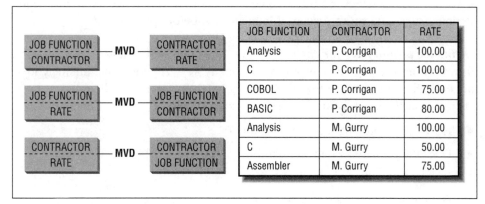

Figure 5-5. Fourth Normal Form

NOTE   In addition to these abstract design steps, remember that you must always test every system model with real sample data. By testing your design on current, real data, you'll find that you can often avoid obvious and costly omissions and duplications in your data. This involves obtaining such items as purchase orders and other forms, and making sure that every field on these forms is covered in your data analysis.

Defining entities

An entity is any person, place, or thing in your system. Entities are related to each other and have attributes. During this first phase of analysis, determine which entities are within the scope of the system or within a particular module of the system. Remember that you do not necessarily need to include every known piece of information in your database tables. For example, there might be a great deal of information that could be maintained on every student who attends a university. However, not every piece of data might need to be included in your database tables—only data that need to be available for retrieval or processing. If you aren't sure what falls in the scope of your system, verify your initial database design by running your application against sample data. The steps in the following sections explain how to define the entities in your system.

Identify all entities in your system. Entities may be tangible (employees, trucks) or intangible (departments, budgets). To be defined as an entity, an entity must exist in or by itself and must not be dependent upon, or subordinate to, other entities. You must construct a table describing each entity in your system. Often, minor entities do not become apparent until they are identified as attributes of initial entities. Whenever you become aware of the existence of a new entity during analysis, be sure to record it immediately, before proceeding.

Define the primary key for each entity. By definition, an entity—and the table that represents that entity—must have a primary key. The key must uniquely identify each element of the entity. The primary key can never be null and must never change over time. Ask yourself these questions:

- How can the key be uniquely identified?

- Does the primary key always exist?

- Is there only one primary key?

- Is there only one entity per primary key?

- Is the primary key subject to change?

Don't define as a primary key any data whose contents have embedded or implied meaning—sometimes known as an intelligent key. If you want to define such a key, break it down into its component parts, and define the whole as a composite key. For example, instead of defining as a primary key an account number whose individual columns have significance, define individual REGION_ID, CATEGORY, and SEQUENCE_NO columns, all making up a composite ACCOUNT_ID.

Verify the scope of the entities. Using simple sample data, test the scope, or domain, of the entity. You need to figure out the values, or range of values, that are valid for each entity. Here we are talking about logical testing, not the thorough testing of the database and code you'll perform later on. At this point, make sure that your sample data thoroughly test the limits of your domain (for example, the smallest value, the largest value). During this step, define the scope by specifying values or ranges for each entity, as in the following:

DATE_OF_BIRTH
    Make sure the date is not in the future.

EMP_NO
    Make sure employee numbers are in the range 1000 through 9999 available for this organization.

LOC_KEY
    If there are currently 250 locations for this organization, make sure this field is three digits.

Document your findings. Document all findings, restrictions, and limitations that you discover while you are defining entities. If you're using a formal design methodology such as a CASE tool, most of this documentation will be created automatically. If you're using other, less sophisticated methods, you should keep a project notebook that documents your findings, in accordance with your own organization's standards. (Refer to Chapter 4, *Defining System Standards.*) Remember that if a point is worth noticing, it must be worth remembering, even if all you are doing is noting that a particular topic needs to be revisited and rehashed at a later date. For each entity, you document, at the very least:

- The name of the table
- The primary key
- The set of sample data you used for testing

All of this information will be invaluable during later, more detailed design phases.

Defining relationships

Once you have defined all entities in your system in tables, determine exactly what relationships exist between these entities. Then verify all relationships by testing with sample data, as directed in the following sections.

Identify all relationships. Relationships are direct, logical associations between two or more entities that have already been defined. Not every relationship needs to be stated, only those of concern to your system. One possible relationship is that between a student table and a homeroom table. Another is that between a bank account table and an interest rate table.

Determine each relationship type. What is the type of relationship? As we've mentioned, the following are supported:

- One-to-one (1:1)
- One-to-many (1:M)
- Many-to-many (M:M)

Verify the scope of the relationships. Verify that all of the relationships you've defined are actually relevant to your system. Verify that the association has been correctly identified (1:1, 1:M, M:M). This can be proven only with real sample data, provided by your users. For example, suppose you have specified a one-to-one relationship between an employee and her children. If there are two children in the test data, the relationship will fail. You'll need to specify a 1:M relationship instead. Test data may raise other questions as well about this relationship. What happens if an employee has twins? Will the relationship break down (along with the employee!)? Do you need to put an expanded primary key in the CHILDREN table to qualify child sequencing? Is the relationship actually of any importance to the system? These are the kinds of questions that should come up when you are logically testing a relationship.

Document your findings. Document all findings, restrictions, and limitations of each relationship. For each relationship, define the keys (both primary and foreign) and any constraints on the keys (e.g., non-null). Include the set of sample data that you used in testing.

Defining attributes

Finally, you must define attributes (characteristics) for all entities and relationships. Derivable data (data that are calculated from existing data, such as the sum of other data, a running total, etc.) are not an attribute. Make sure that you don't include any derivable data in your original (normalized) database design. As we'll see later in this chapter, you may find that in certain situations, you will choose to include derivable data in particular tables to increase performance. However, during this initial stage, we are creating a fully normalized database design. Follow these steps:

Identify all attributes of your entities. An attribute is a characteristic or quality of an entity or a relationship of concern to the user. Attributes are simply pieces of information that you need to display, correlate, or maintain within the system. In theory, every column of a table is an attribute. Attributes can be directly related to entities (employee name), or associations (years an employee has been a member of a department).

Verify the scope of the attributes. Attributes must be of value to the user and the project. Again, sample data must be carefully correlated to demonstrate the correctness of the attribute. Attribute ownership is not always straightforward. It is normally during the defining of attributes that new (minor) entities and associations are discovered. These new attributes are attributes of the new entity. You'll need to keep looping through the normalization process until all entities, relationships, and attributes have been completely defined. Now the analysis phase should return to step 1: Define, record, and test the new entity and its associations, before proceeding.

Document your findings. Document all findings, restrictions, and limitations of each attribute. Include the set of sample data you used in testing.

Tuning Indexes

Indexes provide a powerful way to speed up the retrieval of data from an Oracle database. Yet indexes are often neglected as a performance tool by both designers and programmers. During the system design phase, analysts and designers typically spend many weeks, even months, identifying entities, relationships, and attributes. They extract primary keys, propagate foreign keys, and define one-to-one, one-to-many, and many-to-many relationships. These initial steps are vital, of course, to developing a sound database design. But designers too frequently omit one final step in database design: the defining of indexes. By defining and using indexes properly, you can get much better performance out of your Oracle system.

In theory, you should define all indexes during the system design phase, well before programming begins. If developers know what indexes exist, they will keep these retrieval paths in mind as they code; this will result in better-tuned programs. In practice, there will be cases in which developers discover that they can tune existing SQL statements by specifying indexes. Make sure developers know that they must check out all decisions with the DBA or project leader to avoid defining duplicate indexes or indexes that actually end up degrading system performance.

What Is an Index?

An index is a conceptual part of a database table that may be used to speed up the retrieval of data from that table. (Internally, Oracle uses a sophisticated, self-balancing B-tree index structure.) If an index is defined for a table, via a CREATE INDEX clause on a column of the table, the index associates each distinct value of a column with the rows in the table that contain the value.

Indexes provide a number of benefits. Indexed retrieval of data from a database is almost always faster than a full table scan. The Oracle optimizer uses the indexes defined for a table when it figures out the most efficient retrieval path for a query or update statement. (The optimizer is described in Chapter 6, *Tuning SQL.*) Oracle also uses indexes in performing more efficient joins of multiple tables. Another benefit of indexes is that they provide a way to guarantee the uniqueness of the primary key in a table. (You must create an index with the UNIQUE option if you want to enforce uniqueness.)

When is an index helpful? If one or two columns in your table are the most likely to be used as criteria for retrieval, those are the columns you'll want to index. For example, consider an employee rating system in which employee performance is rated on a one-to-ten scale.

```
SELECT name, dept, rating
FROM   emp
WHERE  rating = 10;
```

To speed up the retrieval of employees with the highest ranks, you might want to create an index on the RATING column. Without an index, the application will have to scan through every row of the table until it finds matches.

You can index any column in a table except those defined with data types of LONG or LONG RAW.

Indexes are not all equal. Large numbers of indexes specified over stable tables that mainly perform queries are not as resource-hungry as are those that are specified over volatile tables. In general, indexes are most useful when they are specified on large tables. If small tables are frequently joined, however, you'll find that performance improves when you index these tables too.

Indexes aren't always the solution to database performance problems. Although indexes usually provide performance gains, there is a cost to using them. Indexes require storage space. They also require maintenance. Remember that every time a record is added to or deleted from a table, and every time an indexed column is modified, the index(es) itself must be updated as well. This can mean four or five extra disk I/Os per INSERT, DELETE, or UPDATE for a record. Because indexes incur the overhead of data storage and processing, you can actually degrade response time if you specify indexes that you don't use.

Although it is wise not to create indexes unless your application can benefit from them, you should be aware that the internal overheads for indexes are not huge. We have done some benchmark testing that showed that a row could be inserted into the EMP table in less than 0.11 second. After we added eight indexes to the table (many more than are normally recommended), the row INSERT was increased to only 0.94 second. Although more than eight times the original overhead, this timing is still well within acceptable overall response time limits.

Some sites have firm standards controlling the maximum number of indexes that can be created for a table. This maximum is usually between four and six indexes per table. In reality, a hard-and-fast rule for indexes is unworkable. Our recommendation: Do keep the number of indexes over a single table to a minimum; but if an index is useful, and response times can be kept below the agreed-upon limit for your site, then don't hesitate to create the index. We know of a site that has created 16 indexes on a table! This particular table is actually an extract table that is downloaded from another application each night and can never be modified by the application, just queried. This is a case in which all of the indexes are useful and incur no ongoing overheads, only the initial overheads associated with creating the index and its required disk space.

An Indexing Checklist

These are the questions you'll need to answer before you assign any indexes. The section "Using Indexes to Improve Performance" in Chapter 6 explains the SQL performance reasons behind these choices.

Should I index the primary key of a table?

Is the primary key unique?
> If yes, define an index; indexes can enforce uniqueness.

Is the primary key used in table joins?
> If yes, define an index (usually).

What is the table's expected volume?
> If the volume is fewer than 250 items and not used within SQL JOIN statements, do not define an index. If the volume is greater than or equal to 250, or the table is used within SQL JOIN statements, define an index.

Should I index the foreign keys of a table?

Is the foreign key used as an online access path?
> If yes, ask the primary key questions. If no, do not define an index.

Is the foreign key used within table joins?
> If yes, define an index (usually).

Does the foreign key have an even table spread, or do the foreign key values in question (those needing to be queried) make up less than about 20% of the table?
> If yes, define an index. If no, an index may or may not help.

Is the foreign key frequently updated?
> If yes, the index will add overhead. If no, the index will add minimal overhead.

Is the foreign key usually part of a WHERE clause?
> If yes, define an index. If no, do not define an index.

Is the foreign key used in table joins?
> If yes, define an index.

Is the foreign key used for Version 7 referential integrity?
> If yes, define an index. If no, an index may or may not help.

Should I index composite columns of a table?

Will it give me improved data spread?
> Two or more columns can often be united to get better selectivity, which might not be available from the poorer data spread of individually indexed columns.

Are all queried columns indexed?

If all queried columns are held within the actual index, no database read is needed; this is particularly useful in SQL*Forms' list of values functions.

What is the table's expected volume?

If the table has many thousands of entries, extra indexes will help you to avoid lengthy full table scans.

Can index numbers be reduced by combining LIKE indexes?

Consider this example:

```
TABLE_IDX1 LOAN_NUM
TABLE_IDX2 LOAN_NUM TRAN_ID
```

These two indexes can be combined into one if the first index is non-UNIQUE. (Uniqueness will otherwise be lost):

```
TABLE_IDX2
```

How can you enforce the use of indexes?

Coordinate index definition and use with the DBA, the programmer, and the QA team.

How Many Indexes?

The actual number of indexes that makes sense for a table depends on the application and how the table is used in it. If a table is the hub of an application and is queried from many different directions, you'll have no choice but to define a large number of indexes for it. As we mention earlier in the section "What Is an Index?" some sites have firm, though often unworkable, standards for the maximum number of indexes that can be created for a table.

Here is an example of indexing a table that is vital to the work of the application. The EMPLOYEE_MASTER table is a core table. Most of the work of the application involves accessing and updating this table. You'll have to specify indexes if your users are going to be able to display online information quickly and in the desired format. The overhead incurred by all these indexes is clearly outweighed by the need to meet user requirements.

```
EMPLOYEE_MASTER
emp_no          INDEXED     PK
emp_name
emp_type        INDEXED     FK
emp_class
emp_sex
dept_code       INDEXED     FK
salary_grade    INDEXED     FK
salary_amt
date_of_birth
hire_date
```

```
next_of_kin
no_of_children
super_fund       INDEXED     FK
bank_account     INDEXED
marital_status
addr_line1
addr_line2
addr_line3
post_code
appraisal_due    INDEXED
home_phone
business_phone
tax_file_no      INDEXED
```

Oracle actually imposes its own internal controls on the number of indexes allowed. In any one SQL statement, Oracle evaluates a maximum of five indexes over each table. The system merges rows from each index and individually validates all other predicate conditions.

One way in which you can reduce the number of indexes specified over a table is to combine similar indexes. For example, suppose you need to specify these two indexes:

```
emp.emp_type
emp.emp_type, emp.emp_class
```

If EMP_TYPE is not a unique column of the EMP table, then you can omit the first index because Oracle will still use the first part of the second index if the second field is not referenced. If EMP_TYPE is a unique column, omit the second index. It is superfluous.

Using Indexes to Improve Performance

Developers can code their SQL statements to take best advantage of the indexes that have been specified for the tables in the application. The section "Using Indexes to Improve Performance" in Chapter 6 describes how Oracle uses indexes to help develop the most efficient execution plan and how you can modify your indexes to further tune SQL performance.

Testing the Data Model for Performance

Now that you have produced a normalized data model and added your indexes, you must investigate the resulting data model to ensure that it is workable from a performance perspective. There are a number of high-level goals that must be employed as part of your investigation:

- Every program must perform within the response times specified in the tuning service agreement for the site.

- You must minimize database activity without sacrificing functionality. System activity includes selects, inserts, updates, and deletes against your tables and indexes. The more indexes the tables have, the more work that needs to be performed to maintain them. Joining many tables usually creates more activity than joining fewer tables.

- Every program must have its design checked against the data model to ensure that it is able to provide the response times specified in the tuning service agreement.

- Every table must be questioned. Is it required? Does it need to be as large as specified? Could it be structured differently to provide better performance without sacrificing functionality.

- Every index must be checked. Is it required? Are any indexes missing?

Requirements for Tuning the Physical Data Model

To accurately check your data model's ability to produce acceptable performance, you need the background information listed below. You need clear documentation on the tables, columns, indexes, constraints, sizing, and detailed usage.

- A detailed physical data model diagram.

- The number of rows per table and the average size of the rows.

- All index and constraint information.

- All proposed database triggers and their functions.

- All program design specifications.

- Which programs are run at which times? How many users will be running each program?

- What are the transaction volumes per second in peak load times? Translate the transaction volumes into selects, inserts, updates and deletes against each of the tables.

- Documentation on purging strategies.

Program Performance Checking

Using the method documented below, you can check on a program's ability to perform without having to develop a prototype. Before you do this, it's essential that you have performed full normalization of your data model. Every program in your application must be checked against the data model because one untuned program has the ability to cause poor performance to all of your application users. Oracle provides development tools that allow you to rapidly produce prototypes to test an application's ability to perform acceptably against your normalized data model. We suggest that you perform ongoing checks on each program's performance as it moves through the development life cycle.

Most disks have a maximum disk I/O rate of 50+ per second. Sites usually have a standard that all online screens must return a response in 2.5 seconds or less. If this is translated into disk reads, no screen should access more than 125 disk reads.

In Figure 5-6, if the account balance calculation reads more than 125 transaction rows, the response time is not likely to be maintained. This is an oversimplification of what actually happens, but it's an excellent starting point. It assures you that the screen will be at least be able to operate with acceptable response times in single-user mode.

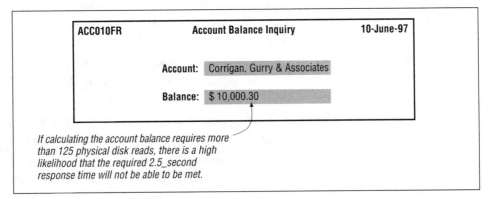

Figure 5-6. Account balance inquiry

When the program moves into production, multiple users will be accessing the same disk as the disk from which the account transactions are being read. The data file containing the disk that contains the tables and indexes may also be striped across several disks. There is also some likelihood that the data being read may already reside in the buffer cache in memory.

Tell-Tale Signs of an Untuned Data Model

Data models that provide poor performance have a number of common characteristics, which we list below. We don't mean to suggest that if any of the characteristics in the list do exist, you will definitely have poor performance. But as you are designing your programs, check to make sure that these common problems won't cause your programs to provide poor performance.

- *One-to-one relationships.* Strict logical data modeling can legitimately create one-to-one relationships. From a performance perspective, however, the one-to-one relationship causes an unnecessary table join. One valid use of a one-to-one relationship is when a table has many columns, one of which is a LONG datatype. If the LONG column rarely needs to be displayed online, the LONG could be stored in a separate table. Note that Oracle8 has a LONG tablespace type that speeds up processing of LONG columns.

- *Exceedingly large tables in an online transaction-processing application with many inserts, updates, and deletes per second.* The question must be asked: "Is it necessary for the application to generate such a large amount of activity?" Multiple rows are often inserted into a table when a single row could provide the same functionality. An example is when you may have a number of static transaction types, such as an administration fee, interest, bank fee, state tax, federal tax, and transaction amount. In such a case, five separate transaction rows could be inserted, with a transaction row for the administration fee, one for the interest, and so on. Each transaction type could be a separate column in a single table, and so only one row would need to be inserted.

- *Many SQL statements are required to join more than five tables.* This can often be remedied by introducing some denormalization into your data model using one or more of the methods described in the next section.

- *Your application has many SQL statements that include a SUM.* This is also often remedied by storing running totals, as we describe later in this chapter.

- *Your application has many SQL statements that contain a MAX or MIN in nested SELECTs.* This is usually cured by storing the latest of the earliest data redundantly in your data model.

- *All of your tables have only single-column indexes.* This usually causes long index scans and merges. It is rare to see a site at which a number of multiple column indexes would not provide significant performance improvements.

Denormalizing a Database

Normalization of data is always the goal of database design. In general, good design calls for a database that has no redundant data—that is, a database that is fully normalized. But a fully normalized database—one that stays normalized over time—is something of a Platonic ideal. In the real world, a world in which performance may be more important than abstract perfection, you may find that you need to compromise your commitment to normalization and be flexible about dealing with real data. In other words, you may need to embrace the necessary evil of denormalization.

You'll need to know how to denormalize in order to optimize certain types of transactions and to help achieve minimally acceptable physical response times on certain systems. In a number of cases, you can substantially improve response times (by reducing physical disk I/Os) by *not* enforcing system design to the Third Normal Form.

It's important to go about denormalization in the proper way. Make sure that the data model is fully normalized before you contemplate denormalization. And don't assume that you will always need to denormalize. Consider each case on its own merits. Some of the aspects of system operation that you'll have to consider are data volumes, query frequency, update frequency, and minimum required retrieval times.

When should you denormalize? There are a number of situations in which you may improve performance by denormalizing your data. If you find that your application is performing repetitive SQL table joins and sort/merges on large tables, you may be able to avoid or reduce the need for these operations if you denormalize some parts of your database.

Denormalization isn't a panacea. Whenever you denormalize, you must accept the consequences:

- Denormalization makes coding more complex.
- Denormalization often sacrifices flexibility.
- Denormalization will speed up retrieval but slow updates.

Figure 5-7 shows how you need to weigh these two types of activities (retrieval and update).

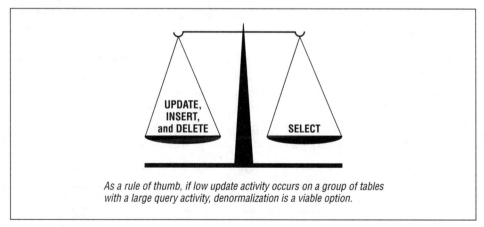

As a rule of thumb, if low update activity occurs on a group of tables with a large query activity, denormalization is a viable option.

Figure 5-7. Denormalization as an option

In the following sections, we outline a number of cases in which denormalizing your data will substantially improve your system's performance. We're not arguing for the general case. In most situations, a fully normalized database is clearly the way to go. But in these specific cases, try these denormalization tricks and watch your system fly.

Including Children in the Parent Record

In most cases, when your data have a parent-child relationship, you'll define separate records for the parent and each of the children. For example, consider the case of a bank account table. The basic information about the account (ID, name, etc.) would typically be stored in the parent record. Each of the quarterly balances might appear in a separate child record. Each of the child records would contain a key and a balance field.

But in a case like this, you will often find that you'll get better performance not by specifying individual child records but by including a set of columns, one for each of the quarterly balances, in the parent record, as shown in Figure 5-8.

It doesn't always make sense to incorporate child columns into the parent record. In general, you should consider doing this when your data meet three criteria:

1. The absolute number of children for a parent is known (in this case, you know that there are four quarterly records).

2. This number will not change over time, that is, it is static (the number of quarters in a year is not going to change!).

3. The number is not very large. "Large" is a hazy notion. Somewhat arbitrarily, we'll say that 20 is the limit. To be more precise, though, the fact that the number is fixed and will not increase over time is more important than the absolute number.

Storing child, or subordinate, data in the parent record in this way reduces the overhead that is required to perform table joins and propagated keys. The total performance improvement is, of course, a function of how many records you are processing and what you are doing with them. You'll realize the biggest performance gains if, by including subordinate data in this way, you avoid having to join thousands of parent and child records during application processing.

EMP#	NAME	QRT_1	QRT_2	QRT_3	QRT_4
0012745	Smith	1,000	1,500	1,750	2,500
0017346	Jones	12,400	12,700	14,000	15,500

Figure 5-8. Storing child data in the parent record

NOTE   There is a downside to incorporating child records into a parent record. You will note an increase in the complexity of your data manipulation and retrieval statements. You'll have to assess the relative advantages and disadvantages of denormalizing your data before making a decision about what to do.

Storing the Most Recent Child Data in the Parent Record

Now consider the case in which a parent record is associated with a series of child records, each arranged in a kind of sequence. For example, the parent record might contain information about a particular bank account whose interest rate fluctuates over time (perhaps each month or quarter). Each child record might contain an effective date and a particular interest rate. Although in this case it makes sense to maintain the individual child records, you can improve performance quite a bit by storing the most recent child record (the record containing the interest rate currently in effect) in the parent record, as shown in Figure 5-9. Because it's very likely that data retrieval will request the current rate, you'll be able to satisfy something like nine out of ten queries without ever needing to access a child record.

Storing the most recent child record in the parent is an appropriate choice when there is an unknown number of children and when each child has a sequencing attribute of some kind (in this case, an effective date). Of course, there are cases in which data retrieval will require access to additional child records (history data). In these cases, a normal table join is performed. But, if few such accesses are expected, you'll find that storing the most recent child record will satisfy most of your access needs.

What's the downside? Your database will have to contain an additional child record (the record containing the data that is duplicated in the parent record), and you'll have to maintain duplicate update routines for this record.

Hard-Coding Static Data

Every good relational analyst shudders at the terms "hard-coding," that is, including specific values in your program code, rather than references to table entries that may contain those values—and for good reason. There are few examples in which hard-coding makes sense.

EMP#	NAME	CURRENT_RATE
0012745	Smith	15.75
0017346	Jones	10.75

EMP#	EFFEC_DATE	RATE
0012745	10-Jan-91	21.00
0012745	30-Jun-91	19.50
0012745	16-May-92	17.25
0012745	01-Jan-93	15.75
0017346	16-Dec-92	12.50
0017346	01-Feb-93	11.75
0017346	01-Jul-93	11.00
0017346	26-Sep-93	10.75

Figure 5-9. Storing the most recent child data in the parent record

But there are a few. When the codes that your programs will test for are very common and very simple—for example, "Yes" and "No"—you'll find that hard-coding these codes into your programs (rather than creating a separate table for them) improves performance and doesn't create any problems for your clean relational design.

If we were to follow the rules of normalization in slavish fashion, we'd have to create a table to contain the "Yes" and "No" codes. A program would have to search the table each time it needed to test for a response. But Third Normal Form isn't always the preferred choice. You may not think of a simple Yes/No or Male/Female test as a denormalization of data, but technically it is. When your programs are going to be testing frequently for such simple choices, you'll find that you can improve performance by hard-coding such choices. Here is an example of such hard-coding:

```
IF :blk.sex NOT IN ('M','F','N') THEN
    message ('INVALID INPUT - (M)ALE, (F)EMALE OR (N)EITHER!');
    RAISE form_trigger_failure;
END IF;
```

Storing Running Totals

Earlier in this chapter, we told you never to store derivable data in a database table. Derivable data is data that can be computed from other data in the table—for example, a total of some values in that table or some other statistical result. It is an axiom of relational design that we don't store derivable data. Because all necessary information is already contained in the system, it's considered unnecessary overhead—a duplication of effort and storage—to keep a total in a record.

But there are cases in which you can greatly improve the performance of online inquiries by storing a running total in a record. For example, in the denormalized table on the left in Figure 5-10, we've stored AMT_TO_DATE as a running total. These data were derived from the normalized SALES table on the right. This example is a trivial one, but remember that the SALES table could contain hundreds of thousands of records, so the savings you gain by keeping running totals in the other denormalized table may be substantial.

EMP Table

EMP#	NAME	AMT_TO_DTE
0012745	Smith	6,750
0017346	Jones	54,600

SALES Table

EMP#	QRT_NO	AMOUNT
0012745	1	1,000
0012745	2	1,500
0012745	3	1,750
0012745	4	2,500
0017346	1	12,400
0017346	2	12,700
0017346	3	14,000
0017346	4	15,500

Figure 5-10. Storing running totals in a table

What's the downside of storing derivable data? You do incur additional storage and data manipulation overhead. Storing running totals also opens up a potential can of worms. You may sometimes run into data consistency problems (inconsistencies may occur between the total you've stored and the total you've calculated), and tracking down the cause of such inconsistencies can be a real nightmare. You'll have to decide whether your expected performance gains compensate for these risks.

Using System-Assigned Keys as Primary Keys

When you create database data, you may decide that you don't want to use any of the entities defined in the table as the primary key. Instead, you can ask Oracle to assign an internally generated unique key to use as the primary key. The internal primary key is stored as another column of the table. Typically, it is indexed. (See the discussion of indexing in Chapter 6.)

The system-assigned key is known as an internal primary key or a surrogate key, whereas the traditional primary key is known as the natural key. Table and column names, which may be very long, are compressed to unique numeric identifiers in a one-to-one relationship. Each record is identified by a system-assigned number, typified by Oracle's own data dictionary tables *col$* and *tab$*, which have system-assigned primary keys (*col#* and *tab#*, respectively), in addition to the natural primary keys (*col$.name* and *tab$name*).

In Figure 5-11, notice that a table is referenced three times (in disk storage areas 1, 2, and 3). Rather than using the original name, APPROPRIATION_BALANCES_MTD, for each row, the system assigns key 1 instead. The physical table name becomes simply a label for the real primary key.

TNAME Table			STORAGE Table				
TABLE#	TABLE_NAME		TABLE#	EXTENT#	FILE#	SIZE	TYPE
1	Appropriation_Balances_MTD		1	1	1	50	M
2	Appropriation_Balances_YTD		1	2	1	25	M
			1	3	3	25	K

Figure 5-11. Using system-assigned keys

In addition to guaranteeing the uniqueness of the primary key, using a system-assigned key also avoids the problems that can occur if an external primary key is null or if, for some reason, the external primary key needs to be changed.

There is another potential benefit to using internal keys. Because a system-assigned number is so much smaller than a typical table or column name (up to 30 alphanumeric characters), you'll potentially save a lot of storage, particularly if your internal key is propagated as a foreign key throughout large tables in the database.

The downside of using system-assigned primary keys is that these keys require storage, programming, and maintenance and that an extra table column and index has to be carried for the surrogate key. There will also be extra overhead associated with having to query through the natural key rather than through a more efficient surrogate key on subordinate tables. Natural keys are preferable when there is a definite performance improvement in accessing subordinate tables using the natural key and when the values in the natural key are not frequently modified. Do not store both natural keys and surrogate keys on subordinate tables!

Combining Reference or Code Tables

Just about every application contains quite a few small, referential validation tables, or code tables; a typical application might have between 10 and 100 such tables. Code tables are used for lookups and usually contain a small handful of records describing such information as country codes, interest category codes, education standards, and other reference information. Typically, each record contains only a single primary key and a description. Figure 5-12 shows two such tables.

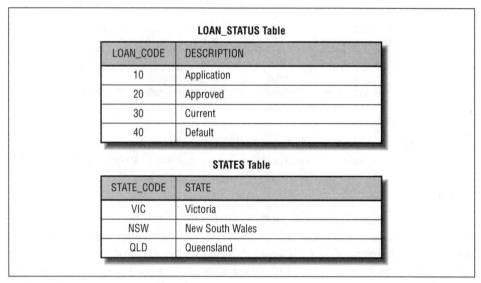

LOAN_STATUS Table

LOAN_CODE	DESCRIPTION
10	Application
20	Approved
30	Current
40	Default

STATES Table

STATE_CODE	STATE
VIC	Victoria
NSW	New South Wales
QLD	Queensland

Figure 5-12. Original code tables

Although, in theory, combining such code tables is considered to be a serious breach of normalization policy, you can often improve system performance by doing so. These tables are accessed quite frequently, usually to look up descriptions (for example, the name of a state or the type of bank loan) so that they can be displayed. You will find that if you combine all such code tables implemented for your system into a single global table, you'll improve performance in a number of ways.

In your combined global table, you'll need to create a concatenated primary key, as shown in Figure 5-13 (the CODE_CODE column) because the primary keys of the original tables are no longer likely to be unique.

The performance benefits of combining small code tables in this way can be substantial. Because only one table definition, only one synonym and grant (for the unified code table), and only one index definition need to be loaded into memory, there is a substantial savings in data dictionary cache (DC).

The code table approach that we have described almost guarantees that all code tables will be resident (cached) in memory at any time. With the other approach (separate code tables), only the more frequently referenced tables will tend to be in memory. You can also realize additional performance gains by reducing the

CODE_TYPE	CODE_CODE	DESCRIPTION
Loan_Status	10	Application
Loan_Status	20	Approved
Loan_Status	30	Current
Loan_Status	40	In Default
States	VIC	Victoria
States	NSW	New South Wales

Figure 5-13. Combining code tables

programming overhead needed to deal with combined code tables. You can create generic lookup and referential integrity routines, store them as standard library procedures, and access them by passing a table identifier plus primary key value(s).

A reduced number of data DB_BLOCK_BUFFERS is needed with this approach. Oracle must store a minimum of one Oracle block per table and one per index. Several (and perhaps all) of these minor code tables can fit into a single Oracle block buffer. This can lead to substantial savings. Suppose you have defined 25 individual code tables. What physical tables, cache buffers, and possible indexes do you need?

- 25 physical tables

- 25 possible indexes

- Up to 50 Oracle cache buffers

Now, suppose you combine the 25 small code tables into one. What do you need?

- One physical table

- One physical index

- A maximum of two Oracle cache buffers

You can see that the savings are significant.

Creating Extract Tables

An important benefit of a relational system is the ability to create reports containing up-to-date information that can combine values from various individual tables and create summary data from them. Despite the enormous benefits of accessing fully normalized data in this way, you will find that some reports are a huge performance drain on the system. Consider the case in which a number of users in your system need to create high-level management reports on a regular basis. The information that is needed to produce such a report is consolidated; it comes from many tables and involves a good deal of calculation and combination of data. Producing the report requires a large number of table joins, as well as quite a bit of repetitive and expensive table summing.

Although timely information is beneficial, you may find that in your organization, it's not imperative that a report reflect the most recent updates to the database. In a case like this, you can improve system performance by completely denormalizing your relational tables and creating a single, consolidated extract table, a type of spreadsheet that actually duplicates the information in the database that the management report needs.

Figure 5-14 shows an abbreviated example of the kind of information a consolidated table (extracted from various other tables—EMP, DEPT, MGR, etc.) might contain.

DEPT#	DEPT_NAME	MGR#	MGR_NAME	EMP#	CLASS	CLASS_NAME
0010	Accounts	04562	Smith	134	A	Profitable
0020	Sales	05664	Brown	180	A	Profitable
0030	Purchasing	34529	Jones	56	A	Profitable
0040	Systems	45230	Green	36	D	Huge Money Pit

Figure 5-14. Creating extract tables

The most common method for producing such an extract table is to run an automated process overnight, when system performance needs are not so pressing, to populate the table. The major advantage of such an approach is that you incur the overhead of table joins and data summation only once, instead of each time a user of a management report needs to look at the consolidated data. The more report and query users, the greater your performance gains will be. You'll also find that this approach is especially beneficial, from a performance point of view, if users typically use GUI interfaces for their management reporting. Once the extract table has been created, programs that use it can do very simple and highly efficient table scans of that table only. Ensure that you add indexes to the extract table as required.

In helping sites to tune their systems, we've found the "denormalized extract" approach very helpful. At one site, we reduced the amount of time needed for overnight processes by several hours. We also made managers very happy when the response time for their consolidated online queries decreased from 40 minutes to 45 seconds!

So what's the downside? The obvious drawback to the use of extract tables for consolidated queries is that the data is not current. Remember that if you populate an extract table during an overnight process, the queries and reports performed during the next day will be using data that are many hours old. Other reports—and decisions—based on these data may suffer as a consequence. Only you, in conjunction with your users, can decide whether the performance gains that you'll realize by using extract tables are worth the risk of using data that may have aged in this way.

However, even if the extract tables are used only for the overnight reporting routine, they will almost certainly provide significant performance gains over individual reports traversing through the database, across the same data, time and time again.

Duplicating a Key Beyond an Immediate Child Record

A principle of relational design is that a table never contains more information than it needs. In particular, when you are working with parent and child records, you must be sure that child, and other subordinate, records do not duplicate information that properly belongs only in the parent record.

But there's always an exception. In some cases it is desirable to actually carry a primary key down even beyond the child record to the record of the child's child. In general, this approach is advantageous only in cases in which multitable joining may frequently be needed to satisfy queries.

For example, suppose that you have three tables: ORDERS, PARTS, and CLASS. In a normalized relational database, these tables contain only the data they need to contain. When an order needs to be printed, your application typically needs to access both the ORDERS table and the PARTS table so that it can print both the part number and the part description. But in quite a few cases, the CLASS code for the part must also be included on the invoice. In these cases, you need to do a three-table join: From the ORDERS table you go to the PARTS table to pick up the part description and, in these cases, the CLASS code. Then you need to go to the CLASS table to get the CLASS description. If the ORDERS table has many thousands (or even many hundreds) of records, and if orders are frequently reported within class, then you will improve performance by duplicating the CLASS code on the individual child record, as shown in Figure 5-15. Having it available on that record speeds up response time.

PARTS Table				ORDERS Table		
PART#	DESCRIPTION	CLASS		PART#	ORDER#	CLASS
A1284	Front Widget	A+		A1284	01237	A+
A345/1	Rear Widget	B-		A1284	00546	A+
				A345/1	00002	B-

Figure 5-15. Duplicating a key

Here is the SQL code that does the retrieval. For the normalized database:

```
SELECT  part_no, order_no, class, class_desc
FROM    class c,
            part p,
            order o
WHERE   o.part_no = p.part_no
AND     p.class = c.class;
```

For the denormalized database:

```
SELECT  part_no, order_no, class, class_desc
FROM    class c,
            order o
WHERE   o.class = c.class;
```

Note that you do incur additional overhead for the duplicated data within the PART table, so it makes sense to denormalize in this way only if you do this kind of retrieval frequently.

Constraints

Oracle constraints provide you with a mechanism for placing intelligence into your database definition without the need for any programming. Because they work independently of application programs, at the sub-SQL level, constraints are extremely efficient. If the rule that is placed into the constraint needs to be modified, it is changed only once, with no program changes required. The Oracle query optimizer uses constraints to assist with query optimization. We strongly recommend that you use constraints extensively, but first be sure that you have a thorough understanding of their performance implications.

Enforcing data integrity through the use of constraints does come with a performance cost. Oracle Corporation tells us that the cost is similar to that of executing the SQL statement into which the integrity constraint would translate. There are a few other performance implications that you must be aware of to use design constraints effectively.

There are four major types of constraints: primary key, unique key, foreign key, and check. The following sections describe each, along with how they may affect your site's performance.

Primary Key Constraints

A primary key constraint enforces uniqueness and ensures that a value is entered for each column in the primary key. It is extremely rare for a table not to require a primary key constraint. Adding a primary key to a table creates an index. Be sure to provide sizing details on the index in your design specification.

Unique Key Constraints

A unique key constraint also checks for uniqueness but does allow the columns in the key to be null. Oracle enforces the unique constraint through the use of an index. Be sure to provide sizing for the index in your design document.

Foreign Key Constraints

A foreign key constraint checks that the dependent (child) table has a row in the referenced (parent) table. An example is when the DEPT_NO column in the EMP table must have a corresponding entry for the same DEPT_NO is the DEPT table. A foreign key constraint can create some severe locking problems on the parent table if it has not been set up with appropriate indexing. See Chapter 8, *Selecting a Locking Strategy*, for a comprehensive explanation of the foreign key locking problems.

In Figure 5-16, unless there is an index on the child table EMP(DEPT_NO), any insert, update, or delete of a row in the EMP table places a SHARE lock on the DEPT table. A share lock will allow many users to read from the DEPT table but will not allow any one of them to perform updates, deletes, and inserts until the share lock has been released. If a transaction is inserting, updating, or deleting from the DEPT table, the foreign key constraint is forced to wait before it can apply the share lock on DEPT. This scenario can cause severe locking problems.

The solution is to have indexes on all foreign key columns in the child table. However, this strategy can go too far. We have observed some sites that specify as many as 20 indexes on tables in an effort to overcome the foreign key locking problem. Most of the indexes are on foreign key columns that have a small reference table as a parent. The result is a database that is full of integrity but performs abysmally. If the reference tables are not going to have their data changed during prime uptime, foreign keys may be able to applied without having the share lock cause any waits as a result of locking problems.

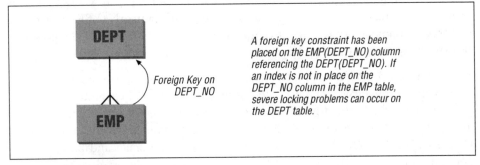

Figure 5-16. Foreign key constraint

If the parent table is heavily updated, we recommend that the foreign key constraint be applied if there is an index on the foreign key columns in the child table. We also recommend that the index and the foreign key constraint be applied only if the index assists queries against the table. You must also put a rule in place that the parent table must not be able to be deleted or have the foreign key column modified during prime working hours.

Foreign key constraints further degrade performance when large numbers of rows are loaded into a table. Every row is checked to ensure that the foreign key columns exist in the parent table. To keep this problem from degrading your performance, consider disabling the foreign key constraint until after the data load is complete. Then enable it once again.

Check Constraints

A check constraint is placed on a column or columns in a table to specify a condition that must be true. A typical example is the case in which a column FLAG has only two valid values: ON or OFF. If a row is inserted into the table with a value other than ON or OFF, the statement is rolled back. Check constraints pose little performance overhead, so you should use them frequently.

Check constraints do have some limitations. They do not allow queries to values in other rows in this table or others. They also cannot use the functions SYSDATE, UID, USER, and USERENV, and they cannot use the pseudocolumns CURRVAL, NEXTVAL, LEVEL, and ROWNUM. You can have multiple check constraints on a single column and refer to other columns in the same row.

Triggers

Triggers are another good option in your application design. Triggers are placed against a table. Depending on how triggers are written, they may be executed either before or after an insert, update, or delete on the table. You have the option of running triggers once per statement or once per row. Triggers can provide substantial performance benefits by reducing network traffic in a client-server environment. They can also guarantee that the PL/SQL code gets run, despite the source of the DML statement.

Before Oracle7.3, database triggers were not compiled like procedures and packages. When a trigger was first executed, it was compiled and cached in the shared pool in memory. If the trigger was flushed from memory and then requested again, it had to be recompiled. For this reason, if you are using a version of Oracle earlier than Oracle7.3, design your triggers to be small and have the triggers call stored packages and procedures that are precompiled.

Triggers are often used to maintain an audit trail, enforce complex business rules, and enforce access security on your tables. Row-level triggers have been known to cause severe performance degradation when they are used inappropriately. Keep your triggers simple! Be careful of triggers that perform updates on other tables that also contain triggers. Figure 5-17 shows sample trigger use.

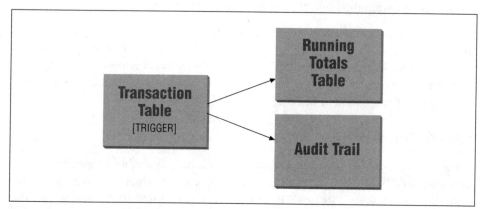

Figure 5-17. Typical trigger usage

Encourage your programmers to use the WHEN clause (similar to a WHERE clause), which keeps triggers from performing unnecessarily. Be aware of triggers that cause other triggers to get called. They can destroy your performance.

NOTE   Constraints are optimized for performing data integrity checks. Do
              not use a trigger to perform the work that a constraint can perform.

Note the following restrictions on triggers:

* You cannot specify triggers on the Oracle dictionary tables.

* Triggers take effect on rows that are modified in the table after the trigger has been added.

- A trigger cannot read or modify rows in the table that contains the trigger.

- Triggers cannot contain COMMIT, ROLLBACK, or SAVEPOINT statements.

- Triggers cannot perform DDL statements, such as CREATE TABLE.

- A row trigger is not allowed to modify a table that has a foreign key pointing to it from the table with the trigger on it.

Packages, Procedures, and Functions

Oracle packages, procedures, and functions (stored objects) compose compiled PL/SQL code that is stored in the database. During the design stage, consider carefully how you can use these objects to improve performance. Your DBA has a facility that allows him or her to pin the objects into memory; be sure that the DBA takes advantage of it. A major benefit of the stored objects is that they can improve your performance, especially in a client-server environment, by reducing the amount of network traffic used. They also provide you with an efficient method of modularizing your code. The code may be shared by all of the users who have access rights to run the objects.

A package comprises one or more procedures and/or functions. Packages provide a number of performance advantages over stored procedures. An entire package is loaded into memory when a procedure or a function within the package is called for the first time. When another procedure in the package is run, no additional I/Os need be performed. If the procedures were stored standalone, rather than in a package, that second procedure would need to be read from disk.

Another benefit of using packages instead of procedures is that if a table has a modification (e.g., a column added to it), all procedures that use the table will need to be individually recompiled. If a standalone procedure calls another procedure, the procedures must be compiled in dependency order. The procedure that is called by the other procedure must be compiled first.

Designing a Very Large Database Application

This section describes the special design considerations for very large database applications. Very large Oracle databases tend to be used for data warehousing and decision support applications. Very large databases can also emerge when an adequate purging strategy is not in place for OLTP applications. (You should have a purging design for any large database.) This avoids having the database become unmanageable and unable to provide adequate performance.

A decision support database design needs to be easy for the DBA to administer and must also provide acceptable performance for all of the database users. It must present its users with a database structure that is simple to access and easily understandable. Decision support database users are not interested in having to understand complex data models. You will usually need to create redundant summary and aggregate tables or use views to assist with the ease of access for end users.

Some sites have a technically magnificent database that is unworkable for end users. Others have a database that is a design masterpiece but unmanageable for the DBA. The major reason that a DBA has trouble maintaining a database is exceedingly large table sizes. If a table is dropped or is corrupted, it can't be rebuilt through export and import.

Improving Extract and Load Performance

When you extract data into the database, you must try to have as little impact on the database being extracted from as possible. This is especially true if the database that is being extracted from is an OLTP database. Make sure that you benchmark the data extraction process. Many of the traps in large database design remain the same from database to database (although all sites have slightly different needs). Here we include a case study from a site that has many common problems.

Case study

This particular site had decided to use snapshot logs across all tables to transfer data from the main OLTP database to the decision support database. They were running snapshots from the receiving database every 10 minutes. The 2,200 online users weren't very happy when they discovered that the response times on all of the heavily used transactions had doubled.

Further investigation revealed that the users were happy to process data that were extracted last night and that the transfer of data every 10 minutes was overkill. The snapshot log and its associated trigger were removed, and the data were extracted nightly using a MODIFIED_DATE and an ACTION column. The ACTION column had three valid values: I for insertions, M for modifications, and D for deletions. The online tables were indexed on (MODIFIED_DATE, ACTION). Rows were logically deleted from the main online database and were not physically deleted until a later date. The online indexes were rebuilt as part of the cleanout of the rows. This overcame the index range scan performance problems that can occur when blocks contain a high percentage of deleted index entries.

The decision support database had been receiving data from all of the tables contained in the online database. The data that had been inactive for more than five years could be removed from the decision support database. The decision support database had all integrity constraints (including foreign key constraints) in place, which was markedly slowing down the data loading. By removing the foreign key constraints, we more than halved the time taken to load the data.

We also discovered that many audit tables were being loaded into the decision support database and would never be used. Therefore we took them out of the list of the tables to be transferred. Many of the columns in the online database tables were also not required for the decision support database, and we also removed them from the extract.

Another problem that the site experienced (one that's common at many sites) was that the values in reference data tables could be modified over time. This meant that Code 10 in the COST CENTER reference table might have contained HAWTHORN in 1995 but was changed to RICHMOND in 1996. Therefore, reference tables were stored once in the decision support database and updated, and if the transaction tables in the decision support database were using the reference tables as lookups, they would be reporting incorrect information. We denormalized decision support tables to store the code value rather than the code. This helped performance by avoiding table joins.

We also looked at the problems the site was having trying to handle updates and deletes. We used the MODIFIED_DATE and ACTION columns on the tables in the online database, and transferred data from the online database very quickly overnight using database links. The transfer inserted, updated, or deleted the rows in the decision support database. Indexes had to be put into place on the tables in the decision support databases to speed up the updates and deletes. Logic also had to be put into place to handle rows that had been added and modified in the online database on the same day. Such rows had an action of M (modified), even though they didn't yet exist in the decision support database.

Extract and load design considerations

Several problems that we encountered at the case study site are common at other sites as well. We suggest that you read the section called "Creating Very Large Databases" in Chapter 9, *Tuning a New Database*. This section provides some insight from the database administration perspective into how to administer a very large database. Several additional data extract and load design considerations are:

- Extensively benchmark any proposed method of transferring data. Don't just read about a feature in the manual and start implementing it in production. Pay particular attention to the performance impact of the transfer on the online user databases, especially if the transfer takes place during prime online usage times.

- When transferring data from the main online database, be cautious about using snapshot logs and database triggers on tables that are extremely volatile. Consider overnight data loads using SQL*Net database links instead.

- Be totally aware of how up to date the data in the decision support database need to be. End users don't realize the potential consequences of asking for data that are "as of 10 minutes ago" or "as of now." Some requirements for the current data can often be met by developing existing screens or fast-running reports against the online database.

- Remove foreign key constraints from the decision support database, especially when the loading is taking place. It is usually better to develop scripts using the MINUS command, as shown below, and run the scripts directly after loading the data.

```
SELECT project_name
FROM   transaction
MINUS
SELECT project_name
FROM   project;
```

- Split your tables into subtables; for example, the TRANSACTION table may be split into TRANSACTION_97, TRANSACTION_98, and so on. You can then create a partitioned view (described in the next section, "Improving Query Performance").

- If the data loads do not run frequently and the amount of data loaded is significant, consider dropping the indexes, loading the data, and then rebuilding the indexes using the UNRECOVERABLE and parallel query options. UNRECOVERABLE does not write redo entries and allows the table to be created at least 10% faster. The parallel query option allows multiple processes to create the index simultaneously. (See Chapter 13, *Tuning Parallel Query*, for more information.)

- Use summary tables in a decision support database. It is often faster to recreate the summary tables using the UNRECOVERABLE and parallel query options.

- Ensure that data being loaded from the other database(s) are actually required for the decision support database. For example, question the need to extract security and audit data from the other databases and to load them into the decision support database.

- Consider storing the code value (e.g., NEW YORK) rather than the code (e.g., 10) for all tables that access reference data. You will usually find that users will search the transaction tables on the code value (NEW YORK) rather than the code. Having the value in the transaction table will avoid having to join tables.

- If you are using SQL*Loader to load your data, consider using the direct load option.

- If you are using IMPORT, increase the BUFFER parameter 2 megabytes or more, and use the DIRECT option.

- Consider running multiple load jobs in parallel, one load job per processor. Ensure that the tables on the disks being read from and written to are not on the same disks as other tables being loaded. This will cause a disk I/O bottleneck and may give a slower run-time than loading the tables serially.

- Be aware of all of the options available to your DBA to improve transferring a very large database. (See the section "Creating Very Large Databases" in Chapter 9.)

- If you are using Oracle8, take advantage of parallel inserts and updates.

Improving Query Performance

You may find it difficult to provide your users with acceptable performance because it's hard to envision the types of inquiries that users will make against the database. Decision support users tend to require multidimensional analysis and to drill down into more detailed information after obtaining high-level details. Most decision support user requirements can be broken down into a clearly defined set of reports, with some unknown ad hoc reporting needs. If you can tune the known reports and preempt the types of ad hoc reports that most users will request, you can structure your data model to provide the absolute best performance to your users.

Decision support users tend to perform most of their multidimensional analyses on their local PCs. You must design a mechanism for retrieving data from your decision support database in both a delimited format (which suits products like Excel and Access) and a standard report format. Transferring the data onto the PC also helps to provide acceptable performance by taking some of the processing load off the main database. However, be sure that the data transfers to the user PCs do not flood the local networks. It is usually best to transfer the data overnight.

Very few decision support databases perform well without some degree of denormalization using summary or aggregate tables. The trade-off is that maintaining denormalized tables requires extra storage and extra processing time when the data is being extracted into the decision support database. You must ensure that the query response time improvements that are obtained from each of the denormalized tables justify the time taken to create these tables. Many sites produce a delimited report directly from the summary tables and download it onto the end users' PCs for local processing.

Figure 5-18 shows the situation at an actual site that has successfully produced a manageable 120-gigabyte decision support database that fulfills user needs and provides excellent performance. (This site also has a powerful but simple purging strategy.) The PROJECT_LOCATION_TRANSACTION table is a summary table created by summarizing the TRANSACTION table. Oracle's parallel query option allows the summary table and its indexes to be created in approximately 20 minutes. Almost all of the users' reports run using the summary table.

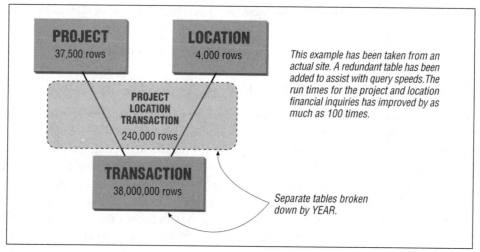

Figure 5-18. Large database example

The site decided to break the TRANSACTION table and the summary table into separate tables stored by year. Oracle has many features that support this table structure, including Oracle7.3 partitioned views and Oracle8 partitions. The summary table is recreated nightly from the current year's transaction information only. The summary table is heavily indexed, but it is relatively small, and the indexes are created very quickly. It also contains redundant information, such as the PROJECT_NAME and LOCATION_NAME, rather than the PROJECT_NO and LOCATION_NO. Because the majority of users' inquiries were on LOCATION_NAME and PROJECT_NAME rather than LOCATION_NO and PROJECT_NO, appropriate indexes were put into place.

Oracle7 introduced the UNION ALL operator, which allows you to scan across multiple (partitioned) tables and return all rows that satisfy your selection criteria.

You can also create a view to simplify the SELECT statement for the end users, as shown below:

```
CREATE VIEW   transactions AS
     SELECT *
     FROM   transactions_95
     UNION  ALL
     SELECT *
     FROM   transactions_96
     UNION  ALL
     SELECT *
     FROM   transactions_97
     UNION  ALL
     SELECT *
     FROM   transactions_98
/
```

Having separate tables allows index creation to be performed only on the stand-alone table. Partitioned tables also allow your summary tables to be rebuilt without the need to read through a huge table. They can be broken down into sizes that allow you to rebuild the table using Oracle's EXPORT and IMPORT facility if the table is mistakenly dropped or corrupted. Another advantage of the EXPORT and IMPORT facility is that the files are much more transportable to later releases of the database. You can import an Oracle7.2 export file into Oracle8, but you can't simply add an Oracle7.2 data file.

Analyzing partitioned tables and their indexes also takes considerably less time, because once the historical tables are analyzed, they will not have to be reanalyzed. As new rows are loaded into the table for the current period, the current table is all that needs to be analyzed, not the tables that contain the previous years' data. The tables that contain the previous period are backed up once. On export, they are placed into read-only tablespaces and don't have to be backed up again.

The view can provide excellent performance for SQL statements if the WHERE clause has the appropriate indexes on the subordinate tables. Having separate transaction tables for each financial year allows you to create a new table, TRANSACTIONS_99. Then you can recreate the view to contain the TRANSACTIONS_99 table and remove the TRANSACTIONS_95 table. End users also have the option of selecting the transactions for one financial year by selecting the underlying tables directly.

You can also place your summary tables into a UNION ALL view. In the view below, the tables summarize the TRANSACTIONS_year tables by location. The original transactions table contained 38,000,000 rows in total. The PROJECT_LOCATION_TRANSACTION table contains 240,000 rows.

```
CREATE VIEW project_location_transaction AS
     SELECT *
```

```
FROM    project_location_transaction_95
UNION ALL
SELECT *
FROM    project_location_transaction_96
UNION ALL
SELECT *
FROM    lproject_location_transaction_97
UNION ALL
SELECT *
FROM    project_location_transaction_98
/
```

Oracle7.3 introduced partitioned views. You can place a check constraint on the tables to assist in the performance of many of the queries. The query will not read any underlying tables that are outside the range of the selection criteria. The optimizer has the intelligence to decide on either an indexed or a full table scan lookup, depending on the cost of performing the operation. If the constraints below were put into place and the user specified WHERE trans_date > '05-JUL-98', only the TRANSACTIONS_98 and TRANSACTIONS_99 tables would be read from; this improves performance significantly.

```
ALTER TABLE transactions_95 ADD CONSTRAINT
   trans_95_check_cons  (trans_date BETWEEN '01-jan-95' AND '31-dec-
95');
ALTER TABLE transactions_96 ADD CONSTRAINT
   trans_96_check_cons  (trans_date BETWEEN '01-jan-96' AND '31-dec-
96');
ALTER TABLE transactions_97 ADD CONSTRAINT
   trans_97_check_cons  (trans_date BETWEEN '01-jan-97' AND '31-dec-
97');
ALTER TABLE transactions_98 ADD CONSTRAINT
   trans_98_check_cons  (trans_date BETWEEN '01-jan-98' AND '31-dec-
98');
ALTER TABLE transactions_99 ADD CONSTRAINT
   trans_99_check_cons  (trans_date BETWEEN '01-jan-99' AND '31-dec-
99');
```

If you use partitioned views prior to Oracle8, you must observe the following limitations:

- Applications that perform inserts, updates, and deletes on the view must refer to the individual table names.

- There must be only one table in the FROM clause.

- The view must list all columns from each table.

- The query used to create the partitioned view cannot use a WHERE clause, Group BY, DISTINCT, ROWNUM, or CONNECT BY START WITH.

Parallel Query

Oracle7.1 introduced the parallel query option, which can speed up index creation, data loading into the database, and queries against the database. It speeds up processing by allocating multiple query server processes to perform these tasks. The parallel query option can assist only SQL statements that perform at least one full table scan. To use the parallel query option, you will need to use either Oracle striping or operating system striping, and you must have multiple processors.

Developing a Purging Strategy

As we mentioned earlier, be sure to put a purging strategy in place when you begin to create any large database. We usually recommend that you break up your tables, including summary tables, by date. Then place a partitioned view across the tables. This will help your purging strategy. You'll be able to add a new table into the database for the current time period and drop the tables for the period that has become obsolete. You may decide to drop your larger transaction tables and keep the denormalized summary tables online for the obsolete period. Figure 5-19 illustrates this strategy.

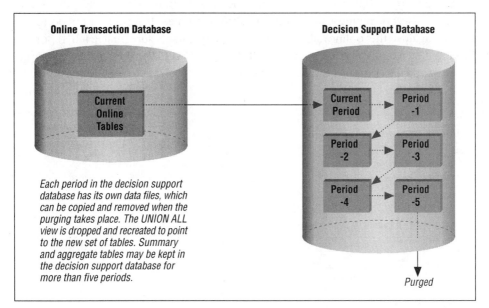

Figure 5-19. Typical purging strategy

Miscellaneous Design Considerations

This section lists a number of additional ways of improving the performance of your applications.

- Oracle Pro*3GL languages offer array processing. This is particularly important in a client-server environment, because it can cut down on the number of packets transferred across the network and improve performance considerably.

- Deleting rows from a table is very resource consuming. It can also leave many data and blocks that contain very few rows. This can markedly slow down your performance. If you do have a table that is often deleted from, consider logically deleting the row using a DELETE_FLAG column. Purge out of normal work hours and consider rebuilding your indexes after the purge. Indexes that contain blocks that contain very few rows can slow down index range scans significantly—for example, WHERE surname LIKE 'GUR%'.

- Apply a MODIFIED_DATE to all of your tables to help in monitoring the frequency of inserts, updates, and deletes. Doing this can also assist with table growth predictions, and with purging and propagation to other systems.

- Design your application so the ad hoc report users don't access the same tables as your online users during peak usage times. If reports do need to be run against the online tables during the day, make sure that each report is tuned to run under 1 or 2 minutes. If the report will take longer than a couple of minutes to run, run the report overnight.

IV

Tuning for Programmers

Part IV describes what Oracle programmers need to know about tuning. It looks at how statements can be tuned in the SQL and PL/SQL environments, and it takes a look at the special tuning considerations presented by different locking strategies.

6

Tuning SQL

Structured Query Language (SQL) is the heart of the Oracle system. Developed originally by IBM in the mid-1970s, SQL has become a standard for database query, retrieval, and reporting. The American National Standards Institute (ANSI) has adopted SQL as a standard (X3.135-1986, with substantial enhancements in 1989), as has the International Standards Organization (ISO) (9075). SQL-2 is the lowest common ANSI standard that has been implemented within the RDBMS engine. SQL is also a U.S. Federal Information Processing Standard (FIPS 127). Oracle, along with many other database vendors, has extended the SQL standard by adding features to its implementation of SQL. For example, functions such as DECODE and CONNECT BY PRIOR are extensions that are beyond the scope of the original standard.

Oracle's SQL is a very flexible language. You can use many different SQL statement variants to reach the same end. Yet, although dozens of differently constructed query and retrieval statements can produce the same result, only one statement will be the most efficient choice in a given situation.

As a programmer, your responsibility for tuning revolves around SQL (and related tools such as PL/SQL). Too many programmers forget that SQL choices are within their power. They somehow believe that as long as a SQL statement returns the expected result, it must be correct. Wrong! A SQL choice is correct only if it produces the right result in the shortest possible amount of time without impeding the performance of any other system resource. You have the ability, and the responsibility, to tune every SQL statement so that it works as efficiently as it can in each application. In each case, you'll have to consider the purpose of your application, where the bottlenecks are, and what your choices of statements and options might be. This section outlines the major performance problems that we see in SQL statements, whether they are entered via SQL*Plus or are embedded in PL/SQL block(s). Refer to Chapter 7, *Tuning PL/SQL*, for specific suggestions on tuning SQL within PL/SQL. Note the following:

Don't expect SQL to work miracles!
> Even the best programmer cannot compensate for more fundamental machine problems. You must protect your application and your SQL by trying to reduce all associated overheads. This "protection" includes tuning the machine, tuning the operating system, tuning the database, and safeguarding the network from excess data traffic.

Do not become complacent about SQL!
> Regardless of how well tuned your hardware and other software resources might be, a single badly constructed SQL statement can decimate the performance of your system.

How can you tell which SQL statement or option results in the best performance for your system? With Oracle7, the cost-based optimizer makes the most of these decisions. If you are still using the rule-based optimizer, you will need to do a lot more manual tuning. Analyzing the physical execution of an individual SQL statement can be a complex process. To judge a statement's performance, you need to examine data volumes, alternative WHERE clauses, the role that might be played by indexes, optimizer hints, user privileges, application environment (distributed or local), and the optimizer mode.

SQL Standards

Before beginning to code any application, you must define programming standards. Having moved beyond the rigors of 3GLs and their particular constraints, people question the need for such tight programming controls. However, they are still necessary—perhaps even more so—in working with SQL.

Why Have SQL Standards?

Large applications may have many programmers all furiously churning out SQL code. Every programmer has his or her own style, preferences, and tendencies. Even if each developer is producing efficient application code, your future maintenance overhead can kill you. Non-uniform application coding standards often mean that the only person who can understand the code is the one who wrote it.

This is not a very nice situation to be in when an application requires major enhancements or amendments.

Coding standards for individual SQL statements are particularly important because of the way that the RDBMS engine handles the statements internally. When a SQL statement is parsed within the database the following steps are performed:

Check syntax
> Is the SQL correctly structured? Do all the opening parentheses match the closing parentheses?

Search shared SQL area
> Does a parsed copy of the same statement (i.e., in pcode form) already exist?
>
> Version 6—Searches the calling session's program global area (PGA).
> Oracle7—Searches a common area of the System Global Area (SGA) known as the *shared buffer pool*.

Search data dictionary
> Performs object resolution (checks views, synonyms, etc.). Checks security privileges.

Calculates search path
> Rule-based *or* cost-based optimizer.

Saves execution plan
> Execution plan is stored in the SGA (Oracle7) or PGA (Version 6). (See Figure 6-1.)

The critical factor is the second step of SQL parsing, "Search shared SQL area." This is where SQL standards for individual statements become important. SQL cannot be shared within the SGA unless it is absolutely identical. Statement components that must be the same include:

- Word case (uppercase and lowercase characters)
- Whitespace
- Underlying schema objects

The following SQL statements are not the same and will not be shared within the SGA:

```
sql> SELECT  NAME  FROM  S_CUSTOMER  WHERE  ID = 212;
sql> SELECT  NAME  FROM  S_CUSTOMER  WHERE  ID = 213;
sql> SELECT  NAME  FROM  S_CUSTOMER  WHERE  ID = :b1;
sql> SELECT  name  FROM  s_customer  WHERE  id = 212;
sql> SELECT  NAME  FROM  S_CUSTOMER  WHERE  ID=212;
sql> SELECT  NAME
        FROM  S_CUSTOMER
       WHERE  ID=212;
```

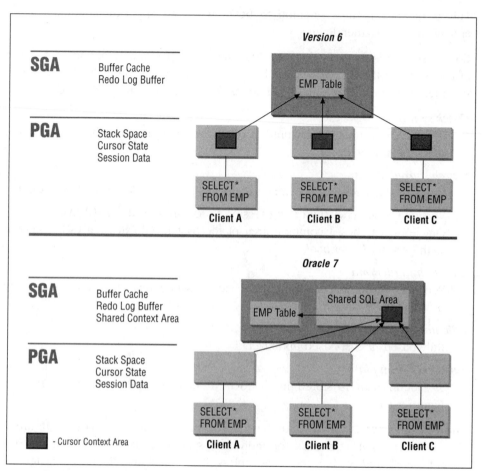

Figure 6-1. SQL context areas

SQL Statement Structure

You do not have to be Einstein to work out that when two statements are identical, they will be shared and, ultimately, contribute to a more efficient application. So why aren't SQL standards promoted and enforced (policed) at every Oracle site?

SQL structure standards are the easiest thing in the world to set up. There is no right or wrong way to structure SQL; you just need consistency. For example:

- Put all SQL verbs in one case.

- Begin all SQL verbs on a new line.

- Right- or left-align verbs with the initial SQL verb.

• Separate all statement "words" by a single space.

The following example illustrates these principles:

```
SELECT   emp_no, emp_name, emp_salary
FROM     emp
WHERE    sal_grade > 10
AND      ( emp_salary >= 10000
OR       tot_staff > 100 )
```

Remember that statements are classified as equal only when the underlying objects are the same. If two users both select the same data from the EMP table, both must be referencing the exact same physical table. Synonyms cannot be used to reference different tables, and users cannot have their own local copy of the table.

To save confusion and mistakes, we always instruct our developers to code all SQL in a single case. No need to distinguish between uppercase verbs, lowercase text, uppercase bind variables, etc. All whitespace is limited to a maximum of one black character. This approach does not necessarily generate the most attractive code to look at but does help to share more SQL resources in the shared pool and reduces "lazy" programming mistakes. Here is an example:

```
SELECT emp_no, emp_name, emp_salary
FROM    emp
WHERE   sal_grade > 10
AND     (emp_salary >= 10000 or tot_staff > 100)
```

(Note that we don't practice what we preach in this book. In the book, we use a mixed-case approach because we believe that it better illustrates the different components of statements.)

Encourage Bind Variables

The values of bind variables do not need to be the same for two statements to be considered identical. If the *bind variable references* are the same, the parsed forms of the statements are considered to be the same. Bind variable values are not actually substituted until a statement has been successfully parsed. The actual values of the bind variables are not considered when selecting a statement's execution plan, and the parsed form of the statement is shared in the context area. For example:

```
Sharable SQL:      SELECT * FROM emp WHERE emp_no = :B1;   Bind value: 123
                   SELECT * FROM emp WHERE emp_no = :B1;   Bind value: 987

Non-Sharable SQL:  SELECT * FROM emp WHERE emp_no = 123;
                   SELECT * FROM emp WHERE emp_no = 987;
```

In general, encourage programmers to use bind variables in favor of hard coding the variable values. This may mean extra coding effort and should be attempted only when you are sure that a particular SQL statement will be used repetitively, the only difference being bind variable values.

NOTE   For static application interfaces such as SQL*Forms, Pro*C, etc., statement case, whitespace, and bind variables will always be the same for the same statements. All users execute the identical SQL statement when using the same program, regardless of the bind variable name or value supplied.

Using Table Aliases

You also need to formulate a standard approach to table aliases. If two identical SQL statements vary because an identical table has two different aliases, then the SQL is different and will not be shared.

Use table aliases, and prefix all column names by their aliases when more than one table is involved in a query. This will reduce parse time and prevent syntax errors from occurring when ambiguously named columns are innocently added to a table at a later time. Consider the following example:

```
SELECT E.emp_no, name, tax_no, C.comp_code, comp_name
FROM   company C,
       emp E
WHERE  E.comp_code = C.comp_code;
```

This SQL will work properly until, without your knowledge, the TAX_NO column is added to the COMPANY table:

```
ALTER TABLE company ADD (tax_no VARCHAR2(20));
```

Many programs will now begin to fail. You'll see messages such as the following:

```
ORA-00918 : COLUMN AMBIGUOUSLY DEFINED
```

To avoid problems of this kind, use table aliases as shown below:

```
SELECT E.emp_no, E.name, E.tax_no, C.comp_code,C.comp_name
FROM   company  C,
       emp E
WHERE  E.comp_code = C.comp_code;
```

The SQL Optimizer

The Oracle optimizer is a hidden but extremely important system resource. A part of the Oracle kernel, the optimizer examines each SQL statement it encounters in your application and chooses the optimal execution plan, or retrieval path, for the statement. The execution plan is the sequence of physical steps the RDBMS must take to perform the operation (e.g., retrieval, update) that you've specified.

To figure out the optimal path, the optimizer considers the following areas:

- The details of the syntax you've specified for the statement
- Any conditions that the data must satisfy (the WHERE clauses)
- The database tables your statement will need to access
- All possible indexes that can be used in retrieving data from the table
- Oracle RDBMS version
- The current optimizer mode
- SQL statement hints
- All available object statistics (generated via the ANALYZE command)
- Physical table location (distributed SQL)
- INIT.ORA settings (parallel query, async I/O, etc.)

On the basis of this information, the optimizer figures out the most efficient retrieval path for the SQL statement that is being executed.

In most situations, the optimizer's efforts remain hidden from your view. But it is possible for you to look more closely at how the optimizer works. If you're trying to improve the performance of your system, you'll want to work closely with the optimizer to structure the most efficient SQL statements. The EXPLAIN PLAN diagnostic statement gives you an inside look at how the optimizer is planning to process your SQL statements. By running EXPLAIN PLAN and examining its output for several alternative SELECT statements, for example, you should be able to determine which statement is the most efficient. See Chapter 10, *Diagnostic and Tuning Tools,* for a discussion of how you can use EXPLAIN PLAN and other diagnostics to tune your Oracle system.

Oracle7 brings you even closer to the inner workings of the optimizer by giving you a choice of two optimizing alternatives: the rule-based optimizer (the only optimizer available in Version 6 and earlier) and the more intelligent cost-based optimizer. How do these optimizers differ?

Regardless of which optimizer you use, you need to realize that neither optimizer knows as much as you do about how the database is constructed and what you and your users want to do with that database. In many key application modules, you will need to supplement the optimizer's work by manually tuning SQL statements, using the suggestions that we provide in this chapter.

Rule-Based Optimizer

The rule-based optimizer uses a predefined set of precedence rules to figure out which path it will use to access the database. The rule-based optimizer was the only optimizer available before Oracle7. Life was easier back then—there were fewer decisions to make.

The rule-based optimizer is driven primarily by 20 condition rankings, or golden rules, shown in Table 6-1. These rules instruct the optimizer on how to determine the execution path, when to choose one index over another, and when to perform a full table scan. These rules are fixed, predetermined, and, in contrast with the cost-base optimizer, not influenced by outside sources (table volumes, index distributions, etc.). For these reasons, most DBAs and programmers are more comfortable with this optimizer; life is a lot more predictable and a lot more controllable.

Table 6-1: Condition Rankings

Rank	Condition
1	ROWID = constant
2	Cluster join with unique or primary key = constant
3	Hash cluster key with unique or primary key = constant
4	Entire unique concatenated index = constant
5	Unique indexed column = constant
6	Entire cluster key = corresponding cluster key of another table in the same cluster
7	Hash cluster key = constant
8	Entire cluster key = constant
9	Entire non-UNIQUE concatenated index = constant
10	Non-UNIQUE index merge
11	Entire concatenated index = lower bound
12	Most leading column(s) of concatenated index = constant
13	Indexed column BETWEEN low value and high value or indexed column LIKE "ABC%" (bounded range)
14	Non-UNIQUE indexed column between low value and high value or indexed column like 'ABC%' (bounded range)
15	UNIQUE indexed column or constant (unbounded range)
16	Non-UNIQUE indexed column or constant (unbounded range)
17	Equality on nonindexed = column or constant (sort/merge join)
18	MAX or MIN of single indexed columns
19	ORDER BY entire index
20	Full table scans

NOTE   The rankings shown here may not be the same as those shown in your Oracle manuals, but they represent our best information about the actual current state of the optimizer, as detailed in the Oracle release notes. Oracle is continually enhancing the optimizer. You should be aware that this process of enhancement will continue, so it will be difficult to be absolutely sure of the exact details of these conditions for every Oracle release on every platform. The DBA at your site must stay aware of all optimizer changes by reading the README notes that accompany each version upgrade.

These rules have not changed greatly since they stabilized at about Oracle6.0.33. Additions have been made to cater to additional Oracle7 features, but the basic rules and techniques have remained constant.

The RDBMS kernel defaults to using the rule-based optimizer under a number of conditions, including:

- Oracle Version 6 or lower

- INIT.ORA: OPTIMIZER_MODE = RULE (Oracle7 and higher)

- INIT.ORA: OPTIMIZER_MODE = CHOOSE (Oracle7 and higher); no statistics exist for any table involved in the statement

- ALTER SESSION SET OPTIMIZER_MODE = RULE

- ALTER SESSION SET OPTIMIZER_MODE = CHOOSE (Oracle7 and higher); no statistics exist for any table involved in the statement

- SELECT /*+ RULE */. . .

Cost-Based Optimizer

The Oracle7 cost-based optimizer is a more sophisticated facility. It uses database information (e.g., table size, number of rows, key spread) rather than rigid rules. This information is available once the table has been analyzed via the Oracle7 ANALYZE command. If a table has not been analyzed, the cost-based optimizer can use only rule-based logic to select the best access path. The ANALYZE function collects statistics about tables, clusters, and indexes, and stores them in the data dictionary. Because the ANALYZE command incurs substantial overhead of its own, it is not always the best option.

A SQL statement will default to the cost-based optimizer if any one of the tables involved in the statement has been analyzed. The optimizer makes an educated guess as to the best access path for the other tables based on information in the data dictionary.

The RDBMS kernel defaults to using the cost-based optimizer under a number of situations. The following list details a few:

- INIT.ORA: OPTIMIZER_MODE = CHOOSE (Oracle7 and higher); statistics exist for *at least one* table involved in the statement

- ALTER SESSION SET OPTIMIZER_MODE = CHOOSE (Oracle7 and higher); statistics exist for *at least one* table involved in the statement

- ALTER SESSION SET OPTIMIZER_MODE = FIRST_ROWS (Oracle7 and higher); statistics exist for *at least one* table involved in the statement

- ALTER SESSION SET OPTIMIZER_MODE = ALL_ROWS (Oracle7 and higher)

- SELECT /*+ FIRST_ROWS */. . .

- SELECT /*+ ALL_ROWS */. . .

ANALYZE command

Database objects need to be analyzed before statistics are available for the cost-based optimizer. The DBA must choose how often to analyze a database and which analyze option to select. Obviously, analyzing an object comes at a price. Analyzing an entire database schema can be very demanding on computer resources.

The basic syntax of the ANALYZE statement is

```
ANALYZE
    TABLE    xxxxx    COMPUTE STATISTICS
    INDEX             ESTIMATE STATISTICS    {SAMPLE nn [ROWS|PERCENT]}
    CLUSTER           DELETE STATISTICS
```

where xxxxx is the table, index, or cluster name. Chapter 10 illustrates additional statement options.

WARNING   Oracle tells us not to analyze objects owned by user SYS. This can cause database deadlocks (while performing the ANALYZE command) and will deteriorate normal day-to-day database performance. Internal database operations on SYS tables have been tuned to use the rule-based optimizer. Analyzing these objects will cause the database to use the cost-based optimizer while parsing the statements and possibly selecting a less efficient execution plan.

CREATE TABLE privileges are sufficient for a user to analyze his or her own tables. A user requires ANALYZE ANY privilege to analyze another user's objects.

Never underestimate the overhead associated with analyzing database objects. Analyzing a table is equivalent to building an index. An exclusive lock is taken on the table, preventing any DML updates until the ANALYZE has completed. The table must be available (no current update activity) for the ANALYZE to be able to begin. When analyzing a table or cluster, all subsequent indexes are also included. The time taken to perform the ANALYZE function is roughly equivalent to the time to perform a full table scan of the table or cluster and all the indexes. More surprising is the amount of temporary disk space required. Sufficient temporary disk storage must be available to simultaneously hold a copy of the table and all associated indexes. A 500-megabyte table with three 100-megabyte indexes requires 800 megabytes of temporary disk space to analyze a table with the COMPUTE STATISTICS option.

Because of these overheads, multiplied by a large number of tables, a full ANALYZE of every schema table can take between 12 and 24 hours for large applications. This is clearly not possible for many applications that cannot afford this type of unavailability. We use the following SQL script to automatically analyze all schema objects. The key to this script is physical table size. Any table less than 10 megabytes in total size has statistics computed, while tables larger than 10 megabytes have statistics estimated. This approach reduces our total lapsed time to less than 2 hours. For example:

```
# analyze.sql
SET PAGES  0
SET LINES  132
SET TERM   OFF
SET RECSEP OFF
SPOOL /tmp/statistics.tmp

SELECT 'analyze table '||owner||'.'||table_name||' '||
       DECODE(SIGN(10485760 - initial_extent),1,'compute statistics;',
                           'estimate statistics;')
FROM   sys.dba_tables
WHERE  owner != 'SYS'
/
SPOOL  OFF
SPOOL  /tmp/statistics.log
@/tmp/statistics.tmp
SPOOL OFF
EXIT

ANALYZE TABLE SCOTT.emp COMPUTE STATISTICS;
ANALYZE TABLE SCOTT.dept COMPUTE STATISTICS;
ANALYZE TABLE SCOTT.sales ESTIMATE STATISTICS;
ANALYZE TABLE SCOTT.sales_history ESTIMATE STATISTICS;
```

Estimating statistics is something you will need to experiment with. In estimating a table, a random 1064 records are read and used to generate key statistics (distribution spreads, total number of rows etc.). A 19th-century Russian statistician was apparently responsible for determining that a sample base of 1064 random elements is sufficient to calculate statistics with an overall accuracy of over 99%.

What statistics are calculated?

A diverse and complete set of statistics is calculated and recorded by the ANALYZE function. These statistics are incorporated as part of the normal Oracle object schema that is used to hold table, index, and cluster definitions. The usual data dictionary views can be used to view these statistics. These views include DBA_TABLES, DBA_INDEXES, DBA_CLUSTERS, USER_TABLES, etc.

Statistics that are calculated by the ANALYZE command are detailed below:

- DBA_TABLES STATISTICS (sys.tab$)

Num_Row	Number of rows
Blocks	Number of blocks*
Empty_Blocks	Number of unused blocks
Avg_Space	Average available free space per block
Chain_Cnt	Number of chained rows
Avg_Row_Len	Average row length

- DBA_TAB_COLUMNS STATISTICS (sys.col$)

Num_Distinct	Number of distinct values per column
Low_Value	Second lowest column value
High_Value	Second highest column value
Density	Column density factor

- DBA_INDEXES STATISTICS (sys.ind$)

Blevel	Index depth (always exact)
Leaf_Blocks	Number of leaf blocks
Distinct_Keys	Number of distinct keys
Avg_Leaf_Blocks_Per_Key	Average number of leaf blocks per key
Avg_Data_Blocks_Per_Key	Average number of data blocks per key
Clustering_Factor	Clustering factor

Inner workings of the cost-based optimizer

Unlike the rule-based optimizer, the cost-based optimizer does not have hard and fast path evaluation rules. The cost-based optimizer is flexible and can adapt to its environment. This adaptation is possible only once the necessary underlying object statistics have been refreshed (reanalyzed). What is constant is the method by which the cost-based optimizer calculates each possible execution plan and evaluates its cost (efficiency).

The cost-based optimizer cost evaluation centers on the total number of logical reads to process the entire SQL statement. By default, the goal of the cost-based

---

* Statistics are collected only during COMPUTE and are always exact.

optimizer is best throughput, that is, to minimize the resource usage necessary to process all rows accessed by the statement (i.e., ALL_ROWS). The goal can be altered to best response time. This means selecting an execution plan that will minimize the total resource usage necessary to process the first row accessed by the statement (i.e., FIRST_ROWS).

The cost-based optimizer can use only statistics that are derived from the last ANALYZE operation and will estimate statistics for tables and indexes that have none (i.e., have not been analyzed). These estimations are based on fixed information that can be derived from the existing data dictionary details (i.e., total object size, etc.). The cost-based optimizer functionality can be (loosely) broken into the following steps:

- Parse the SQL (check syntax, object privileges, etc.).

- Generate a list of all potential execution plans.

- Calculate (estimate) the cost of each execution plan using all available object statistics, eliminating all expensive plans as early as possible.

- Select the execution plan with the lowest cost.

NOTE   The cost-based optimizer will be used only if at least one table within the SQL statement has statistics (unanalyzed table statistics are estimated). If no statistics are available for any table involved in the SQL, the RDBMS will resort to the rule-based optimizer (unless the cost-based optimizer is forced via statement level hints or an optimizer goal of ALL_ROWS or FIRST_ROWS).

To understand how the cost-based optimizer works and ultimately, how to exploit it, we need to understand how it thinks. You need to know what is important to the optimizer and what is not. This assessment centers on the selectivity assumptions and cost computations made in calculating the cost of each possible execution path. The following points detail each data access method and how selectivity is determined:

Primary key and/or UNIQUE index equality
   A UNIQUE index's selectivity is recognized as 100 percent. No other (indexed) access method can be more precise. For this reason, a unique index is always used. For example:

```
SELECT ...
FROM    emp
WHERE   emp_no = 1234;
```

Non-UNIQUE index equality

For non-UNIQUE indexes, index selectivity is calculated. The cost-based optimizer does make the assumption that the table (and subsequent index) has uniform data spread. As we all know, this is not always true, and assumptions based on this principle can be misleading. For example:

```
SELECT ...
FROM    emp
WHERE   dept_no = 0020;
```

$$\text{Selectivity} = \frac{\text{DBA\_Tab\_Columns.Num\_Distinct}}{\text{DBA\_Tables.Num\_Rows}} = \frac{4111}{75421} = 5.52\ \%$$

Range evaluation

For indexed range execution plans, selectivity is evaluated. This evaluation is based on a column's last high-value and low-value statistics. Again, the cost-based optimizer does make the assumption that the table (and subsequent index) has uniform data spread. For example:

```
SELECT ...
FROM    emp
WHERE   emp_no < 1000;
```

$$\text{Selectivity} = \frac{\text{Upper Range Value} - \text{Lower Range Value}}{\text{DBA\_Tab\_Columns.High\_Value} - \text{DBA\_Tab\_Columns.Low\_Value} + 1}$$

$$= \frac{1000 - 0}{9000 - 100 + 1} = 11.24\ \%$$

Range evaluation over bind variables

For indexed range execution plans, selectivity is guessed. Because bind variable values are not available at parse time (values are passed to the cursor after the execution plan has been decided), the optimizer cannot make decisions based on their value. The optimizer assumes a rule of thumb of 25% for unbounded bind variable ranges and 50% for bounded ranges. For example:

```
SELECT ...
FROM    emp
WHERE   dept_no = :b1;      Selectivity = 25 %

SELECT ...
FROM    emp
WHERE   dept_no > :b1
AND     dept_no < :b2;      Selectivity = 50 %
```

Combining the information provided by the selectivity rules with other database I/O information, we are now able to calculate the cost of an execution plan. The COST computation workings for each SQL plan execution method are detailed as follows:

Full table scan

The cost of a full table scan is one of the simplest and most accurate of the lot. It is based primarily on the DB_FILE_MULTIBLOCK_READ_COUNT parameter.

$$\text{Cost} = \text{ceil}\left(\frac{\text{DBA\_Tables.Blocks}}{\text{MultiBlock Read Count}}\right) = \text{ceil}\left(\frac{320}{8}\right) = 40$$

Indexed scan

The cost calculation of an indexed scan starts to become a little less accurate and a little more presumptuous. The statements selectivity is combined with physical index information to derive an overall execution cost. For example:

```
Cost = Index Cost + Table Cost
     = ceil (DBA_Indexes.Avg_Leaf_Block_Per_Key x 'Selectivity')
         + (DBA_Indexes.Custering_Factor x 'Selectivity')
```

Indexed range scan

The cost calculation of an indexed range scan is even more dubious:

```
Cost = Index Cost + Table Cost
     = ceil (DBA_Indexes.Avg_Leaf_Block_Per_Key x 'Selectivity')
         + (DBA_Indexes.Custering_Factor x 'Range Selectivity')
```

EXPLAIN PLAN extensions for the cost-based optimizer

Now that you know how to calculate and compare alternative execution plan costs, you can promptly file it. Oracle provides this information via the EXPLAIN PLAN facility described in Chapter 10. EXPLAIN PLAN can be used to display the calculated execution cost(s) via some extensions to the utility. For example:

```
SELECT     LPAD(' ', 2 * level) || operation || ' ' ||
           DECODE(id, 0, 'Cost = ' || position) Operation,
           options, object_name
FROM       plan_table
CONNECT BY prior_id = parent_id
START WITH id = 0
ORDER BY   id;

SELECT /*+ FULL (emp) */ .....
FROM    emp
WHERE   emp_no = 1234;

Operation                    Options      Object_Name
-------------------------    ----------   -----------
Select Table Cost = 25
Table Access                 Full         EMP

select /*+ INDEX (emp emp_PK) */ .....
from    emp
where   emp_no = 1234;
```

```
Operation                    Options        Object_Name
------------------------     -----------    -----------
Select Table Cost = 35
Table Access                 Rowid          EMP
   Index                     Unique Scan    EMP_PK
```

By manipulating the cost-based optimizer (i.e., via inline hints or creating/removing indexes), we can see the real differences in the actual execution cost as calculated by the optimizer.

NOTE   So far in this chapter, we've tried to give you a better feel for the techniques that the cost-based optimizer uses when making its calculations. The optimizer cost and selectivity calculations are susceptible to change by Oracle Corporation at any time. From the early days of Oracle7.0 to the more mature offerings of Oracle7.2/3, we have seen a marked improvement in the decision-making capabilities of the cost-based optimizer. There is no reason to assume that this trend will not continue.

SQL Tuning

Tuning individual SQL statements is probably one of the easier jobs within an application development and/or support life cycle. After all, the hard work is in isolating a problem to a single SQL statement or group of statements. Even if your tuning skills are light or your knowledge of the application is weak, miracles have been performed with simple trial-and-error tuning.

The following sections cover a number of common SQL pitfalls that we encounter in nearly every application we have to tune. The fact that a single SQL statement can be written in more than a dozen different ways (all returning one result) complicates the tuning process. Common sense tells us that only one could actually be the best. It is that one statement variant that we are striving for.

Oracle provides us with a number of ways of communicating with the RDBMS optimizer. We should use this communication window as a way of passing on special application knowledge to the optimizer. DBAs, team leaders and even some application users have knowledge of the application data, its contents, key data spreads, future changes, and the like, that the optimizer will never be aware of. We must pass on these valuable details whenever possible.

Some Preliminary SQL Questions

Before you begin to tune individual SQL statements, there are a few general questions that need to be answered. Be sure to do your homework by answering these questions and studying your database design with care. A little knowledge is a dangerous thing—here as elsewhere. If you don't really know how your data and programs are constructed or whether those structures are likely to change in the near future, then you might find that by applying the tuning suggestions included in this chapter, you'll actually degrade performance rather than improving it.

A reminder: Make sure that your statements all work before you start trying to tune them. Although producing working code is only the first step to a well-tuned system, it is an important step.

How long is too long? Before you can improve system performance by reducing the amount of time your SQL statements take to retrieve data, you must figure out how long the retrieval *should* take. That's a rather ambiguous question. You'll need to take a look at comparable systems, examine your own system's needs, and do some testing of alternative statements. You'll also need to consult with your organization's management to find out what response time policies are in effect for your system.

Is the statement running over real production volumes? The common, plaintive cry of developers everywhere is, "But it worked during testing." Poor database queries are often due to poor testing environments. To produce well-tuned SQL statements, you must take the time to test your statements thoroughly with (close to) production data volumes. Smaller columns are viable as long as the results can be safely extrapolated to demonstrate production response times.

Too often, developers do their testing with a development database that's simply too small to be realistic. Many problems are revealed only when you test with a large enough amount of data. If your test database is unrealistically small, you won't really be putting your statements through their paces. For example, full table scans are usually a major drain on performance. But if you test using a master table containing only 10 records, you'll never see a true full-table scan in action. Performance problems will remain dormant until your application goes live with real data.

Is the optimal retrieval path being used? Figuring out the optimal path for retrieval is a joint effort between you and the optimizer. Let the optimizer figure out a retrieval path. Then, examine your statements yourself, using the EXPLAIN PLAN utility to confirm the best choice of a retrieval path.

Will future events and/or database changes have an effect on optimization? Optimization may not be forever. Remember that a SQL statement is parsed every time it is encountered. For example, if you add or delete an index for an associated table or reanalyze statistics, you might find that your carefully tuned SQL statements no longer work as efficiently as they did. You'll need to keep testing, checking, and tuning for the life of your database and application.

Rule-Based Optimizer Tuning

The rule-based optimizer provides a good deal of scope for tuning. Because its behavior is predictable, governed by the 20 condition rankings that we presented earlier in this chapter, we are able to manipulate its choices. Although this manipulation can be very rewarding, it is generally difficult and confusing to the uninitiated. The first thing to do is to become familiar with the normal workings of the rule-based optimizer. Investigate and understand how the optimizer makes its decisions; how the creation and/or removal of an index influences the decision process, why a UNIQUE index has precedent over a non-UNIQUE index, etc. This information is all explained in your basic Oracle tuning manuals. But you can go still further. The following sections describe how to communicate with the rule-based optimizer and influence it to perform beyond its default capabilities.

Selecting the most efficient table name sequence

Obviously, if your SQL statement references only a single table, then table sequencing is not an issue. If you have more than one table referenced (in a single FROM clause), then a *driving table* must be chosen by the optimizer.

One of the most important ways you can tune SQL statements under the rule-based optimizer is to make sure your SELECT statements reference tables in the most efficient sequence. Although this discussion is less relevant for the cost-based optimizer, in which the optimizer makes its own determination of the driving table(s), you may encounter situations in which you'll need to do manual tuning, using the suggestions we include here.

NOTE   The sequence of conditions in your WHERE clause (described a bit later in this chapter in the section called "Efficient WHERE clause sequencing") is of higher priority to the rule-based optimizer than the FROM sequence. If two index paths over two tables have different rule-based rankings, then the table with the lowest numeric ranking will be the driving table. Only when the two tables have equal query path rankings does the FROM sequence come into play.

If you specify more than one table name in the FROM clause of a SELECT statement—for example:

```
SELECT COUNT (*)
FROM   emp,
       dept
```

the order in which you specify the tables may have a significant impact on performance.

Regardless of the order in which you specify table names, the optimizer tries to reorder table processing on the basis of what is most efficient. It takes into account such factors as the indexes specified for the tables. However, if you are running the rule-based optimizer and the optimizer cannot make an intelligent decision (because it doesn't have enough extra information), then Oracle simply executes the statement in the order in which the tables are parsed. Because the parser processes table names from right to left, the table name that you specify *last* (e.g., DEPT in the example above) is actually the *first* table processed (driving table).

Because indexes need to be correctly specified in a (well-designed) Transaction Processing Option (TPO) system, table name sequence is usually less of an issue for online jobs than it is for overnight updating and reporting routines. Programs producing reports during lengthy overnight runs tend to scan entire tables, simultaneously joining many objects.

If you suspect that a SQL statement referencing multiple tables is taking longer than is acceptable, you should examine the effects of table sequence on your retrievals. Chapter 10 describes the TKPROF and EXPLAIN PLAN facilities, which can help to localize table sequencing problems.

The driving table

The object of all your SQL query and update statements is to minimize the total physical number of database blocks that need to be read and/or written. If you specify more than one table in a FROM clause of a SELECT statement, you must choose one as the driving table. By making the correct choice, you can make enormous improvements in performance.

Consider the following example of two tables processed by the Version 6 optimizer:

```
Table TAB1  has 16,384   rows
Table TAB2  has 1        row.
```

Suppose you select TAB2 as the driving table (by specifying it second in the FROM clause):

```
SELECT COUNT (*) FROM TAB1, TAB2 0.96 seconds elapsed
```

	count	phys	cr	cur	rows
	------	-----	-----	-----	------
Parse	1	0	0	0	
Execute	1	95	100	4	0
Fetch	1	0	0	0	1

Now suppose that you select TAB1 as the driving table:

```
SELECT COUNT (*) FROM TAB2, TAB1                    26.09 seconds elapsed
```

	count	phys	cr	cur	rows
Parse	1	0	0	0	
Execute	1	95	49247	32770	0
Fetch	1	0	0	0	1

You can see that specifying the correct driving table makes a huge difference in performance (0.96 versus 26.09 seconds). What's going on? When Oracle processes multiple tables, it uses an internal sort/merge procedure to join the two tables. First, it scans and sorts the first (driver) table (the one specified *second* in the FROM clause). Next, it scans the second table (the one specified *first* in the FROM clause) and merges all of the rows retrieved from the second table with those retrieved from the first table.

The 95 physical reads shown on the Execute line in the examples above are the minimum number of database "block reads" needed to read all rows from the two tables. The large overhead differences arise from the ensuing number of consistent buffer reads ("cr") and current mode buffer reads ("cur").

If TAB1 is processed first, then all 16,384 rows (from TAB1) must be read first. These records are sorted, but cannot fit into the area of memory allocated for each user's sort/ merges (specified in the INIT.ORA parameter SORT_AREA_SIZE). Consequently, these records are sorted in small runs with the data stored in temporary segments on disk. After all runs are completed, Oracle merges your data to produce the sorted data. The single piece of TAB2 data is read and joined with the TAB1 data.

By comparison, if TAB2 is processed first, only one row needs to be read (from TAB2), and this row can be sorted within the sort area. The TAB1 table is then joined with the TAB2 table.

Now consider an example in which the number of rows in TAB2 is slightly greater—four instead of one. The performance differential is not quite as extreme in this case.

```
Table TAB1   has 16,384   rows.
Table TAB2   has 4         rows.
```

```
SELECT COUNT (*) FROM TAB1, TAB2                    4.00 seconds elapsed
```

	count	phys	cr	cur	rows
Parse	1	0	0	0	
Execute	1	384	386	10	0
Fetch	1	0	0	0	1

```
SELECT COUNT (*) FROM TAB2, TAB1 37.32 seconds elapsed
```

	count	phys	cr	cur	rows
	------	-----	-----	-----	------
Parse	1	0	0	0	
Execute	1	95	49247	32770	0
Fetch	1	0	0	0	1

Joining three or more tables

If three tables are being joined, try to select the *intersection* table as the driving table. The intersection table is the table that has the most dependencies on it. In the following example, the EMP table represents the intersection between the LOCATION table and the CATEGORY table. This first SELECT:

```
SELECT    . . .
FROM      location L,
          category C,
          emp E
  WHERE   E.emp_no BETWEEN 1000 AND 2000
    AND   E.cat_no = C.cat_no
    AND   E.locn   = L.locn
```

is more efficient than this next example:

```
SELECT    . . .
  FROM    emp E,
          location L,
          category C
  WHERE   E.cat_no = C.cat_no
    AND   E.locn   = L.locn
    AND   E.emp_no BETWEEN 1000 AND 2000
```

Efficient WHERE clause sequencing

The way in which you specify conditions in the WHERE clause(s) of your SELECT statements has a major impact on the performance of your SQL. In the absence of any other information, the rule-based optimizer must use the WHERE clause sequencing to help determine the best execution path within the database. If you are able to specify the most efficient indexed conditions early in your WHERE clauses, the optimizer will be more likely to choose the most efficient execution path. The following sections detail some of the more common index resolution rules.

Two or more equality indexes. When a SQL statement has two or more equality indexes over different tables (e.g., WHERE = value) available to the execution plan, Oracle uses both indexes by merging them at run-time and fetching only rows that are common to both indexes. If two indexes exist over the same table in a WHERE clause, Oracle ranks them.

A UNIQUE index ranks higher than a non-UNIQUE index. If both indexes are of the same type (and same rule-based ranking), the outcome depends on whether the indexes were specified over the same or different tables. If the two (equal) indexes are over two different tables, the statement table sequence determines which will be queried first; the table that is specified *last* in the FROM clause outranks those specified earlier. If the two (equal) indexes are over the same table, the index that is referenced *first* in the WHERE clause ranks higher than the index referenced second. There is no logical performance reason for this decision. Its reasoning is based on the fact that a decision had to be made, and this was as good as any!

Consider the following example; there is a non-UNIQUE index over DEPT_NO, and a non-UNIQUE index over EMP_CAT:

```
SELECT   emp_name
FROM     emp
WHERE    dept_no  =   0020
AND      emp_cat  =   'A' ;

Explain Plan   Query Plan
------------------------------------------------------------------
Table Access By Rowid on EMP
    And-Equal
        Index Range Scan on Dept_Idx
        Index Range Scan on Cat_Idx
```

The DEPT_NO index is retrieved first, followed by (merged with) the EMP_CAT indexed rows. Reversing the WHEN clauses gives us the opposite result.

```
SELECT   emp_name
FROM     emp
WHERE    emp_cat  =   'A'
AND      dept_no  =   0020 ;

Explain Plan   Query Plan
------------------------------------------------------------------
Table Access By Rowid on EMP
    And-Equal
        Index Range Scan on Dept_Idx
        Index Range Scan on Cat_Idx
```

Many programmers share the misconception that unique (and non-unique) comparative WHERE clauses rank very high on the optimizer's ranked list. This is true only when they are compared against constant predicates. If they are compared against indexed columns from other tables, such clauses are much lower on the optimizer's list. For example, consider the statement:

```
SELECT   . . .
FROM     dept D, emp E
WHERE    E.emp_cat = 'A'           Non-unique index;  rank 6
AND      E.name LIKE 'SMITH%'      Indexed range;     rank 9
AND      E.dept_no = D.dept_no     Sort/merge join;   rank 10
```

People assume that because DEPT has a UNIQUE index over DEPT_NO, it will rank very high. This is true, however, only in comparing against constants (or bind variables).

Equality and range predicates. When indexes combine both equality and range predicates over the same table, Oracle cannot merge these indexes. In such cases, it uses only the equality predicate. Each row is individually validated against the second predicate. For example, in the following there is a non-UNIQUE index over DEPT_NO and a non-UNIQUE index over EMP_CAT:

```
SELECT   emp_name
FROM     emp
WHERE    dept_no > 0020
AND      emp_cat = 'A' ;

Explain Plan Query Plan
-----------------------------------------------------------
Table Access By Rowid on EMP
    Index Range Scan on Cat_Idx
```

The EMP_CAT index is used, and then each row is validated manually.

No clear ranking winner. When there is no clear index "ranking" winner, Oracle will use only one of the indexes. In such cases, Oracle uses the first index referenced by a WHERE clause in the statement (Version 6.0.33 and after). For example, in the following there is a non-UNIQUE index over DEPT_NO and a non-UNIQUE index over EMP_CAT:

```
SELECT   emp_name
FROM     emp
WHERE    dept_no > 0020
AND      emp_cat > 'B' ;

Explain Plan Query Plan
-----------------------------------------------------------
Table Access By Rowid on EMP
    Index Range Scan on Dept_Idx
```

The DEPT_NO index is used, and then each row is validated manually.

Automatic index suppression. Under certain circumstances, the RDBMS kernel will actually omit particular indexes from the query plan. Assume that a table has two (or more) available indexes and that one index is unique and the other index is not unique. In such cases, Oracle (wisely) uses the unique retrieval path and completely ignores the second option. In the following example, there is a unique index over EMP_NO and a non-UNIQUE index over EMP_DEPT.

```
SELECT    emp_name
FROM      emp
WHERE     emp_no   = 2362
AND       emp_dept = 0020 ;


Explain Plan Query Plan
------------------------------------------------------------
Table Access By Rowid on EMP
      Index Unique Scan on Emp_No_Idx
```

The EMP_NO index is used to fetch the row. The second predicate (EMP_DEPT = 0020) is then manually evaluated (no index used).

Cost-Based Optimizer Tuning

When using the cost-based optimizer, you can manually tune individual SQL statements, overriding the optimizer's decisions by including your own optimization hints within the SQL statement. By including your own optimization hints as "comments" within the SQL statement, you force the statement to follow your desired retrieval path, rather than the one calculated by the optimizer. In the following example, including /*+ RULE */ inside the SELECT statement instructs the optimizer to use the rule-based optimizer, rather than the cost-based optimizer:

```
# sql_jhint.sql
SELECT     /*+ RULE */  . . . .
  FROM     emp, dept
  WHERE    . . .
```

The optimizer hint(s) can be included only immediately after the initial SQL "action" verb and are ignored when included in INSERT statements.

```
SELECT  /*+ hint text */  . . . .
DELETE  /*+ hint text */  . . . .
UPDATE  /*+ hint text */  . . . .
```

Each hint is operational only within the *statement block* for which it appears. A statement block is one of the following:

- A simple SELECT, DELETE, or UPDATE statement

- The parent portion of a complex statement

- The subquery portion of a complex statement

- Part of a compound query

Consider these examples:

```
SELECT  /*+ RULE */  . . . .
FROM    emp
WHERE   emp_status = 'PART-TIME'
AND     EXISTS     ( SELECT  /*+ FIRST_ROWS */  'x'
                     FROM    emp_history
                     WHERE   emp_no = E.emp_no
                     AND     emp_status != 'PART-TIME' )

SELECT  /*+ RULE */  . . . .
FROM    emp
WHERE   emp_status = 'PART-TIME'
UNION
SELECT  /*+ ALL_ROWS */  . . . .
FROM    emp_history
WHERE   emp_status != 'PART-TIME'
```

NOTE The RULE hint is a particularly helpful option if you have manually tuned some (but not all) of your core application SQL statements using the rule-based optimizer and now wish to move the application to the cost-base optimizer.

Including optimization hints as comments is a somewhat clumsy way to tune, but this feature does provide a better way to do manual tuning than anything available in earlier versions.

Cost-based optimizer hints

Valid hints that you can include as comments in SQL statements are:

ALL_ROWS

Optimizes for best throughput to execute all rows. Statistics do not have to be available for *any* table involved in the SQL statement; statistics are estimated by the optimizer. Other access path hints can be included with the ALL_ROWS hint and override the ALL_ROWS decisions.

FIRST_ROWS

Optimizes for best response time to execute the FIRST rows. Statistics do not have to be available for any table involved in the SQL statement; their statistics are estimated by the optimizer. Other "access path hints" can be included with the FIRST_ROWS hint and override the FIRST_ROWS decisions. This hint:

- Will always choose an index over a full table scan.

- Uses nested loop joins over sort/merge joins, where possible.

- Uses an index to satisfy an ORDER BY clause, where possible.

The optimizer ignores this hint for DELETE and UPDATE statement blocks and any SELECT statement block that contains a "grouping" operation (UNION, INTERSECT, MINUS, GROUP BY, DISTINCT, MAX, MIN, SUM, etc.) or a FOR UPDATE clause. These statements cannot be optimized for best response time because all rows must be accessed by the statement before the first row can be returned.

CHOOSE

Uses the cost-based optimizer if statistics are available for at least one table; otherwise, uses the rule-based optimizer. This hint is valid only for the current statement block.

RULE

Uses the rule-based optimizer for the current statement block.

The following cost-based hints are used to influence a SQL statement's access method(s). Specifying one or more of these hints causes the optimizer to select the specific access path only if it is valid and available for a particular table or cluster within the SQL statement.

FULL (table)

Forces the use of a full table scan for the specified table.

ROWID (table)

Forces a table scan by ROWID for the specified table.

CLUSTER

Forces the use of a cluster scan for the specified table.

HASH (table)

Forces the use of a hash table scan for the specified table.

INDEX (table [index])

Forces the use of an indexed table scan for the specified table. The hint can optionally include one or more indexes. If no indexes are included, the optimizer calculates the cost of all indexes for the table and uses the most efficient (several indexes may be used in tandem). If several indexes are listed, the optimizer calculates the cost of only those indexes and uses the most efficient (several indexes from the list may be used in tandem). If a single index is specified, the optimizer performs a scan of that index.

INDEX_ASC (table [index])

Forces the use of an ascending indexed table scan for the specified table. Oracle cannot guarantee that it will, by default, scan indexes in any specific order, especially when using the parallel query facility. This hint guarantees that the index will be traversed in ascending order. The hint can optionally include one or more indexes. These index entries behave the same as described for the INDEX hint.

INDEX_DESC (table [index])

Forces the use of a descending indexed table scan for the specified table. Oracle cannot guarantee that it will, by default, scan indexes in any specific order. (Normally, Oracle scans indexes in ascending sequence.) This hint guarantees that the index will be traversed in descending order. The hint can optionally include one or more indexes. These index entries behave the same as described for the INDEX hint.

AND_EQUAL (table index)

Explicitly chooses an execution plan that merges the scan on several single-column indexes. A minimum of two indexes must be specified, and no more than five are allowed.

USE_CONCAT

Forces the optimizer to combine OR conditions in the WHERE clause to be converted to a compound UNION ALL query operation.

ORDERED

Forces the optimizer to join tables in the same order as that in which they are specified in the FROM clause (left to right). This hint is very similar to the table sequencing rule-based tuning technique that we described earlier, but (unfortunately) in the reverse order.

USE_NL (table)

Forces the optimizer to join the specified table to another table (or subquery) using a nested loop join. The specified table is joined as the inner table of the nested loops. Nested loop joins are regarded as faster than a sort/merge join at retrieving the first row of a query statement. The first row can be displayed after reading the first selected row from one table and the first matching row from the next. For this reason, nested loop joins are utilized when the FIRST_ROWS hint is selected.

USE_MERGE (table)

Forces the specified table to use a sort/merge join when joining with another table or subquery.

CACHE (table)

Instructs the optimizer to position all blocks retrieved via a full table scan at the most recently used end of the LRU list in the buffer cache.

NOCACHE (table)

Instructs the optimizer to position all blocks fetched for the specified table at the least recently used end of the LRU list in the buffer cache when performing a full table scan. This is the normal behavior for a full table scan.

PUSH_SUBQ

Forces the nonmerged subqueries to be evaluated as early as possible in the execution plan. Nonmerged subqueries are normally executed as the last step of the execution plan. This hint has no effect if the subquery is over a remote table (distributed SQL statement) or the subquery uses a merge join.

The following cost-based hints are explicitly used to communicate with the parallel query facilities of the optimizer. The parallel query option needs to be installed within your database before these hints can be operative.

PARALLEL (table [,interger] [,integer])

Explicitly specifies the actual number of concurrent query servers that will be used to service the query. The first optional value specifies the degree of parallelism (number of query servers) for the table, and the second value specifies the number of parallel servers to divide the query into. If no parameters are specified, the default (calculated) parallel degree and number of parallel servers is sourced from the parameters specified in the INIT.ORA file.

NOPARALLEL (table)

Disables all parallel options for a statement block.

When are hints ignored?

A very important feature of in-line SQL hints is that they are statement comments, not part of the statement itself. This means that the optimizer cannot distinguish a bad hint from a programmer comment. An incorrectly structured or misspelled hint will be ignored rather than reported as an error. What should be a simple process of adding a SQL hint can turn into hours of complex tuning. SQL statement execution plans need to be generated and analyzed to prove that the hint is operable. This lengthy cycle may have to be repeated over and over again. For example:

```
SELECT /*+ RULE */ ...   is equivalent to  SELECT   /* ..comment.. */ ...
    FROM    emp                                 FROM     emp
    WHERE   ......                              WHERE    ......
```

Hints that used to work might not work anymore. Simple schema changes that should have no direct effect on a SQL statement, such as indexes being retitled or a table added to a cluster, can invalidate carefully placed hints. These hints are simply treated as comments—no error, no warning, no recognition at all!

The following list covers some of the more common mistakes people make when programming with hints:

Misspelled hint

As was mentioned earlier, all misspelled hints are ignored. Never assume that a hint is correct until you have inspected the SQL EXPLAIN PLAN output.

Inappropriate hint

When a correctly structured hint is inappropriate within the context of the statement, it is also ignored. For example, if an index is specified for a table that is not part of the statement, it will be ignored:

```
SELECT /*+ INDEX(dept dpt_PK) */ ... wrong table
FROM    emp
WHERE   emp_no = 12345
```

Conflicting hint

Hints that conflict with the statement structure are also ignored. For example: if an index reference is for the correct table but bears no connection to the SQL WHERE clause criteria, it will be discounted.

```
SELECT /*+ INDEX(emp dpt_idx) */ ... wrong index; not over "emp_no" column
FROM    emp
WHERE   emp_no = 12345
```

Invalid table identification

All hints that require a TABLE parameter must correctly specify the table. This means that if the table is referenced via an alias within the SQL statement, the hint must also reference it via the alias. For example:

```
SELECT /*+ INDEX(emp emp_PK) */ ... wrong table; must use "E" alias
FROM    emp E
WHERE   E.emp_no = 12345
```

Invalid hint location

Hints can appear only immediately after the first SQL verb of the statement block. If you position a hint anywhere else in the SQL, it will be ignored. For example:

```
SELECT /*+ hint text */ . . . .
DELETE /*+ hint text */ . . . .
UPDATE /*+ hint text */ . . . .

SELECT /*+ RULE */ . . . .
FROM    emp
WHERE   emp_status = 'PART-TIME'
UNION
SELECT /*+ ALL_ROWS */ . . . .
FROM    emp_history
WHERE   emp_status != 'PART-TIME'
```

Older PL/SQL versions

Versions of PL/SQL prior to PL/SQL 2.0 ignore all inline SQL hints. This includes the Oracle tools SQL*Forms 3.0 and SQL*Forms 4.0; SQL*Forms 4.5 can correctly handle hints.

Cost-Based Versus Rule-Based Optimizers

With the introduction of Oracle7 and the cost-based optimizer came that famous Oracle quote: "The cost-based optimizer generally chooses an execution plan that is as good as or better than the plan chosen by the rule-based optimizer." This is hardly a glowing endorsement for the cornerstone of all future application tuning. Which one do we choose? Should we rush out and enable the cost-based optimizer for all existing applications? One interesting issue for this discussion is Oracle Corporation's commitment to phase out all support of the rule-based optimizer in the coming releases. Oracle8 will continue to provide rule-based support, but no promises have been made beyond that release level.

Existing rule-based applications that are correctly designed and tuned are probably best left alone. Set the database to either rule-based optimization (i.e., INIT.ORA OPTIMIZER_MODE = RULE) or to CHOOSE mode (i.e., INIT.ORA OPTIMIZER_MODE = CHOOSE) and do not analyze any of the application objects. Once you have tuned an application module and its SQL to optimal performance, switching it to the cost-based optimizer cannot make it run any faster. The most efficient execution plan for the rule-based optimizer must also be the most efficient for the cost-based optimizer. At best, the cost-based optimizer will choose the same execution plan.

Poorly written applications that have never been tuned and have unacceptable performance delays should be investigated under the cost-based optimizer. The cost-based optimizer gives the best results for the least effort when applied to poorer applications.

The cost-based optimizer is particularly suited to applications with large queries over multiple tables and indexes. In general, you should use the cost-based optimizer for all new application development. This allows us to tune (manipulate) all SQL as we write it. Complex, core application modules can be tuned via inline SQL hints. The support of these hints allows us to default to the cost-based optimizer for the majority of the application processing while explicitly overriding its choice for the more complicated core modules.

Note the following about the cost-based optimizer:

- Tuned SQL cannot be magically improved by the cost-based optimizer.

- Best results from the cost-based optimizer are seen with untuned applications.

- The cost-based optimizer cannot distinguish grossly uneven key data spreads. If your data is not uniformly distributed, use inline hints to assist the execution path choices.

- The cost-based optimizer will be used if *at least one table* involved in the SQL has been analyzed. This means that multitable SQL statements that were never meant to use the cost-based optimizer do so by accident.

- The cost-based optimizer assumes that you are the only person accessing the database. A full table scan may be the most efficient path when you are the only person executing the routine, but this might not be so for 100 simultaneous users.

- When a table is analyzed, so are all associated indexes. If an index is subsequently dropped and recreated, it must be reanalyzed.

- The cost-based optimizer can make poor execution plan choices when a table has been analyzed but its indexes have not.

- The database should not be forced to use the cost-based optimizer via inline hints when no statistics are available for any table involved in the SQL.

- Using old (obsolete) statistics can be more dangerous than estimating the statistics at run-time.

- Analyzing large tables and their associated indexes will take a long, long time, requiring lots of CPU, I/O, and temporary tablespace resources.

- It is not uncommon for application developers to exploit the best of both optimizer worlds. While the database defaults to rule-based optimization, the programmers enhance the execution plan decision making process with inline hints.

Common Sense in SQL

A number of the more productive tuning techniques that we suggest to people involve nothing more than having the developer exercise a little common sense. The more experienced the programmer is, the more common sense he or she tends to exhibit. The following sections explain some of the techniques that every programmer should be aware of.

Using Efficient Nonindex WHERE Clause Sequencing

WHERE clause sequencing can play an even more important role in dealing with nonindexed equations (those that must be evaluated manually). The behavior of the Oracle optimizer for older versions of the RDBMS (both rule-based and cost-based) is somewhat strange under these circumstances but, thankfully, predictable. Oracle evaluates unindexed equations, linked by the AND verb in a bottom-up fashion. This means that the first clause (last in the AND list) is evaluated, and if it is found true, the second clause is then tested. Always try to position the most expensive AND clause first in the WHERE clause sequencing.

The following example selects all managers who earn more than $50,000 *and* have more than 25 staff reporting to them:

```
# and_or.sql
SELECT    . . . .                    Total CPU = 156.3 Sec
FROM      emp E
WHERE     emp_salary > 50,000
AND       emp_type   = 'MANAGER'
AND       25          < ( SELECT   COUNT(*)
                          FROM      emp
                          WHERE     emp_mgr = E.emp_no )
```

Simply alter the order of the AND clauses:

```
SELECT    . . . .                    Total CPU = 10.6 Sec
FROM      emp E
WHERE     25          < ( SELECT   COUNT(*)
                          FROM      emp
                          WHERE     emp_mgr = E.emp_no )
AND       emp_salary > 50,000
AND       emp_type   = 'MANAGER'
```

Now that you have come to terms with the secrets of the AND behavior, let's move on to SQL statements that contain unindexed OR clauses. Oracle evaluates unindexed equations, linked by the OR verb in a top-down fashion—that's right, in the exact opposite manner of the AND clause! This means that the first clause (first in the OR list) is evaluated, and if it is found false, the second clause is then tested. Always try to position the most expensive OR clause last in the WHERE clause sequencing.

The following example selects all managers who earn more than $50,000 *or* have more than 25 staff reporting to them.

```
SELECT    . . . .                    Total CPU = 28.3 Sec
FROM      emp E
WHERE   ( emp_salary > 50,000
    AND emp_type   = 'MANAGER' )
OR        25          < ( SELECT   COUNT(*)
                          FROM      emp
                          WHERE     emp_mgr = E.emp_no )
```

Simply alter the order of the OR clauses:

```
SELECT    . . . .                    Total CPU = 101.6 Sec
FROM      emp E
WHERE     25          < ( SELECT   COUNT(*)
                          FROM      emp
                          WHERE     emp_mgr = E.emp_no )
OR      ( emp_salary > 50,000
    AND emp_type   = 'MANAGER' )
```

NOTE   Newer versions of the Oracle optimizer have addressed this ineffi-
          cient behavior and always evaluate a simple predicate condition be-
          fore a complex subquery block.

Using ROWID When Possible

The ROWID of a record is the single fastest method of record retrieval. ROWID is actually an encoded key representing the physical record number within an actual Oracle database block on the database. Use ROWID whenever possible to get the best performance out of your data access requests.

You can improve performance by selecting a record before updating or deleting it and including ROWID in the initial SELECT list. This allows Oracle to perform a much more efficient second record access. Remember, when you first query the record, to select the record FOR UPDATE. This prevents another process from being able to update the selected record. For example:

```
SELECT  ROWID,  .  .  .
INTO    :emp_rowid,  .  .  .
FROM    emp
WHERE   emp.emp_no = 56722
FOR UPDATE;

UPDATE emp
SET    emp.name = .  .  .
WHERE  ROWID = :emp_rowid ;
```

Before Oracle7, it was mandatory to select the record FOR UPDATE before being able to update it via its ROWID. This was necessary because Oracle could not guarantee that the ROWID would not be changed via another UPDATE statement (i.e., it could be migrated to another physical block when it grows in size). This restriction has been lifted since Oracle7.

Reducing the Number of Trips to the Database

Every time a SQL statement is executed, Oracle needs to perform many internal processing steps; the statement needs to be parsed, indexes evaluated, variables bound, and data blocks read. The more you can reduce the number of database accesses, the more overheads you can save. Reducing the physical number of trips to the database is particularly beneficial in client-server configurations in which the database may need to be accessed over a network.

The following examples show three distinct ways of retrieving data about employees who have employee numbers 0342 or 0291. Method 1 is the least efficient, method 2 is more efficient, and method 3 is the most efficient of all.

Method 1 shows two separate database accesses:

```
# same_ciur.sql
SELECT emp_name, salary, GRADE
FROM    emp
WHERE   emp_no = 0342;


SELECT emp_name, salary, grade
FROM    emp
WHERE   emp_no = 0291;
```

Method 2 shows the use of one cursor and two fetches:

```
DECLARE
        CURSOR C1 (E_no  number)  IS
        SELECT emp_name, salary, grade
        FROM    emp
        WHERE   emp_no = E_no;
BEGIN
        OPEN    C1 (342);
        FETCH   C1 INTO ..., ..., ...;
          .

          .

          .

        OPEN    C1 (291);
      FETCH   C1 INTO ..., ..., ...;
        CLOSE   C1;
END;
```

Method 3 shows a SQL table join:

```
SELECT    A.emp_name, A.salary, A.grade,
                    B.emp_name, B,salary, B.grade
FROM      emp A,
               emp B
WHERE     A.emp_no = 0342
AND       B.emp_no = 0291 ;
```

In this last example, the same table is identified by two aliases, A and B, that are joined by a single statement. In this way, Oracle uses only one cursor and performs only one fetch.

NOTE   One simple way to increase the number of rows of data you can fetch with one database access, and thus reduce the number of physical calls needed, is to reset the ARRAYSIZE parameter in SQL*Plus, SQL*Forms, and Pro*C. We suggest a setting of 200.

Using Null Values

When inexperienced programmers first encounter a null valued column or an equation involving a null constant, they are generally surprised and confused by the outcome. Programmers, developers, and analysts should all have a complete understanding of the null value and its properties. Once understood, null is no different from (or more mystical than) any other database column.

In general:

- Null is never equal to (=) anything (including zero, space, or null).
- Null is never NOT equal to (!= or <>) anything.
- Null is never less than (<) or less than or equal to (<=) anything.
- Null is never greater than (>) or greater than or equal to (>=) anything.

Programmers should never directly compare null to anything else. If you perform a comparison to a null value, the record will be rejected.

None of the following SQL statements will return a row:

```
SELECT   'X'
FROM     DUAL
WHERE    'X'   =    NULL ;

SELECT   'X'
FROM     DUAL
WHERE    'X'   <>   NULL ;

SELECT   'X'
FROM     DUAL
WHERE    NULL  =    NULL ;

SELEC    'X'
FROM     DUAL
WHERE    NULL  <>   NULL ;

SELECT   'X'
FROM     DUAL
WHERE    NULL IN ('A','B',NULL);

SELECT   'X'
FROM     DUAL
WHERE    NULL NOT IN ('A', 'B', NULL);
```

Each of the following SQL statements *will* return one row:

```
SELECT   'X'
FROM     DUAL
WHERE    'X'   =    NVL(NULL, 'X');
```

```
SELECT   'X'
FROM     DUAL
WHERE    'X'  <>   NVL(NULL, 'Y');

SELECT   'X'
FROM     DUAL
WHERE    NULL IS NULL;

SELECT   'X'DECODE (sex,'M','Male','F','Female',NULL,'Unknown')
FROM     DUAL
WHERE    'X'  IS NOT NULL  ;
```

As with all good rules, there are a few exceptions. Null is in fact equal to null in the following limited situations:

- DECODE parameters (where NULL is a value within the comparison list)

```
SELECT   DECODE (sex,'M','Male','F','Female',NULL,'Unknown') Sex
FROM     emp
WHERE    emp_no = 1234

EMP_NO     SEX
------     -----
  1234     Male
```

- GROUP BY parameters (where several of rows have a column with a null value)

```
SELECT   sex, count(*)
FROM     emp
GROUP BY sex

SEX      Count(*)
-----    --------
M            3214
F             956
null           12
```

- DISTINCT parameters (where a number of rows have a column with a null value)

```
SELECT   count(DISTINCT sex)
FROM     emp

Count(distinct *)
-----------------
        3
```

- UNION/MINUS/INTERSECT columns (where a number of rows have a column with a null value)

```
SELECT   emp_no,   sex
FROM     emp
MINUS
SELECT   emp_no,   null
FROM     emp_history

sql> No rows selected
```

NOTE   Oracle's treatment of null conforms to ANSI standards.

Using DECODE

Programmers often need a way to count and/or sum variable conditions for a group of rows. The DECODE statement provides a very efficient way of doing this. Because DECODE is rather complex, few programmers take the time to learn to use this statement to full advantage. This section describes some common ways you can use DECODE to improve performance.

Using DECODE to reduce processing

The DECODE statement provides a way to avoid having to scan the same rows repetitively, or to join the same table repetitively. Consider the following example:

```
# decode.sql
SELECT COUNT(*), SUM(salary)
FROM    emp
WHERE   dept_no   =   0020
AND     emp_name LIKE 'SMITH%' ;

SELECT COUNT(*), SUM(salary)
FROM    emp
WHERE   dept_no   =   0030
AND     emp_name LIKE 'SMITH%' ;
```

You can achieve the same result much more efficiently with DECODE:

```
SELECT COUNT(DECODE(dept_no, 0020, 'X',    NULL)) D0020_kount,
       COUNT(DECODE(dept_no, 0030, 'X',    NULL)) D0030_kount,
       SUM  (DECODE(dept_no, 0020, salary, NULL)) D0020_sal,
       SUM  (DECODE(dept_no, 0030, salary, NULL)) D0030_sal
FROM    emp
WHERE   emp_name LIKE 'SMITH%';
```

Remember that null values are never included in, nor do they affect the outcome of, the COUNT and SUM functions.

Using DECODE in ORDER BY and GROUP BY clauses

You may need to specify many varying ORDER BY clauses to get the result you want. Rather than coding many identical queries, each with a different ORDER BY clause, you can specify a DECODE function such as the following:

```
# decode.sql
SELECT . . .
 FROM    emp
 WHERE   emp_name LIKE 'SMITH%'
 ORDER
         BY DECODE(:BLK.SEQN_FLD 'E', emp_no, 'D', dept_no);
```

This approach can be extended further to include the GROUP BY clause:

```
SELECT . . .
FROM    emp
WHERE   emp_name   LIKE   'SMITH%'
GROUP
        BY DECODE(:INPUT,'E',emp_no,'D',dept_no);
```

NOTE   DECODE verbs within ORDER BY and GROUP BY statements can-
              not use indexes. Instead, an internal sort is required. Because this is
              a slow process, use DECODE within ORDER BY only for online
              statements in which the number of rows returned by the WHERE
              clause is small. For reports, you need not worry about limits.

Table Alias Shortcuts

The dynamic SQL column reference (*) gives you a way to refer to all of the
columns of a table. For example, if you specify:

```
SELECT * FROM emp
```

Oracle references each column in the EMP table in turn. This is a helpful feature
because it keeps you from having to identify every individual field. The SQL
parser handles all the field references by obtaining the names of valid columns
from the data dictionary and substituting them on the command line.

Usually, we recommend that you do not use the * feature because it is a very inefficient one. However, you can use this feature very effectively in some
circumstances such as table auditing. Prefix the * operator with a table alias, and
use it with other columns from other tables. For example, you can specify

```
# alias.sql
SELECT 'A', 'B', E.* FROM emp E
```

You cannot specify

```
SELECT 'A', 'B', *    FROM emp
```

You can easily develop a mirror image audit trail of a table, for example:

```
INSERT INTO emp_audit
SELECT USER, SYSDATE, A.*
FROM    emp A
WHERE   emp_no = :emp_no;
```

If two tables are identical (e.g., a source table and a mirrored audit table), you can copy data easily from one to the other this way. There is a big advantage to using the * operator. If you keep the audit table up to date (i.e., identical in field number, type, and sequence to the source table), you will never need to maintain the audit routine(s). If you add a column to the EMP table and the EMP_AUDIT table, the routines that access these tables will continue to work; you won't have to modify all of the routines in the EMP audit procedure that deal with updates.

This simple idea can be extended to simplify many programming situations. Another example is shown in the following code:

```
SELECT E.emp_no, E.emp_name, D.*, C.*
FROM    CAT  C,
        DPT  D,
        EMP  E
WHERE   E.dept_no = D.dept_no  (+)
AND     E.cat_type = C.cat_type (+);
```

Beware of the WHEREs

Some SELECT statement WHERE clauses do not use indexes at all. If you have specified an index over a table that is referenced by a clause of the type shown in this section, Oracle will simply ignore the index. Most often, these WHERE clauses can be rewritten or reshaped to use an index while returning the same answer.

In the following examples, for each clause that cannot use an index, we have suggested an alternative approach that will allow you to get better performance out of your SQL statements.

In the following example, the SUBSTR function disables the index when it is used over an indexed column:

Do not use:

```
# where.sql
SELECT account_name, trans_date, amount
FROM    transaction
WHERE   SUBSTR(account_name,1,7) = 'CAPITAL';
```

Use:

```
SELECT account_name, trans_date, amount
FROM   transaction
WHERE  account_name LIKE 'CAPITAL%';
```

In the following example, the "!=" (not equal) function cannot use an index. Remember that indexes can tell you what is in a table but not what is *not in* a table. All references to NOT, "!=", and *"<>"* disable index usage:

Do not use:

```
SELECT account_name,trans_date,amount
FROM   transaction
WHERE  amount != 0;
```

Use:

```
SELECT account_name,trans_date,amount
FROM   transaction
WHERE  amount > 0 ;
```

In the following example, the *TRUNC* function disables the index:

Do not use:

```
SELECT account_name, trans_date, amount
FROM   transaction
WHERE  TRUNC(trans_date) = TRUNC(SYSDATE);
```

Use:

```
SELECT account_name, trans_date, amount
FROM   transaction
WHERE  trans_date BETWEEN TRUNC(SYSDATE)
                  AND TRUNC(SYSDATE) + .99999;
```

When using dates, note that if more than five decimal places are added to a date, the date is actually rounded up to the next day! For example:

```
SELECT TO_DATE('01-JAN-96') + .99999
FROM   DUAL;
```

returns:

```
'01-JAN-96 23:59:59'
```

and:

```
SELECT TO_DATE('01-JAN-96') + .999999
FROM DUAL;
```

returns:

```
'02-JAN-96 00:00:00'
```

In the following example, | | is the *concatenate* function; it strings two character columns together. Like other functions, it disables indexes.

Do not use:

```
SELECT  account_name, trans_date, amount
FROM    transaction
WHERE   account_name || account_type = 'AMEXA';
```

Use:

```
SELECT  account_name, trans_date, amount
FROM    transaction
WHERE   account_name ='AMEX'
AND     account_type = 'A' ;
```

In the following example, the addition operator is also a function and disables the index. All the other arithmetic operators (-, *, and /) have the same effect.

Do not use:

```
SELECT  account_name, trans_date, amount
FROM    transaction
WHERE   amount + 3000 < 5000;
```

Use:

```
SELECT  account_name, trans_date, amount
FROM    transaction
WHERE   amount < 2000;
```

In the following example, indexes will not be used when the column(s) appears on both sides of the operator. This will result in a full table scan.

Do not use:

```
SELECT account_name, trans_date, amount
FROM   transaction
WHERE account_name = NVL(:acc_name, account_name);
```

Use:

```
SELECT account_name, trans_date, amount
FROM   transaction
WHERE account_name LIKE NVL(:acc_name, '%');
```

SQL Performance Tips and Hints

Tuning a SQL statement or group of statements is often more of a battle than an art form. We have met only a few people who can tune SQL by instinct. This form of programming is based on years of experience and is worth watching. On the other hand, people who tune by the ropes can achieve good results through hard work and persistence. Programmers need to be persistent, dogged, and willing to experiment. After all, how are you supposed to reach the level of instinctive programming if you have not tried every possible alternative, no matter how silly it might seem?

This section describes some alternative (dogged) ways in which you can improve the performance of your SQL statements. These tips are directed more toward overcoming specific application and/or SQL problems than to the usual type of day-to-day tuning.

Combining Simple, Unrelated Database Accesses

If you are running a number of simple database queries, you can improve performance by combining them into a single query, even if they are not related. This approach is particularly suited to client-server applications in which the network needs to be protected from excess data traffic. Combining unrelated SQL statements will not reduce the RDBMS database overheads (all tables still need to be read) but will limit the associated cursor and network overheads. Examples of queries that are well suited to this approach are those that set up default screen headers or report banners by obtaining program initialization information from a number of database tables. The usual approach is to perform one query after another, as shown below:

```
# comb_sel.sql
SELECT name
FROM   emp
WHERE  emp_no = 1234;

SELECT name
FROM   dpt
WHERE  dpt_no = 10;

SELECT   name
FROM   cat
WHERE  cat_type = 'RD'   ;
```

To combine all these separate queries into one SQL statement, you must perform an outer join on each table with a table that will always be valid (i.e., one that will return at least one row). The easiest way to ensure this is to set up a dummy outer join with the system table DUAL as shown in the following example:

```
SELECT E.name, D.name, C.name
FROM   cat   C,
       dpt   D,
       emp   E,
       DUAL X
WHERE  NVL('X', X.dummy) = NVL('X', E.rowid (+))
AND    NVL('X', X.dummy) = NVL('X', D.rowid (+))
AND    NVL('X', X.dummy) = NVL('X', C.rowid (+))
AND    E.emp_no   (+)   = 1234
AND    D.dept_no  (+)   = 10
AND    C.cat_type (+)   = 'RD'
```

This type of processing gives you the best performance payoff on machines that are connected to busy networks. Every time a SQL statement is executed, the RDBMS kernel is visited a number of times: at least once to parse the statement, once to bind the variables, and once to retrieve the selected rows. With this simple example, you reduce network overhead by two-thirds. (See Chapter 15, *Tuning Long-Running Jobs*, for more information about this approach.)

Deleting Duplicate Records

A common problem that many DBAs and programmers face is trying to purge duplicate rows from a single table. These rows may have been inadvertently (re)imported by the DBA, or mistakenly created by a rogue application program.

The following example shows a particularly efficient way to delete duplicate records from a table. It takes advantage of the fact that a row's ROWID must be unique.

```
# dups_del.sql
DELETE FROM emp E
WHERE   E.rowid > ( SELECT MIN(X.rowid)
                    FROM    emp X
                    WHERE   X.emp_no = E.emp_no );
```

Counting Rows from Tables

Contrary to popular belief, COUNT(*) is faster than COUNT(1). If the rows are being returned via an index, counting the indexed column—for example, COUNT(EMP_NO) is faster still. The optimizer realizes from the existence of the index that the column must also exist (non-null). We tested the following statements on several different computers and found that COUNT(*) consistently runs between 15% and 20% faster than COUNT(1) and that COUNT (INDEX_COLUMN) is 5% faster again.

The following runs counted 65,536 rows from a table:

```
SELECT COUNT ( ... indexed column ...)
FROM    transaction;                                        2.43 seconds

    SELECT COUNT (*) FROM transaction;                      2.59 seconds

    SELECT COUNT (1) FROM transaction;                      3.47 seconds
```

Using WHERE in Place of HAVING

In general, avoid including a HAVING clause in SELECT statements. The HAVING clause filters selected rows only after all rows have been fetched. This could include sorting, summing, and the like. Restricting rows via the WHERE clause, rather than the HAVING clause (whenever possible), helps to reduce these over-heads. Consider this example:

```
SELECT region, AVG(loc_size)
FROM   location
GROUP
   BY region
HAVING region != 'SYDNEY'
AND    region != 'PERTH'

Execution Plan
-------------------------------------------------
SELECT STATEMENT   OPTIMIZER HINT: CHOOSE
   FILTER
      SORT (GROUP BY)
         TABLE ACCESS (FULL) OF 'LOCATION'
```

You'll find the following more efficient:

```
SELECT region, AVG(LOC_sIZE)
FROM   location
WHERE  region != 'SYDNEY'
AND    region != 'PERTH'
GROUP
   BY region

Execution Plan
-------------------------------------------------
SELECT STATEMENT   OPTIMIZER HINT: CHOOSE
   SORT (GROUP BY)
      TABLE ACCESS (FULL) OF 'LOCATION'
```

Tuning Views

Many people think that views are untunable. In fact, views are effectively SELECT statements and can be tuned, just as any other type of SELECT statement can be. Remember, though, that views cannot retrieve data any faster than the originating SQL can. Views are not subsets of data, nor are they snapshots of data.

All tuning applicable to any SQL statement (including hints) are equally applicable to views since views are just SQL statements. Consider the following example:

```
SELECT E.emp_no, E.emp_name, M.emp_no, M.emp_name
FROM   emp M,
       emp E
WHERE  E.emp_no = 123456
AND    E.mgr_no = M.emp_no (+);
```

```
Execution Plan
----------------------------------------------------
SELECT STATEMENT    OPTIMIZER HINT: CHOOSE
  MERGE JOIN (OUTER)
    TABLE ACCESS (BY ROWID) OF 'EMP'
      INDEX (UNIQUE SCAN) OF 'EMP_PK' (UNIQUE)
    TABLE ACCESS (BY ROWID) OF 'EMP'
      INDEX (UNIQUE SCAN) OF 'EMP_PK' (UNIQUE)
```

This SQL query can easily be converted into a view:

```
CREATE VIEW emp_mgr (emp_no, emp_name, mgr_no, mgr_name) AS
SELECT E.emp_no, E.emp_name, M.emp_no, M.emp_name
FROM   emp E,
       emp M
WHERE  E.mgr_no = M.emp_no (+);
```

As the following example demonstrates, querying the database via the view yields exactly the same results:

```
select * from emp_mgr where emp_no = 123456;

Execution Plan
----------------------------------------------------
SELECT STATEMENT    OPTIMIZER HINT: CHOOSE
  MERGE JOIN (OUTER)
    TABLE ACCESS (BY ROWID) OF 'EMP'
      INDEX (UNIQUE SCAN) OF 'EMP_PK' (UNIQUE)
    TABLE ACCESS (BY ROWID) OF 'EMP'
      INDEX (UNIQUE SCAN) OF 'EMP_PK' (UNIQUE)
```

Personally, we prefer to avoid views whenever we can. Coding the SQL in full may take longer but gives us a warmer feeling. Tuning is easier, and if we ever have to revisit the code for maintenance, we can immediately see the code that is executing.

At all costs, try to avoid specifying "views of views" and "views within SQL subquery" clauses. These statements tend to confuse the optimizer, resulting in full table scans.

Minimizing Table Lookups in a Query

To improve performance, minimize the number of table lookups (subquery blocks) in queries, particularly if your statements include subquery SELECTs or multicolumn UPDATEs.

For example, instead of specifying:

```
# min_lkup.sql
SELECT  emp_name
FROM    emp
WHERE   emp_cat   = ( SELECT MAX(category)
                             FROM    emp_categories )
AND     sal_range = ( SELECT MAX(sal_range)
                             FROM    emp_categories )
AND     emp_dept  = 0020;
```

specify the following:

```
SELECT  emp_name
FROM    emp
WHERE   (emp_cat, sal_range)
                  = ( SELECT MAX(category), MAX(sal_range)
                      FROM    emp_categories )
AND     emp_dept  = 0020;
```

For multicolumn UPDATE statements, instead of specifying:

```
UPDATE  emp
SET     emp_cat   = ( SELECT MAX(category)
                             FROM    emp_categories ),
        sal_range = ( SELECT MAX(sal_range)
                             FROM    emp_categories )
WHERE   emp_dept  = 0020;
```

try using:

```
UPDATE  emp
SET     (emp_cat, sal_range)
                  = ( SELECT MAX(category), MAX(sal_range)
                      FROM    emp_categories )
WHERE   emp_dept  = 0020;
```

Consider Table Joins in Place of EXISTS

In general, consider joining tables rather than specifying subqueries when the percentage of successful rows returned from the driving table (i.e., the number of rows that need to be validated against the subquery) is high. For example, if we are selecting records from the EMP table and are required to filter those records that have a department category of "A", then a table join will be more efficient.

Consider the following example:

```
# tab_join.sql
SELECT emp_name
FROM   emp E
WHERE  EXISTS ( SELECT 'X'
                    FROM    dept
                    WHERE   dept_no  = E.dept_no
                    AND     dept_cat = 'A');
Execution Plan
---------------------------------------------------
SELECT STATEMENT   OPTIMIZER HINT: CHOOSE
    FILTER
       TABLE ACCESS (FULL) OF 'EMP'
       TABLE ACCESS (BY ROWID) OF 'DEPT'
          INDEX (UNIQUE SCAN) OF 'DEPT_PK' (UNIQUE)
```

To improve performance, specify:

```
SELECT emp_name
FROM   dept D,
       emp  E
WHERE  E.dept_no  = D.dept_no
AND    D.dept_cat = 'A';

Execution Plan
---------------------------------------------------
SELECT STATEMENT   OPTIMIZER HINT: CHOOSE
    NESTED LOOPS
       TABLE ACCESS (FULL) OF 'EMP'
       TABLE ACCESS (BY ROWID) OF 'DEPT'
          INDEX (UNIQUE SCAN) OF 'DEPT_PK' (UNIQUE)
```

Consider EXISTS in Place of Table Joins

Consider breaking some table joins out to separate subqueries when the percentage of successful rows returned from the driving table (i.e., the number of rows that need to be validated against the subquery) is small. When two tables are joined, all rows need to be matched from the driving table to the second table. If a large number of rows can be filtered from the driving table before having to perform the validation against the second table, the number of total physical reads can be dramatically reduced.

Consider the following example:

```
# exists.sql
SELECT . . .                          SELECT . . .
FROM   dept D,                        FROM   dept D,
       emp  E                                emp E
WHERE  E.dept_no = D.dept_no          WHERE  E.dept_no = D.dept_no
AND    E.emp_type = 'MANAGER'         AND    ( E.emp_type = 'MANAGER'
AND    D.dept_cat = 'A';              OR     D.dept_cat = 'A'       );
```

To improve performance, specify:

```
SELECT  . . .
FROM    emp E
WHERE   EXISTS      ( SELECT 'X'
                            FROM    dept
                            WHERE   dept_no  = E.dept_no
                            AND     dept_cat = 'A' )
AND     E.emp_type = 'MANAGER'

SELECT  . . .
FROM    emp E
WHERE   E.emp_type = 'MANAGER'
OR      EXISTS      ( SELECT 'X'
                            FROM    dept
                            WHERE   dept_no  = E.dept_no
                            AND     dept_cat = 'A' )
```

NOTE   The EXISTS clause must be positioned *first* in the WHEN clause
              when using an AND operator and *last* in the WHEN clause when us-
              ing an OR operator.

Consider EXISTS in Place of DISTINCT

Avoid joins that require the DISTINCT qualifier on the SELECT list when you
submit queries that are used to determine information at the owner end of a one-
to-many relationship (e.g., departments that have employees). The SQL will actually fetch all rows satisfying the table join and then sort and filter out duplicate
values.

An example of such a query is shown below:

```
# exists_2.sql
SELECT DISTINCT dept_no, dept_name
FROM    dept D,
        emp E
WHERE   D.dept_no = E.dept_no ;

    Execution Plan
    ---------------------------------------------------
    SELECT STATEMENT    OPTIMIZER HINT: CHOOSE
      SORT (UNIQUE)
        NESTED LOOPS
          TABLE ACCESS (FULL) OF 'EMP'
          TABLE ACCESS (BY ROWID) OF 'DEPT'
            INDEX (UNIQUE SCAN) OF 'DEPT_PK' (UNIQUE)
```

EXISTS is a faster alternative because the RDBMS optimizer realizes that when the subquery has been satisfied once, there is no need to proceed any further, and the next driving row can be fetched.

```
SELECT dept_no, dept_name
FROM   dept D
WHERE  EXISTS ( SELECT 'X'
                FROM    emp E
                WHERE   E.dept_no = D.dept_no );


Execution Plan
--------------------------------------------------
SELECT STATEMENT   OPTIMIZER HINT: CHOOSE
   FILTER
      TABLE ACCESS (FULL) OF 'DEPT'
      TABLE ACCESS (BY ROWID) OF 'EMP'
         INDEX (RANGE SCAN) OF 'EMP_DEPT_IDX'
```

Consider NOT EXISTS in Place of NOT IN

In subquery statements such as the following, the NOT IN clause causes an internal sort. Replacing the NOT IN with an indexed NOT EXISTS can be very beneficial. Study the following example:

```
# not_exist.sql
SELECT . . .
FROM   emp
WHERE  dept_no NOT IN ( SELECT dept_no
                        FROM    dept
                        WHERE   dept_cat = 'A');
```

To improve performance, replace this code with:

```
SELECT . . .
FROM   emp E
WHERE  NOT EXISTS ( SELECT X'
                    FROM    dept
                    WHERE   dept_no  = E.dept_no
                    AND     dept_cat = 'A'   );
```

Consider UNION ALL in Place of UNION

Programmers of complex query statements that include a UNION clause should always ask whether a UNION ALL will suffice. The UNION clause forces all rows returned by each portion of the UNION to be sorted and merged and duplicates to be filtered before the first row is returned to the calling module. A UNION ALL simply returns all rows including duplicates and does not have to perform any sort, merge, or filter.

Most statements that do include a UNION clause can in fact replace it with a UNION ALL. These statements are written in a fashion whereby duplicates cannot be generated (sourced from different tables), so why sort and test for them?

Consider the following example:

```
# unionall.sql
SELECT acct_num, balance_amt
FROM   debit_transactions
WHERE  tran_date = '31-DEC-95'
UNION
SELECT acct_num, balance_amt
FROM   credit_transactions
WHERE  tran_date = '31-DEC-95'


Execution Plan
----------------------------------------------------
SELECT STATEMENT    OPTIMIZER HINT: CHOOSE
PROJECTION
SORT (UNIQUE)
UNION-ALL
TABLE ACCESS (BY ROWID) OF 'debit_transactions'
INDEX (RANGE SCAN) OF 'debit_tran_idx' (NON-UNIQUE)
TABLE ACCESS (BY ROWID) OF 'credit_transactions'
INDEX (RANGE SCAN) OF 'credit_tran_idx' (NON-UNIQUE)
```

To improve performance, replace this code with:

```
SELECT acct_num, balance_amt
FROM   debit_transactions
WHERE  tran_date = '31-DEC-95'
UNION ALL
SELECT acct_num, balance_amt
FROM   credit_transactions
WHERE  tran_date = '31-DEC-95'


Execution Plan
----------------------------------------------------
SELECT STATEMENT    OPTIMIZER HINT: CHOOSE
PROJECTION
UNION-ALL
TABLE ACCESS (BY ROWID) OF 'debit_transactions'
INDEX (RANGE SCAN) OF 'debit_tran_idx' (NON-UNIQUE)
TABLE ACCESS (BY ROWID) OF 'credit_transactions'
INDEX (RANGE SCAN) OF 'credit_tran_idx' (NON-UNIQUE)
```

Consider IN or UNION in Place of OR

In general, always consider the IN and/or UNION verb instead of the OR verb in WHERE clauses. Using the OR predicate on an indexed column causes the optimizer to perform a full table scan rather than an indexed retrieval.

NOTE   Choosing IN or UNION over OR will be effective only if the col-
                umn(s) is indexed. If the column(s) is not indexed, you may actual-
                ly increase overhead by not choosing OR.

In the following examples, both loc_id and region are indexed. Consider the
following:

```
# union_in.sql
  SELECT . . .                    SELECT . . .
  FROM    location                FROM    location
  WHERE   loc_id = 10             WHERE   loc_id = 10
  OR      region = 'MELBOURNE'    OR      loc_id = 20
                                  OR      loc_id = 30
```

To improve performance, replace this code with:

```
  SELECT . . .                    SELECT . . .
  FROM    location                FROM    location
  WHERE   loc_id = 10             WHERE   loc_in IN (10,20,30)
  UNION
  SELECT . . .
  FROM    location
  WHERE   region = 'MELBOURNE'
```

If you do use OR, be sure that you put the most specific indexed clause *first* in
the OR's predicate list and put the index that passes the most records *last* in the
list.

Note that the following:

```
  WHERE key1 = 10         Should return least rows
  OR    key2 = 20         Should return most rows
```

is internally translated to

```
  WHERE key1 = 10
  AND ( key1 NOT = 10 AND key2 = 20 )
```

Using Indexes to Improve Performance

This section explains how Oracle uses indexes to help determine the most efficient execution plan. You can code your SQL statements to take best advantage
of the indexes that have been specified for your tables.

Which Is Faster: Indexed Retrieval or a Full Table Scan?

There is a lively debate in the Oracle community about the relative advantages of indexed retrievals and full table scans. At what point does a full table scan become more efficient than an indexed retrieval? What are the relative costs of the two approaches? When should I use parallel query on a full table scan? How many query slaves (parallel degree) should I use?

There are pros and cons on both sides. Full table scans can be efficient because they require less disk head movement. The disk starts reading at one point and continues reading contiguous data blocks. Because indexes retrieve records in a logical sequence, not in the order in which they are physically located on disk, indexed retrievals may result in a lot of disk head movement—perhaps retrieving only one record per physical disk read.

To a large extent, the choice between an indexed retrieval and a full table scan depends on the size of the table and the pattern of access to that table. For example, if the majority of a large table are being processed, a serial search can actually be faster. If the rows being accessed are randomly dispersed throughout the table, processing them in logical (indexed) sequence might be quite slow. In addition to the disk head movement required to retrieve the records, remember that every read of a row requires an additional read of the index.

If every read of the index and record were performed by a single physical disk read (worst case scenario) and in a contiguous disk sector sequence, the break-even point for reading the entire table would be around 50.1% (one index and one table read per record). Because use of the System Global Area (SGA) cache reduces the number of physical to logical reads necessary, the actual break-even point is not quite so obvious. Where do you draw the line between a full table scan and an indexed retrieval?

Oracle Corporation used to recommend that if tables with fewer than eight data blocks are specified in a query, then a full table scan is more efficient than an indexed retrieval. For larger tables, an indexed retrieval is usually faster. There is a lot of debate about where to draw the line.

We have had advice from Oracle staff members that for very large tables (more than 100 megabytes in size) on SMP and MMP machines, queries returning any more than 5% of the rows should be forced to use a full table scan (via hint /*+ FULL */) with a degree of parallelism up to twice the number of CPUs available. Why? When? Are they sure?

In one article we've read on this topic, the author titled this dilemma the "10, 20, 30 percent rule," because nobody could agree on which percentage was more efficient; but they were all happy to provide their own "rule" to live and die by. Our own investigations have indicated that each of the "10, 20, 30" figures might all be valid under certain circumstances.

We've done a good deal of testing to try to refine these numbers. Our tests have shown that choosing a full table scan over an indexed retrieval depends on a number of factors. Issues such as how many rows of the table can fit into a single Oracle block can directly affect the outcome. Oracle blocks are read, written, and cached in the SGA as entire blocks. The more rows contained within a block, the fewer physical reads are needed to scan the entire table. The more dispersed the (indexed) consecutive rows are throughout the table and the fewer the number of rows that can be contained within an Oracle block, the less the likelihood of the next row's being within the SGA cache.

If the only columns being selected were indexed columns or pseudo SQL columns (USER, SYSDATE, LEVEL, COUNT(*), etc.), an index read would always be the most efficient. In such a case, only the index would need to be read. The physical rows would never actually be retrieved. If data (columns) are required to be retrieved from each row, the break-even point is a combination of the percentage of the table that needs to be read and at least some (and perhaps all) of the following elements:

- Operating system block size
- Oracle block size (e.g., DB_BLOCK_SIZE)
- Shared pool size (e.g., SHARED_POOL_SIZE)
- Parallelism (e.g., PARALLEL_DEFAULT_SCANSIZE, PARALLEL_MIN_SERVERS, PARALLEL_MAX_SERVERS, etc.)
- Oracle data read-ahead size (e.g., DB_FILE_MULTIBLOCK_READ_COUNT)
- Operating system filing system (e.g., BAKED, JOURNALING, RAW...)
- Disk subsystem type (e.g., RAID 0 ... RAID 5)

In the following examples, the leftmost column shows what percentage of the table (number of records) met the SQL selection criteria. The first example shows that if approximately 52% of the table needed to be read, a full table scan performs better.

Note that these results are based on the EMP table, which contains 26,000 rows, with seven rows per Oracle block:

	Index Only	Index Table Read	Full Table Scan
Percentage Of table read	SELECT COUNT(*) FROM emp WHERE EMp_NO > 0	SELECT emp_name FROM emp WHERE emp_no > 0	SELECT emp_name FROM emp WHERE emp_no+0 > 0
8.5 %	0.66 seconds	12.03 seconds	35.70 seconds
15.5 %	1.04 seconds	16.21 seconds	35.70 seconds
25.2 %	1.54 seconds	25.45 seconds	35.70 seconds
50.7 %	**2.80 seconds**	**33.89 seconds**	**35.70 seconds ******
100 %	5.72 seconds	87.23 seconds	35.70 seconds

**** *indicates break-even point*

In the next example, the break-even point for the same database setup and hardware configuration is only 15.5% of the table. This difference is credited to the smaller physical size of each record and, consequently, the larger number of rows that can fit in a single Oracle block. The more rows per block, the less reading is required by a full table scan to read the entire table.

The results below are based on the EMP_SMALL table, which contains 26,000 rows, with 258 rows per Oracle block:

	Index Only	Index Table Read	Full Table Scan
Percentage Of table read	SELECT COUNT(*) FROM emp WHERE emp_no > 0	SELECT emp_name FROM emp WHERE emp_no > 0	SELECT emp_name FROM emp WHERE emp_no+0 > 0
8.5 %	0.66 seconds	02.31 seconds	04.52 seconds
15.5 %	**1.05 seconds**	**04.01 seconds**	**04.52 seconds ******
25.2 %	1.59 seconds	06.37 seconds	04.52 seconds
50.7 %	2.91 seconds	12.69 seconds	04.52 seconds
100 %	6.01 seconds	25.37 seconds	04.52 seconds

**** *indicates break-even point*

Although we've presented some guidelines, remember that you must test each table separately; one rule does not fit all. For those people who insist on quoting a full table scan rule of thumb, it is safer to look at a break-even point based on the combination of the physical number of rows per Oracle block and the percentage of the table that requires reading.

Explicitly Disabling an Index

If two or more indexes have equal ranking, you can improve performance by choosing to use only the index that has the least number of rows satisfying the query. In the following example, concatenating ||" to a character column suppresses the use of the index on that column; concatenating +0 to numeric columns suppresses the use of the index on that column.

```
SELECT . . .
FROM    emp
WHERE   emp_category = 'MANAGING DIRECTOR'
AND     dept_no+0  =  0010
AND     emp_type||'' = 'A';
```

A preferable way of selecting an index is via inline hints.

```
SELECT /*+ INDEX (EMP EMP_CAT_IDX) */ . . .
FROM    emp
WHERE   emp_category = 'MANAGING DIRECTOR'
AND     dept_no    =  0010
AND     emp_type   = 'A';
```

This is a rather dire approach to improving performance because disabling the WHERE clause indexes means not only disabling current retrieval paths, but also disabling all future paths. You should resort to this strategy only if you need to tune a few particular SQL statements individually.

Avoiding Calculations on Indexed Columns

The optimizer does not use an index if the indexed column is a part of a function (in the WHERE clause). In general, avoid doing calculations on indexed columns at all costs. When the optimizer encounters a calculation on an indexed column, it will not use the index and will perform a full table scan instead.

In this example, the optimizer cannot use the index over the MAX_SALARY column:

```
SELECT . . .
FROM    department
WHERE   max_salary * 12 > 25000;
```

Often, you can get around this problem simply by moving the function to the other side of the equation. For example, in the following case, the optimizer can use the index:

```
SELECT . . .
FROM    department
WHERE   max_salary > 25000 / 12;
```

Note that the SQL functions MIN and MAX are exceptions to this rule and will use all available indexes.

Adding Additional Columns to the Indexes

In some cases, you'll gain considerable performance benefits by including additional columns (that is, columns that you would not ordinarily specify for indexing) in a concatenated index. Why would you do this? The short answer is that it may allow you to satisfy queries without having to perform a physical read of the actual table records at all.

Although most of the overhead for record retrieval is incurred simply by having to locate the address (ROWID) of the record, you can still save a substantial amount of overhead by avoiding the subsequent physical read of the record. Because indexes return records in an ordered sequence, not a physical sequence, actually having to retrieve the record will require extensive head movement over the disk and the waste of valuable processing time.

Consider the table definition for the DEPARTMENT table. The primary key is DEPT_ CODE, and an index is created over this column.

```
TABLE department
dept_no              NOT NULL   PRIMARY KEY
dept_description     NOT NULL
dept_type            NULL
```

Now suppose that when the DEPARTMENT table is referenced, the DEPT_TYPE column is almost always retrieved as well. By concatenating DEPT_TYPE with DEPT_NO when creating the index, you'll ensure that *most* retrievals can be satisfied without ever needing to physically read the database record:

```
INDEX (dept_no, dept_type)
```

This approach works best for small, frequently referenced columns. Because each extra index column adds storage and updating requirements, you will realize less overall performance gain by including long (for example, DEPT_DESCRIPTION, a 30-character field) or infrequently referenced fields in the index.

```
SELECT dept_no, dept_type
FROM   department
WHERE  dept_no = 0020;
```

The following is an explain plan with a *normal* index:

```
Execution Plan
--------------------------------------------------------
SELECT STATEMENT   OPTIMIZER HINT: CHOOSE
   TABLE ACCESS (BY ROWID) OF 'DEPARTMENT'
      INDEX (UNIQUE SCAN) OF 'DEPT_PK' (UNIQUE)
```

The following is an explain plan with an *extended* index:

```
Execution Plan
--------------------------------------------------------
SELECT STATEMENT   OPTIMIZER HINT: CHOOSE
   INDEX (UNIQUE SCAN) OF 'DEPT_PK' (UNIQUE)
```

A drawback of including additional fields in an index is that if your index was originally classified as UNIQUE, it will lose that quality. Adding extra columns to the end of an index means that uniqueness cannot be automatically enforced for the first column(s).

Avoiding NOT on Indexed Columns

In general, avoid using NOT when testing indexed columns. The NOT function has the same effect on indexed columns that functions do. When Oracle encounters a NOT, it will choose not to use the index and will perform a full table scan instead. For example, in the following case, an index will be not be used:

```
SELECT . . .
FROM    department
WHERE   dept_no NOT = 0;
```

In the next case, an index will be used:

```
SELECT . . .
FROM    department
WHERE   dept_no > 0;
```

In a few cases, the Oracle optimizer will automatically transform NOTs (when they are specified with other operators) to the corresponding functions. These automatic transformations include:

```
SQL Function From: NOT >     to     <=
                   NOT >=    to     <
                   NOT <     to     >=
                   NOT <=    to     >
```

Avoiding Null in Indexes

As we discussed earlier in this chapter, null has several special properties. Because null can never be equated or compared, avoid using any column that contains a null as part of an index. Oracle can never use an index to locate rows via a predicate such as IS NULL or IS NOT NULL. Indexes are often used to guarantee uniqueness. If a concatenated index has all "nullable" indexed column, you could potentially have two rows with the same key—a situation that could wreak havoc with your application.

In a single-column index, if the column is null, there is *no entry* within the index. For concatenated indexes, if every part of the key is null, no index entry exists. If at least one column of a concatenated index is non-null, an index entry does exist.

The treatment of nulls by Oracle is somewhat quirky. Consider this example. If a UNIQUE index is created over a table for columns A and B, and a key value of

(123, null) already exists, the system will reject the next record with that key as a duplicate. This is a case in which Oracle recognizes that a null does equal a null.

However, if all of the index columns are null (e.g., (null, null)), the keys are not considered to be the same, because in this case, Oracle considers the whole key to be null, and null can never equal null. You could potentially end up with 100 rows all with the same key, a value of null!

Using NULL improperly can hurt performance. Because NULL values are not a part of an index domain, specifying a *null operator* on an indexed column will cause that index to be omitted from the execution plan. For example, the index will be used if you specify the following:

```
SELECT . . .
FROM    department
WHERE   dept_no >= 0;
```

But it will not be used if you specify the following:

```
SELECT . . .
FROM    department
WHERE   dept_no IS NOT NULL;
```

Problems in Casting Index Column Types

In both Oracle6 and Oracle7, Oracle automatically performs a simple column type conversion, or *casting*, when it compares two columns of different types. If a numeric column is compared to an alphabetic column, the character column automatically has its type converted to numeric.

Assume that EMP_NO is an indexed numeric column.

```
# casting.sql
SELECT . . .
FROM    emp
WHERE   emp_no = '123'

Execution Plan
-----------------------------------------------------
SELECT STATEMENT    OPTIMIZER HINT: CHOOSE
  TABLE ACCESS (BY ROWID) OF 'EMP'
    INDEX (UNIQUE SCAN) OF 'EMP_PK' (UNIQUE)
```

In fact, because of the automatic conversion this statement will actually be processed as:

```
SELECT . . .
FROM    emp
WHERE   emp_no = TO_NUMBER('123')
```

Even though a type conversion has taken place, in this example, index usage is not affected. Unfortunately, this is not the case in the next example. Here, assume that EMP_TYPE is an indexed VARCHAR2 column:

```
SELECT . . .
FROM    emp
WHERE   emp_type = 123

Execution Plan
-----------------------------------------------------
SELECT STATEMENT    OPTIMIZER HINT: CHOOSE
   TABLE ACCESS (FULL) OF 'EMP'
```

This statement will actually be processed as

```
SELECT . . .
FROM    emp
WHERE   TO_NUMBER(emp_type) = 123
```

Indexes cannot be used if they are included in a function. Therefore this internal conversion will keep the index from being used. Automatic type conversion can cause strange performance anomalies when the columns are indexed.

NOTE   The EXPLAIN PLAN utility cannot detect or identify casting prob-
            lems; it simply assumes that all module bind variables are of the cor-
            rect type. Programs that are not performing up to expectation may
            have a casting problem. The EXPLAIN PLAN output will report the
            SQL statement as correctly using the index.

SQL Tuning Alternatives

After exhausting all the usual approaches, we may need to look beyond the scope of SQL to reach our goal. There are a number of enhancement, extensions, and alternatives to SQL that we can play with. However, this type of program-ming does come at a price. The level of team expertise needs to be higher; future maintenance may be more expensive; and "alternative" programming techniques are always more susceptible to the elements (i.e., they may be changed or desup-ported in the next Oracle version, may not be available on all Oracle ports, etc.).

The following sections describe some of our experiences in attempting to squeeze the last millisecond out of an application module.

Using PL/SQL

For many complex SQL statements with many table joins and/or subquery blocks, PL/SQL can be a godsend. PL/SQL allows us to tackle these more demanding business rules using a better suited procedural language. SQL is a very powerful language but does struggle to perform efficiently under some circumstances.

You should read Chapter 7 immediately after finishing this chapter—in particular, read the section called "Exploiting the Power of PL/SQL." This will complement your SQL tuning.

Inline SQL Functions

SQL inline functions are also detailed in Chapter 7; read about them there in conjunction with this section. Because of their power, flexibility, and potential SQL savings, we'll also spend time on them here.

Inline SQL functions are one of the most underrated, misunderstood features of the RDBMS. They have been available since Oracle7.1, and we are amazed at the number of experienced programmers who never use them. Why are they so good?

Inline functions permit us to structure database calls in a fashion that is never permitted by normal SQL. Rather than making many separate calls to the database, we can combine these calls into a single database access. This point alone is invaluable in client-server applications. Here are some of the simple examples of how we have exploited inline functions.

Many-to-many table joins

Inline SQL functions are very beneficial in fetching rows from the database with summation conditions on multiple child tables. We all know that trying to sum on more than one table causes a Cartesian table join and massively inflated results. For example:

```
# inl_m2m.sql
Tables : EMP
       : SICK_LEAVE        (4 rows, 6 days sick)
       : HOLIDAY_LEAVE     (2 rows, 20 days leave)

SELECT E.emp_no, E.emp_name,
       SUM(S.days) sick_days,
       SUM(H.days) holidays
FROM   holiday_leave H,
       sick_leave S,
       emp E
WHERE  E.emp_no = :emp_no
AND    E.emp_no = S.emp_no (+)
AND    E.emp_no = H.emp_no (+)
GROUP
    BY E.emp_no, E.emp_name

Result : Emp No    Emp Name    Sick Days  Holidays
         123456    Tom Jones       12          80
```

As you can see, the summed columns are wrong. Rather than coding this SQL as multiple SQL statements, we can utilize the power of in-line SQL functions. For example:

```
# inl_m2m.sql
FUNCTION Sum_Sick_Leave (emp  IN number) RETURN number
AS
  tot_days  number := 0;
  CURSOR C1 IS
  SELECT SUM(days)
  FROM   sick_leave
  WHERE  emp_no = emp;
BEGIN
  OPEN  C1;
  FETCH C1 INTO tot_days;
  CLOSE C1;
  RETURN (tot_days);
END;

FUNCTION Sum_Holiday_Leave (emp IN number) return number
AS
  tot_days  number := 0;
  CURSOR C1 IS
  SELECT SUM(days)
  FROM   holiday_leave
  WHERE  emp_no = emp;
  BEGIN
  OPEN  C1;
  FETCH C1 INTO tot_days;
  CLOSE C1;
  RETURN (tot_days);
END;

SELECT E.emp_no, E.emp_name,
       sum_sick_leave(E.emp_no) sick_days,
       sum_holiday_leave(E.emp_no) holidays
FROM   emp E
WHERE  E.emp_no = :emp_no

Result: Emp No    Emp Name    Sick Days   Holidays
        123456    Tom Jones       6           20
```

Beating the outer-join limitations

We all know the power of SQL's outer-join functionality. Where would we be without it? What does become very frustrating is the rigid limitations to which it has to adhere. We cannot outer-join with more than one source table, we cannot outer-join with a subquery select, and so on. What can we do?

The following example demonstrates how to overcome an outer-join with a subquery SELECT:

```
# inl_outj.sql
SELECT E.emp_no, E.emp_name, H.hist_date, H.Hist_Type
FROM    emp_historty H,
        emp E
WHERE   E.emp_no       = :emp_no
AND     E.emp_no       = H.emp_no (+)
AND     H.hist_date (+) = ( select MAX(hist_date)
                            FROM    emp_history
                               WHERE  emp_no = E.emp_no );
```

We all know that this statement is illegal. As much as we would like it to work, we know that it doesn't. The following code shows how to get around this problem with an elegant, simple solution:

```
# inl_outj.sql
FUNCTION Max_Emp_History (emp IN number) return date
AS
   max_dte DATE;
   CURSOR  C1 IS
   SELECT  MAX(hist_date)
   FROM     emp_history
   WHERE    emp_no = emp;
BEGIN
   OPEN  C1;
   FETCH C1 INTO max_dte;
   CLOSE C1;
   RETURN (max_dte);
END;

SELECT E.emp_no, E.emp_name, H.hist_date, H.Hist_Type
FROM    emp_historty H,
        emp E
WHERE   E.emp_no       = :emp_no
AND     E.emp_no       = H.emp_no (+)
AND     H.hist_date (+) = Max_Emp_History(E.emp_no);
```

Reducing very large table join I/O

We often have to scan very large tables to produce simple, aggregated reports. A table could be several million rows in size. There is nothing we can do about having to read the table, but overheads associated with joining to other "description" tables can be substantially reduced. For example:

```
# inl_ltj.sql
SELECT H.emp_no,     E.emp_name,
       H.hist_type, T.type_desc,
       COUNT(*)
FROM    history_type T,
        emp E,
        emp_history H
```

```
WHERE    H.emp_no    = E.emp_no
AND      H.hist_type = T.hist_type
GROUP
     BY H.emp_no, E.emp_name, H.hist_type, T.type_desc ;
```

This statement will return the correct result and in a fairly efficient manner. If the EMP_HISTORY table is 5 million rows, the optimizer has to join *both* the HIST_TYPE and EMP tables 5 million times to finally return only a few hundred aggregated rows. On top of that, the descriptive columns are included in the output data set that then needs to be written to the temporary tablespace, sorted and aggregated. What can be done? Here is a suggestion:

```
# inl_ltj.sql
FUNCTION Lookup_Hist_Type (typ IN NUMBER) RETURN VARCHAR2
AS
  tdesc    VARCHAR2(30);
  CURSOR   C1 IS
  SELECT   type_desc
  FROM     history_type
  WHERE    hist_type = typ;
BEGIN
  OPEN  C1;
  FETCH C1 INTO tdesc;
  CLOSE C1;
  RETURN (nvl(tdesc,'?'));
END;


FUNCTION Lookup_Emp (emp IN number) RETURN VARCHAR2
AS
  ename    VARCHAR2(30);
  CURSOR   C1 IS
  SELECT   emp_name
  FROM     emp
  WHERE    emp_no = emp;
BEGIN
  OPEN  C1;
  FETCH C1 INTO ename;
  CLOSE C1;
  RETURN (NVL(ename,'?'));
END;


SELECT H.emp_no,    Lookup_Emp(H.emp_no),
       H.hist_type, Lookup_Hist_Type(H.hist_type),
       COUNT(*)
FROM   emp_history H
GROUP
     BY H.emp_no, H.hist_type;
```

The real beauty of this particular approach is that the lookup procedure calls happen only after the EMP_HISTORY table has been scanned and sorted. Only a few hundred, rather than a few million, lookups need to be executed. The amount of data written to the temporary tablespace and sorted is also substantially reduced. When all else fails and sheer table size is your worst enemy, try coding a few well placed inline functions.

NOTE	Inline SQL functions are not the answer to all problems and should be used carefully. If performance is being affected, investigate database views or stored procedures using PL/SQL cursor variables.

Full Table Scans via Parallel Query

The parallel query facility is something that many sites have (and have paid for) and never get around to using. Enabling the parallel query facility is very simple to do. Simply specify

```
ALTER TABLE xxxx PARALLEL(DEGREE n);
```

No coding changes, no database reorganizations, and no embedded SQL hints are required. So what is the problem?

Chapter 13, *Tuning Parallel Query*, describes the parallel query option in detail, so we won't cover it here. All we want to do is stress the importance of understanding this facility and remembering to use it where applicable. The previous example could realize further performance improvements by also using the parallel option, as follows:

```
# para.qry.sql
SELECT /*+ FULL(H) PARALLEL(H, 8) */
       H.emp_no,    Lookup_Emp(H.emp_no),
       H.hist_type, Lookup_Hist_Type(H.hist_type),
       COUNT(*)
FROM   emp_history H
GROUP
    BY H.emp_no, H.hist_type;
```

Discrete Transactions

Although the Oracle RDBMS has supported discrete transactions for quite a while, only recently have they been available for development use. Discrete transactions are very fast and very particular. Their support is provided with a very strict set of caveats. Discrete transactions are allowed only under the following conditions:

- The INIT.ORA parameter DISCRETE_TRANSACTIONS_ENABLED must be set to TRUE.

- The BEGIN_DISCRETE_TRANSACTION operation must be the first statement executed in the transaction state.

- The number of modified data blocks is very small.

- Each data block can be modified only once per discrete transaction state.

- Modified data blocks do not need to be read in their modified form during the discrete transaction state.

- The discrete transaction isn't modifying a table that contains a LONG column.

How does the discrete transaction work? During all discrete transactions, all changes that are made are deferred until the transaction commits. Redo information is generated but is stored in a separate area in memory. This is why you cannot see the updated state of a record during the transaction state (no change has been made) and why the update must be very small (only a few data blocks are reserved for discrete transactions). When the transaction issues the commit, all redo information is written to the online redo log file, and all changes to the database are applied to the data block in the usual manner.

Savings are made from the fact that no "undo" information is written to the rollback segments, since the data blocks are not actually modified until the transaction is committed and the redo information is successfully written to the redo log file.

Because no undo information is written to the rollback segments, any long-running queries that span the time the data was modified by a discrete transaction operation will fail with SNAPSHOT TOO OLD errors. For example, consider this PL/SQL example:

```
# disc_trn.sql
BEGIN
  dbms_transaction.begin_discrete_transaction;
  UPDATE emp
  SET    mo_of_children = NVL(no_of_children,0) + 1
  WHERE  emp_no = :emp_no;
EXCEPTION
  WHEN dbms_transaction.discrete_transaction_failed THEN
      ROLLBACK;
      UPDATE emp
      SET    no_of_children = NVL(no_of_children,0) + 1
      WHERE  emp_no = :emp_no;
END;
```

It is always a safe practice to double-code all discrete transactions so that if the transaction fails, it will be retried using a normal SQL transaction state. If that statement subsequently fails, an error is returned to the calling module.

Using Null to Flag Record Subsets

Although null values frequently cause problems in data retrievals, they can sometimes be used to increase performance.

Consider the case of a very large table (20,000,000 rows) to which new records are added daily (usually about 1,000 of them). Every night, you need to report these additions on an audit trail. Rather than scan the whole table looking for changes, of course you will want to use an index over the TRANSACTION_DATE column. But the index would need to be huge. This is a case in which your index is over the entire table, although you are actually interested only in the 1,000 or so records that were added today. The actual index is physically many times larger than it needs to be, and it uses many more disk I/Os to traverse the binary tree to the leaf data.

Now suppose you add a smaller (one-character) column to the table. This column distinguishes between the records that need to be printed and the records that do not need be printed; the column would contain "U" for unprinted and "P" for printed. This gives you a good way to find the records you are looking for. Although the index isn't as large as was required in the previous example, it still contains 20,000,000 entries. All this just to find the 1,000 that you need to print.

By taking advantage of the special qualities of null, you can avoid having to store and maintain all of these index entries. When the print job actually prints the new records, it prints each record containing a "U" flag. Once the record has printed successfully, the print routine resets this column to null, thus removing all references to those unprinted (and not new) records from the index. The index will never grow any larger than the approximately 1,000 records you have added today. By doing this, you reduce the expected size of the index from approximately 20 megabytes to 20 kilobytes. The reduction in size easily justifies the additional overhead (a new subindex and an extra column update) associated with it.

Using WHERE Instead of an ORDER BY

One common mistake that SQL developers make is to specify an ORDER BY clause when it is not really needed. The SQL ORDER BY clause will always force an implicit record set sort of all rows satisfying the WHERE criteria. Why sort all records (potentially millions of rows) when you know that they will be fetched in the required sequence anyway? How do you guarantee that the records will continue to be fetched in the required sequence?

The optimizer will use an index if no index (or overriding hint) is triggered in the WHERE clause; that is, if no index is going to be used to satisfy the WHERE clause(s) and an index is available and suitable for the ORDER BY clause, it will be used.

ORDER BY clauses use an index only if the following rigid requirements are met:

1. No index is suitable for any part of the WHERE clause(s).

2. All of the columns that make up the ORDER BY clause must be contained within a single index in the same sequence.

3. All of the columns that make up the ORDER BY clause must be defined as NOT NULL within the table definition. Remember that null values are not contained within an index.

These three requirements tend to rule out most indexes.

NOTE　　　　WHERE clause indexes and ORDER BY indexes cannot be used in parallel.

Ordering via the WHERE clause

It is much more efficient to retrieve records via an index than via a manual sort. It is possible to manipulate a SQL statement into fetching rows in the required sequence without having to sort them. This manipulation may involve including a "dummy WHERE" clause as part of the statement.

Here is an example of what goes on behind the scenes when you specify WHERE and ORDER BY clauses. Note that DEPT_TYPE is defined as allowing NULL and has the index over it:

```
TABLE DEPARTMENT

dept_no               NOT NULL   PRIMARY KEY
dept_description      NOT NULL
dept_type             NULL

INDEX dept_type_idx (dept_type)
```

The following statement fetches rows from the department table in the DEPT_TYPE sequence.

```
SELECT    . . .
FROM      department
ORDER BY dept_type

Explain Plan Query Plan
------------------------------------------------------------------
Sort Order By
    Table Access FULL
```

Adding a dummy WHERE clause to the statement triggers an index to be used:

```
SELECT   . . .
FROM     department
WHERE    dept_type > 0

Explain Plan Query Plan
-----------------------------------------------------------------
Table Access By Rowid on DEPARTMENT
     Index Range Scan on Dept_Idx
```

NOTE   This technique returns records only in an ascending sequence. If
                you require data in a descending sequence, try the next suggestion.

Ordering via inline hints

With the advent of the parallel query facilities, we now can scan a table via a full
table scan in preference to an index. Even more complicated is the fact that
Oracle can no longer guarantee an index to fetch rows in an ordered sequence.
Oracle Corporation concedes that indexes do fetch rows in ascending order (for
the current releases) but warns that this may not always be true. Indexes provide
a fast and efficient mechanism for locating a record, not sequencing a table.
Indexes built by using the parallel query utilities build the indexes as multiple
subsets of the raw data. In the future, these indexed subsets may not necessarily
be merged as part of the final step to the index build. What should we do?

Inline SQL hints allow us to force the use of an available index. This method is
more elegant and somewhat safer than the corresponding WHERE clause.

```
SELECT   /*+ INDEX (department dept_type_idx) */ . . .
FROM     department

Explain Plan Query Plan
-----------------------------------------------------------------
Sort Order By
     Index Range Scan on Dept_Type_Idx
```

To heed Oracle's warning and do the correct thing, we should actually use the
INDEX_ASC hint. This hint behaves exactly the same as the INDEX hint but does
protect us from future Oracle changes to the optimizer and/or index structure.

```
SELECT   /*+ INDEX_ASC (department dept_type_idx) */ . . .
FROM     department

Explain Plan Query Plan
-----------------------------------------------------------------
Sort Order By
     Index Range Scan on Dept_Type_Idx
```

One valuable aspect of inline hints is the ability to descend an index tree. This is not available via the (manipulative) WHERE clause.

```
SELECT   /*+ INDEX_DESC (department dept_type_idx) */ . . .
FROM     department

Explain Plan Query Plan
-----------------------------------------------------------------
Sort Order By
    Index Range Scan on Dept_Type_Idx
```

Identifying Poor SQL Statements

The majority of this chapter has been dedicated to writing and tuning SQL statements within the application. This assumes that you already know which statements within your application need attention. But this is not always true; in fact, it is rarely true. How many times has the cry gone up from the trenches, "The system is running too slowly!" When you ask the question, "Which part of the application is slow?" all you get in response is "All of it. Fix it!" Users often do not understand the intricacies of even a simple application, and many believe that a slow-running application can be cured by flicking a switch. If that were so, wouldn't we have done it by now?

So how do we isolate the poorer SQL? Any application of moderate size is made up of many hundreds of thousands of lines of code containing thousands of individual SQL statements. A poorly performing application could be suffering at the hands of a single statement if that one statement runs all day, every day. Imagine if it is run four or five times, simultaneously. Where do we begin?

There are two areas of poor performance when it comes to SQL: CPU-intensive statements and I/O-intensive statements. CPU-intensive programs are fairly easy to locate. All operating systems allow us to view the top CPU-intensive tasks. These tasks can then be traced to a particular user who should be able to identify the application module that he or she was processing. CPU-intensive modules are generally a result of poor program coding and/or structure, rather than poor SQL. Once the module has been identified, you must then attempt to make it more efficient. A possible solution is to move some processing out of the program and into the database (smarter SQL, stored objects, inline functions, array processing, etc.).

The second problem area is I/O-intensive SQL statements. These statements cause high amounts of database I/O (full table scans, sorting, updating, etc.) and can run for several hours at the expense of other database requests. The introduction of Oracle7 has solved many of our SQL identification problems. By carefully querying the database's shared pool area, we can readily identify most I/O-intensive SQL statements.

The following SQL statements demonstrate how to identify SQL statements that have an I/O hit ratio of less than 80 percent. This hit ratio reflects the overall I/O from all executions of this statement since the statement was first parsed into the shared pool. This may be over the last few minutes or the last few days.

```
# sqlarea.sql
sql> SELECT executions, disk_reads, buffer_gets,
               ROUND((buffer_gets - disk_reads)
                  / buffer_gets, 2) hit_ratio,
               sql_text
        FROM    v$sqlarea
        WHERE   executions  > 0
        AND     buffer_gets > 0
        AND     (buffer_gets - disk_reads) / buffer_gets < 0.80
        order by 4 desc ;


EXECUTIONS DISK_READS BUFFER_GETS   HIT_RATIO
---------- ---------- ----------- ----------
SQL_TEXT
----------------------------------------------------------------
       16        180         369         .51
SELECT SKU,PREPACK_IND,CASE_ID,TRANSFER_QTY,UNIT_COST,UNIT_RETAIL,ROWID
FROM TSF_DETAIL WHERE transfer = :1 order by sku
       16         30          63         .52
SELECT TRANSFER,TO_STORE,TO_WH FROM TSFHEAD  WHERE TRANSFER = :b1  AND
TRANSFER_STATUS = 'A'
        2          3           7         .57
SELECT SKU   FROM UPC_EAN  WHERE UPC = :b1
       12         14          35         .60
SELECT SUBSTR(DESC_UP,1,30),DEPT,SYSTEM_IND   FROM DESC_LOOK  WHERE
SKU = :b1
       14         13          35         .63
SELECT UNIT_COST,UNIT_RETAIL,SUBCLASS FROM WIN_SKUS WHERE SKU = :b1
```

Actually, we find this particular SQL a little misleading. It does isolate SQL statements with poor I/O hit ratios, but these statements are not necessarily the offenders. Consider the following v$sqlarea output:

```
Executions Disk_Reads Buffer_Gets Hit_Ratio Sql_Text
---------- ---------- ----------- --------- --------------------
        2          6          19      0.68   SELECT A.EMP_NO, ...
```

This statement has a very poor hit ratio but is actually very efficient. Because the SQL operates via a UNIQUE index, the number of physical disk reads is almost the same as the number of logical reads. The UNIQUE index dramatically reduces the overall amount of physical and logical disk I/O, resulting in a mistakenly poor hit ratio.

In the next example, the hit ratio is exceedingly good. Is it really that good?

```
Executions Disk_Reads Buffer_Gets Hit_Ratio Sql_Text
---------- ---------- ----------- --------- --------------------
        2       3625      178777      0.98   SELECT A.EMP_NO, ...
```

This SQL statement appears to be very efficient. However, when we take a closer look, things are very different. What the hit ratio does not reveal is that the statement is a five-table join and is performing more than 3,600 physical disk reads per execution. Is that a lot? Is that efficient? Neither of these two questions can be answered without further investigation. What was actually happening in this instance was that one of the five tables was incorrectly performing a full table scan. By restructuring the SQL, we were able to reduce physical disk I/O to less than 50 while also substantially reducing logical disk I/O. Coincidentally, the hit ratio also fell to less than 70%.

Our preferred v$sqlarea query is to actually report on physical disk I/O per statement execution. Hit ratios are informative but sometimes misleading. Logical I/O is less relevant. If the statement executes 1,000,000 logical I/Os but still only takes less than one-tenth of a second, who cares? It is the total physical I/O that consumes nearly all the time and identifies the potentially incorrect SQL. For example:

```
# sqlarea.txt
sql> SELECT sql_text, executions,
             ROUND(disk_reads / executions, 2) reads_per_run,
             disk_reads, buffer_gets,
             ROUND((buffer_gets - disk_reads)
                   / buffer_gets, 2) hit_ratio,
             sql_text
     FROM    v$sqlarea
     WHERE   executions  > 0
     AND     buffer_gets > 0
     AND     (buffer_gets - disk_reads) / buffer_gets < 0.80
     ORDER by 3 desc ;
```

The previous two statements would have reported more enlightening results:

Executions	Reads_Per_Run	Disk_Reads	Buffer_Gets	Hit_Ratio	Sql_Text
2	3	6	19	0.68	SELECT ...
2	1812.5	3625	178777	0.98	SELECT ...

From this view of the v$sqlarea table, we can immediately isolate all statements that are performing high numbers of physical reads. These statements might not necessarily be inefficient or poorly written, but they are prime candidates for investigation and further tuning.

Adjusting SQL Statements Over Time

You are not finished after you have tuned your SQL statements for best performance. You'll have to keep monitoring system performance and adjusting your

SQL to take advantage of changing times and situations. Here are some reasons why you may find that today's most efficient SQL statements are not tomorrow's:

Physical table volumes

Driving tables may grow or shrink over time. For example, the table of creditors might have had only 25 records when the system was launched, but now, after five years of recession, the table might contain 25,000 records.

Indexes

The number of indexes available at execution time may change over time. Indexes come and go. Even adding a single index on a minor application table can affect the entire execution plan of crucial statements in your application.

Key field data spread

As data is added to the database over time, an indexed column might turn out to have a very lopsided data key-data spread. In this case, defining an index over a table actually adds overhead to that table. Oracle provides a SQL script, *ONEIDXS.sql* (found in the ..*dbs* directory; the actual directory name is operating system dependent), which actually plots an index spread over the key fields.

Oracle version

As new versions of the Oracle RDBMS and associated tools are released, new features may affect your SQL. For example, the rule-based optimizer has frequently been altered and refined over time. And with Oracle7, a new cost-based optimizer has been introduced.

Physical location

The physical distance between client-server machines makes a big difference in SQL performance. For example, certain statements take only 2 seconds to process on a unitary machine but take 22 seconds to process over the network connecting Sydney and Melbourne.

7

Tuning PL/SQL

PL/SQL (Procedure Language/SQL) is a set of procedural capabilities that extends the power of traditional SQL. PL/SQL statements can be combined with traditional SQL in a variety of Oracle products to increase the ease of application programming, allow SQL to perform control and procedural functions previously beyond its powers, and considerably improve overall system performance.

PL/SQL is essentially a procedural extension of SQL. It allows all of the procedural constructs that are available in traditional third-generation languages to be specified directly within the Oracle SQL environment—for example, conditional control (IF, THEN, ELSE) and local variable and constant declarations, rather than through complex Pro* programs or inline user exits.

Over the years, the functionality and capabilities of PL/SQL have been developing. Following are the milestones in PL/SQL releases:

PL/SQL Version	RDBMS Version
1.0 PL/SQL	6.0.37 RDBMS
2.0 PL/SQL	7.0 RDBMS
2.1 PL/SQL	7.1 RDBMS
2.2 PL/SQL	7.2 RDBMS
2.3 PL/SQL	7.3 RDBMS

PL/SQL is incorporated into all versions of the current Oracle tool library, as shown below:

Oracle Tool	PL/SQL Version
SQL*Forms	Version 3.0 and above
SQL*Reportwriter	Version 2.0 and above
SQL*Plus	Version 3.0 and above
SQL*Menu	Version 5.0 and above
SQL*DBA / SRVMGR	All versions

PL/SQL and SQL

The introduction of PL/SQL has changed the face of programming within the Oracle environment. The most complex of tasks can be broken down to their lowest functions, easing both programming and future maintenance. From our point of view, the most important feature of PL/SQL is its dramatic effect on performance. Database accesses and network communications are usually the slowest aspects of Oracle processing. PL/SQL improves performance by dramatically reducing the number of calls the application must make to the database. Because PL/SQL allows multiple SQL statements to be included in a single block, PL/SQL cuts down on database accesses by passing the whole block of instructions at one time. With one database access, PL/SQL can process many statements that, with traditional SQL, would have to be passed to the database one at a time. In fact, if a PL/SQL block contains no traditional SQL statements at all, the application doesn't even need to call the database.

The reduction in database calls is demonstrated in Figure 7-1.

The inclusion of PL/SQL capabilities in a variety of Oracle tools (e.g., SQL*Forms, SQL*Plus) significantly increases the performance of all of these tools. The greatest performance gains of all are realized when client-server applications are being run.

What Does PL/SQL Offer?

With traditional SQL, each statement is a single entity, with no particular relationship to the other SQL statements that you issue. Oracle executes each SQL statement separately, accessing the database for each distinct SQL statement. With PL/SQL, by contrast, you can group many SQL statements into a single block. Oracle processes this group as a unit, accessing the database only once for each block. The PL/SQL block structure is shown in Figure 7-2.

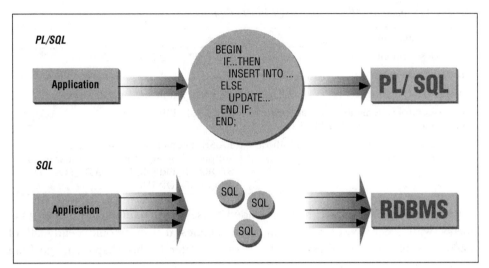

Figure 7-1. Contrast between SQL and PL/SQL

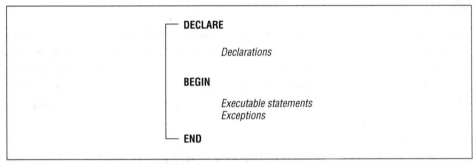

Figure 7-2. PL/SQL block structure

Full ANSI/ISO-Standard SQL Support

The PL/SQL language includes full ANSI/ISO standard support. You can include traditional SQL statements as well as special PL/SQL statements, as shown in Table 7-1.

Table 7-1: Statements Allowed in PL/SQL Blocks

SQL Statements	Type
Query and data manipulation language statements	SELECT, INSERT, UPDATE, DELETE
Cursor control statements	DECLARE, OPEN, FETCH, CLOSE
Transaction-processing statements	COMMIT, ROLLBACK, SAVEPOINT

Table 7-1: Statements Allowed in PL/SQL Blocks (continued)

PL/SQL Statements	Type
Control statements	IF...THEN...ELSE, EXIT, GOTO
Looping statement	FOR...LOOP, WHILE...LOOP
Assignment statements	X := Y + Z and similar statements
Block control statements (you can nest PL/SQL blocks within other blocks)	DECLARE, BEGIN, END
Error exception statements (beyond those supported by SQL)	RAISE statements that handle errors supported by SQL for such conditions as STORAGE_ERROR, NO_DATA_FOUND, and ZERO_DIVIDE.

Current versions of Oracle have extended these more traditional PL/SQL statements with a variety of special in-house utilities that overcome nearly all of PL/SQLs shortcomings. These facilities, covered later in this chapter, range from screen I/O to inline dynamic SQL.

Portability

Like SQL, PL/SQL is completely portable across all Oracle platforms and versions. All PL/SQL functionality is upward-compatible. You can develop applications that incorporate PL/SQL code in SQL*Forms, SQL*Menu, or SQL*Plus applications (as well as others), without regard for whether the final production platform will be a PC running Windows, a Sun workstation running UNIX, or an IBM mainframe running MVS.

PL/SQL in Packages, Procedures, and Functions

All database packages, stored library procedures, and system library functions support PL/SQL. Packages, procedures, and functions are globally stored within the database and are available to all application products. Using PL/SQL, you can code powerful shared routines and reduce the number of application-specific libraries that are needed.

Packages, procedures, and functions (both stored and local) open whole new worlds to the Oracle DBA, analyst, and programmer. These features exploit the capability of application code sharing and common business rule location, regardless of which frontend tool, application, or vendor is being used. A more detailed explanation of procedure and function tuning is included later in this chapter.

PL/SQL in Triggers

RDBMS inline database triggers are written in PL/SQL. Triggers are one of the more powerful RDBMS features. They can be used to guarantee specific business constraints, specify unusual referential integrity requirements, or aid in simple data auditing. All these features are beneath the surface of the application and are inconsequential to the frontend software, business, or software vendor.

Client-Server and Server-Server Remote Procedure Support

PL/SQL supports *client-server* and *server-server* remote procedure calls (RPCs). Database location and commit synchronization (two-phase commit) are handled by PL/SQL as if all objects were local.

Remote procedure calls can be initiated by using either *synchronous* or *asynchronous RPCs*. Synchronous RPCs update as a single transaction within a two-phase commit protocol, guaranteeing database integrity and consistence. Asynchronous RPCs process stored procedures in a store-and-forward (asynchronous) manner.

Enhanced Variable Types, Records, and Constants

PL/SQL extends the traditional SQL data types by supporting a number of additional object types, such as Boolean, tables, records, and arrays. Because the PL/SQL parser and interpreter are incorporated directly into the RDBMS kernel, variables and constants can be linked to RDBMS data dictionary table and column definitions. This means that any variable that is referenced within a PL/SQL block can draw its TYPE definition directly from the database and be incorporated into the actual procedure. For example:

```
# pl_types.sql
DECLARE
    deptno        scott.dept.deptno      %TYPE;
    deptname      scott.dept.dept_name   %TYPE;
    emp_rec       scott.emp  %ROWTYPE;

    CURSOR C1 IS SELECT * FROM sales;
    sales_rec     C1  %ROWTYPE;

    TYPE dept_rec IS RECORD
      ( deptno  scott.dept.deptno%TYPE,
        dname   scott.dept.dept_name%TYPE );

    new_Emp       boolean     := FALSE;
    max_Emp       number      constant:= 999999;
    nxt_Emp       positive    := 1;
BEGIN
```

```
END;
```

Current versions of PL/SQL extend the definition of numeric variables (type NUMBER) to enhance its default range checking capabilities and its compatibility with other languages. For example:

```
BINARY_INTEGER        Signed integer from -2147483657 to +2146483657.
NATURAL               Non-signed integer from 0 to 2146483647.
POSITIVE              Non-signed integer from 1 to 2146483647.
NUMBER                Floating point numeric from 1.0E-129 to 9.99E-
                      125.
```

You can replace NUMBER with any of the following data types. These extra subtypes are included for compatibility with ANS/ISO, IBM SQL/DS, and IBM DB2 types and represent the same range of values as NUMBER.

```
NUMBER       ==>      DEC
                      DECIMAL
                      DOUBLE PRECISION
                      FLOAT
                      INTEGER
                      INT
                      NUMERIC
                      REAL
                      SMALLINT
```

Bind Variables

PL/SQL supports the inclusion of external bind variables. These bind variables provide a link from the PL/SQL block to the outside world. Data variables can be passed and returned.

```
# bind_var.sql
BEGIN
    IF  :emp_sal <= 2000  THEN
        :emp_int := 0;
    END IF;

    IF  :emp_val >= 8001  THEN
        :emp_int := (:emp_val * 25 ) / 100;
    END IF;
END;
```

Processing of PL/SQL blocks does have to continually pause while the bind variable value is retrieved from the source application. The following PL/SQL routine demonstrates how to reduce the number of application variable calls while executing the PL/SQL block. This example performs only one GET of :EMP_SAL, storing it in a local PL/SQL block variable (SAL_VAL), and it performs only one PUT of the calculated result into the :EMP_INT field.

```
# bind_var.sql
```

```
DECLARE
     sal_val  NUMBER;
     tax_val  NUMBER;
BEGIN
 sal_val  :=  :emp_sal;
     IF  sal_val <= 2000  THEN
         tax_val := 0;
     END IF;
     IF  sal_val >= 8001  THEN
         tax_val := (sal_val * 25 ) / 100;
     END IF;
     :EMP_INT := tax_val;
END;
```

Writing this routine as a function would work better; by making use of more efficient reference parameters, you wouldn't have to pass any bind variables.

```
# bind_var.sql
FUNCTION calc_tax  ( sal_val IN NUMBER ) RETURN NUMBER IS
BEGIN
     IF  sal_val <= 2000  THEN
         RETURN (0);
     END IF;
     IF  sal_val >= 2001  AND
         sal_val <= 8000  THEN
         RETURN (sal_val * 15 ) / 100;
     END IF;
     IF  sal_val >= 2001  AND
         sal_val <= 8000  THEN
         RETURN ( (sal_val * 15 ) / 100);
     END IF;
END;
```

Recursive Subcalls

PL/SQL blocks are fully recursive, supporting reentrant PL/SQL routines. Local variable values are retained for each recursive subcall without compromising the value of other code iterations. For example, the following function calculates a factorial algorithm:

```
FUNCTION factorial ( fac INTEGER )  RETURN INTEGER  IS
BEGIN
     IF fac = 1 THEN
         RETURN 1;
     ELSE
         RETURN ( fac * factorial ( fac - 1 ) );
     END IF;
END;
```

Beware that if an incorrect (or missing) break function is coded, a PL/SQL procedure and/or function will eventually use up all free shared buffer pool memory and fail with the exception STORAGE_ERROR.

Error Handling

PL/SQL provide powerful and simple error routines using exceptions, user defined pragma instructions, and error handlers. PL/SQL automatically alters the normal flow control triggered by error conditions, invoking predetermined error handles in the EXCEPTION section(s) of the code block. Unhandled PL/SQL errors are not ignored but are propagated back to the calling program, which may in turn trip another PL/SQL procedure or function.

The following PL/SQL block demonstrates how to code and trap a user-defined pragma:

```
DECLARE
    Insufficient_Tax    Exception;
    PRAGMA Exception_Init (insufficient_privileges, -1031);
BEGIN
    .
    .
    IF Total_Tax > Total_Income THEN
        raise Insufficient_Tax;
    END IF;
    .
    .
EXCEPTION
    WHEN Insufficient_Tax THEN
        BEGIN
        .
        END;
END;
```

PL/SQL includes a number of common Oracle errors and exceptions, defined in the default STANDARD package. The predefined PL/SQL exceptions are as follows:

Exception Name	Oracle Error
Cursor_Already_Open	ORA-06511
Dup_Val_In_Index	ORA-00001
Invalid_Cursor	ORA-01001
Invalid_Number	ORA-01722
Login_Denied	ORA-01017
No_Data_Found	ORA-01403
Not_Logged_On	ORA-01012
Program_Error	ORA-06501
Store_Error	ORA-06500
Timeout_On_Resource	ORA-00051
Too_Many_Rows	ORA-01422
Transaction_Backed_Out	ORA-00061

Exception Name	Oracle Error
Value_Error	ORA-06502
Zero_Divide	ORA-01476

PL/SQL Limitations

Although PL/SQL offers many benefits, it does have some limitations you'll need to be aware of to get the best performance from the product. In this section, we highlight these problem areas and offer some strategies you might need to follow to use PL/SQL to best advantage.

Block Size

PL/SQL blocks do have a size limit. This limitation is dependent on the number and type of PL/SQL commands and the PL/SQL version in use. The size limitation error can be triggered either by the total physical size of the actual block being too large or by a lack of a large enough contiguous piece of free memory in the shared pool within the SGA.

Physical block sizes can now reach many thousands of lines of code. A simple workaround can usually be achieved by breaking the PL/SQL block into smaller subblocks (as shown in Figure 7-3) or by breaking subsections of the routine out into several self-contained stored procedures and/or functions.

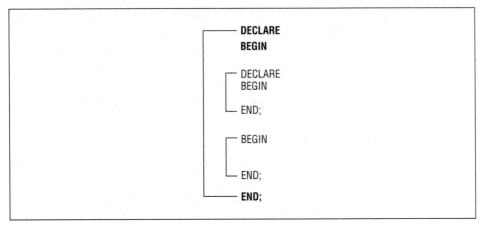

Figure 7-3. Use of subblocks

NOTE   Oracle7.3 has made changes to the way it holds stored procedures and claims to have doubled the maximum size of stored objects.

The most common PL/SQL sizing problem is encountered during object compilation and is annoyingly random. Each PL/SQL block insists on contiguous memory within the shared pool. This is not always possible. The only real alternatives to this scenario are the following:

- Flush the shared pool. This will flush only SGA shared pool memory that is not in use by an open cursor. This still may not provide the sufficient contiguous memory.

- Enlarge the shared pool size. This may only delay the problem for a few hours. As time passes, the shared pool will become more and more full and more and more fragmented. The same error may occur but just take a little longer.

- Pin the procedure into memory. Pinning the object into the shared pool at database startup time is one way to guarantee that the block will be available when required.

- Upgrade to Oracle7.3 or better. This latest version of the RDBMS has changed the way it stores PL/SQL *pcode* (code generated from the PL/SQL compiler) within the SGA, allowing a single PL/SQL block to be stored in many nonconsecutive SGA memory pages.

Interpreted Language

PL/SQL is an interpreted language. This means that the code is not stored or retained in "compiled" form. Interpreted languages are understandably slower than compiled (executable) languages, because they have to parse (check syntax), validate object availability, check user privileges, and evaluate access path(s) before they can even begin processing. Stored procedures and packages are held within the database in a pseudo-compiled form (PL/SQL pcode) but still need to perform low-level code preparation and object security before execution.

Poor Debugging Facilities

PL/SQL has always been a nightmare to debug. Even simple syntax errors are reported in generic, unhelpful error messages. A new GUI tool introduced by Oracle as part of the Developer/2000 suite called Oracle Procedure Builder can provide client-side PL/SQL debugging. Debugging functions include single instruction set walkthrough, inline variable interrogation/modification, code break points, and others.

NOTE   PL/SQL version 2.2 (Oracle7.2) has built-in support for server-side stored procedure, function, package, and trigger debugging.

No Direct Support Of DDL or DCL

PL/SQL is a procedural engine only. It does not support SQL statements that manipulate the data dictionary, including CREATE TABLE, CREATE INDEX, DROP TABLE, ALTER TABLE, and CREATE SEQUENCE.

PL/SQL does not support such data control language (DCL) statements as CONNECT, GRANT, SET ROLE, and REVOKE.

NOTE   All of these shortcomings have been addressed via special RDBMS procedure utilities that are discussed later in this chapter (e.g., DBMS_SQL).

No Direct Support of Screen or Printer I/O

PL/SQL does not support screen or printer I/O. In fact, PL/SQL has no ability to communicate outside its block except via table updates, updates of application variables, and error exceptions. Although this might seem to be a major limitation, in practice it is rarely an issue. Just remember that the fundamental function of PL/SQL is to group many SQL statements into a single processing unit. Any other function (e.g., I/O) can be handled via the more global tool you're using (e.g., SQL*Forms and user exits, Pro*C, etc.)

NOTE   Support for reading and writing directly to/from an operating system via PL/SQL by a special RDBMS utility is introduced in Oracle7.3. This utility is discussed later in this chapter.

Limited LONG Support

PL/SQL does not directly support LONG or LONG RAW data types. These fields can be up to 2 gigabytes within the RDBMS, but PL/SQL can address only the first 32,760 bytes. If you select a LONG defined field into a PL/SQL variable defined as LONG, you will not get an error message, but your data may be truncated. LONG variables defined in PL/SQL are no different from variables defined as VARCHAR2

(32760). PL/SQL does support the updating of RDBMS LONG fields, but again, only up to 32,760 characters in length.

Proprietary Language

Oracle developed the PL/SQL language as an extension to the common SQL data interface. However, SQL is ANSI/ISO compliant, while PL/SQL is not. As you read this book, committees are in place trying to nail down an industry standard foundation. Until this is achieved (and PL/SQL complies), use of the PL/SQL language locks you into the Oracle environment and its associated tools. Many large companies base their application development on total software and hardware independence. One of the big selling points of the Oracle RDBMS is that you can (almost) painlessly change the underlying hardware at any time. Many applications are basing their frontend application development on the same principles, allowing the client to choose and/or change the backend database vendor. Locking an application into PL/SQL can make changes to the underlying database software very difficult. If this is a possible problem at your site, developers should try to hold most or all of their PL/SQL as stored packages, procedures, and triggers, rather than as local inline code. Linking the PL/SQL code with the backend database environment rather than the frontend application software will help to create a more generic application.

Annoying PL/SQL Behavior

PL/SQL has a number of annoying attributes that can be very surprising when they are first encountered. The following are just a few of the idiosyncrasies that you need to remember when coding PL/SQL.

Problems with duplicates

PL/SQL allows you to declare local variables. If you inadvertently give a local variable the same name as a column from a table that you are referencing, the PL/SQL routine compiles successfully and no error is reported. If in your code the local variable is compared or referenced within a SQL statement, undesirable results may occur.

The following example of such a situation might seem an obvious and simplistic one, but it's one that actually occurred, disrupting an organization's processing for many weeks. Be careful that you don't make the same mistake.

```
PROCEDURE SYSTEM_ERROR (msg_no IN NUMBER) IS
BEGIN
    DECLARE
        CURSOR C1 IS
        SELECT msg_text
```

```
                FROM SYSTEM_MESSAGES
                WHERE msg_no = msg_no;
                        ↑           ↑
                                                    table
    column              procedure variable

        BEGIN
                .
                .
                .
        END;
    END;
```

Problems with GOTO

Many programmers have complained to us about the behavior of the PL/SQL
GOTO macro. This macro provides a valuable way of breaking loops, and you'll
often find that you want to use it to simplify processing of complex routines.
However, you can't GOTO the end of a PL/SQL block directly. You must include
a NULL statement in your block immediately following the exit label and
preceding the END statement. If you insert the NULL, as shown, following
<<EXIT_LABEL>> in the following example, you won't run into trouble.

```
    DECLARE
        loop_no NUMBER := 0;
    BEGIN
        WHILE loop_no <= 10 LOOP
            .
            .
            IF  ABC > XYZ   THEN
                GOTO EXIT_LABEL;
            END IF;
        END LOOP;
        .
        .
        <<EXIT_LABEL>>
        NULL;
    END;
```

PL/SQL version inconsistencies

PL/SQL surprises some Oracle users by operating somewhat differently from one
Oracle tool to another. Even when you use the same product on a multiplatform
network, you may even find that the PL/SQL on one platform (e.g., a PC running
OS/2) operates differently from the PL/SQL on another platform (e.g., a Sun workstation running UNIX). You may also find that there are subtle differences
between versions of PL/SQL.

PL/SQL is incorporated into different tools in different ways. PL/SQL is bound
directly into the Oracle RDBMS kernel and also into the SQL*Forms executable.

To achieve the best performance, some SQL functions use the RDBMS SQL engine, while others access the local SQL*Forms PL/SQL engine (the TO_DATE macro is coded in this way). So you need to be aware that behavior in PL/SQL statements may differ and test all of your implementations thoroughly.

For example, all of the following statements are invalid in SQL*Forms, but all are valid in RDBMS (via SQL*Plus) and return 01-JUN-96.

```
SELECT TO_DATE ('01JUN96', 'DD-MON-YY') FROM DUAL;
SELECT TO_DATE ('01JUN96', 'DD/MON/YY') FROM DUAL;
SELECT TO_DATE ('1JUN96',  'DD-MON-YY') FROM DUAL;
```

A second, even worse anomaly occurs when two Oracle tools return different results altogether. The SQL statement:

```
SELECT TO_DATE ('10011996', 'DD/MM/YYYY') FROM DUAL;
```

returns the date 10-OCT-1996 in SQL*Plus and 10-JAN-0096 in SQL*Forms!

PL/SQL Coding Standards

Application analysts and DBAs must implement and enforce standards for PL/SQL as they would for any other programming language. Many common PL/SQL errors and shortcoming can be averted by good coding standards.

Most conventional 3GL coding standards apply equally to the PL/SQL language. In reality, the hard part of coding standards is enforcement rather than definition. The following sections detail some of these standard practices.

Conventional Programming Standards

Companies should not throw away all the hard-earned experience they have gained with older 3GL languages. The same standards are just as suited to PL/SQL. For example:

Module naming standards

Remember to define, refine, and document rigid programming naming standards. This simple task is too often overlooked. Permitting programmers to invent their own program names might seem harmless but can lead to mass confusion for larger projects.

PL/SQL modules can be shared by many frontend products (stored procedures, packages, and functions), indirectly invoked from seemingly unrelated actions (stored triggers) or simply sourced from common library routines (Forms 4.5 libraries). Naming standards become exceedingly important when you are trying to track/debug application problems. More important, because PL/SQL supports module scoping, a local PL/SQL library could be accidentally executed in place of the global database procedure if both PL/SQL blocks have the same names.

Prefixing or suffixing each module with a predefined literal will help to guarantee the uniqueness of modules throughout your application. For example, consider using names such as these:

Pub_Create_Audit_Rec_**Prc**	Global/public database procedure
Pub_Create_Audit_Rec_**Pck**	Global/public database package
Pub_Create_Audit_Rec_**Fnc**	Global/public database function
{table name}_I_R_**T1**	Row-level, insert-only, trigger number 1
F4L_Create_Audit_Rec_**Prc**	Forms 4.5 library procedure
Lcl_Create_Audit_Rec_**Fnc**	Local/private module function
Prv_Create_Audit_Rec_**Prc**	Private procedure, accessible only within the current package or PL/SQL module

Variable naming standards

You need to define strict PL/SQL variable naming and type casting conventions. Variable names should reflect their purpose, scope, and usage. Encourage programmers to use type casting where possible, rather than hard-coding field dimensions. This leads to fewer programming errors and can help to substantially reduce later application maintenance. For example:

```
DECLARE
     deptno         scott.dept.deptno%TYPE;
     deptname       scott.dept.dept_name%TYPE;
     emp_rec        scott.emp%ROWTYPE;
     tmp_emp_seqn   NUMBER;
BEGIN
     .
     .
END;
```

Coding standards

Each site should put together a detailed manual of PL/SQL coding standards before beginning any major development. PL/SQL standards will differ from site to site, largely depending on the personal taste of the person who wrote them. This is not a problem. What is important is that all PL/SQL modules be written with the same flavor and style. Coding standards help to reduce the number of silly mistakes and ease the maintenance learning curve for developers who are confronted with debugging someone else's code.

Common coding standards include:

* Case sensitivity
* Text alignment

- Cursor type (explicit or implicit)
- Preferred (maximum) module size
- Preferred module type (package or procedure)

Code modularity

Encourage developers not to code large, complex PL/SQL blocks. All elaborate programming tasks should be broken down to smaller, simpler, self-contained blocks. This will simplify the job, reduce programming errors, and help with module debugging and future maintenance tasks. Holding common PL/SQL code segments as standalone PL/SQL stored procedure/packages and/or sharable libraries will also simplify coding tasks while improving a programmer's productivity.

PL/SQL-Specific Programming Standards

Your application development team also needs to adopt a number of PL/SQL specific programming standards. These standards need to be identified at the beginning of the project and enforced for the duration.

Explicit and implicit cursors

Standards must be put in place to decide which cursor definition is preferred: explicit or implicit. Explicit cursors are more efficient, whereas implicit (inline) cursors tend to be more readable (the cursor is located within the code where it is actually used). (See the section called "Using Explicit and Implicit Cursors in PL/SQL" later in this chapter for more details).

Nested block and subblock routines

Break up large PL/SQL code blocks into several smaller subblocks. This allows the developer to reuse rather than rewrite common code, concentrates specific error handing/trapping, and assists block debugging, while presenting modules in a more readable fashion.

Utilize the power of PL/SQL functionality

Get to know the power of PL/SQL. Nearly all SQL functions are available (no DECODE?), as well as many common 3GL statement flow constructs. GOTO, WHILE/FOR, IF-THEN-ELSE, and so on, all exist for a purpose. Used in the correct way, they can help make to clearer, more accurate modules.

Exploit Oracle packages

Over the years, PL/SQL has matured with Oracle's assistance. Many perceived deficiencies have been overcome by the addition of special enhanced packages. Screen I/O, file I/O, dynamic SQL, job scheduling and event alerts are just a few. (These packages are described in more depth later in this chapter.) I have seen many thousands of lines of code written to "compensate" for a supposed lack of functionality that is now available. Get to know these routines intimately. You will be pleasantly surprised at what is available.

Tuning PL/SQL

All good programming practices apply equally well to the PL/SQL language; after all, it's the closest link Oracle has to the 3GL past. Don't throw away your hard-earned knowledge and experience. The following sections expand on PL/SQL-specific tuning issues that go beyond the more traditional rules of thumb.

Exploiting SQL

Never underestimate the supremacy of SQL. We have seen many programmers so overwhelmed by the idea of PL/SQL (finally, a structured programming language!) that they forget basic SQL. Simple tasks that are better suited to pure SQL are coded in PL/SQL, using many times more lines of code than are actually necessary. In general, SQL is easier to code, easier to understand, and *much more efficient*. For example, the following PL/SQL:

```
# pl_sql.sql
DECLARE
        CURSOR C1 IS
        SELECT  fld1, fld2
        FROM    summary_table
        WHERE   fld3 =  1234;

        xfld1        NUMBER;
        xfld2        NUMBER;
        xfld_tot     NUMBER;
    BEGIN
        OPEN C1;
        FETCH C1 INTO xfld1, xfld2;
        xfld_tot := xfld1 + xfld2;

        UPDATE  summary_table
        SET     fld1 = 0,
                fld2 = 0,
                fld3 = xfld_tot
        WHERE   fld4 = 1234;
    END;
```

should be coded as

```
# pl_sql.sql
  BEGIN
        UPDATE  summary_table
```

```
SET      fld1 = 0,
         fld2 = 0,
         fld3 = fld1 + fld2
WHERE    fld4 = 1234;
END;
```

Using Explicit and Implicit Cursors in PL/SQL

Two types of cursors are available to PL/SQL programmers: explicit and implicit. When Oracle processes a SQL statement, PL/SQL opens a work area called the context area. A cursor gives you a way to access a portion of this context area.

You can define an explicit cursor by specifying it in a DECLARE statement. You include this DECLARE in your PL/SQL code (before you specify any BEGIN blocks). Then, within the block you may include OPEN, FETCH, and CLOSE statements. OPEN opens and parses the cursor and is required. FETCH fetches the cursor's current row and is also required. CLOSE closes the cursor after all fetches have been completed and is optional. For example:

```
# explicit.sql
DECLARE
CURSOR C IS
SELECT      emp_name
   FROM     emp
   WHERE    emp_no = 1234;

BEGIN
   OPEN   C;
   FETCH  C INTO . . . ;
   CLOSE  C;
END;
```

If you do not specify an explicit cursor for a SELECT statement, PL/SQL will implicitly open a cursor to use when it processes each SQL statement, as shown below.

```
# explicit.sql
SELECT      emp_name
   INTO     :emp_name
   FROM     emp
   WHERE    emp_no = 1234;
```

You will get better performance if you declare explicit cursors. PL/SQL handles the two types of cursors differently. When PL/SQL is handling implicit cursors, it performs a second fetch for each row to be sure that nothing else meets the SQL selection criteria. For instance, in the preceding example, suppose there is a second employee with an EMP_NO of 1234. If a second row is found (fetched), PL/SQL will raise the message "MORE THAN ONE ROW RETURNED," as required by ANSI standards.

The savings associated with using explicit, rather than implicit, cursors are significant. Suppose that an application needs to perform 100 SELECTs using an implicit
cursor within a session. The application would perform 100 unnecessary extra
FETCHes. (Remember though, that although each FETCH is performed twice, the
parse is performed only once.) Use of explicit cursors is especially important in
the client-server environment, as we describe in Chapter 16, *Tuning in the Client-
Server Environment.*

Removing Unnecessary SQL Overheads

Never lose sight of the hidden overheads that are associated with SQL. In this
book we sing the praises of SQL and stress the importance of tuning underlying
SQL before anything else. However, after you've exhausted all the normal
avenues of SQL tuning, PL/SQL can provide an alternative. By replacing some of
the data processing from a complex SQL statement with PL/SQL code, you can
achieve significant performance gains. These types of improvements are usually
associated with SQL statements that perform large table joins. For example:

```
# pl_ohead.sql
  DECLARE
      CURSOR C1 IS
          SELECT  E.dept_no,
                  E.category,
                  D.description,
                  count(*)
          FROM    dept D,
                  emp E
          WHERE   D.dept_no = E.dept_no
          GROUP
              BY  E.dept_no,
                  E.category,
                  D.description;
      BEGIN
          for XX in C1 loop
              ...
              ...
          end loop;
      END;
```

If EMP has 1,000,000 rows, 1,000,000 table joins need to be performed with the
DEPT table. This seems rather excessive, considering that only 2,000 rows are
actually fetched after the GROUP BY clause is actioned. Consider the following
alternative:

```
# pl_ohead.sql
  DECLARE
      Xdept   NUMBER;
      Xdesc   VARCHAR2(60);
```

```
        CURSOR C1 IS
        SELECT E.dept_no,
               E.category
               count(*)
        FROM   emp E
        GROUP
            BY E.dept_no,
               E.category;
        CURSOR C2 IS
        SELECT D.description
        FROM   dept D
        WHERE  D.dept_no = Xdept;
    BEGIN
        FORXX in C1 LOOP
            . . .
            Xdept := XX.dept_no;
            OPEN C2;
            FETCH C2 into Xdesc;
            . . .
        END LOOP;
    END;
```

We have now managed to reduce the number of table joins with the DEPT table from 1,000,000 to 2,000. Common sense tells us that of the 2,000 DEPT lookups, we must be repeating ourselves a number of times. Recognizing that the GROUP BY clause performs an implied data sort (forcing rows to be returned in DEPT_NO/CATEGORY sequence), we can reduce the number of DEPT lookups even further. Consider the next alternative:

```
    # pl_ohead.sql
    DECLARE
        Xdept   NUMBER := -9999;
        Xdesc   VARCHAR2(60);

        CURSOR C1 IS
        SELECT E.dept_no,
               E.category
               COUNT(*)
        FROM   emp E
        GROUP
            BY E.dept_no,
            E.category;

        CURSOR C2 IS
        SELECT D.description
        FROM   dept D
        WHERE  D.dept_no = Xdept;
    BEGIN
        FOR XX IN C1 LOOP
            . . .
            IF Xdept != XX.dept_no
               Xdept := XX.dept_no;
               OPEN   C2;
```

```
              FETCH C2 INTO Xdesc;
         END IF;
         . . .
      END LOOP;
   END;
```

Simple PL/SQL logic has further reduced the number of table joins with the DEPT table to 12 (12 is the total number of distinct department numbers returned by the table join). This simple example shows how overall SQL execution time can be improved many times over.

Database Triggers

Database triggers, first introduced in Oracle7.0, stretch the power of PL/SQL to the next dimension. This powerful server-side functionality opens up a whole new world to application developers.

More often than not, database triggers are used for the wrong reasons—as a functionality afterthought, a quick bug fix, or even a crude, postimplementation auditing control. While all these reasons may be sound and particularly suited to database triggers, they were not part of the original schema design. Triggers are like any other application object and should be identified during initial database design. Hastily adding triggers at the end of a project invariably backfires.

Trigger advantages

When database triggers are used in the correct way, they have many wonderful features. You can reduce application coding and testing many times over with a few well-placed database triggers. The following points touch on the strengths of database triggers and how to exploit them.

Code sharing

Database triggers are probably the easiest way to guarantee common code sharing. Regardless of tool, language, or DML statement origination, all updates to a table (or row of a table) will execute a predetermined code module. The code needs testing only once; it does not have to be retested every time it is used in a new program.

Retrospective business rules

Database triggers allow the retrospective fitting of new or modified business rules. If a business function changes, you don't have to modify all affected programs. Instead, a database trigger can be used to add the new functionality. Database triggers can also be used to enforce new business requirements. If a data rule has been violated, the database trigger can raise an error, forcing all database changes for that transaction state to be rolled back. For example:

```
Create or Replace Trigger Check_Salary_T1 on EMP
After Insert OR Update
On EMP For Each Row
BEGIN
    IF :NEW.salary > 100,000
    AND:NEW.sal_grade < 10 THEN
        RAISE form_application_error ( -20001,
            'Salary cannot excede 100,000 for this Job Grade');
    END IF;
END;
```

Before and after column values

How much code have you had to write to hold on to the old value of a column so that you can calculate the difference between an old and a new amount? Now it comes for free. Triggers allow you to programmatically reference (and update) table columns as they are being written to the database. For example:

```
Create or Replace Trigger Update_Sum_T1
After Update
On EMP For Each Row
BEGIN
    IF :OLD.salary != :NEW.salary THEN
        UPDATE   emp_summary
        SET      tot_salary = tot_salary + :NEW.salary - :OLD.salary
        WHERE    dept_no = :NEW.dept_no;
    END IF;
END;
```

DML operation identifiers

Triggers can tell what type of DML statement they are performing. This helps you to write a single generic insert/update/delete trigger, rather than having to write three. For example:

```
# trg_tune.sql
Create or Replace Trigger Update_Sum_T1
After Insert OR Update OR Delete
On EMP For Each Row
DECLARE
    offset number := 0;
BEGIN
    IF NVL(:OLD.salary, 0) != NVL(:NEW.salary,0) THEN
        IF INSERTING
            offset := :NEW.salary;
        ELSIF UPDATING
            offset := :NEW.salary - :OLD.salary
        ELSE
            offset := 0 - :OLD.salary;
        END IF;
        UPDATE   EMP_Summary
        SET      Tot_Salary = Tot_Salary + offset
```

```
          WHERE    Dept_No = :NEW.Dept_no;
      END IF;
   END;
```

Multiple triggers of the same type

RDBMS Oracle7.1 and later versions support multiple triggers of the same type (before-insert, after-insert, before-update, etc) on one table. This has the advantage of simplifying database triggers for smaller tasks, rather than having very large trigger modules performing many unrelated functions.

Suited to client-server applications

Database triggers are very efficient in a client-server environment. PL/SQL modules fire automatically, independent of the calling process, thus cutting down on client-to-server network communication and assisting in the laborious task of software distribution. Only one copy of the source needs to exist, and it is held in the database, not at 200 or more client workstations.

Trigger disadvantages

Triggers are not without their disadvantages. Here we discuss the most important ones. One of the ways that we judge the quality of an application's physical design is to query the number, size, and types of database triggers that are incorporated into the application. If there are fewer than 10 database triggers, this usually indicates that an older application has been migrated from an Oracle6 environment. Fifty or more database triggers indicate functionality indecision by the users during the build phase and probable performance issues. A number between 10 and 50 leads us to believe that the application was carefully designed and developed for Oracle7 deployment. On the basis of the quality of the trigger code, we can usually judge the quality of the application. Of course, these observations are all rules of thumb and are occasionally incorrect, but they do help us to form an immediate opinion of an application before committing our time and energy to that application's future.

Not compiled

Unlike stored procedures and packages, triggers are not held in the database in a compiled (PL/SQL pcode) form. Every time a trigger is fired, the code must be recompiled. However, overheads will be reduced if the trigger is already in the shared buffer pool. One alternative to this repetition is for each trigger to call a stored procedure to perform the work. The procedure is precompiled, and the trigger code is reduced to a handful of lines.

For example:

```
New command: sql> alter trigger Summary_Emp_T1 compile;
```

NOTE   Oracle7.3/PL/SQL 2.3 does now support precompiled PL/SQL trig-
                ger code.

No SELECT trigger support

Database triggers work only for DML operations. A trigger cannot be attached
to a SELECT SQL statement. We have seen a number of instances in which an
Access Validation trigger would have been invaluable on a business-sensitive
table. This problem of restricting who can read what, where, and when can
be handled via views, roles, and access grants, but it becomes very difficult
when you are trying to retrofit a business enhancement. Obviously, allowing
DML triggers for SELECT statements would not be practical (or even possible)
with locking, rollback, and transaction state conflicts, but read-only triggers
would be handy.

Complete trigger failure

When a database update fails, the offending statement and all previous trigger
updates are also rolled back. Programmers often try to use data validation triggers to write an error message to a logging table before "failing" the
transaction. They cannot understand why, when the transaction is aborted, no
error log is found in the logging table. What has really happened is that the
error message has been written to the logging table and then immediately
rolled back by the very same trigger when it raises application failure. To
inexperienced programmers, this behavior is more surprising than annoying.
The only way to achieve this type of activity is to report the error via a nonupdate activity, such as a database pipe.

Disabled triggers

Database triggers can be accidentally disabled or dropped by a person with
sufficient privilege. This is actually nothing new. The problem is that there is
no practical way of writing application code to guarantee that a trigger actually exists. If your application uses database triggers to audit sensitive data or
accumulate summary tables, a disabled trigger can compromise the integrity
of your whole system. The bad part is that nothing will be obviously wrong.
The trigger is only performing a subtask; the originating action will still
proceed. We design applications in which integrity is guaranteed by database
triggers but cannot guarantee that the trigger actually exists or is enabled.
DBAs must be aware of, and alert to, this potential problem.

No version control

Either database triggers exist or they don't; they are enabled or they are not. Other than building complex logic into the trigger text, we have no way to support multiple trigger versions on the one table.

Update OF COLUMN

The database trigger syntax includes an OF COLUMN extension that refines the sensitivity of the trigger. The trigger will execute only when that particular column (or columns) is updated. The problem with this approach is that the database thinks that setting a column back to its current value constitutes a change. The pros and cons of this approach can be debated long into the night, but what is annoying is the number of available application tools that insist on updating all table columns if any one of the columns has been modified. SQL*Forms is a prime example. All base table columns are updated back to the database, regardless of which column(s) were physically modified. For example:

```
Create or Replace Trigger Update_Sum_T1
After Update OF salary
On EMP For Each Row
BEGIN
    IF NVL(:OLD.salary, 0) != NVL(:NEW.salary,0) THEN
        .
        .
    END IF;
END;
```

No support of SYS table triggers

Oracle has decided that a database trigger cannot be associated with any table owner by user SYS. This is sound reasoning for all internal database tables (e.g., the V$ and X$ tables) but a little annoying for other noncritical SYS objects. For example, we've had situations in which trigger support for a a table such as SYS.AUD$ would have been handy. In this case, we wanted to check every user logging in to the database with a number of complex business rules (e.g., multiple connections, valid terminal IDs, client-server support for some database accounts and not for others). By enabling database auditing on the CONNECT function, I could have trapped the connect with an ON-INSERT TRIGGER on the SYS.AUD$ table, but it wasn't supported. (Note that moving the AUD$ table (with trigger) to another user account and creating a synonym in the SYS account is also not supported!)

Mutating triggers

Database triggers are permitted to do almost anything except reference the table that instigated the trigger. This type of "loop" is known as a mutating trigger. Not being able to read or modify the record in question is understandable, and not being able to update any other record in the table is plausible—but not being able to read any other record in the table is a real nuisance.

Earlier implementations of database trigger mutation could be circumnavigated via views, but this hole has now been plugged. The only legal way to achieve a mutating update now is to replicate all required data into a second mirror table and query the necessary information from that table via the trigger. The trigger would also need to be extended to maintain this mirrored table.

Hidden behavior

The power of database triggers can also be its downfall. One of the most dangerous attributes of a database trigger is its hidden behavior. Updates can take far longer than they should or can generate strange, seemingly unrelated database errors. How many times have you heard the developer cry, "I only inserted a single row into table xxx; it can't be my fault!"? In such cases, you should immediately ask whether a trigger is involved. Poor developers are desperately trying to tune their 20-line programs, absolutely devastated when the programs take 4 hours to run. Little do they know that for every row they insert, 100 rows may be getting inserted into seven different distributed databases, worldwide! They might not know that their organization *had* a Hong Kong office.

Tuning database triggers

Having examined the strengths and weaknesses of PL/SQL database triggers, let's look now at how to put them to more effective use.

Exploit the power of SQL and PL/SQL

All of the SQL and PL/SQL tuning tips and techniques detailed in the previous chapter apply directly to database triggers.

Move trigger code to stored procedures

As was described earlier, database triggers are not held in a compiled form until PL/SQL 2.3 (Oracle7.3). As a consequence, it is more efficient to move trigger logic to a stored procedure and simply call the procedure from the trigger. This may mean passing all necessary trigger information (NEW and OLD column values, DML statement type, etc.) to the procedure because it does not have access to the information.

```
Create or Replace Trigger Update_Sum_T1
After Update OR INSERT OR DELETE
On EMP For Each Row
BEGIN
    Update_Sum_Prc (:OLD.salary, :NEW.Salary, :NEW.rowid);
END;
```

Do not use triggers

The most efficient trigger is no trigger at all. Often triggers are incorrectly used to initialize default table columns, perform simple data integrity checking, or enforce referential integrity rules. All of these trigger components can now be replaced by DDL table constraints and referential integrity. These actions operate below the user level (internal to the RDBMS kernel) and are always more efficient than row-level triggers. For example, this example:

```
# trg_tune.sql
Create or Replace Trigger Validate_EMP_T1 on EMP
After  InsertOn EMP For Each Row
DECLARE
    CURSOR C1 IS
    SELECT 'x'
    FROM    dept
    WHERE   dept_no = :NEW.dept_no;
    --
    xdummy  VARCHAR2(1);
BEGIN
    IF :NEW.salary <= 0 THEN
        RAISE form_application_error ( -20000,
            'Salary must be greater than $0.00');
    END IF;
    --
    IF :NEW.salary > 100,000
    AND :NEW.sal_grade < 10 THEN
        RAISE form_application_error ( -20001,
            'Salary cannot excede 100,000 for theis Job Grade');
    END IF;
    --
    OPEN C1;
    FETCH C1 INTO xdummy;
    IF C1%notfound THEN
        RAISE form_application_error ( -20002,
        'Invalid Department Number Entered');
    END IF;
    --
    :NEW.last_upd_date := sysdate;
    :NEW.last_upd_user := user;
END;
```

would be better coded as

```
# trg_when.sql
CREATE TABLE EMP
(
emp_no          NUMBER(6)NOT NULL,
....
dept_no         NUMBER(4)       CONSTRAINT EMP_dept_FK
                                REFERENCES dept(deptno),
salary          NUMBER(12,2)    CHECK (salary > 0),
sal_grade       NUMBER(2),
```

```
last_upd_date   DATE              DEFAULT SYSDATENOT NULL,
last_upd_user   VARCHAR2(10)      DEFAULT USERNOT NULL,
CONSTRAINT      check_sal
                CHECK (salary < 100000 OR sal_grade >= 10)
)
```

Note that DDL DEFAULT values column definitions can often be confusing because default functionality changes depending on how the row column is inserted into the table. We have always assumed that default values would be applied if no column values (NULL) were provided on initial row insertion. But it turns out that not referencing the column during row creation and inserting it with a value of null are two separate things. For example:

```
Table Tab1
(fld1   VARCHAR2(20),
 fld2   VARCHAR2(10)  DEFAULT USER )

INSERT INTO tab1        values  ('ABC', NULL);
INSERT INTO tab1 (fld1) values  ('ABC');

Fld1           Fld2
------------   -------------
ABC            NULL           <-- Default did not activate
XYZ            SCOTT          <-- Default did activate
```

Exploit the WHEN clause

Oracle has always boasted that DDL-defined referential integrity, check constraints, and default column settings are more efficient than application-level coding. Oracle claims that this built-in functionality operates one level below any user-defined SQL code (whatever that means!). These claims are quite true, and the WHEN clause associated with a table trigger is no exception.

Always use the WHEN clause before you resort to inline trigger coding. With versions before Oracle7.3 (triggers are precompiled in Oracle7.3), this is even more important. More often than not, the first line of the trigger code is of the form

```
IF :NEW.column1 = 'A' THEN
```

For every row updated, this trigger is to be compiled and executed, and yet the very first line of PL/SQL code excludes the trigger processing. All this expensive processing can be avoided by a well-written WHEN clause. Remember that WHEN clause has access to everything to which a trigger has access, including full SQL functionality. The following example:

```
# trg_when.sql
Create or Replace Trigger Validate_EMP_T1 on EMP
After Insert OR Update
On EMP For Each Row
BEGIN
    IF  UPDATING THEN
```

```
        IF  :NEW.salary    !=   :OLD.salary
        OR  :NEW.dept_no    !=   :OLD.dept_no THEN
             .
        END IF;
    ELSIF INSERTING THEN
        IF  :NEW.salary    !=   0 THEN
             .
        END IF;
    END IF;
END;
```

would be better coded as

```
# trg_when.sql
Create or Replace Trigger Validate_EMP_T1 on EMP
After Insert OR Update
On EMP For Each Row
WHEN ( UPDATING  AND (  NEW.salary  != OLD.salary
                     OR NEW.dept_no != OLD.dept_no )
    OR INSERTING AND    NEW.salary  != 0                )
BEGIN
    IF  UPDATING THEN
         .
    ELSIF INSERTING THEN
         .
    END IF;
END;
```

Increase the size of the shared pool

Because trigger code is repeatedly parsed and reparsed when it is executed multiple times, retaining the "parse tree" in memory helps performance. Monitor the activity within the shared buffer pool and increase the size of the pool (physical memory permitting) if you think that it is not retaining cursor information long enough.

Stored Procedures and Functions

Stored procedures and functions, first introduced in Oracle7.0, use the full capabilities of PL/SQL. Stored procedures and functions are just a natural progression from the sharable procedural libraries supported by tools such as SQL*Forms 3 for Oracle 6 databases.

NOTE   The following sections refer to both procedures and functions and, for the purposes of this discussion, assume that these two objects are interchangeable. For simplicity, we refer only to procedures below.

Procedure and function advantages

When database procedures and triggers are used correctly, they have many
wonderful features. Application coding and testing can be reduced many times
over by a few stored database objects. The following list summarizes the strengths
of database procedures and describes how to exploit them.

Code sharing

Stored procedures guarantee common code sharing, regardless of tool,
language, or DML statement origination. The code needs testing only once; it
does not have to be retested every time it is used in a new program.

Object security

EXECUTE privilege is granted to a database user for the stored procedure, not
for the tables that the procedure may reference. This means that a DBA does
not have to grant DML access on database objects for a user to be able to
update those objects. Obviously, the owner of the stored procedure needs the
correct privileges on the underlying objects, but the calling user does not. The
calling user does not even have to know the procedure tables exist. The user
needs only to be concerned about the fact that a result is achieved when he
or she calls a procedure, not how that result is arrived at.

Variable parameter passing

One valuable feature of stored procedures (and library procedures) is their
ability to pass values to and receive results from them. This functionality can
be exploited by providing variable defaults (e.g., := NULL), named notational
variables (e.g., Param =>), or a combination of both, to pass a nonuniform
number of parameters to the same procedure. This flexibility allows us to
extend the functionality of an older procedure by adding more command line
information to the procedure while supporting all of the previous procedure
calls. Consider the following, for example:

```
# prc_parm.sql
PROCEDURE Value_List (Fld  IN char,            Val1 IN char := NULL,
                      Val2 IN char := NULL,Val3 IN char := NULL,
                      Val4 IN char := NULL,Val5 IN char := NULL,
                      Val6 IN char := NULL,Val7 IN char := NULL,
                      Val8 IN char := NULL,Val9 IN char := NULL)
    IS
    BEGIN
      IF Fld in (Val1,Val2,Val3,Val4,Val5,Val6,Val7,Val8,Val9) THEN
        NULL;
      ELSE
        RAISE form_application_error ( -20001,
        'Invalid Value Entered : Not Found within select list');
      END IF;
    END;
```

This procedure can be executed by any of the following calls:

```
# prc_parm.sql
value_in_list ('A','B','C','D','F','G','H','I','J','H');
value_in_list (val,'B','C','D','F','G','H','I','J');
value_in_list (val,b1, b2, b3, b4);
value_in_list (val);
```

by passing positional and/or named notation parameters:

```
# prc_parm.sql
value_in_list ('A','B','C','D','F','G','H','I','J','H');
value_in_list (Fld => val, Val1 => b1, Val2 => b2);
value_in_list (Val1 => b4, Val2 => b7, Fld => val);
value_in_list (val, b1,b2, Val8 => b2, Val9 => b2);
```

Procedure overlaying

Procedure overlaying is another powerful extension of stored procedures (and library procedures) that developers should exploit. This overlaying can be a very elegant way to retrospectively alter and/or extend business functionality. Overlaying allows the developer to define a procedure with several alternative definitions to choose from. Each definition is checked until a parameter list type match is found. For example:

```
PROCEDURE  Chk_Value (Fld  IN date) IS
BEGIN
    IF Fld NOT BETWEEN to_date('01-JAN-80')
                    AND to_date('31-DEC-99') THEN
        RAISE form_application_error ( -20001,
            'Invalid Date Value Entered');
    END IF;
END;

PRCEDURE Chk_Value (Fld  IN char) IS
BEGIN
    IF Fld NOT BETWEEN 'A' AND 'ZZZZZZZZ' THEN
        RAISE form_application_error ( -20001,
            'Invalid Alpha Value Entered');
    END IF;
END;

PROCEDURE Chk_Value (Fld  IN number) IS
BEGIN
    IF Fld NOT BETWEEN 0 AND 99999999 THEN
        RAISE form_application_error ( -20001,
            'Invalid Numeric Value Entered');
    END IF;
END;
```

These procedures can be called (overlaid) by any of the following:

```
# prc_olay.sql
BEGIN
    Chk_Value ( SYSDATE );
```

```
        Chk_Value ( 'PETER' );
        Chk_Value ( 4723764 );
    END;
```

Automatic dependency tracking

Oracle automatically tracks all object interdependencies for every PL/SQL stored object. Object dependencies include all tables, views, sequences, and synonyms in both local and remote databases that a procedure may reference. Whenever an object that is referenced in a stored procedure is altered (dropped and/or re-created, column definitions changed, or new columns added), that procedure is marked as INVALID. Oracle automatically recompiles the procedure the next time it is called. If the compilation is successful, processing proceeds as usual; otherwise an error is reported back to the calling application.

Retrospective business rules

Stored procedures allow the retrospective fitting of any new or modified business rules. You can retrofit in several different ways, which we've already described. First, if the original functionality is contained in a single, global stored procedure, any modification to that procedure will automatically be applied to the hundreds of application modules that may be using it. Second, use procedure overlaying to modify the functionality of an existing stored procedure by adding option procedure parameters.

Suited to client-server applications

Stored procedures are very efficient in client-server environments. Stored procedures are executed with a single procedure call, potentially processing thousands of lines of PL/SQL code rather than transmitting all the code across the network. Only one copy of the source, held in the database, needs to exist.

Procedure and function disadvantages

Procedures and functions do have some disadvantages.

Disabled procedures

Database procedures can be accidentally dropped by a person with sufficient privilege. This is nothing new, except that there is no practical way of writing application code to detect inoperable procedure(s). Since SQL and PL/SQL are interpreted languages, an invalid or missing stored procedure is not detectable until module run-time. When the error is encountered, a confusing, cryptic database error results that is of very little help to the average application user.

Automatic dependency tracking

Dependency tracking is a vital feature of stored procedures. Without dependency tracking and automatic module recompilation, application errors would quadruple. The downside of dependency tracking is that it all happens behind the scenes, and no obvious alarm bells ring. When a simple DDL operation, such as adding a new column to an existing table, is performed, many stored procedures are marked as needing recompilation. What is not provided is the ability to recompile all these dependencies in a single action or to ascertain which procedures are, in fact, invalid. Other than compiling each object one at a time and checking its results, we have no way of determining the effect of a DDL modification.

Restricted overloading functionality

Procedure and function overloading is available only within database packages or as PL/SQL sub-blocks. Database stored procedures cannot be overloaded. If you try to add a second overloaded stored procedure with the same procedure identifier, an error will result. The following shows an example of overloading:

```
DECLARE
    PROCEDURE Chk_Value ( val IN date ) IS
    BEGIN
        . . .
    END;
    PROCEDURE Chk_Value ( val IN number ) IS
    BEGIN
        . . .
    END;
    PROCEDURE Chk_Value ( val IN varchar2 ) IS
    BEGIN
        . . .
    END;
BEGIN
    Chk_Value ( SYSDATE );
    Chk_Value ( 'PETER' );
    Chk_Value ( 4723764 );
END;
```

No version control

Either database procedures exist or they don't. Other than building logic into the procedure text, we have no way of supporting multiple procedure versions.

Tuning procedures and functions

Procedures are a key building block of every new application. They provide the flexibility, efficiency, and performance advantages that all complex Oracle applications require. With the increases in their number, size, complexity, and functionality, greater care and diligence must be given to their tuning.

Exploit the power of SQL and PL/SQL

All of the SQL and PL/SQL tuning tips and techniques detailed in the previous chapters apply directly to database procedures.

Increase the size of the shared pool

All executing stored procedures are resident (in parsed pcode form) in the shared buffer pool. Once a procedure has finished executing, it is eligible to be swapped out of memory. Increasing the size of the shared pool will also increase the likelihood of a common stored procedure remaining in memory from one execution to the next. Monitor the shared buffer pool and increase it (physical memory permitting) if you think that it is not retaining commonly used SQL and PL/SQL code segments long enough.

Group like procedures into a stored package

It is often a good idea to group common procedures into a single package procedure. This is most appropriate when you have a number of procedures that are always referenced together or that physically call each other. Rather than having to call each procedure into memory as required, a common set of procedures is loaded into memory on the initial reference of any procedure within that group (package).

Pinning procedures into memory

Once a stored procedure has been loaded into the shared buffer pool, it can be "pinned" into the buffer pool via a special Oracle database package procedure. Pinning large, frequently accessed procedures into memory can be very beneficial. Pinned procedures can never be swapped out of memory until the database is shut down or until they are explicitly unpinned. (Note that flushing the shared pool will not release a pinned object.)

```
sqlplus> execute dbms_shared_pool.keep  ('scott.Chk_Value_Prc');
         execute dbms_shared_pool.unkeep('scott.Chk_Value_Prc');
```

Be careful not to pin too many of your application procedures and functions into memory, or you will use up all available shared buffer space and the performance of the remainder of the application will suffer. (See the section "Pinning objects into memory" for more details.)

Stored Packages

Stored packages are sets of related procedures and functions grouped together into a single PL/SQL module. Packages allow us to create library-like modules similar to those in 3GL languages.

Package advantages

The following summarizes the advantages of stored packages:

Structured environment

Large complex applications could conceivably have many thousands of stored procedures and functions in the database. This leads to a complex production (and development) environment, making source control very difficult and prone to error. Grouping all related database objects into database packages can help to alleviate this problem. For example, all general ledger procedure and functions go into the GL_Package, security modules in the SEC_Package, and so on.

Object security

EXECUTE privilege is granted to a database user for the database package, not for the tables that procedures and functions within the package may reference. This means that a DBA does not have to grant DML access on database objects for a user to be able to update those objects. Obviously, the owner of the package needs the correct privileges on the underlying objects, but the calling user does not. The calling user does not even have to know that the tables exist. The user needs only to be concerned about the fact that a result is achieved when he or she calls a package object, not how that result is arrived at.

Pre-loading related procedures and functions

The first reference to any element within a stored package module triggers the entire package to be loaded and parsed for execution. Preempting the loading of like procedures can help to ease overall application overheads (reducing disk I/O) for databases that have many, large stored procedures and functions. In practice, every time an overloaded procedure is referenced by an application, all overloaded procedures may need to be inspected to decide which one has a parameter match. Loading all these related procedures into memory via a package is the most efficient approach.

Local/private package procedures and functions

Packages may contain local/private procedures and/or functions within the package body that are not available to the general user base. This means the procedures and functions can be referenced only by other procedures and/or functions of that package. This feature allows us to code "private'" modules that perform a specific function that is not generally available. The "public" modules within the procedure must decide whether the caller has the privileges to perform the private operation.

Grouping overloading procedures

Overloaded procedures (described earlier) can be misleading when you are trying to debug application problems. Overloaded procedures and functions are not always obvious and may often perform completely unrelated tasks. Trying to debug the wrong module can be difficult! Combining all overloaded procedures into their own packages will make debugging and/or future maintenance a lot simpler.

No dependency chain reactions

Automatic dependency tracking is based on the package header definition. Any changes to a package body will not cause a dependency invalidation chain reaction. Changes to a standalone stored procedure can cause many or all other stored procedures, functions, and packages to be marked as invalid and to require recompilation.

Static package variable

Packages support the definition of static variables. These variables are local to each user session, retaining their value for the duration of the session. This means that repetitive calls to the same package can access package variables defined or initialized during previous calls. Static package variables are held in each programmer's global area (PGA) within the System Global Area (SGA).

Suited to client-server applications

Stored packages are very efficient in a client-server environment. Packages are executed with a single call, potentially processing thousands of lines of PL/SQL code rather than transmitting all the code across the network. Only one copy of the source needs to exist (in the database, not at the many client workstations).

Package disadvantages

Stored packages do have some disadvantages:

Unnecessary module loading

Many applications that we have seen insist on grouping all stored procedures and functions of each major business line into packages. These packages can be very, very large. The first person to reference any module of these packages has to wait several minutes for a response. This time is spent preloading and parsing a package of 10,000+ lines. This seems like a high price to pay just to execute a five-line procedure within that package!

When large packages are being loaded into the shared buffer pool, other packages and procedures may also need to be flushed, creating a vicious circle. The flushed packages are called in and cause other modules to be flushed. This action yields no benefits in grouping multiple procedures and functions (they never remain in memory long enough to be used) and results only in higher than necessary parse times for very simple procedure calls.

Unable to load packages

Very large packages may not be able to be loaded into memory at all. Packages, procedures, and functions all insist on contiguous shared buffer pool memory (until Oracle7.3). This is not always possible, especially when the database has been up for a long period of time. The longer the database has been running, the more checkered the shared pool becomes. The only alternative is to shut down the database to clear out the shared buffer pool.

NOTE   Flushing the shared pool via the ALTER SYSTEM FLUSH SHARED_
              POOL command releases only unused objects. Free, contiguous buff-
              er space still might not be large enough.

Unable to compile large packages

We have encountered packages that were too large to compile by using the normal rollback segments. When a package is compiled (via the create or replace package), the old package text is deleted from the database and the new one is inserted, all in the one transaction state. On recompilation of a large package we would encounter the error UNABLE TO EXTENT ROLL-BACK SEGMENT. Setting a rollback segment before package compilation (via SET TRANSACTION USE ROLLBACK SEGMENT) is of little help. All DDL statements execute in their own transaction state, thus ignoring any preset rollback segment. The only alternatives are to drop the old package before compiling the new version (this still may not work) or to increase the size and/or number of your rollback segment extents.

Lack of synonym support

Database synonyms can be used to identify only packages, not package procedures. This particular behavior is very frustrating. Application designers must make a conscious decision at the beginning of a project where and when to use packages and where and when to use stored procedures and functions. DBAs cannot pick and choose between package procedure and stored procedure functionality via synonyms. Developers must code the physical procedure or package procedure inline. For example, the following procedure calls cannot be transposed via synonyms:

```
scott.Chk_Value_Prc ( .... );
scott.GL_Pck.Chk_Value_Prc ( .... );
```

No version control

Either database packages exist or they don't; they are enabled or they are not. Other than building logic into the package text, we have no way to support multiple package versions.

Tuning packages

Let's look at how to use packages in the most efficient way.

Exploit the power of SQL and PL/SQL

All of the SQL and PL/SQL tuning tips and techniques detailed in the previous chapters apply directly to database packages.

Increase the size of the shared pool

All executing packages are resident (in parsed pcode form) in the shared buffer pool. Packages can be very large and must be loaded into memory in their entirety to execute its smallest subprocedure. Once a package has finished executing, it is eligible to be swapped out of memory. Increasing the size of the shared pool will increase the likelihood that a common package will remain in memory from one execution to the next. Monitor the shared buffer pool and increase it (physical memory permitting) if you think it is not retaining commonly used SQL and PL/SQL code segments long enough.

Pinning packages into memory

Once a package has been loaded into the shared buffer pool it can be pinned into the buffer pool via a special database package procedure. Pinning large, frequently accessed packages into memory can be very beneficial. Pinned packages can never be swapped out of memory until the database is shut down or until they are explicitly unpinned.

```
sqlplus> execute dbms_shared_pool.keep  ('scott.Chk_Value_Prc');
sqlplus> execute dbms_shared_pool.unkeep('scott.Chk_Value_Prc');
```

Be careful not to pin too many of your application packages into memory and use up all of your available shared buffer space or the performance of the remainder of the application will suffer. (See the section called "Pinning objects into memory" later in this chapter for more details.)

Exploiting the Power of PL/SQL

This section describes some special features of PL/SQL that we've found especially helpful in improving performance at many sites. Don't be limited by our suggestions. Although use of these features can result in substantial performance gains, others that we haven't yet envisioned may bring you performance gains as well. Use your imagination!

Expanding the Functionality of Other Tools

By incorporating PL/SQL into Oracle tools such as SQL*Forms and SQL*Plus, you expand the capabilities of these tools by allowing them to perform functions that are not normally available to them. For example, SQL*Forms ordinarily does not allow DML statements (UPDATE, INSERT, DELETE, COMMIT, ROLLBACK) to be specified outside the scope of a commit phase (the normal scope is between pre-COMMIT and post-COMMIT). You can get around these limitations by including such statements in PL/SQL blocks.

In the following example, SQL*Forms updates information when a user enters the form. Within the KEY-STARTUP trigger, you cannot specify a COMMIT statement directly. However, by including COMMIT inside a PL/SQL block (delimited by BEGIN and END), you can get around this limitation.

```
KEY-STARTUP :    BEGIN
                     UPDATE user_form
                     SET     curr_form = `XXXXXX',
                             form_time = SYSDATE
                     WHERE   user_code = USER;

                     :SYSTEM.MESSAGE_LEVEL   := 25;
                     COMMIT;
                     :SYSTEM.MESSAGE_LEVEL   := 0;
                 END;
```

NOTE   SYSTEM.MESSAGE_LEVEL needs to be set to level 25 to suppress
              the message NO OUTSTANDING COMMITS. This message is a side
              effect of having no outstanding basetable commits. The PL/SQL up-
              date proceeds regardless of the message.

Using PL/SQL to Speed Up Updates

PL/SQL provides especially noticeable performance gains when you are running a large batch update job in which parent/child updating plays a part. Consider a system in which the ACCOUNT_TOTALS table is updated every night from various systems to post each account's current expenditures against its budget. There are approximately 10,000 rows in the ACCOUNT_TOTALS table and about 200 rows in the TRANSACTION table (containing the day's transactions). The system is not an integrated one in which data loaded into the TRANSACTION (child) table automatically update the ACCOUNT_TOTALS (parent) table. You need to run a program that posts the updates to ACCOUNT_TOTALS as a separate step.

Using SQL only, you would update as follows. This type of update would take several minutes to run.

```
# pl_upd.sql
UPDATE ACCOUNT_TOTALS A
SET current_exp = current_exp + ( SELECT daily_exp
                                  FROM   TRANSACTION T
```

```
                                          WHERE T.acc_no = A.acc_no )
    WHERE EXISTS ( SELECT 'X'
                   FROM    TRANSACTION T
                   WHERE   T.acc_no = A.acc_no  );
```

Now suppose you used PL/SQL to achieve the same result. You would accomplish the update in seconds!

```
# pl_upd.sql
DECLARE
    CURSOR read_tran  IS
    SELECT acc_no, daily_exp
    FROM   TRANSACTION;
    --
    acc_no_store      NUMBER (6);
    daily_exp_store   NUMBER (9,2);
BEGIN
    OPEN read_tran;
    LOOP
        FETCH read_tran INTO acc_no_store, daily_exp_store;
        EXIT WHEN read_tran%NOTFOUND;
        --
        UPDATE account_totals A
        SET    current_exp = current_exp + daily_exp_store
        WHERE  aCC_NO      = acc_no_store ;
    END LOOP;
END;
```

Although using PL/SQL instead of traditional SQL may result in a substantial performance gains, PL/SQL does not always produce such results. What if the TRANSACTION table contains 1,000 or more rows, rather than 200. If a daily child transaction table updates more than about 10% to 15% of the parent table (ACCOUNTS_TABLE, in the example), PL/SQL will actually make the update run more slowly. PL/SQL uses the table's indexes and performs more physical reads against the database than the SQL method, which performs a full table scan in this case. Always experiment with alternatives, benchmark the options, and question the results.

Exploiting Stored Packages, Procedures, and Functions

Stored PL/SQL objects can also be exploited in a variety of ways that will give you the kinds of features you've always wanted but never had access to before in PL/SQL. The following sections provide a starting point.

Exploiting package variables

We all know that packages support static variables that retain their values for the duration of the session. Why don't programmers use them? These variables are invaluable in helping to reduce application overheads.

Every application we have ever been involved with has a package (or stored procedure) that returns the operating system account code of the current user. This routine can be called many hundreds of times in a very short interval. But why look up the V$SESSION table every time? After all, you cannot change the usercode in mid-session. Exploiting the fact that a package variable is NULL on the first call of the routine, we are able to avoid subsequent table reads.

```
# pkg_vars.sql
FUNCTION get_osuser RETURN VARCHAR2 AS
   Xosuser VARCHAR2(30);
BEGIN
   SELECT   v.osuser
   INTO     Xosuser
   FROM     v$session v
   WHERE    v.audsid = userenv('SESSIONID');
   RETURN   (Xosuser);
END;


>> :osuser := get_osuser;
```

This function should be coded as follows:

```
# pkg_vars.sql
PACKAGE get_user_details
AS
   FUNCTION osuser RETURN VARCHAR2;
END;


PACKAGE BODY get_user_details
AS
   Xosuser  varchar2(30);
   FUNCTION osuser RETURN VARCHAR2 AS
      CURSOR C1 IS
      SELECT v.osuser
      FROM   v$session v
      WHERE  v.audsid = userenv('SESSIONID');
   BEGIN
      IF Xosuser IS NOT NULL THEN
         OPEN  C1;
         FETCH C1 INTO Xosuser;
         CLOSE C1;
      END IF;
      RETURN   (Xosuser);
   END;
END;


>> :osuser := get_user_details.osuser;
```

This simple sample can be used in many different ways, such as for code validation. Users often concentrate their work on one department at a time, processing all invoices from each department as a batch. Why validate the same department over and over again when it is the same one as last time? For example:

```
# pkg_vars.sql
PACKAGE validate_code
AS
  FUNCTION dept (dpt IN number);
  Xdept  NUMBER := -9999;
  Xdesc  VARCHAR2(30);
END;

PACKAGE BODY validate_code
AS
   FUNCTION dept (dpt IN number) RETURN VARCHAR2 AS
     CURSOR C1 IS
     SELECT dept_desc
     FROM   dept
     WHERE  dept_no = dpt;
   BEGIN
     IF Xdept != dpt THEN
        Xdesc := NULL;
        OPEN  C1;
        FETCH C1 INTO Xdesc;
        CLOSE C1;
        Xdept := dpt;
     END IF;
     IF Xdesc IS NULL THEN
        raise_application_error (-20101, 'Invalid Dept Entered');
     ELSE
        RETURN  (Xdesc);
     END IF;
   END;
END;

>> :dept_desc := validate_code.dept (:dept_no);
```

Exploiting the package initialization section

An often overlooked feature of database packages is the support of an initialization code section. This means that a predefined block of code will be executed the first time the package is referenced. If package variables need to be initialized before they are referenced, this is the ideal place to do it. The previous section described how to supply the current operating system usercode without having to look it up every time. That procedure could be streamlined even further by use of the initialization section.

This function should be coded as follows:

```
# pkg_init.sql
PACKAGE get_user_details
```

```
AS
  .....
  .....
  Xosuser   VARCHAR2(30);
END;

PACKAGE BODY get_user_details
AS
  CURSOR C1 IS
  SELECT v.osuser
  FROM   v$session v
  WHERE  v.audsid = userenv('SESSIONID');
  .....
  .....
  BEGIN            -- Package Initialization Section
    OPEN  C1;
    FETCH C1 INTO Xosuser;
    CLOSE C1;
  END;
END;


>> :osuser := get_user_details.Xosuser;
```

Exploiting package variable constants

Static package variables can be taken one step further. Most applications have a number of constant variables or static "data sets" that are almost constant for the life of the application. This information must be held in a database table and carry the same overheads as normal application data. Other than hard coding these near-constants in every application module that requires them, we've had few other alternatives in the past. Consider using a package to hold nearly static application variables and treat the package as a type of *include .h* file. The results can be rewarding. For example:

```
# pkg_cons.sql
PACKAGE fixed
  AS
    sex               VARCHAR2(1);
    --
    male              CONSTANT fixed.sex%type := 'M';
    female            CONSTANT fixed.sex%type := 'F';
    --
    true              CONSTANT NUMBER(1)    := 1;
    false             CONSTANT NUMBER(1)    := 0;
    min_school_age    CONSTANT NUMBER(2)    := 5;
    max_child_dep     CONSTANT NUMBER(12)   := 29,490;
  END;
```

What is interesting about package constants is that they can be referenced from anywhere inside a PL/SQL block, including within SQL code. Referencing a packaged constant can save a 1,000,000 row table(s) join with a table that has one row. Package variables can also be used as system-wide "type" definitions. (Note that these package variables cannot be constant.)

```
# pkg_cons.sql
DECLARE
     sex    fixed.sex%type;
   BEGIN
     IF :tot_sal <= fixed.max_child_dep THEN
        SELECT COUNT(DECODE(C.gender, fixed.male,   'x','')),
               COUNT(DECODE(C.gender, fixed.female,'x',''))
        INTO   :tot_males, :tot_females
        FROM   emp_children C
        WHERE  C.age >= fixed.min_school_age;
     ELSE
        ....
     END IF;
   END;
```

NOTE   No package body is required, but a copy of every package static
                variable will be held in the SGA for every user session that has refer-
                enced a variable. This could cause excessive memory overheads for
                an application with many users and a shortage of real memory.

Avoiding passing large parameters

PL/SQL tables and records are supported as parameters in procedures, functions, and packages. PL/SQL tables in particular can be very large, being limited only by the amount of memory you have available. PL/SQL always works on a local copy of each parameter rather than on the actual parameter itself. (This is necessary to preserve the value of the original parameter if the called procedure/package fails.) When a parameter is passed to a procedure that uses an IN or IN OUT reference, the actual parameter value is copied to a local variable reference within the procedure. If the parameter is returned from the procedure that uses an IN OUT or OUT reference, the local variable reference has to be copied back to the actual parameter itself. This type of activity can quickly use up large amounts of memory and CPU time. Remember that every user session has its own copy of an object's local variables.

What to do? As described earlier, package variables are available to all interested parties. Rather than passing, copying, and returning large parameters, use the one package variable as the common variable definition. This will save on memory and variable initialization overheads.

Using SQL inline functions

Stored database functions and packaged functions can be directly accessed from within a SQL SELECT statement. This powerful functionality is often overlooked by developers, who prefer to code extra processing outside the SQL statement. Functions can be called from wherever expressions are allowed in a SQL statement (e.g., SELECT, SET, WHERE, START WITH, GROUP BY, HAVING, ORDER BY.). Developers and DBAs are now able to extend the power of SQL to meet their exact requirements. Oracle7 servers using the Parallel Query Option can evaluate in-line functions in parallel. This behavior alone can yield performance gains way beyond any other alternatives.

Many application modules incur extra interprocess communication and client-server network overheads because they are forced to perform a second database query to retrieve related information. A single PL/SQL block can be used to perform all processing in a single database visit, but cannot (easily) return multiple records to the calling process. For example, inline SQL functions are very beneficial in fetching rows from the database with summation conditions on multiple child tables. We all know that trying to "sum" on more than one table causes a cartesian table join and massively inflated results.

```
Tables : emp
       : sick_leave       (4 rows, 6 days sick)
       : holiday_leave    (2 rows, 20 days leave)

# pkg_inl.sql
  SELECT E.emp_no, E.emp_name,
         sum(S.days) sick_days,
         sum(H.days) holidays
  FROM   holiday_leave H,
         sick_leave S,
         emp E
  WHERE  E.emp_no = :emp_no
  AND    E.emp_no = S.emp_no (+)
  AND    E.emp_no = H.emp_no (+)
  GROUP
      By E.emp_no, E.emp_name

  Result : Emp No     Emp Name     Sick Days   Holidays
           123456     Tom Jones       12          80
```

As you can see, the summed columns are wrong. Rather than coding this SQL as multiple SQL statements, we can use the power of inline SQL functions, as shown below.

```
# pkg_inl.sql
  FUNCTION Sum_Sick_Leave (emp  IN NUMBER) RETURN NUMBER
  AS
    tot_days  number := 0;
    CURSOR C1 IS
```

```
   SELECT  SUM(days)
   FROM    sick_leave
   WHERE   emp_no = emp;
BEGIN
   OPEN  C1;
   FETCH C1 INTO tot_days;
   CLOSE C1;
   RETURN (tot_days);
END;

FUNCTION  Sum_Holiday_Leave (emp IN number) RETURN NUMBER
AS
   tot_days  NUMBER := 0;
   CURSOR C1 IS
   SELECT sum(days)
   FROM   holiday_leave
   WHERE  emp_no = emp;
BEGIN
   OPEN  C1;
   FETCH C1 INTO tot_days;
   CLOSE C1;
   RETURN (tot_days);
END;

SELECT E.emp_no, E.emp_name,
       sum_sick_leave(E.emp_no)    sick_days,
       sum_holiday_leave(E.emp_no) holidays
FROM   emp E
WHERE  E.emp_no = :emp_no
```

```
Result:  Emp No    Emp Name    Sick Days  Holidays
         123456    Tom Jones       6          20
```

One of the major drawbacks of inline SQL functions is the fact that they can return only one value. What do we do when we need to fetch more than one value? Calling the inline function more than once per row would be very expensive and would defeat the purpose—or would it? Actually, by encapsulating the function into a package, we can exploit some package variables to call the function twice but execute it only once. For example:

```
SELECT E.emp_no, E.emp_name,
       SUM(S.days)     sick_days,
       COUNT(S.rowid) sick_occasions,
       SUM(H.days)     holidays,
       COUNT(H.rowid) holiday_occasions
FROM   holiday_leave H,
       sick_leave S,
       emp E
WHERE  E.emp_no = :emp_no
AND    E.emp_no = S.emp_no (+)
And    E.emp_no = H.emp_no (+)
```

```
                              ----- Sick ----    --- Holidays --
            Result :  Emp No   Emp Name   Days Occasions   Days Occasions
                      123456   Tom Jones   12      8         80     8
```

This SQL statement is still incorrect, but translating it to inline functions is a bit more complex.

```
# pkg_inl.sql
PACKAGE Sum_Emp
AS
  FUNCTION Sum_Sick_Leave (emp  IN number) RETURN number;
  FUNCTION Sum_Sick_Occasions (emp  IN number) RETURN number;
  FUNCTION Sum_Holiday_Leave (emp  IN number) RETURN number;
  FUNCTION Sum_Holiday_Occasions (emp  IN number) RETURN number;

  PRAGMA restrict_references (Sum_Sick_Leave,        WNDS, WNPS);
  PRAGMA restrict_references (Sum_Sick_Occasions,    WNDS, WNPS);
  PRAGMA restrict_references (Sum_Holiday_Leave,     WNDS, WNPS);
  PRAGMA restrict_references (Sum_Holiday_Occasions, WNDS, WNPS);
END;

PACKAGE BODY  Sum_Emp
AS
  last_sick_emp      NUMBER;
  sick_days          NUMBER;
  sick_occasions     NUMBER;
  last_holiday_emp   NUMBER;
  holidays           NUMBER;
  holidays_occasions NUMBER;

  CURSOR C1 (emp IN number) IS
  SELECT SUM(days), COUNT(*)
  FROM   sick_leave
  WHERE  emp_no = emp;

  CURSOR C2 (emp IN number) IS
  SELECT SUM(days), COUNT(*)
  FROM   holiday_leave
  WHERE  emp_no = emp;

  FUNCTION Sum_Sick_Leave (emp  IN number) RETURN number
  AS
  BEGIN
    If NVL(Last_Sick_Emp,-1) != emp THEN
      OPEN  C1;
      FETCH C1 INTO sick_days, sick_occasions;
      CLOSE C1;
      Last_Sick_Emp := Emp;
    END IF;
    RETURN (sick_days);
  END;

  FUNCTION Sum_Sick_Occasions (emp  IN number) RETURN number
```

```
  AS
  BEGIN
    IF NVL(Last_Sick_Emp,-1) != emp THEN
      OPEN  C1;
      FETCH C1 INTO sick_days, sick_occasions;
      CLOSE C1;
      Last_Sick_Emp := Emp;
    END IF;
    RETURN (sick_occasions);
  END;


  FUNCTION Sum_Holiday_Leave (emp  IN number) RETURN number
  AS
  BEGIN
    IF NVL(Last_Holiday_Emp,-1) != emp THEN
      OPEN  C2;
      FETCH C2 INTO holidays, holiday_occasions;
      CLOSE C2;
      Last_Holiday_Emp := Emp;
    END IF;
    RETURN (holidays);
  END;


  FUNCTION Sum_Holiday_Occasions (emp  IN number) RETURN number
  AS
  BEGIN
    IF NVL(Last_Holiday_Emp,-1) != emp THEN
      OPEN  C2;
      FETCH C2 INTO holidays, holiday_occasions;
      CLOSE C2;
      Last_Holiday_Emp := Emp;
    END IF;
    RETURN (holiday_occasions);
  END;
END;

SELECT E.emp_no, E.emp_name,
       sum_emp.sum_sick_leave(E.emp_no)          sick_days,
       sum_emp.sum_sick_occasions(E.emp_no)    sick_occasions,
       sum_emp.sum_holiday_leave(E.emp_no)       holidays
       sum_emp.sum_holiday_occasions(E.emp_no) holiday_occasions
FROM   emp E
WHERE  E.emp_no = :emp_no
```

			----- Sick ----		--- Holidays --	
Result :	Emp No	Emp Name	Days	Occasions	Days	Occasions
	123456	Tom Jones	**6**	**4**	**20**	**2**

NOTE Packages that contain in-line SQL functions must define those functions as read-only via the RESTRICT_REFERENCES pragma. Inline functions can never perform update operations, and this pragma defines the function as read-only to the outside world. Packaged functions that occur in the SELECT list need pragma WNDS (described below). Functions that appear within the WHERE clause require WNPS.

WNDS: Writes No Database State

Does not modify database tables. This pragma is mandatory for all inline package functions.

WNPS: Writes No Package State

Does not modify package variables within other packages

RNPS: Reads No Database State

Does not query database tables

RNPS: Reads No Package State

Does not reference package variables from other packages

Pinning objects into memory

By default, the RDBMS handles all loading and flushing of SQL information from the shared buffer pool. The database uses a least-recently-used algorithm to prioritize shared pool memory. Database objects are loaded into the shared pool (in compiled pcode form) the first time they are referenced and are immediately available for removal once all references to that object have finished. Pinning database objects into the SGA shared pool is very important to tuning large TPO-based applications. Database packages, functions, procedures, and individual cursors can all be pinned into memory. For example:

```
# pkg_pin.sql
PACKAGE dbms_shared_pool IS
     PROCEDURE Keep (pkg_name varchar2);
END;

sql >> execute dbms_shared_pool.keep ('scott.GL_package');
```

When a database object is pinned into memory and it is not already in the shared pool, the object is queued to be kept when it is first referenced. Note that the keep function mentioned earlier does not compile and load the object into the SGA.

NOTE   To permit an object to be pinned into memory, EXECUTE privilege must be granted to the Oracle user account that owns the DBMS_ SHARED_POOL package (normally SYS). This is necessary because packages and procedures are executed with the privileges of their creator, not the initiator.

Some users pin objects in the SGA in a preemptive way before they are actually loaded. Doing this can overshadow any possible gains. Once the object is referenced, the responsible session will bear the cost of loading and compiling the object. In the case of very large packages and procedures, this can be several minutes. Even worse, the object may not be able to be loaded because of insufficient or checkered memory within the shared buffer pool. We recommend that you always load (reference) an object before pinning it into the SGA. This is best done on database startup by the startup routine itself. How do you reference a package or procedure without executing it? You can't. What happens if the object updates the database or deletes rows from a table? Our preference is to pin only packages into memory and include a dummy variable definition in every package that can be referenced safely. For example:

```
# pkg_pin.sql
PACKAGE GL_Package IS
    Load_Me    NUMBER;
    PROCEDURE ABC;
    . . .
END;
PACKAGE AP_Package is
    Load_Me    NUMBER;
    PROCEDURE MNO;
    . . .
END;
PACKAGE AR_Package IS
    Load_Me    NUMBER;
    PROCEDURE XYZ;
    . . .
END;
```

The database startup routine should execute the following script after opening the database:

```
# pkg_pin.sql
sql >> execute scott.GL_package.Load_Me := 0;
sql >> execute dbms_shared_pool.keep ('scott.GL_package');

sql >> execute scott.AP_package.Load_Me := 0;
sql >> execute dbms_shared_pool.keep ('scott.AP_package');

sql >> execute scott.AR_package.Load_Me := 0;
sql >> execute dbms_shared_pool.keep ('scott.AR_package');
```

Oracle Corporation recommends that the following packages always be pinned into the shared pool at database startup (if you have installed them into the database):

```
SYS.STANDARD              SYS.DBMS_LOCK
SYS.DBMS_STANDARD         SYS.DBMS_PIPE
SYS.DBMS_DESCRIBE         SYS.DBMS_OUTPUT
SYS.DBMS_UTILITY
```

Using dynamic version control

A number of application rollouts have suffered from the lack of stored object version control. What do we mean by this? Wouldn't it be nice to be able to have two versions of a database procedure in the one application schema? We have been involved with sites that have had between six and eight physical database schemas (including full data volumes), all required to support a single application rollout. For example:

```
1)   Production    - Release 2.0
2)   QA Testing    - Release 2.1
3)   Training      - Release 2.1
4)   Unit Testing  - Release 2.2
5)   Regression    - Release 1.2
6)   Development    - Release 2.1
7)   Development    - Release 2.2
8)   Prd Support    - Release 2.0
```

This type of database redundancy might seem excessive to smaller development sites but is a fairly common occurrence with large, multi-phase applications. The total number of databases in this example was limited to eight because deployment was only on one hardware platform. Try supporting four or five platforms, and see how many separate databases you will need.

How do we overcome this DBA nightmare? Version control helps. By using an inter-connecting package procedure, we are able to call variant copies of the one stored object within the one database schema. The following example demonstrates this principle. Note that the Upd_Payroll procedure was changed from a standalone stored procedure to be part of the Payroll package when version 2.0 of the application was deployed. This type of structural schema change is possible with this approach.

```
# pkg_vers.sql
PROCEDURE Upd_Payroll_V10 ( Emp_No IN number) AS
BEGIN
....
END;

PROCEDURE Upd_Payroll_V11 ( Emp_No IN number) AS
BEGIN
....
```

```
END;

PACKAGE Payroll_V20 AS
    PROCEDURE Upd_Payroll ( Emp_No IN number) AS
    ....
END;
```

Developers should reference the procedure only via a special version control package, which is responsible for determining which copy of the object should be executed. For example:

```
BEGIN
    ....
    Ver_Cntl.Upd_Payroll ( 12345 );
    ....
END;
```

The application package to control object versioning can be driven by a number of approaches. The user's current application version could be held in the database as normal data; it could be initialized at application entry and held as a special package variable constant; or it could even be hard-coded in the version control package itself. For example:

```
# pkg_vers.sql
PACKAGE Ver_Cntl AS
    PROCEDURE Upd_Payroll ( Emp_No IN number) AS
    ....
END;


PACKAGE BODY Ver_Cntl AS
    PROCEDURE Upd_Payroll ( Emp_No IN number) AS
    BEGIN
        IF    fixed.version = 1.0 THEN
                Upd_Payroll_V10 (Emp_No);
        ELSIF fixed.version = 1.1 THEN
                Upd_Payroll_V11 (Emp_No);
        ELSIF fixed.version = 2.0 THEN
                Payroll_V20.Upd_Payroll (Emp_No);
        ELSE
                raise_application_error (-20001, '.....');
        END_IF;
    END;
    ....
    ....
END;
```

Once your application has moved into production and is in a stable state, you can happily delete all older versions of each object and alter the version control package to call only the one remaining object.

Getting schema flexibility via packages

We always recommend that the team leader of each new project pass a rule prohibiting the use of stored procedures and functions. These objects should be supported only via database packages. This recommendation is not a performance issue but one of schema flexibility. We support this argument for the following reasons:

- Database synonyms can reference a procedure, function, or package, but not a procedure or function *within a package*. This means that once a procedure is referenced by an application module, without having to undergo extensive back-coding, it must remain as a procedure. The object name can be altered and a synonym created to support references to the original name, but the object type cannot. The DBA loses the power to make decisions on whether a stored object should be a procedure or a package-procedure once coding begins.

  For example, the following procedures cannot be transposed by the DBA with synonyms:

  ```
  PROCEDURE scott.Upd_Payroll (...);
  PACKAGE PROCEDURE scott.GL_Pck.Upd_Payroll (...);
  ```

- Automatic dependency checking by the RDBMS is easier to control when dealing with packages. The dependency is based on the package header definition. Any changes to actual procedure code within the package body will not cause the dependency chain reaction that a procedure or function alteration could.

- Stored procedures and functions cannot support object overloading. Overloading is a vital weapon in the developer's toolkit. Restricting all stored objects to packages will mean that overloading will always be possible in the future.

- Dividing an application into many small module groups at the beginning of the project can have a real benefit. Rather than ending up with very large packages because things grew as the project progressed, small packages will provide additional flexibility. Small packages can always be collapsed into one another to form larger, more efficient modules via database synonyms. But large packages cannot be broken up into smaller modules with application back-coding. For example, the following packages:

  ```
  PACKAGE scott.GL_Pck;    PROCEDUREs: Ins_GL; Upd_GL; Del_GL;
  PACKAGE scott.AP_Pck;    PROCEDUREs: Ins_AP; Del_AP;
  PACKAGE scott.AR_Pck;    PROCEDUREs: Ins_AR; Del_AR;
  PACKAGE scott.FA_Pck;    FUNCTION:   Deprec_Asset;
  ```

  could be collapsed into a single package without having to change a single line of code:

  ```
  PACKAGE scott.FIN_Pck;   PROCEDUREs: Ins_GL; Upd_GL; Del_GL;
  ```

```
                                  Ins_AP; Del_AP;
                                  Ins_AR; Del_AR;
                     FUNCTION:    Deprec_Asset;

CREATE SYNONYM scott.GL_Pck FOR scott.FIN.Pck;
CREATE SYNONYM scott.AP_Pck FOR scott.FIN.Pck;
CREATE SYNONYM scott.AR_Pck FOR scott.FIN.Pck;
CREATE SYNONYM scott.FA_Pck FOR scott.FIN.Pck;
```

- Forcing all standalone procedures and functions to be part of a package does not reduce the potential of the module. If a developer explicitly requires the module to be small and compact, then the package could be a single module package (containing only one procedure or one function). This will not noticeably increase the size of the original module and will still provide the power of the package for later use.

- Packages make available static session variables that are an invaluable asset to the developer. Forcing all objects to be part of a package makes package variables available to the procedure or function at all times. This encourages their use and increases the coding alternatives for the module(s).

Using PL/SQL wrappers

One of the best assets of PL/SQL's stored objects is possibly also one of its worst. The fact that a PL/SQL module is available to all external tools and developers means that its source is, too. This source code could be confidential and dangerous in the wrong hands.

The PL/SQL wrapper is a standalone utility introduced with Oracle7.2 (PL/SQL 2.2) that allows you to provide your application to a third party in an encrypted mode. This is similar to providing an application in object or executable form rather than in raw source code. The wrapper converts the PL/SQL code into intermediate object code that can be read and loaded by the PL/SQL compiler. Wrapper PL/SQL code has the same attributes and advantages as normal PL/SQL code. It is portable, is platform independent, has automatic dependency checking, and is compatible with all Oracle tools and utilities. Oracle Corporation itself provides a number of stored objects that are encoded (wrapped) to protect intellectual property. You can wrap code as follows under UNIX:

```
wrap iname={input file} [oname={output file}]
```

Wrapping a PL/SQL block does perform syntax checks on the PL/SQL code, reporting any basic coding errors. As you would expect, semantic checking can be performed only at compilation time. External object references can be resolved only against the destination database schema.

The PL/SQL wrapper does have some minor disadvantages:

- Anonymous PL/SQL blocks and triggers cannot be wrapped. This restriction will possibly be addressed in a future release.

- Wrapped PL/SQL output is generally two to three times the size of its original source code.

Cursor Variables

The support of database cursors within stored RDBMS objects was introduced in Oracle7.2 (PL/SQL 2.2) and was a long awaited breakthrough. Cursor-variables provide a handle between an application module and a multiple record result set. A complex SQL statement can be defined within a database procedure and used by a number of application modules and/or tools. Developers no longer need to know how the table(s) is structured, how it inter-relates with other tables, or for that matter, what the table name is.

One record or multiple result sets can be passed or returned to the calling module. As with any other stored object, the calling user needs only EXECUTE privilege on the stored object; no SELECT privileges are necessary on any of the underlying tables. With a careful choice of parameters and a little more application coding, we can now communicate between stored database objects and the calling programs via multirow array fetches rather than via single rows. This one feature alone makes cursor variables invaluable to client-server environments. For example:

```
# pkg_curs.sql
Pro*C Module
...
struct emp_rec {
   char    name [31];
   double emp_no;
} emp_rec;
...
SQL_CURSOR c;
EXEC SQL ALLOCATE :c;
EXEC SQL EXECUTE
     BEGIN  Emp_Pck.Open_Cur (:c);   END;
END-EXEC;
...
while (1)
{  ...
   EXEC SQL FETCH :c into :emp_rec;
   ...
   break;
}
...
EXEC SQL CLOSE c;
```

```
. . .

Stored Procedure
. . .
Create or Replace Package Emp_Pck IS
    TYPE emp_rec IS RECORD (name     emp.name%type,
                            emp_no emp.emp_no%type);
    TYPE emp_cur IS CURSOR   RETURN emp_rec;
    PROCEDURE Open_Cur ( C1 IN OUT emp_cur);
    . . .
END;

Create or replace Package body Emp_Pck IS
    PROCEDURE Open_Cur ( C1 IN OUT emp_cur);
    BEGIN
      OPEN C1 FOR Select name, emp_no FROM EMP;
    END;
    . . .
END;
```

The important characteristics of PL/SQL cursor variables can be summed up as follows:

Multirow SELECT

Communication between client and server is not limited to single record fetches.

Centrally defined SQL

Large complex SQL is held in the database, hidden from developers. The only information a developer needs to know is the name of the cursor package and the structure of the data it is returning.

Schema flexibility

The database schema can be altered, and only the packaged cursor variables need to be altered. Hundreds of application modules will not need maintaining.

Data security

Each client needs only EXECUTE privilege on the package. The underlying tables and their data can be hidden from the outside world.

Oracle PL/SQL Function Extensions

Over the last few years, Oracle have provided a number of special PL/SQL macros that can perform functions that are not generally available to the ordinary developer. These functions overcome most of the common PL/SQL shortcomings. All members of your application team should investigate these functions before beginning any development. You cannot use a feature if you do not know that it exists.

Every new version of the RDBMS seems to include another utility or function extension. These PL/SQL macros can usually be found in the *$ORACLE_HOME/rdbms/admin* directory. Never assume that you know them all. Keep looking and keep investigating. The following sections cover the most commonly used functions and utilities.

DBMS_OUTPUT: dbmsotpt.sql

This utility provides valuable communication between a PL/SQL block and the outside world. DBMS_OUTPUT is best suited for debugging procedures and packages or for simple reporting. The package needs to be enabled before messages will be retained within the output buffer. Any calls to the put_line and/or get_line procedures without first enabling the package will be lost. The following procedure calls are available:

dbms_output.enable ({buffer_size})	Enables output
dbms_output.put_line ('Error processing step ' I I to_char(:step))	Displays buffer message
dbms_output.get_line (:buffer, :status)	Gets message
dbms_output.disable	Disables output

The DBMS_OUTPUT package is much simpler to use from the SQL*Plus or SQL*DBA tools. Extensions have been made to these tools to support direct PL/SQL I/O to the screen. For example:

```
sql*plus>>    set serveroutput on size 10000
              execute test_plsql_block;
              ...... dbms output .....
```

NOTE   All put_line calls from this block are written directly to the output buffer. All messages are stored in this buffer until the PL/SQL block completes (or fails) and are then directed to the screen. Once the buffer fills, all subsequent messages are lost. The maximum output buffer size is 1,000,000 bytes. (The default is 2000 bytes.)

DBMS_SHARED_POOL: dbmspool.sql

This package allows the DBA to query the size of objects within the shared pool and/or mark those objects to be retained (keep) or released (unkeep) from the shared pool. DBAs should use this macro to pin all large database objects into the shared pool at database startup. The following procedure calls are available:

dbms_shared_pool.sizes (*size*);	Displays all objects currently in the shared pool that are larger than the specified size (in kilobytes)
	Remember to specify *set serveroutput on* before executing this procedure from SQL*Plus
dbms_shared_pool.keep ('scott.GL')	Marks a database object to be kept (or queued to be kept) in the shared pool
dbms_shared_pool.unkeep('scott.GL')	Releases a pinned object from the shared pool

DBMS_TRANSACTION: dbmsutil.sql

This package provides a number of transaction level commands to a PL/SQL block, stored procedure, function or package. The following procedure calls (and SQL equivalents) are available:

dbms_transaction.read_only	sql> set transaction read only
dbms_transaction.read_write	sql> set transaction read write
dbms_transaction.commit	sql> commit
ddbms_transaction.savepoint	sql> savepoint
dbms_transaction.rollback	sql> rollback
dbms_transaction.rollback_savepoint	sql> rollback to savepoint

DBMS_SQL: dbmssql.sql

This package supports dynamic SQL from within a PL/SQL block of a stored object. This one utility opens up an enormous range of possibilities to the DBA or developer. Consider using it at all stages of development. Using dynamic SQL means that large application objects can be substantially reduced in size by combining repetitive SQL code into a single dynamic statement. Numerous similar PL/SQL objects/blocks can be collapsed into a few well-written generic routines. A single stored procedure could perform a host of functions all within the same dynamic cursor. The following procedure calls are available:

dbms_sql.open_cursor	Opens a new cursor
dbms_sql.is_open (*cur*)	Returns TRUE if the *cur* cursor is OPEN
dbms_sql.close_cursor (*cur*)	Closes the cursor
dbms_sql.parse (*cur, stmt, lang*)	Parses *stmt* using the *cur* cursor
dbms_sql.bind_variable (....)	Binds program variables to the cursor

dbms_sql.define_column (....)	Defines a column to be selected
dbms_sql.execute (*cur*)	Executes the *cur* cursor
dbms_sql.fetch_rows (*cur*)	Fetches rows from the *cur* cursor
dbms_sql.execute_fetch (*cur, boolean*)	Executes and fetches from the *cur* cursor
dbms_sql.column_value (....)	Gets a value for the identified column
dbms_sql.variable_value (....)	Gets a value for the identified variable

The following example demonstrates the possibilities of dynamic SQL. Here it is used to purge records from any table (tab_owner.tab_name) with values for a column (col_name) between two dates (date_fm & date_to):

```
# dyn_sql.sql
create or replace package RTS_purge
AS
PROCEDURE purge
  ( tab_owner IN VARCHAR2,
    tab_name  IN VARCHAR2,
    col_date  IN VARCHAR2,
    date_fm   IN DATE,
    date_to   IN DATE       DEFAULT SYSDATE,
    roll_back IN VARCHAR2   DEFAULT NULL
  );
END ;

create or replace package body RTS_purge
AS
  sql_curs        INTEGER;
  sql_text        VARCHAR2 (2000);
  --
  PROCEDURE purge
  (
    tab_owner IN VARCHAR2,
    tab_name  IN VARCHAR2,
    col_date  IN VARCHAR2,
    date_fm   IN DATE,
    date_to   IN DATE       DEFAULT SYSDATE,
    roll_back IN VARCHAR2   DEFAULT NULL
  )
  IS
    rows_deleted integer := 0;
  BEGIN
    IF roll_back IS NOT NULL THEN
        dbms_transaction.use_rollback_segment ( roll_back );
    END IF;
    --
    sql_text := 'delete from ' || tab_owner || '.' ||
                tab_name || ' WHERE ' || col_date ||
                ' BETWEEN :fm_date AND :to_date';
    --
    sql_curs := dbms_sql.open_cursor;
    dbms_sql.parse (sql_curs, sql_text, dbms_sql.v7);
```

```
        dbms_sql.bind_variable (sql_curs, 'fm_date', date_fm);
        dbms_sql.bind_variable (sql_curs, 'to_date', date_to);
        rows_deleted := dbms_sql.execute (sql_curs) + rows_deleted;
        dbms_sql.close_cursor (sql_curs);
        --
        COMMIT;
    EXCEPTION
        WHEN others THEN
            IF dbms_sql.is_open (sql_curs) THEN
                dbms_sql.close_cursor ( sql_curs );
            End IF;
            dbms_output.put_line (sql_text);
            RAISE;
    END purge;
END;

sqlplus>> execute RTS_purge.purge ('scott',
                                   'GL_transactions',
                                   'tran_date',
                                   to_date('01-jan-90'),
                                   to_date('31-dec-92'));

        execute RTS_purge.purge ('scott',
                                 'GL_jrnl_lines',
                                 'jrnl_date',
                                 to_date('01-jan-90'),
                                 to_date('31-dec-92'));
```

DBMS_PIPE: *dbmspipe.sql*

This package allows two database sessions to communicate via a database pipe. This means that a process does not have to write information to the database to talk to another process. Database pipes work on much the same principle as UNIX files system pipes. They provide a very efficient way for two application programs to trigger events or send messages between themselves without incurring the high cost of database updating. The following procedure calls are available:

dbms_pipe.send_message (...)	Sends a message to a named pipe
dbms_pipe.receive_message (...)	Receives a message for a named pipe
dbms_pipe.pack_message (...)	Packs a message item into a named pipe
dbms_pipe.unpack_message (...)	Unpacks a message item from a named pipe
dbms_pipe.purge (...)	Purges a named pipe

DBMS_ALERT: *dbmsalrt.sql*

This package allows a process to block or wait on another process without having to continually poll the database for an event or to update the database to hold and/or release locks. Database alerts are a very efficient way of having a process (indefinitely) wait for an event to occur. The following procedure calls are available:

dbms_alert.register (*alert*)	Registers an *alert* identifier
dbms_alert.signal (*alert, message*)	Signals the *alert* with an associated message
dbms_pipe.remove (*alert*)	Removes an *alert* from the registration list
dbms_pipe.removeall	Removes all alerts from the registration list
dbms_pipe.waitone (*alert*)	Waits for an *alert* to occur
dbms_pipe.waitany	Waits for any *alert* to occur

DBMS_SESSION: dbsmutil.sql

This package provides access to all ALTER SESSION SQL commands from within a PL/SQL block, stored procedure, function, or package. Take special notice of the function that lets you enable or disable SQL tracing. You can now use the trace facility for any stored package, procedure, or function or any third party development tool without having to enable it for the entire database. The following procedure calls (and SQL equivalents) are available:

dbms_session.set_role (*role_command*)	sql> set role all sql> set role none sql> set role XXX identified by YYY
dbms_session.set_sql_trace (*boolean*)	sql> alter session set sql_trace true sql> alter session set sql_trace false
dbms_session.set_close_database_link (*db_link*)	sql> alter session close database link *db_link*

DBMS_DDL: dbmsutil.sql

This package provides access to some of the SQL DDL commands from within stored procedure, functions, and packages. The following procedure calls are available:

dbms_ddl.alter_compile (*type, schema, object*)	sql> ALTER *type schema.object* COMPILE
dbms_ddl.analyze_object (*type, schema, object, method {, est_rows} {, est_perc}*)	sql> ANALYZE *type schema.object method* STATISTICS {SAMPLE *est_rows* ROWS} sql> ANALYZE *type schema.object method* STATISTICS {SAMPLE *est_perc* PERCENT}

DBMS_UTILITY: *dbmsutil.sql*

This macro extends the functionality of the DBMS_DDL packages by allowing the DBA to compile or analyze an entire database schema. The macro actually makes calls to the DBMS_DDL package procedures. It also provides some important added functions.

dbms_utility.compile_schema (*schema*)	Compiles all objects of a particular *schema*
dbms_utility.analyze_schema (*schema, method*)	Analyzes all objects of a particular *schema* using the specified *method*
dbms_utility.is_parallel_server	Indicates whether the database is currently running in parallel server mode
dbms_utility.get_time	Returns the system clock time in 100ths of seconds
dbms_utility.name_resolve (...)	Resolves the physical schema object identified by an input name; this resolution includes synonym translation and authorization validation

DBMS_JOB: *dbms_job.sql, catjobq.sql*

This package is a major milestone in the lifecycle of the Oracle RDBMS. DBMS_JOB allows us to schedule processes from inside the database rather than via the operating system. Those of us who lean toward UNIX say, "What's wrong with *cron*?; it has performed a good job so far." This is a valid question with an equally valid answer. Submitting jobs (calling a stored procedure and package) allows us to skip the whole login/password problem. No longer do we need to hard-code passwords or grant "superuser" privileges to an OPS$ account. No password is required. Even better, if the database is down at the point of invocation, there is no problem; the job is executed as soon as it is back up.

Creating database jobs provides a neat catalog for the DBA of all scheduled batch processing. He no longer needs to search through all user *cron* accounts. Jobs can be invoked once and then can disappear or be executed in a repetitive fashion (e.g., every 2 hours, every 7 days). Database jobs can even modify their own characteristics from within the called routine. The stored procedure/package could decide that waking up every 10 minutes is too demanding during peak usage periods and drop itself back to every 30 minutes.

Database jobs are executed with the same privileges as the user account that scheduled them. The user environment is recreated with the same default roles and profiles. When a job is started, a new session is invoked, so ALTER SESSION commands can be executed and trace files can be generated.

The *catjobq.sql* script provides two extra database views that allow us to interrogate the database job queue. These views are as follows:

dba_jobs_running	All jobs that are currently executing
dba_jobs	All jobs currently recorded in the database

A number of INIT.ORA parameters need to be set up to use database jobs:

JOB_QUEUE_PROCESSES=n	Maximum number of concurrent background processes permitted (0-9)
JOB_QUEUE_INTERVAL=n	Interval in seconds to check the job queue (1 to 3600 [1 hour])
JOB_QUEUE_KEEP_ CONNECTONS=*boolean*	Whether or not a background process remains after the job ends

The following procedure calls are available:

dbms_job.submit (...)	Submit a new job into the job queue
dbms_job.isubmit (...)	Submits a new job with a unique job number
dbms_job.remove (...)	Removes a job from the job queue
dbms_job.change (...)	Changes the details of a scheduled job
dbms_job.broken (...)	Disables a job from executing
dbms_job.run (...)	Performs ad hoc job execution (even when broken)
dbms_job.user_export (...)	Exports job definition text

DBMS_APPLICATION_INFO: dbmsutl.sql

This package allows us to register the name of a transaction before executing it. The transaction name can later be used to identify resource-hungry application activities.

The following procedure calls are available:

dbms_application_info.set_module (...)	Sets current module name
dbms_application_info.set_action (...)	Sets current module action
dbms_application_info.set_client_info (...)	Sets client information field
dbms_application_info.read_module (...)	Reads module and action data
dbms_application_info.read_client_info (...)	Reads client information field

For example:

```
PROCEDURE Calc_Tax (...)
AS
BEGIN
    dbms_appliaction_info.set_module ('Calc_Tax',Look Up Salary');
    ...
    ...
    dbms_application_info.set_action ('Checking Dependants');
    ...
    ...
    dbms_application_info.set_action ('Checking Deductions');
    ...
    ...
    dbms_appliaction_info.set_module ('','');
END;
```

Module and action names may be queried via the V$SQLAREA view or by calling the READ_MODULE function. Client information can be queried via the V$SESSION view or calling the READ_CLIENT_INFO function. For example:

```
SELECT sql_text, executions, disk_reads, module, action
FROM   v$sqlarea
WHERE  module like 'GL%'
```

NOTE   This package is available with Oracle7.2 and later versions.

8

Selecting a Locking Strategy

How well your application performs often depends directly on the data locking strategies you adopt. Yet, unlike many performance decisions, locking decisions are often overlooked by designers and unappreciated by application users. If you plan carefully what row and table locking strategies your application will use, your smart thinking will tend to go unnoticed. Your application will simply chug along, performing efficiently and keeping users happy. If you make the wrong choices, however, your application may be completely crippled.

Time and time again, we've found that poor performance is linked directly to poor selection of locking strategies. We've also found that application designers and developers tend to overlook locking as a critical issue. When application modules are being developed—and even into the acceptance phases of a project—testing is too often limited to looking at modules and programs as single, independent units, not as small pieces of the larger application jigsaw. Unfortunately, locking problems often remain hidden until full and rigorous system testing puts all the pieces together by simultaneously executing all of the programs that make up an application. Until they are revealed, locking problems will linger in your application as potential time bombs that threaten to cripple your application's performance when that performance is most critical.

What Is Locking?

Oracle is a large, multiuser system. Many users are issuing many transactions—perhaps concurrently. What if two or more users are trying to update the same table or row simultaneously? Oracle's locking facilities keep concurrent users and transactions from clashing. If updating isn't controlled in some way, you might find your data changed out from under you; even as you are updating a value in the database, another user might be changing that value too. The integrity of the data is at risk.

The basic idea of locking is a simple one: when one transaction is issued, it acquires a lock on the data it needs to modify. Locking has two purposes. The first purpose of locking is to keep data from being modified by multiple users. Until the lock is released, no other transaction can modify those data. This is known as *data concurrency*. The second purpose of locking is to ensure that all processes can always access (read) the original data as they were at the time the query began (uncommitted modifications). This is known as *read consistency*. But, the reality of locking can be more complex. Because performance will obviously suffer if locks are maintained for too long, it's in the interest of overall system performance to lock the smallest amount of data for the shortest amount of time.

The Oracle RDBMS supports a number of lock types, each necessary for a particular type of job. These lock types include the following:

- *DDL locks:* Used to protect object definitions.

- *DML locks:* Used to protect data concurrency.

- *Internal locks:* Used to protect shared data structures.

- *Internal latches:* Used to protect data dictionary entries, data files, tablespaces and rollback segments.

- *Distributed locks:* Used to protect data concurrency in a distributed and/or parallel server environment.

- *PCM locks:* Parallel cache management locks used to protect the buffer cache in a parallel server environment.

Although locks are vital to enforcing database consistency and performance, they can create performance problems. Every time one process issues a lock, another user may be shut out from processing the locked row or table. Oracle allows you to lock whatever resources you need—a single row, many rows, an entire table, even many tables. But, the larger the scope of the lock, the more processes you potentially shut out.

Oracle provides two different levels of locking:

Row-level locking

When one transaction updates a table, only the table row that is actually being updated is locked to other transactions. Other transactions can continue to update other rows in the table but can't access the particular row that is locked by the first transaction until the row lock is released. To use row-level locking, your system must have installed the Transaction Processing Option (TPO).

Table-level locking

When one transaction updates a table, the entire table is locked to other transactions. Other transactions can't update any of the table's rows until the table lock is released.

With either level of locking, although one transaction may have an update lock on a particular table or row, other transactions can still read that table or row. They just can't update it.

As you would expect, your application realizes substantial performance gains with row-level, as opposed to table-level, locking because a row lock ties up only one row of a table. Row-level locking is especially effective for large, online transaction processing (OLTP) applications because it allows many users to simultaneously update, insert, and delete different rows in the same table. By contrast, with table-level locking, the entire table is locked (although briefly) during the time that an actual update takes place.

Releases of Oracle prior to Version 6 supported only table-level locking. Current releases allow the selection of either strategy (TPO or non-TPO). Although row-level locking tends to provide far better performance, there are certain situations in which you'll want to select table-level locking or will want to issue explicit table locks for certain transactions. These special situations are described in this chapter.

Row-Level Locking

With a row-level locking strategy, each row within a table can be locked individually. Locked rows can be updated only by the locking process. All other rows in the table are still available for updating by other processes. Of course, other processes continue to be able to read any row in the table, including the one that is actually being updated. When other processes do read updated rows, they see only the old version of the row prior to update (via a rollback segment) until the changes are actually committed. This is known as a *consistent read*.

When a process places a row level lock on a record, what really happens? First, a data manipulation language (DML) lock is placed over the row. This lock prevents other processes from updating (or locking) the row. This lock is released only when the locking process successfully commits the transaction to the database (i.e., makes the updates to that transaction permanent) or when the process is rolled back. Next, a data dictionary language (DDL) lock is placed over the table to prevent structural alterations to the table. For example, this type of lock keeps the DBA from being able to remove a table by issuing a DROP statement against the table. This lock is released only when the locking process successfully commits the transaction to the database or when the process is rolled back.

Table-Level Locking

With table-level locking, the entire table is locked as an entity. Once a process has locked a table, only that process can update (or lock) any row in the table. None of the rows in the table are available for updating by any other process. Of course, other processes continue to be able to read any row in the table, including the one that is actually being updated.

If you have not installed the TPO in your system, table-level locking is the default. If TPO is installed (and row-level locking is the default), you can globally select table-level locking by default by setting the INIT.ORA parameter, ROW_ LOCKING, to INTENT. This setting overrides the default of ROW_LOCKING = ALWAYS.

How does table-level locking work? The first DML operation that needs to update a row in a table obtains what's called a Row Share Exclusive lock over the entire table. All other query-only processes needing access to the table are informed that they must use the rollback information for the locking process. The lock is released only when the locking process successfully commits the transaction to the database or when the process is rolled back.

Releasing Locks

Many users believe that they are the only users on the system—at least the only ones who count. Unfortunately, this type of attitude is what causes locking problems. We've often observed applications that were completely stalled because one user decided to go to lunch without having committed his or her changes. Remember that all locking (row or table) will prevent other users from updating information. Every application has a handful of central, core tables. Inadvertently locking such tables can affect many other people in a system.

Many users, and some programmers, don't understand that terminating a process does not always release locks. Switching off your workstation before you go home does not always release locks. Locks are released only when changes are committed or rolled back. A user's action is the only thing that distinguishes between committing, aborting, and rolling back changes. Make it a priority to train your users to commit or roll back all outstanding changes before leaving their current screens.

A number of alternatives are available to help reduce the length of time a process may inadvertently hold a database resource lock. It is the DBA's responsibility to do everything within his or her power to ensure the smooth running of the database(s), and this includes the management of resource locking. The following sections describe two lock management alternatives.

SQL*Net Dead Connection Identification

A common problem within a client-server environment (especially for UNIX) is dead database connections inadvertently retaining resource locks after the client process has terminated (died). Client process termination is usually caused by a network failure or by a user's turning off his or her PC without cleanly logging off. (Won't they ever learn?)

SQL*Net 2.1 has introduced a new configuration option that instructs the database to periodically *poll* the client connection, making sure the process is still active. If the remote client connection does not respond, the database session is terminated, all changes are rolled back, and resource locks are released. You set this option as follows:

```
Sqlnet.ora Configuration file:
    . . .
    sqlnet.expire_time = 10
    . . .
```

WARNING   The polling period is in whole minutes and should not be set too low. This value designates how often every client (SQL*Net) connection is polled. If you have several thousand PC clients and have set an expire_time of 1 minute, the network traffic involved in verifying an active connection will keep anything else from ever getting done.

Resource Profiles

Another valuable option that can help the DBA to reduce the number and duration of database locks is to activate resource profiles (process governors). This facility allows us to configure a number of options to pick and choose which users can consume what resources. Setting maximum values for these profile parameters allows us to influence how many resources a particular session can lock and/or how long they can retain these resources.

A maximum value can be assigned to a single machine/database resource or a group of these resources, governing when a process will be automatically terminated by the database. An individual user can have a particular profile or can adopt a system-wide default profile. Profiles can be enforced at either the session level or the individual statement level.

Session-level profiles
> These limit the resources per connection (session). Once a limit has been reached, the Oracle connection is automatically aborted; all uncommitted changes are rolled back, and resource locks are released.

SQL statement profiles
> These limit the total resources available to an individual database access. If this limit is exceeded, the offending statement is aborted; all uncommitted changes are rolled back, and resource locks are released.

Profiles provide us with low-level resource control and a viable way of managing excessive locking periods. Table 8-1 shows the available resource profiles.

Table 8-1. Resource Profiles

Resource	Description
SESSIONS_PER_USER	Total concurrent sessions per username
CPU_PER_SESSION	Maximum CPU per session
CPU_PER_CALL	Maximum CPU per call
CONNECT_TIME	Maximum continuous connect time per session
IDLE_TIME	Maximum allowable idle time before user is disconnected
LOGICAL_READS_PER_SESSION	Maximum database blocks read per session
LOGICAL_READS_PER_CALL	Maximum database blocks read per database call
PRIVATE_SGA	Maximum number of bytes of private space within SGA
COMPOSITE_LIMIT	Maximum weighted sum of: CPU_PER_ SESSION, CONNECT_TIME, LOGICAL_READS_ PER_SESSION, and PRIVATE_SGA

Avoiding the Dreaded Deadlock

Locking—in particular, row-level locking—is an excellent way to preserve database consistency while improving performance. But locking itself can occasionally cause performance problems by creating *deadlocks*.

What is a deadlock? In rare cases, each of two (or more) processes holds resources that the other process requires. For example, suppose process A needs to update the EMP table and then the DEPT table. It acquires a lock on the EMP table and maintains that lock until the next resource it needs to lock, the DEPT table, is free. Concurrently, process B needs to update the DEPT table and then the EMP table. It acquires a lock on the DEPT table and maintains that lock until the EMP table is free. Because neither process can lock the other resource that it needs, neither will release the lock it holds. The processes could wait forever for the necessary resources to become available. This situation, illustrated in Figure 8-1, is known as a deadlock.

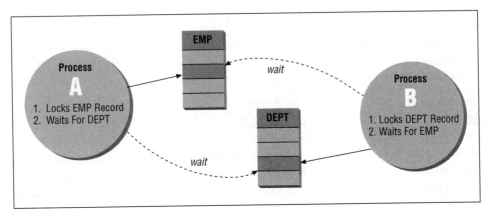

Figure 8-1. Deadlock situation

Oracle doesn't let deadlocks stop your applications dead in their tracks. It has its own strategy for dealing with the deadlocks it encounters. It picks one of the contending processes and rolls back the updating that it has already performed for that process's locked resources. How does Oracle decide which process to roll back? It automatically aborts the process requiring the least amount of rollback activity and informs that process about the failure. The aborted process can simply retry the action again.

Handling Deadlocks Explicitly

When you use certain third-generation language interfaces (Pro*C, Pro*COBOL, etc.), you need to be aware that these products do not automatically handle deadlock detection. They leave the handling of deadlocks and other types of database errors up to the programmer. If you use these tools, your programs will have to include logic that explicitly detects errors of various kinds.

With some very serious errors, you'll have to abort program execution. Deadlocks, although a nuisance, are not intrinsically serious problems. When your program detects such an error, it should respond by explicitly rolling back changes to the database and beginning the update routine again.

Establishing a Locking Sequence

Even when you use standard Oracle tools, which provide automatic deadlock detection, you should do all you can to minimize the chances of deadlocks occurring. The best way to prevent deadlocks is to establish a strict locking sequence for tables. It is the job of the DBA to specify, during the initial system design, the physical locking sequence and to document and distribute information about this sequence. It is the job of the application developer to make sure that the program code carries out the locking policy. Both DBA and developer must share in policing these policies within the organization to make sure they adhere to table-locking rules.

To specify a locking sequence, you assign a table ranking to each table. Program statements must lock tables strictly in this order. When a process locks a resource, it can do so only by ascending or descending table ranking order.

Although alphabetic ordering is simple and usually effective (e.g., DEPT before EMP), alphabetic locking is not always suitable for more complex applications in which many tables are updated in a single transaction state. In general, when you devise table locking rankings, make sure that each table has a higher ranking than any table referenced via a foreign key connection. The following example illustrates only one of many ranking possibilities. The most important thing you can do here is to enforce carefully whatever schema has been adopted for your own application. For example:

```
    TABLE EMPLOYEE                    Ranking 1
        . . .
        . . .
        . . .
    DEPARTMENT                        Ranking 4
        . . .
        . . .
        . . .
    CATEGORY                          Ranking 12
    CLASS                             Ranking 13
    DEPT_TYPE                         Ranking 14
```

Locking Considerations for Oracle Features

Several of Oracle's newer features have the potential to cause locking problems that are unlikely but worth knowing about. For complete information about the features, consult your standard Oracle documentation.

Process Priorities

The Oracle environment is a very complicated one. Many processes work in tandem, all simultaneously accessing the shared memory resources in the SGA. Oracle has always preached the importance of all database processes, both user and kernel, having the same machine priority (the default operating system priority). We are amazed at the number of sites that blatantly ignore this warning and proceed to juggle user priorities on the basis of the user's stature and/or application activities. (Incidentally, we have never found a site that can actually prove or quantify any productivity gain from priority juggling, but several have experienced degradation.)

Unfortunately, assigning different priorities to the Oracle processes can magnify the effects of data and latch contention. A higher priority task may require a memory resource that is currently held by a lower priority task. In such a case, the higher task cannot get the resource, and the lower task cannot get the CPU time to finish its transaction and release the resource.

Referential Integrity

With the introduction of automated referential integrity (RI) came a whole new suite of locking problems. What seems at first to be a DBA's blessing can turn out to be an absolute nightmare when the DBA doesn't fully understand the implications of this feature. Why is this so?

RI constraints are validated by the database via a simple SELECT from the dependent (parent) table in question—very simple, very straightforward. If a row is deleted or a primary key is modified within the parent table, all associated child tables need to be scanned to make sure no orphaned records will result. If a row is inserted or the foreign key is modified, the parent table is scanned to ensure that the new foreign key value(s) is valid. If a DELETE CASCADE clause is included, all associated child table records are deleted. Problems begin to arise when we look at how the referential integrity is enforced.

Oracle assumes the existence of an index over every foreign key within a table. This assumption is valid for a primary key constraint or even a unique key constraint but a little presumptuous for every foreign key. Most applications that we have been involved with have a small number of core tables. These core tables can have 100 or more columns, of which 10 or 20 columns will be foreign keys. For example, the EMP table could have many foreign keys: emp_category, emp_type, salary_range, post_code, dependency_code, mgr_emp_no, dept_code—and the list goes on. It would not be practical to have 20 or more indexes over each of these core tables. If no index exists over these foreign keys, what happens? You might assume that if a row were deleted from the department table, the worst that could happen would be a full table scan on the EMP table, validating that the department in question was in fact unused. Unfortunately, it is not this simple. (Never assume anything!)

If an index exists on the foreign key column of the child table, no DML locks, other than a lock over the rows being modified, are required. If the index is not created, a share lock is taken out on the child table for the duration of the transaction. The referential integrity validation could take several minutes or even hours to resolve. The share lock over the child table will allow other users to simultaneously read from the table, while restricting certain types of modification. The share lock over the table can actually block other normal, everyday modification of other rows in that table.

Oracle versions prior to 7.1.6 are more restrictive and uncompromising when it comes to enforcing RI constraints when indexes were missing. Many of these locking clashes have been overcome with the introduction of Oracle7.1.6. Table 8-2 demonstrates a number of DML locking variants on the EMP and DEPT tables and their resulting locking restrictions applied.

```
TABLE DEPT                          (parent table)
( Dept_No    NUMBER(5)    PRIMARY KEY,
  . . . )

TABLE EMP                           (child table)
( Emp_No     NUMBER(6)    PRIMARY KEY,
  Emp_Name   VARCHAR2(30),
  Dept_No    NUMBER(4)    REFERENCES dept(dept_no),
  . . . )
```

The EMP table has a referential integrity association with DEPT, but no index over the EMP.dept_no foreign key.

Table 8-2. Referential Integrity Locking

Locking DML Statement	DML Request	V7.1.4 (and prior)	V7.1.6 (and after)	DML Request	V7.1.4 (and prior)	V7.1.6 (and after)
INSERT dept	INSERT dept	OK	OK	INSERT emp	WAIT	OK
	UPDATE dept	OK	OK	UPDATE emp	OK	OK
	DELETE dept	OK	OK	DELETE emp	WAIT	OK
				UPDATE emp.dept_no	WAIT	OK
UPDATE dept	INSERT dept	OK	OK	INSERT emp	WAIT	OK
	UPDATE dept	OK	OK	UPDATE emp	OK	OK
	DELETE dept	OK	OK	DELETE emp	WAIT	OK
				UPDATE emp.dept_no	WAIT	OK
DELETE dept	INSERT dept	OK	OK	INSERT emp	WAIT	WAIT
	UPDATE dept	OK	OK	INSERT emp	WAIT	WAIT
	DELETE dept	OK	OK	DELETe emp	WAIT	WAIT

Table 8-2. Referential Integrity Locking (continued)

Locking DML Statement	DML Request	V7.1.4 (and prior)	V7.1.6 (and after)	DML Request	V7.1.4 (and prior)	V7.1.6 (and after)
				UPDATE emp.dept_no	WAIT	WAIT
UPDATE dept.dept_no	INSERT dept	OK	OK	INSERT emp	WAIT	WAIT
	UPDATE dept	OK	OK	UPDATE emp	WAIT	WAIT
	DELETE dept	OK	OK	DELETE emp	WAIT	WAIT
				UPDATE emp.dept_no	WAIT	WAIT
INSERT emp	INSERT dept	WAIT	OK	INSERT emp	WAIT	OK
	UPDATE dept	WAIT	OK	UPDATE emp	OK	OK
	DELETE dept	WAIT	WAIT	DELETE emp	OK	OK
				UPDATE emp.dept_no	OK	OK
UPDATE emp	INSERT dept	OK	OK	INSERT emp	OK	OK
	UPDATE dept	OK	OK	UPDATE emp	OK	OK
	DELETE dept	WAIT	WAIT	DELETE emp	OK	OK
				UPDATE emp.dept_no	OK	OK
DELETe emp	INSERT dept	WAIT	OK	INSERT emp	OK	OK
	UPDATE dept	WAIT	OK	UPDATE emp	OK	OK
	DELETE dept	WAIT	WAIT	DELETE emp	OK	OK
				UPDATE emp.dept_no	OK	OK
UPDATE emp.dept_no	INSERT dept	WAIT	OK	INSERT emp	OK	OK
	UPDATE dept	WAIT	OK	UPDATE emp	OK	OK
	DELETE dept	WAIT	WAIT	DELETE emp	OK	OK
				UPDATE emp.dept_no	OK	OK

Referential integrity has been responsible for bringing many good applications to their knees. Well-meaning DBAs try to make their jobs easier by implementing every conceivable RI constraint possible. They assume that this will guarantee the integrity of the data. However, creating every conceivable foreign key index is obviously out of the question. What are the alternatives?

The only viable workarounds to this locking behavior are the following:

- Enable referential integrity and create all associated indexes for the *core* RI constraints of the application.

- Replace embedded RI constraints with row-level stored triggers for those important RI constraints that are not practical to index.

- Omit all referential integrity for the less important RI application constraints, leaving the validation up to the application code itself.

Parallel Server Locking

Any DBA who supports a parallel-server environment must have a clear understanding of how it operates and how it performs its lock management. Parallel server locking differs from any normal locking in that it must support Parallel Cache Management (PCM) locks. These locks are managed by the distributed lock manager and are necessary to maintain data block consistency between various instance SGAs. The distributed lock manager is a specialized software module that is provided by your hardware vendor. These PCM locks work in addition to the standard row-level locking, each lock controlling one or more database block.

For a complete description of parallel server technology and its special locking requirements, see Chapter 12, *Tuning Parallel Server*.

Stored Database Triggers

Stored triggers are fired at table or row level (for both pre and post INSERT, UPDATE, and DELETE). If a table has 100 rows updated by a user, 100 more row-level triggers may be executed, and neither the user nor the programmer will be aware of it. Each of these hidden actions could update other tables and fire other stored triggers. What was supposed to be a simple database update may end up propagated to vast, multitable transactions, possibly spanning multiple databases. This behavior in itself is fairly harmless but becomes a concern when you are trying to enforce a locking sequence strategy. Because we do not have any control over the firing sequence of multiple database triggers, we have little or no control over when resources will be locked and the sequence in which they will be locked.

Mutating Database Triggers

A very annoying side effect of database triggers is the way that Oracle handles a mutating trigger. A *mutating trigger* is identified as one that attempts to read or modify the same table that initiated the trigger in the first place. At first glance, trigger mutating does not seem to be much of an issue. It is not until you begin programming some more complex business rules and/or associations that mutation becomes a problem.

The most disappointing feature of trigger mutation is the fact that it can be caused by a simple referential integrity constraint. For example, suppose that we have a normal RI constraint between a parent and child table combination. A row-level trigger exists on the parent table to insert an audit record for every change to the master table. The child table also has a standard RI association back to the parent table. This RI check will automatically reference the parent table and, in doing so, cause a mutating trigger. What can you do?

Consider this example:

```
TABLE emp
( emp_no      NUMBER(6)       PRIMARY KEY,
  emp_name    VARCHAR2(30),
  . . . )

TRIGGER emp_trg
After Insert On empFor Each Row
BEGIN
  INSERT INTO emp_history
  VALUES(:OLD.emp_no, SYSDATE, :OLD.emp_name, .... );
END;

TABLE emp_history
( emp_no      NUMBER(6)       REFERENCES emp(emp_no),
  eff_date    date,
  . . .
  PRIMARY KEY (emp_no, eff_date) )

INSERT INTO emp
VALUES (12345, 'Bill Smith', . . . );
ERROR at Line 1
ORA-04091: table SCOTT.EMP is mutating, trigger/function may not see it
ORA-06512: al line 2
ORA-04088: error during execution of trigger 'SCOTT.EMP_TRG'
```

The only way of circumnavigating a mutating trigger while still achieving the desired results is to remove the referential integrity check from the child table and enforce the integrity via a synthetic trigger level constraint. This method is more involved to program and maintain, less efficient, and a nuisance!

Interestingly enough, Oracle's own referential integrity does not raise a mutating error. If we define a table with a RI reference back to itself, the "cyclic" reference is allowed. Even though Oracle triggers its RI constraints in the same fashion as application triggers, they do not come under the same restrictions. For example:

```
CREATE TABLE emp
( emp_no      NUMBER(6) PRIMARY KEY,
  emp_name    VARCHAR2(30),
  mgr_emp_no NUMBER(6)    REFERENCES emp(emp_no)
);
```

```
INSERT INTO emp
VALUES(123456, 'Bill Smith', 42365);
1 row inserted
```

DELETE CASCADE

Oracle7 allows us to enhance a referential integrity definition to included cascading deletion. If a row is deleted from a parent table, all of the associated children will be automatically purged. This behavior obviously will affect an application's locking strategy, again circumnavigating normal object locking, removing control from the programmer. For example:

```
TABLE emp_history
( emp_no      number(6)      REFERENCES emp(emp_no) ON DELETE CASCADE,
  eff_date    date,
  . . .
  PRIMARY KEY (emp_no, eff_date)
)
```

What is so dangerous about a cascading delete? A deleted child table might, in turn, have its own child tables. Even worse, the child tables could have table-level triggers that begin to fire. What starts out as a simple, single-record delete from a harmless table could turn into an uncontrollable torrent of cascading deletes and stored database triggers, as shown in Figure 8-2.

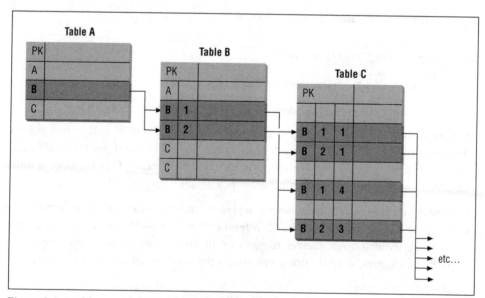

Figure 8-2. Problems with DELETE CASCADE

TRUNCATE Table

The TRUNCATE command is the quickest and most efficient way of purging all rows from a table or cluster. Resource overhead and associated locking requirements are independent of the size of the table; tables containing one million rows can be truncated just as quickly as tables with ten rows. The locking advantage of the TRUNCATE command is the fact that it does not need to write any rollback information. A TRUNCATE command is immediate; either it will work or it won't. Locks are not required to be held for any period of time.

Two words of warning in truncating a table: First, remember that there is no turning back; no rollback or detailed redo information is generated. Second, remember is that no table triggers will be executed when truncating a table.

Rollback Segment Selection

It is always advisable to encourage the application designer(s) to plan for at least one larger rollback segment in their specifications. This larger rollback segment is reserved for abnormal transactions that require a large amount of rollback segment space. This helps to prevent transaction failure (and rollback) for the longer running tasks, while helping to avoid the error SNAPSHOT TOO OLD. For example:

```
SET TRANSACTION USE ROLLBACK SEGMENT rbs_large;
```

Correct selection of a rollback segment helps in the overall locking strategy of an application. Transactions have more of a chance of succeeding in a quicker time frame, holding resources for a shorter period. Other tasks requiring a consistent view of older data also have a much better chance of succeeding, with the rollback information more likely to be retained for a longer period of time.

Distributed Databases

Version 6 supports distributed database queries, while Oracle7 supports full distributed updating. The two-phase commit process provides automatic, transparent updates that guarantee that all databases are updated via a single distributed transaction and either commit or rollback as a single unit. In effect, *global referential integrity* is always maintained.

Distributed update transactions are more susceptible to failure than are single database transactions. Coupled with this extra exposure to network and database failure is the problem of distributed locking failure. If a distributed update does fail and at least one node has already been updated, those nodes continue to hold resources via an IN-DOUBT distributed transaction lock. These locks will remain in place until one of the following occurs:

- The offending network problem is rectified and transaction recovery completes (or rolls back).

- The offending database is corrected and transaction recovery completes (or rolls back).

- The DBA forces a commit or rollback of all IN-DOUBT database locks.

There is another locking problem that you should consider if you are updating a record in another database on the other side of the world: You have had no input into the database design and have no way of preempting any resulting actions. The remote database could trigger a stored trigger, for example, which could then perform a remote update back at the originating database.

Overriding the Default Locking Strategy

By default, Oracle locks a table or row only when it needs to. Oracle executes the lock only when a DML statement of some kind (UPDATE, INSERT, DELETE) actually executes an update, not when a query is issued against that table or row.

Because Oracle does not lock the table or row any sooner than it actually needs to, this default locking strategy usually provides the best performance. For example, suppose that a user selects 100 rows from the database but updates only one. It would be inefficient to lock the entire set of rows.

Sometimes, though, relying on Oracle's default locking strategy does not result in the best performance. Oracle provides statements that allow you to override the default strategy and lock a table or row explicitly. You'll want to use these statements if it is important to your application to lock a table or row before you update the database.

When default locking is in effect, the lock occurs when the database update or deletion is actually performed, not when the query is issued. You'll have to consider your own system needs carefully before selecting an appropriate strategy—row locking, table locking, or the hybrid pseudo-code form that we discuss at the end of this section.

SELECT...FOR UPDATE: Locking a Row Explicitly

The SELECT statement, through the FOR UPDATE OF clause, allows you to explicitly lock a row, or more likely a set of rows, before you perform an update to these rows. This statement is useful if you need to process a number of rows as a single unit. Consider the case in which Oracle has, by default, locked only one of the rows in your unit, and you've successfully updated it, but another process has acquired a lock on the next row in your unit, changing the data in it before you've been able to lock and update it. Having another process change data out from under you in this way may result in an inconsistency in the data or even a corrupted database.

Using the FOR UPDATE OF clause in the SELECT statement that selects your desired group of rows issues a preemptive lock. It prevents other processes from locking a row that you will need access to in order to complete your work.

Here's an example of explicitly locking a row in the emp table:

```
SELECT . . .
FROM    emp
FOR     UPDATE OF emp_no;
```

Remember that even if you have locked several rows of a table, other processes will still be able to lock and update the rows that you have not locked.

Here is an example of using SQL*Forms to lock specific "detail" rows of a table, when the "master" row is locked:

```
TRIGGER ON-LOCK

SELECT 'X'
FROM    emp
WHERE   emp_no = 1234
FOR     UPDATE OF emp_no;

SELECT 'X'
FROM    emp_history
WHERE   emp_no = 1234
FOR     UPDATE OF emp_no;
```

SQL*Forms allows you to override default locking. If you choose to do this, you disable all normal locking routines, and your code is completely responsible for all locking. You must be aware of all of the operations that would otherwise be handled by default. For example, if you are simply locking a second associated table in your code, you must also manually perform the original table lock that would otherwise have been handled by default.

LOCK TABLE: *Locking a Table Explicitly*

Row locking is not always the most efficient approach to updating a table. If you are updating a large number of rows in a table, you might end up locking, in sequence, each of many thousands of rows. In a case like this, you'll find that an exclusive table lock is more efficient than successive row locks.

The LOCK TABLE statement allows you to lock a table before performing an update on it. This statement prevents other processes from exclusively locking the entire table. You might need to use the LOCK TABLE statement if many rows in a table need to be updated together as a single unit or if several tables must be treated as a unit. If you have tables with referential connections, such as master/detail relationships, you might want to lock the associated rows of the detail table explicitly when their master record is reserved for deletion.

There are two types of table locks: exclusive and shared. Here is an example of explicitly locking a table with an exclusive lock:

```
LOCK TABLE emp  IN EXCLUSIVE MODE NOWAIT;
```

What does this statement do?

1. It exclusively locks the table. This means that other processes cannot update any part of the table, even rows that your program will not be updating.

2. It takes out a DDL lock, preventing the DBA from dropping or modifying the table structure.

3. NOWAIT means that if exclusive mode cannot be acquired (usually because some other process is currently accessing the table), the program reports an error. It does not wait for the offending locks or processes to complete. If a lengthy table is undergoing updating, the wait could take hours!

Here is an example of explicitly locking a table with a shared lock:

```
LOCK TABLE emp, emp_history IN ROW SHARE MODE NOWAIT;
```

What does this statement do?

1. It locks the table in shared mode. This allows other processes to update the rows of the table that are not affected by this process, and it prevents other processes from locking the table exclusively.

2. It takes out a DDL lock, preventing the DBA from dropping or modifying the table structure.

3. When the process actually updates a row in the locked table, that row has a DML lock placed over it.

4. NOWAIT has the same effect as in the previous example.

Here is an example of locking a table when you're using PL/SQL:

```
LOCK TABLE emp, emp_history IN SHARE MODE NOWAIT;
    . . .
    . . .
    . . .
DELETE FROM emp
WHERE  emp_no = 1234;
```

```
   .  .  .
   .  .  .
   .  .  .
DELETE FROM emp_history
WHERE   emp_no = 1234;
   .  .  .
   .  .  .
   .  .  .
COMMIT;
```

Using Pseudo-Code to Lock a Large Table

There are some situations in which neither locking an entire table nor locking all of the affected rows in that table, seems to be a good choice. Suppose that a large table (e.g., one with more than 1,000 rows) is being updated during online access. The obvious way to handle such an update would be to put an exclusive lock on the entire table. Even if row locking is the default for your system, you can explicitly lock the table using the LOCK TABLE statement described in the previous section. The problem with this approach is that it stops other processes from accessing the table, potentially for a very long time. For large tables, this is a major problem. Updating a table containing 50,000 rows might take many hours.

Now suppose you lock individual rows of the table instead. Although we generally advise you to lock rows, not whole tables, row locking for a large table may also be problematic. When you use a SELECT statement, you'll need to explicitly mark 50,000 distinct rows for locking (50,000 row latches) before starting the update.

What you need is a way to allow several thousand row updates while allowing other users to continue to have online access to the table. One solution that we've used successfully is to write pseudo-code that batches database locking and updating.

In the program example shown below, the SELECT statement for cursor C1 (the driving statement) selects all records for department 20. This cursor assembles all of the rows that meet the first selection criterion (EMP_DEPT = 0020) before the first row is fetched. It does this to enforce consistency in the read. No matter how many rows are selected, the data in the rows represent a consistent snapshot of the table as it was when the first row was selected.

Note, however, that although we have selected all of the rows, we have not locked them. (To do so with a very large table, in which we might be selecting 100,000 records, for example, would cause serious performance problems for the whole system.) Therefore it is possible that the actual data in one of the selected rows might have been modified by another process after cursor C1 selected it, but before cursor C2 locked it.

To get around this problem, we simply reapply the original condition:

```
SELECT . . .
WHERE  emp_dept = 0020;
```

as well as specifying the unique WHERE clause:

```
SELECT . . .
WHERE emp_no = :xemp_no;
```

when we lock and fetch the row.

Here is the full example:

```
# pl_lock.sql
DECLARE
    CURSOR C1 IS
      SELECT  emp_no
      FROM emp
      WHERE emp_dept = 0020;
    CURSOR C2 IS
      SELECT ROWID
      FROM emp
      WHERE emp_no    = :xemp_no
      AND emp_date = 0020
      FOR UPDATE;
  BEGIN
    kounter = 0;
    OPEN C1;
    LOOP
      FETCH C1 INTO :semp_no;
      OPEN C2;
      FETCH C2 INTO :XROWID;
      IF C2%FOUND THEN
         UPDATE empP
         SET     . . . =  . . .
         WHERE  ROWID = :XROWID;
         kounter = KOUNTER + 1;
         IF kounter = 200 THEN
            COMMIT;
            kounter = 0;
         END IF;
       END IF;
     END LOOP;
   CLOSE C1;
   CLOSE C2;
  END;
```

A major advantage of this approach is that it dramatically reduces the overhead that would be incurred by single-row processing. By incrementing counter and committing the update to the database only every 20 records, rather than every one, performance increases a good deal. This practice does run the risk of having large update processes fail when they have only partially completed. Make sure that such update processes are restartable and be sure to commit only "complete" units, never violating the referential integrity of the application.

Internal Lock Contention

As mentioned previously, a number of internal lock types exist that can result in poor database performance. These internal locks are commonly referred to as *latches* and *events*. Locking problems resulting from latch and event problems are harder to identify but often simpler to correct. Rather than having to rewrite a whole section of application code, you may be able to rectify the problem by changing an INIT.ORA parameter. The following sections cover some of the more common internal lock contention problem areas. For further details on tuning these contention areas, consult Chapter 11, *Monitoring and Tuning an Existing Database.*

Rollback Segment Contention

Every time a user modifies the database, rollback information needs to be written to the rollback segments. This information is required for transaction rollback integrity, point-in-time read consistency, and database recovery. Applications that have many users all performing updates simultaneously (any medium to large TPO application) may suffer from rollback segment contention.

The following SQL script demonstrates how to identify rollback segment contention:

```
# rbk_segs.sql
SELECT name, gets, waits,
          ((gets - waits) * 100) / gets hit_ratio
   FROM   v$rollstat S,
          v$rollname R
   WHERE  S.usn = R.usn
```

Name	Gets	Waits	Hit_Ratio
SYSTEM	572	0	100.00
RBS1	222579	37	99.98
RBS2	516112	237	99.95
RBS3	1157698	2198	99.81
RBS4	389975	418	99.89

If your hit_ratio from this query is less than 99%, then you have rollback contention. This could be attributed to too few rollback segments or rollback segments that are too small. Another possible cause could be applications that have explicitly assigned all large transactions to a larger rollback segment. Even though this is a good practice (and we do recommend it), you must always be careful not to overload this bigger segment. You may need to increase the number of extents the segment has or to add another larger rollback segment.

Another way of identifying and dissecting rollback segment contention is via the v$waitstat view. This view allows us to break up the waits by latch class:

```
# rbk_cont.sql
SELECT class, count(*)
FROM   v$waitstat
WHERE  class IN  ('system undo header', 'system undo block',
                  'undo header',        'undo block')


Class                  Count
------------------     -------
system undo header        1
system undo block         1
undo header               1
undo block                1
```

Rollback Shrinkage Contention

Another potential area of rollback contention is during the shrinkage of rollback extents. You can specify an optimal rollback size in the OPTIMAL parameter, and the database will automatically shrink the segment back (as close as possible) to this value. This task is performed by the SMON process. If you have selected a optimal rollback size that is too small, the database will be continually shrinking the rollback segment after every transaction completes. This can lead to serious contention problems.

The following SQL script demonstrates how to identify rollback shrinkage:

```
# rbk_shrk.sql
SELECT name, extents, waits, shrinks, extends, hwmsize,
FROM   v$rollstat S,
       v$rollname R
WHERE  S.usn = R.usn
```

Name	Extents	Waits	Shrinks	Extends	HWMsize
SYSTEM	3	0	0	0	237568
RBS1	4	37	0	0	209707008
RBS2	4	237	0	0	209707008
RBS3	4	2198	1	1	262135808
RBS4	4	418	1	3	366993408

We try to encourage developers to size their rollback segments correctly, rather than relying on the OPTIMAL parameter to clean up afterward. Using OPTIMAL in conjunction with a correctly sized rollback segment is the best solution.

Redo Log Buffer Contention

The redo log buffers are used to hold database changes before writing them to the on-line redo logs. These buffers operate in a circular fashion and are controlled via internal database latches. Applications that perform several simultaneous update transactions can experience poor performance if these buffers are not large enough to keep up.

The following SQL script demonstrates how to identify redo buffer contention:

```
# log_cont.sql
SELECT name, gets, misses, immediate_gets, immediate_misses
FROM    v$latch
WHERE   name in ('redo allocation', 'redo copy')

Name                 Gets   Misses Immediate_Gets Immediate_Misses
---------------- -------- ------- -------------- ----------------
redo allocation  28303493  304304              0                0
redo copy            1441    1093        2918590             1458
```

If the ratio of gets to misses or immediate_gets to immediate_misses exceeds 1%, you should consider tuning the redo buffer. Here are some suggestions for helping to reduce redo buffer latch contention.

- Increase the size of the redo buffer. An OLTP system should be able to cope with a buffer size of around 256 kilobytes, and as a batch application can benefit from a redo buffer as large as 2 megabytes. Applications with a mixture of OLTP and batch application should set their redo buffer to approximately 1 megabyte.

- Decrease the size of the INIT.ORA parameter LOG_SMALL_ENTRY_MAX_SIZE to reduce contention for the redo allocation latch for multi-CPU machines.

- Increase the value of the INIT.ORA parameter LOG_SIMULTANEOUS_COPIES to reduce contention for the redo copy latches for multi-CPU machines.

Latch Spin Count

Multi-processor machines can improve overall database performance and reduce latch contention by tuning the INIT.ORA parameter SPIN_COUNT. This parameter controls the number of times a process will loop, trying to lock a busy latch before going to sleep and trying again later. Internal database latches are never held for very long. Machines that have spare CPU resource can be better served by spinning on a latch for a longer period, rather than going to sleep.

Free List Contention

Applications that have many processes simultaneously inserting into a single database table can experience free list contention. Every table, index, and cluster header maintains a free list chain of all blocks that have some free space available. By default, objects are created with only one free list chain. INSERT-intensive applications can experience contention on the object header block while trying to scan the free list chain. The simplest way of fixing this type of contention is to increase the number of free lists for the object in question.

```
CREATE TABLE emp ( . . . )   STORAGE  ( ...  FREELISTS 4)
```

NOTE   The number of free lists chains can be allocated only at object creation (not supported as part of the ALTER TABLE syntax), and its maximum number is dependent on the Oracle block size.

Lock Detection Scripts

The following section contains some of the scripts we use to track and identify database locks. These scripts can be very handy in helping to identify application locking problems.

who.sql

The *who.sql* script details who is currently logged on to the database. It distinguishes operating system and Oracle usercodes, and identifies both the foreground and background process ID (PID) numbers.

```
# who.sql
SELECT NVL(S.OSUSER,S.type) OS_Usercode,
       S.usernameOracle_Usercode,
       S.sidOracle_SID,
       S.processF_Ground,
       P.spid  B_Ground
FROM   V$SESSION S,
       V$PROCESS P
WHERE  NVL(UPPER(S.OSUSER),'?')   LIKE NVL(UPPER('&OS_User'),'%')
AND NVL(UPPER(S.Username),'?') LIKE NVL(UPPER('&Oracle_User'),'%')
AND s.paddr  = p.addr
ORDER s.sid

sql>    @who
        Enter value for OS_User:
        Enter value for Oracle_User:
```

OS_Usercode	Oracle_Usercode	Oracle_SID	F_Ground	B_Ground
BACKGROUND		1		8639
BACKGROUND		2		8640
BACKGROUND		3		8641
BACKGROUND		4		8642
BACKGROUND		5		8643
BACKGROUND		6		8644
BACKGROUND		7		8645
oracle	SYSTEM	13	28292	28294
s6	S6	16	3829:01	15829
oracle	SCOTT	18	28359	28360
s4	S4	28	7445:01	26605
oracle	SCOTT	31	28359	2366
oracle	SCOTT	32	28359	2367

NOTE	The foreground process IDs (those ending in *:01*) are actually client-server connections to the database with the PID belonging to the client host. This explains why the two PIDs appear to be unrelated.

When a number of Oracle processes have same foreground PID; it means that the statement is currently using the parallel query option. In the above case, SID 18 is actually the user process, and SID 31 and 32 are the parallel query slaves. When a parallel query slave is used by a statement, it adopts the requesting processes environment (logs on as the same user) and sets its parent ID to the controlling process.

table_locks.sql

The *table_locks.sql* script helps to identify which users currently have what objects locked (both DML and DDL). This is one way of identifying what a process might be doing or what step a multistep program may be running.

```
# tab_lcks.sql
SELECT s.osuser, s.username, s.sid, a.object tablename, a.owner,
       DECODE (a.ob_typ,2,'DDL','DML') lock_mode
FROM sys.v_$session S,
       sys.v_$access A
WHERE a.sid = s.sid
AND a.object   LIKE NVL(UPPER('&TableName'||'%'),'%')
AND s.osuser   LIKE NVL(lLOWER('&OS_User'||'%'),'%')
AND s.username LIKE NVL(LOWER('&UserName'||'%'),'%')
AND a.ob_typ in (2,4)
ORDER
   BY 1, 2, 3, 4
```

```
sql>    @table_locks
        Enter value for TableName:
        Enter value for OS_User: oracle
        Enter value for Username:

OS Usercode    Oracle Usercode  Sid Tablename      Owner    Lock_Mode
-------------  ---------------- --- ------------- -------- ---------
oracle         SYSTEM            13 STOCK_ON_HAND SCOTT    DDL
                                    PRODUCTS      SCOTT    DDL
                                    SOH_HISTORY   SCOTT    DML

               SCOTT             18 EMP           SCOTT    DLL
                                    DEPT          SCOTT    DDL
                                    SALES         SCOTT    DML
```

rollback_locks.sql

The *rollback_locks* script helps to identify which users are currently updating the database. This information is invaluable in trying to determining how far a multi-step program has progressed, and whether a rollback will be necessary if the process is terminated.

```
# rbk_lcks.sql
SELECT r.usn,  r.name,  s.osuser,
       s.username, s.sid,   x.extents,
       x.extends,  x.waits, x.shrinks,
       x.wraps
FROM sys.v_$rollstat X,
       sys.v_$rollname R,
       sys.v_$session S,
       sys.v_$transaction T
WHERE t.addr = s.taddr (+)
AND x.usn (+)  = r.usn
AND  t.xidusn (+) = r.usn
ORDERr
   BY r.usn


sql>    @rollback_locks
```

```
ID Name   OSuser Username SID Extents Extends Waits Shrinks Wraps
-- ------ ------ -------- --- ------- ------- ----- ------- -----
   SYSTEM
 2 RBS1   oracle SYSTEM    13       4       0    37       0     2
 3 RBS2
 4 RBS3
 5 RBS4   s6     S6        16       4       3   418       1     3
```

NOTE   Rollback segments are allocated in a cyclic round-robin fashion. By executing this query over and over again, you should be able to see whether an updating program is progressing. Each time the program commits a change, it will skip to the next rollback segments. This may not seem to be a lot of information, but when a program has been running for 20 hours straight, knowing that it is performing commits on a regular basis at least gives you a warn feeling!

waiters.sql

The *waiters.sql* script is our favorite when users are complaining of spasmodic application performance. "Sometimes it takes 3 seconds, but other times it takes 20 minutes," they tell us. This type of behavior is indicative of application locking conflicts. Running this scripts allows us to pinpoint who is blocking whom.

```
# waiters.sql
SELECT SUBSTR(s1.username,1,12)    "WAITING User",
       SUBSTR(s1.osuser,1,8)  "OS User",
       SUBSTR(to_char(w.session_id),1,5)    "Sid",
       P1.spid  "PID",
       SUBSTR(s2.username,1,12)    "HOLDING User",
       SUBSTR(s2.osuser,1,8)          "OS User",
       SUBSTR(to_char(h.session_id),1,5)    "Sid",
       P2.spid  "PID"
FROM sys.v_$process P1,    sys.v_$process P2,
       sys.v_$session S1,    sys.v_$session S2,
       sys.dba_locks w,      sys.dba_locks h
WHERE  h.mode_held       = 'None'
AND h.mode_held        = 'Null'
AND w.mode_requested   != 'None'
AND w.lock_type (+)    = h.lock_type
AND w.lock_id1   (+)   = h.lock_id1
AND w.lock_id2   (+)   = h.lock_id2
AND w.session_id       = S1.sid  (+)
AND  h.session_id       = S2.sid  (+)
AND  S1.paddr           = P1.addr (+)
AND  S2.paddr           = P2.addr (+)

sql>    @waiters

WAITING User OS User  Sid  PID    HOLDING User OS User  Sid  PID
------------ -------- ---- -----  ------------ -------- ---- -----
SYSTEM       oracle   13   28294  SCOTT        oracle   18   28360
SCOTT        oracle   18   28360  S6           s6       16   15829
S4           s4       28   26605  S6           s6       16   15829
```

NOTE   This script references views from the Oracle-supplied script *cat-block.sql*. This script can be located in the directory *$ORACLE_HOME/rdbms/admin*.

---

what.sql

Once you have determined who is blocking whom via the *waiters.sql* script, we are now able to drill down and query what the offending user is actually doing. By identifying who is causing the locking and the actual SQL statement they are executing, we can define the application module that needs to be reviewed.

```
# what.sql
SELECT   /*+ ORDERED */
        s.sid, s.username, s.osuser,
        NVL(s.machine, '?') machine,
        NVL(s.program, '?') program,
        s.process F_Ground, p.spid B_Ground,
        X.sql_text
FROM sys.v_$session S,
        sys.v_$process P,
        sys.v_$sqlarea X
WHERE s.osuser       LIKE LOWER(NVL('&OS_User','%'))
AND s.username       LIKE UPPER(NVL('&Oracle_User','%'))
AND s.sid            LIKE NVL('&SID','%')
AND s.paddr          = p.addr
AND s.type           != 'BACKGROUND'
AND s.sql_address    = x.address
AND s.sql_hash_value = x.hash_value
ORDER BY S.sid

sql>    @what
        Enter value for OS_User:
        Enter value for Oracle_User:
        Enter value for SID: 16

Sid Username OSUser  Machine Program      F_Ground B_Ground
--- -------- ------- ------- ------------ -------- ---------
SQL_Text
------------------------------------------------------------------
16  s6       S6      thor    sqlplus      3829:01  15829
Udate EMP set emp_salary = least(nvl(emp_salary,0) * 1.135, 36000)
where dept_no = '0020' and sal_range between 10 and 20
```

V

Tuning for Database Administrators

Part V describes what Oracle database administrators (DBAs) need to know about tuning: how can you tune a new database to best advantage, what can you do to improve the performance of an existing database, what diagnostic and tuning tools are available to you, what are the special issues presented by parallel server, parallel query, and backup and recovery?

9

Tuning a New Database

Since publication of the first edition of this book, there have been rapid performance improvements in parallel processing and in disk I/O load sharing through RAID (Redundant Arrays of Inexpensive Disks) technology. Nevertheless, our rule remains the same: "The way you create your database has a significant impact on your site's performance." Not only do programs run faster against a well-tuned database, the database structure also makes it easier for you to monitor performance. The importance of database performance ranks right behind your first database goal: making sure you'll be able to recover data in case of a system crash or data integrity problem. Keep these two goals in mind as you tune your new database.

What does your database contain? There are four main types of files; they are the following:

Database files

Contain tables, indexes, clusters, sequences, the Oracle data dictionary, temporary segments, and rollback segments.

Redo log files

Contain both before-image information (rollback segment data) and after-image information—the new values that the database will contain after updates have completed.

Archive logs

Historical copies of the redo logs.

Control files

Used to check the consistency of data files from a recovery perspective.

Remember that you are responsible for creating and tuning all of the databases at your site—not only the production database, but also the developers' database, the quality assurance database, and the training database. Tuning is important for all of these databases. Your programmers will be better able to meet deadlines and provide good response times if they are doing their work on a well-tuned database. Your QA staff will be able to do accurate response time testing only if the database is properly tuned. And your users will be better able to learn how to use the production system if they are working on a database that behaves the way it will in production. Remember, too, that many organizations have tuning service agreements for specific response times that enforce a certain level of performance.

Your specific hardware configuration determines how much flexibility you will have in tuning your database—in particular, the amount of memory and the size and number of disks. If you don't have enough memory to satisfy demands, memory bottlenecks will occur. The CPU will be consumed by moving whole processes or parts of processes into and out of memory. If one or more of your disk controllers are operating above their recommended maximum, you'll encounter disk bottlenecks too. Make sure you know how to use the memory and disk-monitoring commands that are available for your own particular operating system so that you can keep close tabs on memory and disk availability.

WARNING   Never put any part of your database on the operating system disk.

Although, as the database administrator, you have primary responsibility for database tuning, the entire tuning process is a team effort. Make sure you work closely with the system administrator and the analysts, designers, and developers at your site.

What do you need from your system administrator? He or she is responsible not only for Oracle but also for other non-Oracle applications such as electronic mail. This person maintains the system hardware and software and makes sure you have enough contiguous disk space for your database files. The system administrator sets up many items that affect disk I/O performance such as striping, mirroring, raw devices, and logical volumes. He or she also creates user accounts in your system and assigns memory to these users (in operating systems like VMS that support per-user memory assignments). Be aware that if the amount of memory assigned is too low, CPU will be consumed when the system needs to obtain additional memory increments. If the amount of memory assigned is too large, memory is wasted that might be sorely needed by other products. Make sure the system administrator knows what your database needs are.

What do you need from your analysts, designers, and developers? They will provide valuable information on the expected size and usage patterns of the various tables, which help to determine the types of indexes you need and how much storage to allocate to tables and indexes. This information will also help you to spread the disk load across disks to avoid disk I/O bottlenecks. Analysts and designers should also be able to help you determine the number of expected users and what they will be doing in the system. Your developers will advise you on the appropriate optimizer settings—whether to choose the rule-based optimizer, the cost-based optimizer, or a combination of the two. They will also advise you on which packages, procedures, triggers, and functions are required; which ones should be pinned; and what the constraint requirements are.

Steps in Setting Up a Database

Here are the basic steps to follow when you set up your database:

1. Obtain from analysts, designers, and/or user representatives background information on the numbers of users, their usage patterns, and the expected increase in the number of users.

2. Check with the system administrator to make sure there is adequate memory and disk space. Also, make sure that the disk space is contiguous. This helps performance when you are reading to and writing from database files.

3. Provide information on RAID usage, raw device requirements, and logical volume manager, where appropriate, to your system administrator.

4. With the help of the system administrator, develop comprehensive backup and recovery procedures.

5. Create the INIT.ORA parameter file, and set the most efficient values for the parameters.

6. Obtain the required optimizer settings from your development teams, along with a list of commonly used packages, procedures, triggers, and functions.

7. Create the database and tablespaces, with their default storage allocations,

8. Create the users who will own the tables, indexes, clusters, sequences, views, triggers, packages, procedures, and functions.

9. Create tables, indexes, and clusters with the appropriate storage parameter. Also create the views, foreign key constraints, snapshots, and sequences.

10. Import the data into the tables (if you are transferring data from an existing Oracle application). If you are creating a large database, you might consider creating your indexes and constraints after the import. (See the section called "Creating Very Large Databases" at the end of this chapter.)

11. Create packages, procedures, functions, and triggers.

12. Create all other users and roles with their appropriate grants and synonyms.

Tuning Memory

This section describes the layout of memory and briefly discusses how you can tune memory areas. Because most of the memory tuning that you will perform occurs once your system is running (and perhaps experiencing bottlenecks), Chapter 11, *Monitoring and Tuning an Existing Database*, describes memory tuning in greater detail.

Memory Components

The general layout of memory in the Oracle system is shown in Figure 9-1. Figure 9-2 shows a simplified diagram of the SGA structure.

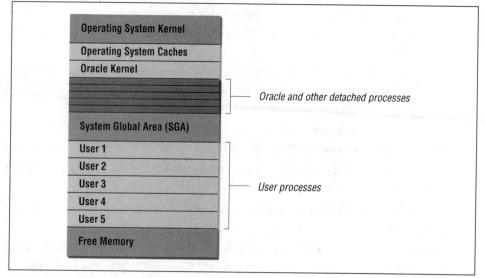

Figure 9-1. Oracle memory layout

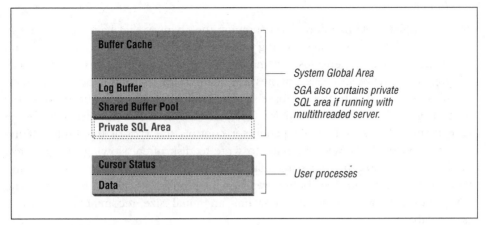

Figure 9-2. SGA and user processes

By tuning these memory areas (primarily by setting the appropriate INIT.ORA parameters), you can improve performance in your Oracle system. All of the parameters that affect performance are included in the list in the section called "INIT.ORA Parameter Summary" later in this chapter.

You can tune the following areas:

- **Buffer cache**: Holds copies of database blocks for tables, indexes, rollback segments, and clusters. Each buffer holds one Oracle data block.

- **Log buffer**: Holds copies of redo log buffers.

- **Private SQL and PL/SQL areas**: Hold the SQL and PL/SQL statements that are not shared.

- **Shared pool**: Holds the library cache (for shared SQL statements being executed), the dictionary cache, and some session information.

Buffer cache

The buffer cache holds copies of database blocks for tables, indexes, rollback segments, sort data, dictionary data, and clusters. Each buffer holds one Oracle data block. The more blocks you can hold in memory, the better your performance will be. You control the size of the buffer cache with the DB_BLOCK_ BUFFERS parameter. The description of this parameter in "INIT.ORA Parameter Summary" contains an initial size recommendation for a new database. Chapter 11 describes how you can monitor the buffer cache over time and adjust this size to suit your own site's needs.

Log buffer

The log buffer contains information showing the changes that have been made to database buffer blocks. When the log buffer reaches one-third full (two-thirds full in Oracle7.3), a user performs a commit, or a write takes place to the database, the log writer (LGWR) process writes the contents of the buffer out to the redo log files associated with the database. It also writes from the log buffer every few seconds if there has been no activity. (Chapter 11 describes these files and how to tune them.) The LOG_BUFFER parameter controls the size of this buffer. If the buffer is too small, LGWR may have to write to disk often, slowing performance, particularly with batch processing that tends to have less frequent commits and write each time the log buffer reaches one-third (or two-thirds) full. The "INIT.ORA Parameter Summary" contains an initial size recommendation for a new database.

Shared buffer pool

The shared buffer pool contains the library cache, the dictionary cache, and, if you are running Oracle's multithreaded server, some session data. You control the size of the shared buffer pool with the SHARED_POOL_SIZE parameter. The description of this parameter in the "INIT.ORA Parameter Summary" contains an initial size recommendation for a new database. Chapter 11 describes how you can monitor the shared buffer pool over time and adjust this size to suit your own site's needs. Figure 9-3 shows the contents of the shared buffer pool.

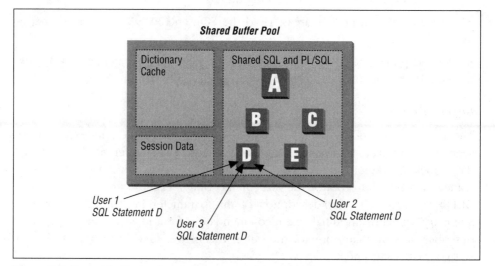

Figure 9-3. Shared buffer pool

There is a single library cache (sometimes called the shared SQL area) in the shared buffer pool of the SGA. (Remember, this pool also contains dictionary information and some session information.) Figure 9-4 illustrates these context areas.

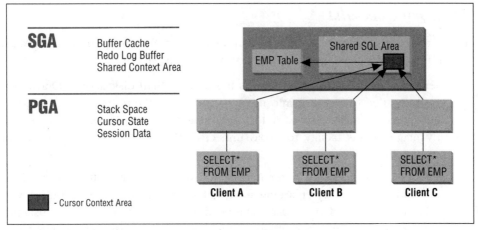

Figure 9-4. SQL context areas

The dictionary cache is a part of the shared buffer pool. To tune the dictionary, you simply set the SHARED_POOL_SIZE large enough to accommodate information about the dictionary, as well as shared SQL statements and session information. Dictionary tuning has a major effect on overall system performance. We have found in testing that poorly tuned dictionaries can result in as much as a 50% performance degradation in an Oracle system. If you are using the earlier versions of Oracle7, you may observe poor dictionary cache performance (Chapter 11 shows how to detect dictionary cache performance). Don't despair; each new version of Oracle7 has shown marked improvements in dictionary cache performance.

Private SQL and PL/SQL areas

As we mentioned previously, the library cache contains shared SQL statements. Included in this area are the parse tree and the execution plan for these statements. Another separate area contains the bind variables and run-time buffers associated with these statements for each user. In the following statement, :1 is a bind variable:

```
SELECT name
  FROM emp
 WHERE id = :1
```

The location of the private SQL area depends on whether you are running with the multithreaded server. If you are, the private SQL area is in the shared buffer pool, along with the dictionary cache. If you are running with a dedicated server, this private area is in the user's own PGA. The number of private SQL areas that an individual user can process is determined by the OPEN_CURSORS parameter, which has a default of 50.

Memory Checklist

Here are some guidelines to help you optimize your memory performance. We'll expand on each of these points in the rest of this chapter:

*   Memory access is tens of thousands times faster than disk access. Oracle lets you bring items from disk into memory and cache them there for subsequent use. Memory caching saves a lot of disk access time. Make sure you take advantage of this facility to avoid unnecessary disk I/Os and slowdowns in performance.

*   Memory is also used to buffer information that is being written to the database and redo logs. By enlarging such buffer areas as the redo log buffer, you will reduce the number of times data need to be written. This will also significantly reduce the number of disk I/Os, particularly when performing batch processing.

*   Make sure you keep some free memory available (but not too much). Performance suffers drastically if you run out of memory. When additional processes request memory, your CPU will be forced to spend almost all of its cycles managing paging and swapping activities.

*   Make sure you know how to use the memory-monitoring commands provided by your operating system, and use them regularly to ensure that you have free memory.

*   If your operating system allows you to install the Oracle executables as shared, take advantage of this facility. In this way, executables such as *iap30* (SQL*Forms), *dmu50* (SQL*Menu), and SQL*Plus will be stored once in memory and shared between many users, rather than requiring each user process to store its own copy. Unfortunately, many operating systems don't allow shared executables. Check your own system's *Oracle Installation and Users Guide* to find out whether it offers the shared executable facility.

*   If you are running in a client-server environment, be aware of your memory usage levels at both the client and server ends. There are ways you can use your memory to reduce the number of packets being transferred across the network. See Chapter 16, *Tuning in the Client-Server Environment.*

*   Be aware of any memory usage by other Oracle or non-Oracle applications that may affect the level of free memory on your machine.

- If your users log on second and subsequent times running products like SQL*Forms Version 3, they are likely to use between 1 and 3 megabytes per logon. Client-server users will use between 500 kilobytes and 1 megabyte at the server end. Make sure that you have planned for this when calculating free memory. You can control your users' use of memory by setting the INIT.ORA parameter, RESOURCE_LIMIT.

- Pin your SYS-owned packages DBMS_STANDARD, STANDARD, DBMS_UTIL-ITY, DBMS_DESCRIBE, DBMS_OUTPUT, and any other heavily used packages, procedures, functions, and triggers in your database. You will need to consult with your development team to find out which are the most commonly used objects.

Setting INIT.ORA Memory Parameters

As we mentioned previously, you control memory in your Oracle database by assigning values to the memory parameters in the INIT.ORA file for your system. The location of this file varies, depending on the operating system you're using. Consult your *Oracle Installation and Users Guide* for information. Make sure to read all README files as well, to check for any new INIT.ORA parameters or any changes to existing ones.

In some systems, there will be multiple INIT.ORA files; this allows different databases to have their own parameter settings. For example, *INITDEV.ORA* may control the developer database, *INITQA.ORA* the QA database, and *INITPROD.ORA* the production database.

The section later in this chapter called "INIT.ORA Parameter Summary" lists all of the INIT.ORA parameters that affect memory tuning, along with default values and recommended values. In addition, there are a few operating system-specific parameters; for example, the SPIN_COUNT parameter applies only to UNIX systems. For information on these parameters, see Chapter 18, *Tuning for Specific Systems*. Don't set the INIT.ORA parameters lower than the defaults, or your database creation may fail. In the next chapter, we'll describe a few situations in which you may be able to decrease the values of these parameters later on. We have yet to see a site that performs well with the default values. Consider each value carefully.

Pinning Objects in the Shared Pool

Pinning objects can improve your performance by preventing the objects from being removed from the shared pool to make way for new objects that need to be run. The ability to pin objects was first made available in Oracle7.1. If you do pin your packages, you will usually need to increase your SHARED_POOL_SIZE because the unpinned objects will have less memory to fit into. It is essential that your development team tell you which are the commonly used objects so that you'll know which objects to pin.

You should always pin your packages and other objects immediately after starting up your database or after flushing the shared pool. It would be very nice if Oracle would automatically work out the objects to pin and pin them for us. The word is that an automatic pinning functionality will be arriving in a future version of Oracle. In the meantime, it is up to you to do the pinning.

To pin a package, use the syntax as shown below. You need to run the SQL script *dbmspool.sql* to be able to execute the procedure dbms_shared_pool.

```
execute dbms_shared_pool.keep('SYS.STANDARD');
```

When you perform the keep, it does not place the package into the shared pool area unless you execute or recompile the package. The SYS.STANDARD, SYS.DBMS_STANDARD, and SYS.DIUTIL packages are automatically loaded by Oracle. Be aware that when you pin packages owned by users other than SYS, you will have to GRANT EXECUTE ON package TO PUBLIC for the keep to work. Interestingly, once you have pinned your objects, they can be removed only by unkeep or by shutting your database down. ALTER SYSTEM FLUSH SHARED POOL will not remove the object from the shared pool.

In production, always pin the SYS packages STANDARD, DBMS_STANDARD, DBMS_UTILITY, DBMS_DESCRIBE, and DBMS_OUTPUT. If you use DBMS_LOCK, DBMS_SNAPSHOT, and DBMS_ALERT, they should also be pinned. It is also advisable to pin all of the larger and more executed packages and procedures. In development, you should also pin the PIDL, DIANA, and DIUTIL packages.

Before Oracle7.1.6, you could pin only packages, but you could place procedures and functions into packages and have triggers call packaged procedures. With Oracle7.1.6 and later, you can pin both packages and procedures with the syntax

```
execute dbms_shared_pool.keep('owner.pname');
```

Oracle7.1.6 and later versions allow triggers to be pinned with the syntax shown below. Prior to Oracle7.3, triggers have to be reparsed each time they are run, so it can be beneficial to pin some of the more heavily used and larger triggers.

```
execute dbms_shared_pool.keep('owner.triggername','R');
```

You can also pin PL/SQL blocks by replacing the "R" with any other letter. We suggest that you read the documentation in *dbmspool.sql* for a comprehensive set of examples. To determine which objects are pinned in your database, run the following SQL script:

```
# kept.sql
SELECT name, type, kept
    FROM v$db_object_cache
  WHERE kept ='YES';
```

Tuning Disk I/O

You can improve performance a great deal by setting up your disks and your disk parameters carefully. Remember, though, that your primary obligation is to set up your disk files in a way that guarantees database recovery. Performance comes second. There are two basic disk performance rules: Keep disk I/Os to a minimum, and spread your disk load across disk devices and controllers. (This will avoid contention, which is caused when disks operate above their maximum I/O rates per second.)

Figure 9-5 shows the basic disk components in an Oracle system.

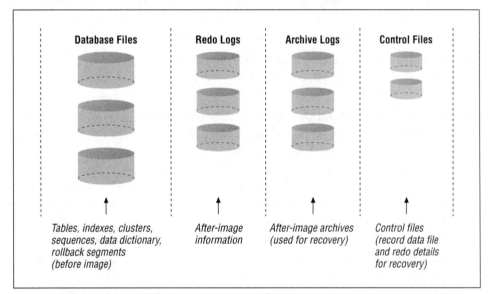

Figure 9-5. Disk components

Disk I/O Checklist

Here are some guidelines to help you optimize your disk performance. We'll expand on these points in the rest of this chapter.

- Don't allow developers to develop programs on the machine in which the production database is running or to make large ad hoc queries against your production database. Programmers typically use many resource-intensive tools (e.g., SQL*Forms generation, linking user exits into RUNMENU and RUN-FORM). They also have an unfortunate tendency to head straight to the production database and perform the dreaded full table scans on tens of thousands, hundreds of thousands, or even millions of rows of data! Make sure the programmers at your site know that they must ask you to approve any access to the production database. Otherwise, chaos will reign.

- Don't allow QA staff to test their programs on the machine that is running the production database. Untested programs may also be poorly tuned and may slow your production machine down by causing excessive disk I/Os. This is obviously not as severe if the testers have their database stored on different disks.

- Know your applications, the tables and indexes defined for them, their usage patterns, and the amount of storage they will require. You'll need to get information from your analyst, designer, and/or user representatives. If the sizes of tables and index extents have not been computed correctly, performance will be seriously affected. A personal note here: We have never seen an Oracle database in which the default sizes were adequate.

- Be aware of the optimizer (cost- or rule-based) that the coders used when they tuned their code. If you select the incorrect setting, your response times may be abysmal.

- Separate redo logs and the database files onto different drive (that includes multiplexed redo logs). You should have at least four redo logs, each 5 megabytes or larger in size. The availability of four redo logs allows your site to turn archiving on, and usually ensures that the redo that is being written to the archive log will have time to be written before Oracle needs to write more redo information to it. In general, 5 to 10 megabytes is adequate to allow sites to operate efficiently, but you'll have to assess this estimate for your own site. Many sites use more and larger redos very effectively.

- Consider ping-ponging your redos to allow the LGWR to write to a different disk from the disk the ARCH is reading. For example, DiskA might contain redo1 and redo3, while DiskB might contain redo2 and redo4. (We describe this in the section "How Many Redo Logs and What Size?" later in the chapter.)

- Take advantage of multiplexed redo logs, or mirror your redo logs using RAID technology. You must ensure that your multiplexed or mirrored redo logs are on different disks from your primary redo logs, your archive logs, and your data files.

- Consider striping (RAID1) and mirroring (RAID0) your redo logs. Also, if you are using UNIX, consider using raw devices or async_io for your redo logs. If you stripe your redo logs, you must use a small stripe size.

- If you have a large number of long-running updates, consider striping and mirroring your archive logs to help the ARCH process keep up with the LGWR process.

- Make sure that the archive logs reside on a different disk from that used for any database file or redo log. It is important to get tape backups of your archives after they have been written to disk. You should consider compressing all except the last two archive logs, using your operating system compression commands. This will assist by speeding up the copying of the archive logs to tape.

- Do not store any database files on the operating system disk. The operating system disk is normally heavily used for operating system functions such as hard page faulting and swapping.

- Make sure that you have more than one control file and that each one resides on a different disk device and disk controller.

- If you are backing up database files from disk to disk, don't place your backup on the same disk as the one that is used to store the same database file. Obvious, you say? We've seen a number of sites do this.

- If one of your tables has high insert, update, or delete activity, with many indexes continually being modified, consider splitting the indexes for the table onto different disks.

- Split tables and indexes into separate tablespaces. Because indexes and tables are often inserted into and read from simultaneously, splitting them minimizes disk head movement and allows concurrent access.

- Split commonly used tables into separate tablespaces (logical parts of the database). For example, if the users typically access the EMP and DEPT tables together, it may pay to separate EMP and DEPT into separate tablespaces. Also, mix frequently used indexes in the same tablespace as infrequently used ones to avoid constant demand on a particular tablespace.

- If your system has mixed transaction sizes, create one rollback segment for every four concurrent users (if you have up to 40 users) or every eight concurrent users (if you have up to 100 users). If all transactions are small, consider assigning one 10 kilobyte rollback segment per user process to allow rollback segments to be stored in buffer cache. Most sites create a number of rollback tablespaces and use these exclusively for rollback segments.

- Create one or more separate tablespaces for temporary segments. If you are using Oracle7.3 or later, create the tablespace using the command CREATE TABLESPACE tspace TEMPORARY. All users must have this tablespace defined as their temporary tablespace. This tablespace must be at least the size of your largest table. It can be used to monitor temporary table activity (for example, to determine whether the size of the SORT_AREA_SIZE parameter is adequate) when your database is running. Ensure that the tablespace's INITIAL and NEXT extent sizes are a multiple of the SORT_AREA_SIZE.

- Make sure you have enough free space in your database to rebuild your largest table. You must also have enough free storage in your temporary tablespace to create your largest index.

- Spread your disk I/O load across as many disks and as many disk controllers as possible. Many medium-sized disks are preferable to a few very large files. A disk spread keeps one disk from getting overworked. Consider using Oracle striping or operating system striping to spread your I/O load. If you plan to use the parallel query option effectively, you must stripe (See Chapter 13, *Tuning Parallel Query.*)

- Maintain the system tablespace as a separate tablespace of at least 30 megabytes, or as high as 120 megabytes or larger if you have a large number of stored packages, procedures, functions, and triggers.

- Ensure that the space available on the disk where database files are to be placed is physically contiguous. You may have to ask your system administrator to do a disk reorganization before creating the database. If you are using UNIX, consider using raw devices.

- Don't be rigid about where to put database files. Some sites have such inflexible standards that they can't get decent performance. We worked at one site that was experiencing disk I/O problems on all disks except one. That disk contained the system tablespace. Because a site standard stated that the system tablespace must reside on its own disk, everybody was suffering the consequences. Although standards are a good idea, sometimes they can unnecessarily restrict performance.

- If you are performing disk-to-disk-image backups of database files, do not allow the backup devices to contain only backed-up database files. You can use these devices more fruitfully.

- If you are using snapshots, don't forget the storage allocations. Make sure that you specify a disk that is separate from the table for snapshot logs. When you create the SNAP$_ table at the receiving database, specify the USING INDEX clause to apply proper storage allocation. Snapshot logs should be created with a PCTFREE of 0.

- Store very large objects in their own tablespace. If a large object exceeds the maximum allowable for export (2 gigabytes on many UNIX systems), break it into smaller objects and use partitioned views (Details are provided in the section called "Creating Very Large Databases" at the end of this chapter). Every table must be able to be rebuilt via the EXPORT/IMPORT facility.

- If the creation of your new database requires you to delete a lot of rows from one of your tables, rebuild the table using EXPORT and IMPORT. If you don't have time to rebuild the entire table, rebuild the indexes using the parallel query option. (You must be using striping to do this effectively.) Oracle7.3 also has an option, ALTER INDEX indexname REBUILD, which provides large reductions in index creation time.

- If you have mistakenly oversized your table and are using Oracle7.3 or later, take advantage of the ALTER TABLE tname DEALLOCATE UNUSED [KEEP (integer)] command, which allows you to remove the unused blocks from the table after the high-water mark. You can also free index space using the ALTER INDEX command and free cluster space using the ALTER CLUSTER command.

- Oracle8 has tablespaces especially set up for LONG datatypes. Place all of your tables that contain LONG data into a tablespaces especially set up for LONG row processing.

Setting Disk Storage Parameters

When you create a table, index, tablespace, cluster, or rollback segment, you tell Oracle how much disk space to allocate for it. With some database objects, such as tablespaces and clusters, you specify a STORAGE clause in the CREATE statement used to create the object—for example, in CREATE CLUSTER and CREATE TABLESPACE. You can change these via the various versions of the ALTER statement. If you do not specify a STORAGE clause, the tables, indexes, and clusters are given the default storage of the tablespace in which the objects are being created.

You might specify a STORAGE clause in the form:

```
CREATE TABLE . . .
STORAGE (INITIAL 5M NEXT 1M MAXEXTENTS UNLIMITED
    MINEXTENTS 1 PCTINCREASE 0)
```

You can also specify values for OPTIMAL (rollback segments only) FREELISTS, and FREELIST GROUPS in this clause. The following list summarizes the STORAGE parameters; the sections that follow describe the specifics of using these parameters with particular database objects.

INITIAL
Default: 10 kilobytes
Values: OS-dependent
> Size of the first extent (a contiguous piece of database storage) allocated to the object. Ideally, the entire amount of data in the table or other object should fit in this extent. The default is 10 kilobytes. The minimum size varies

by object. For tables it is one Oracle block; for indexes, it is two Oracle blocks.

NEXT

Default: 10 kilobytes

Values: OS-dependent

Size of the next extent to be allocated after the extent specified in INITIAL has been filled. Set the NEXT parameter to minimize the number of extents in the object while ensuring that there is enough space to create the extent.

PCTINCREASE

Default: 50

Values: 0 to 100

Percentage by which the NEXT storage parameter is increased for the next extent. If you set this value to 0, every additional extent is the same as the value of NEXT. (Leaving it at the default causes each of the additional extents to be 50% larger than the previous one.) If your table is sized correctly, set the parameter to 0.

Be careful not to set this parameter indiscriminately. Think of how quickly the extent sizes can grow and how little of the last extent may actually be used.

One particular site that we visited complained that its database was now using 1 gigabyte more storage space than they had estimated. (They had planned that the 2.5 gigabytes they initially allocated would allow for 12 months' growth.) But now the conversion run was using all 2.5 gigabytes and was screaming for more as it crashed. It turned out that they had set PCTIN-CREASE to 50. When they carefully sized the tables and set PCTINCREASE to 0, they reduced the amount of storage needed to 1.5 gigabytes.

You cannot set PCTINCREASE for rollback segments.

MAXEXTENTS

Default: OS-dependent

Values: 1 to OS-dependent maximum (and Oracle version-dependent)

Maximum number of extents allowed for this object. Set this parameter to a few extents lower than the maximum allowable number of extents in your database prior to Oracle7.3 and UNLIMITED for Oracle7,.3 and later. The particular value that you can specify depends on your operating system and the size of its blocks. Each table extent must be recorded in the table header block. A 1-kilobyte header block (DB_BLOCK_SIZE) allows about 57 extents, 2 kilobytes allows about 121 extents, 4 kilobytes allows about 249 extents, and 8 kilobytes allows about 505 extents.

Oracle7.3 has removed the upper limit on the number of extents for a table or index. The MAXEXTENTS is no longer driven by the DB_BLOCK_SIZE parameter. You can now specify MAXEXTENTS UNLIMITED, which places no limit on the number of extents your object can contain. We don't recommend that you have thousands of extents on every object in your database, however, because throwing extents does cause a performance overhead. There are some other implications that you should be aware of before setting all of your objects to MAXEXTENTS UNLIMITED:

- SYS-owned dictionary tables cannot be altered to have their MAXEX-TENTS larger than the values prior to Oracle7.3. For example, if your DB_BLOCK_SIZE is 4 kilobytes, you can't have any more than 249 extents.

- Rollback segments must be off-line before you can convert them to have unlimited extents.

- The minimum extent size for rollback segments in unlimited format is four blocks.

- Tablespaces created under Oracle7.3 do not have MAXEXTENTS UNILIM-ITED set by default. You must change them manually, using the ALTER TABLESPACE tspace DEFAULT STORAGE (MAXEXTENTS UNLIMITED) command.

Prior to Oracle7.3, we recommend that you specify a few less than the maximum number of extents. This allows you the opportunity to allocate a NEXT extent of an optimal size to the table or index. If the table or index exceeds MAXEXTENTS and MAXEXTENTS equals the maximum allowable machine limit, you have no choice but to rebuild the table and all its indexes with a new storage allocation. This may take a long time if the table is extremely large and has many indexes. If the MAXEXTENTS parameter is several less than the maximum number of possible extents on your machine, you can find the largest free extent size available to you and resize your table dynamically, using a statement like the following one:

```
ALTER TABLE ACCOUNT STORAGE (NEXT 5M);
```

Do not set MAXEXTENTS too low. If you are using Oracle7.3, set your MAX-EXTENTS to UNLIMITED. Too often, a long-running job fails because a DBA tried to cut the number of extents too close, and a minor miscalculation resulted in disaster.

NOTE   Prior to Oracle7.3 you will fail with an error if you specify a value higher than the maximum value for your selected DB_BLOCK_SIZE.

MINEXTENTS

Default: 1 (for rollback segments, default is 2)

Values: 1 to OS-dependent maximum

> Minimum extents allocated to the table. Leave this parameter at its default value unless the storage allocation is for an Oracle striped table, in which case MINEXTENTS must be equal to the number of files across which the table has been striped. With Oracle7.2 and later, striping is particularly effective for data warehousing applications because Oracle is aware of the locations of the files in the stripe and can allocate parallel query servers accordingly, one per disk.

OPTIMAL

Default: Null

Values: Default value to OS-dependent maximum

> Optimal size for a rollback segment. Oracle will automatically shrink the segment back to this setting to maintain the optimal size after the segment has expanded beyond its specified optimal size. We usually recommend that you don't set this parameter because of the performance degradation we have seen it cause during benchmarks. We have also seen it cause SNAPSHOT TOO OLD errors, when a rollback has shrunk in the middle of a large batch update. It does lessen administration, but if you do wish to set it, make it high. As an alternative, use the ALTER ROLLBACK SEGMENT segment SHRINK command if you are using Oracle7.3 or later.

FREELISTS

Default: 1

Values: 1 to block-dependent maximum

> Number of free lists for each free list group. Free lists are lists of data buffers allocated for table or index extents. Increase this parameter if your programs are performing a lot of inserts. This avoids contention because multiple transactions can insert into the same table or index via different buffers. You should set FREELISTS to the number of concurrent inserts you would expect against your table.

FREELIST GROUPS

Default: 1

Values: 1 to block-dependent maximum

> Number of groups of free lists. You set this parameter only if you are using the parallel server option (in parallel mode) for tables or clusters. FREELIST GROUPS allows each database instance to have its own specified number of free lists so that multiple inserts can be performed. You cannot specify this parameter for indexes. (See Chapter 12, *Tuning Parallel Server*.)

Creating the Database

You create a database with the CREATE DATABASE statement. In this statement, you specify the files to be used for the database, the files to be used as redo log files, and a number of other options. Try to structure your database so that it minimizes disk I/O by spreading I/O evenly across disk drives. The ideal database also can easily be monitored for I/O bottlenecks and easily changed if an I/O bottleneck does occur.

At many sites, the hardware configuration is dictated ahead of time; for example, you may be assigned three disks: one for the operating system and two for your own use. Other sites in which you have more control of the configuration may support many disks. At such sites, you can split the database across disks to get the best possible performance, or you can stripe your data files or both. In general, it is better to have many medium-sized disks rather than a few very large disks, because this type of configuration allows the database load to be shared across disks.

An Oracle database may have one or more tablespaces, as described later in this chapter called "Creating the Tablespaces."

How Many Data Files Should You Create?

Under normal circumstances, create one contiguous database file per tablespace. This is not always feasible for very large databases, but you should always take the approach of divide and conquer. If you have a single table that is 40 gigabytes in size, consider breaking it into subordinate tables that are under 2 gigabytes in size with a UNION ALL view across it. The tablespaces you choose must allow you to spread I/O across disks and to cope with all forms of transactions that may be run against the database. If a disk is overworked with excessive I/O and you are convinced that your SQL statements are tuned and the most appropriate indexes are in place, you will find it helpful to move the data files from disk to disk to share the load. (What is considered "excessive" depends on your hardware, but on most computers anything approaching 50 I/Os per second on a consistent basis is regarded as excessive.).

What Should You Name Your Data File?

What has naming got to do with tuning, you ask? Obviously, names are a site standard, but to be able to monitor file activity easily, you must have names that indicate the type of file, the application, and the database the file belongs to. Even if you are using a symbolic link against raw devices, you should name the link to indicate the purpose of the data file. For example, INDEX_ ACCT1_

PROD.DBF is an index (INDEX) accounting (ACCT1) file that is part of the production (PROD) database (DBF).

At many sites that we tune, the files are named FILE1.DBS, FILE2.DBS, FILE3.DBS, and so on. When we are investigating I/Os per file, those names don't help us to determine whether the file that has excessive I/Os is a rollback segment data file, a temporary segment data file, a system tablespace data file, or perhaps an index data file.

What Size Should You Make the Data File?

When you are figuring out the optimal size for your total database, be aware that there is more to an Oracle database than just the data stored in tables. There are also the Oracle data dictionary; stored objects, such as packages, procedures, functions, and triggers; the tables required to store Oracle products such as SQL*Forms; temporary tables used for sorting; rollback segments used to store before-image data; and the indexes placed on tables.

Also keep in mind that even though you may have the physical disk capacity to hold your entire database, it may be on too few disks or disk controllers to provide satisfactory performance. An Oracle database must be sized to allow the flexibility for future changes in case of poor performance. For example, you might need to add a new index, recreate a table to avoid a chaining problem, or move a tablespace to a different disk device.

You must also plan for growth. Some sites shortsightedly create databases that allow for only a few months of growth. When they suddenly run out of space, their tables and indexes have to expand onto small extents on noncontiguous parts of disk. Undersized extent allocations often causes dynamic extension problems that can seriously affect performance.

How Many Redo Logs and What Size?

Redo log files are separate from the database itself but are necessary to its operation. You must protect these files just as you protect the control files. If you lose or damage the redo log files, your only recourse will be to recover the database to its last full backup.

You specify the number of redo log files by setting the LOG_FILES parameter in the INIT.ORA file. The maximum value you can specify is the value of the MAXLOGFILES parameter in the CREATE DATABASE statement. As we've mentioned, most sites get the best performance if they create four or more redo logs, each at least 5 to 10 megabytes or larger.

However, sites that have an extremely heavy update activity and are having problems with the archive writer ARCH not being able to keep up with the log writer LGWR, can often overcome this problem by having up to eight redo logs of 30 megabytes spread across four disks. Disk1 will contain Redo1, Disk2 will contain Redo2, Disk3 will contain Redo3 and so on, as shown in Figure 9-6. The purpose of doing this is to ensure that the LGWR is not writing to the same disk as the ARCH is reading from, to avoid a disk I/O bottleneck.

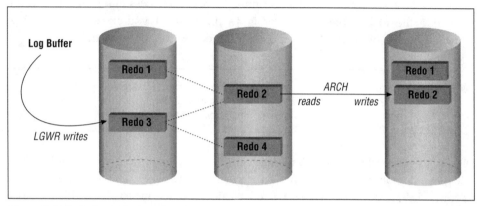

Figure 9-6. Redo log ping-ponging

You also can help the archiver to keep up by increasing the LOG_ARCHIVE_ BUFFERS and LOG_ARCHIVE_BUFFER_SIZE to the maximum allowable on your machine. You can also write a script that will wake up at regular intervals and issue the command ALTER SYSTEM ARCHIVE LOG ALL, which will spawn processes to archive any unarchived log in the thread. If you have fine-grained striping, you may stripe (RAID0 NOT RAID5) disks where your archive logs are to be placed. You must use small stripe sizes and mirror your archives (RAID1) if you are striping.

You must have a minimum of two redo log files to allow a database to operate. In this mode, the two files alternate as the current log file. As soon as the system finishes writing one file, it immediately starts writing to the next file. There is usually no advantage in having each of the two or three redo log files defined for your database on a separate disk if you are not running in archivelog mode (which we don't recommend). The system writes to only one file at a time, and only the current log file is needed for recovery.

The physical size of each log file is fixed at the time you create the file. The minimum size is 50 kilobytes. You don't gain anything by setting redo log files to varying sizes because all log files are used in a cyclical fashion under system control; a transaction cannot select a particular log file. Having several small redo logs and a much larger redo log will often cause the LGWR to wait for the larger redo log to be written to the archive log. This occurs because the log switches will occur quickly between the smaller redos and attempt to write to the larger redo while the ARCH process is still copying the larger redo log to the archive log.

If you are running under UNIX, there is an advantage to placing redo log files on the fastest disk drive available and using raw devices. However, don't make them run so fast that the archiver can't keep up. Never locate a redo log file on the same disk as a database file. The current log file is always required for instance recovery. If a disk crash occurs, you must be able to access either the database or the redo file to be able to recover it. In this case, if you have ARCHIVE LOG enabled, we recommend that you copy the archives to tape regularly.

| *NOTE* | If you do encounter the unfortunate experience of losing your current redo log, do not shut your instance down. Give the DBWR a chance to clear the dirty (modified) buffers to the database. |

Often, the redo file disk will have more I/O activity than the data and index disks. Be sure to monitor the I/O rates on a per-file basis when the database is active. To get the information that you need to figure out how to share the I/O load, double-check which files are performing what amount of activity.

The multiplexed redo log facility allows the log writer process (LGWR) to enhance recovery by writing to multiple redo logs simultaneously, as shown in Figure 9-7. This can be achieved equally effectively by using operating system mirroring. These features provide you with great recovery benefits; but if not managed correctly, they can pose some performance problems. The system writes heavily to the redo log files, and we recommend that each redo log file group be on a distinct disk. If you don't have enough disk devices, the next best thing is to put one redo log group on its own disk device and the other on the device that has the least amount of activity. In Figure 9-7, Redo1a file in Group 1 is written to at the same time as Redo1b in Group 1; Redo2a in Group 2 is written to at the same time as Redo2b in Group 2, and so on.

Creating the Tablespaces

Tablespaces are logical divisions of the database. You create a tablespace with the CREATE TABLESPACE command. A tablespace may contain one or more database files, specified in the DATAFILE clause of the command. These files may reside on any disk drive. You can also specify default storage for the tablespace in the DEFAULT STORAGE clause. Your tables, indexes, the Oracle data dictionary, and

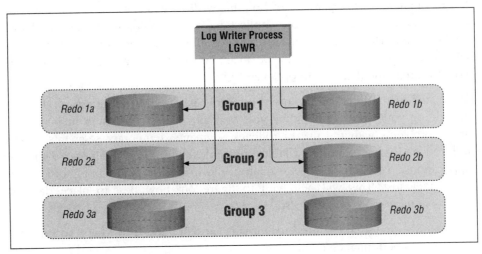

Figure 9-7. Multiplexed redo logs

temporary segments will use this default if they don't have specific storage parameters assigned to them.

When you create a table, index, cluster, or rollback segment, it will be created in a tablespace. If you don't specify which tablespace should be used for an object, the system uses the default for the user who owns the object.

To structure tablespaces for best performance:

- Spread the I/O load across disk devices and controllers.

- Allow the monitoring of the use of various parts of the database.

- Apply default storage allocations to speed up certain database options.

- Allow the flexibility to easily move objects from disk to disk if you encounter an I/O bottleneck.

- Take a particular application offline without affecting other applications.

- Reduce contention for database objects; for example, new rows can be inserted into the table while the indexes for the table use different tablespaces located on different disk devices.

- Provide logical data separation; for example, accounting data is separate from personnel data.

Do not let data files exceed 1 gigabyte unless absolutely necessary. We have seen performance drop on a number of minicomputer systems when files exceeded 1 gigabyte. Larger files may also stop you from being able to move database files from one disk to another.

We recommend that, regardless of how many disks you now have available, you create your tablespaces as if your applications were running in an ideal, multidisk environment. This allows you to monitor the load and spread it between tablespaces with the eventual aim of obtaining more disks and the knowledge of how to spread the database to optimize I/O.

Make sure that before you go into production, when your developers and testers are testing your applications, they give you all of the information they uncover about problems with the use of rollback segments, temporary segments, tables, indexes, and usage patterns of tables and indexes by the major programs in the applications. You can also get valuable information by monitoring disk usage while they test. This will help you to figure out how best to place database objects in the various tablespaces.

Figure 9-8 shows a tablespace breakdown that will allow you to spread your I/O load and do performance monitoring.

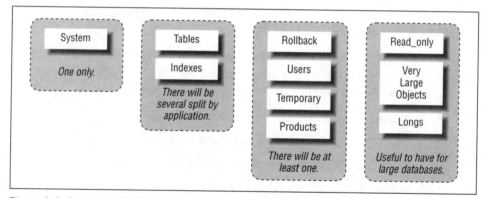

Figure 9-8. Recommended tablespaces

System Tablespace

When you create an Oracle database, that database is initialized with a system tablespace. The system tablespace contains the Oracle data dictionary, which holds information on tables, indexes, clusters, views, grants, synonyms, rollback segments, database files, tablespaces and their default storage parameters, valid users, and other information. The system tablespace is also the default home for all tables, indexes, rollback segments, and temporary tables that have not been explicitly directed to another tablespace. The only other information that you may store in the system tablespace is the small rollback segment that must exist before additional tablespaces can be added. Make sure that you don't allow any of your database objects to be stored in the system tablespace. If you do, this will limit your option to move different components of your database from one disk to another in order to spread disk I/O evenly and to set variable default storage parameters from one tablespace to the next.

A system tablespace usually requires only a small percentage of the overall database storage requirements. You must ensure, however, that enough free space is left for growth in the data dictionary and the deferred rollback segments. When you create the system tablespace, make sure it has about 75% free space. Give it a storage allocation of at least 50–100 megabytes for a medium- to large-size site. The tablespace stores packages, procedures, functions, and stored triggers in the system tables. If Oracle products such as SQL*Forms are going to be stored in the system tablespace (which is not recommended), make the system tablespace even larger.

A good policy is to not allow any database objects to be created in the system tablespace after its initial creation. You must remember to set all new users' default and temporary tablespaces to alternate tablespaces. If you don't, they will default to the system tablespace.

NOTE   It is important that you leave Oracle's default storage settings for the system tablespace intact. We have visited a few sites that have made the PCTINCREASE 0 on the system tablespace and, as a result, have extremely fragmented dictionary tables and associated poor performance. One site exceeded the maximum allowable extents on the tables that store packages and procedures. An alternative is to alter the storage setting in the SQL.BSQ files, which is the file where Oracle sets its dictionary table sizing. You must alter the file before you create your database. Use the sizes of your TEST database as a guide, and add on a percentage for the additional users you are likely to have in your production database.

Table Tablespaces

Table tablespaces store tables and clusters. If you have a large database, you will probably have more than one such tablespace. Tables that are commonly used together should ideally be split across multiple tablespaces. For even better performance, place the tablespaces on separate disk devices. It is also a good idea to balance the load by storing some commonly accessed tables in the same tablespace as some of those less commonly accessed.

You can improve performance a lot by splitting application tables into separate table tablespaces. This allows the application to be taken offline by taking the tablespace offline. Tables that are shared between applications can be stored in a separate tablespace. It is good practice to place very large tables into their own tablespace for performance and recoverability reasons. This allows you to carefully monitor I/Os on your larger tables as well as stripe the tables according to their usage.

Index Tablespaces

An index tablespace contains the indexes defined for a table. Try to put the tablespace for a particular index on a different disk device from the one that holds that index's table.

Some sites create one index tablespace per application. As with table tablespaces, it is a good idea to put frequently used indexes in the same tablespace as some that are less frequently used. If one of your tables has a high rate of insertions, you might consider placing some of that table's indexes on one disk and the other indexes on a different tablespace on another disk device. As with large tables, it is often beneficial to place large indexes into their own tablespaces.

Temporary Tablespace

It is important that you put temporary segments in their own separate tablespace. There are two main reasons for this: First, it lets you modify more easily the default table storage allocation so that you can make sure large, long-running jobs (for example, those that create indexes on very large tables) do not fail because they cannot acquire enough temporary segments. Second, it gives you a handy way to monitor the effectiveness of the SORT_AREA_SIZE parameter, which assigns memory to each user for sorting data. It is often handy to have a temporary tablespace set up for batch users TEMP_BATCH and an OLTP temporary tablespace TEMP_OLTP. Assign the appropriate users by using the TEMPORARY TABLESPACE clause of the CREATE USER and ALTER USER statements.

As we describe in the section in Chapter 11 called "Reducing Disk I/O by Increasing the Sort Area," Oracle tries to sort in memory; however, if SORT_AREA_SIZE is not large enough, some sort activity has to be moved to the temporary tablespace. By looking at the disk activity on the temporary tablespace, you will be able to figure out how much larger SORT_AREA_SIZE must be.

With tables, indexes, and rollback segments, you create tablespaces via the appropriate version of the CREATE command. You can't use this command for temporary tablespaces. The size of temporary segments depends entirely on the default storage setting you assign to the temporary tablespace using the command

```
ALTER TABLESPACE temp-tspace DEFAULT STORAGE [storage parameters]
```

Compute the most effective default storage size as follows:

1. Allocate one block for the segment header.

2. Add to that a size which is a multiple of the SORT_AREA_SIZE.

For example, if you have a DB_BLOCK_SIZE of 4 kilobytes and a SORT_AREA_ SIZE of 64 kilobytes, you may set the INITIAL and NEXT extents of 64K + 4K = 68K, or 128K + 4K =132K, or any other multiple.

WARNING   Never set your INITIAL extent size lower than your SORT_AREA_ SIZE. If it is smaller, you will be throwing additional extents before you even begin your sort.

Some sites have two temporary tablespaces: one with small INITIAL and NEXT extent sizes for high-volume online transaction processing users and a second temporary tablespace for longer-running jobs requiring larger sort areas and therefore larger INITIAL and NEXT extents. In Chapter 15, *Tuning Long-Running Jobs*, the section called "Resizing Temporary Tables" describes a procedure that you can follow to define daytime and nighttime temporary tablespaces.

Oracle7.3 introduced a new temporary tablespace type especially designed to tune Oracle sorting. It achieves this by eliminating serialization of space management. To use this facility, specify:

```
CREATE TABLESPACE oltp_tspace TEMPORARY;
```

Temporary tablespaces cannot contain permanent objects. To change a tablespace back to a tablespace that is able to store objects, use the command

```
ALTER TABLESPACE tspace PERMANENT;
```

You can also alter a tablespace from a PERMANENT tablespace to a temporary tablespace using the command

```
ALTER TABLESPACE tspace TEMPORARY;
```

All sorts in a temporary tablespace use a single sort segment and allocate space using a table called the sort segment table that coordinates disk access.

You can monitor the performance of your TEMPORARY tablespace by viewing the entry "sort extent pool latch" in the V$LATCH table. If the latch contention is significant, consider increasing swapping some of the usage across to another temporary tablespace, as well as adjusting the INITIAL and NEXT storage parameters on your temporary tablespace. There is a table called V$SORT_SEGMENTS that contains information about all of the sort segments that have been produced.

User Tablespaces

In some systems, your users can create their own tables. However, you might want to monitor these tables to make sure performance won't suffer because users are creating an excessive number of tables. If you find that users are indiscriminately creating tables and performance is suffering, separating this activity into a user tablespace gives you the option to move this activity to a separate database using an extract from the production database or to encourage users to do their work during nonpeak hours.

GUI users often make ad hoc requests for application data. To accommodate such users you can create extract tables (which resemble spreadsheets) in overnight batch procedures and place them in the users' tablespaces. These extract tables eliminate the need for the GUI users to have a detailed understanding of complex data models and avoids having to requery the same foundation tables over and over again. Placing extract tables in the user tablespaces also allows you to monitor all ad hoc GUI queries against your database.

Rollback Segment Tablespace

Because rollback segments usually have such a high level of activity, we recommend that you spread them across a number of disks and put them in separate tablespaces or stripe the rollback segment across the disk using a striped tablespace or operating system striping. If you are using operating system striping, it is best to use RAID0 and RAID1 (striping without parity and mirroring) rather than RAID5 (striping with parity).

Another method that sites use to distribute rollback I/O across disks is to have a number of rollback segment tablespaces. If you create three rollback segment tablespaces, you then create your rollbacks in the sequence ROLLB_1 in tablespace ROLLB_TSPACE1, ROLLB_2 in ROLLB_TSPACE3, ROLLB_3 in ROLLB_TSPACE3, ROLLB4 in ROLLB_TSPACE1, ROLLB_5 in ROLLB_TSPACE2, and so on. Oracle assigns transactions to rollbacks in a round-robin fashion, with transaction1 getting the rollback segment created first, transaction2 getting the rollback created second and so on, as shown in Figure 9-9.

You can monitor rollback segment activity by means of the DBA monitoring screen that you invoke via the SQL*DBA function or by using the V$ROLLSTAT table:

```
SQLDBA> MON R
```

(See the discussion of MONITOR in the section in Chapter 10, *Diagnostic and Tuning Tools*, called "MONITOR: Monitoring System Activity Tables.")

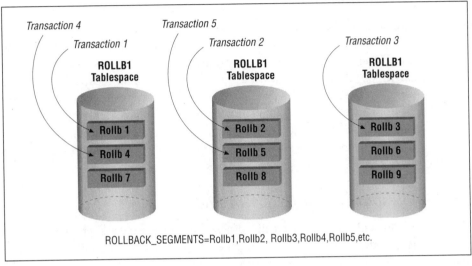

Transaction 4   Transaction 5

Transaction 1   Transaction 2   Transaction 3

ROLLB1   ROLLB1   ROLLB1
Tablespace   Tablespace   Tablespace

Rollb 1   Rollb 2   Rollb 3

Rollb 4   Rollb 5   Rollb 6

Rollb 7   Rollb 8   Rollb 9

ROLLBACK_SEGMENTS=Rollb1,Rollb2, Rollb3,Rollb4,Rollb5,etc.

Figure 9-9. Rollback segment splitting

If you make sure that rollbacks are put in their own tablespaces, you keep the rollback activity from interfering with the activity of the other tablespaces (for example, a tablespace containing tables that are being monitored).

Products Tablespace

If you don't tell Oracle where to place products such as SQL*Forms and SQL*Menu, the system will put them in the system tablespace. If you have not allocated enough space for these products, serious performance problems can occur. These problems will have an impact both on the programmers who are trying to generate programs using product tables and on QA staff and production users who are using products such as SQL*Menu. Sites that put their products in the system tablespace find themselves struggling for contiguous extents because product tables expand quickly.

For performance reasons, define a separate products tablespace, at least in the development database. Loading large SQL*Forms library forms, SQL*Reportwriter programs, and SQL*Menu menus can cause product tables and indexes to grow in size very quickly. It is quite common to see a table or index exceed the maximum number of extents. For best results, assign a storage allocation of INITIAL 200K and NEXT 200K to the products tablespace.

If you want to move your products tables from the system tablespace, export them and rebuild them with new sizes that allow for growth. Then, re-import the product data on a regular basis to maintain acceptable performance.

Large Object Tablespaces

As we mentioned earlier, placing very large tables and indexes in their own tablespaces can provide significant advantages in terms of both performance and recoverability. From the performance perspective, it allows you to closely monitor the I/O activity of the table by viewing the tablespace's data files read and write statistics using the V$FILESTAT view. It allows you to stripe the object for absolute best performance, using Oracle striping or operating system striping. It also avoids your having to rebuild a huge table and its indexes into new tablespaces if you find that the tablespace containing the large table or index and other objects has excessive I/Os.

LOB Tablespaces and External Files

Oracle8 has dramatically improved the processing of long data, such as video text and images, with the introduction of the BLOB, CLOB, NCLOB, and BFILE datatypes. The columns can be up to 4 gigabytes in size. The BLOB and CLOB datatypes can be stored in a separate tablespace from the rest of the table. The BFILE columns can be stored in a file external to the database, which can provide a huge performance boost. If your database has a large number of LOB columns, create your database with a DB_BLOCK_SIZE of 8 or 16 kilobytes (if allowable on your operating system) to avoid the possibility of chaining. You must set the DB_BLOCK_SIZE when you first build your database.

Number of Database Files per Tablespace

Ideally, you should place each tablespace into a single data file and make sure the data file is contiguous on the disk. The exception to this rule occurs when you are using table striping. With striping, you create a tablespace with a number of database files where each file is the same size and is placed onto a separate disk. You then create the table to be striped with its minimum number of extents set to the same number as the number and size of database files. The table is assigned the tablespace containing the multiple files. This is particularly useful for very large objects in decision support systems. The parallel query option in Oracle7.2 and later is able to recognize that the table is spread across multiple Oracle extents on different disks and to optimize the number of parallel query servers assigned to the task. (See Chapter 13.)

If you are forced to add a data file to a tablespace, try to add it to the same disk device as the disk that contains the original data file of the tablespace. The reason for this is that usually, the major purpose of creating the tablespace is to spread I/O across disk devices. If the second data file is placed onto a different disk device, this will make it difficult to predict how much of the tablespace load will go onto each disk device. Placing your second data file onto a second disk device may be unavoidable because of the free space available. If several tablespaces contain data files that are spread across multiple disks, consider restructuring your database.

Striping Your Data Files

Disk I/O has always been a sore point in tuning databases. As symmetric multi-processing (SMP) and, to a lesser extent, massively parallel processing (MPP), have had an increasing impact on users, these technologies have placed more and more pressure on disks to perform quickly. Disk striping can improve disk I/O substantially. However, if it's used inappropriately, it has the potential to make your disk I/O run considerably more slowly. Worse still, it may also leave you in a vulnerable position if you need to recover your database. Pay close attention to the guidelines in the following sections.

NOTE   You can use the operating system to stripe files that have been creat-ed by using Oracle striping. This structure produces pleasing perfor-mance improvements with the parallel query option available in Oracle7.2.

Operating system striping and mirroring

Operating system striping and mirroring have revolutionized disk storage. RAID has become extremely popular because it provides you with recoverability capa-bilities as well as the potential for performance improving. The following provides a brief description of the various RAID levels that can assist performance:

RAID 0

Stripes a file across disks without performing any parity or redundancy checks. If the file is spread across four disks and any one of the four disks has a failure, the data file is destroyed and requires recovery. RAID 0 provides excellent performance improvements by spreading I/O load across disks, but ideally, you should combine it with RAID 1 (mirroring).

RAID 1

This implementation of RAID mirrors disks, with each disk drive storing iden-tical information. Each disk operation writes to each disk. RAID 1 provides excellent recovery and can also speed up query response times because the data can be read from both sides of the mirror to avoid disk I/O bottlenecks. There is an overhead in maintaining two copies of the data; the amount of overhead varies in its effect on performance, depending on hardware platform.

RAID 5

This implementation offers striping with the addition of parity. This means that you can stripe your file over multiple disks, lose a disk, and the file will still be able to continue to be used. RAID5 does not require mirroring. RAID 5 tends to cause a performance degradation if your applications have a high number of inserts, updates, and deletes and assist with the performance of queries. It will usually degrade performance on rollback segment tablespaces, redo logs, temporary tablespaces, and archive logs, as well as any other data file that experiences a high number of inserts, updates, and deletes. The degradation is caused by the fact that an additional parity block write is required for each write to the file.

General RAID recommendations

Follow these guidelines to get the best results from the use of RAID technology:

*   Use RAID 0 (striping no parity) and RAID 1 (mirroring) on your redo logs. Redo logs are hit extremely heavily and are prone to disk I/O bottlenecks. These bottlenecks result from changes being written to your database, and the fact that the changes are read from heavily at checkpoint time by the archive process. It is important that the stripe size be very small (e.g., 8, 16, or 32 kilobytes), because of the way that Oracle writes serially from the log buffer to the redo logs. Oracle writes when the log buffer reaches one-third full (two-thirds in Oracle7.3 and later), which is the norm for batch processing and for OLTP processing if you have an undersized LOG_BUFFER. It usually writes as a result of a transaction issuing a commit in OLTP applications if the amount of data is much less than one-third (or two-thirds) of the log buffer. Oracle can write several committed transactions in a single write, however. This tells us that batch applications will benefit more from having the redo logs striped, but only if the stripe size is divisible into one-third (or two-thirds) of the log buffer size. OLTP applications are often not able to take full advantage of the striping because the size of the changes being written may be too small to spread beyond the first disk being striped.

WARNING   If you have archivelog enabled, you may find that speeding up your redo logs by using striping and using raw devices (if you are using UNIX) creates a problem. Your redos will switch so quickly that your ARCH process won't be able to keep up, and you will continually have waits. The LGWR process will have to wait for the ARCH process to clear an old redo log that is yet to be archived. Some sites prefer not to stripe their redos for this reason.

- RAID 0 (striping without parity) works very well on all machines that we have used, for both OLTP and batch processing data files. It assists query response times, as well as update, insert, and delete response times. To avoid disk I/O bottlenecks, you must stripe if you are using the parallel query option, and RAID 0 provides the ideal striping architecture. It does not provide you with recoverability, however, so it should ideally be used with mirroring (RAID 1). Remember that your data file is lost if any one of the disks in the stripe is lost. And don't forget to run in archivelog mode. You can still mistakenly drop or corrupt a table in the striped file!

- If you are using mirroring (RAID 1) as your backup/recovery strategy, we usually recommend that you run your database in archivelog mode as an alternative recovery strategy. If you drop a table in your database or remove a data file by mistake, the mirrored copy will also be removed. We have seen sites improve their query times by mirroring, because Oracle users can read from both sides of the mirror to avoid disk I/O bottlenecks.

- RAID 5 (striping with parity) can cause performance degradation if your system has a high rate of inserts, updates, and deletes. It provides recoverability capabilities by allowing the database to continue operating even if you have lost one of the disks in the stripe set. If you happen to lose a disk, performance will be so slow that it is best to recover the system using Oracle's recovery procedures. Make sure that you benchmark the types of response times that you will receive if you lose a disk to make sure that it is acceptable to your users. If you remove a file or a table in a RAID 5 data file, remember that you can potentially lose huge amounts of data unless you have archivelog enabled in your database. RAID 5 is a popular choice in decision support databases, where nightly data loads can be run overnight without affecting your users. During the day, the users are query-only. We don't recommend RAID 5 for OLTP databases. *Please* don't use it on your redo logs!

- Ideally, you should benchmark your selected RAID configuration from a performance, as well as a recoverability, point of view. RAID 5, in particular, should be carefully benchmarked. Don't use RAID for RAID's sake. Often, a properly configured non-RAID database will provide performance superior to that of a RAID database.

- Ensure that the people implementing RAID have a good knowledge of all of the Oracle database components, and make sure they don't stripe redo logs across the same disks where the database files are located—or, worse still, place the archive logs onto the same disks as the database files.

Oracle striping

Oracle striping can best be described as the "forgotten striping." Very few sites use it, and it provides very few performance improvements. However, with the release of the parallel query option (PQO) and Oracle7.2 (which introduced intelligent PQO usage across Oracle stripes), we are bound to see an increased use of Oracle striping. Benchmarks indicate that PQO using Oracle striping can provide better response times than can operating system striping. You can even have the best of both worlds, using operating system striping to stripe the Oracle striped files.

To set up Oracle striping, use the following syntax:

```
CREATE TABLESPACE acctrans_history_tspace
        DATAFILE '/disk1/database/ACCTRANS_HISTORY_1' size 500000K,
                 '/disk2/database/ACCTRANS_HISTORY_1' size 500000K,
                 '/disk3/database/ACCTRANS_HISTORY_1' size 500000K,
                 '/disk4/database/ACCTRANS_HISTORY_1' size 500000K,
                 '/disk5/database/ACCTRANS_HISTORY_1' size 500000K;
CREATE TABLE acctrans_history
        (account_no       number(10) not null,
         trans_date         date,
         trans_descn        varchar2(1000),
         trans_amount    number(14,2),
         trans_type         varchar2(2))
 TABLESPACE acctrans_history_tspace
 STORAGE (INITIAL 499995K NEXT 499995K
         MINEXTENTS 5       PCTINCREASE 0);
```

Setting the MINEXTENTS equal to 5 forces all five data files, one on each disk, to be used immediately. Notice that the extents are marginally smaller than the extents. This is to allow for table extent overheads. Some sites have also achieved good I/O spread by creating their rollback segments, so each fits nicely into the Oracle stripes.

Coalescing Tablespaces and Deallocating Unused Space

Oracle7.3 introduced a new command, ALTER TABLESPACE tspace COALESCE, which improves space management and the performance of objects that require additional extents. This command coalesces free extents in the tablespace into larger contiguous extents on a per file basis. A new view DBA_FREE_SPACE_COALESCED has been introduced to monitor the percentage of free extents in the tablespace have been coalesced. The lower the percentage of coalesced extents, the greater the need to perform the ALTER TABLESPACE command.

```
# coalescd.dql
SELECT tablespace_name, total_extents, extents_coalesced,
```

```
percent_extents_coalesced
FROM dba_free_space_coalesced;
```

Oracle7.2 introduced a useful feature that allows you to release unused space in a segment and return it for use by other segments. This was performed by a package called DBMS_SPACE. Oracle7.3 went one better by introducing the following command:

```
ALTER TABLE tablename DEALLOCATE UNUSED [KEEP (integer)];
```

which allows you to deallocate space for the selected table, keeping the integer value number of free bytes as specified in the KEEP clause. Unfortunately, the space is freed only after the high-water mark, that is, the furthest point in the table that the inserts have reached. You can also deallocate space in an index, which will often avoid a huge index rebuild using the command

```
ALTER INDEX indexname DEALLOCATE UNUSED [KEEP (integer)];
```

You can free space from a cluster using the command

```
ALTER CLUSTER clustername DEALLOCATE UNUSED [KEEP (integer)];
```

Setting Default Storage for Tablespaces

Before you assign storage allocations for your tablespaces via the DEFAULT STORAGE clause, make sure you understand extents: contiguous pieces of database storage that may contain data or may be free to be used by a table, an index, or another object that needs more storage. When a tablespace is first created, it will have one extent that will be equal in size to the tablespace. Figure 9-10 illustrates how extents are used.

When a segment (e.g., a table) is dropped from the database, all of its extents become available for other segments. Because this space is a multiple of all other segment storage sizes, when a smaller segment uses the space, a usable fragment still remains.

If the minimum application storage size is set to 50 kilobytes, all subsequent (larger) storage clauses should only be multiples of this base (e.g., 100 kilobytes, 500 kilobytes, 750 kilobytes, 10 megabytes, 20 megabytes). This prevents the creation of smaller, useless fragments of database storage that cannot be used until the database is rebuilt.

Setting default storage parameters

There is no need to assign storage parameters individually on very small tables. Simply leave them with the default storage settings if they have been created

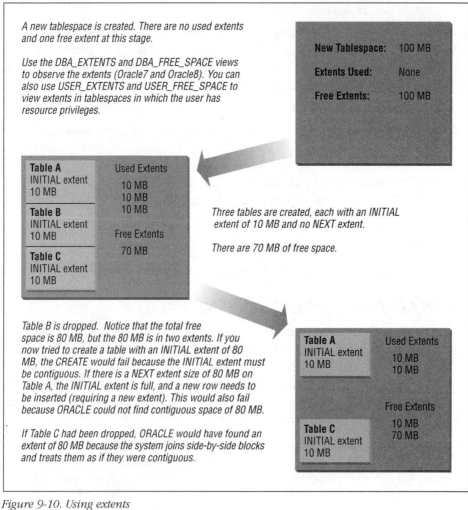

A new tablespace is created. There are no used extents and one free extent at this stage.

Use the DBA_EXTENTS and DBA_FREE_SPACE views to observe the extents (Oracle7 and Oracle8). You can also use USER_EXTENTS and USER_FREE_SPACE to view extents in tablespaces in which the user has resource privileges.

New Tablespace:	100 MB
Extents Used:	None
Free Extents:	100 MB

Table A
INITIAL extent
10 MB

Used Extents
10 MB
10 MB
10 MB

Table B
INITIAL extent
10 MB

Free Extents
70 MB

Table C
INITIAL extent
10 MB

Three tables are created, each with an INITIAL extent of 10 MB and no NEXT extent.

There are 70 MB of free space.

Table B is dropped. Notice that the total free space is 80 MB, but the 80 MB is in two extents. If you now tried to create a table with an INITIAL extent of 80 MB, the CREATE would fail because the INITIAL extent must be contiguous. If there is a NEXT extent size of 80 MB on Table A, the INITIAL extent is full, and a new row needs to be inserted (requiring a new extent). This would also fail because ORACLE could not find contiguous space of 80 MB.

If Table C had been dropped, ORACLE would have found an extent of 80 MB because the system joins side-by-side blocks and treats them as if they were contiguous.

Table A
INITIAL extent
10 MB

Used Extents
10 MB
10 MB

Free Extents
10 MB
70 MB

Table C
INITIAL extent
10 MB

Figure 9-10. Using extents

appropriately at the tablespace level. All table, system, user, and index tablespaces could have the following default:

```
STORAGE    (INITIAL      10K
            NEXT          10K
            MINEXTENTS    1
            MAXEXTENTS    100
            PCTINCREASE   1 )
```

Prior to Oracle7.3, you cannot exceed the maximum possible extents on your machine. If you have a DB_BLOCK_SIZE of 2 kilobytes, you will have 121 maximum extents, whereas if your machine has a 4 kilobyte block size, you will have 249 maximum extents. If you are using Oracle7.3 or later, you can now set MAXEXTENTS UNLIMITED.

Set your temporary tablespace default storage parameters as a multiple of the SORT_AREA_SIZE parameter plus one block for the online transaction processing. If your block size is 4 kilobytes and your sort area size is 64 kilobytes, you may specify:

```
4K + (64K * 4) = 260K
```

as both your INITIAL and NEXT extents. With this size, the block is used for the segment header and the multiple of the SORT_AREA_SIZE because this allows a resource-efficient transfer of the sort area memory buffer to the temporary segment. Some sites set the PCTINCREASE to 100, which doubles the size of each NEXT extent.

To help prevent database fragmentation, make sure all segment storage classes have a common denominator. INITIAL extent and NEXT extent values must all be divisible by this denominator.

Setting PCTINCREASE

By setting the PCTINCREASE STORAGE parameter to 0% or 100%, you can prevent accidentally generating storage extents that are not a multiple of the application base. In Figure 9-11 the INITIAL extent is 1.5 megabyte, and the first NEXT extent is 1 megabyte. Because PCTINCREASE has been set to 50%, each additional NEXT extent will be 50% larger than the previous one.

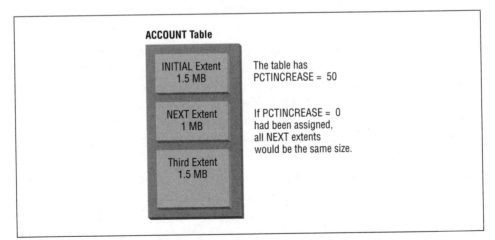

Figure 9-11. Adjusting the PCTINCREASE variable

To appreciate why a PCTINCREASE of 50 is so dangerous, look at the figures in the following table. Assume that we have a table that has an INITIAL extent of 5 megabytes and a NEXT extent of 1 megabyte. Note that each NEXT extent is rounded up to the nearest five blocks.

Extent	Megabytes
Extent 1	5
Extent 2	1
Extent 3	1.5
Extent 4	2.25
Extent 5	3.37
Extent 6	5
Extent 7	7.5
Extent 8	11.2
Extent 9	16.8
Extent 10	25.2
Extent 11	37.7
Extent 12	55.7
Extent 13	83.5
Extent 14	125.2

Leaving PCTINCREASE at its default of 50 can be dangerous. If you add one row of data after the 13th extent, you will require more than 125 megabytes of contiguous extent space. There is a very strong possibility that a contiguous extent of 125 megabytes will not be available. This will produce an Oracle error message and will disallow the extension. It's also a huge waste of database space, because the last extent will often contain very few rows.

Segment extents are issued from the free extent list according to a first-fit algorithm. The first free space block that is large enough to accommodate the extent requirement is used, and any unused portion of the extent is returned to the free space list. If a free extent cannot be located, a second pass of the free list is made, attempting to join side-by-side blocks into a single extent. Having all database extents as a multiple of the common denominator means joining free blocks to prevent generating useless fragments.

Another interesting effect of the PCTINCREASE is the impact on the SMON process, which coalesces adjoining extents. If the PCTINCREASE is set to 0, SMON will not automatically coalesce the adjoining extents. This is a bonus at some sites, because the SMON process can be the largest consumer of disk I/O. If the PCTINCREASE is set to a value greater than 0, it will coalesce extents. We recommend that you set your PCTINCREASE to 1 unless your SMON process is too active, in which case you should set it to 0. If you are using Oracle7.3 or later, you can leave the value at 0 and use the ALTER TABLESPACE COALESCE command during low activity times on your database. Other sites can set the PCTINCREASE to 1 overnight and set it to 0 for peak processing times using the ALTER TABLESPACE DEFAULT STORAGE clause.

Creating Rollback Segments

Rollback segments enforce read consistency within your database. They store data as they existed before an update. These data can be used to restore the database to a consistent state, as it was at an earlier point in time. If you are changing data and decide in midstream that you don't want to commit the changes after all, rollbacks give you a way to "roll back" the changes and return the data to their original form. If other users want to read the data you are in the midst of changing, rollbacks give them a way of reading the data as they were before the changes.

You create a rollback segment with the CREATE ROLLBACK SEGMENT statement. You specify the size allocation for a rollback segment in the STORAGE clause of the statement. You can subsequently modify a rollback statement with the ALTER ROLLBACK SEGMENT and DROP ROLLBACK SEGMENT statements. Oracle also provides public rollback segments that are designed to be used for shared disk systems—those in which multiple instances access one database. Public rollback segments are created, altered, and dropped by adding the word PUBLIC after the CREATE, ALTER, and DROP keywords; for example:

```
CREATE PUBLIC ROLLBACK SEGMENT
```

Rollback segments exist inside database files assigned to a tablespace. If you incorrectly structure your rollbacks, you can seriously degrade the performance of your system by causing excessive disk I/Os or by allowing user transactions to suffer contention for rollback segment headers. Rollbacks are very I/O-intensive in databases in which a lot of data changes occur. If this I/O is not distributed evenly across disk devices, there is potential for I/O bottlenecks. Contention for rollbacks occurs because every time writes are made to a rollback segment, the rollback header segment is locked. The header is freed after the write is completed. This contention is avoided by having sufficient rollback segments.

Rollback segments are the most difficult storage components to understand and tune. Figure 9-12 shows a single rollback segment that may have one or many transactions writing to it. When a transaction makes a change to data, all of the before-image data must be written into the rollback extents. In the figure, if there is insufficient space in the four existing extents, another extent is allocated to the rollback. This now becomes part of the rollback ring that Oracle will loop around and use for future changes.

It is possible to set the optimal size for the rollback to shrink back to. To force the rollback to shrink back to its original four extents, specify an OPTIMAL 40-kilobyte clause in the CREATE ROLLBACK statement. We recommend strongly that you do not use the OPTIMAL clause if the number of shrinks is significant. If you are using Oracle7.3, use the ALTER ROLLBACK SEGMENT SHRINK command as an alternative, and shrink the rollbacks outside prime usage times.

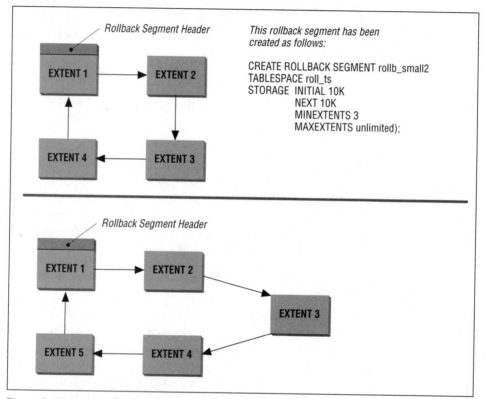

Figure 9-12. Using rollback segments

Oracle offers a way to change the storage of a rollback segment dynamically by using the command:

```
ALTER ROLLBACK rollb_10 STORAGE (NEXT 100M MAXEXTENTS 100);
```

You cannot modify the INITIAL or MINEXTENTS parameters without recreating the rollback segment. You can take the rollback offline, drop the rollback, and then recreate it to its optimal size and specify:

```
ALTER ROLLBACK rollb_10 ONLINE;
```

If you plan to set the MAXEXTENTS UNLIMITED using the Oracle7.3 functionality, you must take the tablespace offline first. You must also have at least four blocks for each rollback segment extent.

To structure your rollback segments correctly, you must perform some background research on the number and types of transactions that are performed at your site. You must know the number of concurrent Oracle transactions and the type of transaction (online transaction with short, sharp updates or larger, long-running updates or queries).

You must be flexible in your choice of rollback segments. If your site has one type of transaction during prime daily working hours and another type of transaction for overnight jobs, you may use smaller rollback segments for daily processing and enlarged rollback segments for overnight processing.

We recommend that you place the rollback segments into one or more tablespaces set up specifically for rollback segments.

Be aware of the following:

- One rollback is created automatically in the system tablespace when the database is first created.

- You must have at least one nonsystem segment, as well as the system rollback segment that is created at the time of database creation to add additional tablespaces.

- Every rollback segment that is created must have at least two extents.

- Transactions cannot write to multiple rollback segments at once.

- A transaction can write to only one extent at any given time.

- You can specify the rollback segment that you wish to use in a transaction by issuing the SET TRANSACTION USE ROLLBACK statement. Take advantage of this but be aware of its limitations. The SET TRANSACTION USE ROLLBACK statement must be the first statement that is issued after connecting to Oracle or immediately following a ROLLBACK, COMMIT or DDL (CREATE TABLE, CREATE INDEX etc.) statement. If you connect as another user, perform a rollback, or perform a commit, you will have to reissue the command.

- Oracle will share rollback segments among the various transactions if you don't specifically assign the transaction to a rollback segment.

How Many Rollback Segments?

As the amount of data being modified in a table increases, the amount of rollback space required increases proportionately. There must be enough space in your tablespace to store your rollback segment data.

The number of rollback segments must be large enough to eliminate contention for rollback segment usage. When you are figuring out how many rollback segments you need, take into account the number of active transactions, the type of transactions, and the transactions per rollback segment.

If you have 20 rollback segments and 20 transactions, Oracle will use all 20 rollbacks, assigning one transaction to each rollback. A reasonable rule of thumb is one rollback segment per four transactions for online transaction processing. Although this recommendation provides acceptable performance, for some sites you might want to allocate more. Our tests have shown minor improvements in response times of 5% to 10% when we allocated one 10-kilobyte rollback segment to all transactions. When the transactions are all online transaction processing performing small numbers of database updates, smaller rollback segments increase the chance that a particular rollback is available in the buffer cache in the SGA.

Creating a large number of rollback segments carries an administrative overhead. If you have a large number of small rollback segments (e.g., 8 kilobytes), Oracle warns that long-running queries, such as online reports that may run for several minutes, may experience problems if transactions frequently update records that are required by the query. The message "SNAPSHOT IS TOO OLD" is displayed because all queries must obtain the data as they were when the query started.

Consider the following example: Suppose that a change has been made to a large table that is currently being queried on, and the change has been committed. Committed changes are no longer required and can be overwritten in the rollback segment. Many other updates have also occurred using the same rollback segment. Eventually, the extent that contained the data as they were before the committed change are overwritten by another transaction requiring rollback space in the rollback ring. The query can't obtain the data for the long-running query as they existed when the query started, and the query fails and must be rerun.

We have discovered that sites that perform large numbers of updates get considerably better performance (often improvements of more than 50%) when they assign larger rollback segments. We recommend that you use fewer, larger rollback segments for overnight processing because such overnight jobs are more likely to contain long-running updates that will speed up considerably by avoiding dynamic extension.

If your mix of jobs includes a few long-running jobs and many smaller transactions, you will get better performance if you have one or more larger rollbacks, as shown in Figure 9-13. Figure out how large the rollback segment needs to be by looking at the results of QA testing. You can specify the SET TRANSACTION USE ROLLBACK SEGMENT command to set at least one rollback segment to the largest size taken from the production simulation. If you use this statement consistently for all long-running jobs, you will avoid the chance that larger transactions will use rollbacks that are too small and thus need many extents, which would result in bad performance. By using this version of the SET TRANSACTION statement, you will effectively assign the larger transactions to the larger rollbacks. The smaller transactions will then have a high probability of running against the smaller rollbacks, although it can't be guaranteed because rollbacks are blindly assigned in round-robin fashion, regardless of their size. For smaller rollback segments, assign 8 kilobytes or something similar to increase the possibility that these segments will be able to be held in cache.

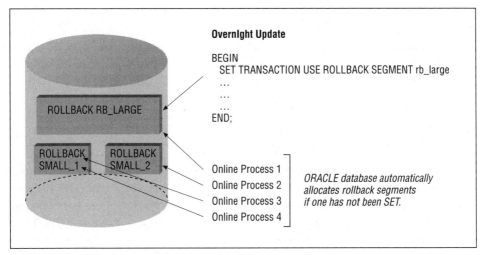

Figure 9-13. Rollback segment for overnight jobs

Rollback segment usage can be extremely high at some sites. At such sites, some DBAs prefer to place the rollbacks into one or two separate tablespaces. Others prefer to place the rollbacks into other tablespaces, such as those set up to store tables. We recommend very strongly that you place your rollbacks into tablespaces that are set up especially to store rollback segments.

Remember that from a performance point of view, your main goals are to spread I/O evenly across disk drives, avoid dynamic extension, and eliminate contention for rollback segments. You can check to see how effective your rollbacks are by examining the disk I/Os on the tablespaces and disk devices that contain rollback segments. You can detect rollback contention by looking for excessive I/O, the "buffer busy waits" statistic, the V$ROLLSTAT WAITS column, and the V$WAIT-STAT table. (See Chapter 11.)

Setting Rollback Segment Size

Picking the right size for your rollback segments can have an important effect on performance. You'll reduce dynamic extension and increase the chances that rollbacks will be stored in the buffer cache when needed.

To specify the size of your rollback segments, use the same STORAGE parameters that you use for any other data object.

```
CREATE ROLLBACK SEGMENT rolb_onight
    TABLESPACE rolb_large_tspace
    STORAGE (INITIAL        5M
             NEXT           5M
             MINEXTENTS     4
             MAXEXTENTS     UNLIMITED)
```

In this example, MINEXTENTS 4 indicates that the rollback is to be created with 4 * 5 megabytes per extent, or a total of 20 megabytes. This is a typical setting for four transactions.

Note the following:

- The PCTINCREASE parameter is not allowed for rollback segments. Oracle effectively forces a PCTINCREASE value of 0.

- Prior to Oracle7.3, the MAXEXTENTS parameter may not exceed the extents allowable by the DB_BLOCK_SIZE setting. For example, if your DB_BLOCK_SIZE is 2K, you will have a MAXENTENTS of 121. Oracle7.3 and later versions of the RDBMS allow an unlimited number of extents using MAXEXTENTS UNLIMITED. This does not mean that you should be profligate in the use of extents in your database! Throwing many extents means poor performance.

- The OPTIMAL parameter specifies the size that the rollback will shrink back to after it has expanded beyond its specified optimal size. In the preceding example, the ideal optimal size is 20 megabytes, which is the value you'd get by multiplying MINEXTENTS * extents. We recommend that you don't set OPTIMAl if you have a high rate of shrinkage.

  You might specify:

```
CREATE ROLLBACK SEGMENT rolb_onight
    TABLESPACE rolb_tspace
    STORAGE (INITIAL        5M
             NEXT           5M
             MINEXTENTS     4
             MAXEXTENTS     UNLIMITED
             OPTIMAL        40M)
```

If the database that you are creating is a production database and you're loading an application that has been tested in a QA environment containing a reasonable amount of data, try running a transaction mix that is similar to the one the application will use in production, and note the rollback segment sizes. This ensures that the rollback segments will be able to provide satisfactory performance regardless of the rollback selected. It also means, however, that you may be wasting database space on rollbacks.

If your application is an online transaction-processing system with only small transactions, keep your rollback segments to 10 kilobytes in size to increase the chances that they will be able to be stored in cache. If the rollbacks are small, it is common to have one rollback segment per transaction. If you have long-running queries that are querying large amounts of data that are being changed, you may get the error "SNAPSHOT TOO OLD."

Like other segments, rollback segments must be able to acquire enough space to hold their data. From an application perspective, if many extents are required to place the data, serious performance problems will often result. Be sure that you set INITIAL and NEXT parameters high enough to reduce the number of extents. Set MAXEXTENTS high enough to ensure that rollback segments do not exceed the maximum extents. In Oracle7.3 and later, set MAXEXTENTS UNLIMITED.

Rollback Checklist

The following list summarizes the main guidelines to follow in creating rollback segments:

- Use large rollbacks for long-running updates.

- Use small rollbacks for online transaction processing systems.

- Do not have too many transactions per rollback segment because this significantly increases the chance of rollback segment header contention.

- As a rule of thumb, assume four concurrent transactions per rollback for acceptable performance. This setting may need to be modified to suit the usage of your database. Use the recommendations in Chapter 11 to obtain the optimal number of rollback segments for your site.

- Use the SET TRANSACTION USE ROLLBACK SEGMENT statement to assign users to large rollback segments for all long-running updates. Keep all other rollback segments small to increase their chances of being held in buffer cache.

- Consider taking advantage of the OPTIMAL option in the STORAGE clause that allows rollbacks to shrink back in size. Be aware that if the number of shrinks per day exceeds a handful, there can be a negative effect on performance during the shrinking back process and its associated locking. We usually leave the OPTIMAL setting at its default null, which does not shrink your rollback segments.

- Never set MAXEXTENTS higher than your maximum allowable. Prior to Oracle7.3 you will get an error if the amount is exceeded. Use UNLIMITED with Oracle7.3 or later.

Creating Tables

Setting appropriate sizes for your tables boosts performance in your system. If you don't allocate enough space for a table, Oracle will be forced to perform dynamic extension on your tables (i.e., allocate more extents for them during processing). Dynamic extension, described in the section later in this chapter called "Reducing Dynamic Extension," has an extremely bad effect on performance.

You create a table with the CREATE TABLE statement. In this statement, you specify a size allocation in a series of parameter clauses, described in the text that follows. You can associate a table with a tablespace via the TABLESPACE clause. You can later modify a table via the ALTER TABLE statement or by dropping the table via DROP and then recreating it. Note that the INITIAL extent size and the tablespace assigned to the table cannot be changed via the ALTER command. To change these, you must drop and recreate the table with the new storage parameters.

You can change the NEXT extent size on the fly using the command:

```
ALTER TABLE tname STORAGE (NEXT 100M);
```

This ensures that you find an extent size that exists in your tablespace and that the extent is large enough to avoid exceeding maximum extents. You can also adjust your PCTFREE, using the ALTER TABLE command to avoid chaining problems for all new blocks added to your table. You can use this option when you have detected chaining on a table and wish to keep future rows being inserted into the tables from suffering the same fate.

NOTE   Oracle7.3 allows an unlimited number of extents per object.

Specifying the Tablespace

When you create a table, you can specify its tablespace in the TABLESPACE clause of the CREATE TABLE statement. If tables are frequently joined during processing (e.g., EMP and DEPT), separating these tables into separate tablespaces on different disks will usually improve performance, especially if the tablespaces can be placed onto separate devices. Place all of your tables into a dedicated table tablespace (that is, a tablespace that is used only for table storage).

Calculating the Size of the Table

If at all possible, size your tables so each table fits into one contiguous extent, and with no row chaining or row migration. (Figure 2-7 in Chapter 2, *What Causes Performance Problems?*, shows an example of chaining.) Be sure to set up the table so that it can grow over time and still fit in the single extent. The exception is if you wish to use Oracle's parallel query option and Oracle striping. If you do wish to use PQO, set the number of extents over the number of disks that you wish to spread your I/O across (See Chapter 13). A rule of thumb is to allow for 12 months' growth, but be prepared to rebuild the table every nine months or so.

To be able to allocate the proper size for a table, you must know the following: how many rows the table will contain when the database is first created, how much the rows will expand after the row has been created, and the expected growth in number of rows over the next year. Try to estimate as well how many rows are likely to be deleted from the table. By looking at the results of QA testing at your site, you should be able to get a more precise estimate of how quickly a row is likely to grow. Find out the length of the rows when first created and after processing. For example, if a row grows in length by 40%, on average, make sure you set the PCTFREE parameter on the table to 50% to avoid chaining.

Here is a simple example of a row analysis. Assume that the APPLICATION table has four columns:

```
APPLIC_ID        NUMBER(6)
CATEGORY         CHAR(10)
CHANGED_DATE     DATE
DESCR_LINE       CHAR(80)
```

When the row was first inserted, it had all this information except for DESCR_ LINE. This line is always filled in, but only after the initial insertion of the row. To obtain the length of the rows before and after the DESCR_LINE update, perform this query to calculate the average row length:

```
SELECT AVG ((NVL(VSIZE(APPLIC_ID),0)+1)
       +   (NVL(VSIZE(CATEGORY),0)+1
       +   (NVL(VSIZE(CHANGED_DATE),0)+1)
       +   (NVL(VSIZE(DESCR_LINE),0)+1)) +5
       FROM APPLICATION;
```

Ideally, the table will contain only the rows that have been updated, with the query being run once before the update to the DESCR_LINE column and then after the update.

In the CREATE TABLE statement, you can specify the following storage parameters. You can also specify a STORAGE clause to set the same values available to other data objects at tablespace level (e.g., ALTER TABLESPACE DEFAULT STORAGE

(INITIAL, NEXT, MINEXTENTS, MAXEXTENTS)). Remember that MAXEXTENTS is no longer an issue with Oracle7.3 and later and should be set to UNLIMITED.

INITRANS

Default: 1 for tables, 2 for indexes

Values: 1 to 255

> Initial number of transactions that can simultaneously update a block of data. Increase the default value if many transactions are likely to be simultaneously accessing a single block in the table. Each transaction has 23 bytes reserved for it. If there is more than one transaction accessing a single block for update, a new 23-byte slot will be created in the block to store the second transaction's identifier. This will cause a wait. It can also lead to chaining if the number of new transaction identifier slots is significant.

MAXTRANS

Default: OS-dependent

Values: 1 to OS-dependent maximum

> Maximum number of transactions that can simultaneously update a block of data. There is no performance advantage to changing this default. If you lower the MAXTRANS, you may encounter a problem when one transaction is forced to wait before performing its own update until another transaction completes its updates.

PCTFREE

Default: 10

Values: 0 to 99

> Percentage of space Oracle will leave in the current block when inserting a row into a table. PCTFREE + PCTUSED must not exceed 100. Set PCTFREE to allow for row expansion and its associated chaining and migration.

PCTUSED

Default: 40

Values: 0 to 99

> Percentage minimum of available space in a block that has to be reached before Oracle can start inserting rows into it again. PCTFREE + PCTUSED must not exceed 100.

FREELISTS

Default 1

Values: 1 to DB_BLOCK_SIZE dependent

> Number of buffers that will be made available in the buffer cache for transactions to simultaneously insert into. For optimal performance, set the parameter to the number of transactions that are likely to insert into a table simultaneously. You can specify this parameter in the CREATE TABLE, CREATE CLUSTER, and CREATE INDEX commands. Unfortunately, you can't

alter an object to have a new FREELIST setting unless you totally rebuild the object. This has always surprised us!

FREELIST GROUPS

Default 1

Values: 1 to number of instances

Used with parallel server to indicate the number of groups of FREELISTS; set to one for each instance running against your database.

Determining INITIAL

In a perfectly tuned system, the initial extents allocated for a table (specified in the INITIAL parameter in the STORAGE clause) will contain all of a table's data (unless striping is being performed). To work out the size of the INITIAL extent, you will need to determine the number of rows the table will contain and its likely growth rate over the next 12 months.

Use the following formula to determine the INITIAL value:

$$\text{Size(bytes)} = \text{blocksize} \times \frac{(\text{rows in 12 months} \times \text{average row length})}{(\text{blocksize} - 90) \times (1 - \text{PCTFREE}/100)}$$

In this calculation, "average row length" is the average row length from the previous calculation. Notice that each block has an overhead of 90 bytes.

Determining PCTFREE

PCTFREE is the percentage of the block that must be left free when rows are being inserted into a table. This free space is set aside for future row expansion. DBAs too often neglect to set an appropriate value for PCTFREE.

If you set a high value for PCTFREE, more physical reads will be required if full table scans are made on the table. A low PCTFREE may cause chaining and migration; that is, a single row may span several physical blocks. In general, avoid chaining and migration at all costs. (See Chapter 11 for more information on identifying and repairing chained rows.) Some sites modify PCTFREE to a low value when they do a reorganization of the table and change PCTFREE back to a larger value after the table has been rebuilt. This method can be used to minimize storage and avoid chaining at the same time. There are fewer physical blocks in the table for Oracle to read because every block that has a PCTFREE specified above 0 has to reserve that amount of free space for row expansion.

Chapter 11 describes a chaining situation. In one example an update involving 8,000 rows with a chained table took 58.82 seconds to complete processing. On the other hand, a table with an appropriately sized PCTFREE, and therefore no chaining, took 27.24 seconds. Queries of chained rows take approximately twice the time it takes to query unchained rows.

When a table grows, each column it grows by requires 1 byte of overhead; each row requires 5 bytes of overhead. By looking at the average length before and after the update, you'll determine the percentage by which the rows are going to increase. This supplies a value for PCTFREE. For example, growing from an average of 30 characters to an average of 100 characters indicates a growth rate of 70%. Set PCTFREE as follows:

$$\text{growth rate} = \frac{\text{end row length} - \text{start length}}{\text{end row length}} \times 100$$

where:

`end row length`
  is 100 in the above example or the length of the row after the update.

`start length`
  is the length of the row when it is first inserted.

Determining PCTUSED

The previous section showed how to select a value for PCTFREE that reduces the possibility of chaining and migration. Most applications will perform optimally with a PCTFREE set high enough to avoid all chaining and migration, but there are some exceptions. One exception occurs when there are many full table scans against the table and very few updates or indexed lookups of individual rows. There are fewer physical blocks in the table for Oracle to read because every block that has a PCTFREE specified above 0 has to reserve that amount of free space for row expansion.

The PCTUSED value that you specify can also have an impact on performance. PCTFREE is reserved for row expansion, whereas PCTUSED attempts to keep the PCTUSED percentage of the block filled with data. If the percentage that is used in the block falls below the PCTUSED value, Oracle is informed that there is free space and new rows may be added. A high PCTUSED indicates that the data will be stored very efficiently in terms of space usage, but the likelihood of chaining or migration is increased.

Note that the sum of PCTFREE + PCTUSED cannot exceed 100.

Determining INITRANS and MAXTRANS

The INITRANS and MAXTRANS parameters that are specified at the time of table creation control the number of transactions that are able to access a block. INITRANS specifies the minimum number of concurrent transactions per block for which space is reserved. MAXTRANS is the maximum number of transactions that a block will support. Each entry for a transaction that is currently accessing a block uses about 23 bytes of free space. The INITRANS parameter is set at 1 and should be increased to the number of transactions that will be accessing a single block in the table simultaneously. If more transactions simultaneously access a block for update than the value set for INITRANS, a wait will occur as a new 23-byte slot is allocated for the transaction identifier. This slot will never be removed from the block; in addition to using space, it can also cause row chaining and migration, caused by not allowing for the extra storage required for the slots. We recommend that you leave MAXTRANS at its default of 255 and set INITRANS to the maximum number of transactions that are likely to update a single block simultaneously.

Determining FREELISTS

If a table is likely to have a large number of insertions from many simultaneous processes, check the value of FREELISTS. A free list is a list of data blocks in a table that contains free space. This list is checked before new rows are inserted. We recommend that you set the free lists to the number of transactions that will be simultaneously inserting into your table. Ideally, set free lists for each table that has the number of simultaneous inserts greater than 1.

You specify the FREELISTS parameter in the STORAGE clause. If you experience free list contention, you will have to rebuild your table using an increased FREELISTS parameter. This can be very time-consuming on a large table with several indexes. We recommend that you make every effort to put the appropriate FREELISTS parameter in place at the time you create the table.

Understanding the High-Water Mark

The high-water mark is the furthest point in a table in which you've placed data. If you have a table that is 10 megabytes in size and data have been inserted up to the 5-megabyte point, the high-water mark is at 5 megabytes. Why is this important? Full table scans will always read up to the high-water mark, even if all of the rows in the table have been removed. This has the effect of loading the buffer cache with blocks that don't contain rows. It also causes table scans to take significantly longer than you would expect. We recommend that you rebuild tables that have a high number of deletes as frequently as practical. Oracle7.3 and later versions have a command to truncate after the high-water mark and to let unused space in the table be allocated to other objects in the tablespace. (It would have been a lot nicer if Oracle had provided us with a means of truncating up to the high-water mark.) To free the unused blocks, run the following command:

```
ALTER TABLE tname DEALLOCATE UNUSED [KEEP (bytes)];
```

Caching Tables

Oracle7.1 introduced the CACHE parameter for the CREATE TABLE, ALTER TABLE, and CLUSTER statements. It allows you to place data on the most-recently-used end of the least-recently-used chain. What does all this mean? As we've mentioned before, Oracle keeps in the buffer cache the data that were accessed most recently in memory. This greatly improves the chance of a table's being found in the buffer cache, rather than having the number of blocks specified in the INIT.ORA parameter _SMALL_TABLE_THRESHOLD be placed at the most-recently-used (MRU) end of the chain and the rest at the least-recently-used (LRU) end of the chain. Note, however, that the data have to be specifically read into the buffer cache by using the statement SELECT COUNT(*) FROM table_name to be resident in memory. Data can also be removed from cache if they are not accessed and reach the least-recently-used end of the LRU chain.

Reducing Dynamic Extension

Dynamic extension is the process of acquiring more extents of disk space for tables and indexes that have not been allocated a large enough INITIAL extent to begin with. When you first create a database object such as a table or an index, Oracle determines the size to be allocated by looking for a STORAGE clause in the CREATE command or by assigning a default allocation from the tablespace in which the object is created. When the INITIAL extent size is exceeded for that object, Oracle must dynamically create an extent based on the NEXT parameter in the STORAGE clause. This creation of additional extents is referred to as dynamic extension.

In almost all cases, you'll get far better performance if the disk allocation for a table or any other object is in one contiguous extent. With one large extent available, Oracle is able to read a large amount of data from disk in a single multiblock read with less disk movement.

If a table consists of many discontiguous areas of data scattered across the disk, Oracle is forced to scan all of these areas, as well as having to access the table segment header before obtaining each extent. The database functions that suffer the most from discontiguous extents are full table scans, table drops, deletes of many rows from tables, and inserts of many rows into tables. If the table or index is small and has a large number of extents, the impact is much greater.

Be sure to think carefully when you first create your database about how big your tables and indexes are likely to be, and assign storage parameters that allow for enough contiguous space, and as few extents, as possible. Figure 9-14 shows the way a table can be distributed around the disk when dynamic extension occurs. Extent information is stored in two system tables, UET$ (used extents) and FET$

(free extents). When extents are thrown, the information is written immediately to disk to maintain database address consistency. Throwing many extents can cause a bottleneck against these tables.

Dynamic extension is a particularly serious problem with long-running jobs, as described in Chapter 15. Another common cause of poor performance is when the DEFAULT STORAGE clause on the tablespaces set up for temporary segments is smaller than the SORT_AREA_SIZE. As soon as the SORT_AREA_SIZE fills and the sorted data is required to be written to disk, damaging extents will be thrown.

Consider the following example of how much more quickly an operation can be performed on a contiguous, rather than a fragmented, table:

Operation	Contiguous	Fragmented
Inserting 4,000 rows	0.76 second	3.62 seconds
Dropping the table	5.29 seconds	1 minute, 31 seconds

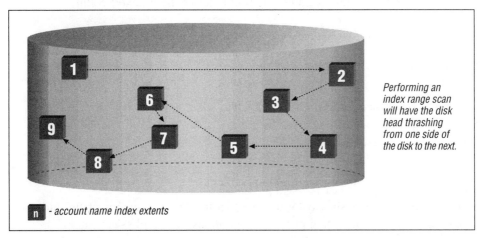

Performing an index range scan will have the disk head thrashing from one side of the disk to the next.

n - *account name index extents*

Figure 9-14. Dynamic extension

The section "Reducing Dynamic Extension" in Chapter 11 describes how you can monitor activity in an existing database to·detect dynamic extension and how you can tune your database to avoid dynamic extension as much as possible.

Creating Indexes

As we discussed in earlier chapters, specifying the appropriate indexes over columns in your tables can greatly increase performance in your system. Oracle Expert has impressed us greatly with its ability to help set the most appropriate indexes. (See Appendix D, *Oracle Performance Pack.*) You create an index and allocate its size with the CREATE INDEX statement.

Specifying the Index Tablespace

Place all indexes in tablespaces that are dedicated to use by indexes. If possible, place index tablespaces on their own disk drive or, at the very least, on a different drive from the one that is used by the corresponding table tablespace.

Calculating the Size of an Index

Sizing indexes, like sizing tables, requires knowledge of the number of rows in the table (with growth for the next 12 months allowed) and the average length of the columns. The following calculation determines the size of the index, assuming that the APPLICATION table is being indexed on the APPLIC_ID and CATEGORY columns:

```
SELECT AVG((NVL(VSIZE(applic_id),0)+1)
   + (NVL(VSIZE(category),0)+1))
   FROM application;
```

This calculation gives the average length in bytes of the indexed columns:

$$\text{leaf size = Bsize} \times \frac{(\text{rows in 12 months}) \times (11 + \text{average row length})}{(\text{Bsize} - 90) \times (1 - \text{PCTFREE}/100)}$$

where:

Bsize
  is the block size set in the INIT.ORA file.

index size
  approximately equals leaf size * 1.1.

1.1
  is the overhead for storing the branch blocks.

This is the value that should be assigned to the INITIAL extent of the index. As with tables, make every attempt to store the index in one physical extent.

You can also use the VALIDATE INDEX command to determine the size of the index, particularly when you are sizing a production database and have a test database at your disposal that contains sound information that could be used for sizing. This command places index information into a table called INDEX_STATS. You can specify:

```
VALIDATE INDEX index_name;
```

NOTE   The VALIDATE INDEX command places index information into a
              table called INDEX_STATS.

You can also use the ANALYZE command described in Chapter 12. Specify:

```
ANALYZE INDEX index_name
     VALIDATE STRUCTURE;
```

To obtain information on the index, select from the view INDEX_STATS
containing the following definitions:

INDEX_STATS Statistic	Description
HEIGHT	Height of B-tree
BLOCKS	Blocks allocated to the index
NAME	The name of the index
LF_ROWS	Number of leaf rows
LF_BLKS	Number of leaf blocks in the B-tree
LF_ROWS_LEN	Sum of the lengths of all leaf rows
LF_BLK_LEN	Usable space in leaf block
BR_ROWS	Number of branch rows
BR_BLKS	Number of branch blocks in the B-tree
BR_ROWS_LEN	Sum of lengths of all branch rows
BR_BLK_LEN	Sum of lengths of all branch blocks
DEL_LF_ROWS	Number of deleted leaf rows in the index
DEL_LF_ROWS_LEN	Total length of all deleted rows in the index
DISTINCT_KEYS	Number of distinct keys in the index
MOST_REPEATED_KEY	How many times most repeated key is repeated
BTREE_SPACE	Total space allocated to B-tree
USED_SPACE	Total space currently used
PCT_USED	Percent of space allocated being used
ROWS_PER_KEY	Average rows per distinct key
BLKS_GETS_PER_ACCESS	When a row is searched for, using the index, the number of blocks read to satisfy that search

Two columns of particular interest in this view are the HEIGHT and DEL_LF_
ROWS columns. If either of these figures become too large (that is, if HEIGHT is
greater than 4 or if DEL_LF_ROWS is greater than 25%), the index is a candidate
for dropping and recreating. Pay particular attention as well if you have only a
handful of rows in the index (LF_ROWS) but you have a significant number if LF_

BLOCKS. This tends to occur when you have many deleted rows and indicates that the index should be rebuilt for optimal performance.

To obtain the storage allocated, storage used, and percentage used, perform the following calculation. Remember to attempt to store the index in one contiguous extent and to allow for 12 months' growth.

```
SELECT name  "INDEX NAME",
    blocks * 4096 "BYTES ALLOCATED",
    btree_space "BYTES UTILIZED",
    (btree_space / (blocks * 4096)) * 100 "PERCENT USED"
  FROM index_stats;
```

NOTE   The 4096 in this calculation refers to the DB_BLOCK_SIZE setting on the database from which you are selecting. You can obtain similar output by observing the PCT_USED statistic in the INDEX_STATS view.

You must closely monitor all space usage within dynamic indexes. Ideally, make sure that INITIAL extent sizing is always large enough to hold all indexed rows. Once this has been established, index growth needs to be monitored. Indexes do not release space when a row is deleted from the table. Index leaf blocks will be released only when all indexed rows within a leaf block have been deleted. Space is reused if a new row is added to the table with a record key that causes the index entry to be placed within the same index leaf block.

Volatile tables can become a space management problem when rows are spasmodically deleted from tables. Under certain conditions, the physical size of the index can even exceed the physical size of the table that owns that index.

Oracle7.3 had been expected to introduce bitmapped indexes, which can provide dramatic performance boosts on queries. Bitmapped indexes are suited to indexes that have low cardinality, that is, very few distinct values, such as MALE and FEMALE, or ON and OFF. They have another distinct benefit in using significantly less storage and are a must for both OLTP and data warehousing databases.

Oracle7.3 promised and produced a mechanism that speeds up the building of an index from an existing index. Specify

```
ALTER INDEX index_name REBUILD
```

This provides significant build time improvements and is vital for very large indexes. If you are rebuilding your index to free space left by deleted index entries, you can speed up the operation using ALTER INDEX REBUILD and UNRE-COVERABLE. You may also consider using the DBMS_SPACE package (if you are using Oracle7.2) and the ALTER INDEX indexname DEALLOCATE UNUSED [KEEP (integer)] command to simply remove the unused blocks from your index.

Oracle7.2 introduced a mechanism to speed up index creation when the index can't be recovered:

```
CREATE INDEX index_name UNRECOVERABLE
```

This command provides you with a build time improvement of up to 50%. Every minute counts when you are building large indexes. We recommend that you build very large indexes using Oracle's parallel query option and using the UNRE-COVERABLE option. You lose recovery with the option, but indexes can always be rebuilt if the table is in place.

Oracle8 introduced index-only tables, which can save a huge amount of storage for very large databases and have the added luxury of providing the data to you in the order of the index keys. You can save a very large amount of storage using this facility; inserts, updates, and deletes will run faster because the only object being updated is the index, not the index and the table.

Analyzing Tables and Indexes

Be sure to communicate with your project team about the optimizer requirements of your SQL code. If you are running the cost-based optimizer, you will have to analyze your tables and indexes. If OPTIMIZER_MODE=RULE is currently set, but you now plan to use the cost-based optimizer, you must change the parameter to CHOOSE, FIRST_ROWS, or ALL_ROWS. You must then ANALYZE all of your tables. If some of your tables are not analyzed, they will be accessed by using the rule-based optimizer. If you happen to join a table that is running the rule-based optimizer with a table that has been analyzed by using the cost-based optimizer, a full table scan usually results for the table using the rule-based optimizer. Not surprisingly, the phone begins ringing with complaints of poor performance!

We recommend that you compute your statistics on *all* tables unless the time needed to analyze your tables is impractical or unless your code has been especially tuned for the rule-based optimizer. Oracle provides a packaged procedure that you should use that analyzes an entire schema. To analyze all of the tables owned by the user SCOTT, for example, run the command:

```
EXECUTE dbms_utility.analyze_schema('scott', 'compute');
```

The sample command will compute the statistics.

If you have very large tables, and you find that analyzing your tables is taking too long, try to estimate at least 40% of your rows. We have seen inconsistent results when tables have been analyzed with less. Never analyze the indexes and not the tables; we have seen this cause some very unusual and inefficient access paths. If the data in your indexes are skewed, that is, they have a few rows for one value and many rows for another value, you must analyze your index to produce a histogram. If you don't. Oracle will assume an even spread of rows for each value in the index, and a full table scan will often result.

Creating Views

Too often, DBAs don't create and tune views with the same enthusiasm with which they tune tables and indexes. This is unfortunate, because untuned views can badly damage performance in your system. You create a view with the CREATE VIEW statement.

Check that the statements that create the view have been written efficiently. A fast way of checking the effectiveness of views is to specify:

```
SELECT   *
FROM     VIEW_NAME
WHERE    ROWNUM < 5;
```

If the view contains a GROUP BY, such as the one in the following statement:

```
CREATE   VIEW RUNNING_TOTALS
SELECT   D.NAME, SUM(T.FIGURE)
FROM     DOMAIN D, TRANSACTION T
WHERE    D.ACC_NO = T.ACC_NO
GROUP    BY D.NAME;
```

the entire transaction table will be scanned because there are no qualifying conditions. In reality, the view will always have an ACC_NO provided. To test a view that contains a GROUP BY simply dissect the statement as follows:

```
SELECT   d.name
FROM     domain d, transaction t
WHERE    d.acc_no = t.acc_no
AND      ROWNUM < 5;
```

If the view or the statement above does not return the rows instantly, the chance of the view being badly tuned is high. Remember that views are simply SQL statements and should be tuned as such. The most common performance problems with views are caused by the use of an incorrect driving table or a missing index. A more sophisticated method of checking a view is to extract the SQL that is used in the view and run it through the EXPLAIN PLAN or TKPROF facilities to ensure that all the necessary indexes are being used. (See Chapter 10 for a discussion of these facilities.)

Creating Users

When you create a user via the CREATE USER statement, you create a user account that has certain specific privileges and storage allocations. When you create your users, you can assign them resource privileges that allow them to create tables. You can also assign them a default tablespace for any tables and indexes that they create and a temporary tablespace where their sort processing will be performed if it can't be done in memory.

It is good practice to assign all of your users to a default tablespace dedicated to end users so that you can monitor the processing they do. By assigning a space quota to this tablespace, you can prevent the indiscriminate creation of large, ad hoc tables.

Issue this command:

```
ALTER USER gurry DEFAULT TABLESPACE user_tspace
    TEMPORARY TABLESPACE oltp_temp_tspace;
ALTER USER gurry QUOTA 5M ON user_tspace;
```

You can also take advantage of resource profile limits, which let you control the resources you assign a user. You can set the following resource limits for a user profile:

Resource Limit	Description
SESSIONS_PER_USER	Total concurrent sessions per username
CPU_PER_SESSION	Maximum CPU per session
CPU_PER_CALL	Maximum CPU per call
CONNECT_TIME	Maximum continuous connect time per session
IDLE_TIME	Maximum allowable idle time before user is disconnected
LOGICAL_READS_PER_SESSION	Maximum database blocks read per session
LOGICAL_READS_PER_CALL	Maximum database blocks read per database call
PRIVATE_SGA	Maximum number of bytes of private space within SGA
COMPOSITE_LIMIT	Maximum weighted sum of:
	CPU_PER_SESSION, CONNECT_TIME, LOGICAL_READS_PER_SESSION, and PRIVATE_SGA.

Note that it is possible to impose explicit resource limits on some parameters, combined with the composite limit on other parameters. To impose the resource limits, issue the CREATE PROFILE or ALTER PROFILE statements or the SQL*DBA ALTER PROFILE facility. To assign a user to a profile with a resource limit, use the CREATE USER or ALTER USER commands or the SQL*DBA dialogue to create and alter users. The following example creates the AD_HOC profile and then assigns user *gurry* to it:

```
CREATE PROFILE AD_HOC
LIMIT
SESSIONS_PER_USER            2
CPU_PER_SESSION              20000
CPU_PER_CALL                 20000
CONNECT_TIME                 120
IDLE_TIME                    30
LOGICAL_READS_PER_SESSION    UNLIMITED
LOGICAL_READS_PER_CALL       UNLIMITED;

ALTER USER gurry PROFILE ad_hoc;
```

INIT.ORA Parameter Summary

This section summarizes the INIT.ORA parameters that allow you to tune memory and disk performance. For a complete discussion of these and the other INIT.ORA parameters, see Oracle's standard DBA documentation.

Starting with Oracle7.3, you can modify certain parameters dynamically using the command:

```
ALTER SYSTEM SET parameter = value;
```

You can also set the parameters for a user session using the command:

```
ALTER SESSION SET parameter = value;
```

Oracle7.3.2 has made the HASH_AREA_SIZE, HASH_JOIN_ENABLED, and HASH_MULTIBLOCK_IO_COUNT parameters dynamically changeable. Later versions of the RDBMS make many more parameters changeable dynamically.

ALWAYS_ANTI_JOIN (parallel query option, Oracle7.3 and later)
Default: Null
Values: NESTED_LOOPS, MERGE, HASH
    Set the parameter to HASH to allow parallel processing of the NOT IN clause (a real resource hog). If you set the parameter to NESTED_LOOPS, the NOT IN is evaluated the same way it was as Oracle7.2 and earlier (which will not please you). MERGE uses the SORT MERGE algorithm to process the NOT IN, which is faster than NESTED_LOOPS but not as fast as HASH.

BITMAP_MERGE_AREA_SIZE (Oracle7.3 and later)
Default: 1048576
Values: 0 to OS-dependent
    Merges bitmapped indexes. Typically, a large installation that has many bitmapped indexes will increase this parameter to 10 megabytes. The parameter is measured in bytes. (See CREATE_BITMAP_AREA_SIZE as well.)

CHECKPOINT_PROCESS

Default: FALSE

Values: TRUE or FALSE

Turns the new background process, CKPT, on (TRUE) or off (FALSE). Checkpoints can have a negative impact on performance, typically causing a 1- or 2-second delay, as the DBWR process writes data to the database and the LGWR updates the database and control files to record the current log sequence number (required for archive recovery) and writes entries from the redo log buffer to the redo log file. CKPT updates the database and control files; this takes a load off the LGWR process and allows it to concentrate on the task of clearing the log buffer to the redo log. CHECKPOINT_PROCESS has a greater influence if the frequency of checkpoints is high and there are numerous database files. We strongly recommend that you set the parameter to TRUE.

COMPATIBLE (parallel query option)

Default: Null

Values: Any Oracle RDBMS Release (e.g., Oracle7.2.3)

Set to the release of the Oracle RDBMS that you are currently running to take full advantage of any new features provided in the release. This inappropriately named parameter can provide you with huge performance improvements. Oracle7.1.5 introduced the ability to bypass the buffer cache (direct reads) for table scans and sorts (COMPATIBLE=7.1.5). Oracle7.3 introduced temporary tablespaces that improve the performance of sorts and hash joins (COMPATIBLE=7.3.1).

CREATE_BITMAP_AREA_SIZE (Oracle7.3 and later)

Default: 8388608

Values: 0 to OS-dependent

Number of bytes of memory used to create bitmapped indexes. For the creation of very large bitmapped indexes, consider increasing this value.

CURSOR_SPACE_FOR_TIME

Default: FALSE

Values: TRUE or FALSE

Turns waiting for application cursors on (TRUE) or off (FALSE). Setting this parameter to TRUE gives you a minor performance improvement by pinning SQL areas in the shared context area and stopping private SQL areas from being deallocated until the application cursors are closed. If the parameter is set to FALSE, a check has to be made to see whether the SQL statement is contained in a shared SQL area in the library cache. You must allocate a shared pool that is large enough (see the SHARED_ POOL_SIZE parameter). If it is not large enough and this parameter is set to TRUE, Oracle will display a message telling you that it can't parse the statement. If it can't maintain the private SQL area because of insufficient memory, Oracle displays a message telling you that it has run out of memory.

DB_BLOCK_BUFFERS
Default: 32
Values: 4 to unlimited

Sets the size of the database buffer cache in memory. You must set this parameter, as well as the SHARED_POOL_SIZE and LOG_BUFFER described later, to get optimal performance by caching data from the database in memory. The buffer cache stores tables, indexes, clusters, sort data, dictionary data, and rollback segments. Our testing shows that the higher the number of block buffers, the less I/O and the better your system will perform. If excessive paging and swapping activity occurs for user processes or if any paging or swapping of the SGA occurs, you will have to reduce DB_BLOCK_ BUFFERS to free memory. You should enlarge this parameter only after you are certain that the SHARED_POOL_SIZE parameter (dictionary and library caches) has been adequately tuned.

For a typical medium-sized system, set this parameter to 10 megabytes or more; for a larger system, set it to 20 megabytes or more. We have observed that many sites achieve performance improvements by setting their buffer cache well over 100 megabytes. The size of your buffer cache can be obtained by multiplying the DB_BLOCK_BUFFERS parameter by DB_BLOCK_ SIZE.

DB_BLOCK_CHECKPOINT_BATCH
Default: 8
Values: 0 to derived

Number of blocks the DBWR background process writes at any one time. You can increase this parameter to allow checkpoints to complete faster. The setting is often too small on a heavily used system. We recommend that you leave this parameter at its default unless you are experiencing delays during checkpointing.

DB_BLOCK_LRU_LATCHES (Oracle7.3 and later)
Default: CPU_COUNT/2
Values: 1 to the number of CPUs

LRU latch contention has always been a source of frustration on multiprocessor machines; this parameter relieves much of the pain. Set it to your number of CPUs, and watch the MISSES and IMMEDIATE_MISSES columns in the V$LATCH table diminish.

DB_BLOCK_LRU_STATISTICS
Default: FALSE

Values: TRUE/FALSE

Disables (FALSE) or enables (TRUE) the compilation of statistics on the effect of having fewer buffers in the buffer cache. Don't leave this parameter set to TRUE in your production database because it can increase your latch contention significantly and cause poor performance. See Chapter 10 for more information on how to use this parameter.

DB_BLOCK_LRU_EXTENDED_STATISTICS
Default: 0

Values: 0 to unlimited

Forces statistics to be gathered on the effect of increasing the buffer cache. Use this parameter very sparingly; we've seen it cause performance degradation. See Chapter 10 for more information on how to use this parameter.

DB_FILE_SIMULTANEOUS_WRITES
Default: 4

Values: 1 to 24

Number of write batches written by the database writers. If you are experiencing problems getting buffers written to your disks during checkpoints, try increasing the value. It is applicable only to operating systems that support more than one write to your disk devices.

_DB_BLOCK_MAX_SCAN_CNT (will become obsolete)
Default: 30

Values: 0 to value of DB_BLOCK_BUFFERS

Maximum number of buffers that the user will scan before DBWR is invoked. This parameter can use an excessive amount of CPU if it is set too high, particularly for a database that has a very high percentage of queries and very few updates. DBWR scanning will continue until either the number of modified blocks specified in _DB_BLOCK_WRITE_BATCH has been found or the _DB_ BLOCK_MAX_SCAN_CNT number of blocks has been scanned. The default value is adequate for most sites. If you have a DB_BLOCK_BUFFER size greater than 10 megabytes, though, consider increasing this parameter, especially if you are experiencing CPU problems.

_DB_BLOCK_WRITE_BATCH (will become obsolete)
Default: 8

Values: 1 to OS-dependent

Number of blocks DBWR passes at one time to the operating system for writing. Setting this parameter higher allows the operating system to write to different disks in parallel and to write adjacent blocks in a single I/O (if your operating system allows these features). If your buffer cache is small, having a high value will increase the wait time to modify a block that is in the batch being written.

DB_BLOCK_SIZE

Default: OS-dependent (often 2048)

Values: OS-dependent (normally 1 kilobytes to 8 kilobytes)

Size of each database buffer. Oracle recommends that you set the parameter to a minimum of 4 kilobytes. We performed several tests, creating a small database on a UNIX system with a DB_BLOCK_SIZE twice the default size. (The default was 2048, and we set it to 4096.) There was no improvement in OLTP response times, but there was a slight improvement (less than 10%, in batch processing times). We have read other benchmark figures that have indicated much greater response time improvements. We recommend that you set the parameter to 4 kilobytes for OLTP databases and up to 16 kilobytes for decision support databases. This parameter takes effect only at the time the database is created. Remember that if you adjust the parameter, the sizes of other parameters are also changed (e.g., DB_BLOCK_BUFFERS).

DB_FILES

Default: OS-dependent

Values: MAXDATAFILES for the database being mounted to O/S dependent.

Number of database files that can be open when the database is running. Set this value lower than the default if you are not using 32 data files (to reduce the space used in the SGA). You can increase this value by shutting down your database, changing the parameter value, and restarting the database. All instances must be set to the same value if you are using the parallel server.

DB_FILE_MULTIBLOCK_READ_COUNT

Default: OS-dependent but usually a function of DB_BLOCK_BUFFERS and PROCESSES.

Values: OS-dependent (normally 1 to either the DB_BLOCK_BUFFERS / 4 or the operating systems Maximum I/O size / DB_BLOCK_SIZE)

Number of blocks read into the buffer cache at once when performing a sequential scan. Be sure to explicitly set this parameter, because the default is inappropriate for many sites. This parameter is often set higher for full table scans performed by overnight runs and is then adjusted back for high-volume daily processing. At the time the database is created, there will often be sequential scans of tables to create indexes.

For best performance, it is usually best to set the parameter to 8 for OLTP application and either 16 or 32 for decision support databases and batch processing.

DISCRETE_TRANSACTIONS_ENABLED

Default: FALSE

Values: TRUE or FALSE

Enables (TRUE) or disables (FALSE) discrete transactions. Such transactions are available for nondistributed systems and can be used only for the following types of transactions:

- Transactions that update only a small number of blocks (ideally, one).

- Transactions that will not change an individual database block more than once and will not insert more than one row into the same table.

- Transactions that will not modify data and commit the changes against the same data that long-running queries are running against (this will cause an abort on the query with the message "SNAPSHOT TOO OLD").

- Transactions that do not have to refer to the data they have changed.

- Transactions that do not modify a table containing a long column.

Discrete transactions can be run with nondiscrete (normal) transactions. The reason why discrete transactions run faster is that no undo (rollback) information is stored. Instead, the redo information is stored in a separate location in memory, and all changes made to the data is committed when data is transferred to the redo log buffer and updates to the database are performed as usual.

Use discrete transactions only when you are absolutely certain that the transaction falls into the category specified here and only when your database is experiencing excessive rollback activity.

DML_LOCKS

Default: 4* value of TRANSACTIONS

Values: 20 to unlimited or 0

Maximum number of data manipulation language (DML) locks. If three users are modifying data on two tables, you will need six DML locks. If this value is set to 0, enqueues are disabled and performance is improved, particularly if you are using parallel server. The downside is that you cannot use DDL statements, such as CREATE INDEX, and you also can't perform LOCK TABLE tname in EXCLUSIVE MODE. If you do set the parameter to 0, which we recommend that you do for a parallel server, you must set DML_LOCKS equal to 0 for all instances.

ENQUEUE_RESOURCES

Default: Depends on SESSIONS parameter

Values: 10 to 65535

Sets the number of resources that can be locked by the operating system lock manager. Enqueues are a locking mechanism that is platform-specific. With latches, the first one to try to get a latch may be the last one to obtain the latch if the latch is busy. Enqueue users must wait their turn for the resource. Each enqueue wait is more damaging than a single latch wait. If you have many tables in your database, consider increasing the parameter to the number of tables in your database plus 30%. If you continue to get timeouts, increase your ENQUEUE_RESOURCES until the timeouts disappear (see Chapter 11).

GC_DB_LOCKS (parallel server)

Default: 0

Values: 1 to unlimited

Controls locks on table and index data blocks. The total number of PCM locks is specified by the parameter GC_DB_LOCKS. All instances must have the same value set for this parameter. PCM locks are distributed evenly among all data files if you do not set the GC_FILES_TO_LOCKS parameter. You must almost always set the numbers of locks per data file using the GC_FILES_TO_LOCKS parameter to obtain the best performance.

This parameter and GC_FILES_TO_LOCKS are the most critical parameters in tuning parallel server. GC_DB_LOCKS needs to be equal to or larger than the number of locks in GC_FILES_TO_LOCKS.

The advantage of setting the number of PCM locks high is that it lessens the chance of damaging PCM lock contention. The disadvantages are that it may take considerably longer to start and recover your database and that the locks may use a substantial amount of memory. This is a substantial difference for very large tables that have a large potential for cross-instance locking. You must have the identical GC_DB_LOCKS for all instances.

GC_FILES_TO_LOCKS (parallel server)

Default: Null

GC_FILES_TO_LOCKS assigns locks on a per data file basis, which affects table and index data blocks within the data file. If you add a data file to your tablespace, don't forget to add the GC_FILES_TO_LOCKS settings to the data file. GC_FILES_TO_LOCKS protects only data blocks, not rollback segment blocks. Don't assign locks to tablespaces that contain only rollback segments or tablespaces used exclusively for temporary segments. Group read-only tables/indexes together and assign only one lock to that data file. Make the tablespace read-only (Oracle7.1 and later) to ensure that no updates occur to the tablespace.

Use the following syntax to set the parameter settings.

```
GC_FILES_TO_LOCKS = "<file#> = <#locks> [!<Blocking Factor>]
    [EACH]........"
```

file# is the internal database file number. To obtain the appropriate file# from your database, use the command

```
SELECT * FROM DBA_DATA_FILES;
```

You can have a number of files with the same definitions by using the format 1,2,3 representing file1, file2, and file3. The same can be achieved by specifying 1-3.

#locks is the number of PCM locks to have against the data file.

Blocking Factor is an optional parameter that dictates the mapping of PCM locks to data files. If it is not specified, it defaults to 1. As a simple example, imagine that you have data file with 32 blocks. If you specify a locking factor of four blocks, the mapping will look like this:

PCM Lock	Database Blocks							
1	1	2	3	4	17	18	19	20
2	5	6	7	8	21	22	23	24
3	9	10	11	12	25	26	27	28
4	13	14	15	16	29	30	31	32

If the optional parameter EACH is specified, each of the data files specified will be allocated the specified locks and mapping.

GC_TABLESPACES (parallel server)

Default: 5

Affects locking on the header block for the deferred rollback segment. This segment is used when a rollback is requested on a tablespace that is offline. When the tablespace comes back online, the rollback is applied to the tablespace automatically. Unless you are taking a number of files offline concurrently, don't change the parameter from its default.

GC_SEGMENTS (parallel server)

Default: 10

Controls segment header blocks. A segment header block is the first block of a table or index. It contains the extents within the table or index as well as other information. Your aim should be to set the value of this parameter to cause the least possible number of pings. The default parameter can cause a lot of false pings. The segment header blocks are usually accessed in Shared mode for full table scans (SELECT) and in Exclusive mode for bumping up the high-water mark (INSERT). The parameter must have the same setting across all instances.

GC_SAVE_ROLLBACK_LOCKS (parallel server)

Default: 20

> Also affects locking on the header block for the deferred rollback segment. As for GC_TABLESPACES, unless you are taking a number of files offline concurrently, don't change the parameter from its default. If you are taking tablespaces offline, increase the setting to 10 per instance.

GC_ROLLBACK_SEGMENTS (parallel server)

Default: 20

> Controls the locking on the rollback segment header block sometimes referred to as the transaction table. Set this parameter to the total number of rollback segments in your database including the SYSTEM rollback segment. If you add rollback segments to your database, don't forget to adjust this parameter.

GC_ROLLBACK_LOCKS (parallel server)

Default: 20

Values:

> Controls the locks on rollback segment blocks. If you see a lot of pinging on undo blocks, you should increase the value of this parameter. Each rollback segment gets GC_ROLLBACK_LOCKS assigned to it, regardless of the rollback segment sizes. It is useful to have rollback segments equally sized.

HASH_JOIN_ENABLED (parallel query option, Oracle7.3 and later)

Default: TRUE

Values: TRUE/FALSE

> Introduced in Oracle7.3 to enable hash joins. Hash joins are a new innovation that provides a performance enhancing alternative to sort merge joins. They perform considerably faster when the number of rows being joined for the two sides of the join are significantly different. Set HASH_JOIN_ENABLED=TRUE. You can dynamically modify the value of this parameter and it will take effect without the need to shut down and restart the database. Use ALTER SYSTEM SET parameter=value; to change the parameter at system level or ALTER SESSION SET parameter=value; to set it for one session only.

HASH_AREA_SIZE (parallel query option, Oracle7.3 and later)

Default: 2 * SORT_AREA_SIZE

Values: Any integer

> Introduced in Oracle7.3 to provide memory for each process performing a hash join. According to Oracle, this parameter can be increased considerably in size and continue to provide excellent performance improvements. Remember that it is used on a per-process basis and that there is potential for damaging paging and swapping if it is set too high. You can dynamically modify the value of this parameter, and it will take effect without the need to

shut down and restart the database. Use ALTER SYSTEM SET parameter=value; to change the parameter at system level or ALTER SESSION SET parameter=value; to set it for one session only.

HASH_MULTIBLOCK_IO_COUNT
Default: 1
Values: 1 to 65536 / DB_BLOCK_SIZE

Controls how many blocks each hash join reads and writes simultaneously. You must increase this value above its default to obtain optimal performance. For a 2-kilobyte DB_BLOCK_SIZE, increase the value to 16 or 32; for a 4-kilobyte DB_BLOCK_SIZE, make it 8 or 16; and for an 8-kilobyte DB_BLOCK_SIZE, set it to 4 or 8. You can dynamically modify the value of this parameter, and it will take effect without the need to shut down and restart the database. Use ALTER SYSTEM SET parameter=value; to change the parameter at system level or ALTER SESSION SET parameter=value; to set it for one session only.

LOG_ARCHIVE_DEST
Default: OS-dependent
Values: OS-dependent

Specifies the location of the archive log. For recovery purposes, be sure to keep this log separate from all database files and redo logs. The writing of the archive logs can have some impact on the performance of lower-end machines (for example, when the archive logs are being written to a disk using the same disk controller as database files or redo logs). It is essential that you keep the destination on a separate disk (and controller) from the database files.

LOG_ARCHIVE_BUFFERS
Default: OS-dependent
Values: OS-dependent

Number of buffers to allocate for archiving. This parameter can be adjusted, along with LOG_ARCHIVE_BUFFER_SIZE, to tune the archiving process so that it has as little impact as possible on your site's performance. The more buffers you allocate, the faster the archiver will run. But this parameter will also take a larger slice of your site's CPU resources, which could otherwise be used for other functions such as writing to or querying your database.

As a rule of thumb, the faster the device being written to, the larger the number of buffers you can have. Typically, a value of 4 is appropriate if you are archiving to disk or a high-speed tape device. Reduce the number of buffers if archiving is having an impact on performance. If you are experiencing problems in which a redo log switch cannot occur because the archiver process ARCH can't keep up, increase this parameter to the maximum allowable on your operating system.

LOG_ARCHIVE_BUFFER_SIZE

Default: OS-dependent

Values: OS-dependent

> Buffer size for archive log. This parameter is used with the LOG_ARCHIVE_ BUFFER parameter to tune the archiving process. If you specify a larger number, more archive data is stored in the archive buffer before writes are performed. If you specify a smaller number, you increase archive write activity. We recommend that you increase the buffer size to the maximum possible (operating system dependent). At one site, increasing this parameter from 32 kilobytes to 64 kilobytes decreased the overnight batch processing from 50 waits for the ARCH process per night to fewer than 10.

LOG_ARCHIVE_START

Default: FALSE

Values: TRUE or FALSE

> Enables (TRUE) or disables (FALSE) archiving.

LOG_BUFFER

Default: 4 * block size

Values: OS-dependent

> Number of bytes allocated to the redo log buffer in the SGA. The log buffer can affect the performance of the RDBMS by buffering information before writing to the redo logs. If you are experiencing I/O bottlenecks on the disks that contain the redo logs, increase this parameter. For high-volume, intensive-update applications, we have noticed response improvements of 50% by increasing the buffer size from 8 kilobytes (the default value) to 1 megabyte. There were no advantages to increasing beyond 1 megabyte.

> The trade-off is that if you specify a larger value, more memory is used in the SGA. You must keep in mind that relative to the SHARED_POOL_SIZE and DB_BLOCK_BUFFERS, the amount of memory used is relatively tiny. However, if your system is tight on memory and is likely to experience paging and swapping activity, reduce it down to a figure such as 64 kilobytes. If there is abundant memory, set the buffer size at about 1 megabyte and monitor its performance.

> For a typical medium-sized system, set this parameter to 64 kilobytes; for a larger system, set it to somewhere between 640 kilobytes and 1 megabyte. You specify this value in operating blocks. Under VMS, your block size is 2048 (so the LOG_BUFFER default would be 8192); on a Sun workstation, the block size is also 8192; on an Amdahl, it is 16384; and on HPs, it is 4096.

LOG_CHECKPOINT_INTERVAL

Default: OS-dependent

Values: 2 to unlimited

Number of new redo log file blocks needed to trigger a checkpoint. Note that these blocks are operating system blocks, not Oracle blocks. If you set this parameter smaller than the sizes of the redo log files, it will cause a checkpoint to occur prior to a log switch. A checkpoint causes all modified database buffers to be written to disk and stores the location from the redo log where checkpointing has occurred in the control file and database files.

Keep in mind that Oracle writes modified buffers regardless of checkpointing, so many of the buffers in the redo log since the last checkpoint have probably already been written to the database. If your database writer DBWR is not active enough, a checkpoint can cause a delay as all dirty (modified) buffers are written to the database. Typical response delays are between 1 and 2 seconds to end users, although the checkpoint itself can take much longer, depending on the size of your buffer cache.

If fast recovery time is required and you have redo logs greater than 50 megabytes, keep the LOG_CHECKPOINT_INTERVAL at a value lower than the size of the redo logs and at a size that is a whole fraction of the redo log size. If performance is the more important consideration, make your LOG_CHECKPOINT_INTERVAL equal to or greater than the size of the redo logs; this will force less frequent checkpoints and will minimize the amount of I/O in your system caused by the checking and writing required to perform the checkpoint. Typically, this parameter is set to a high value (e.g., 100,000). If you have very large redo logs (perhaps greater than 50 megabytes) consider setting this value to 25 megabytes.

LOG_CHECKPOINT_TIMEOUT

Default: 0

Values: 0 to unlimited

Forces more frequent checkpoints. If you set this parameter to a nonzero value, checkpoints will occur more often than when a redo log fills and the associated redo log switch takes place. You can achieve the same effect by setting the LOG_CHECKPOINT_INTERVAL to a size less than the redo log file size. The difference is that the timeout parameter works in seconds since the last checkpoint; the LOG_CHECKPOINT_INTERVAL parameter, on the other hand, uses the number of buffers filled as its indicator of when to throw a checkpoint.

You'll get the best performance by leaving the LOG_CHECKPOINT_TIMEOUT parameter at its default value of 0, which causes a checkpoint only on a change of redo log. The exception to the rule may be to set it to every 10 minutes or so if you are experiencing very long delays when a log switch is occurring. This does not always solve the problem, because there are many potential causes. Make sure that you also set LOG_CHECKPOINT_INTERVAL to a size larger than that of the redo log.

LOG_SIMULTANEOUS_COPIES
Default: CPU_COUNT
Values: 0 to unlimited

Maximum number of redo buffer copy latches that can write log buffers simultaneously. Specify this parameter only for multiple-CPU systems. We recommend that you set this parameter to twice the number of CPUs in systems that have high transaction rates. This reduces contention for the redo allocation latch, which is the only latch available if you leave this parameter at its default of 0. Note that if you set this parameter to zero, redo copy latches are turned off.

LOG_SMALL_ENTRY_MAX_SIZE
Default: OS-dependent (usually 800)
Values: OS-dependent

Size in bytes of the largest copy to log buffers that may occur without obtaining a redo copy latch. The redo allocation latch will be used for all changes greater than LOG_SMALL_ENTRY_SIZE bytes. This parameter applies only when the LOG_SIMULTANEOUS_ COPIES is greater than zero. If the entry to be written to the buffer is larger than 0, user processes will release the latch after allocating space in the log buffer and getting a redo copy latch. If the entry to be written is smaller than this size, the user process releases the redo allocation latch after the copy.

We have seen pleasing throughput improvements by setting this parameter down as low as 80 for OLTP applications. It may need to be decreased later if you are experiencing redo allocation latch contention. (See the discussion of this point in Chapter 11.)

LOG_ENTRY_PREBUILD_THRESHOLD (reappears with Oracle7.3 and later)
Default: 0 bytes
Values: 0 to unlimited

Causes redo copy latch entries to be prebuilt in readiness for writing to the log buffer via the redo copy latches. This once undocumented parameter is now an official parameter again. If you have LOG_SIMULATANEOUS_COPIES greater than 1, you can increase this value to 65,536 or larger to get a performance boost.

MTS_DISPATCHERS

Default: null

Values: Not applicable

Number and type of dispatcher processes to be created when a database or database instance starts up. You must specify a string that shows your network protocol, for example:

```
MTS_DISPATCHERS = TCP,4
MTS_DISPATCHERS = DECNET,4
```

MTS_MAX_DISPATCHERS

Default: 5

Values: OS-dependent

Maximum number of dispatchers that can run simultaneously.

MTS_MAX_SERVERS

Default: 0

Values: OS-dependent

Maximum number of server processors that can run simultaneously.

OPEN_CURSORS

Default: 50

Values: 1 to O/S dependent

Maximum number of cursors that a user session can have open at any one time. If the number of cursors being held by users is frequently near the maximum, increase the OPEN_CURSORS value for a performance boost. If the setting is too high, you will be wasting memory. A typical setting for users of a large application is between 200 and 300.

OPTIMIZER_MODE

Default: CHOOSE

Values: CHOOSE, RULE, FIRST_ROWS, ALL_ROWS

Selects the cost-based optimizer (CHOOSE, FIRST_ROWS, or ALL_ROWS) or the rule-based optimizer (RULE). The parameter is used to select the most efficient retrieval path for your SQL statements. We recommend that all sites have a plan in place to take advantage of the performance improvements you'll get from the cost-based optimizer with Oracle7.3 and later. However, if you are transferring a fully tuned application from rule to cost, you will probably want to start out by setting OPTIMIZER_MODE to RULE and then take your time testing the performance of your application with the new optimizer. FIRST_ROWS causes the optimizer to start returning rows quickly and is well suited to OLTP. ALL_ROWS is more designed for batch, and provides an overall better response time.

If you have analyzed your tables and you have the parameter set to RULE, the rule-based optimizer will be used. If you have set your parameter to

CHOOSE, FIRST_ROWS, or ALL_ROWS and you have not analyzed your tables, the rule-based optimizer is also used. If you have some tables analyzed and others not analyzed, and if you are using CHOOSE, FIRST_ROWS, or ALL_ROWS and the analyzed tables are being joined with tables that are not analyzed, you stand a very good chance of getting abysmal response times. Either analyze all of your tables and use either FIRST_ROWS or ALL_ROWS, or use the rule-based optimizer.

OPTIMIZER_PERCENT_PARALLEL

Default: 0

Values: 0 to 100

Determines the level of parallelism that the optimizer will use in its costing calculations. If you set the value to 100, the optimizer will use an object's degree of parallelism when computing the cost of a full table scan. Simply put, low values will use indexes, and high values will make more use of the parallel query option in preference. We recommend that you use the default setting for OLTP applications and set it to 100 for decision support applications, where you have multiple processors and would like to make use of the parallel query option. Note that the cost-based optimizer will always be used for an object that has a nonzero degree of parallelism.

PARALLEL_MAX_SERVERS (parallel query option)

Default: OS-dependent

Values: 0 to 256

Maximum number of servers that are allowed to exist concurrently. If you set your maximum servers to 20 and you have five SQL statements requesting a degree of parallelism of 5 each, the fifth statement will be forced to run the full-table scan using a single server. Set the value to (maximum number of PQO users * their maximum degree of parallelism * 2).

PARALLEL_MIN_SERVERS (parallel query option)

Default: 0

Values: 0 to PARALLEL_MAX_SERVERS

Number of servers created when an instance starts. Oracle will spawn more server processes as required, which does provide a small overhead on performance. The performance overhead is most noticeable when you are processing a small table. The number of servers can be reduced as queries complete and the server is idle for the amount of time specified in the PARALLEL_SERVER_IDLE_TIME parameter. The number of servers running never falls below the value specified in PARALLEL_MIN_SERVERS.

PARALLEL_SERVER_IDLE_TIME (parallel query option)

Default: OS-dependent

Values: 0 to unlimited

Number of minutes that a server remains idle before Oracle can terminate it. There can be a few seconds of startup time for servers, so we usually leave the parameter at its default to avoid frequent shutdown.

PARALLEL_MIN_PERCENT (parallel query option)

Default: 0

Values: 0 to 100

Introduced in Oracle7.3. If a query has a degree of parallelism requirement and is unable to obtain the percentage of query servers specified in this parameter, the query will terminate with an error. The default value for this parameter is 0, which allows your query to run with whatever resources are available. If you have long-running jobs that run considerably faster if they are able to run with the full quota of query servers, it may pay to set this parameter to 50 or higher and restart the query when the required number of servers becomes available.

PARTITION_VIEW_ENABLED (Oracle7.3 and later)

Default: FALSE

Values: TRUE and FALSE

Decision support databases will often use partitioned views to ease the administration of huge tables and improve the performance of queries that join several of the partitions. If you have tables (partitions) that have been divided into financial years 1990, 1991, 1992, 1993, 1994, 1995, 1996, and 1997, for example, and you would like to query a view across all of the tables for dates in the range January 1, 1996 to December 31, 1997, setting this parameter to TRUE will provide the intelligence to just have the last two tables read from if you have the appropriate check constraints on the tables. Set the value to TRUE if you are using partitioned views.

RESOURCE_LIMIT

Default: FALSE

Values: TRUE and FALSE

Limits (TRUE) or does not limit (FALSE) a user's database resources to those defined in his or her profile. Your setting takes effect after the database has been shut down and restarted. You can enable resource limits by issuing the command:

```
ALTER SYSTEM SET RESOURCE_LIMIT TRUE
```

After you issue this command, the resource limits are returned to the INIT.ORA value after the database has been shut down and restarted. (See the section earlier in this chapter called "Creating Users" for information.)

We strongly recommend that you set RESOURCE_LIMIT to TRUE (and manage the way users are using your site's resources). Our testing indicates that setting this parameter to TRUE does not slow performance.

SEQUENCE_CACHE_ENTRIES
Default: 10
Values: 10 to 32,000

Number of sequences that will be cached in memory (in the SGA). Set this parameter to the number of sequences that will be used by your instance at one time. Setting this parameter too low affects response times because a disk read is required to obtain each sequence number.

If you have the NOCACHE option set when you create the sequence in the CREATE SEQUENCE command, the sequence will not reside in this cache; it will have to be brought in from disk. Many sites use the NOCACHE option, however, because they cannot skip sequence numbers that can occur when the sequence cache facility is used.

To obtain the exact setting for your database, perform the following query:

```
SELECT SUM(CACHE_SIZE) from ALL_SEQUENCES;
```

The summed total provides you with the exact number of cache entries that are required if all of your sequences are being used.

SESSION_CACHED_CURSORS (obsolete in Oracle7.3 and later)
Default: 0
Values: 0 to OS-dependent maximum

Specifies the number of session cursors to cache. Introduced with Oracle7.1, this parameter can improve performance of OLTP applications when you frequently switch between the same group of forms and would like to have your cursors remain cached. Storing the cursors in this cache will avoid them having to be reopened. A typical setting is 150.

SHARED_POOL_SIZE
Default: 3.5 megabytes
Values: 300 kilobytes to OS-dependent maximum

Size of the shared buffer pool in the SGA. This pool stores shared SQL and PL/SQL blocks, packages, procedures, functions, triggers, the data dictionary cache, and (if your site is using a multithreaded server architecture) some session information.

Make the shared pool large enough, but not too large. If your shared pool is too large, you are wasting memory that could otherwise be used to enlarge the buffer cache. If you set it too low, you'll need to do too many disk accesses as objects are reloaded into memory, and performance will suffer— sometimes as much as 50%. Make sure you have some free memory after increasing this parameter, or the resulting paging and swapping will seriously degrade performance. Tune this parameter before you tune the buffer cache (see the DB_BLOCK_BUFFER parameter) because having an undersized shared pool will degrade performance even more than an undersized buffer cache will.

The maximum size allowed for the shared pool in your own system is shown in your *Oracle Installation and User's Guide.*

For a small system, we recommend that you reduce the default value to about 10 megabytes. For a small- to medium-sized system, 25 to 30 megabytes is usually adequate. For a medium- to large-sized system, it is usually optimally set at between 60 and 80 megabytes. We have observed that sites with large applications using many packages and procedures achieve improved performance when the SHARED_POOL_SIZE is enlarged beyond 100 megabytes. You must monitor the performance of the shared pool cache regularly and adjust the shared pool size to optimize your site's performance (see Chapter 11).

_SMALL_TABLE_THRESHOLD (will become obsolete)
Default: 5
Values: 0 to OS maximum

Number of blocks that will be stored in the most-recently-used end of the buffer cache during a full table scan before the rest of the blocks from the same table will be stored in the least-recently-used end of the list and will be overwritten by new data coming into the buffer cache.

This parameter keeps the data blocks read using full table scans in the buffer cache for a longer time. If you perform a query that uses a full table scan and then repeat the query, the same or a similar number of physical reads from the database will occur in both situations. The reason is that, for a full table scan, Oracle assumes that the data will be needed only briefly. It places the first five blocks (as specified by this parameter) into the most-recently-used end of the list and all data after the first four blocks read into the least-recently-used end of the list. As new data is read from the table, the new data replace the least-recently-used blocks in the buffer.

Oracle recommends that you keep the default for this parameter. We have tested the impact of increasing the value and have found that increasing the value can improve performance. Oracle7.1 and later introduce another facility, ALTER TABLE tname CACHE (described earlier in this chapter), which also assists with the caching of data.

SORT_AREA_SIZE

Default: OS-dependent

Values: Two database blocks to OS dependent

Size in bytes that a user process has available for sorting. If the machine on which the database is being created has an abundance of memory, you can increase this parameter beyond the default (for example, 2,097,152).

The performance improvements can be substantial, especially when your site is running long-running overnight jobs such as sorted reports or creating large indexes after a table reorganization. Some sites adjust this parameter upward for overnight processing (when there are fewer users logged on to the system and more free memory). They then set it back to its smaller number for daytime processing after the nightly runs complete. Because SORT_AREA_SIZE is allocated on a per-user process basis, free memory will disappear very quickly if the parameter is left high during peak system usage times. All users are allocated SORT_AREA_RETAINED_SIZE memory for sorting by default. The amount of memory a user can use for a sort can increase up to SORT_AREA_SIZE. If the SORT_AREA_SIZE cannot accommodate the entire sort, the use of temporary segments is required on disk.

SORT_AREA_RETAINED_SIZE

Default: value of SORT_AREA_SIZE

Values: 0 to value of SORT_AREA_SIZE

All users are given the number of bytes specified in this parameter for sorting. If the user requires some more memory for sorting, the user's memory allocation can increase up to SORT_AREA_SIZE. This parameter is the size in bytes to which Oracle will reduce your sort area if sort data is not being referenced. Memory is reduced only after all of the rows have been fetched from the sort space. Sometimes, a number of concurrent sorts may be required, and each is given its own memory allocation of a size that is determined by this parameter.

SORT_DIRECT_WRITES (Oracle7.2 and later)

Default: FALSE Oracle7.2 and AUTO in Oracle7.3

Values: AUTO, TRUE, FALSE

Can improve your sort performance by up to six times if you have adequate memory. Setting the parameter to TRUE or AUTO forces sorts that would normally be written to disk via the buffer cache to write directly from other areas of memory, bypassing the buffer cache. If you set the value to TRUE, Oracle uses the parameters SORT_WRITE_BUFFERS and SORT_WRITE_BUFFER_SIZE to allocate the sort area used to transfer sorted data in memory to disk. If you set the value to AUTO, Oracle derives the settings for SORT_WRITE_BUFFERS and SORT_WRITE_BUFFER_SIZE from the SORT_AREA_

SIZE. We recommend that you set the parameter to TRUE and tune your SORT_WRITE_BUFFERS and SORT_WRITE_BUFFER_SIZE to suit your site.

SORT_WRITE_BUFFERS

Default: 2

Values: 2 to 8

Used with SORT_WRITE_BUFFER_SIZE to determine the memory allocation used for sort direct writes. Sort direct writes occur when you have SORT_DIRECT_WRITES set to TRUE or AUTO. Each user process will have its own memory allocation calculated as (SORT_WRITE_BUFFERS * SORT_WRITE_BUFFER_SIZE). If you are running your query using the parallel query option, the memory that is required will be (number of query processes * SORT_WRITE_BUFFERS * SORT_WRITE_BUFFER_SIZE). We recommend that you adjust this parameter to the maximum allowable on you machine as well as increasing the SORT_WRITE_BUFFER_SIZE, but only if you have sufficient memory.

SORT_WRITE_BUFFER_SIZE

Default: 32,768

Values: 32,768 to 65,536

Used with SORT_WRITE_BUFFERS to determine the memory allocation that is used for sort direct writes. Sort direct writes occur when you have SORT_DIRECT_WRITES set to TRUE or AUTO. Each user process will have its own memory allocation calculated as (SORT_WRITE_BUFFERS * SORT_WRITE_BUFFER_SIZE). If you are running your query using the parallel query option, the memory required will be (number of query processes * SORT_WRITE_BUFFERS * SORT_WRITE_BUFFER_SIZE). If you have very large sorts and sufficient memory, you can set this parameter up as high as your machine allows and continue to receive good improvements in response time.

SORT_READ_FAC (Oracle7.2 and later)

Default: OS-dependent

Values: OS-dependent

Assists with sort merges. The setting of this parameter influences a sort's internal memory allocation and optimizer decisions. We recommend that you set it to 25%, 50%, or equal to the DB_BLOCK_MULTIBLOCK_READ_COUNT parameter.

SORT_SPACEMAP_SIZE
Default: OS-dependent
Values: OS-dependent

Adjust this parameter upward to reduce the run time involved in building very large indexes. You can set the parameter back to its default after you have completed. Oracle recommends that you set the parameter to:

((total sort bytes / (SORT_AREA_SIZE)) + 64

where total sort bytes = (number of records) * (average row length + (2 * # columns))

SQL_TRACE
Default: FALSE
Values: TRUE or FALSE

Enables (TRUE) or disables (FALSE) the SQL trace facility. Make this parameter FALSE when creating your new database; setting it to TRUE slows down database creation. We recommend that you leave SQL_TRACE set to FALSE. Some sites leave SQL_TRACE on in QA databases and then run TKPROF against all trace files and interrogate the output nightly to identify any poorly tuned statements. It is better to use the V$SQLAREA table and oradbx for a production database rather than using this parameter. Setting this parameter to TRUE not only causes the disk identified by USER_DUMP_DEST to fill up quickly, but also degrades response times markedly. In tests we have run, turning on SQL_TRACE has degraded our performance by as much as 27%. See Chapter 11 for information on tuning your application code using V$SQLAREA and oradbx.

TIMED_STATISTICS
Default: FALSE
Values: TRUE and FALSE

Enables (TRUE) or disables (FALSE) timed statistics from certain SQL*DBA MONITOR screens. If you set this parameter to TRUE, it provides needed CPU timing information on your SQL statements and by user session. Unfortunately, it degrades performance by up to 10%, so use it in small doses.

USER_DUMP_DEST
Default: OS-dependent
Values: OS-dependent

Specifies the directory to which to write user process trace files. Usually, output is placed into a subdirectory of the Oracle RDBMS's home directory. This default is acceptable for use during database creation.

NOTE In addition to the standard INIT.ORA parameters, there are several "hidden parameters." These parameters are not displayed by the SQL*DBA SHOW PARAMETERS command, nor are they shown in the V$PARAMETERS view. These parameters are all prefixed by an underscore (_) and are used primarily for internal testing and support. We describe only the performance-related hidden parameters in this chapter. If you are curious about other hidden parameters, you can connect as SYS and run the following query to display them:

```
# undoc.sql
SELECT  KSPPINM FROM X$KSPPI
WHERE   SUBSTR (KSPPINM, 1,1) = '_';
```

Do not attempt to change any hidden parameter (except for those we mention in this chapter) unless Oracle support advises you to.

Creating Very Large Databases

More and more Oracle sites now need to store huge amounts of data in their databases. Many of the databases are data warehouses, which have data fed into them from an OLTP application. Some OLTP databases are very large indeed, with several thousand users and hundreds of gigabytes of storage. Many sites with such databases plan to purge data from the main OLTP database. Time passes, and the purging plan is always considered to be low priority. Before they know it, they are confronted with a huge database, with hundreds or even thousands of online users busily adding data to a database that has become unmanageably large.

Our rule is that you should always be able to rebuild your largest table through the EXPORT and IMPORT facility. If you can't, your database is unworkable. Remember that most UNIX installations have a maximum file size of 2 gigabytes. You should also separate your batch decision support users from your OLTP users into different instances using Oracle parallel server or into completely separate databases. Decision support users can devastate the response times of online users if they are allowed to access the same instance and share the same tables and indexes. Don't leave your purging strategy until it's too late.

There are several key performance considerations for very large databases. In addition to the information presented here, please refer to Chapter 5, *Designing for Performance*; Chapter 12, *Tuning Parallel Server*; and Chapter 13, *Tuning Parallel Query*.

Loading Data

How can you load the data into your database as quickly as possible, in a way that causes as little downtime as possible for the users of the application from which data is being transferred?

- Create your database with either an 8-kilobyte or 16-kilobyte DB_BLOCK_SIZE, whichever is the largest allowable for your operating system.

- Use an SMP or MPP computer.

- Use async_io or raw devices if they can be used on your machine.

- Stripe your data files using Oracle or operating system striping so that you can take advantage of the parallel query option. You can then perform parallel data loads and parallel index creation.

- Size your objects correctly to avoid throwing performance-damaging extents. Keep in mind that 10 extents for a 1.5-gigabytes table are far less damaging than 10 extents on a 100-kilobyte table.

- Load your data into your database first, and then create your indexes. Make sure that you have a large SORT_AREA_SIZE, perhaps 2 megabytes (or larger if you can fit the entire index in memory), when you rebuild your indexes. Ensure that your INITIAL and NEXT extent sizes in your temporary tablespace are larger than, and are a multiple of, the SORT_AREA_SIZE (e.g., 10 megabytes or larger).

- With Oracle7.3, make sure that the user performing the sort is assigned to a tablespace that has been created as TEMPORARY. For Oracle7.2 and later, make sure that you have SORT_DIRECT_WRITES, SORT_DIRECT_BUFFERS, SORT_DIRECT_BUFFER_SIZE, and COMPATIBLE set appropriately.

- If your database requires foreign key constraints or triggers, apply them after the data have been loaded into your tables. You will need to have scripts to apply the changes that the triggers perform, because if the trigger applies database changes, the changes will be applied only for rows that are added after the trigger was added.

- Create your indexes using the UNRECOVERABLE option to achieve approximately 10% performance improvements. You can always recreate your indexes if your tables are in place.

- Create your indexes using the parallel query option. Be sure to build your smaller indexes first, because the parallel query option does not always release memory.

- If you are importing your data, import with a large buffer size, perhaps 2 megabytes. Also, if you are using UNIX, consider using the single-task

IMPORT executable, which needs to be created in the *$ORACLE_HOME/rdbms/lib* directory. To make the executable, you must specify

```
make -f oracle.mk impst
```

You can also make the single-task EXPORT executable if you are exporting from an existing Oracle database. Specify:

```
make -f oracle.mk expst
```

Our benchmarks indicate that the single-task executables run between 15% and 30% faster.

- Run your exports (if applicable) and imports on a per-table basis for your larger tables. This allows you to export and import multiple tables at once. To get the absolute best performance from doing this, you must have one IMP for each CPU. In addition, each table that is being imported must be on a separate disk, or the tables that are being inserted into must be striped across at least as many disks as there are processors. Similarly, your rollback segments must also be on separate disks or striped.

- Set up your rollback segments to have very large extents to accommodate the large data loads. If you have huge rollbacks and you are using IMP to load the data, you can set COMMIT=N for a marginal performance improvement.

- If you are using SQL*Loader, use the DIRECT option as load in parallel, as specified in Chapter 13.

- If you are using Oracle8 or later, and your table is always being accessed by a strict access path, consider using INDEX ONLY tables.

- If the rows in your large database are not going to be updated, set PCTFREE to 0 and PCTUSED to 99 in your tables and indexes.

- Oracle8 provides parallel insert, update, and delete. Take advantage of it!

Tuning After Creation

Once you have created your database, you will need to be able to run frequent data loads from your core OLTP database. If you notice that your massive data loads cause severe archiver waits (a result of the ARCH process not being able to write redo logs quickly enough to stay in front of the LGWR writing to redo logs), you can do the following:

- Increase the LOG_ARCHIVE_BUFFERS and LOG_ARCHIVE_BUFFER_SIZE to the maximum allowable on your machine.

- Increase the number of online redo logs and the size of the redo logs. This will help only if the redo logs are large enough to overcome the LGWR catching its tail. We are aware of decision Support databases that have redo logs that are 500 megabytes or larger.

- Write a script to *wait* at regular intervals; this will issue the command ALTER SYSTEM ARCHIVE LOG ALL, which will spawn processes to archive any unarchived log in the thread.

- If you have fine-grained striping, you may stripe disks where your archive logs are to be placed. You must use small stripe sizes and must also mirror your archives if you are using this implementation.

- If you perform the snapshot across to your decision support database, consider dropping the indexes that you may have added (not the index created by Oracle) on the snapshot table, and recreate them after the data load.

- When you create any snapshot tables (SNAP$_) in the decision support database, make sure that you create them with the USING INDEX clause to ensure that the index is sized adequately to avoid dynamic extension.

- It is likely that you will need to add indexes to your SNAP$_ table to achieve acceptable performance. Ensure that they are sized adequately and separated from the table.

How can you provide the best overall performance to the users of your very large database?

- If your very large database is a decision support database, set your database up for the parallel query option. You will need to stripe your tablespace data files by Oracle striping, operating striping, or both.

- More heavily user and critical data files may be striped by using RAID 0 and 1 (striped data files with no parity that are mirrored). Less critical data files may be striped with RAID 5 or Oracle striping. Striping is required to make the best use of the parallel query option.

- Be aware that the decision support databases that perform best are those that allow the download of data to a PC that enables local processing and has several summary tables. The decision support users can access these tables and thus avoid scanning hundreds of millions of rows over and over.

- Place your very large tables and indexes into their own tablespaces. This allows you to easily back up tables, move them across disks to get the best performance, stripe them in the most appropriate manner, and monitor the activity on the table.

How can you reduce the amount of time taken to administer your database, for example, if you are forced to recover your database?

- If you export your tables and you are using Oracle7.3 or later, use the DIRECT option on the EXP command, which bypasses the buffer cache and speeds up the table export. Set the BUFFER parameter of the export to 2 megabytes.

- Break your tables up into subtables, preferably separated by date. For example, you might have an ACCOUNTS table broken into ACCOUNTS_91, ACCOUNTS_92, ACCOUNTS_93, ACCOUNTS_94, ACCOUNTS_95, ACCOUNTS_96, ACCOUNTS_97, and so on. This allows you to create a UNION ALL view across the tables.

```
CREATE VIEW ACCOUNTS AS
SELECT * FROM ACCOUNTS_91
UNION ALL
SELECT * FROM ACCOUNTS_92
UNION ALL
SELECT * FROM ACCOUNTS_93
UNION ALL
SELECT * FROM ACCOUNTS_94
UNION ALL
SELECT * FROM ACCOUNTS_95
UNION ALL
SELECT * FROM ACCOUNTS_96
UNION ALL
SELECT * FROM ACCOUNTS_97
/
```

- An application that performs inserts, updates, and deletes into the view must refer to the individual table names.

- There is only one table (not a view) in the FROM clause.

- The SELECT list contains all columns of each table.

- The query does not use a WHERE, GROUP BY, DISTINCT, ROWNUM, or CONNECT BY START WITH clause.

- Make use of Oracle's READ ONLY(Oracle7.1), TEMPORARY (Oracle7.3), and LONG tablespaces (Oracle8).

WARNING   Prior to Oracle8 (which introduces partitions), the partitioned view approach has several limitations:

Purging Data

Large databases can't grow forever. They must have data purged at some stage, usually on a periodic basis. How can data be purged with as little effect as possible on the database users?

- If you use partitioned views, you can simply drop the view and recreate it to UNION ALL a new set of tables. In the previous example, you would drop ACCOUNTS_91 out of the view and add a new table, ACCOUNTS_98. If a table becomes corrupted (your worst nightmare), the rebuild time for the table is a fraction of what it would have been with the larger table.

- Remember that no object should exceed the maximum export size on your machine!

- Place all objects for a particular period into separate tablespaces that are especially set up for that period, for example, PERS_TABLES_91, PERS_INDEXES_91, PERS_TABLES_92, PERS_INDEXES_92, and so on. This allows you to take entire tablespaces online and offline as required.

10

Diagnostic and Tuning Tools

This chapter describes a number of Oracle database monitoring and diagnostic tools that help you to examine system and database statistics so that you can tune more effectively. Chapter 9, *Tuning a New Database*, introduced the memory and disk tuning issues that you can address with these tools. Chapter 11, *Monitoring and Tuning an Existing Database*, shows how you can use the tools in specific tuning situations. For complete information about tuning tools and their options, consult standard Oracle documentation.

These are the major tools:

MONITOR

A SQL*DBA facility that lets you look at various system activity and performance tables

SQL_TRACE

A utility that writes a trace file containing performance statistics

TKPROF

A utility that translates the SQL_TRACE file into readable output and can also show the execution plan for a SQL statement

EXPLAIN PLAN

A statement that analyzes and displays the execution plan for a SQL statement

ORADBX

An undocumented tool that allows you to track a running process and create a trace file in the same format as the SQL_TRACE trace file. You can then run TKPROF against the trace file to obtain the execution plan details, as well as disk I/O, parsing, and CPU usage.

ANALYZE

A statement that compiles statistics for use by the cost-based optimizer to construct its execution plan. The statement also produces other useful information that can be used to detect chained rows and help with capacity planning.

UTLBSTAT (begin) and UTLESTAT (end)

Scripts that produce a snapshot of how the database is performing from the time you start UTLBSTAT until you run UTLESTAT

Oracle scripts

A number of additional diagnostic and tuning scripts provided by Oracle

Custom scripts

A number of diagnostic and tuning scripts that we have developed ourselves

Enterprise Manager/Performance Pack

An Oracle product introduced with Oracle7.3 that provides some excellent tuning tools, including Oracle Performance Manager, Oracle Trace, and Oracle Expert, which are documented in Appendix D, *Oracle Performance Pack.*

Diagnostic and tuning tools are also available for the various operating systems that support Oracle. For example, in a UNIX environment, you might use *iostat* to look at disk activity in your system. In VMS, you might use **MON PAGE** to examine memory. For information about these system-specific tools, consult your operating system documentation.

In addition to the standard Oracle and operating system facilities, every database administrator develops his or her own set of handy scripts and modified utilities. As was mentioned above, we've included a few of our own favorites in this chapter. We encourage you to save any diagnostic and tuning scripts that you develop in your own system toolbox so that they will be available next time you need them. If you think Oracle DBAs or other users could benefit from what you've learned about improving system performance, we encourage you to send us a copy, and we'll include the best scripts and other tools in the next edition of this book.

The tools described in this chapter help you to identify potential and real database problems. By using them on a regular basis to monitor system activity and performance, you can detect when a potential problem is becoming a real one and when a real problem is turning into a true disaster. You'll notice that some of the tools overlap in function. Choose the tools and options that best suit your style and your system, and use them on a regular basis to monitor system, memory, and disk usage. Things can change rapidly in a dynamic system like Oracle.

MONITOR: Monitoring System Activity Tables

The SQL*DBA MONITOR facility allows you to monitor activity and performance in your system by looking at the views of a variety of read-only system performance tables that are held in memory. The way you use this facility depends on your particular platform, but its function is consistent across platforms. If you are using a command line interface (e.g., VMS), you'll type a command line in response to the SQLDBA prompt, such as

```
SQLDBA> MON FILES
```

to display information about file activity. If you're running a GUI (e.g., Macintosh), you'll select a MONITOR function, such as Files, from a pull-down menu. Table 10-1 shows the available MONITOR displays.

This chapter and Chapter 11 show how you can use the MONITOR facility to look at memory and disk performance. For complete information about that facility and how you invoke it in your own system, refer to the *Oracle Database Administrator's Guide.*

Table 10-1: MONITOR Displays

Monitor Option	Description
FILE IO	Read/write activity for database files in the system. You can select an individual file or set of files. Pay particular attention to the "Request Rate" columns.
SYSTEM IO	Logical and physical reads in writes, cumulative figures, and interval.
LATCH	Internal latches in the system. Pay particular attention to "No Wait Request Misses," which must be kept as low as possible.

Table 10-1: MONITOR Displays (continued)

Monitor Option	Description
LOCK	Locks in the system. We recommend that you use the locking scripts instead because for a reasonably sized system, it is impossible to see all of the locks on the screen at once.
PROCESSES	Process IDs for Oracle and operating system, username, terminal, and executing program.
ROLLBACK SEGMENTS	Extents, transactions, size, writes, and waits for rollbacks. Pay attention to extents (should be as low as possible) and waits (should not be any).
STATISTICS	Run-time statistics on system or session use and performance (includes user, enqueue, cache, and redo).
TABLE	Table statistics. You can display an individual table and its owner.
SESSION	Session ID for user ID, process ID, session status, username, and most recent SQL statement executed.
CIRCUIT	(Multithreaded server only) Status, currently active queue, number of messages, and total bytes transferred for each path.
DISPATCHER	(Multithreaded server only) Total messages, bytes, idle time, busy time, and load.
LIBRARYCACHE	Parts of the cache and the hit ratio. Pay particular attention to the "Gets" ratio, which must be kept as close to 1 as possible.
QUEUE	(Multithreaded server only) Current number of messages in dispatcher queue, total messages, and average wait time.
SHARED SERVER	(Multithreaded server only) Requests from server, idle time, and load (which should be kept balanced).
SQLAREA	SQL statements being executed and contained in cache. Pay attention to whether almost identical statements are in the cache.

NOTE   All MONITOR displays have a default of 5 seconds, which means that the information in the tables is refreshed every 5 seconds. To change the default, issue the following command:

SQLDBA > MON CYCLE *number*

where *number* is the number of seconds, in the range 1 to 3600.

SQL_TRACE: Writing a Trace File

The SQL trace facility writes a trace file containing performance statistics for the SQL statements being executed. These include:

- Number of parses, executes, and fetches performed
- Various types of CPU and elapsed times
- Number of physical and logical reads performed

- Number of rows processed

- Number of library cache misses

This trace file provides valuable information that you can use to tune your system. You should be sparing about running it, however. When you have globally enabled SQL_TRACE by setting the appropriate parameters in the INIT.ORA file, your overall response times are likely to degrade as much as 20% to 30%, as well as quickly filling your disk with trace files.

The exact form of the trace file name written by SQL_TRACE is system dependent, but usually it is in the form *filename.TRC.* You can read this file directly, but it is best to run the TKPROF utility against it to produce an output with more useful tuning information. (TKPROF is discussed later in this chapter; that section shows the particular statistics collected by SQL_TRACE.)

To globally enable SQL_TRACE, you must set a number of INIT.ORA parameters:

Parameter	Setting	Description
SQL_TRACE	TRUE	Enables the trace for all application users. A setting of FALSE disables the trace. FALSE is the default.
USER_DUMP_DEST	directory	The directory where SQL_TRACE writes the trace file. The default is system dependent but generally is the directory that holds your system dumps (e.g., *$ORACLE_HOME/rdbms/log*).
TIMED_STATISTICS	TRUE	Causes the RDBMS to collect additional timing statistics. These timing statistics are useful to SQL_TRACE and also to the SQL*DBA MONITOR command. The default is FALSE.
MAX_DUMP_SIZE	number	Limits the physical size of the trace file to the specified number of bytes. If you enable the SQL_TRACE parameter for the entire database, this option helps control the amount of disk space used. To find out what size to specify, find out the number of operating system blocks available in your system. If SQL_TRACE runs out of space, it will truncate your output; you'll have to allocate more space and start again.

The way you invoke SQL_TRACE for individual Oracle tools and user sessions depends on the Oracle program you are running:

For:	Do This:
SQL*Forms	RUNFORM *formname usercode/password* -S (Version 3 and later)
SQL*Plus	ALTER SESSION SET SQL_TRACE TRUE

For:	Do This:
SQL*Reportwriter	Create a field called SQL_TRACE and a group report with an attribute of CHAR(40). Specify the following statement against the column: &SQL ALTER SESSION SET SQL_TRACE TRUE
Pro* tools	EXEC SQL ALTER SESSION SET SQL_TRACE TRUE

Turning on SQL_TRACE for a Running Session

A great new feature that snuck in with the Oracle7.2 release is the ability to turn SQL_TRACE on for a user session other than your own. One catch is that you must be logged on as Oracle to run it. This feature can be used in the same way as ORADBX; you identify a problem user and create a trace file of all of his or her database activities. You can run TKPROF against the trace file to obtain the SQL statements execution plans, as well as many run-time statistics such as disk I/Os, number of reads from Oracle's buffer cache, and CPU utilization.

To turn on SQL_TRACE for another user, you must provide the SID and the serial number of the problem user from the V$SESSION table. If you know the operating system user, you can perform the following query.

NOTE   The process ID is obtained because most machines have the process ID as part of the trace file name. For example, most UNIX machines have the format *ora_23526.trc*, where 23526 is the operating system process ID.

```
# usersid.sql
SELECT  sid, serial#, osuser, process
   FROM v$session
  WHERE osuser='gurrym';
SID          SERIAL#              OSUSER     PROCESS
------------------------------------------------------
20              26               gurrym      23526
```

You can also pick out the user that has the most disk I/Os and trace what statements they are running using the command

```
# maxsidio.sql
 SELECT ses.sid, ses.serial#, ses.osuser, ses.process
   FROM v$session ses, v$sess_io sio
  WHERE ses.sid = sio.sid
    AND nvl(ses.username,'SYS') not in ('SYS', 'SYSTEM')
    AND sio.physical_reads = (SELECT MAX(physical_reads)
                                FROM v$session ses2, v$sess_io sio2
                               WHERE ses2.sid = sio2.sid
                                 AND ses2.username
                                  NOT IN ('SYSTEM', 'SYS'));
```

SID	SERIAL#	OSUSER	PROCESS
41	46	corriganp	12818

You can now turn SQL_TRACE on for the troublesome user with the following command; 41 is the SID and 46 is the serial number.

```
EXECUTE dbms_system.set_sql_trace_in_session(41,46,TRUE);
```

The SQL_TRACE output is automatically turned off when the user being traced logs off the database. To to turn it off explicitly, specify

```
EXECUTE dbms_system.set_sql_trace_in_session(41,46,FALSE);
```

You will find the trace file in the directory specified by the INIT.ORA parameter USER_DUMP_DEST. You can run TKPROF against the trace output file to obtain the EXPLAIN PLAN details and run-time statistics. (See the next section for more details on using TKPROF.)

TKPROF: Interpreting the Trace File

The TKPROF utility translates a trace file to a readable format. You can run TKPROF against a trace file that you have previously created using SQL_TRACE or ORADBX, or you can run it while the program that is creating the trace file is still running. You can optionally tell TKPROF to invoke the EXPLAIN PLAN statement (described in the next section) for the statements being analyzed.

You invoke TKPROF by issuing the command

```
TKPROF tracefile listfile [SORT = parameters] [PRINT = number]
       [INSERT =  FILENAME] [SYS = YES/NO] [TABLE = schema.table]
       [EXPLAIN = username/password] [RECORD = filename]
```

where

tracefile
> Is the name of the trace file containing the statistics gathered by the trace facility. The trace file is stored in the directory specified by the INIT.ORA parameter USER_DUMP_DEST

listfile
> Is the name of the file where TKPROF writes its output.

SORT=parameters
> Is the order in which to display output. You can specify, as parameters, any of the statistics collected by SQL_TRACE. (These are listed in Table 10-3.) TKPROF outputs statistics in the descending order of the values of these parameters. For example, if you specify

```
SORT = EXECPU
```

TKPROF first displays statistics for the statements that had the worst EXECPU values (that is, required the most CPU time).

If you specify more than one parameter, for example,

```
SORT = (FCHPHR, PRSCPU)
```

TKPROF adds the statistics you specify. The output that appears first is for statements in which the sum of these two statistics was the worst.

PRINT = *number*

Is the number of statements included in the output. You might want to limit the amount of output to the worst-performing statements.

INSERT = *filename*

Creates a SQL script that can be used to store the trace file statistics in the database. The script name is identified by filename.

SYS = *yes/no*

Allows you to include Oracle's own dictionary statements. Including these statements makes your output considerably longer. It is usually best to set SYS=NO.

TABLE = *schema.table*

If many users are using TKPROF at the same time, you may get situations in which the users are interfering with each other's output. This is because TKPROF uses a single table in the database to store its EXPLAIN PLAN details. The table is called PROF$PLAN_TABLE. If the table doesn't exist, TKPROF creates it for you, uses the table, and then drops it. If the table does exist, TKPROF removes the rows from the table, which can create problems if there are multiple users. This option allows you to specify another table name, for example, MARKG_PLAN, to avoid conflicts.

RECORD = *filename*

Allows you to store a SQL script from your trace file so that you can replay your commands and test the effect of changing indexes and changing the optimizer. The recursive calls are removed from the script automatically.

EXPLAIN = *username/password*

Runs the EXPLAIN PLAN statement on all of the statements in the trace file, logging in under the account specified.

For example, you might specify

```
TKPROF 12_12626.TRC TRACE.LIS SORT=(EXECPU)
   EXPLAIN = username/password SYS=NO
```

When you run TKPROF, it interprets the trace file and puts the readable output in the file you specify. TKPROF produces a formatted listing. The rows and columns in the TKPROF output have the meanings shown in Table 10-2.

Table 10-2: TKPROF Output Rows and Columns

Row/Column	Description
Parse	Statistics for the parse steps performed by SQL statements. Parsing checks for security, and the existence of tables, columns, and other objects being referenced by your SQL.
Execute	Statistics for the execute steps performed by SQL statements. UPDATE, DELETE, and INSERT statements show the number of rows processed here. SELECT statements list the number of selected rows.
Fetch	Statistics for the fetch steps performed by SQL statements. SELECT statements show the number of rows processed here. UPDATE, INSERT, and DELETE do not return rows for this value.
count	Number of times a SQL statement is parsed or executed, plus the number of times a fetch is performed in order to carry out the operation.
cpu	CPU time for all parses, executes, and fetches in seconds.
elapsed	Elapsed time for parses, executes, and fetches in seconds.
disk	Number of data blocks read from disk for each parse, fetch, or execute. If a single multiblock read returns eight blocks, this figure is incremented only once for the physical read. Most disks operate at 50+ I/Os per second, so if you divide the figure by 50, you can usually get a good idea of the time taken to perform the disk reads.
query	Number of times a buffer was returned in consistent mode, that is, the data is for query only and has not been modified since the SELECT statement started.
current	Number of times a buffer was retrieved for INSERT, UPDATE, or DELETE.
rows	Number of rows processed by a SQL statement (only queries, not subqueries). Unfortunately, this figure does not include the rows returned by subqueries. The number of rows returned appears in the fetch step for the SELECT statement and in the execute step for the INSERT, UPDATE, and DELETE statements.

Following is an example of TKPROF output illustrating the rows and columns shown in Table 10-2. Notice that the cpu and elapsed times are 0.00. This is because the INIT.ORA parameter TIMED_STATISTICS is set to FALSE. If you set it to TRUE, you get more information, but it does have a 5% to 10% performance drag on your machine.

```
    SELECT    D.dept_name, E.surname
      FROM    emp e , dept D
     WHERE    D.dept_no like 'ACC%'
       AND    D.dept_no = E.dept_no
  ORDER BY    D.dept_name, E.surname;
```

```
              count     cpu   elapsed   disk    query    current    rows
  Parse:         1      0.00    0.00       3      11         0         0
  Execute:       1      0.00    0.00       0       0         0         0
  Fetch:         1      0.00    0.00       9      29         4        90

Misses in library cache during parse: 1
Parsing user id: 8
      Rows     Execution Plan
  ---------    -------------------------------------------------------------
        90     MERGE JOIN
         4         SORT                        JOIN
         4            TABLE ACCESS             BY ROWID          DEPT
         4               INDEX                 RANGE SCAN        DEPY_IDX2
        86         SORT                        JOIN
        86            TABLE ACCESS             BY ROWID          EMP
        86               INDEX                 RANGE SCAN        EMP_IDX2
```

You can select any of the statistics shown in Table 10-3, computed by SQL_
TRACE and interpreted by TKPROF, in the SORT clause. Of these, EXECPU (if
you have set TIMED_STATISTICS=TRUE), PRSDSK, FCHDSK, and EXEDSK are
probably the most useful. EXECPU shows the total CPU time spent executing the
statement; and PRSDSK, FCHDSK, and EXEDSK record the number of disk reads.

Table 10-3: TKPROF SORT Parameters

Parameter	Description
PRSCNT	Number of times parsed
PRSCPU	CPU time spent parsing
PRSELA	Elapsed time spent parsing
PRSDSK	Number of physical disk reads during parse
PRSQRY	Number of consistent mode reads during parse
PRSCU	Number of current mode block reads during parse
PSRMIS	Number of library cache misses during parse
EXECNT	Number of executes
EXECPU	CPU time spent executing
EXEELA	Elapsed time spent executing
EXEDSK	Number of physical disk reads during execute
EXEQRY	Number of consistent mode block reads during execute
EXECU	Number of current mode block reads during execute
EXEROW	Number of rows processed during execute
EXEMIS	Number of library cache misses during the execute
FCHCNT	Number of fetches
FCHCPU	CPU time spent fetching
FCHELA	Elapsed time spent fetching
FCHDSK	Number of physical reads during fetch

Table 10-3: TKPROF SORT Parameters (continued)

Parameter	Description
FCHQRY	Number of consistent mode blocks read during fetch
FCHCU	Number of current mode blocks read during fetch
FCHROW	Number of rows fetched

TKPROF formulates its output first for each individual SQL statement and then at the user session level. It often pays to look at the "Overall Totals for All Statements" before you examine individual statement performance. The overall totals will tell you what general problems exist. Another time saver is to scan the TKPROF output file for keywords. For example, in UNIX, you can scan the file using *grep FULL trace.lis*. The word FULL is for full table scans.

Here are some rules for interpreting these statistics; these rules apply to all types of systems and jobs:

- If the cpu, elap, and disk figures in the Parse row are high relative to those in the Execute and Fetch rows, you probably need to enlarge your SHARED_POOL_SIZE so that you'll be able to store more of the dictionary in memory. This will reduce the required amount of disk I/O.

- If the library cache misses are greater than 5% of the count, you should tune your shared pool (see Chapter 11). The library cache misses are listed between the statistics and the EXPLAIN PLAN details in your TKPROF output.

- If the Parse count figure is relatively high, you may need to do open cursor tuning on the application.

- If the sum of Execute disk + Fetch disk is more than 10% of the sum of Execute query + Execute current + Fetch query + Fetch current, the hit ratio of finding data in the cache is too low. Consider tuning the statement by adding an index or by using a more appropriate index, by rewriting the statement, by using a hint, or by using a different optimizer option (e.g., FIRST_ROWS instead of ALL_ROWS for an online system). You will often get a further improvement by increasing the buffer cache using the INIT.ORA parameter DB_BLOCK_BUFFERS.

- If the Fetch count is about twice Fetch rows, and if PL/SQL is being used, it's likely that implicit cursors are in use. (Implicit cursors are SQL statements that are not declared; they are less efficient than explicit cursors.) Ask your analysts/programmers to investigate.

- If the total of the elap column is greater than 2.5 seconds, and if the query is an interactive, online one, investigate the SQL statements. The response times indicated by these statistics exceed the standards for most sites.

- If Execute query is high, and Execute rows and Execute current are markedly lower, investigate your indexes. Your tables probably do not have enough indexes or have inadequate indexes defined for them.

The following additional rules apply only to online transaction processing systems that require excellent response time (e.g., 2.5 seconds elapsed for all online queries):

- Make sure all Execute cpu times are less than 1 second.

- Make sure Parse cpu times are less than 1 second. If not, tune your shared pool, as documented in Chapter 11.

- Allow full table scans only on small tables. Don't allow them on tables with more than 200 rows or on tables that are frequently used in multiple-table joins.

- Remove all unnecessary calls to the system table, DUAL.

- Declare all PL/SQL SELECTs.

- Make sure Oracle chooses the appropriate driving table (described in the section called "The driving table" in Chapter 6, *Tuning SQL*).

Take Care in Using TKPROF

TKPROF has a few traps that you'll want to avoid:

- If any changes have occurred to the schema, such as adding an index or reanalyzing tables and/or indexes, the EXPLAIN PLAN results may be different from what they were when the trace file was created.

- If you have obtained your trace file from the production database and you are running TKPROF against your test or development database, the execution plans may be different from what they were when the trace file was created. This is the result of different statistics on tables and indexes. Other factors that may cause the cost-based optimizer to act differently are the DB_BLOCK_SIZE and DB_FILE_MULTIBLOCK_READ_COUNT setting; the latter is used to determine whether a full table scan is preferable to an index search.

- TKPROF does not know what data type bind variables are. It assumes VARCHAR2. This may cause your EXPLAIN PLAN to appear as though an index is not being used when in fact it is.

- The optimizer behavior can change from one release of Oracle to the next, so you must make sure that you are running your TKPROF against the same version of Oracle that was used to create the trace file.

- Do not use a different optimizer mode from the one that was used when the trace file was created. RULE acts differently in the cost-based optimizer. FIRST_ROWS also behaves differently from ALL_ROWS.

EXPLAIN PLAN: Explaining the Optimizer's Plan

EXPLAIN PLAN is a statement you can include in your SQL to explain the execution plan, or retrieval path, that the optimizer will use to do its database retrieval. The execution plan is the sequence of physical operations that Oracle must perform to return the data requested. (See the discussion of the optimizer in the section called "The SQL Optimizer" in Chapter 6.) By looking at the execution plans for SQL statements, you can see which ones are inefficient, and you can compare alternatives to find out which will give you better performance.

If you are going to issue the EXPLAIN PLAN statement, you need to create a table called PLAN_TABLE that will hold the data to be displayed. You do this by running a script. The name of this script is system dependent but is likely to be *UTLXPLAN.sql.* (You can use your own table instead, if you define it to be identical to the PLAN_TABLE and reference it in the INTO clause described below.)

Use the following syntax to run an explain:

```
EXPLAIN PLAN [SET STATEMENT_ID [=] string literal>]
[INTO table_name]
FOR sql_statement
```

where

STATEMENT_ID

Is a unique optional identifier for the statement

INTO

Allows the user to save the results of the analysis in the specified table. The table must conform to the format for the table used to store the analysis (see the description of the table format below). If this clause is not specified, the system will then attempt to store the information in a table named <user_id>.PLAN_TABLE. If the explicit or implicit table does not exist, the EXPLAIN command will fail.

sql_statement

Is an INSERT, DELETE, UPDATE, or query statement

The table that is used to represent the plan information consists of the following fields:

STATEMENT_ID

An identifier associated with the statement. If this identifier is not set by the user, it will be null. Note that a user can identify a statement by the timestamp field.

TIMESTAMP

The date and time when the statement was analyzed

REMARKS

Any comment the user wishes to associate with this step of the analysis

OPERATION

The name of the operation being performed. The following table lists the operations described by the facility. The operation column on the first row of the EXPLAIN PLAN contains one of the following: DELETE STATEMENT, INSERT STATEMENT, SELECT STATEMENT, or UPDATE STATEMENT.

The operation shown when counting the number of rows returned by a query (i.e., SELECT COUNT(*)) is SORT. Note, however, that the table will not really be sorted. This is because of the way that COUNT is implemented internally.

OPTIONS

Option that modifies the operation (e.g., OUTER option on join operations, rationale for sorting, type of index scan, type of filter, etc.). Table 10-4 provides a list of the options for the operations that have options.

OBJECT_NODE

Name of the node that owns the database object. The column may also contain the database link. For the parallel query option, it describes the order in which the output from the query servers is processed.

OBJECT_OWNER

Name of the schema (user) that owns the database object.

OBJECT_INSTANCE

Number corresponding to the ordinal position of the object as it appears in the original query. Numbering proceeds from left to right, from outer to inner, with respect to the original query text.

OBJECT_NAME

Name of the table or index.

OBJECT_TYPE

Modifier that provides descriptive information about the database object (e.g., NON-UNIQUE for indexes).

OPTIMIZER

Current mode of the optimizer: RULE, CHOOSE, FIRST_ROWS, ALL_ROWS.

SEARCH_COLUMNS

Not used for the later releases of Oracle7 and 8.

ID

Number assigned to this operation in the tree. Corresponds to a preorder traversal of the row source tree.

PARENT_ID

Number assigned to the previous operation that receives information from this operation. This field combined with the ID field allows users to do a tree-walk of the specified plan with the CONNECT BY statement.

POSITION

Position this database object occupies for the previous operation. Prior to Oracle7.3, the first row returned contained the cost of the statement (if the statement used the cost-based optimizer). The lower the cost, the more chance there is that your statement will perform well. The rule-based optimizer has a null in this column on the first row. To get the cost, add DECODE(id, 0, 'Cost = '|| position) to your SELECT statement on the plan_ table.

COST

Stores the cost of the statement if you are using the cost-based optimizer. This column replaces the value that was stored in the position column prior to Oracle7.3.

CARDINALITY

Used by the cost-based optimizer. It stores the number of distinct values that are likely to be returned, which will assist with determining whether to use a full table scan or an index lookup.

BYTES

Used by the cost-based optimizer to determine how many bytes are likely to be returned by the statement. The optimizer uses this information when determining the optimal access path.

OTHER_TAG

Introduced in Oracle7.3 to assist with parallel query tuning. The values and their meanings are shown in the following table. See Chapter 13, *Tuning Parallel Query*, for a detailed explanation of each option.

SERIAL or NULL
    The SQL is executed locally using the parallel query option.

SERIAL_FROM_REMOTE
    The SQL is executed at a remote site.

PARALLEL_COMBINED_WITH_PARENT
    The table is scanned in parallel; the next step will be handled by the same parallel process.

PARALLEL_COMBINED_WITH_CHILD
    The child process will scan the table in process and also perform the next step (e.g., a sort).

PARALLEL_TO_SERIAL

The table is scanned by using multiple processes, but the data is passed to a single process.

PARALLEL_TO_PARALLEL

The table scan is performed by a number of processes running in parallel, and the data is passed to a number of processes, also running in parallel.

PARALLEL_FROM_SERIAL

Many processes perform the table scan and hand the output to a single process.

OTHER

Other information specific to the row source that a user may find useful—for example, the SELECT statement to a remote node, or (with the parallel query option) the statement that is performed for each of the query servers.

Table 10-4. EXPLAIN PLAN Operations

Operation	Option	Description
AND-EQUAL		A retrieval using the intersection of rowids from index searches. Duplicates are eliminated. This operation is used for single-column accesses.
CONNECT BY		A retrieval that is based on a tree walk. The SQL will contain a CONNECT clause.
CONCATENATION		This is essentially a UNION ALL operation of the sources. Used for OR operations.
COUNT		This is a node used to count the number of rows returned from a table. Used for queries that use the ROWNUM meta-column.
	STOPKEY	Rows are counted and the WHERE clause contains a ROWNUM < *number*, where *number* is any digit.
FILTER		A restriction of the rows returned from a table.
FIRST-ROW		A retrieval of only the first row.
FOR UPDATE		A retrieval that is used for updating. The SQL will contain a FOR UPDATE clause.
INDEX		A retrieval from an index.
	UNIQUE SCAN	A single rowid returned from a unique or primary key index.

Table 10-4. EXPLAIN PLAN Operations (continued)

Operation	Option	Description
	RANGE SCAN	One or more rows returned from an index in ascending order.
	RANGE SCAN DESCENDING	One or more rows returned from an index in descending order.
INTERSECTION		A retrieval of rows common to two tables.
MERGE JOIN		A join using merge scans. Two or more selects are performed. The rows from each select are individually sorted and then merged.
	OUTER	A merge join that contains an outer join.
MINUS		A retrieval of rows in source 1 table, not in source 2 table. Duplicates are eliminated.
NESTED LOOPS		A join using nested loops. Each value in the first subnode is looked up in the second subnode. Often used when one table in a join is indexed and the other is not. Use this in preference to a merge join for online systems.
	OUTER	A nested loop that contains an outer join.
PROJECTION		A retrieval of a subset of columns from a table.
REMOTE		A retrieval from a database other than the current database.
SEQUENCE		An operation involving a sequence table.
SORT		A retrieval of rows ordered on some column or group of columns.
	AGGREGATE	A single row is retrieved from a GROUP BY function.
	UNIQUE	Rows are sorted, and duplicates are eliminated.
	GROUP BY	Rows are sorted, and one or more rows are returned to satisfy a GROUP BY clause.
	JOIN	Rows are sorted in readiness for merging rows in a merge join.
	ORDER BY	Rows are returned in a particular order using ORDER BY.
TABLE ACCESS		A retrieval from a base table.
	FULL	A full table scan.

Table 10-4. EXPLAIN PLAN Operations (continued)

Operation	Option	Description
	CLUSTER	A selection of rows from a table based on the key of an indexed cluster.
	HASH	A selection of rows from a table based on the key of an indexed cluster.
	BY ROWID	A retrieval of a row from a table using a rowid. This usually implies an index lookup in which the rowid is obtained from the index.
UNION		A retrieval of unique rows from two tables.
VIEW		A retrieval from a virtual table.

EXPLAIN PLAN Table Definition

The following example shows the CREATE TABLE statement definition for the EXPLAIN PLAN table.

```
CREATE TABLE plan_table

statement_id       VARCHAR2(30)
timestamp          DATE,
remarks            VARCHAR2(80),
operation          VARCHAR2(30),
options            VARCHAR2(30),
object_node        VARCHAR2(128),
object_owner       VARCHAR2(30),
object_name        VARCHAR2(30),
object_instance    NUMERIC
object_type        VARCHAR2(30),
optimizer          VARCHAR2(255),
search_columns     NUMERIC
id                 NUMERIC,
parent_id          NUMERIC,
position           NUMERIC
cost               NUMERIC,
cardinality        NUMERIC,
bytes              NUMERIC,
other_tag          VARCHAR2(255),
other              LONG);
```

Interpreting EXPLAIN PLAN Output

After you have run the EXPLAIN PLAN, it's important to interpret the results correctly. For the most usable output format, run the following statement against your PLAN_TABLE:

```
# plan.sql
SELECT LPAD(' ', 2*level) || operation ||' ' ||
```

```
              options ||' ` || object_name "Execution Plan"
   FROM plan_table
CONNECT BY PRIOR ID = parent_id
   START WITH ID = 1;
```

Figure 10-1 shows the effect.

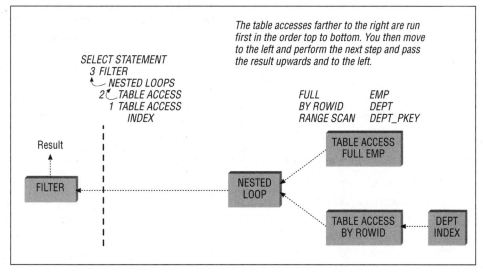

Figure 10-1. Interpreting EXPLAIN PLAN output

Some of the more common EXPLAIN PLAN outputs are described in the following sections.

Primary or UNIQUE key index lookup

Primary and UNIQUE key lookups, shown in the example below, are extremely efficient. Use them whenever possible.

```
SELECT surname
   FROM emp
  WHERE emp_no = 12111;
SELECT STATEMENT
           TABLE ACCESS        BY ROWID        emp
               INDEX           UNIQUE SCAN     emp_pk
```

Non-UNIQUE index lookup

It is usually better to use an index than to perform a full table scan. Make sure that the most appropriate index on the table is being used.

```
SELECT surname
   FROM emp
  WHERE dept_no = 30;
```

```
SELECT STATEMENT
        TABLE ACCESS              BY ROWID        emp
            INDEX                 RANGE SCAN      emp_idx2
```

Index-only lookup

For an index-only lookup, all of the columns in the SELECT statement and the WHERE clause have to be contained in the index. This is a very efficient way of accessing data. The data is also returned in the order of the index (ascending by default). In the following statement, the data would be returned in dept_no order:

```
SELECT dept_no
  FROM emp
 WHERE dept_no = 30;
SELECT STATEMENT
    INDEX               RANGE SCAN      emp_idx2
```

ORDER BY without using an index to order the data

As was mentioned, using an index to sort your output is the most efficient way to produce sorted data. This is not always possible, given the column being selected and the column in the ORDER BY. The following output performs a separate sort process. If the statement read ORDER BY dept_no, surname, and the dept_no index was expanded to include the surname column (dept_no, surname), the sort could be avoided.

```
SELECT surname
  FROM emp
 WHERE dept_no = 30
 ORDER BY surname;
SELECT STATEMENT
    SORT (ORDER BY)
        TABLE ACCESS        ROWID           emp
            INDEX           RANGE SCAN      emp_idx2
```

Full table scan

Avoid full table scans unless you are using the parallel query option, you are retrieving 15% or more of the rows in the table, or the table has very few rows. For example,

```
SELECT surname
  FROM emp
 WHERE dept_no = 30;
SELECT STATEMENT
        TABLE ACCESS        FULL            emp
```

Sort merge

Sort merges are usually best suited to batch processing, not online screens. Sort merges obtain all of the rows from two or more tables and then sort and merge all of the data before returning them to the transaction that is running the query. Online screens run better using nested loops, where rows are joined and presented to the transaction one at a time. If you set the OPTIMIZER_MODE parameter to ALL_ROWS, sort merges will usually be performed. If you set it to FIRST_ROWS, nested loops will usually be performed. This enables online screens to receive one buffer full of information (perhaps about 20 rows) without having to sort and merge all of the rows in the table.

The USE_MERGE hint will force a merge join to be used.

```
SELECT dept.dept_name, emp.surname
  FROM emp, dept
 WHERE dept.dept_no  = 30
   AND emp.dept_no    = dept.dept_no;
SELECT STATEMENT
    MERGE JOIN
        SORT                    JOIN
            TABLE ACCESS        BY ROWID        dept
                INDEX           RANGE SCAN      depy_idx2
        SORT                    JOIN
            TABLE ACCESS        BY ROWID        emp
                INDEX           RANGE SCAN      emp_idx2
```

Nested loop

As was mentioned, a nested loop is usually preferable to a merge join when many rows are going to be returned to an online screen. You can use the USE_NL hint in your statement to force a nested loop to be used.

```
SELECT dept.dept_name, emp.surname
  FROM emp, dept
 WHERE dept.dept_no  = 30
   AND emp.dept_no    = dept.dept_no;
SELECT STATEMENT
    NESTED LOOP
        TABLE ACCESS        BY ROWID        dept
            INDEX           RANGE SCAN      depy_idx2
        TABLE ACCESS        BY ROWID        emp
            INDEX           RANGE SCAN      emp_idx2
```

Running EXPLAIN PLAN Against Problem Statements

The following script detects all SQL statements that will have an expected run time of greater than 2.5 seconds and runs EXPLAIN PLAN against them. Assume that approximately 50 I/Os can be performed per second. Before you can run your main query, you will have to create a file called *explain.sql* as follows:

```
# explain.sql
SELECT LPAD(' ', 2*level) || operation ||' ' ||
```

```
       options ||' ' || object_name "Execution Plan"
   FROM plan_table
CONNECT BY PRIOR id = parent_id
   START WITH ID = 1;
```

Now run the main script, which creates a temporary file called *expstat.sql*. That script is run to create a file called *expstat.lis*, which you can view using your favorite editor.

```
SET LINESIZE 2000
SET ARRAYSIZE 1
SPOOL expstat.sql
COLUMN nl NEWLINE
SELECT 'delete from plan_table;' nl,
       'explain plan for ' nl,
       sql_text||';' nl,
       'start explain.sql' nl
 FROM   v$sqlarea
WHERE   disk_reads / executions > 250
ORDER   BY disk_reads / executions desc;
SPOOL   OFF
SPOOL   expstat.lis
START   expstat.sql
SPOOL   OFF
```

ORADBX: Listing Events

ORADBX is an undocumented Oracle product that is available on most Oracle platforms used by Oracle consultants and Oracle support. Be careful with this product, and don't experiment with it. If you use it incorrectly, it can totally screw up your database. If you use the event 10046, you can get some valuable tuning information. You can obtain a full list of all the events that can be set by viewing the file *oraus.msg*. Most of the 10000-10999 range of events may be set using ORADBX. Please don't set any other event except for 10046 without permission from Oracle support.

The 10046 event has the ability to track the SQL statements that a user is running. If you spot an Oracle user on your database who is using a large amount of CPU, you can trace him or her to see exactly what SQL is being run, as well as the translated bind variable values being used. This event also provides the full execution path of the statement and which indexes, if any, are being used. It will also provide you with CPU usage if you have set the TIMED_STATISTICS parameter to TRUE.

Before you can use ORADBX, you must make the executable. Under UNIX, use the following *make* command. You will find that *oradbx.o* and *oracle.mk* are required to make the *oradbx* executable in the *$ORACLE_HOME/rdbms/*

admin/lib directory. You may wish to copy the *oradbx* executable across to the *$ORACLE_HOME/bin* directory to place it into your own path.

```
make -f oracle.mk oradbx
```

You can now start using ORADBX. To run the statement, select an Oracle shadow process of one of your users, typically the user who is using the most CPU or the most disk I/Os. For example, obtain the users in question for the PERS database instance on some UNIX systems, you'll run an operating command such as the following:

```
ps -ef | grep oracle | grep PERS > all_PERS_users.lis
```

This will list all the shadow processes, as well as other Oracle processes for the PERS database instances, and place them into a file called *all_PERS_users.lis*. You can now sort the file to see the largest CPU users first:

```
sort +6 -r all_PERS_users.lis > high_PERS_cpu_first.lis
```

You identify the process ID of the shadow process and run ORADBX against it. The following example assumes that the process ID that you have identified is 8972:

```
oradbx
debug 8972
event 10046 trace name context forever, level 12
exit
```

A trace file is created in the directory as specified by the INIT.ORA parameter USER_DUMP_DEST. The name of the file varies across operating systems but it usually contains the process ID and has a *trc* suffix (for example, *ora_PERS_8972.trc*). You run the TKPROF utility (described earlier) against the file to obtain the SQL statements, their execution path, and a range of statistics.

```
tkprof ora_PERS_8972.trc 8972.lis explain=owner/pass sys=no
```

In this example, *ora_PERS_8972.trc* is the trace file in the USER_DUMP_DEST directory; *8972.lis* is the output list file, which you can name according to any naming convention that suits you; *explain=owner/pass* is the owner name and password of the owner of the database objects being used (or a user that has grants and synonyms to the tables); and *sys=no* tells TKPROF to include only the user SQL statements and not those performed against the Oracle dictionary tables.

To turn ORADBX off for the process, specify

```
oradbx
>debug 8972
>event 10046 trace name context off
>exit
```

NOTE   If you start ORADBX on a process that has already parsed the un-
              tuned SQL, you will not get the details of the statement. The state-
              ment must be parsed and run after ORADBX has been turned on for
              the process ID.

If you are using UNIX, you'll find the next script useful in quickly turning the
tracing on and off for a selected process ID:

```
# oradbx.sh

#!/bin/ksh
#
#  This script turns on/off tracing a selected use shadow process.
#  You must have oradbx installed before this script will run.
#
#  usage: trace.sh pid <off>
#
if [ "$2" != "off" ]; then

oradbx <<EOD
debug $1
event 10046 trace name context forever, level 12
exit
EOD

else
oradbx <<EOD
debug $1
event 10046 trace name context off
exit
EOD

fi
```

ANALYZE: Validating and Computing Statistics

The ANALYZE statement introduced in Chapter 6 is a SQL*Plus statement that
allows you to validate and compute statistics for an index, table, or cluster. These
statistics are used by the cost-based optimizer when it calculates the most efficient
plan for retrieval. In addition to its role in statement optimization, ANALYZE also
helps in validating object structures and in managing space in your system. You
issue ANALYZE as follows:

```
ANALYZE  object-clause operation STATISTICS
    [VALIDATE STRUCTURE [CASCADE]]
    [LIST CHAINED ROWS [INTO table]]
```

where

object-clause

TABLE, INDEX, or CLUSTER, followed by a name. You can run ANALYZE on any one of these.

operation

You can choose one of these operations:

COMPUTE

Calculates each value. This option provides the most accurate statistics but is the slowest to run.

ESTIMATE

Estimates statistics by examining data dictionary values and performing data sampling. This option provides less accurate statistics but is much faster. The default estimate number of rows is 1064, which is usually far too few. You should use COMPUTE if you have sufficient time to run the analysis of use the SAMPLE command (see below).

DELETE

Removes all table statistics (freeing space), for example, ANALYZE TABLE EMP DELETE STATISTICS

Earlier versions of Oracle7 produced unpredictable results when the ESTIMATE option was used. It is best to compute your statistics using the following:

```
ANALYZE TABLE emp COMPUTE STATISTICS
```

If you don't have time to compute the statistics and you are using a version of Oracle earlier than Oracle7.3, estimate at least 50% of your rows using

```
ANALYZE TABLE emp ESTIMATE STATISTICS SAMPLE 50 PERCENT
```

If you are using Oracle7.3 or later, analyze at least 33% of your rows.

Oracle provides you with a procedure that allows you to analyze an entire schema. Specify the following:

```
EXECUTE DBMS_UTILITY.ANALYZE_SCHEMA('SCOTT','COMPUTE');
```

where SCOTT is the owner of the tables, clusters, and indexes, and COMPUTE is the type of analysis that you require.

ANALYZE produces the following statistics; depending on whether you have specified COMPUTE, or ESTIMATE, these statistics will be exact or estimated.

For tables

Number of rows
Number of blocks that have been used
Number of blocks unused

Average available free space
Number of chained rows
Average row length

For indexes
Index level
Number of leaf blocks
Number of distinct keys
Average number of leaf blocks/key
Average number of data blocks/key
Clustering factor
Minimum key value (exact only)
Maximum key value (exact only)

For columns
Number of distinct values per column
Second smallest value per column
Second largest value per column

For clusters
Average cluster key chain length

ANALYZE stores these statistics in the views, USER_TABLES, USER_TAB_ COLUMNS, USER_INDEXES, and USER_HISTOGRAMS. (The last view is available only in Oracle7.3 and later.)

ANALYZE has many uses. In addition to its use in optimization, ANALYZE can look for chained rows (a performance drain on the system). See Chapter 11 and consult your documentation for complete information.

UTLBSTAT.sql and UTLESTAT.sql: Taking Snapshots

Oracle provides the SQL scripts *UTLBSTAT.sql* and *UTLESTAT.sql*. They allow you to take a snapshot of how the database is performing. They provide information that may help you to identify problems and give you guidance about what needs tuning. The scripts are sometimes criticized because they identify performance problems but do not give very much advice on how to repair the problem. UTLB-STAT tells Oracle to start writing system statistics into a table. UTLESTAT stops this writing and displays the report. Keep in mind that the statistics that these scripts provide are system-wide, but only for the interval between UTLBSTAT and UTLESTAT.

Be sure to run these scripts when your system is doing ordinary processing. If you run them when there are no users on the system, they will give unrealistic and misleading results. You may also get distorted results if you run them all day (24 hours) on a system in which users are normally logged on for only the work day (8 hours). Most sites run UTLBSTAT and UTLESTAT from 10:00 a.m. to 12:00 p.m. and again from 2:00 p.m. to 4:30 p.m. These periods normally reflect peak production load and consistent application transaction activity.

You should run UTLBSTAT and UTLESTAT logged on as INTERNAL in SQL*DBA. *UTLBSTAT.sql* creates a set of tables and views that contain a snapshot of database performance statistics. The table and view names are as follows:

```
View/Table Name          Description
---------------          -----------
stats$begin_dc           Dictionary cache statistics from v$rowcache
stats$begin_event        System wait statistics from v$system_event
stats$begin_file         Table of file i/o statistics from stats$file_view
stats$begin_latch        Latch statistics from v$latch
stats$begin_lib          Library cache statistics from v$librarycache
stats$begin_roll         Rollback segment statistics from v$rollstat
stats$begin_stats        System stats from v$sysstat
stats$file_view          File I/O statistics from v$filestat,
                            v$datafile, ts$, file$
stats$dates              Contains beginning date and time
```

In addition, *UTLBSTAT.sql* creates a set of tables that contain the ending snapshot of the database performance statistics:

```
Table Name               Description
----------               -----------
stats$end_dc             Dictionary cache stats from v$rowcache
stats$end_event          Wait statistics from v$system_event
stats$end_file           File I/O stats from stats$file_view
stats$end_latch          Latch statistics from v$latch
stats$end_lib            Library cache statistics from
                            v$librarycache
stats$end_roll           Rollback segment stats from v$rollstat
stats$end_stats          System stats v$sysstat
```

UTLESTAT.sql populates the end statistics tables and creates an additional set of tables that contain the difference between the beginning statistics and the ending statistics:

```
Table Name               Description
----------               -----------
stats$dc                 Dictionary cache statistics
stats$event              Systemwide wait statistics
stats$files              File I/O statistics
stats$latches            Latch statistics
stats$lib                Library cache statistics
stats$roll               Rollback segment statistics
stats$stats              System statistics
stats$dates              Contains ending date and time
```

UTLESTAT.sql creates a report in your current directory with the following database performance statistics:

```
Library Cache Stats
System Wide Statistic Totals
System Wide Event Stats
Average Length of Dirty Buffer Write Queue
File I/O Stats
Tablespace I/O Stats
Willing-To-Wait Latch Stats
No-Wait Latch Stats
Rollback Segment Stats
Init.ora Parameters
Dictionary Cache Stats
Date/Time of executing utlbstat/utlestat
```

In testing, we have found that UTLBSTAT and UTLESTAT incur no system overhead.

To start the snapshot, type

```
SQLDBA> @UTLBSTAT
```

Let UTLBSTAT run for as long as you want to gather information. Then end the snapshot by typing

```
SQLDBA> @UTLESTAT
```

Note that you must set the INIT.ORA parameter TIMED_STATISTICS to TRUE (the default is FALSE) to produce the timing statistics (e.g., "current lock get time") shown in the output. We have found that TIMED_STATISTICS does incur a 5% to 10% performance overhead, so don't leave it on in your production database for a prolonged period.

```
SQLWKS> Rem The total is the total value of the statistic between the time
SQLWKS> Rem bstat was run and the time estat was run.  Note that the estat
SQLWKS> Rem script logs on as "internal" so the per_logon statistics will
SQLWKS> Rem always be based on at least one logon.
SQLWKS> select n1.name "Statistic",
               n1.change "Total",
               round(n1.change/trans.change,2) "Per Transaction",
               round(n1.change/logs.change,2)  "Per Logon",
               round(n1.change/(to_number(to_char(end_time,    'J'))
                 *60*60*24 - to_number(to_char(start_time, 'J'))
                   *60*60*24 + to_number(to_char(end_time,    'SSSSS'))
                     - to_number(to_char(start_time, 'SSSSS'))), 2) "Per
                       Second"
          from stats$stats n1, stats$stats trans, stats$stats logs,
               stats$dates
         where trans.name='user commits'
           and  logs.name='logons cumulative'
           and  n1.change != 0
         order by n1.name;
```

The "Statistics Definitions" section contains comments suggesting simple things you can do to improve performance when you notice suspicious statistics. The following sections show specifically how to interpret UTLBSTAT/UTLESTAT output. Chapter 11 expands on this discussion and suggests other ways to tune the areas of memory and disk mentioned below. The statistics shown in the table are from an Oracle7.3 database.

Statistic	Total	Per Transaction	Per Logon	Per Second
CR blocks created	34	34	.03	0
DBWR buffers scanned	127210	127210	95.72	1.6
DBWR checkpoints	18	18	.01	0
DBWR free buffers found	127068	127068	95.61	1.59
DBWR lru scans	12721	12721	9.57	.16
DBWR make free requests	12707	12707	9.56	.16
DBWR summed scan depth	127210	127210	95.72	1.6
DBWR timeouts	26529	26529	19.96	.33
SQL*Net round trips to/from	23	23	.02	0
background checkpoints comp	1	1	0	0
background checkpoints star	1	1	0	0
background timeouts	54395	54395	40.93	.68
bytes received via SQL*Net	2556	2556	1.92	.03
bytes sent via SQL*Net	1121	1121	.84	.01
calls to get snapshot scn:	2269	2269	1.71	.03
calls to kcmgas	20	20	.02	0
calls to kcmgcs	272	272	.2	0
calls to kcmgrs	2336	2336	1.76	.03
cleanouts and rollbacks	17	17	.01	0
cleanouts only - consistent	4	4	0	0
cluster key scan block gets	408766	408766	307.57	5.13
cluster key scans	247051	247051	185.89	3.1
commit cleanout failures	1	1	0	0
commit cleanout number succ	49	49	.04	0
consistent changes	45	45	.03	0
consistent gets	1406646	1406646	1058.42	17.64
cursor authentications	3	3	0	0
data blocks consistent read	45	45	.03	0
db block changes	265	265	.2	0
db block gets	3263	3263	2.46	.04
deferred (CURRENT) block cl	8	8	.01	0
enqueue releases	4935	4935	3.71	.06
enqueue requests	4929	4929	3.71	.06

Statistic	Total	Per Transaction	Per Logon	Per Second
execute count	1970	1970	1.48	.02
free buffer requested	104896	104896	78.93	1.32
immediate (CR) block cleano	21	21	.02	0
logons cumulative	1329	1329	1	.02
messages received	12764	12764	9.6	.16
messages sent	12764	12764	9.6	.16
no work - consistent read	830715	830715	625.07	10.42
opened cursors cumulative	8867	8867	6.67	.11
parse count	7547	7547	5.68	.09
physical reads	104849	104849	78.89	1.32
physical writes	146	146	.11	0
recursive calls	66561	66561	50.08	.83
redo blocks written	81	81	.06	0
redo buffer allocation retr	1	1	0	0
redo entries	147	147	.11	0
redo log space requests	1	1	0	0
redo size	35833	35833	26.96	.45
redo small copies	146	146	.11	0
redo synch writes	1	1	0	0
redo wastage	4744	4744	3.57	.06
redo writes	26	26	.02	0
rollbacks only - consistent	23	23	.02	0
session logical reads	1409864	1409864	1060.85	17.68
session pga memory	183515664	183515664	138085.53	2301.89
session pga memory max	183515664	183515664	138085.53	2301.89
session uga memory	3671736	3671736	2762.78	46.06
session uga memory max	15301296	15301296	11513.39	191.93
sorts (memory)	1335	1335	1	.02
sorts (rows)	512	512	.39	.01
summed dirty queue length	312	312	.27	.01
table fetch by rowid	28	28	.02	0
table scan blocks gotten	291430	291430	219.29	3.66
table scan rows gotten	629956	629956	474.01	7.9
table scans (long tables)	472	472	.36	.01
table scans (short tables)	265	265	.2	0
total number commit cleanouts	50	50	.04	0
user calls	1352	1352	1.02	.02
user commits	1	1	0	0
write requests	24	24	.02	0

Note that Oracle provides a number of other ways you can derive this same information on system activity, as described later in this chapter and in Chapter 11.

Statistics Definitions

The following are some of the more important tuning statistics:

consistent changes

Number of times a block has been changed, and number of times that the rollback entry had to be read for a transaction has to obtain a consistent read. If this figure is high on your system, make sure that no long-running updates are running during prime online usage times. Also be wary of SNAPSHOT TOO OLD errors.

consistent gets

Number of times a block was acquired in a consistent mode, that is, with the correct time stamp to provide read consistency. The figure is incremented by 1 for each block read during a full table scan. It is incremented by the (height of the index + (2 * index key entries)) for indexed table lookups and is incremented once for each block read during an index-only lookup.

db block changes

Total number of dirty blocks that have resided in the buffer cache. "Dirty" in this case implies that an update or a delete has been applied to the block. The more "db block changes," the more redo activity will be generated. If a block is changed once for each row within the block, the "db block changes" is incremented only by 1.

db block gets

Number of blocks read for update. These also include updates to rollback segment headers, temporary segment headers, and table and index segment headers. The figure is also incremented during extent allocation and when an update to the high-water mark takes place.

DBWR checkpoints

Number of times that checkpoints were sent to the database writer process DBWR. The log writer process hands a list of modified blocks that are to be written to disk. The dirty buffers to be written are pinned, and the DBWR begins writing the data out to the database.

It is usually best to keep the DBWR checkpoints to a minimum, although if there are too many dirty blocks to write out to disk at one time because of a "lazy" DBWR, there may be a harmful effect on response times for the duration of the write. See the parameters LOG_CHECKPOINT_INTERVAL and LOG_CHECKPOINT_TIMEOUT, which have a direct effect on the regularity of checkpoints.

The size of your redo logs can also have an effect on the number of checkpoints if the LOG_CHECKPOINT_INTERVAL is set to a size larger than your redo logs, or if the LOG_CHECKPOINT_TIMEOUT is longer than the time it takes to fill a redo log or has not been set.

DBWR timeouts

Number of times that the DBWR looked for dirty blocks to write to the database. Timeouts usually occur every 3 seconds if the DBWR is idle, but the frequency depends on the operating system.

DBWR make free requests

Number of messages received requesting DBWR to make the buffers free. This value is a key indicator as to how effectively your DB_BLOCK_BUFFERS parameter is tuned. If you increase DB_BLOCK_BUFFERS and this value decreases markedly, there is a very high likelihood that the DB_BLOCK_BUFFERS was set too low.

DBWR free buffers found

Number of buffers that the DBWR found on the least-recently-used chain that were already clean. You can divide this value by the "DBWR make free requests" value to obtain the number of buffers that were found that were free and clean (i.e., did *not* have to be written to disk).

DBWR lru scans

Number of times that the database writer scans the least-recently-used chain for more buffers to write. The scan can be invoked either by a "DBWR make free requests" or by a checkpoint.

DBWR summed scan depth

Can be divided by "DBWR lru scans" to determine the length of the scans through the buffer cache. This is *not* the number of buffers scanned. If the write batch is filled and a write takes place to disk, the scan depth halts.

DBWR buffers scanned

Total number of buffers scanned in looking for dirty buffers to write to disk and create free space. The count includes both dirty and clean buffers. It does *not* halt as the "DBWR summed scan depth" does.

free buffer waits

Number of times a free buffer was requested in the buffer cache and none was available because the buffers in the buffer cache had been modified and needed to be written to disk first. This can cause sizable delays and is often caused by having the DB_BLOCK_BUFFERS set too small.

physical reads

Number of requests to the operating system to read a database block into the buffer cache. Even if the parameter DB_FILE_MULTIBLOCK_READ_COUNT is set to more than 1, the physical reads' incremented only by 1. Reading from the temporary segments does not increment this figure.

physical writes

Number of writes by LGWR and DBWR to the disk I/O subsystem. The figure is incremented by 1 regardless of whether the write is a single-block or multi-block write.

recursive calls

Number of times a change is made to Oracle's own internal tables. It is often an indication of too many extents being thrown on your database objects (e.g., tables) or an undersized library cache

redo entries

Number of times changed data is copied into the redo log buffer

redo log space requests

Number of times a user process has to wait for space in the redo log buffer. This wait is often caused by the archiver being lazy and the log writer not being able to write from the log buffer to the redo log because the redo log has not been copied by the ARCH process. One possible cause of this problem is when hot backups are taking place on files that are being written to heavily. For the duration of the hot backups, an entire block is written out to the log buffer and the redo logs for each change to the database, as compared to just writing the characters that have been modified. This figure should ideally be zero and is a key performance indicator.

redo synch writes

When a commit occurs, the log buffer must have all of its contents written to the redo logs. When this occurs, the redo sync writes is incremented by 1.

sorts (disk)

Indicates that the SORT_AREA_SIZE allocated to a user is not large enough to complete a sort and that the user has been forced to complete the sort in the temporary tablespace. It measures the number of disk writes. Increasing the SORT_AREA_SIZE may solve this problem.

sorts (memory)

Indicates that a sort that has been performed entirely in memory. This is the ideal situation for sorting from a performance perspective.

table fetch by rowid

Number of rows accessed by an index or as the result of explicitly stating the ROWID in the WHERE condition.

table fetch continued row

Number of additional blocks that have had to be read to read a single row after the first block has been accessed. The problem is caused by either having a PCTFREE that is too low or having very long rows. You can issue the command ALTER TABLE tname STORAGE (PCTFREE 40), where 40 is the figure most likely to avoid row migration for all future rows inserted into the table. To find the offending tables, look in the CHAIN_CNT column of DBA_TABLES or USER_TABLES. The long column chaining problem can often be solved by setting a higher DB_BLOCK_SIZE. Unfortunately, this is going to require a database rebuild.

table scan blocks gotten
Number of blocks read using full table scans

table scan rows gotten
Number of rows read using full table scans

table scans (long tables)
Number of rows read from tables using a full table scan, where the number of blocks read is greater than the parameter _SMALL_TABLE_THRESHOLD, which has a default of 5

table scans (short tables)
Number of rows read from tables using a full table scan, where the number of blocks read is less than or equal to the parameter _SMALL_TABLE_THRESHOLD, which has a default of 5

user calls
Is incremented by 1 each time a user logs on, parses a statement, or executes a statement

user commits
Number of times users have committed their transactions

user rollbacks
Number of times users have rolled back changes that they have made

write requests
Number of times the DBWR writes dirty buffers to disk, including tables, clusters, indexes, rollback segments, dictionary data, and sort data. You can tell how effective the DBWR has been for each request by dividing "physical writes" by "write requests."

Tuning the Buffer Cache Hit Ratio

The goal of this performance test is to find as much application data in memory as possible. If you tune the buffer cache correctly, you can significantly improve database performance. The hit ratio computed below is the rate at which Oracle finds the data blocks it needs already in memory. The closer the hit ratio approaches 100%, the better your system will perform. Use the statistics from UTLBSTAT/UTLESTAT to do the following calculation:

```
Hit ratio = (logical reads - physical reads) / (logical reads)
Logical reads = consistent gets + db block gets = 1406646 + 3263 = 1409909
Hit ratio = (1409909 - 104849) / (1409909) = (1305060) / (1409909) = 92%
```

The general rule of thumb is this: if the hit ratio is below 95% for online transaction processing applications and 85% for batch applications, if the SHARED_POOL_SIZE has been tuned, and if you have been careful to tune your SQL, then you should increase the buffer cache value to the point at which at least 5% free memory remains available during peak usage. The online transaction processing system being monitored in this example has a hit ratio of 92%, which is not hopeless, but we discovered that the site had several untuned SQL statements. The statements were tuned, and the hit ratio went to 95%. The buffer cache was then tuned, and the hit ratio exceeded 99%. We usually consider anything below 60% very poor and believe that any OLTP application below 95% can be improved, given sufficient free memory. The particular threshold for your system depends on your application transaction mix and on the amount of free memory you have available.

What can you do to solve this problem? Enlarge the amount of buffer cache in your system by increasing the INIT.ORA parameter, DB_BLOCK_BUFFERS, but make sure you keep 5% of your memory free. Also make sure that your SQL is tuned and the appropriate indexes are in place.

For another example of computing the hit ratio via the MONITOR statistics, refer to Chapter 11.

Tuning Buffer Busy Wait Ratio

The goal of this performance test is to reduce contention for database data and rollback blocks. Use the UTLBSTAT/UTLESTAT statistics to perform this calculation:

```
Buffer busy waits ratio=(buffer busy waits) / (logical reads)=(1) / (39414)
          = 0.00002
```

If the ratio is greater than 5%, there is a problem. In this sample, the figure is close to 0%, which is an ideal situation. We have found that a high percentage usually indicates a wait for a rollback segment buffer. You should add rollback segments to the rollback tablespace. If there are any "undo header waits" in the V$WAITSTAT table, add more rollback segments until the "undo header waits" is 0. If there are high "segment header waits," you may find that adding free lists helps. Check V$SESSION_WAIT to get the addresses of the actual blocks having contention.

NOTE   Depending on your version of Oracle, the "buffer busy waits" will
              come from either the V$SYSSTAT view or the V$SESSION_WAIT
              and V$WAITSTAT views. UTLBSTAT and UTLESTAT reports from all
              three views. Be sure to determine your buffer busy waits ratio, be-
              cause if this is not repaired, it can cause major damage to your per-
              formance.

Tuning the DBWR

The database writer (DBWR) process handles all writes to the database. The aim
of this performance test is to ensure that free buffers are available in the buffer
cache as needed. Read-only buffers can always be swapped out, but dirty buffers
need to be retained until they have been successfully written to the database.
User processes that require DBWR must be functioning efficiently. The following
query provides you with the average length of the dirty queue. Anything above
100 indicates that the DBWR is having real problems keeping up.

```
# dirtque.sql
SELECT  DECODE (name, 'summed dirty queue length', value)
                       /
         DECODE (name, 'write requests', value) "Write Request Length"
   FROM  v$sysstat
  WHERE  name IN ( 'summed dirty queue length', 'write requests')
    AND  value > 0;
```

If there were a problem, you could increase the number of free buffers by
increasing the INIT.ORA parameters DB_BLOCK_BUFFERS, DB_WRITERS, and _
DB_BLOCK_WRITE_BATCH. For a more detailed discussion of this process, see
the section called "Tuning the Database Writer" in Chapter 11.

Tuning Table Access Method

The goal of this performance test is to increase the effectiveness with which data
is accessed by indexes. If the result of the following calculation is greater than
10%:

```
Table scans (long tables) / (table scans (short tables) + table scans
       (long tables))
```

you must evaluate your use of indexes. This rule may vary depending on the
nature of your site's transaction mix. For databases that are used primarily for
reporting, full table scans are sometimes preferable to indexed table lookups,
especially if you are using the parallel query option. You'll have to select the right
approach for your own particular site.

In our example, the calculation is

```
472 / (472 + 265) = .64
```

This indicates that a large percentage of the tables accessed were not indexed lookups. You need to investigate this situation. Refer to the section called "Identifying Untuned Application Code" in Chapter 11 for details on how to locate the resource-consuming SQL statements.

What can you do about this problem? Ensure that the appropriate indexes are in place. Also ensure that the best use is being made of the optimizer. For online transaction processing systems, investigate all full table scans to determine whether you can use an index to avoid the need to scan this way. Note, however, that if a particular report or update requires that every row of a table be read, it is more efficient to do a full table scan. This is because the system needs to read the index (to find out the row's physical address on disk) for each row and then do a physical read of the database block. With a full table scan, one table block may contain more than 100 rows, which can all be read with one physical read. (Chapter 6 describes a number of other indexing and data access considerations.)

Tuning I/O Spread

Check the output of the following query from the UTLBSTAT/UTLESTAT temporary tables to observe how well the I/O load is distributed across the disk devices in your system.

```
SQLDBA> set charwidth 48;
SQLDBA> set numwidth 12;
SQLDBA> rem  I/O should be spread evenly across drives. A big difference
SQLDBA> rem  between PHYS_READS and PHYS_BLKS_RD implies table
SQLDBA> rem  scans are going on
SQLDBA> select * from stats$files;
```

TABLE_SPACE	FILE_NAME	PHYS_ READS	PHYS_ BLKS_RD	PHYS_ RD_TIME	PHYS_ WRITES	PHYS_ BLKS_WR	PHYS_ WRI_TIM
ROLLBACK	/db/datafile1.ora	0	0	0	78	78	2034
TEMP	/db/datafile2.ora	0	0	0	0	0	0
DATA1	/db/datafile3.ora	202	766	1330	54	54	1058
DATA2	/db/datafile4.ora	62	391	720	29	29	1112
INDEX1	/db/datafile5.ora	37	37	117	3	3	39
SYSTEM	/db/datafile0.ora	740	3353	6779	44	44	1619

6 rows selected.

In the example shown, the system tablespace was the most active, which is not a healthy scenario. The previous tuning steps have uncovered the fact that quite a few unindexed searches have been taking place. The tablespace table shown here indicates that there might be sort activity going on in the system tablespace. To identify the users who will perform their disk sorting in the SYSTEM tablespace, run the following command:

```
SELECT username FROM dba_users WHERE temporary_tablespace = 'SYSTEM';
```

What can you do about this problem? Create a separate tablespace for temporary table activity. With the ALTER USER *username* TEMPORARY TABLESPACE *tablespace* command, you can assign each user to this new temporary tablespace. If users do not have a temporary tablespace explicitly assigned, they default to the SYSTEM tablespace, which should not be allowed. If you cannot add a new temporary tablespace because there isn't enough free disk space on your system, assign your users elsewhere—perhaps to the DATA1 tablespace.

Reducing Contention for Internal Latches

If a user process is going to perform an operation such as accessing data in the SGA, it must first obtain a latch from the table and then own the latch. If the process is forced to wait for a latch because there aren't enough available, a slow-down occurs. Additional CPU is also needed to keep interrogating the latch queue.

This query asks whether internal latch contention is going on:

```
REM Latch statistics. Latch contention will show up as a large value for
REM the 'latch free' event in the wait events above.
REM Sleeps should be low.  The hit_ratio should be high.
SELECT name latch_name, gets, misses,
       ROUND(DECODE(gets-misses,0,1,gets-misses)/decode(gets,0,1,gets),3)
          sleeps,
          ROUND(sleeps/DECODE(misses,0,1,misses),3) "SLEEPS/MISS"
   FROM stats$latches
  WHERE gets != 0
  ORDER BY name;
```

LATCH_NAME	GETS	MISSES	HIT_RATIO	SLEEPS	SLEEPS/MISS
cache buffer handl	2	0	1	0	0
cache buffers chai	2358869	7	1	10	1.429
cache buffers lru	117619	132	.999	185	1.402
dml lock allocatio	113	0	1	0	0
enqueue hash chain	9840	0	1	0	0
enqueues	22701	0	1	0	0
ktm global data	265	0	1	0	0
library cache	79594	0	1	0	0
library cache load	10	0	1	0	0
list of block allo	35	0	1	0	0
messages	146844	3	1	3	1
modify parameter v	1329	0	1	0	0
multiblock read ob	7756	0	1	0	0
redo allocation	26712	0	1	0	0
row cache objects	45471	0	1	0	0
session allocation	6406	0	1	0	0
session idle bit	4566	0	1	0	0

session switching	1263	0	1	0	0
shared pool	17561	0	1	0	0
sort extent pool	265	0	1	0	0
system commit numb	2604	0	1	0	0
transaction alloca	587	0	1	0	0
undo global data	3255	0	1	0	

If the hit ratio of any of the key latches ("cache buffers lru chain", "enqueues", "redo allocation", "redo copy", or "library cache") is lower than 99%, there is substantial latch contention. For example, "cache buffer lru chain" has a ratio of 99.9%.

The sections in Chapter 11 called "Monitoring for redo log latch contention," "Reducing Buffer Cache Latch Contention," and "Reducing Library Cache Latch Contention" show how to deal with latch problems. Chapter 18, *Tuning for Specific Systems*, also contains a discussion of how to handle this problem in a UNIX system.

Reducing Rollback-Related Transactions

This query asks whether transactions are waiting for rollback segments to be released by other transactions:

```
REM Waits_for_trans_tbl high implies you should add rollback segments.
SELECT * from stats$roll;
UNDO_SEGMENT    TRANS_TBL_GETS      TRANS_TBL_WAITS
------------    ------------------  -------------------
0                    17                     0
2                  12273                   212
```

If the TRANS_TBL_WAITS is more than 0, it usually means that you must add rollback segments. In our example, the DBA has forgotten to create the necessary number of rollback segments. Adding more rollback segments ensures that each transaction can get a rollback segment without having to wait for another transaction to release it.

System Waits

Various types of system waits can occur in your Oracle database. Each type of wait may indicate that contention that may be occurring on your machine.

```
REM System wide wait events for background processes (PMON, SMON, etc)
SELECT n1.event "Event Name",
     n1.event_count "Count",
n1.time_waited "Total Time",
ROUND(n1.time_waited/n1.event_count, 2) "Avg Time"
  FROM stats$bck_event n1
WHERE n1.event_count > 0
  ORDER BY n1.time_waited desc;
```

Event Name	Count	Total Time	Avg Time
control file parallel write	17	0	0
control file sequential read	19	0	0
db file parallel write	26	0	0
db file scattered read	2166	0	0
db file sequential read	67	0	0
db file single write	4	0	0
latch free	9	0	0
log file parallel write	30	0	0
log file sequential read	1	0	0
log file single write	2	0	0
log file sync	4	0	0
pmon timer	26535	0	0
rdbms ipc message	65602	0	0
smon timer	265	0	0
rdbms ipc reply	9	0	0

15 rows selected.

From a performance perspective, the "db file scattered read" usually indicates too many full table scans; "db file sequential read" often indicates disk I/O contention caused by indexed table searches; "latch free" indicates latch contention; and "db file parallel write" may indicate that checkpoints are not occurring frequently enough. The various log file waits may mean that checkpoints are occurring too frequently.

Other Oracle Scripts

Oracle provides a variety of SQL scripts in each system release. In addition to UTLBSTAT and UTLESTAT, several others allow you to diagnose system problems and tune for better performance. In this section, we describe the most commonly used Oracle tuning scripts.

ONEIDXS.sql: Testing an Individual Index

The *ONEIDXS.sql* script allows you to test a particular index to find out how effective it is. Use this script to identify columns on which you might index in the future, to evaluate how selective a current index is, and to evaluate whether an existing index is still useful.

This output, from an application master table, shows the column spread for a particular index:

Table_Name	Column_Name	Stat_Name	Stat_Value
LOAN_MASTER	MGR_CODE	Rows - Total	26062
LOAN_MASTER	MGR_CODE	Rows - Null	23991
LOAN_MASTER	MGR_CODE	Total Distinct Keys	34
LOAN_MASTER	MGR_CODE	Rows per key - avg	60.91176

```
LOAN_MASTER      MGR_CODE      Rows per key - min              1
LOAN_MASTER      MGR_CODE      Rows per key - max            751
LOAN_MASTER      MGR_CODE      Rows per key - dev       125.7822
LOAN_MASTER      MGR_CODE      db_gets_per_key_miss     313.0116
LOAN_MASTER      MGR_CODE      db_gets_per_key_hit       156.916
```

You can see from this output that the indexed column (MGR_CODE) may not have been the best choice of a column. Nearly all the rows of the table (more than 92%) have a null value as the key. Of the 2071 non-null keys, only 34 distinct key values exist. This means that there are, on average, 60.9 rows per key value. To make matters even worse, one key value has 751 rows, more than 36% of the non-null records.

All this tells us, though, is that we need to investigate this index further. In fact, when we looked more carefully, we found out that the indexed column, MGR_ CODE, was only the first column of a concatenated index; that accounted for the reporting of poor key spread. But the large number of null rows did in fact turn out to be a problem that had to be followed up.

CATBLOCK.sql and UTLOCKT.sql: Showing Locking Information

The *CATBLOCK.sql* scripts creates a number of views showing information about locks held in the database.

DBA_LOCKS

Has a row for each lock and latch that is being held and one row for each outstanding request for a lock or latch

DBA_DML_LOCKS

Has one row for each DML lock held and one for each outstanding request for a DML lock

DBA_DDL_LOCKS

Has one row for each DDL lock held and one for each outstanding request for a DDL lock

DBA_WAITERS

Shows all sessions waiting for locks and the session that holds that lock

DBA_BLOCKERS

Shows all sessions that are holding a lock required by another process

The following example shows the DBA_LOCKS view:

```
ID LOCK_TYPE        HELD        RQST  LOCK_ID1                     LOCK_ID2
-- ---------------  ----------  ----  ---------------------------  --------
2  Media Recovery   Share       None  6                            0
2  Media Recovery   Share       None  2                            0
2  Media Recovery   Share       None  1                            0
2  Media Recovery   Share       None  2                            0
```

```
3  Redo Thread             Exclusive    None  1                                        0
6  Transaction             Exclusive    None  196640                                   129
8  DML                     Row-X (SX)   None  1456                                     0
8  Transaction             Exclusive    None  327726                                   152
8  DML                     Row-X (SX)   None  1460                                     0
8  DML                     Row-X (SX)   None  1462                                     0
6  Cursor Definition Lock Null  None SELECT SYSDATE FROM SYS.DUAL            0070E210
6  Cursor Definition Lock Null  None SELECT USER FROM SYS.DUAL               0072F8A0
6  Cursor Definition Lock Null  None SAVEPOINT IAP_1                         00825214
6  Cursor Definition Lock Null  None SAVEPOINT IAP_1                         008254B0
6  Cursor Definition Lock Null  None SELECT 'C' FROM GROUP_USERS G,          00877F7C
                                  MENU_GROUPS M  WHERE M.MENU_
                                  CODE = :b1  AND M.GROUP_CODE = G.
                                  GROUP_C  AND G.USER_CODE = :b2
                                  AND M.UPD_LEVEL <= G.ACCESS_LVL
6  Cursor Definition Pin Share  None SELECT 'C' FROM GROUP_USERS G,          00877F7C
                                  MENU_GROUPS M  WHERE  M.MENU_
                                  CODE = :b1  AND M.GROUP_CODE = G.GR
                                  OUP_CODE  AND G.USER_CODE = :b2
                                  AND U.UPD_LEVEL <= G.ACCESS_LVL
```

DBMSLOCK.sql: Requesting, Converting, and Releasing Locks

The *DBMSLOCK.sql* script makes use of the available packages and functions. With this script, you can request, convert, and release locks managed by the RDBMS lock management service. Such locks have the "UL" identifier, when they appear on the SQL*DBA MONITOR LOCK function and in various views, to avoid confusion with real Oracle data locks.

NOTE   These are manual locks, not real Oracle data locks. Be careful with this script, though, because if you are not, you might release or modify Oracle locks, resulting in unpredictable and possibly disastrous outcomes.

Deadlock detection is performed on these manual user locks, and all locks are released automatically when the owning session terminates. Services provided by this package include the following:

Allocate_Unique
    Allocates a unique lock identified for a lock name

Request
    Requests a lock for a given mode

Convert
> Converts a lock from one mode to another

Release
> Releases a database lock (Oracle or user)

Sleep
> Sleeps for a specified time

We generally avoid using this script. We did use it once to release the resource locks of a terminated session that had inadvertently failed and continued to hold vital resources. These locks were only over the table schema, not individual table rows. Nevertheless, they prevented us from performing a table ALTER that was required by another area of this application.

SYNC.sql: Synchronizing Processes

The *SYNC.sql* script helps you to tune SQL statements. Often, these statements do not reveal their tuning flaws until they are run in conjunction with other processes. The *SYNC.sql* script allows you to activate many other processes and synchronize them so that they work concurrently. These processes can be different SQL statements or (for testing purposes) the same one multiple times. This script also generates a number of functions (libraries) that you can call via SQL*Plus to coordinate the resulting information.

In the following example, we are synchronizing three user processes in order to process three separate SQL statements at exactly the same time.

Process 1	Process 2	Process 3
EXECUTE SYNC.INIT (3)	EXECUTE SYNC.INIT (3)	EXECUTE SYNC.INIT (3)
EXECUTE SYNC.WAIT	EXECUTE SYNC.WAIT	EXECUTE SYNC.WAIT
. . . SQL statement . . .	. . . SQL statement . . .	. . . SQL statement . . .

Some Scripts of Our Own

Through the years, we've been writing scripts to do all kinds of things. The ones included in this section are our favorite database tuning scripts—developed, begged, and borrowed over the last few years. These scripts aren't definitive in any way; they could have been, and probably have been, written in a dozen alternative ways. But they do get the work done. (You will find all of these scripts on the floppy disk in the back of this book.)

What Version of Oracle?

The version of Oracle that you are running can have a significant impact on your performance. Use the following command to show version information:

```
SELECT *
    FROM v$version;
-------------------------------------------------------------
Oracle7 Server Release 7.2.3.2.0 - Production Release
PL/SQL Release 2.2.2.2.0 - Production
CORE Version 2.3.7.1.0 - Production (LSF Alpha)
TNS for SVR4: Version 2.1.6.0.0 - Production
NLSRTL Version 2.3.6.0.0 - Production
```

What Are the INIT.ORA Settings?

In addition to the standard INIT.ORA parameters, Oracle also has a number of undocumented parameters, that appear with an underscore in front of them in parameter displays. Several of the undocumented parameters, such as _DB_ BLOCK_WRITE_BATCH and _LOG_ENTRY_PREBUILD_THRESHOLD, can be used to improve your performance. (See the discussion of such parameters in Chapters 9 and 11.)

Run this script to show your system's parameter setting; then compare your settings to the recommendations in this book.

```
# undoc.sql
SELECT name, value
  FROM v$parameter;
SELECT ksppinm, ksppivl
  FROM x$ksppi
 WHERE SUBSTR(ksppinm,1,1) = '_';
```

We don't show the output from this script because of its excessive length.

Looking Inside the SGA

This script shows details of the System Global Area in memory. The most significant information is the reading for "free memory," which may indicate that the SHARED_POOL_SIZE INIT.ORA parameter should be reduced if the free memory is excessive. If the parameter setting is low, you should *not* be decreasing the SHARED_POOL_SIZE.

WARNING   Oracle tends to maintain some free memory even when the shared pool size is flooded with activity and needs to be made larger.

Other figures that are useful are the "db_block_buffers," size of the buffer cache, which is usually required to be at least 20 megabytes for optimum performance;

the "sql area," which is where all of the shared SQL is placed; the dictionary cache, which is where Oracle's dictionary is placed; and the "log buffer," which is where all changes are written prior to writing to your redo logs.

The log buffer should typically be at least 32,078 bytes or larger. The "shared_sql" and "dictionary cache" sizes are affected by the size of your SHARED_POOL_SIZE INIT.ORA parameter. Unfortunately, the dictionary cache is tuned automatically and not very well by the kernel. The majority of sites operate most efficiently with a shared pool size of at least 30,000,000 bytes.

```
# sgastat.sql
SELECT *
FROM v$sgastat
WHERE name IN ('free memory', 'db_block_buffers', 'log_buffer'
               'dictionary cache', 'sql area', 'library cache');
```

NAME	BYTES
free memory	88652
db_block_buffers	20480000
log_buffer	512000
dictionary cache	2528868
sql area	43658416
library cache	13177800

Identifying Database Extents

One of the most common activities you'll find yourself doing as a DBA is scanning the physical database, looking for new table and index extents. You ought to do this on a regular basis, ideally as part of an automated daily or weekly overnight procedure. Your goal is to minimize the number of extents on disk. Access to contiguous areas of disk is much faster than access to noncontiguous areas. In one test that we did on a 4,000-row table, we found that when the entire table fit on one extent, it took 0.76 second to scan it; when the table was spread over 10 extents, it took 3.62 seconds.

We have found that the existence of a small number of such extents (fewer than five) doesn't seem to affect performance very much, but it is still good practice to store your objects in a single extent. (In the next section, we describe how to size the table for the reorganization while not wasting valuable disk space.)

The following script assumes that the operating system Oracle block size is 4 kilobytes and that all ROLLBACK segments were created with 10 initial extents (MINEXTENTS parameter).

```
# objstor.sql
SELECT SUBSTR(s.segment_name,1,20) OBJECT_NAME,
       SUBSTR(s.segment_type,1,5) TYPE,
       SUBSTR(s.tablespace_name,1,10) T_SPACE,
```

```
        NVL(NVL(t.initial_extent, i.initial_extent),r.initial_extent)/ 4096
            FST_EXT,
        NVL(NVL(t.next_extent,i.next_extent),R.NEXT_EXTENT) / 4096 NXT_EXT,
            s.extents - 1  tot_ext,
            s.blocks  tot_blks
        FROM
            dba_rollback_segs R,
            dba_indexes I,
            dbs_tables T,
            dba_segments S
    WHERE s.segment_name     LIKE  UPPER('&S_NAME')  || '%'
      AND s.tablespace_name  LIKE  UPPER('&T_SPACE') || '%'
      AND s.extents            >  1
      AND s.owner            =   t.owner (+)
      AND s.segment_name     =   t.table_name (+)
      AND s.tablespace_name  =   t.tablespace_name (+)
      AND s.owner            =   i.owner (+)
      AND s.segment_name     =   i.index_name (+)
      AND s.tablespace_name  =   i.tablespace_name (+)
      AND s.owner            =   r.owner (+)
      AND s.segment_name     =   r.segment_name (+)
      AND s.tablespace_name  =   r.tablespace_name (+)
    ORDER BY s.segment_name,   s.segment_type;
```

OBJECT_NAME	TYPE	T_SPACE	FST EXT	NXT EXT	TOT EXT	TOT BLKS
ALL_TRAN_AUDX_INDX	INDEX	DEV_IDX	125	63	2	251
OBJ$	TABLE	SYSTEM	13	13	1	26
PRODUCT_PROFILE	TABLE	SYSTEM	13	13	1	26
RBACK1	ROLLB	RBK	25	25	9	300
RBACK2	ROLLB	RBK	25	25	9	525
RBACK_BIG	ROLLB	RBK	256	256	9	2560
XREF$	TABLE	SYSTEM	13	13	1	26

Performing Database Table Sizing

This section contains several scripts that we use to size a database.

Looking for tablespace space shortages

When tables, indexes, and rollback segments are created, they are preassigned a storage allocation (extent), which is reserved and cannot be used by any other object. Although the objects may not use all of the space allocated at the start, as more information is placed into the area the amount of available free space diminishes. This query helps you instantly find application problems resulting from space shortages. Run it at regular intervals for the best information. Note that this script assumes that you have Oracle data blocks of 4 kilobytes (4,096 bytes). This size is operating system dependent, and you will have to modify the query if your block sizes differ.

```
# tspuse.sql
SELECT  SUBSTR(D.tablespace_name,1,15)                    TSPACE,
              D.file_id                                   FILE_ID
              D.bytes / 1024 / 1024                       TOT_MB,
              D.bytes / 4096                              ORA_BLKS,
              SUM(E.blocks)                               TOT_USED,
              ROUND(SUM(E.blocks) / (D.bytes / 4096), 4) * 100  PCT_USED,
    FROM    sys.dba_extents    E,
            sys.dba_data_files D
    WHERE   D.file_id = E.file_id (+)
    GROUP   BY D.tablespace_name, D.bytes
```

TSPACE	FILE_ID	TOT_MB	ORA_BLKS	TOT_USED	PCT_USED
DEV	4	250	64000	36633	57.2
DEV_AUD	6	100	25600	3691	14.4
DEV_IDX	5	300	76800	61317	79.8
HST	7	200	51200	38400	75.0
INV	8	80	20480	13739	67.1
INV_IDX	9	50	12800	7673	59.9
RBK	3	25	6400	4110	64.2
SYSTEM	1	20	5120	2366	46.2
TMP	2	50	12800		

Looking for tablespace fragmentation

This query of the database gives a detailed breakdown of the fragmentation of each tablespace file within the database.

```
# fragment.sql
SELECT      SUBSTR(ts.name,1,10)                               TSPACE,
                tf.blocks                                      BLOCKS,
                SUM(f.length)                                  FREE,
                COUNT(*)                                       PIECES,
                MAX(f.length)                                  BIGGEST,
                MIN(f.length)                                  SMALLEST,
                ROUND(AVG(f.length))                           AVERAGE,
                SUM(DECODE(SIGN(f.length-5), -1, f.length, 0)) DEAD
        FROM    sys.fet$          F,
                sys.file$         TF,
                sys.ts$           TS
        WHERE   ts.ts#  =  f.ts#
        AND     ts.ts#  =  tf.ts#
        GROUP BY ts.name, tf.blocks;
```

Tspace	Blocks	Free	Pieces	Biggest	Smallest	Average	Dead
DEV	64000	27366	9	25614	105	3041	0
DEV_AUD	25600	21908	1	21908	21908	21908	0
DEV_IDX	76800	15482	16	175	4	968	2
HST	51200	12799	1	12799	12799	12799	0
INV	20480	6740	12	6740	6740	6740	0
INV_IDX	12800	5126	4	2565	63	1282	0

RBK	6400	2289	1	2289	2289	2289	0
SYSTEM	5120	2753	74	487	3	16	12
TMP	12800	12799	41	1536	11	312	0

The last column, "Dead," is based on the assumption that any contiguous block smaller than five Oracle blocks (20 kilobytes for the operating system that we used for testing) cannot be used. That is, no table or index has an INITIAL or NEXT extent size less than 20 kilobytes.

Looking at space use by individual tables

This query reports how full a particular table actually is. It compares the number of Oracle blocks that have at least one record against the total number of blocks allocated to the table extent(s). You can use this query to interrogate table after table; the table name replaces the name &TAB_NAME in each statement execution.

```
# tabused.sql
SELECT    BLOCKS                                          ALLOCATED_BLKS,
               COUNT(DISTINCT SUBSTR(T.ROWID,1,8)
                       || SUBSTR(T.ROWID,15,4))           USED,
               (COUNT(DISTINCT SUBSTR(T.ROWID,1,8)
                       || SUBSTR(T.ROWID,15,4))
               / BLOCKS) * 100                            PCT_USED
      FROM    SYS.DBA_SEGMENTS E,
               &TAB_NAME T
      WHERE   E.SEGMENT_NAME = UPPER ('&TAB_NAME')
      AND     E.SEGMENT_TYPE = 'TABLE'
      GROUP BY E.BLOCKS;


ALLOCATED_BLKS            USED        PCT_USED
--------------            ----        --------
2560                      1728        67.50
```

Looking at the average number of records per block

This query reports the number of rows physically residing in Oracle blocks of a table. This query can be used to calculate how much space a table will ultimately require.

```
# blokrows.sql
SELECT    SUBSTR(T.ROWID,1,8)  || '-' ||SUBSTR(T.ROWID,15,4)      BLOCK,
               COUNT(*)                                           ROW_CNT,
      FROM    &TAB_NAME T
      WHERE   ROWNUM < 2000
      GROUP BY SUBSTR(T.ROWID,1,8) || '-' || SUBSTR(T.ROWID,15,4);
```

Output from this query is as follows:

```
BLOCK                    ROW_CNT
-------------            -------
00001F52-0002            93
00001F53-0002            85
00001F54-0002            82
```

```
00001F55-0002          100
00001F56-0002          83
00001F57-0002          71
00001F58-0002          82
00001F59-0002          91
00001F5A-0002          93
00001F5B-0002          91
00001F5C-0002          63
00001F5D-0002          69
00001F5E-0002          75
00001F5F-0002          1
00001F60-0002          4
00001F61-0002          5
```

Putting it together

By looking at the results of the set of scripts that are included in this section, you can do a good job of calculating future table requirements:

Script 1

Tells us that the DEV tablespace is only 43% used. Of the initial 250-megabyte allocation, more than 107 megabytes are still free. This tablespace should not be a problem for some time.

Script 2

Tells us that the 107 megabytes of free space within the DEV tablespace comprise only nine contiguous segments and no dead blocks. This tells us that the free space is indeed free and usable.

Script 3

Tells us that the table being analyzed currently has consumed only 67% of its current extent allocations.

Script 4

Tells us that the table being analyzed can store an average of 80 to 90 records per Oracle block (4 kilobytes per block). Therefore the current volume represents one year of growth and is already 40,000 records in size. What storage will be needed for 10 years' growth?

We advise you to be relatively conservative in making estimates so that you don't consume needless amounts of disk space, while being sensible enough not to run out of space too soon. This is not always an easy task! Our calculation is as follows:

```
Total records      = 40,000 x 10
                   = 400,000 records  (adjust to 500,000)

Records Per Block  = 80 . . . 90      (adjust to 75)
```

```
Space Requirements = (Total Records / Records Per Block) x Block Size
                   = ( 500,000 / 75 ) * ( 1024 * 4 )
                   = 27,306,667 bytes
                   = 26.4 megabytes
```

Checking Extent Sizes and PCTINCREASE

If the default extent sizes and PCTINCREASE on your tablespaces are set incorrectly, these can have a marked impact on your performance. The SYSTEM tablespace has a default PCTINCREASE of 50%. If you decrease that value to 0, as many sites do, the number of extents on the dictionary objects becomes excessive and degrades performance. The default INITIAL and NEXT parameters on your temporary tablespace can also cause a lot of extents to be thrown if they are set to a value smaller than the SORT_AREA_SIZE. Ideally, the NEXT extent sizes should be equal to, or a multiple of, the SORT_AREA_SIZE.

```
SELECT SUBSTR(tablespace_name, 1,18), initial_extent,
       next_extent, pct_increase
  FROM dba_tablespaces
 ORDER BY tablespace_name;
```

Another troublesome problem that can affect performance is when a user other than SYSTEM or SYS has his or her default tablespace set to the SYSTEM tablespace. Use the following query to ensure that all of your users have been assigned to an appropriate tablespace:

```
SELECT username
  FROM dba_users
 WHERE username NOT IN ('SYS', 'SYSTEM')
   AND (default_tablespace = 'SYSTEM'
               OR
        temporary_tablespace = 'SYSTEM');
```

Looking at Objects That Can't Throw an Extent

Some scripts list all objects that will not have a free extent that is large enough, assuming that the object has filled its current space allocation and is forced to throw an extent. The following script provides the same information but runs 20 times faster:

```
# exent.sql
SELECT seg.owner, seg.segment_name,
       seg.segment_type, seg.tablespace_name, t.next_extent
  FROM sys.dba_segments seg, sys.dba_tables   t
 WHERE (seg.segment_type = 'TABLE'
 AND          seg.segment_name = t.table_name
 AND          seg.owner        = t.owner
 AND          NOT EXISTS
          (SELECT tablespace_name
```

```
              FROM dba_free_space free
                 WHERE free.tablespace_name =  t.tablespace_name
                    AND bytes                 >=  t.next_extent    ))
     UNION
     SELECT seg.owner, seg.segment_name,
            seg.segment_type, seg.tablespace_name,
            DECODE (seg.segment_type,
                          'CLUSTER',   c.next_extent)
        FROM sys.dba_segments seg,
             sys.dba_clusters c
     WHERE(seg.segment_type = 'CLUSTER'
     AND          seg.segment_name = c.cluster_name
     AND          seg.owner        = c.owner
     AND          NOT EXISTS
              (SELECT tablespace_name
                                 from dba_free_space free
                    WHERE free.tablespace_name =  c.tablespace_name
                       AND bytes                >=  c.next_extent    ))
     UNION
     SELECT seg.owner, seg.segment_name,
     seg.segment_type, seg.tablespace_name,
        DECODE (seg.segment_type,
                         'INDEX',    i.next_extent )
     FROM sys.dba_segments seg,
          sys.dba_indexes  i
     WHERE   (seg.segment_type = 'INDEX'
     AND          seg.segment_name = i.index_name
     AND          seg.owner        = i.owner
     AND          NOT EXISTS
           (SELECT tablespace_name
          FROM dba_free_space free
             WHERE free.tablespace_name =  i.tablespace_name
                AND bytes                >=  i.next_extent      ))
     UNION
     SELECT seg.owner, seg.segment_name, seg.segment_type,
            seg.tablespace_name,
            DECODE (seg.segment_type, 'ROLLBACK', r.next_extent)
     FROM sys.dba_segments seg, sys.dba_rollback_segs r
     where  (seg.segment_type = 'ROLLBACK'
     AND        seg.segment_name = r.segment_name
     AND        seg.owner        = r.owner
     AND        NOT EXISTS
             (SELECT tablespace_name
           FROM dba_free_space free
              WHERE free.tablespace_name =  r.tablespace_name
                 AND bytes                >=  r.next_extent     ));
```

Determining Archive Log Disk Location

From both a performance and recovery perspective, it's important to put the archive logs on a different disk from that used by your other data files and redo logs. If the archive logs are on the same disk as other data files or the redos, there is a high likelihood of disk I/O bottlenecks.

```
# datafile.sql
SELECT value
FROM    v$parameter
WHERE   name like 'log_archive_dest'
UNION
SELECT name
FROM    v$datafile
UNION
SELECT member
FROM    v$logfile
/
```

Which User Is Using the CPU?

The following query lists four users' usage of the CPU, ordered by largest usage first. You must have TIMED_STATISTICS set to TRUE for the readings to appear. If TIMED_STATISTICS is set to FALSE, all of the readings will be zero.

```
# sesscpu.sql
SELECT SUBSTR(name,1,30) parameter,
       ss.username||'('||se.sid||') ' user_process, value
FROM    v$session ss, v$sesstat se, v$statname sn
WHERE   se.statistic# = sn.statistic#
AND     name  like '%CPU used by this session%'
AND     se.sid = ss.sid
ORDER BY substr(name,1,25), value DESC
/
```

Computing the Hit Ratio

Throughout this book, we have emphasized how proper sizing of the Oracle cache buffers can help to reduce I/O. Computing the hit ratio is a very helpful way to do this sizing. The hit ratio tells us how many times Oracle has needed to retrieve a database block and has found it in memory (rather than having to access it on disk). Because memory access is so much faster than disk access, the higher the hit ratio, the better your performance.

You can ordinarily obtain the hit ratio for your application only by looking at either the UTLBSTAT/UTLESTAT statistics or the DBA MONITOR screens, as described earlier in this chapter. The script included below shows how to get the hit ratio from SQL*Plus. If you do this, you can automatically schedule hit ratio queries and can direct the output to a report or another database table. That table can then be used to produce application statistics or management reporting.

```
# hitrate.sql
SELECT
   SUM(DECODE(name, 'consistent gets',value, 0))   "Consis Gets",
   SUM(DECODE(name, 'db block gets',value, 0))     "DB Blk Gets",
```

```
        SUM(DECODE(name, 'physical reads',value, 0))    "Phys Reads",
      (SUM(DECODE(name, 'consistent gets',value, 0))
        + SUM(DECODE(name, 'db block gets',value, 0))
        - SUM(DECODE(name, 'physical reads',value, 0)))
                        /
      (SUM(DECODE(name, 'consistent gets',value, 0))
        + SUM(DECODE(name, 'db block gets',value, 0))  )  * 100 "Hit Ratio"
FROM v$sysstat;
```

The following output is taken from an actual site. Before the buffer cache was increased and a handful of SQL statements were tuned, the hit ratio was at 26%.

Consis Gets	DB Blk	Gets	Phys Reads	Hit Ratio
436987321	877262	2142974	99.	5105852

The next step you must take is to find out which user is causing the poor hit ratio.

```
# userhit.sql
SELECT se.username||'('|| se.sid||')' "User Session",
  SUM(DECODE(name, 'consistent gets',value, 0))   "Consis Gets",
  SUM(DECODE(name, 'db block gets',value, 0))     "DB Blk Gets",
  SUM(DECODE(name, 'physical reads',value, 0))    "Phys Reads",
  (SUM(DECODE(name, 'consistent gets',value, 0))
    + SUM(DECODE(name, 'db block gets',value, 0))
    - SUM(DECODE(name, 'physical reads',value, 0)))
                    /
  (sum(DECODE(name, 'consistent gets',value, 0))
    + SUM(DECODE(name, 'db block gets',value, 0))  )  * 100 "Hit Ratio"
  FROM  v$sesstat ss, v$statname sn, v$session se
WHERE  ss.sid    = se.sid
  AND   sn.statistic# = ss.statistic#
  AND   value != 0
  AND   sn.name IN ('db block gets', 'consistent gets', 'physical reads')
GROUP BY se.username||'('|| se.sid||')' ;
```

User Session	Consis Gets	DB Blk Gets	Phys Reads	Hit Ratio
(5)	27679	8934	11012	69.92
(6)	36	272	24	92.21
CORRIGANP(16)	173176	385	521	99.70
GURRYM(18)	1265544	2187	11959	99.06
OREILLYT(21)	22705	149	21	99.91
RUSSELLD(61)	128754	317	185	99.86

Looking at the Dictionary Cache

This script lets you interrogate the Oracle data dictionary performance tables via SQL*Plus. These tables give you information about all the objects stored in your dictionary (tablespaces, files, users, rollback segments, constraints, synonyms, etc.). This information is available in other ways, but getting at it through SQL*Plus lets you automate your queries, as we described for the hit ratio in the previous section.

If the dictionary cache is perfectly tuned, the query below would return no rows. When entries are loaded into the dictionary cache for the first time, the "Getmisses" figure is incremented by one. If the "Count," which is the number of entries set aside for each dictionary cache type, is set too small, entries will have to be thrown out to make way for new dictionary entries being read from disk into memory. This will cause rows to appear in the following query.

```
# rowcache.sql
SELECT parameter, count, getmisses
FROM    v$rowcache
WHERE getmisses > count;

          Dictionary Cache (Part of Shared Buffer Pool)
PARAMETER                              COUNT     GETMISSES
------------------------------------   --------- ----------
dc_free_extents                           41        172
dc_used_extents                           18        150
dc_segments                              125        202
dc_objects                              1798       1815
dc_columns                              4428       4639
```

Some people prefer to work with ratios and percentages. The dictionary cache miss ratio should ideally be less than 1%, although when the database is first started, the miss ratio will be higher because each dictionary item loaded into memory will record a miss. If the miss ratio is greater than 2% and you have spare memory, increase your SHARED_POOL_SIZE. If the ratio has decreased, you should have improved your performance.

```
# rowcache.sql
SELECT SUM(gets) "Gets", SUM(misses) "Misses",
   TO_CHAR(SUM(getmisses) / SUM(gets) * 100 , '999.99')||'%' "Miss
Ratio"
 FROM v$rowcache;

  Gets                     Misses                       Miss Ratio
---------------------------------------------------------------------
119,929,181                314,100                        2.61%
```

Looking at Rollback Segment Usage

It is sometimes useful to know which users are accessing the rollback segments. This is important information when a user is continually filling the rollbacks and causing extents to be thrown.

```
# rolbusrs.sql
SELECT r.name "Rollback Segment Name ",
            p.spid "System Process Id ",
            s.username||'('||l.sid||')' "Oracle User Pid"
FROM v$lock l, v$process p, v$rollname r, v$session s
WHERE  l.sid = p.pid(+)
AND s.sid=l.sid
```

```
AND TRUNC (l.id1(+)/65536) = r.usn
AND l.type(+) = 'TX'
AND l.lmode(+) = 6
ORDER BY r.name
/
```

Finding Foreign Key Relationships

It's useful to know the foreign keys and the unique or primary keys to which they relate. Foreign keys produce potentially damaging locking problems if the foreign key columns on the child table are not indexed, as we describe in Chapter 8, *Selecting a Locking Strategy*. The first query below lists all of the foreign keys and the parent table and columns to which they relate.

```
# forgnkey.sql
SELECT    a.owner , a.table_name , c.column_name ,
          b.owner , b.table_name , d.column_name
FROM      dba_constraints a, dba_constraints b,
          dba_cons_columns c, dba_cons_columns d
WHERE     a.r_constraint_name = b.constraint_name
  AND     a.constraint_type = 'R'
  AND     b.constraint_type = 'P'
  AND     a.r_owner=b.owner
  AND     a.constraint_name = c.constraint_name
  AND     b.constraint_name=d.constraint_name
  AND     a.owner = c.owner
  AND     a.table_name=c.table_name
  AND     b.owner = d.owner
  AND     b.table_name=d.table_name;
```

The second query lists all of the foreign keys that do not have the appropriate indexes in place on the child table. It shows the foreign key constraints that cause locking problems.

```
# forgnkey.sql
SELECT acc.owner||'-> '||acc.constraint_name||'('||acc.column_name
       ||'['||acc.position||'])'||' ***** Missing Index'
  FROM  all_cons_columns acc, all_constraints ac
 WHERE  ac.constraint_name = acc.constraint_name
   AND  ac.constraint_type = 'R'
   AND  (acc.owner, acc.table_name, acc.column_name, acc.position)
            IN
 (SELECT acc.owner, acc.table_name, acc.column_name, acc.position
    FROM   all_cons_columns acc, all_constraints ac
   WHERE  ac.constraint_name = acc.constraint_name
     AND   ac.constraint_type = 'R'
   MINUS
   SELECT table_owner, table_name, column_name, column_position
     FROM all_ind_columns)
 ORDER BY acc.owner, acc.constraint_name,
          acc.column_name, acc.position;
```

Listing Columns with Inconsistent Data Types or Lengths

The following query lists all columns that have differing lengths or data types but that have the same column name. For example, ACCOUNT_NO may be NUMBER(9) in one table and VARCHAR(9) in another. Having different data types can cause data casting problems and result in indexes not being used. (See Chapter 6 for details on data casting.)

```
# coldiffs.sql
SELECT owner, column_name
     , table_name||' '||data_type||'('||
       DECODE(data_type, 'NUMBER', data_precision, data_length)||')'
       "Characteristics"
  FROM all_tab_columns
 WHERE (column_name, owner)
   IN
   (SELECT column_name, owner
     FROM all_tab_columns
    GROUP BY column_name, owner
    HAVING MIN(DECODE(data_type, 'NUMBER', data_precision,
        data_length))
          < MAX(DECODE(data_type, 'NUMBER', data_precision,
        data_length)) )
   AND  owner NOT IN ('SYS', 'SYSTEM')
```

Listing Tables That Are Cached

Oracle7.1 and later provide a mechanism for caching tables in the buffer cache, using the command

```
ALTER TABLE tablename CACHE
```

Caching tables will speed up data access and improve performance by finding the data in memory and avoiding disk reads. To determine which tables have been cached, run the following command:

```
# tabcache.sql
SELECT owner, table_name, cache
FROM   all_tables
WHERE  owner not in ('SYS', 'SYSTEM')
AND    cache not like 'N%';
```

Listing Invalid Objects

Having invalid objects in your database usually indicates that your underlying tables have been altered to add a new column or have had DDL operations performed on them. The most common objects that become invalid are views, packages, and procedures. Invalid packages and procedures can cause a long response delay because they have to be recompiled. The user is forced to wait for the recompilation to complete. If you do alter your tables, you should always recompile your invalid packages and procedures to avoid user frustration. To obtain a list of all of the invalid objects, run the following query:

```
# invalobj.sql
SELECT owner, object_type, object_name, status
FROM   all_objects
WHERE  status = 'INVALID'
ORDER BY owner, object_type, object_name
/
```

Listing All Triggers

Triggers can significantly affect performance. They can cause major problems if the trigger has been disabled and someone has forgotten to reenable the trigger. In this case, the changes that the trigger was to have made will be difficult to recreate, since it is difficult to determine what updates have been applied to the table after the trigger was disabled. To obtain a list of all of the triggers and their status, run this query:

```
# triggers.sql
TTITLE 'List All Triggers'
SELECT table_name, trigger_name, status
    FROM all_triggers
 ORDER BY table_name, trigger_name;
```

Doing Latch Analysis

Latches are low-level locking mechanisms that are used to protect Oracle data and memory structures, such as the least-recently-used list in the buffer cache or the redo allocation of space in the log buffer. (We describe latch tuning in Chapter 11.) The following script investigates who is holding the latches:

```
# latchhld.sql
SELECT l.name "Latch Held", p.username "User Holding the Latch"
  FROM v$process p,v$latchholder l
 WHERE l.pid  = p.pid;
```

Checking the Number of Objects

This listing provides you with a list of the number of objects on a per-user basis. It can be run regularly to make sure that your database is operating as you expect it to.

```
# objcount.sql
SELECT   username,
         COUNT(DECODE(o.type, 2, o.obj#, '')) Tab,
         COUNT(DECODE(o.type, 1, o.obj#, '')) Ind,
         COUNT(DECODE(o.type, 5, o.obj#, '')) Syn,
```

```
            COUNT(DECODE(o.type,  4, o.obj#, '')) Vew,
            COUNT(DECODE(o.type,  6, o.obj#, '')) Seq,
            COUNT(DECODE(o.type,  7, o.obj#, '')) Prc,
            COUNT(DECODE(o.type,  8, o.obj#, '')) Fun,
            COUNT(DECODE(o.type,  9, o.obj#, '')) Pck,
            COUNT(DECODE(o.type,12, o.obj#, '')) Trg,
            COUNT(DECODE(o.type,10, o.obj#, '')) Dep
     FROM   sys.obj$ o,  sys.dba_users U
     WHERE  u.user_id = o.owner# (+)
     GROUP  BY username;
```

Oracle Performance Manager

The Oracle Enterprise Manager, released with Oracle7.3, contains many new products that assist with performance tuning, as well as backup/recovery capabilities and a number of other impressive functions. An extra-cost piece of software, the Oracle Performance Pack can be run from the Enterprise Manager frontend and incorporates a variety of performance products, including the Performance Manager, Oracle Lock Manager, Oracle Topsessions, Oracle Tablespace Manager, Oracle Expert, and Oracle Trace, all described in Appendix D.

11

Monitoring and Tuning an Existing Database

As we described in Chapter 9, *Tuning a New Database*, database tuning has an enormous effect on overall system performance. Tuning a newly created database is only the start. As time goes on, you'll need to monitor your database to make sure it continues to work efficiently. As a database administrator, there is a great deal you can do to keep the database tuned as the amount of data, the number of users, and the complexity of queries increase over time. This chapter builds on the concepts introduced in the previous two chapters, describing how you can monitor and tune in four areas: untuned application code, memory, disk I/O, and contention (a situation in which several of your users vie for system resources). Be sure to read Appendix F, *Tuning Case Studies*, which documents case studies of sites that we have tuned using the methods provided in this chapter.

Oracle provides a number of tools that allow you to observe database performance, diagnose performance problems in the making, and remedy problems when they occur. These tools were introduced in Chapter 10, *Diagnostic and Tuning Tools*. This chapter shows in greater detail how to use the tools with an existing database. Oracle has introduced a new set of tuning tools, called Oracle Performance Pack, that may be purchased as an additional option with Oracle Enterprise Manager (see Appendix D, *Oracle Performance Pack*). These tools contain tuning features that are unique to the Oracle database. Not only do they reveal performance problems, but they also assist greatly by suggesting how to remedy these problems.

Although the DBA does have the primary responsibility for overall database performance, performance tuning is a joint effort. The need to work as a team has become even more important with the increased usage of RAID technology, logical volume management, raw devices, the choice of two optimizers (cost-based and rule-based), and a heavy reliance on stored database procedures, packages, functions, triggers, and constraints. As the DBA, you must be aware of where the data files are physically located through the RAID and logical volume jungle and must have input into the type of RAID being used at the site. You must also be aware of which optimizer the application expects to be in place. Many applications are dependent on triggers and constraints to operate correctly. You need to be on top of this so you can ensure that all of the required objects remain valid in the database. We have high hopes for DBAs and their ability to make a difference. Our goal, in this book and in the systems we tune, is to achieve as close as possible to the ideally performing Oracle system. For that reason, our recommendations are often more stringent than Oracle's own.

Identifying Untuned Application Code

At most sites, our tuning audits typically identify several SQL statements that are the major cause of poor performance. To get the full benefit from your database tuning, you must tune your users' SQL statements before proceeding with overall database tuning. Not only do untuned SQL statements cause the program containing them to perform poorly, but they usually cause all the other users to get poor performance as well. This is because the data that the statements process can flood the buffer cache, which stores tables, indexes, sort data, rollback data, and Oracle dictionary information and is shared among all users. Troublesome SQL also has the ability to thrash the disk on which the object(s) being read reside.

Oracle offers a number of tools that you can use to proactively identify untuned SQL, including the V$SQLAREA table, SQL_TRACE, and ORADBX. None of these tools require you to have a detailed knowledge of the application. To get a full understanding of how to tune SQL statements, read Chapter 6, *Tuning SQL*.

Tuning Using V$SQLAREA

The V$SQLAREA table contains the statements currently residing in the shared pool area in memory, as well as information on the numbers of disk reads that have been performed by the statements and the number of times that the statements have been executed. The table provides you with valuable information that you can share with your application development teams to help tune SQL statements. (For more information about the shared pool, see the section "Tuning the Shared Pool," later in this chapter.)

Use a V$SQLAREA statement similar to the one shown below to report on untuned statements. The statement lists all SQL statements that have an average number of disk reads exceeding 200, which is equivalent to about a 4-second response delay to the user in real terms, assuming 50 I/Os per second. The response time shown in the query is response time in seconds. We recommend that you run this script regularly to identify and repair problem statements before they have a crippling long-term effect on your performance.

```
# diskread.sql
COLUMN "Average"  FORMAT 999,999,999.99
COLUMN "Response" format 999,999,999.99
TTITLE 'List Statements in Shared Pool with the Most Disk Reads'
SELECT  sql_text, disk_reads ,
        executions ,
        disk_reads / decode(executions, 0,1,executions) "Average",
        ' Estimated Response = ',
        disk_reads / decode(executions, 0,1,executions) / 50 "Response"
  FROM  v$sqlarea
 WHERE  disk_reads / decode(executions, 0,1,executions) > 200;
```

The following output is from an actual site that had chronic performance problems caused mainly by faulty SQL statements, one of which is shown in the example.

```
Fri Apr 26                                       page    1
List Statements in Shared Pool with the Most Disk Reads
SQL_TEXT
----------------------------------------------------------------------

DISK_READS EXECUTIONS    Average
---------- ----------- ---------------
SELECT 'X' FROM   job_desc WHERE   jd_event = DECODE(jd_subtype, 'P',
&evt_ppm, &evt_no) AND    jd_subtype in ('J', 'P', 'R') ORDER BY jd_
subtype desc
268672         243       1,105.65     Estimated Response = 22.11
```

The output tells us that the statement had been performed 243 times at an average of 1,105.65 disk reads, which is usually a 20-second or more response delay. This particular statement was one of 25 pages of statements that we received from the database. At this particular site, the database had been running for about 2 hours, which means that the statement had been running more than 100 times per hour. No wonder the production users weren't very happy with the response times. Strangely enough, the application development teams informed us that the response times weren't too bad!

To determine the execution path that the statement is using, spool your output to a file and edit it to obtain the EXPLAIN PLAN details.

```
DELETE FROM plan_table
/
EXPLAIN PLAN
FOR
SELECT   'X'
  FROM   job_desc
 WHERE   jd_event = DECODE(jd_subtype, 'P', &evt_ppm, &evt_no)
```

```
    AND    jd_subtype IN ('J', 'P', 'R')
  ORDER BY jd_subtype desc
  /
  SELECT LPAD(' ', 2*level) || operation ||' ' || options || ' ' ||
         object_name  "Execute Plan"
    FROM plan_table
  CONNECT BY PRIOR ID = parent_id
    START WITH id = 1
```

You can then obtain the indexed columns on the table in question using the following statement:

```
  # i.sql
  BREAK ON index_name SKIP 1
  SELECT index_name, column_name
    FROM user_ind_columns
   WHERE table_name = UPPER('&Enter_Table_Name')
   ORDER BY index_name, column_position
```

The cause of the poor performance in the preceding example was that although there was an index on subtype, it wasn't used because the subtype has only 11 distinct values in a 970,000-row table. There was an index on the jd_event column, but it was the second column in the index. There was also an index on (jd_subtype, jd_centre). The subtypes that were being searched on ('J', 'P', 'R') had a total of 19 rows in the table, but the Oracle7.1.6.2 cost-based optimizer decided to do a full table scan. Interestingly, other statements that had WHERE clauses on both jd_subtype and jd_centre actually used the index correctly.

Our major observation was that the cost-based optimizer is not aware of skewness of data—that is, how many rows exist for each value. Oracle7.3 overcame this problem by dealing with skewness through the use of histograms. Prior to Oracle7.3, you can make use of hints or use the rule-based optimizer to get around the problem.

Common SQL problems

These are some of the more common problems you may encounter in your SQL:

- Work practices at your site are not conducive to good performance. For example, large batch updates and reports are being run during prime online usage times. Some sites run a report 10 times to get 10 copies rather than running it once and using the photocopier. Another site that we visited was quite happy running hot backups during prime online usage times.

- The design has not taken performance into perspective. For example, consider the case in which a trial balance has to track through a huge amount of financial data to come up with running totals for each account. If you know that trial balances are a commonly requested item, you might provide a table that maintains running totals on a per-account basis; this would provide response times that are significantly faster. (See Chapter 5, *Designing for Performance*.)

- Indexes are missing. This may occur either as the result of a design oversight or after a table has been rebuilt and the indexes were forgotten. Indexes can also often have an inappropriate column sequence, which may force a longer scan through the index or may cause the index not to be used at all.

- As we've mentioned, the cost-based optimizer prior to Oracle7.3 is aware only of cardinality, that is, how many distinct values exist in the table. It is not aware of how many rows exist for each value. The most typical example of this is the situation in which you have a flag that has two values in a very large table. There may be 10 rows with a value of 'Y' and 1,000,000 with a value of 'N'. This type of index is often handy when you may wish to select rows that may need to be printed overnight (i.e., those with a value of 'Y'). You will then print the row and set the flag to 'N'. Prior to Oracle7.3 the cost-based optimizer assumes that the split of rows will be 50% for 'Y' and 50% for 'N'. Oracle7.3, however, is aware of skewness of data through the use of histograms. It will use the index if you select 'Y' because it realizes that 'Y' has only a handful of rows. The rule-based optimizer will also use the index.

- There is a function against the column, which disables the index usage. For example,

```
WHERE TRUNC(trans_date) = TRUNC(SYSDATE)
```

should be replaced by

```
WHERE trans_date BEWEEN TRUNC(SYSDATE) + .99999
```

- A key column is on both sides of the WHERE condition, as shown below:

```
SELECT fields
  FROM accounts
 WHERE key_id1 = NVL(:param,key_id1)
   AND key_id2 = NVL(:param2,key_id2)
```

This should read

```
SELECT fields
  FROM accounts
 WHERE key_id1 = :param1
 UNION ALL
SELECT fields
  FROM accounts
 WNERE key_id2 = :param2
```

- Performing joins using the cost-based optimizer with one table analyzed and the other table not analyzed is not advisable. This invariably causes a full table scan of the table that is not analyzed.

NOTE   When you are using the cost-based optimizer, be aware that the EX-
                PLAIN PLAN against a particular statement in your development en-
                vironment may not produce the same execution path as it would
                during production. This is due to the differing statistics that the opti-
                mizer has to work from. Also be aware that the execution path may
                change each time a table is reanalyzed. It is good practice to run EX-
                PLAIN PLAN for critical statements against the production tables if
                you are using the cost-based optimizer prior to Oracle7.3. You don't
                want your production users telling you that your code is untuned.

After the statement has been tuned, you must determine whether your tuning
efforts have been successful. To get the statement used in the example, add the
WHERE condition that will obtain the problem statement and remove the conditions that search only for long-running statements. The following example is the
result of our tuning:

```
SELECT  sql_text, disk_reads ,
        executions ,
        disk_reads / decode(executions, 0,1,executions) "Average",
        ' Estimated Response = ',
        disk_reads / DECODE(executions, 0,1,executions) / 50 "Response"
   FROM  v$sqlarea
  WHERE  UPPER(SQL_TEXT) LIKE '%FROM %JOB_DESC%';
```

The output is

```
SQL_TEXT
---------------------------------------------------------------------------
DISK_READS EXECUTIONS    Average
---------- ---------- ---------------
select 'X' from    job_desc where    jd_event = decode(jd_subtype, 'P', &evt_
ppm, &evt_no) and    jd_subtype in ('J', 'P', 'R') order by jd_subtype desc
294         263        1.12       Estimated Response = 0.02
```

There has been response improvement of more than 20 seconds each time the
statement is run.

Checking the buffer cache

Many sites have very large buffer caches. For these, scripts that check disk reads
do not catch all poorly performing SQL. A column that we can look at is the
BUFFER_GETS column in the V$SQLAREA table. A SQL statement may be scan-
ning hundreds of thousands of buffers in the buffer cache. To capture these types
of statements, use the following script. Note that the number of buffers scanned
to achieve our timings is 500 per second.

```
# bufgets.sql
COLUMN "Response" FORMAT 999,999,999.99
TTITLE 'List Statements in Shared Pool with the Most Buffer Gets'
```

```
SELECT  sql_text, buffer_gets ,
        executions ,
        buffer_gets / DECODE(executions, 0,1,executions) "Average",
        ' Estimated Response = ',
        buffer_gets / DECODE(executions, 0,1,executions) / 500
        "Response"
  FROM  v$sqlarea
 WHERE  buffer_gets / DECODE(executions, 0,1,executions) > 2000;
```

Checking for tables without indexes

The following script lists all tables that don't have indexes. A lot of sites leave indexes off smaller tables, expecting them to be stored in the buffer cache. You can force a table to be cached in Oracle7.1 using the statement ALTER TABLE tname CACHE, to guarantee that it's in the buffer cache. The problem is that having the unindexed table cached does not always guarantee the best performance. When an unindexed small table is joined to a larger table, the smaller table will often become the driving table because the smaller table has a full table scan performed on it. This situation provides much slower performance than having the larger table being the driving table. Also, a table without an index cannot be guaranteed of uniqueness unless it is done through application code.

```
# noindex.sql
TTITLE 'Report on all Tables Without Indexes'
SELECT owner, table_name
  FROM all_tables
MINUS
SELECT owner, table_name
  FROM all_indexes;
```

Oracle Expert documents the usage of current indexes as well as recommending additional indexes. We strongly recommend that you use this facility if you have purchased the Enterprise Manager Performance Pack.

Listing tables with many indexes

The next script lists all tables that have more than six indexes. There are no hard-and-fast rules for the number of indexes a table has to have to maintain optimal performance. At the very least, though, tables with more than six indexes should have their indexes justified. Observe the output from the query taken from an actual site. After we've checked the need for each index, ACCODES now has two indexes, ACCNAME and ACREACT have six, and ACENTRY has seven indexes. Inserts, updates, and deletes are running four times as fast as they were on the tables, and all queries are being provided with at least the same response times as before the change. One heavily used SQL inquiry is running more than 10 times faster, because it wasn't using the most effective index. However, if 10 indexes are required on a table to make all your SQL running against it have response times that are within the performance service agreement, then that's the way it has to be!

```
# 6index.sql
TTITLE  'Tables which have > 6 Indexes'
SELECT  owner, table_name, COUNT(*)
  FROM  all_indexes
 WHERE  owner NOT IN ('SYS', 'SYSTEM')
 GROUP  BY owner, table_name
HAVING  COUNT(*) > 6
```

```
Tue May 7                                          Page 1
           Tables which have > 6 Indexes


ACCTS                 ACCCODES               7
                      ACCNAME                9
                      ACRECACTS             10
                      ACENTRY               18
```

Checking index columns

The next inquiry gives you a list of indexes that have the same column as the leading column in the index. These indexes can cause queries to use the inappropriate index; in other words, Oracle will use the index that was created most recently if two indexes are of equal ranking. This can cause different indexes to be used from one environment to the next (e.g., from DEV to TEST to PROD). Each environment may have had its indexes created in a different sequence. We strongly recommend that you use hints in your programs, where necessary, to force specific queries to use a specified index.

The following information does not automatically indicate that an index is incorrect; however, you'll need to justify the existence of each of the indexes. The script lists all tables that have more than one index with the same leading column. If you run EXPLAIN PLAN on your SQL statements, you will be surprised at how many times a statement is not using the most appropriate index and the index is one of the indexes provided by the following script.

NOTE   Multiple indexes on a table with the same leading column may be totally legitimate, so you can't always assume that they will cause a problem.

```
# superind.sql
COLUMN table_owner FORMAT a20;
COLUMN table_name  FORMAT a26;
COLUMN column_name FORMAT a26;
TTITLE 'Indexes which may be Superfluous'
SELECT table_owner, table_name ,column_name FROM  all_ind_columns
WHERE  column_position =1
```

```
      GROUP  BY table_owner, table_name, column_name
      HAVING  COUNT(*) > 1;
```

Picking the optimizer

Many sites that we tune use the incorrect optimizer (for example, rule instead of cost). We recommend that every site aim to use the cost-based optimizer with Oracle7.3. If application developers are not skilled in writing SQL that is tuned for the rule-based optimizer, the cost-based optimizer can provide more acceptable response because it selects more appropriate driving tables and sometimes performs full table scans on tables that have a high percentage of rows for the value you are searching on. The cost-based optimizer offers many performance advantages such as the parallel query option, which makes more intelligent decisions on load sharing across processors, distributed queries being able to use indexes that aren't used with the rule-based optimizer. Oracle's new performance-monitoring tool Oracle Expert operates with and provides advice based on the cost-based optimizer.

The cost-based optimizer's biggest problem is that it can often cause applications that have been tuned for the rule-based optimizer, to run abysmally when they are transferred to the cost-based optimizer prior to Oracle7.3. The main cause of the problem is that indexes are avoided because the optimizer is not skewness aware. This can be overcome by using hints, but adding hints takes time and it is usually thought best to transfer with the arrival of Oracle7.3.

The DBA must tell the application development team which optimizer to use. We often visit sites where the DBA has not realized that he or she has to analyze a new table. Perhaps a table has been rebuilt, and the DBA has forgotten to reanalyze it. If the table is not analyzed and is joined to a table that has been analyzed, an inefficient full table scan often results for the table not analyzed. The following script checks which tables have been analyzed. If some are analyzed and some aren't, you will almost always experience some performance problems. If you are supposed to be running the cost-based optimizer, you must have your tables analyzed!

```
   # analyzed.sql
   COLUMN owner FORMAT a16
   COLUMN "Chained Rows" FORMAT 99,999
   COLUMN table_name FORMAT a26
   COLUMN analyzed   FORMAT a16
   TTITLE 'Tables that Are Analyzed (Summary by Owner)'
   SELECT owner,
          SUM(DECODE(NVL(num_rows,9999), 9999,0,1)) "Tables Analyzed"
          SUM(DECODE(NVL(num_rows,9999), 9999,1,0)) "Tables Not Analyzed"
     FROM all_tables
    WHERE owner NOT IN ('SYS', 'SYSTEM')
    GROUP BY owner;
```

The next script provides you with a table-by-table account of which tables are analyzed. We recently visited one site that had none of its tables analyzed. The application developers had told the DBA to analyze indexes only. Don't do this! It caused the cost-based optimizer to make some bad decisions. The ideal is to analyze your table and compute statistics on all tables. For very large tables, however, this may take too long. If this the case, we recommend that you estimate 40% or more of the rows in your tables and analyze compute statistics on the indexes. One other item that you should be aware of is that the optimizer path can change with new versions of the Oracle RDBMS. It may also change if you reanalyze tables on a periodic basis. Your site needs a way of testing code for efficiency in both of these cases.

Notice that this script also lists the number of chained rows in each table. See the section called "Chained and migrated rows" later in this chapter for information on how to eliminate chained rows.

```
# chained.sql
TTITLE 'Tables that Are Analyzed'
SELECT owner, table_name,
       DECODE(NVL(to_char(num_rows), '** Not Analyzed' ),
       '** Not Analyzed', '**> Not Analyzed' , 'OK') "Analyzed"
       , NVL(chain_cnt,0)      "Chained Rows"
  FROM all_tables
 WHERE owner NOT IN ('SYS', 'SYSTEM')
 ORDER BY owner, table_name ;
```

Tuning Using SQL_TRACE

SQL_TRACE is an INIT.ORA parameter that creates trace files in the directory specified in the parameter USER_DUMP_DEST. You run the TKPROF utility (described in Chapter 10) against the trace files to obtain each SQL statement that has been run, the number of times executed, the number of logical and physical reads by each statement, and the amount of CPU that the statement has consumed. To obtain the CPU usage, you must have the parameter TIMED_STATISTICS set to TRUE; doing so will degrade performance on your system by about 5% to 10%. We recommend that you set TIMED_STATISTICS to FALSE in the production database.

We recommend that for a production system that you use the SQL_TRACE facility sparingly and use the V$SQLAREA table and ORADBX instead. The reason for this is the large number of trace files that SQL_TRACE creates, many of which will contain SQL that has no problem statements at all.

Tuning Using ORADBX

ORADBX is a mostly undocumented facility that is offered on most releases of Oracle. It is used largely for debugging, and Oracle support people use it extensively. ORADBX can also help you with tuning. It lets you look into an Oracle process and determine what statements it is performing, the number of times each is executed, and the number of logical and physical reads performed. It also shows the full execution path of the statement and which indexes, if any, are being used. It will also provide you with CPU usage if you have set TIMED_STATISTICS=TRUE. See Chapter 10 for details on how to use it.

Identifying Users Running Untuned SQL

The following script lists CPU usage on a per-user basis. You must have set TIMED_STATISTICS to TRUE to obtain meaningful results from the script. If TIMED_STATISTICS is FALSE, all CPU usage will equal zero. If a user process has a considerable amount of CPU usage, it is worth investigating. The causes include untuned SQL statements, indexes missing, cursors being closed too often, or an ad hoc user running rampant. In certain cases, high CPU usage may be acceptable, depending on the type of tasks the person is performing.

```
# sesscpu.sql
TTITLE ' CPU Used By Session Information '
SELECT SUBSTR(name,1,30) parameter,
       ss.username||'('||se.sid||') ' user_process, value
FROM v$session ss, v$sesstat se, v$statname sn
 WHERE  se.statistic# = sn.statistic#
    AND  name  LIKE '%CPU used by this session%'
    AND  se.sid = ss.sid
 ORDER  BY value, SUBSTR(name,1,25) desc;
```

Tuning Memory

You have a lot of control over the use of memory in an Oracle system, and it is up to you to monitor its use and make sure your Oracle instance and your user processes are using memory as efficiently as they can. Memory access is vastly faster than disk access, so the more you are able to keep information in memory, rather than having Oracle seek it on disk, the better your response time and your overall system performance will be. This section describes four particular tunable areas of memory and makes recommendations for tuning each of them. The SORT_AREA_RETAINED_SIZE and SORT_AREA_SIZE are two other tunable memory allocation parameters that are documented later in this chapter in the section called "Reducing Disk I/O by Increasing the Sort Area."

- Buffer cache

- Log buffer

- Shared buffer pool (contains library cache, dictionary cache, and session information)

- Private SQL and PL/SQL areas

System Global Area (SGA)

As was mentioned in Chapter 9, the System Global Area (SGA) is an area in memory that is shared among all users. It contains the buffer cache, the log buffer, and the shared pool area. For a full list of the contents of the SGA, run the query shown below. The listing gives details of the SGA breakdown in memory. One particularly significant piece of information is the reading for "free memory," which indicates that the SHARED_POOL_SIZE INIT.ORA parameter may be reduced if the free memory is excessive. If it is low, you should *not* be decreasing the SHARED_POOL_SIZE. Be careful, however, because Oracle tends to maintain some free memory even when the shared pool is flooded with activity and should be made larger.

Other figures that are useful are the size of the buffer cache "db_block_buffers," which is usually required to be at least 20 megabytes for optimum performance; the "sql_area," which is where all of the shared SQL is placed; the "dictionary cache," which is where Oracle's dictionary is placed; and the "log buffer," which is where all changes are written prior to writing to your redo logs. User cursor usage is the value shown in "library cache," which was over 13 megabytes at the site measured in this example.

The log buffer should typically be 32,078 or larger. The "shared_sql" and "dictionary_cache" sizes are affected by the size to which you set the SHARED_POOL_SIZE INIT.ORA parameter. Unfortunately, the dictionary cache is tuned automatically (and not very well) by the earlier versions of the Oracle7 kernel. Each new release of Oracle7 has shown marked improvement in the dictionary cache performance. Most sites operate most efficiently with a shared pool size of at least 30,000,000.

```
# sgastat.sql
TTITLE ' SGA Statistic Listing '
SELECT  *
  FROM  v$sgastat;

Fri Apr 26                                       page    1
SGA Statistic Listing
NAME                                 BYTES
-------------------------------- ---------
free free memory                     88652
miscellaneous                        36788
fixed_sga                            48260
```

```
db_block_buffers                   20480000
log_buffer                           163840
db_block_multiple_hashcha             90348
db_multiblock_read                    14400
distributed_transactions               1440
kxfp subheap                          67184
SYSTEM PARAMETERS                      4096
PL/SQL DIANA                          228796
transaction_branches                   1680
trigger defini                         5192
fixed allocation callback               160
UNDO INFO                              4720
gc_*                                 1013252
PL/SQL MPCODE                         25536
db_files                              56992
DML locks                             88000
transactions                          59840
PLS non-lib hp                         2096
enqueue_hash                           3800
enqueue_locks                         96800
ENQUEUE STATS                          6940
dictionary cache                    2528868
event statistics                      20116
messages                              25600
enqueue_resources                      4800
table definiti                          840
processes                             95200
sql area                           43658416
sessions                             243760
SEQ S.O.                              17600
library cache                      13177800
db_block_hash_buckets               1604024
```

System-Specific Monitoring and Tuning Tools

In addition to the Oracle memory monitoring and tuning tools described in this section, there are a number of operating system facilities that you and your system administrator can use to improve memory usage. Oracle facilities cannot provide you with such system-specific information as the available memory on your machine, the amount of memory currently free on your machine, and the amount of memory being used by non-Oracle applications. You must become familiar with the operating system commands and utilities that allow you to do memory monitoring. These differ from system to system. Under VMS, for example, you'll issue the command *MON SYS* or *SH MEM*. Under UNIX, you'll use *vmstat* or *sar -M*. Consult your operating system documentation for the facilities that are available in your own system.

Tuning the Shared Pool

The SGA contains a shared buffer pool that holds the following:

- Library cache, which contains shared SQL and PL/SQL statements
- Dictionary cache, which stores data dictionary information
- Some session information (only if you have a multithreaded server architecture)

To tune this pool most effectively, you need to set several INIT.ORA parameters: SHARED_POOL_SIZE, SHARED_POOL_RESERVED_MIN_ALLOC, and SHARED_POOL_RESERVED_SIZE. You should also be making use of a packaged procedure, *dbms_shared_pool.keep('user.object')*, that allows you to maintain a selected package, procedure, trigger, or other code object in memory.

This section describes each of these components and suggests how to monitor the shared buffer pool to make sure you have allocated enough space for this area.

Tuning the library cache

How can you get the best performance out of the library cache area? There is only a certain amount of memory in this cache. If no more room is available in the cache for new entries, old statements are removed to make room. Then, if the statement that was removed from the cache is needed again, Oracle will have to parse it again before putting it back into the shared area. This will consume CPU and I/O resources. To avoid this, be sure that the value of SHARED_POOL_SIZE is large enough, and use packages, procedures, and functions wherever possible. The advantage of using packages, procedures, and functions is that they do not need to be parsed when they are loaded into the database. Database triggers do not have to be parsed for Oracle7.3 and later versions.

How can you figure out the optimal size for the library cache? One good way is to monitor your system to find out how often Oracle is looking for statements in the cache that have been removed because of inadequate memory. There are several ways to find this out. You can use SQL*DBA to look at the MONITOR displays; you can run a query against the V$LIBRARYCACHE table; you can examine the V$SGASTAT; or you can examine the V$SQLAREA table.

NOTE Oracle always has some free memory in the shared pool area, which it sets aside for incoming objects, so having free memory does not give you an immediate instruction to decrease the size of the shared pool. Oracle is also quite wasteful of memory, allocating larger chunks of memory to objects than they actually require. It does this to reduce the CPU overhead of allocating memory chunks to the many objects being loaded into and flushed from the shared pool.

There are two SQL*DBA MONITOR displays that provide information about the shared SQL area: SQLAREA and LIBRARYCACHE. Different versions of Oracle have different display screens that display similar information. We suggest that you become familiar with where to locate the information on your version of SQL*DBA. Remember that, unless SQL statements are absolutely identical, the parser will not know that they can be shared.

Looking at the V$LIBRARYCACHE table

The V$LIBRARYCACHE table contains a column called RELOADS whose value gives you valuable tuning information. If the sum of this column is greater than zero, Oracle has been forced to reparse a statement or reload a statement that has been removed because of a lack of memory (even though it might still be required by a process). You can issue a query against the table, for example,

```
# libloads.sql
SELECT SUM(reloads)
   FROM V$LIBRARYCACHE;
```

If RELOADS is too large, increase the SHARED_POOL_SIZE parameter. You may also need to increase the OPEN_CURSORS parameter, which specifies the maximum number of cursors allowed for each session. Typically, OPEN_CURSORS should not exceed 300 because these cursors use memory on per-user session basis. In addition to setting the parameters that are under your control, you will need to enlist the support of others in your organization by adhering to application standards. There are several rules about consistency that will help performance a great deal:

- SQL statements can be shared in the cache only if they are identical. "Identical" means just that. There must be no variation. For example, if one letter is uppercase in one statement, it must be uppercase in the other. (See Chapter 6 for details.)

- Encourage developers to make use of shared packages, procedures, and functions. (These shared objects also have the advantage of being stored in parsed form.)

- Encourage developers to use bind variables whenever possible. For example, use this statement:

```
SELECT acct_name, acct_limit
   FROM account
  WHERE acct_no = :accno;
```

instead of these:

```
SELECT acct_name, acct_limit FROM account WHERE acct_no = 10301;

SELECT acct_name, acct_limit FROM account WHERE acct_no = :accno;

SELECT acct_name, acct_limit
   FROM account
  WHERE acct_no = :accno;
```

The following script provides information in SQL that is a prime candidate for the use of bind variables. Hand the output to your developers, and check to see whether bind variables can be used; if so, they will avoid duplicate parsing of the statements, save memory in your library cache, reduce the number of reloads, and reduce fragmentation and latch contention of your shared pool. The output below is from an actual site. The database had been up for only 3 hours. Notice that one statement alone had 2102 statements similar to it stored in the shared pool. Each would have been reparsed; each would have to be loaded into the shared pool; and each would use memory in the shared pool. If bind variables were used, on the other hand, only one statement would need to be parsed and stored in the shared pool.

```
# sametext.sql
TTITLE ' SQL Statements that are Similar in Shared Pool Area'
SELECT SUBSTR(sql_text,1,30) sql , count(*)
   FROM v$sqlarea
  GROUP BY SUBSTR(sql_text,1,30)
  HAVING COUNT(*) > 200;
```

```
Tue 7 May                                    page    1
SQL Statements that are Similar in Shared Pool Area
SELECT ACTION_EVENT,ACION_NO,ACT             548
SELECT EVT_FREQUENCY,EVT_TYPE,EV             204
SELECT EVT_SUBTYPE,EVENT_NO,EVT_             701
SELECT CTL_CLASS,CTL_PROMPT,ROLE            1234
SELECT UVC_MAX    FROM USER_VALIDA          1278
select count(event_no) from events           363
select location_desc from location         2102
```

Another parameter that you should be aware of is CURSOR_SPACE_FOR_TIME. This parameter causes statements to be deallocated from the shared SQL area only when the program cursors requiring the statements are closed. This provides some performance improvements of execution calls. We usually recommend that you set it to FALSE and rely on pinning only the heavily used packages and procedures using *dbms_shared_pool.keep*. You must make sure that the library cache is large enough to store all required statements; if it is not, and CURSOR_SPACE_ FOR_TIME is set to TRUE, an error will occur. Most sites do not have enough memory to store every object run in the shared pool area.

Looking at the V$SQLAREA table

You can also examine the V$SQLAREA table to observe which statements are currently stored in your shared SQL area. To identify which statements are being used against the ACCOUNT table, for example, issue the statement

```
SELECT sql_text
  FROM v$sqlarea
  WHERE UPPER(sql_text) LIKE '%FROM%ACCOUNT%'
                  OR
        UPPER(sql_text) LIKE '%INSERT%ACCOUNT%'
                  OR
        UPPER(sql_text) LIKE '%UPDATE%ACCOUNT%SET%'
                  OR
        UPPER(sql_text) LIKE '%DELETE%FROM%ACCOUNT%';
```

The following figures are the reloads required for SQL, PL/SQL, packages, and procedures. The ideal is to have zero reload. Why? By definition, a reload occurs when the object could not be maintained in memory, Oracle was forced to throw it out of memory, and then a request has been made for it to be brought back in. If your reload figures are very high, try enlarging the SHARED_POOL_SIZE parameter and recheck the figures. Most medium to large sites require a SHARED_ POOL_SIZE of between 30 and 60 megabytes. We are aware of one site that achieved excellent performance improvements by increasing its SHARED_POOL_ SIZE up to 120 megabytes. If your figures continue to come down, continue to increase the SHARED_POOL_SIZE in increments of 5 megabytes.

```
# reloads.sql
TTITLE ' Total Shared Pool Reload Stats '
SELECT namespace, reloads
  FROM v$librarycache;
```

The following output is from a production site that had the database running for just over 5 hours. The number of reloads of objects is excessive. After tuning using the information in this section, we gathered the same information and found that the reloads were 1/50th of the untuned figures.

```
Fri Apr 26                                      page    1
Total Shared Pool Reload Stats
NAMESPACE          RELOADS
---------------  ----------
SQL AREA              3816
TABLE/PROCEDURE       5173
BODY                    37
TRIGGER                187
```

```
INDEX                     0
CLUSTER                   0
OBJECT                    0
PIPE                      0
```

The following three queries obtain information on the contents of the shared pool area. The first query lists the packages, procedures, and functions in the order of largest first. The second query lists the number of reloads. Reloads can be very damaging because memory has to be shuffled within the shared pool area to make way for a reload of the object. The third query lists how many times each object has been executed.

Oracle has introduced several new features to help you achieve acceptable shared pool performance. Both are documented in more detail later in this section. The first is a package that is stored in *$ORACLE_HOME/rdbms/admin* called *dbmspool.sql* on UNIX machines. The SQL program produces three procedures: keep, unkeep, and size. The keep procedure (i.e., *dbms_shared_pool.keep*) can be run to pin a procedure in memory; this ensures that it will not have to be reloaded. The unkeep procedure removes objects from the shared pool. The size procedure checks the sizes of objects in the shared pool.

Oracle7.1.5 and later offers two new parameters that allow space to be reserved for procedures, packages, and other objects above a selected size. This gives greater control over the avoidance of fragmentation in the SHARED POOL. See the parameters SHARED_POOL_RESERVED_SIZE and SHARED_POOL_RESERVED_ MIN_ALLOC later in this section.

```
# spoolsiz.sql
SET PAGESIZE 999
COLUMN owner format a16
COLUMN name    format a36
COLUMN sharable_mem FORMAT 999,999,999
COLUMN executions   FORMAT 999,999,999
TTITLE ' Memory Usage of Shared Pool Order - Biggest First'
SELECT  owner, name||' - '||type name, sharable_mem FROM v$db_object_cache
 WHERE sharable_mem > 10000
    AND type IN ('PACKAGE', 'PACKAGE BODY', 'FUNCTION', 'PROCEDURE')
ORDER BY sharable_mem desc;
```

```
Fri Apr 26                                          page    1
    Loads Into Shared Pool - Most Loads First
OWNER               NAME                                SHARABLE_MEM
---------------     ---------------------------------   ------------
SYS                 STANDARD - PACKAGE                   144,035
SIRPROD             SIRS_ND - PACKAGE BODY                47,201
SIRPROD             SIRS_ND - PACKAGE                     41,101
SIRPROD             SIRS_PACK4 - PACKAGE                  38,919
SYS                 STANDARD - PACKAGE BODY               31,887
SIRPROD             SIRS_PACK - PACKAGE BODY              17,730
SIRPROD             SIRS_PACK - PACKAGE                   16,446
```

```
SIRPROD          PAR_PROCS_FROM_SP - PROCEDURE      15,159
SYS              DBMS_STANDARD - PACKAGE            11,700
```

The sharable memory used by the various objects often vary. Memory will be allocated from the shared pool as quickly as possible to avoid shared pool latch contention. The end result is that objects are often allocated more memory than they require to run. If you pin your larger objects, size your SHARED_POOL_SIZE, and take advantage of the SHARED_POOL_RESERVED_SIZE and SHARED_POOL_RESERVED_MIN_ALLOC parameters, you will find that objects will tend to use less memory.

```
# spooload.sql
TTITLE ' Loads into Shared Pool  - Most Loads First'
SELECT  owner, name||' - '||type name, loads , sharable_mem
  FROM v$db_object_cache WHERE loads > 5
    AND type IN ('PACKAGE', 'PACKAGE BODY', 'FUNCTION', 'PROCEDURE')
  ORDER BY loads desc;


Fri Apr 26                                          page    1
     Loads Into Shared Pool - Most Loads First
OWNER            NAME                                   LOADS
SHARABLE_MEM
---------------- ------------------------------------ ------ -----------
SIRPROD          SIRS_ND - PACKAGE BODY                  25      47,201
SIRPROD          SIRS_ND - PACKAGE                       25      41,101
SIRPROD          SIRS_PACK - PACKAGE BODY                24      17,730
SIRPROD          SIRS_PACK - PACKAGE                     24      16,446
SIRPROD          SIRS_PACK4 - PACKAGE                    22      38,919
SIRPROD          PAR_PROCS_FROM_SP - PROCEDURE           23      15,159
SYS              STANDARD - PACKAGE BODY                 20      31,887
SYS              STANDARD - PACKAGE                       20     144,035
SYS              DBMS_STANDARD - PACKAGE                 19      11,700
```

The number of times all of these packages and procedures have been loaded is excessive. This is a clear reason for the poor performance at this site (where the database has not been running for very long). The reload of the SYS-owned packages is particularly damaging; note how dependent the database is on them in the next output.

```
# mostexec.sql
TTITLE ' Executions of Objects in the  Shared Pool-- Most Executions First'
SELECT  owner, name||' - '||type name, executions
FROM v$db_object_cache
WHERE executions  > 200
    AND type IN ('PACKAGE', 'PACKAGE BODY', 'FUNCTION', 'PROCEDURE')
ORDER BY executions  desc;


Fri Apr 26                                             page   1
Executions of Objects in the  Shared Pool  - Most Executions First
OWNER            NAME                              EXECUTIONS
---------------- ------------------------------- ----------
SYS              STANDARD - PACKAGE BODY             165,977
```

```
SYS              STANDARD - PACKAGE                  165,977
SYS              DBMS_STANDARD - PACKAGE              83,416
SYS              DBMS_STANDARD - PACKAGE BODY         83,416
SYS              DBMS_UTILITY - PACKAGE                8,416
SYS              DBMS_DESCRIBE - PACKAGE               8,405
SYS              DBMS_UTILITY - PACKAGE                8,106
SYS              DBMS_DESCRIBE - PACKAGE BODY          8,016
SIRPROD          SIRS_ND - PACKAGE BODY               5,977
SIRPROD          SIRS_ND - PACKAGE                    4,101
SIRPROD          SIRS_PACK - PACKAGE BODY             3,730
SIRPROD          SIRS_PACK - PACKAGE                  2,446
SIRPROD          SIRS_PACK4 - PACKAGE                 1,919
SIRPROD          PAR_PROCS_FROM_SP - PROCEDURE        1,159
```

The output highlights how many times the packages are performed. The packages STANDARD and DBMS_STANDARD are obvious candidates for pinning, as are the rest of the packages and procedures in this list. The next section describes how objects are pinned.

Pinning objects in the shared pool

Oracle7.1.x and later versions provide a mechanism for pinning objects into the shared pool (placing them there in a way that keeps them from being swapped or paged out), which can improve your performance markedly. If you do pin your packages, you will often need to increase your SHARED_POOL_SIZE because unless you do, the unpinned objects will have less memory to fit into, and their performance will degrade. When a user loads a large package or procedure into the shared pool, it has to search for a large contiguous pieces of memory. If not enough memory is available, it has to make the free memory available by removing other objects on a least-recently-used basis. This is particularly damaging to performance.

Always pin your packages and other objects immediately after starting up your database or after flushing the shared pool. It would be very nice if Oracle would automatically work out the objects to pin and pin them for us; in fact, we've heard that automatic pinning will be arriving in a future version of Oracle. In the meantime, it is up to you to do the pinning.

You can run the following script and spool the output to a file to help with creating the command to pin objects. The script selects the packages and procedures in most-frequently-used order first.

```
# mkkeep.sql
SELECT 'execute dbms_shared_pool.keep('''||owner||'.'||name||''');'
  FROM v$db_object_cache
 WHERE type IN ('PROCEDURE', 'PACKAGE')
 ORDER BY executions desc;
EXECUTE dbms_shared_pool.keep('SYS.STANDARD');
```

Don't forget the ' or you'll get an error. When you perform the keep, it does not place the package into the shared pool area, unless you execute or recompile the package. Oracle automatically loads the SYS.STANDARD, SYS.DBMS_STANDARD, and SYS.DIUTIL packages. Oracle provides an example of how to execute packages and place them into the shared pool, as shown below. In this example, pk1 is a package with a variable called dummy. Assigning dummy to a package and executing it loads it into the shared pool, so you can now pin it. Why didn't Oracle place it into the shared pool and keep it without all this having to happen? A very good question!

```
BEGIN
    pk1.dummy:=0;
END;
```

Be aware that when you pin packages that are owned by users other than SYS, you will have to GRANT EXECUTE ON package TO PUBLIC for the keep to work. Interestingly, once you have pinned your objects, they can be removed only by unkeep or by shutting your database down. ALTER SYSTEM FLUSH SHARED POOL will not take effect.

In production, you should always pin the SYS packages STANDARD, DBMS_STANDARD, DBMS_UTILITY, DBMS_DESCRIBE, and DBMS_OUTPUT. If you use DBMS_LOCK and DBMS_ALERT, they should also be pinned. It is also advisable to pin all of the larger and more executed packages and procedures. In development, also pin the PIDL, DIANA, and DIUTIL packages.

We advise you to package your procedures and functions to make better use of memory in the shared pool area and avoid the dependency tree problems when compiling. Prior to Oracle7.0.15, your packages could not exceed 64 kilobytes. You should always try to keep your packages less than 100 kilobytes because there are still situations in which larger packages won't compile.

Before Oracle7.1.6, you could pin only packages, but you could place procedures and functions into packages and have triggers call packaged procedures. With Oracle7.1.6 and later, you can pin both packages and procedures by specifying

```
EXECUTE dbms_shared_pool.keep('owner.pname');
```

Oracle7.1.6 and later versions allow triggers to be pinned with the syntax shown below. Prior to Oracle7.3, triggers have to be reparsed each time they are run, so it can be beneficial to pin some of the more heavily used and larger triggers.

```
EXECUTE dbms_shared_pool.keep('owner.triggername','R');
```

You can also pin PL/SQL blocks by replacing the 'R' with any other letter. We suggest that you read the documentation in DBMSPOOL.SQL for a comprehensive set of examples.

To determine which objects are pinned in your database, run the following SQL script:

```
# pinned.sql or #objremov.sql
SELECT name, type, kept
  FROM v$db_object_cache
 WHERE kept ='YES';
```

Some sites experience problems with large objects, especially when they are running a release of Oracle7.1.6. If you get error ORA-4031, try to identify the object on which it is occurring. If that is not obvious from the error message, add the following line:

```
event="4031 trace name errorstack level 10"
```

to your INIT.ORA file. You will now have a trace file, which you can search for the text "load=x". A few lines below that you will see the name of the package or procedure. You should pin it to avoid having this problem occur again.

Oracle has a table called X$KSMLRU, which provides interesting information on how many objects are being removed from the shared pool area for an object that is being loaded in. The "ksmlrcom" column is the object, and the "ksmlrnum" column is the number of object cleared out to make way for the new objects. Specify the following:

```
SELECT ksmlrcom, ksmlrnum
  FROM x$ksmlru;
```

Splitting the shared pool

Two new parameters introduced in Oracle7.1.5, SHARED_POOL_RESERVED_SIZE and SHARED_POOL_RESEVED_MIN_ALLOC, allow you to separate large objects from small objects. Enough memory is reserved for the loading of large packages and procedures without having too disruptive an effect on the shared pool area performance. Smaller objects will not be able to fragment the area because all objects smaller than the size specified in the parameter SHARED_POOL_ RESERVED_MIN_ALLOC will be placed into a shared pool area that is especially reserved for the smaller objects.

The total amount of space given to the larger area is specified by the parameter SHARED_POOL_RESERVED_SIZE. The amount of space assigned to the small objects is the SHARED_POOL_SIZE less the SHARED_POOL_RESERVED_SIZE. There is also a new procedure that controls the amount of flushing from the shared pool to make way for new objects being moved into the pool. The RDBMS will continue to flush unused objects from the buffer pool until enough free memory is available to fit the object into the shared pool. If not enough memory is available even after all of the objects have been flushed, Oracle reports a 4031 error. Unfortunately, getting far enough to discover that there is not enough memory can be very resource-consuming.

The DBMS_SHARED_POOL.ABORT_REQUEST_THRESHOLD parameter sets the limit on the size of objects allowed to flush the shared pool if the free space is not sufficient to satisfy the request size. All objects larger than the setting (the valid range is 5,000 to 2,147,483,647) will immediately return an error 4031 if sufficient free space is not available.

As a rule of thumb, if a site is using a lot of packages and procedures, we set the SHARED_POOL_RESERVED_SIZE to half the size of the SHARED_POOL_SIZE. Typically, for a large production system, the SHARED_POOL_SIZE will be set to 60 megabytes and the SHARED_POOL_RESERVED_SIZE will be set to 30 megabytes. We then set the size of the SHARED_POOL_RESERVED_MIN_ALLOC to 2,500. These are settings that we start with on benchmarks. However, each site is different, and there is no guarantee that our settings will be the ideal for your site. Oracle assists your tuning of the SHARED_POOL_RESERVED_SIZE with the following three scripts:

```
# respool.sql
TTITLE ' The Reserve Pool Settings for the Shared Pool Area'
SELECT SUBSTR(name,1,32) "Parameter", substr(value,1,12) "Setting"
  FROM v$parameter
 WHERE NAME LIKE '%reser%'
              OR
       name = 'shared_pool_size';
```

The output from this script provides you with the current settings from your database.

```
# poolfail.sql
COLUMN next_line FORMAT a60 newline
TTITLE ' Shared Pool Reserved Size Recommendation'
SELECT 'You may need to increase the SHARED_POOL_RESERVED_SIZE' next_line,
  '
       Request Failures = '||request_failures
  FROM v$shared_pool_reserved
 WHERE request_failures > 0
   AND 0 != ( SELECT to_number(value)
                FROM v$parameter
               WHERE name = 'shared_pool_reserved_size' );
```

This script tells us whether larger objects have failed to obtain memory in the portion of the shared pool reserved for larger objects. Increasing the size of the SHARED_POOL_RESERVED_SIZE will often overcome this problem. You should increase your SHARED_POOL_RESERVED_SIZE in 20% increments.

```
# rdsdecr.sql
SELECT 'You may be able to decrease the SHARED_POOL_RESERVED_SIZE'
       next_line,
```

```
            'Request Failures = '||request_failures
   FROM v$shared_pool_reserved
WHERE request_failures < 5
   AND 0 != ( SELECT to_number(value)
             FROM v$parameter
             WHERE name = 'shared_pool_reserved_size' );
```

The output from this query tells you that you may decrease the SHARED_POOL_RESERVED_SIZE. Decreasing in 20% chunks is a reasonable starting point.

What some sites prefer to do is to sum all currently running objects that are larger than the size of the SHARED_POOL_RESERVED_MIN_ALLOC. The following script assumes that you have set you SHARED_POOL_RESERVED_MIN_ALLOC to 2,500:

```
# resersiz.sql
SELECT SUM(sharable_mem)
  FROM v$db_object_cache
 WHERE sharable_mem > 2500;
```

This is the total memory of packages, procedures, triggers, views, functions, and other objects stored in the database.

```
SELECT SUM(sharable_mem)
  FROM v$sqlarea
 WHERE sharable_mem > 2500;
```

This output is the amount of storage required for SQL. If you add the two values together, you have an approximate sizing for the SHARED_POOL_RESERVED size. It is best to add on some contingency, perhaps 40%, for factors such as dynamic SQL, which is not counted in the second query, and for all statements that are not currently running. The same methods can be used to calculate the total shared pool size. You simply remove the WHERE sharable_mem > 2500 clause.

When you are estimating the total shared pool size, you have to take into account user cursors, which also use memory. You need about 250 bytes of shared pool memory per user for each cursor that the user has open. To obtain the total cursor usage, either run the following query or get the figure from the "library cache" from the V$SGASTAT table.

```
SELECT SUM(250 * user_opening)
  FROM v$sqlarea;
```

The SHARED_POOL_SIZE must also include memory for the dictionary cache (usually around 4 megabytes) and a collection of areas that are required to compile database objects and other miscellaneous areas shown in the V$SGASTAT.

After all of these computations, you may decide to start with our rule of thumb of 60 megabytes, pin your objects, take advantage of SHARED_POOL_RESERVED_

SIZE and SHARED_POOL_RESERVED_MIN_ALLOC, and monitor and tune the shared pool on an ongoing basis.

Tuning cursor usage

The next query lists the number of open cursors that each user is currently using. Each SQL statement that is executed is stored partly in the shared SQL area and partly in the private SQL area. The private area is further broken into two parts: the persistent area and the run-time area. The *persistent area* is used for binding information. The larger the number of columns in a query, the larger the persistent area. The size of the *run-time area* depends on the complexity of the statement. The type of statement is also a factor. An INSERT, UPDATE, or DELETE statement will use more run-time area than a SELECT statement will.

For INSERT, UPDATE, and DELETE statements, the run-time area is freed immediately after the statement has been executed. For a query, the run-time area is cleared only after all rows have been fetched or the query is canceled.

What does all this have to do with open cursors?

A private SQL area continues to exist until the corresponding cursor is closed. Note that the run-time area is freed but the persistent (binding) area remains open. If the statement is re-used, leaving cursors open is not bad practice if you have sufficient memory on your machine. However, leaving cursors open that are not likely to be used again is bad practice, particularly if you are short of memory. The number of private areas is limited by the setting of the INIT.ORA parameter OPEN_CURSORS. The user process will continue to operate, despite having reached the OPEN_CURSORS limit. Cursors will be flushed and will need to be re-parsed the next time they are accessed. Recursive calls are used to handle the reloading of the cursors if they have to be rebound after being closed.

The data in the following query list each user process, the number of recursive calls (the lower the better), the total cumulative opened cursors, and the current opened cursors. If the number of current opened cursors is high (> 200), ask why cursors are not being closed. If the number of cumulative opened cursors and recursive calls is significantly larger for some of the users than for others, determine what transaction they are running and whether they can leave cursors open to avoid having to rebind the statements and avoid the associated CPU requirements. Most sites run well with OPEN_CURSORS set to 300.

```
# usercurs.sql
DROP VIEW user_cursors;
CREATE VIEW user_cursors as
 SELECT
ss.username||'('||se.sid||') ' user_process, SUM(DECODE(name,'recursive
calls',value)) "Recursive Calls",
```

```
SUM(DECODE(name,'opened cursors cumulative',value)) "Opened Cursors",
SUM(DECODE(name,'opened cursors current',value)) "Current Cursors"
    FROM v$session ss, v$sesstat se, v$statname sn
 WHERE  se.statistic# = sn.statistic#
        AND (    name  LIKE '%opened cursors current%'
             OR name   LIKE '%recursive calls%'
             OR name   LIKE '%opened cursors cumulative%')
        AND  se.sid = ss.sid
        AND ss.username IS NOT NULL
GROUP BY ss.username||'('||se.sid||') ';

TTITLE 'Per Session Current Cursor Usage '
COLUMN USER_PROCESS FORMAT a25;
COLUMN "Recursive Calls" FORMAT 999,999,999;
COLUMN "Opened Cursors"  FORMAT 99,999;
COLUMN "Current Cursors"  FORMAT 99,999;
SELECT * FROM user_cursors
 ORDER BY "Recursive Calls" desc;


Fri Apr 26                page    1
Per Session Current Cursor Usage
USER_PROCESS            Recursive Calls Opened Cursors Current Cursors
---------------------- --------------- -------------- ---------------
SO32617(17)             14,541          7,339          99
SO32128(44)             13,854          5,404          97
SO32012(45)             12,071          5,395          99
```

This particular site had its OPEN_CURSORS set to 100, which was too small. Believe it or not, the database had only been running for a few hours. The applications had also made little use of bind variables and were frequently not closing cursors.

Tuning the dictionary cache

You need to set only one parameter, SHARED_POOL_SIZE, to control the amount of space allocated for the entire dictionary cache. You need to monitor the number of times Oracle tried but failed to find items in the dictionary. You can view the amount of memory set aside for the dictionary cache by viewing the V$SGASTAT dictionary cache row. You can still view the DC* parameters as you could with Version 6, but you cannot adjust the individual parameters.

We have observed that earlier releases of Oracle7 appeared to have exceedingly high "getmisses." A getmiss occurs each time a dictionary entry (e.g., a column) or table is brought up from disk and placed into memory. The number of slots set aside for each type of entry is shown in the count column in the output below. Ideally, the count should be high enough to never have the getmisses exceed it, especially considering that we are speaking of only a few megabytes in total for the dictionary cache (compared with hundreds of megabytes for the shared pool and buffer cache). Having an untuned dictionary cache can have a devastating effect on your performance.

```
#dicthits.sql
SELECT count, getmisses
   FROM v$rowcache
 WHERE getmisses > count;
```

The following output is from an Oracle7.2.3 database. If you are running a 7.0.x database, you will observe figures that are much worse than those shown. This output is from a medium-sized production site. If you have a large disparity between the count and getmisses, try enlarging your SHARED_POOL_SIZE parameter and rerun the query. Ideally, no rows should appear in this report.

```
Fri Apr 26                                      page    1
       Dictionary Cache (Part of Shared Buffer Pool)
PARAMETER                        COUNT     GETMISSES
------------------------------   ---------- ----------
dc_free_extents                      41        172
dc_used_extents                      18        150
dc_segments                         125        202
dc_objects                         1798       1815
dc_columns                         4428       4639
```

Each new release of Oracle7 appears to have improved dictionary cache tuning.

Tuning session data

If you are using Oracle's multithreaded server, you may need to allocate a larger-than-usual SHARED_POOL_SIZE. This is because for such systems, the shared pool stores the user process's private SQL area and sort areas.

To gauge how much larger to make your shared pool size to accommodate session data access, query the V$SESSTAT table as follows:

```
# mtsmem.sql
SELECT SUM(value)
   FROM v$sesstat
 WHERE name = 'session uga memory'
```

The result indicates the memory that is currently allocated to all sessions. You can use this figure to increase the shared pool size if you are planning to use the multithreaded server. The following script also lets you obtain the maximum amount of memory that the server sessions have used:

```
SELECT SUM(value)
   FROM v$sesstat
 WHERE name = 'session uga memory max'
```

It is usually best to use the latter calculation and add on a 30% contingency.

Tuning the Buffer Cache

The buffer cache is an area in memory that stores copies of database blocks for tables, indexes, rollback segments, clusters, sort data (if SORT_DIRECT_WRITES=FALSE and COMPATIBLE is not set), and Oracle dictionary data. Each buffer holds a single Oracle data block as set in the DB_BLOCK_SIZE INIT.ORA parameter. The buffer cache significantly reduces disk I/O and improves performance. By simply increasing one INIT.ORA parameter, DB_BLOCK_BUFFERS, you can often realize better than 60% performance improvements for both long-running update jobs and online transaction-processing systems. In general, the larger the buffer cache, the faster Oracle runs on most systems. This is obviously not the case if enormous tables are being serially scanned on a continual basis, but it is true for the more common online transactions.

In DB_BLOCK_BUFFERS, you specify the number of Oracle database blocks that will fit in the buffer cache. To make this change take effect, you must shut down the database or database instance and then restart it. Typically, a serious production database cannot perform with a buffer cache that is under 10 megabytes, and most perform at their optimum with a buffer cache 50 megabytes or larger.

Oracle recommends that you gauge the performance of the buffer cache by looking at the hit ratio—how often the data being retrieved are available in memory (rather than having to be retrieved from disk). We find, however, that the hit ratio is only one part of the performance story. The other consideration is how effectively the database writer (DBWR process) is writing to your database. When a user process reads data into the buffer cache, it has to find free buffers to place the data into. If the buffers are dirty, it has to wait for the DBWR process to write the dirty buffers to disk before the user data can be loaded in. This task can increase response times markedly.

We have found that when using the hit ratio as a measure, many of the sites we have tuned have improved long-running jobs by as much as 50% reduction in run-time with a hit ratio improvement of less than 10%; for online transaction processing, they have realized a better than 25% improvement in response times, with the hit ratio improving by less than 1%. There are a number of other ways to test the effectiveness of the buffer cache.

As a guide, you should aim for as high as 95% for OLTP applications and 85% for batch applications. The main reason for the higher allowance for the OLTP applications is that dictionary tables, rollback data, and indexes range data are often accessed, boosting the figure up. Sort through the buffer cache (not setting SORT_DIRECT_WRITES and COMPATIBLE), and note that physical reads are accumulated into the hit ratio but logical reads aren't, which forces the hit ratio down.

NOTE Increase the buffer cache only after you have tuned the shared pool size.

Remember that you must have at least 5% free memory on your machine. If you have closer to 10%, ask yourself whether you would benefit from adding this memory to your buffer cache. The answer is almost always yes. Make sure you include the planned memory usage of new users coming on to your system!

Our advice is to keep an open mind about what size buffer cache is right for your site. Test and then decide.

There are several ways to test how effective the current hit ratio of the buffer cache is; these are described below.

- Use the SQL*DBA MONITOR I/O function.
- Set INIT.ORA parameters on a test basis, and assess the results.
- Look at the SQL_TRACE and TKPROF output for information.
- Look at the snapshot created by running the UTLBSTAT and UTLESTAT scripts.
- Use the V$SYSSTAT for the instance hit ratio and the V$SESSTAT for individual user session hit ratios.

Looking at SQL*DBA MONITOR I/O

Look at the MONITOR I/O display and observe the current hit ratio. This is the rate at which Oracle finds the data blocks it needs already in memory. It is computed by

```
(logical reads - physical reads)  /  (logical reads)
```

The closer the hit ratio approaches 1.00, the better your system will perform. If you have already tuned your dictionary cache, you still have free memory, and the hit ratio is below 95% for OLTP and 85% for batch, try increasing the value of DB_BUFFER_BLOCKS. Make sure that you always have at least 5% free memory.

You may need to buy more memory if the following conditions are true:

- Your ratio is below 60%.
- You have no untuned SQL in your application.
- You have already tuned your shared pool area and not oversized your SHARED_POOL_SIZE, SORT_AREA_RETAINED_SIZE, and SORT_AREA_SIZE.
- Your response times are poor.
- You have no free memory.

In fact, this situation sounds pretty grim; buy that memory today!

Testing INIT.ORA parameters for the effect of increasing buffer cache

Sometimes, the best way to figure out whether the buffer cache needs to be increased or decreased is to try it out on a test basis. With this method, you make changes to the INIT.ORA parameters and then assess the results. When you use this method in production, make sure to turn it off as soon as you have gathered your results. Do not leave this function activated as an ongoing check on your production database. The function will continue to degrade your response times by about 20% as a result of buffer cache latch contention.

Even if enlarging certain parameters shows only marginal increases, these may equate to significant improvements in response times. Even a 5% improvement may make a big difference in your system. Be sure to monitor during periods of peak usage, not over the course of an entire day. Daily figures that average times of high and low activity may give you unrealistic results. If you change your buffer cache to suit these results, your performance may suffer significantly.

To measure the effect of increasing the buffer cache, set the INIT.ORA parameter DB_BLOCK_LRU_EXTENDED_STATISTICS (specified in Oracle blocks) to the value that you are considering as an increase to the buffer cache. Shut down the database instance and restart it. Statistics will be placed in the SYS.X$KCBRBH table. You can query this table to see the effect of increasing the buffer cache. For example, to see the effect of increasing the cache in chunks of 250, perform the following query:

```
# decbcach.sql
SELECT 250 * TRUNC(indx / 250) +1 || 'to' ||250 *
    (TRUNC(indx / 250) +1 interval,
    SUM(count) cache_hits
    FROM sys.x$kcbrbh
        GROUP BY TRUNC(indx / 250);
```

To test a different interval, change 250 to the next increment you want to test. You'll see output in the following format:

```
Interval          Cache_Hits
_____         _____
1 to 250            21000
251 to 500          15000
501 to 750          10000
751 to 1000         3500
```

This shows that if 250 cache blocks were added to DB_BLOCK_BUFFERS, there would be 21,000 additional cache hits over and above the current DB_BLOCK_ BUFFERS setting. If an additional 250 blocks were added, there would be 21,000 + 15,000 cache hits, or a total of 36,000.

Testing INIT.ORA parameters for the effect of decreasing buffer cache

To measure the effect of decreasing the buffer cache, set the INIT.ORA parameter DB_BLOCK_LRU_STATISTICS to TRUE. Shut down the database instance, and then restart it. Statistics are placed in the SYS.X$KCBCBH table. You can query this table to see the effect of decreasing the cache.

```
# incbcach.sql
SELECT 250 * TRUNC(indx / 250) +1 || 'to' || 250 *
    (TRUNC(indx / 250) +1)    interval,
    SUM(COUNT) cache_hits
  FROM sys.x$kcbcbh
 WHERE indx > 0
 GROUP BY TRUNC(indx / 250);
```

The output produced will be in the following format:

Interval	Cache_Hits
1 to 250	1021000
251 to 500	115000
501 to 750	50000
751 to 1000	9500

If memory is scarce, you can reduce the DB_BLOCK_BUFFERS parameter by 250, which will increase your disk I/O but probably provide better response times by lessening the CPU-intensive paging and swapping operations caused by the lack of memory. If memory is not scarce, do not decrease the parameter. The 9,500 hits in cache eliminate disk I/O that may occur during peak usage times and increase user response times.

Using UTLBSTAT/UTLESTAT for testing

You can use Oracle's UTLBSTAT and UTLESTAT scripts to take a snapshot of program activity, including buffer cache activity. Chapter 10 shows a detailed listing of UTLBSTAT/UTLESTAT output and details a number of performance tests you can run on it.

The following example extracts some statistics from UTLBSTAT/UTLESTAT output and shows the effects of different figures as the buffer cache is enlarged.

Looking at the V$SYSSTAT table

The V$SYSSTAT table contains a variety of performance statistics, including buffer cache statistics. Consider the following query:

```
# hitratio.sql
TTITLE ' The Hit Ratio      '
SELECT
SUM(DECODE(name, 'consistent gets',value, 0))  "Consis Gets",
SUM(DECODE(name, 'db block gets',value, 0))  "DB Blk Gets",
```

```
       SUM(DECODE(name, 'physical reads',value, 0))  "Phys Reads",
       (SUM(DECODE(name, 'consistent gets',value, 0))  +
       SUM(DECODE(name, 'db block gets',value, 0))  -
       SUM(DECODE(name, 'physical reads',value, 0)))
                          /
       (SUM(DECODE(name, 'consistent gets',value, 0))  +
           SUM(DECODE(name, 'db block gets',value, 0))  )  * 100 "Hit Ratio"
       FROM v$sysstat;
```

We ran this query to produce the following output for a site that had been experiencing a hit ratio of 26% prior to tuning. You can imagine the difference in end user response times when the site was tuned to achieve the Hit Ratio below. The improvement was made by increasing the buffer cache from 1 megabyte to 20 megabytes. Many SQL statements were individually tuned and the OPTIMIZER_ MODE was changed from cost-based to rule-based.

```
Fri Apr 26                                   page    1
The Hit Ratio
Consis Gets DB Blk Gets  Phys Reads Hit Ratio
----------- ------------ ---------- ----------
436987321       877262    2142974   99.5105852
```

It is also possible to look at user sessions that are experiencing poor hit ratios. You can delve further by finding out which tables the user is currently using and the cursors that the user is currently running. You are usually better off concentrating on using the V$SQLAREA table from identifying the statements that are performing badly. Knowing which user is experiencing a poor hit ratio can assist you with knowing who to contact to ask what they are running that is causing the poor hit ratio.

NOTE   A process usually appears on this report which does not have a username. This process, SMON, performs system cleanups, joins coalescing extents, and controls sort extent allocation and reclaiming. You can tune this activity if it is harming your response times by having larger extent sizes in your temporary tablespace, making the PCTIN-CREASE 0 on your tablespace default storage, and sizing your objects to avoid segment fragmentation.

The following statement lists all users with a hit ratio of less than 60%:

```
# userhit.sql
TTITLE ' User Hit Ratios'
COLUMN "Hit Ratio" FORMAT 999.99
COLUMN  "User Session" FORMAT a15;
SELECT se.username||'('|| se.sid||')' "User Session",
SUM(DECODE(name, 'consistent gets',value, 0))  "Consis Gets",
SUM(DECODE(name, 'db block gets',value, 0))  "DB Blk Gets",
SUM(DECODE(name, 'physical reads',value, 0))  "Phys Reads",
```

```
(SUM(DECODE(name, 'consistent gets',value, 0)) +
  SUM(DECODE(name, 'db block gets',value, 0))   -
  SUM(DECODE(name, 'physical reads',value, 0)))
                    /
(SUM(DECODE(name, 'consistent gets',value, 0))  +
 SUM(DECODE(name, 'db block gets',value, 0))  )  * 100 "Hit Ratio"
    FROM   v$sesstat ss, v$statname sn, v$session se
WHERE   ss.sid    = se.sid
    AND      sn.statistic# = ss.statistic#
    AND      value != 0
    AND      sn.name IN ('db block gets', 'consistent gets', 'physical
    reads')
GROUP BY se.username||'('|| se.sid||')'
HAVING
(SUM(DECODE(name, 'consistent gets',value, 0)) +
  SUM(DECODE(name, 'db block gets',value, 0))   -
  SUM(DECODE(name, 'physical reads',value, 0)))
                    /
(SUM(DECODE(name, 'consistent gets',value, 0))  +
 SUM(DECODE(name, 'db block gets',value, 0))  )  * 100
       < 60;
```

The following script creates a table that can be used to join to other tables to obtain more details on the cursors currently held by user sessions that have a hit ratio less than 60%. We have created a temporary table, USER_HIT_RATIOS, to achieve this. You can make this a view rather than a table if you wish, and achieve the same results.

```
# lowhits.sql
DROP TABLE user_hit_ratios;
CREATE TABLE user_hit_ratios as
(SELECT se.username||'('|| se.sid||')' "User Session",
SUM(DECODE(name, 'consistent gets',value, 0))   "Consistent Gets",
SUM(DECODE(name, 'db block gets',value, 0))  "DB Block Gets",
SUM(DECODE(name, 'physical reads',value, 0))   "Physical Reads",
(SUM(DECODE(name, 'consistent gets',value, 0)) +
  SUM(DECODE(name, 'db block gets',value, 0))   -
          SUM(DECODE(name, 'physical reads',value, 0)))
                    /
(SUM(DECODE(name, 'consistent gets',value, 0))  +
 SUM(DECODE(name, 'db block gets',value, 0))  )  * 100 "Hit Ratio"
    FROM   v$sesstat ss, v$statname sn, v$session se
WHERE   ss.sid    = se.sid
    AND      sn.statistic# = ss.statistic#
    AND      value != 0
    AND      sn.name in ('db block gets', 'consistent gets', 'physical
    reads')
GROUP BY se.username, se.sid)
HAVING
(SUM(DECODE(name, 'consistent gets',value, 0)) +
 SUM(DECODE(name, 'db block gets',value, 0))   -
          sum(decode(name, 'physical reads',value, 0)))
                    /
```

```
(sum(decode(name, 'consistent gets',value, 0))  +
sum(decode(name, 'db block gets',value, 0))  )  * 100 "Hit Ratio"
         < 85;
```

The following script provides you with information on the objects being utilized by the user sessions that are experiencing poor hit ratios. If the same object appears across all users, it is often the cause of the poor hit ratios.

```
BREAK ON "User Session"
TTITLE 'Objects Being Used by Users with Hit Ratio < 60'
SELECT se0.username||'('|| se0.sid||')' "User Session",
SUBSTR(owner, 1,12) "Object Owner",
               SUBSTR(object,1,30) "Object"
    FROM  v$access ac, v$session se0
WHERE    ac.sid    = se0.sid
   AND   ob_typ    = 2
   AND   60 >
   (SELECT "Hit Ratio" from user_hit_ratios
     WHERE se0.username||'('|| se0.sid||')' = "User Session")
ORDER BY username, se0.sid, owner;
```

The next script lists the cursors currently running for user sessions with a poor hit ratio. If the same statement or same set of tables appears in the output consistently, these are often pointers to untuned SQL and or incorrectly indexed table.

```
COLUMN "User Session"  format a12;
TTITLE 'Cursors that Users currently have Open Where User Hit Ratio < 60%'
SELECT distinct username||'('||sid||')' "User Session",  sql_text
FROM v$open_cursor , v$session
WHERE v$session.saddr       = v$open_cursor.saddr
    AND   60 >
    (SELECT "Hit Ratio" from user_hit_ratios
        WHERE username||'('|| sid||')' = "User Session")
ORDER BY username, sid;
```

At one site, we enlarged the buffer cache from 10 megabytes to 40 megabytes and achieved a fourfold response time improvement. The V$SYSSTAT values that had an associated improvement are listed in the table below. See Chapter 10 for a more detailed explanation of many more of the VYSYSTAT parameters.

Table 11-1. V$SYSSTAT Parameters After Enlarging Buffer Cache

Parameter	10 Meg Buffer Cache	40 Meg Buffer Cache
Physical Reads	42150	5970
Physical Writes	49680	30740
Write Requests	2740	1420
Summed Dirty Queue Length	16530	0
Free Buffers Requested	72590	39050
Dirty Buffers Inspected	3970	0
Free Buffer Waits	2080	0

Table 11-1. V$SYSSTAT Parameters After Enlarging Buffer Cache (continued)

Parameter	10 Meg Buffer Cache	40 Meg Buffer Cache
Free Wait Time	58570	0
DBWR Make Free Requests	2440	0
DBWR Free Buffers Found	169960	0
DBWR Summed Scan Depth	248170	6100
DBWR Buffers Scanned	210890	6100
redo wastage	1199070	208280
redo write time	76750	48020

There are a number of interesting observations about these parameters:

- There are significantly fewer physical reads with the larger buffer cache. We have read that reading from disk uses between five and eight times the amount of CPU that reading from the buffer cache uses. Our figures support such findings, so reducing disk reads is a telling factor for good performance.

- When the buffer cache is too small, the DBWR has to write in panic mode to free buffers from new data being read into the buffer cache. Physical writes have been reduced by around 40%.

- Redo write time has increased. The interaction between the redos and the log buffer is an important one. Each time the DBWR writes to the data files, a corresponding write also takes place by the LGWR to the redo logs. From the other perspective, when a checkpoint occurs, the LGWR instructs the DBWR to clear all dirty buffers from the buffer cache, committed or uncommitted.

- Notice that all of the wait times and numbers of waits is much worse for the smaller buffer cache. See Free Buffer Waits and Free Wait Time.

- Notice that the parameters that clear space in the buffer cache for new buffers being brought in are much higher with the smaller buffer cache.

Looking inside the buffer cache

Oracle provides you with a means of obtaining a summary of the current states in your buffer cache. The following script scans through the buffer cache and counts the number of buffers in the various states. The three main states are:

CUR
> Blocks read but not dirtied

CR
> Blocks that have been read and dirtied and are remaining in cache with the intention of supplying the new values to queries about to start up

FREE
 Buffers that are usable to place new data being read into the buffer cache

You occasionally get buffers in a status of READ, indicating buffers currently being read into the buffer cache.

The most significant information you might get from this query is finding that the FREE count is high, perhaps 40% of overall buffers. In this case, you may consider decreasing the DB_BLOCK_BUFFERS parameter. Note, however, that Oracle attempts to always maintain a free count greater than zero to make way for new data coming into the buffer cache, so consistently having free buffers does not automatically imply that you should lower the parameter DB_BLOCK_BUFFERS.

To create the view v$bh, which is used by this script, you must run the script *$ORACLE_HOME/rdbms/admin/catparr.sql*.

```
# bufcache.sql
TTITLE ' Current Buffer Cache Usage '
SELECT status, count(*)
  FROM v$bh
  GROUP BY status;
```

To obtain the objects in the buffer cache, and the number of buffers each is using, you can run the following script. You have to rerun *catparr.sql* prior to rerunning this script. (See details on *catparr.sql* in Chapter 12, *Tuning Parallel Server*.) This script takes awhile to run, which is why the WHERE clause asks whether you need to run it.

```
# bufcache.sql
TTITLE ' Breakdown of what is Currently Being Stored in the Buffer
Cache'
SELECT kind, name, status, count(*)
  FROM v$cache
  WHERE SUBSTR('&Look_inside_Buffer_Cache?',1,1) in ('y','Y')
  GROUP BY kind, name, status;
```

Remember that the buffer cache stores tables, indexes, dictionary tables, sort temporary tables, and rollback segments. Oracle7.1, 7.2, and 7.3 introduce options to bypass the buffer cache for some of these operations.

See the 7.2 parameter SORT_DIRECT_WRITES, which bypasses the buffer cache and allows sorts to run as much as three times as fast. In 7.1.6 and later, parallel table scans and reading sort data from disk can bypass the buffer cache if you set COMPATIBLE=7.1.6 or later.

In 7.2 Oracle turns off logging (not strictly buffer cache) if you use the UNRECOV-ERABLE option. When building an index, you can bypass writing to redo logs by setting this parameter. The direct load path is used also to bypass the buffer cache. One interesting point is that UNRECOVERABLE is the default when Archiving is not enabled.

You should also be aware that Oracle7.1 and later provides a mechanism for loading an entire object into cache. See the ALTER TABLE tname CACHE; command. The data from the table is placed on to the most recently used end of the Least Recently Used (LRU) list which means that the data is stored in the buffer cache for longer. Having a table with a CACHE setting does not automatically cache the table. You must perform a full table scan to get the data into the buffer cache.

Sharing Executable Images

Some platforms allow you to install the Oracle product executables as shared executable images. For example, products like SQL*Forms may be installed once in memory and shared by all users. This feature can save enormous amounts of memory, but unfortunately it is not available on all platforms. For example, on a VMS system, suppose that you have 50 concurrent Oracle users running RUNFORM (*iap30*). If the RUNFORM executable isn't installed in memory, more than 50 megabytes of memory will be required. Each user will have his or her own copy of RUNFORM residing in memory. If you install RUNFORM as a shared executable, you'll save most of this memory. On VMS, to install the shared executable, you run the utility, *@ORA_INSTALL:ORA_INSUTL*. Check to see if your system supports image sharing and make sure users take advantage of this facility.

Tuning Disk I/O

With the increased usage of logical volume managers and RAID technology at many sites, monitoring your disk I/O has become increasingly difficult. We see complex problems at many of the sites we visit. For example, we see a single Oracle data file experiencing 90% of a site's disk I/Os. We approach the systems administrator to explain the situation, only to find that the data file has been striped across six disks. We walk away relieved. We then perform one last check on the logical-to-physical database translation, and we discover that the redos are on the same physical disk device as the archive logs and the system tablespace. The physical disk is thrashing and, worse still, if we lose the disk, we lose our database. We feel a bad headache coming on, and since we only had one Foster's apiece last night, it can't be the booze!

DBAs must work closely with systems administrators on the database layout not only at the database creation stage, but also on an ongoing basis. Unfortunately, some systems administrators make an art form of moving logical volumes from disk to disk without fully understanding the recovery and performance implications of doing so. Disk tuning is a team effort, and one weak link in the team can cause a disaster!

Oracle provides many ways for you to monitor the use of disk and the number of disk accesses in your system. Because disk access is so much slower than memory access, your focus must be on ways to reduce the amount of disk I/O required. You can do this by allocating large enough areas in memory and by assigning large enough disk space allocations for tables, indexes, and other objects. In this way, you can avoid the problems of disk fragmentation and data row chaining.

Make sure when you monitor disk activity that you sample at the times of day when your system experiences peak usage. You should also be sure to monitor disk activity for long-running overnight batch jobs, which are often poor at sharing the disk load.

System Monitoring and Tuning Tools for Disk I/O

In addition to the Oracle tools for disk monitoring and tuning, your own operating system provides facilities that you and your system administrator can use to improve disk I/O usage. Oracle facilities cannot provide you with information on disk I/O speeds, seek operations, available channels, data transfer rates, and spread across disk devices. You must become familiar with the operating system commands and utilities that allow you to monitor disk access on your machine. These differ from system to system. Under VMS, for example, you'll issue the command *MON DISK*. Under UNIX, you'll run *iostat* in the form:

```
iostat  drives interval count
```

where:

drives
    Drives to be monitored

interval
    Interval in seconds

count
    Number of samples taken

Another common UNIX command is

```
sar -d 1 15
```

which will provide 15 disk I/O statistics at 1 second intervals.

Consult your operating system documentation for the facilities available in your own system.

Using the MONITOR Function to Monitor Disk Activity

You can display information about disk activity for the Oracle database files in your system by invoking the SQL*DBA MONITOR facility as follows:

```
SQLDBA> CONNECT INTERNAL
      >  MON DISK
```

If the I/O rate for a given disk is continually close to its recommended maximum I/O, select one of the following approaches:

1. Break the tablespace down into two data files. Place each on a separate disk device.

2. Place the entire data file on a faster device.

3. If you have memory available, reduce disk I/O by enlarging the buffer cache.

4. If more than one tablespace is sharing a physical disk drive, physically place high-activity tablespaces between the less frequently accessed tablespaces. This can significantly reduce disk seek times.

5. Consider striping the data file using either Oracle striping or RAID technology.

Looking at Disk I/Os per Disk File

V$FILESTAT provides a file-monitoring table that you can query to find out the number of disk I/Os per disk file. The output from this query will show you which files are the most active. However, it does not show you if any disk is exceeding its maximum I/Os per second at any given point in time. If you combine all of the I/Os on data files on a per-disk basis, you can identify the data files most likely to cause a disk bottleneck. You must spread your database differently if you are experiencing disk bottlenecks.

The following script shows the spread of disk I/Os. Ideally, the disk I/Os should be even across disks. If the disk I/O on one of the disks is too high, consider moving one of the data files on that disk to another disk. If you are using raw devices, it is handy to make the raw devices consistent sizes for this purpose. If you can't move one of the data files, consider moving objects into alternate tablespaces on different disks.

If there is a large amount of activity on one of the disks, there is often an untuned query causing the damage. Be aware of which table is causing the problems. As mentioned earlier in this chapter, the V$SQLAREA table has a column called disk_ reads as well as the SQL statement that was performed. If you select all statements with an average greater than 2,500 disk_reads, and order it by disk_reads desc, this is often an indicator of the problem query. The script below was run at an actual production site at which many users complained about poor performance. The database had about 100 online concurrent users who were using the database very heavily, recording details from clients over the phone.

```
# diskperc.sql
DROP TABLE tot_read_writes;
CREATE TABLE tot_read_writes
  AS SELECT SUM(phyrds) phys_reads, sum(phywrts) phys_wrts
        FROM V$FILESTAT;
TTITLE ' Disk I/O s by Datafile '
COLUMN name FORMAT a30
COLUMN phyrds FORMAT 999,999,999
COLUMN phywrts FORMAT 999,999,999
COLUMN read_pct FORMAT 999.99
COLUMN write_pct FORMAT 999.99
SELECT name, phyrds, phyrds * 100 / trw.phys_reads read_pct,
            phywrts,  phywrts * 100 / trw.phys_wrts write_pct
   FROM  tot_read_writes trw, v$datafile df, v$filestat fs
   WHERE df.file# = fs.file#
   ORDER BY phyrds desc;
```

NAME	PHYRDS	READ_PCT	PHYWRTS	WRITE_PCT
/fs04/data/PER/persdata003.dbf	149,065	36.18	384	.40
/fs04/data/PER/persdata005.dbf	94,128	22.85	1,983	2.06
/fs01/data/PER/system01.dbf	22,058	5.35	1,531	1.59
/fs04/data/PER/persdata002.dbf	21,010	5.10	1,611	1.67
/fs04/data/PER/persdata004.dbf	20,922	5.08	3,871	4.01
/fs03/data/PER/persindex002.dbf	20,703	5.03	142	.15
/fs03/data/PER/persindex001.dbf	19,522	4.74	884	.92
/fs04/data/PER/persdata001.dbf	15,404	3.74	934	.97
/fs03/data/PER/persindex003.db	13,470	3.27	4,998	5.18
/fs04/data/PER/perstmp04.dbf	11,057	2.68	1,369	1.42
/fs03/data/PER/persindex004.dbf	9,692	2.35	6,251	6.48
/fs04/data/PER/perstmp03.dbf	8,204	1.99	12,855	13.33
/fs01/data/PER/temp01.dbf	5,633	1.37	48,466	50.26
/fs01/data/PER/system02.dbf	398	.10	0	.00
/fs01/data/PER/rbs02.dbf	387	.09	6,319	6.55
/fs01/data/PER/rbs03.dbf	177	.04	3,870	4.01
/fs01/data/PER/tools01.dbf	78	.02	0	.00
/fs01/data/PER/rbs_load01.dbf	57	.01	961	1.00
/fs01/data/PER/rbs01.dbf	0	.00	0	.00
/fs04/data/PER/perstmp02.dbf	0	.00	0	.00
/fs04/data/PER/perstmp01.dbf	0	.00	0	.00
/fs01/data/PER/users01.dbf	0	.00	0	.00
/fs04/data/PER/perstmp.dbf	0	.00	0	.00

The first observation we made was that the site was using meaningful data file names. We perform tuning at many sites that have meaningless file names such as PROD_File1, PROD_File2, etc. which makes tuning more difficult. The observations from the output are listed below:

- The /fs04 disk is performing about 70% of the total reads and 23% of the writes. The first question that must be asked is "Can one of the data files on /fs04 be moved to another disk to spread I/O load?" Moving data files should wait until we are sure we have tuned our application's SQL and have performed other I/O-saving modifications, such as a larger buffer cache and perhaps a larger SORT_AREA_SIZE.

- About 70% of the reads were being performed on data files that contained tables. The index data files were having 15% of the disk reads performed against them. This was later found to be caused by many full table scans being performed because of missing indexes and ineffective use of the cost-based optimizer.

- For a database that serves OLTP users and had only been running for a few hours, there was an unusually high number of disk I/Os. Further investigation uncovered that the buffer cache was sized at one megabyte, and that a hit ratio of 26% was being achieved. The buffer cache was eventually adjusted upward to 40 megabytes.

- There were a large number of writes to the temporary tablespace, 70%. One solution to this problem would be to increase SORT_AREA_SIZE, but prior to doing that, we discovered that the amount of data being sorted could be greatly reduced by more appropriate index usage. After tuning the application, the use of the temporary tablespace went under 5%.

Changes were put into place to repair the application. In all, there were 40 pages of SQL statements that exceeded 4-second response time, with many exceeding 40 seconds. Changing back to the rule-based optimizer and adding a handful of indexes had all statements running under two seconds. And there was no need to move any data files or adjust the SORT_AREA_SIZE.

Other symptoms of poor performance are when you have almost as many reads as writes on the rollback segment data files. The two major causes of this are an undersized buffer cache, or a batch update running during prime OLTP which is updating tables that are read from heavily by OLTP users. Batch update jobs should be run overnight!

Another situation we have seen at sites that are more batch-oriented is that the disk containing the rollback segments is being written to so heavily that it is causing a disk I/O bottleneck. If you have several users performing heavy updates at the same time, consider alternating rollbacks from one disk to the next by placing them into alternate tablespaces that have data files on different disks; for example, rollback1 will be created on the rollback_disk1 tablespace, rollback2 on rollback_disk2 tablespace, rollback3 on rollback_disk1 tablespace, rollback4 on rollback_disk2 tablespace, and so on. Of course, you must have the rollback_disk1 tablespace on a separate disk drive from rollback_disk2.

For both recovery and performance reasons, it's also important to have your data files on different disks from your redos. The archive logs should be on a different disk from both data files and redo logs. You will be surprised at how often the following simple script will uncover the fact that you have your redo logs on the same disk as your data files, or the archive logs on the same disk as your data files.

```
# allfiles.sql
TTITLE ' Breakup of files across Disks / Check Recovery '
SELECT value
  FROM v$parameter
 WHERE name LIKE 'log_archive_dest'
UNION
SELECT name
  FROM v$datafile
UNION
SELECT SUBSTR(member,1,55)
  FROM v$logfile;
```

Another common occurrence is when the redo logs are multiplexed, with the first redos being placed away from the data files for performance reasons and the multiplexed redos being placed on the same disk as your most heavily hit data files. Instant bottleneck!

Investigating full table scans

A full table scan occurs when every block is read from a table. Full table scans are often a preferred performance option in batch-style applications, such as decision support. We have seen some excellent run-time improvements in decision support systems that use the parallel query option, which relies on full table scans to operate. (See Chapter 13, *Tuning Parallel Query*). However, full table scans at an OLTP site during prime online usage times can create havoc with response times. As mentioned earlier in this chapter, full table scans, even on small tables, can degrade response times because the small table drives the query, and this table is not always the most efficient access path.

The following query provides you with a overview of how many full table scans are taking place. The output following the script is from the same site as that used for the disk I/O example. The database had only been up for a short while and was used for OLTP users.

```
# tabstats.sql
SELECT name, value
  FROM v$sysstat
 WHERE name LIKE '%table %'
 ORDER BY name;
```

```
Fri Apr 26                                    page    1
        Table Access Methods
NAME                              VALUE
----------------------------      ----------------
table fetch by rowid                161,756,289
table fetch continued row             2,996,635
table scan blocks gotten              3,540,450
table scan rows gotten               94,048,914
table scans (cache partitions)                0
table scans (direct read)                     0
table scans (long tables)                   661
table scans (rowid ranges)                  106
table scans (short tables)              160,618
```

The values relating to the full table scans are "table scans (long tables)" (a scan of a table that has more than five database blocks) and "table scans (short tables)" (a count of full table scans with five or fewer blocks). There have been 661 full table scans at this site, in the space of a few hours. If the number of long table scans is significant, there is a strong possibility that SQL statements in your application need tuning or indexes need to be added. As we've mentioned, full table scans have a potentially crippling effect on performance.

To get an appreciation of how many rows and blocks are being accessed on average for the long full table scans, look at this calculation:

```
Average Long Table Scan Blocks
          = (table scan blocks gotten - (short table scans * 5))
                    /       long table scans
          = (3,540,450 - (160,618 * 5)) / 661
          = (3,540,450 - (803,090))  / 661
          = 4,141 blocks read per full table scan
```

Let's face it, 4,141 average disk reads performed on an OLTP application 661 times in the space of a few short hours is not a healthy situation. Tune that application right now! If you can identify the users who are experiencing the full table scans, you can find out what they were running to cause these scans. The script below helps you find the users.

```
# fullscan.sql
DROP VIEW Full_Table_Scans;
CREATE VIEW Full_Table_Scans as
 SELECT ss.username||'('||se.sid||') ' "User Process",
  SUM(DECODE(name,'table scans (short tables)',value)) "Short Scans",
  SUM(DECODE(name,'table scans (long tables)', value)) "Long Scans",
  SUM(DECODE(name,'table scan rows gotten',value)) "Rows Retrieved"
    FROM v$session ss, v$sesstat se, v$statname sn
   WHERE  se.statistic# = sn.statistic#
     AND (name  LIKE '%table scans (short tables)%'
         OR name  LIKE '%table scans (long tables)%'
         OR name  LIKE '%table scan rows gotten%'      )
     AND  se.sid = ss.sid
```

```
      AND    ss.username IS NOT NULL
 GROUP BY ss.username||'('||se.sid||') ';

 COLUMN  "User Process"       FORMAT a20;
 COLUMN  "Long Scans"         FORMAT 999,999,999;
 COLUMN  "Short Scans"        FORMAT 999,999,999;
 COLUMN  "Rows Retrieved"     FORMAT 999,999,999;
 COLUMN  "Average Long Scan Length" FORMAT 999,999,999;
 TTITLE ' Table Access Activity By User '
 SELECT "User Process", "Long Scans", "Short Scans", "Rows Retrieved"
   FROM Full_Table_Scans
  ORDER BY "Long Scans" desc;
 Fri Apr 26                                        page    1
 Table Access Activity By User
 User Process              Long Scans  Short Scans Rows Retrieved
 -------------------- ------------ ------------ -------------
 MAG001(23)                     25           79       780,260
 PGC001(65)                     12        1,190       393,191
 RAY001(10)                      9          102       296,818
 CRT001(101)                     9           40       199,243
```

To obtain the average lengths of the full table scans by user, run the following script.

```
 TTITLE 'AVERAGE SCAN LENGTH OF FULL TABLE SCANS BY USER '
 SELECT "User Process", ( "Rows Retrieved" - ("Short Scans" * 5))
   / ( "Long Scans" ) "Average Long Scan Length" from Full_Table_Scans
   WHERE "Long Scans" != 0
 ORDER BY "Long Scans" desc;
 User Process              Average Long Scan Length
 -------------------- ------------------------
 MAG001(23)                    31194.6
 PGC001(65)                    33103.1
```

We approached the top four users from our list, who quickly pointed out three screens that were performing abysmally. Further investigation revealed that there was an index missing from the production database. Smiles all around!

Reducing Disk I/O by Increasing the Sort Area

A sort area in memory is used to sort records before they are written out to disk. Increasing the size of this area by increasing the value of the INIT.ORA parameter, SORT_AREA_SIZE, lets you sort more efficiently. To allow a new value for SORT_AREA_SIZE to take effect, you must shut down the database and then restart it. Other INIT.ORA parameters that have an effect on sort performance are SORT_DIRECT_WRITES (Oracle7.2 and after), which writes sort data from memory to the temporary tablespace while avoiding the buffer cache, and COMPATIBLE (Oracle7.1.6 and later), which avoids reading sorted data through the buffer cache. Both can have a significant effect on performance.

Most online sorting queries request sorts of only a handful of records at a time, so unless the size of your sort area is unusually small, the whole operation can usually be done in memory. But in large batch jobs the size of the sort area becomes an issue. The problem is that most sites tend to have a mixture of OLTP and batch processing, so you are faced with the dilemma of tuning for both. Oracle provides the SORT_AREA_RETAINED_SIZE parameter (described later) to assist you with allocating smaller amounts of memory for sorting to all users. If required, an indicated user can have his or her memory allocation for sorting increased to the number of bytes specified by the parameter SORT_AREA_SIZE.

If the data being sorted does not fit in memory, Oracle must sort it in small runs. As each run is completed, Oracle stores the data in temporary segments on disk. After all of the runs have completed, Oracle merges the data to produce the sorted data. Of course, this is less efficient than doing the entire sort in memory.

In general, try to allocate as much space in memory as possible for SORT_AREA_SIZE (assuming that your entire sort can fit into memory). Surprisingly, we have found in benchmarks that a two megabyte SORT_AREA_SIZE can often perform faster than a 100-megabyte SORT_AREA_SIZE when your sorted data exceeds 100 megabytes in size. Because SORT_AREA_SIZE is allocated per user, increasing this parameter can exhaust memory very quickly if a large number of users are logged on. You also need to make sure that the temporary segments to which the sort operation will write its output (if it runs out of memory) are large enough, with appropriately sized INITIAL and NEXT extents.

To find out whether sorting is affecting performance in your system, monitor the sorting disk activity in your system and then adjust accordingly. How can you monitor sorting activity? One good way is to define a separate tablespace for temporary tables. By watching the I/O rate on the temporary tablespaces, you can detect how frequently the sort process failed to perform the entire sort in memory. You can monitor the V$SYSSTAT table to observe memory and disk activity. (For information on special considerations when running overnight and other long jobs, see Chapter 15, *Tuning Long-Running Jobs.*

Here is an example of querying the V$SYSSTAT table:

```
# sortlocn.sql
SELECT  name, value FROM v$sysstat
 WHERE name IN ('sorts(memory)', sorts(disk)');
```

```
    Name                                           Value
    ------------------------------------------------------------------
    sorts(memory)                                  1291
    sorts(disk)                                    2
```

The figures in this example raise little cause for concern. The "sorts(memory)" statistic shows the total number of sort operations that could be performed completely within the sort buffer in memory, without using the temporary tablespace segments. The "sorts(disk)" statistic shows the number of sort operations that could not be performed in memory. (Note that this number does not represent the total number of times a temporary table extent was written by a sort process.) Out of a total of 1293 sorts, only two required disk usage.

You may not always realize that your program statements invoke a sort. Sorting is performed by the following statements:

- CREATE INDEX
- DISTINCT
- GROUP BY
- ORDER BY
- INTERSECT
- MINUS
- UNION
- Unindexed table joins
- Some correlated subqueries

If your monitoring shows that you have a sorting problem, follow these suggestions:

1. Before you incur any sort overhead, ask a basic question: Is this sort really necessary? Has an index been inadvertently overlooked? Can a SQL statement be structured more efficiently.

2. Increase the value of the SORT_AREA_SIZE parameter. Because this increase applies to all user processes, this is likely to consume a lot of memory. Make sure you don't increase the value of SORT_AREA_SIZE to the point where you have little free memory. The maximum allowable value is system-dependent.

3. When you create your temporary tablespace(s), make sure that you specify large enough table extents (in the INITIAL and NEXT parameters on the CREATE statement) to allow SORT_AREA_SIZE of memory to be written to disk without having to throw multiple extents. Make your temporary segments a minimum of SORT_AREA_SIZE + 1 block.

4. A less likely, but possible, alternative, is to let users who require larger sorts, such as those who regularly run reports, use a temporary tablespace with larger INITIAL and NEXT default tablespace storage parameters. This will help

reduce the degree of dynamic extension. For example, during daily online transaction processing hours, set your default settings to:

```
ALTER TABLESPACE temp_tspace DEFAULT STORAGE
    (INITIAL 260K  NEXT 260K  PCTINCREASE 0);
```

For overnight processing, you might set the default storage to:

```
ALTER TABLESPACE temp_tspace DEFAULT STORAGE
    (INITIAL 5M  NEXT 5M  PCTINCREASE 0);
```

5. To achieve minor improvements in response times, you might also consider setting your INITIAL and NEXT extent sizes to one block plus a multiple of the sort area size. Assuming that you have a DB_BLOCK_SIZE of 4K and a SORT_AREA_SIZE of 64K, you may consider any of the following sizes or a higher size, depending on your requirements:

```
4K  +  (1 * 64K)  =   68K
4K  +  (2 * 64K)  =  130K
4K  +  (3* 64K)  =  196K
4K  +  (4 * 64K)  =  260K
```

6. Make sure to use the SORT_AREA_RETAINED_SIZE. Oracle will restore the sort area available to user processes to the size specified in this parameter if it believes that the sort area data will not be referenced in the near future. This will save memory. If memory is tight, we highly recommend that you take advantage of this feature by setting your SORT_AREA_RETAINED_SIZE to half the SORT_AREA_SIZE. For example, you might set:

```
SORT_AREA_SIZE          = 131072   (128K)
SORT_AREA_RETAINED_SIZE = 65536    (64K)
```

7. Be sure to use the SORT_DIRECT_WRITES=TRUE and COMPATIBLE=RDBMS version, for example, COMPATIBLE=7.1.6. We have noticed substantial sort run-time improvements (as much as a factor of 10) with the parameters being set.

8. Oracle7.3 introduced a new TEMPORARY tablespace which you should be using as your users' TEMPORARY tablespace. The new tablespace type is tuned especially for sorting and will boost your performance.

Reducing Dynamic Extension

There are many discussions about whether dynamic extension causes poor performance. We performed many benchmarks and can summarize our findings as follows:

Dynamic extension is most damaging when:

*   The extent sizes are small

*   Sorting is taking place from a large SORT_AREA_SIZE against a small INITIAL and NEXT extent size on the TEMPORARY tablespace

- Rollback extents used for batch jobs are small, and OPTIMAL has been set to force continual shrinkage

- A table is being created by selecting from another table; either the table being created is throwing many extents or the table being read from has many extents, or both

- Index range scans are being performed against indexes that have many small extents

- Many extents are thrown during batch processing

It is not so noticeable when:

- Extents are large

- OLTP users are randomly selecting one row

- The extents are on different disks

It is preferable to have multiple extents when:

- You are using the parallel query option and using Oracle striping

- You have rollback segments that are shared among many OLTP users

In this chapter, we introduced the problem of dynamic extension, in which additional extents allocated for a table or an index are on areas of the disk that are not contiguous with the initial allocation. The result of dynamic extension is usually poor performance because disk access is less efficient. This section describes how you monitor for dynamic extension and tune your system to avoid this problem.

There are a few cases in which dynamic extension may be acceptable. Having many extents may be desirable when your tables are striped or when rollback segments have many transactions sharing them. If your database is badly fragmented, and the free storage consists of many small extents, you may need to use many small extents until you are able to perform a database reorganization.

Detecting dynamic extension

You can check for recursive calls by querying the V$SYSSTAT table with the following query:

```
# recursiv.sql
SELECT name, value
  FROM v$sysstat
WHERE name = 'recursive calls';

Name                                                             Value
----------------------------------------------------------------------
recursive calls                                                   1203
```

There are several potential causes of recursive calls including:

- Misses on dictionary cache

- Firing of database triggers

- Execution of DDL statements such as ALTER INDEX and CREATE INDEX

- Execution of SQL statements within stored procedures, functions, packages, and anonymous PL/SQL blocks

- Enforcement of referential integrity constraints

This script checks for segments exceeding five extents:

```
# 5extents.sql
TTITLE ' List All Segments with More than 5 Extents '
SELECT owner, tablespace_name, segment_name||
        DECODE(segment_type,'TABLE','[T]', 'INDEX', '[I]',
                    'ROLLBACK','[R]', '[O]') segment_name,
        SUM(bytes) sizing,
        DECODE(COUNT(*),1,to_char(count(*)),
                        2,to_char(count(*)),
                        3,to_char(count(*)),
                        4,to_char(count(*)),
                        5,to_char(count(*)),
                        to_char(count(*))||' < Re-build') seg_count
    FROM dba_extents
  GROUP BY owner, tablespace_name, segment_name||
        DECODE(segment_type,'TABLE','[T]', 'INDEX', '[I]',
                'ROLLBACK','[R]', '[O]')
HAVING COUNT(*) > 5;
```

You may wish to exclude the rollback segments by specifying WHERE segment type != 'ROLLBACK'.

Rebuilding your segment into a single extent may require a database reorganization. There may not be a single extent large enough to create it. To inquire about available extent sizes, perform the following query:

```
# freespac.sql
SELECT tablespace_name, bytes
  FROM dba_free_space
 WHERE tablespace_name = UPPER('&tspace')
 ORDER BY tablespace_name, bytes desc;
```

where *tspace* is the name of the tablespace on which the segment resides. If you are unable to place the segment into a single extent, the next best thing would be to place the segment into two extents or perhaps rebuild the segment into one extent in a different tablespace.

NOTE   When you rebuild your tables and indexes, you may use more space than the original size. The original amount of free space in each block has to be re-established. The way around this problem is to create the table or index with a lower value for the PCTFREE parameter, and then alter the table's PCTFREE definition to the appropriate size after the table has been created. (See the discussion of PCTFREE and other parameters in Chapter 9.)

To place the data from tables into one contiguous extent, follow these steps; note that if your table contains LONG columns, you must export and import.

- Export the table.
- Drop the table.
- Create the table with the appropriate size.
- Import the table.

Or, if you have sufficient space in your database,

- Drop any foreign key constraints that refer to the table and any grants on the table.
- Rename the table to table_copy.
- Create the table with the new storage definition as SELECT * FROM table_copy.
- Drop the table table_copy.
- Recreate the indexes.
- Recreate the foreign key constraints and reissue the grants.

To place indexes into one contiguous extent,

- Drop foreign constraints that refer to the index.
- Drop the index.
- Create the index with the appropriate size.
- Recreate the foreign key constraints.

Dynamic extension on temporary segments

DBAs often forget temporary segments when they are doing tuning. But by avoiding dynamic extension on temporary segments, you'll often realize performance improvements of more than 50% on large index creation and lengthy sort jobs.

If your temporary tables are the cause of the dynamic extension, the solution is to alter the default TABLESPACE STORAGE parameters on your temporary tables' tablespace. If only certain users are causing the dynamic extension, you have the alternative of placing the users into a second temporary tablespace that has a larger INITIAL extent in its default storage clause. If you cannot determine which users are causing the dynamic extension, you can increase the INITIAL or NEXT extent if space permits. As a rule of thumb, in many of these situations an INITIAL extent of 256 kilobytes plus one block and a NEXT extent of 256 kilobytes plus one block appear to solve the problem.

Untuned tablespace settings

The next query provides you with information on the way your tablespaces have been created. This simple script can provide valuable information on how well your tablespaces are set up for optimal performance. The following output is from an OLTP production site:

```
# defstorg.org
TTITLE 'Tablespace Information '
SELECT SUBSTR(tablespace_name, 1,18), initial_extent,
       next_extent, pct_increase
  FROM dba_tablespaces
  ORDER BY tablespace_name;
```

```
Tue May 7                                          Page 1
                    Tablespace Information
PERS01              20480          8192          0
PERS02              20480          8192          0
PERS03              20480          8192          0
PERS04              20480          8192          0
PERS05              20480          8192          0
PERS06              20480          8192          0
PERS07              20480          8192          0
RBS                 20480          8192          50
SUPS01              20480          8192          50
SUPS02              20480          8192          50
SUPS03              20480          8192          0
SYSTEM              20480          8192          0
TEMP                 8192          8192          0
```

The observations that we made about this site are as follows:

- The system tablespace had its default sizing and PCTINCREASE modified by the DBA without any resizing of the system objects. Several objects had well over 100 extents. The PCTINCREASE should be left at 50% for the SYSTEM tablespace.

- The SORT_AREA_SIZE was set at 256 kilobytes, but the temporary tablespace had extent sizes of 8 kilobytes. Not only did many sorts exceed the maximum number of extents, but they also ran abysmally. The extent sizes were adjusted to INITIAL 260K NEXT 1M.

- The PCTINCREASE on the SUPS01 and SUPS02 tablespaces was set to 50%. Strangely enough, the two tablespaces contained very large tables and were regularly running out of space. The PCTINCREASE was not set on the table create scripts. The PCTINCREASE was altered on all of the objects to zero, as was the default storage on the tablespaces.

- There were no separate tablespaces for indexes and tables. The tables and their indexes were thrown into the same tablespace. It is best to have separate tablespaces for tables and indexes.

Chained and migrated rows

Disk chaining occurs when a row can't physically fit into an Oracle block. Another block is required to store the remainder of the row. Chaining can cause serious performance problems. We have seen many sites experiencing chaining problems, especially those storing multimedia data or large binary objects (blobs). You should pay special attention to the DB_BLOCK_SIZE parameter when you create your database. Block sizes of 4 kilobytes or more are the norm, not the exception.

Migration of an Oracle row occurs when a row is updated in an Oracle block and the amount of free space in the block is not adequate to store all of the row's data. The row is migrated to another physical block in the table. The problem is that the indexes that refer to the migrated row are still pointing to the block where the row used to be, and hence the table reads are doubled. One saving grace is that full table scans will scan blocks as they come and will perform the same number of reads whether the rows are migrated or not.

If a table has chaining problems, you can rebuild the table, specifying a larger value for the PCTFREE parameter. If the bulk of the rows currently in the table have already been updated to their full lengths, a lot of space will be wasted. The free space will be reserved for rows that will not expand any further. To eliminate this waste, you can create the table with a smaller PCTFREE parameter, load the existing data, and then run the ALTER command on the table with a larger PCTFREE.

Oracle7 offers a handy command that lists all of the chained rows in any selected table. To run the query, you must have created a table named CHAINED_ROWS using a script called *utlchain.sql*. First, issue the ANALYZE command to collect the necessary statistics:

```
ANALYZE TABLE account LIST CHAINED_ROWS;
```

Then query the CHAINED_ROWS table to see a full listing of all chained rows, as shown below. (Chapter 10 describes ANALYZE in greater detail and describes a script that you can use to examine chained rows.)

```
SELECT * FROM CHAINED_ROWS
   WHERE TABLE_NAME = 'ACCOUNT';

Owner_name  Table_Name        Cluster_Name   Head_Rowid      Timestamp
-----------------------------------------------------------------------
GURRY        ACCOUNT         00000723.  0012.0004      30-SEP-93
GURRY        ACCOUNT             00000723.    0007.0004        30-SEP-93
CREATE TABLE CHAINED_TEMP AS
SELECT * FROM ACCOUNT
   WHERE ROWID IN (SELECT HEAD_ROWID  FROM CHAINED_ROWS
   WHERE TABLE_NAME = 'ACCOUNT');
DELETE FROM ACCOUNT
   WHERE ROWID IN (SELECT HEAD_ROWID  FROM CHAINED_ROWS
   WHERE TABLE_NAME = 'ACCOUNT');
INSERT INTO ACCOUNT
SELECT * FROM CHAINED_TEMP;
```

When you are convinced that everything has worked properly, you can drop the temporary table:

```
DROP TABLE CHAINED_TEMP;
```

Now clean out the CHAINED_ROWS table:

```
DELETE FROM CHAINED_ROWS
   WHERE TABLE_NAME = 'ACCOUNT';
```

Even when you analyze your tables without the LIST CHAINED ROWS option (i.e., ANALYZE tname COMPUTE STATISTICS;), a column called chain_cnt stores the number of chained and migrated rows at the time the ANALYZE was run. If you are using the rule-based optimizer and you have set OPTIMIZER_MODE to CHOOSE (the default), don't forget to remove the statistics from your tables and indexes using ANALYZE tname DELETE STATISTICS;.

```
# chaining.sql
TTITLE 'Tables Experiencing Chaining'
SELECT owner, table_name,
       NVL(chain_cnt,0)     "Chained Rows"
          from all_tables
  WHERE owner NOT IN ('SYS', 'SYSTEM')
    AND NVL(chain_cnt,0) > 0
  ORDER BY owner, table_name;
```

You can also obtain the overall number of chained and migrated rows read by your instance since startup time using the V$SYSSTAT table.

```
SELECT SUBSTR(name, 1, 30), value
  FROM V$SYSSTAT
  WHERE name = 'table fetch continued row';
```

The chained row output from our problem site was very alarming, as shown below. Remember that the figures are cumulative since the database started up, and it had been started for only a few hours.

```
Fri Apr 26                                        page    1
        Database Wide Chaining Problems
NAME                               VALUE
------------------------------ ----------------
table fetch continued row          2,996,635
```

The major causes of the problems at this site are as follows:

- The DB_BLOCK_SIZE had been left at its default of 2,048. Many of the tables in the database stored long columns with the column data exceeding 2,048 bytes.

- The design of the application involved people entering the bare essentials of the rows first and then adding much more detail later on, as it became available (including the LONG data).

- All tables and indexes had a PCTFREE of 10, which is the default.

The only change that we could make in the very short term was to alter all of the problem tables to have a higher PCTFREE. After some experimentation, we eventually set the PCTFREE to 80 on four tables and set the PCTUSED to 19. The application is now being modified to have the rows created when the LONG data become available. There is also a plan in place to perform a table reorganization of the problem tables. Given how critical the database is, that can't take place for several months.

Tuning the Archive Writing Process (ARCH)

The archive writer process (ARCH) copies your after-image data from the redo logs to the archive logs. With Oracle databases put under more stress with a large number of changes, many sites experience a serious archive bottleneck. The most obvious ways to detect the problem is when your redo log disks are experiencing an I/O bottleneck or when your alert file detects a bottleneck in the archiver and mentions that LGWR is being held up.

To overcome the problem, do the following:

- Ping-pong your redo logs from disk to disk, with redos 1 and 3 on disk A and redo logs 2 and 4 on disk B. This will allow the ARCH process to read from one disk and the LGWR to write to a separate disk. Sites that we have visited have their archive logs on the same disk as active data files or redo logs. This is an absolute no-no from a recovery perspective, as well as from a performance perspective.

- Enlarge the INIT.ORA parameter LOG_ARCHIVE_BUFER_SIZE to a value such as 256 or 512 kilobytes. The parameter has a default on most machines of about 150 operating system blocks, which is often inadequate for a heavily used production system.

- If you are archiving to tape, consider archiving to disk and then copy to tape in background. You may also consider compressing your archive logs (however, not the one currently being written to) to save disk space if it is at a premium.

- Consider placing your archive log files onto a higher-speed disk.

- Consider adding more redo logs; for example, have six disks, with 1, 3, and 5 on disk A and redo logs 2, 4, and 6 on disk B.

- Consider enlarging your redo log sizes. The problem with doing this is that if you lose your instance, you may be off the air for quite some time while your current redo log is being read to ensure that the database is intact.

- Try not to perform hot backups at the same times as overnight jobs—in particular at the same time that batch updates are occurring. Entire blocks are written to your log buffer, redo logs, and, eventually, archive logs, for the duration of the hot backup on the data file being written to. If you must have 24-hour uptime, coordinate your backups so that there is little activity on the data file being backed up. We know of one large site that had its overnight run-times intruding into OLTP times. They stopped performing hot backups and shut the database down, performed a nightly cold backup, and then ran the overnight jobs. They now have 3 hours spare time before the OLTP users commence work.

- Run the command ALTER SYSTEM ARCHIVE LOG ALL, which will add another archive writer.

Avoiding Contention

Contention occurs when one or more of your user processes vies with another process for use of an Oracle or system resource. Since we published the first edition of this book, the fastest-growing contention problem has been latch contention, particularly for the library cache, buffer cache, and log buffer. The growing contention problems have been caused by the increased use of symmetric multiprocessor (SMP) machines.

Tuning the Database Writer

The database writer (DBWR) process handles all writes to the database. This process maintains two lists of buffers. The *dirty list* holds modified buffers that have not yet been written to disk. The *least-recently-used (LRU) list* holds free buffers that are in use or pinned buffers that are waiting on multiblock buffering before writing dirty buffers that have not yet moved to the dirty list. You must be sure that free buffers are available in the buffer cache as needed.

When a user process requires a block that is currently in the cache, it moves it to the most-recently-used end of the LRU list. If the block is not in the cache, a search begins at the least-recently-used end of the LRU list and searches until it finds a free buffer or until the _DB_BLOCK_MAX_SCAN_CNT buffers have been scanned. If your user process finds dirty buffers, it moves them to the dirty list. The DBWR writes dirty buffers to disk under the following circumstances:

- A user process finds that there are _DB_BLOCK_WRITE_BATCH / 2 buffers in the dirty list.

- A user process scans _DB_BLOCK_MAX_SCAN_CNT buffers but doesn't find a free one.

- A timeout occurs (timeouts occur every 3 seconds).

- A checkpoint occurs, and LGWR gives DBWR a list of buffers to write.

A lazy DBWR becomes most noticeable when a checkpoint occurs. The LGWR instructs the DBWR to write all dirty buffers to the datafiles, whether they have been committed or not. We observe a definite spike in performance when a checkpoint occurs during benchmarks. The worse tuned the DBWR, the more severe the spike.

There are many methods of identifying a DBWR that is not writing frequently enough, some described in this section. The following statement detects contention in the buffer cache:

```
# buffwait.sql
SELECT name, value
  FROM V$SYSSTAT
 WHERE name = 'free buffer waits';
```

```
name                                       value
------------------------------------ ------------------
free buffer waits                          120010
```

This output indicates that a process was attempting to read data into the buffer cache and it had to wait for the DBWR to clear dirty buffers from the buffer cache.

To reduce DBWR contention, some implementations of Oracle allow the ability to increase the number of database writer processes. To do this, you must increase the INIT.ORA parameter DB_WRITERS or ASYNC_IO. Both parameters provide the same functionality. Read the *Oracle Installation Manual* for the most appropriate settings for your machine. If you are using DB_WRITERS, do not set the parameter higher than two times the number of disk drives that hold database files that are being written to. Before setting either parameter, check with Oracle to ensure that the parameters do not create any problems on your machine.

Regardless of whether there is DBWR contention, using additional DB_WRITERS processes can improve performance, and we recommend that you take advantage of this parameter. We have found the response time improvements most evident when a checkpoint occurs and LGWR requests that the DBWR clears all dirty buffers from the buffer cache to the database.

Disk I/O load can also be a critical factor for DBWR performance. If the DBWR is continually writing to the one disk or is competing with reads to the same disk it is trying to write to, the DBWR is forever waiting for disk I/O, and a huge backlog of data to be written (dirty list) is often created. Read Chapter 9 for advice on load sharing for performance.

Two parameters used to be available for tuning the DBWR, but both have now become undocumented. We used to be able to decrease the _DB_WRITER_MAX_ SCAN_CNT and increase the _DB_BLOCK_WRITE_BATCH to reduce our DBWR contention. We would often observe decreased performance spikes during check-points. By setting the parameters, you reduce the frequency with which the user process signals the DBWR to write, and you increase the number of blocks that the DBWR attempts to write. With a higher value, the DBWR is better able to use the operating system facilities, writing to different disks in parallel and writing adjacent blocks in a single I/O. Whether the parameters take effect now appears to vary from one version of Oracle to the next. Try them out on your system only if you are experiencing DBWR problems.

An undersized buffer cache can also be a major cause of database writer prob-lems. This is because the DBWR is continually running in "panic mode," cleaning out dirty buffers to make way for new buffers that are being brought into the buffer cache.

Yet another method that we have used with some success to overcome a lazy DBWR is to perform checkpoints more frequently by lowering the LOG_ CHECKPOINT_INTERVAL below the size of the redo logs by giving LOG_ CHECKPOINT_TIMEOUT a value or by making your redo logs smaller. More frequent checkpoints tend to cause more performance spikes as each checkpoint occurs, but each spike is lower than the spike associated with a larger checkpoint.

Some sites have huge redo logs in an attempt to completely eliminate checkpoints until a time when there is little activity on the system. They then perform a log switch. We tried this approach but found that the time to recover an instance was far too long. We also were concerned that if the latest redo log got removed and we lost our instance, data might be lost. We suspect that data loss is very likely. If you ever do lose your current redo log, leave the database running to give the DBWR time to write all of the dirty buffers out to the database.

Another way to monitor the DBWR process is to run the UTLBSTAT/UTLESTAT scripts and examine the output. See Chapter 10 for a discussion of performance tests that you can run with these scripts.

Tuning Rollback Segments

Rollback segments are used by all kinds of transactions for rollback, transaction, read consistency, and recovery. Tuning problems can occur when transactions experience contention for rollback segments. The following statement provides you with details on the overall number of waits that have occurred for rollback segments.

```
# rollbwait.sql
SELECT class, count
  FROM  v$waitstat
 WHERE  class IN  ('undo header', 'undo block');
```

CLASS	COUNT
undo header	1129
undo block	5151

If the number of waits is greater than zero, you have had contention for your roll-back segments. Once again, this output is from an actual site. The site had 100 concurrent users and increased their number of rollbacks from 6 to 12; the counts against both the undo header and undo block are always below 10.

Each rollback segment has a transaction table that controls the transactions accessing the rollback segment. Oracle documentation says that the transaction table has approximately 30 slots in the rollback if your database has a 2-kilobyte block size. The following query lists the number of waits on a slot in the transaction tables. The ideal is to have the waits zero; but in the real world, this is not always achievable. However, they should be as close to zero as possible. At the very worst, the ratio of gets to waits should be around 99%.

```
# rollstat.sql
SELECT usn "Rollback Table", GETS, WAITS , xacts "Active Transactions"
  FROM V$ROLLSTAT;
```

Rollback Table	GETS	WAITS	Active Transactions
0	463	0	0
1	9761	0	1
2	8713	2	0
3	8056	0	0
4	8669	0	0

```
           5    8492         0            0
           6    8755         1            0
           7    9371         0            0
           8    8300         1            0
```

We usually advise sites to create *n* new rollback segments (where *n* equals the number of rollback segments that have experienced waits). In the example above, you would add three rollback segments. This formula has worked well for sites, but we recently came to a site that had a single nonsystem rollback segment that had 3500 waits. A long-running overnight job had been run, and the database had been shut down and restarted with a single huge rollback segment. The DBA then innocently forgot to reinstate the 10 rollback segments that had been there. Our advice in that case was to revert back to the 10 rollbacks. The waits disappeared from all 10 rollback segments.

The two scripts below indicate the number of rollbacks performed on the transaction tables. We don't use these particular scripts very often, but you may find them interesting and useful.

In these scripts, 'transaction tables consistent reads - undo records applied' is the total number of undo records applied to rollback transaction tables only. It should be less than 10% of the total number of consistent changes.

'Transaction tables consistent read rollbacks' is the number of times the transaction tables were rolled back. It should be less than 0.1% of the value of consistent gets. If either of these scenarios occurs, consider creating more rollback segments or a greater number of extents in each rollback segment. A rollback segment equates to a transaction table, and an extent is like a transaction slot in the table.

```
# trantbl.sql
SELECT 'Tran Table Consistent Read Rollbacks > 1% of Consistent Gets'aa,
          'Action: Create more Rollback Segments'
  FROM V$SYSSTAT
 WHERE DECODE (name,'transaction tables consistent read rollbacks',value)
                    * 100
                 /
      DECODE (name,'consistent gets',value) > 0.1
  AND name IN ('transaction tables consistent read rollbacks',
                  'consistent gets')
  AND value > 0;
SELECT 'Undo Records Applied > 10% of Consistent Changes' aa,
       'Action: Create more Rollback Segments'
  FROM V$SYSSTAT
 WHERE DECODE
     (name,'transaction tables consistent reads - undo records applied'
                ,value)
                * 100
                /
      DECODE (name,'consistent changes',value) > 10
  AND name IN
```

```
         ('transaction tables consistent reads - undo records applied',
                  'consistent changes')
   AND value > 0;
```

One common performance problem that we come across is when a long update has taken place and the transactions reading the updated rows seem to take forever to query the new data. This is surprising, because you would assume that the data should have been cached. This is because every time a dirty buffer is read, the query has to find the status of the transaction by looking into the transaction table that is contained in the rollback segment header.

The way to speed this up is to do a SELECT COUNT(*) FROM tname(s);, where the tnames are the tables in which modified and committed blocks occur. This marks the transactions as committed, and later queries do not have to find the status of the transactions in the transaction tables to determine that status. You'll be pleasantly surprised at how much this can speed up the query transaction.

It is important that rollback segments do not extend very often. Dynamic extension is particularly damaging to performance, because each extent used (or freed) is written to disk immediately. See the UET$ and FET$ system tables. Some sites have a large amount of performance degradation when the optimal value is set, because the rollback is continually shrinking and extending. This situation has been improved to make the SMON less active where the PCTINCREASE is set to zero.

NOTE   In this case, free extents will not be coalesced. When a rollback throws extents after it has shrunk back, it will (we hope) find an extent of the correct size. It is often beneficial for all of the rollback segments within a tablespace to have a uniform INITIAL and NEXT extent size. If you would like the coalescing to continue, set the PCTINCREASE on the tablespace to 1.

We usually recommend *not* using the OPTIMAL setting. OPTIMAL eases administration, but it can infringe on performance. The following listing provides figures on how many times each rollback segment has had to extend and shrink. If the amount of shrinks and extends is high, it is likely that you are experiencing poor performance.

```
   # shrink.sql
   SELECT usn, extends, shrinks, hwmsize, aveshrink
     FROM v$rollstat;
```

Large updates

Transactions performing large updates perform better with larger rollbacks because of the minimizing of dynamic extension. Take advantage of the statement

```
SET TRANSACTION USE ROLLBACK SEGMENT
```

Long-running jobs

Long-running overnight-style jobs use very large rollback segments. It is common to swap rollback segments from small to large for overnight processing and back to small for daily processing.

Monitoring and Tuning Redo Log Files

As was discussed earlier, the role of the redo logs is to protect your database against losing a disk, having the processor suddenly go off the air, or suffering any other kind of system failure. The system writes heavily to the redo logs. They contain all of the changes made to your tables, indexes, and rollback segments, as well as information on checkpoint and other administrative information that can be used to recover your database.

It is common for sites to mirror the redo logs because these logs are so critical to the operation of your database. This can be done by using either operating system mirroring or Oracle's own redo log groups. We visit many sites that carefully place their primary redos onto disks that spread the I/O load evenly but then carelessly place the mirrored redos onto disks that contain heavily used data files or operating system files.

Other sites use striping on redo logs, often with disappointing results. Redo log writes are always performed sequentially; they take place when a commit occurs, when the log buffer reaches one-third full (two-thirds full for Oracle7.3 and later), every few seconds if there has been no activity, or when the database writer writes to the datafiles. OLTP applications will usually write to one part of the stripe on a single disk because of the small size of the data being written. Striping is most effective if you make your stripe sizes as small as possible.

Batch processing is when most redo log bottlenecks occur, usually caused by an undersized log_buffer. If this is occurring at your site, you should be increasing your log_buffer. If you do feel that striping will help, make sure that the stripe sizes are tuned to cope with writes of one-third (two-thirds for Oracle7.3 and later) the size of your log buffer. This figure comes from the fact that the most likely condition for LGWR to write for batch jobs is when the buffer is one-third full (two-thirds full in Oracle7.3 and later).

Unfortunately, Oracle does not provide a means of monitoring redo disk I/Os, so you must use your operating system disk monitoring commands, such as *sar* -d 1 15, which monitors the disks 15 times at 1-second intervals on UNIX machines.

One important tuning issue that is directly related to redo processing is the frequency of checkpoints. When frequent checkpoints occur, they can have a marked effect on system performance for the duration of the checkpoint. Another issue is the effect on performance of redo log buffer latch contention. We have seen the increasing impact of this latch contention on performance as machines begin to operate more and more CPUs. This section describes the INIT.ORA parameters that you can set to make the writing of redo log files as efficient as possible.

LOG_CHECKPOINT_INTERVAL

Number of new redo log file blocks needed to trigger a checkpoint. (These are operating system blocks, not Oracle blocks.) This parameter controls the frequency of checkpoints, which has a major impact on performance. Checkpoints occur regardless of archiving method. Each checkpoint forces all modified database buffers in the buffer cache to be written to the database; old log files don't need to be kept for instance recovery. Because database-processing overheads are incurred each time a checkpoint is written, we recommend that you perform checkpoints only as each log file fills and a log file switch occurs. You can cause this to happen by setting LOG_ CHECKPOINT_INTERVAL larger than the size of the redo log file size. All of your redo logs should be set to the same size.

Forcing checkpoints within your redo log files reduces the time taken to do instance recovery, because the amount of work needed to roll forward is not as large. The same effect can be achieved by having very small redo log files, automatically forcing checkpoints every time each one fills. The ongoing performance of the database is a more important consideration than the time taken to perform a recovery of your database, which is a much rarer event.

We have found that having either four or six redo logs of 5 or 10 megabytes each works well for most sites. If you are performing huge once-off data loads into your database, consider increasing the size of your redos (perhaps to 500 megabytes). Other options that you may consider are to use the UNRE-COVERABLE clause in your CREATE TABLE and CREATE INDEX statements. You may also consider taking a cold backup before processing and turning off archiving for the duration of the processing. You then perform your data loads, take a cold backup, and reenable archiving.

It is advisable to ping-pong your redos if you have archiving enabled. This means that redo logs 1, 3, and 5 will be on disk A, and redo logs 2, 4, and 6 will be on disk B. When a redo log switch occurs, having the next redo on an alternate disk allows you to read from one redo (e.g., redo 1), which is written to your archive logs, and write new changes from the log buffer to redo 2, which is located on another disk.

CHECKPOINT_PROCESS

Enables the CKPT process. When a checkpoint occurs, it forces the redo log writer process (LGWR) to update each data file in your database with the latest checkpoint information. This writing momentarily stops the LGWR process from performing its primary role of writing log entries to the redo logs. Setting CHECKPOINT_PROCESS to TRUE causes CKPT to handle the updating of the data files and prevents the LGWR process from being held up while it performs this task. Make sure that you set it to TRUE, especially when you have many data files in your database.

LOG_CHECKPOINT_TIMEOUT

Specifies the frequency, in seconds, with which checkpoints will occur. We recommend that you leave this parameter at its default value of 0. That value forces the LOG_CHECKPOINT_INTERVAL parameter to be the deciding factor on the frequency of checkpoints. We also recommend that you set the LOG_CHECKPOINT_INTERVAL to a value higher than the size of your redo logs. This forces checkpoints to occur when a redo log fills and a redo log switch occurs.

LOG_BUFFER

Number of physical bytes allocated to the redo log buffer in the SGA. Whenever a database buffer block is modified, the redo information is also written to the log buffer pool. Only the modified data are written by the LGWR to the redo log, not the entire database block, unless you are performing hot backups, in which case the entire block is written to the log buffer, redo logs, and archive logs. Whenever a commit occurs, only the changes within the redo buffer need to be written to disk. The actual database blocks can be written by the DBWR from the buffer cache to the data files at a later time.

If the redo log buffer is too small, LGWR will have to write to disk too frequently, causing a disk I/O bottleneck on the redo log disks and potentially a wait for a user process to have its changes placed into the log buffer. If many processes are accessing the log buffer, they will be forced to wait for the write to complete; the result is redo log contention.

You can reduce log file disk I/O overheads and redo log contention by increasing the value of the LOG_BUFFER parameter to at least 64 kilobytes on a busy OLTP database. We have done benchmarks showing that heavily used applications that have a lot of database modifications will often have their response times improved more than 50% by enlarging the LOG_BUFFER to 1 megabyte. Overnight jobs that perform heavy updates may also improve by increasing LOG_BUFFER even more.

WARNING   Do *not* enlarge your log buffer to the point at which you have little free memory available on your machine. But keep in mind that there is only one LOG_BUFFER setting, and it is a critical parameter in providing acceptable response times.

The background process LGWR is activated under any of these circumstances: when a commit is processed, when the redo log buffer is one-third full, when dirty (modified) blocks are written from the buffer cache to the data files, or every few seconds when there is no activity on your database.

To optimize redo log file disk I/O, do the following:

1. Separate redo log files from database data files.

2. Place redo files on faster disks.

3. Increase the LOG_BUFFER parameter, as discussed above; in the next section we tell you how you can determine whether you need to increase this parameter.

4. If you are multiplexing your redo logs using Oracle's redo group facility, put careful thought into where you place your mirrored redos. You must ensure that they are not located on a heavily used data file disk. Ideally, each side of the redo should be on a disk of its own.

5. If you have archivelog enabled, ping-pong your redos.

Monitoring for redo buffer space contention

Perform the following query against the V$SYSSTAT table to monitor for redo buffer space contention. The "redo log space requests" returned by the query indicates the number of times a process could not find space in the redo log buffer and had to wait for space. This is caused because the LGWR process is not able to write to the redo logs fast enough to clear the log buffer for new entries to be written. This should not happen in an efficient system; if the value is much larger than zero, increase the size of your log buffer.

```
# redowait.sql
SELECT name, value
 FROM v$sysstat
 WHERE name IN ('redo log space requests',
               'redo buffer allocation retries');
```

```
Fri Apr 26                                           page    1
              LOG_BUFFER and Redo Log Tuning Information
redo buffer allocation retries               403019
redo log space requests                       19010
```

The "redo log space requests" are often caused by the archiver not being able to keep up and the log writer not being able to write from the log buffer to the redo log because the redo log has not been copied by the ARCH process. One possible cause of this problem is when hot backups are taking place on files that are being written to heavily. Note: For the duration of the hot backups, an entire block is written out to the log buffer and the redo logs for each change to the database, as compared to just the writing of the characters that have been modified.

The output shown below was from a site that had its LOG_BUFFER set to 8 kilobytes on a production database. That site also performed hot backups each night on data files that were being heavily updated. The problems were repaired by increasing the buffer cache from 8 kilobytes to 1 megabyte and by changing the hot backups to run after the overnight processing had completed at 3:00 a.m. After the modifications, the values for the two parameters below were close to zero.

Ideally, the output for redo log space requests should be zero. If it is greater than zero, increase the INIT.ORA parameter LOG_BUFFER to force fewer but larger writes to the redo logs. This will reduce the likelihood of redo log buffer contention. Typically, a large site will have its LOG_BUFFER set to 500 kilobytes or larger.

The _LOG_BLOCKS_DURING_BACKUP parameter is supposed to overcome the hot backup problem. Check to see whether the parameter is functional for your version of the RDBMS with Oracle. It can avoid severe bottlenecks. A sensible approach for overnight processing is to time your hot backups, if they are really required, to occur when the data files being backed up have little or no activity occurring against them. (Many sites seem to have these backups just for the sake of saying that they are running them.)

The "redo buffer allocation retries" returned by the query indicate when the redo writer is waiting for the log writer to complete the clearing out of all of the dirty buffers from the buffer cache. Only then can the redo writer continue onto the next redo log. This problem is usually caused by having the LOG_BUFFER parameter too small, but can also be caused by having the buffer cache too small (see the DB_BLOCK_BUFFERS parameter).

Some other V$SYSSTAT statistics from the problem site are shown in the following table:

Parameter	8-Kilobytes Log_Buffer	1-Megabyte Log_Buffer
change write time	4,063,311	43,900
write wait time	68,023	20,043
redo writes	372,021	73,001
redo write time	6,433,019	465,344

Monitoring for redo log latch contention

A system that has multiple CPUs and performs many updates can often experience contention for redo log buffer latches; this can cause degradation of your system response times. A recent benchmark that we performed surprised us; it provided a startling 20% throughput improvement by eliminating a small number of redo allocation latch misses. As a process performs database changes, it allocates space in your redo log buffer using the redo allocation latch. By default, all changes go through the one latch (the redo allocation latch). SMP and MPP machines usually experience redo allocation latch waits. The more CPUs on the machine, the higher the number of latch waits.

You can reduce the number of waits by setting up multiple copy latches via the LOG_SIMULATANEOUS_COPIES parameter. We recommend that you set that parameter to the number of CPUs on your machine. To more effectively use multiple copy latches, you must also set the LOG_SMALL_ENTRY_MAX_SIZE parameter. If the amount of the redo data to be copied is greater than the value of the LOG_SMALL_ENTRY_MAX_SIZE parameter, the redo allocation latch is released and the data are copied by using a redo copy latch. If the process is unable to obtain a latch, redo latch contention is occurring. The process waits a short amount of time and requests the latch again.

Issue a query against the V$LATCH table as follows. The output below is taken from a site after it had been tuned. Prior to tuning, it had LOG_SIMULTANEOUS_COPIES set to zero and LOG_SMALL_ENTRY_MAX_SIZE set to 800, which are the default settings. The misses had been as high as 6,000 on the redo allocation latch, and the redo copy latch had no activity.

```
# redlatch.sql
SELECT * FROM V$LATCH
  WHERE name LIKE 'redo%';
```

                    Redo Allocation Latch Misses

Latch	Gets	Misses	Immed Gets	Immed Misses
redo allocation	1890138	382	0	0
redo copy	7	7	1616883	7

If the number of misses or immediate misses is not zero, there is contention in your system. Oracle recommends that if the ratio of misses to gets, or the ratio of immediate misses to immediate gets, is greater than 0.1%, you should act to reduce latch contention. We recommend that you eliminate latch contention if the contention exceeds 0.01%.

To reduce contention on your redo allocation latch, decrease the LOG_SMALL_ENTRY_MAX_ SIZE parameter to force more copies to use the copy latches. It will decrease the number and size of redo copies made by using the redo allocation latch. Most OLTP sites run best with a LOG_SMALL_ENTRY_MAX_SIZE of between 150 and 200. The default 800 is usually much too high.

To reduce contention of redo copy latches, increase the parameter LOG_SIMULTANEOUS_COPIES to the number of CPUs on your system. This increases the number of latches available (if you are using a multi-CPU computer). By default, there is only one latch: the redo allocation latch.

Reducing Buffer Cache Latch Contention

Buffer cache latch contention has caused frequent tuning headaches. The latch is used to allocate buffers on the LRU chain of the buffer cache. All user processes are able to read data into the buffer cache. Sites that had many OLTP users combined with multiple CPUs are the worst hit. To identify buffer cache latch contention, run the following statement:

```
# buflatch.sql
SELECT SUBSTR(name,1,25), gets, misses,
        immediate_gets, immediate_misses
  FROM V$LATCH
 WHERE misses > 0 OR immediate_misses > 0
   AND name LIKE 'cache bu%'
 /
```

If your misses or getmisses are greater than 3%, do the following:

- Make sure you have DB_BLOCK_LRU_EXTENDED_STATISTICS turned off. The parameter is used to test the effect of increasing and decreasing the buffer cache. It can cause chronic latch contention, so use it sparingly.

- Increase the size of your buffer cache using the DB_BLOCK_BUFFERS parameter.

- If you are running a UNIX system, check your *Installation and User's Guide* to see the description of the SPIN_COUNT parameter. Decreasing the parameter can often relieve latch contention.

- If you are using Oracle7.3 or later, set the parameter DB_BLOCK_LRU_ LATCHES to the number of CPUs on your machine. This parameter is a huge help in avoiding buffer latch contention.

- Avoid the buffer cache whenever possible by setting parameters such as SORT_DIRECT_WRITES and COMPATIBLE.

- Try not to mix OLTP users with long-running batch and decision support users on the one instance.

- If you are experiencing latch contention on a single CPU system, we have been told that you can increase the value of the _LATCH_WAIT_POSTINGS parameter to 20 or so, and this will reduce latch contention and provide a response improvement. Note the underscore in front of the parameter name; this indicates that it is a secret parameter, as we describe in Chapter 9. Unfortunately, we are never completely sure whether the secret parameters work. They appear to be on-again, off-again from one version of Oracle to the next.

Reducing Library Cache Latch Contention

The library cache latches are used to allocate memory within the shared pool area. The more fragmented the shared pool area and the more reloads required of objects because your shared pool is undersized, the more severe your contention will be. The contention is made worse when multiple users, each running on a separate CPU, require a new package, procedure, function, trigger, SQL statement, or PL/SQL block in memory. To find out the degree of library cache contention in your system, run the following statement:

```
# liblatch.sql
SELECT SUBSTR(name,1,25), gets, misses,
         immediate_gets, immediate_misses
  FROM V$LATCH
 WHERE misses > 0 OR immediate_misses > 0
   AND name LIKE 'library cach%';
```

If your misses or immediate misses are significantly greater than zero, consider taking the following steps:

- Ensure that your shared pool area is adequately sized. Most sites that use packages and procedures extensively require at least a 30-megabyte shared pool area.

- Pin the packages and procedures that are frequently accessed using the dbms_ shared_pool.keep('owner.procedure') utility provided by Oracle.

- Use packages, procedures, functions, and library procedures wherever possible to allow users to share code.

- Get your application coders to use bind variables.

- Use the SHARED_POOL_RESERVED_SIZE and SHARED_POOL_RESERVED_ MIN_ALLOC parameters to separate the larger objects from the smaller objects. This helps to avoid fragmentation of the shared pool area.

Data block and free list contention

The following query displays information on wait contention for an Oracle data block. The figures are taken from an OLTP site that has a transaction rate that rises as high as 200 per second.

```
# blokwait.sql
SELECT class, count
  FROM V$WAITSTAT
 WHERE class IN ( 'data block',  'free list');

                   Data Block Waits

    Class               Waits
  data block          144910
  free list              300
```

The cause of the data block waits is difficult to find. Basically, your transactions are contending for hot data blocks because they are held by another transaction or they are contending for shared resources within the block—for example, transaction entries (set by the INITRANS parameter) and rows. You must set your INITTRANS on a table to the number of transactions that will access a single block within your table or index at the same time.

The INITRANS storage parameter sets the number of transaction slots within each table or index block. The default INITRANS is 1. If more than one transaction is waiting to access a block, a second transaction slot will have to be created. Each transaction slot uses 23 bytes. Having the INITTRANS set too low can cause chaining and migration, because once the new transaction slot is inserted into the block, it stays there. For the duration of the insertion of the transaction slot into the data block, a wait occurs. You may consider increasing the PCTFREE in the table to have fewer rows per block or make a design change to your application to have fewer transactions accessing the same block.

If a background batch job is updating many rows, which the online users require, the number of data block waits can grow quite large, even if the background job has completed some time earlier. This is because the processes have to check the state of the transaction in the rollback segment header prior to proceeding. Another cause of data block waits is when many users are updating different rows, trying to access an updated row in the same data block, or, even worse, updating the same row in a data block.

The ideal count on the data block waits is zero. This is usually not achievable in the real world, because the storage overhead of increasing the INITRANS is usually not justified given the large amount of storage overhead that it will introduce. Data block contention can cause problems, and enlarging INITRANS can improve performance, so don't immediately dismiss the idea of enlarging INITRANS. Potential performance improvements *can* be significant.

Free list contention occurs when a table buffer is inserted into by many transactions simultaneously. By default, only one buffer is available for all transactions to insert into. The number of buffers is specified by the FREELISTS clause, which you apply to a table at creation time. It pays to predict the tables that are likely to have many transactions inserted into them simultaneously. You should set the FREELISTS at table creation stage to the number of simultaneous transactions that you expect to insert into the table. If you discover free list contention after the table has been built, you are left with no option but to rebuild the entire table with the increased FREELISTS setting.

Unfortunately, identifying the exact tables and blocks that are experiencing data block and free list contention is quite difficult. Your best bet is to examine the output from the V$SESSION_WAIT table. This will provide you with the SID of the session that is experiencing waits. You can then examine the V$ACCESS table to determine which tables the process is using; one of those tables is the offending table.

Reducing Multithreaded Server Process Contention

Use of the multithreaded server can greatly reduce the overheads that exist for user processes. To get the full benefit from the multithreaded server architecture, you must reduce contention for the dispatcher processes and shared server processes.

Contention for dispatcher processes is indicated by a high busy rate of dispatcher processes or an increase in the wait time for responses from the dispatcher processes. To find out if there is contention in your system, Oracle recommends that you issue the following query against the V$DISPATCHER table:

```
# mtswait.sql
SELECT network, SUM(busy) / (SUM(busy) + SUM(idle)) "Busy Rate"
  FROM v$dispatcher
  GROUP BY network;


Network          Busy Rate
-----------------------------------------
tcp              .320000978
```

The figures in this output indicate that in your TCP/IP network you are experiencing a 32% busy rate. If you are busy more than 50% of the time, Oracle recommends that you add dispatcher processes. You achieve this by enlarging the number of dispatchers in the INIT.ORA parameter, MTS_DISPATCHERS. For example, to increase the value from two to four TCP/IP dispatchers, specify

```
MTS_DISPATCHERS = TCP, 4
```

You can also increase the number of dispatchers for your instance by adjusting the value of MTS_DISPATCHERS in the ALTER SYSTEM command. Make sure that if you do this, you don't exceed the value specified in the INIT.ORA parameter.

To test the response times of the dispatcher process queues, perform the following query:

```
# mtsresp.sql
SELECT network, DECODE (SUM(totalq), 0 , "No responses",
     SUM(wait)/SUM(totalq) || '   100ths secs') "AVERAGE WAIT "
   FROM v$queue Q, v$dispatcher D
   WHERE Q.type = 'DISPATCHER'
   AND Q.paddr = D.paddr
 GROUP BY network;


   NETWORK                          AVERAGE WAIT
   --------------------------------------------------
   TCP                        .219287726 100THS SECS
```

Oracle recommends that if your wait time increases, you should consider adding dispatcher processes. We suggest that you add dispatcher processes to determine whether the wait times come down. The lower the wait times, the better.

To determine contention for shared server processes, perform the following query:

```
# mtsavwait.sql
SELECT DECODE( totalq, 0, 'NO REQUESTS',
                    wait/totalq ||'  100THS SECS') "AVERAGE WAIT"
     FROM v$queue
     WHERE type = 'COMMON''

   AVERAGE WAIT
   --------------------------------------------------
   .072727622    100THS SECS
```

The wait time for a shared server request is 0.07. If this time is increasing in your system, see if you can solve the problem by increasing the number of shared servers. You can do this by increasing the values of the INIT.ORA parameters MTS_SERVERS and MTS_MAX_SERVERS. You can also adjust these values dynamically with the SQL*DBA MONITOR QUEUE facility.

To make sure that you have the number of query servers running that you expect, you can run the following script. If the number of servers is at the limit specified by the parameter MTS_MAX_SERVERS (which has a default of 20) and you are getting poor performance, try increasing the parameter. Be sure that your database is totally tuned before you do this. We have found that when MTS is used, the database performance problems mentioned in this chapter increase exponentially. A traffic jam effect occurs on one of the servers, so very poor performance is often likely to be due to something other than the number of MTS servers.

```
# mtsrunng.sql
SELECT COUNT(*) "MTS Shared Servers"
  FROM v$shared_servers
 WHERE status != 'QUIT';
```

Reducing Locking Problems

Locking can be extremely destructive to the performance of Oracle applications. Locking creates a situation in which a process has to wait for another process to free the resource before the process lock can proceed. You must make sure that locking situations in your system don't hinder the performance of users as they access data. You can use the following scripts to identify many of your site's locking problems.

To avoid most locking problems, enable the transaction processing option (TPO), which allows you to use row-level locking. Make sure you set the INIT.ORA parameter, ROW_LOCKING, to ALWAYS, in all database instances. (See Chapter 8, *Selecting a Locking Strategy*, for details.)

We have found that the single biggest cause of locking problems is when a user leaves his or her screen in the middle of an update and goes for lunch without committing the changes. You must train your users to commit all transactions and exit the screen back to the menu whenever they are going to leave their terminals for any period of time.

Oracle provides several tools that can help you monitor the locks in your system:

*   Use the *UTLLOCKT.sql* script.

*   Use SQL*DBA or the Enterprise Manager MONITOR LOCKS screens.

*   Be sure to run *CATBLOCK.sql* as part of your database installation. If you haven't, *UTLLOCKT.sql* won't function correctly. Don't despair; you can run *CATBLOCK.sql* now and rerun *UTLLOCKT.sql* to obtain current locking problems.

Other scripts that you can run to detect lock contention in your database are listed below.

You can run the following query to observe the usernames being blocked and the objects involved in a locking situation. The statements listed are the last statement run by each user, which is usually the statement causing the locking problem. The user that has a lockwait of null is the user that the other users are waiting for. That user is not listed in this query. Use *UTLLOCKT.SQL* to find the offending user.

```
# locksql.sql
SELECT ses.username||'('||sid||')'  users, acc.owner owner,
          acc.object object, ses.lockwait, txt.sql_text sqltext
  FROM v$sqltext txt, v$access acc, v$session ses
WHERE txt.address = ses.sql_address
  AND  txt.hash_value  = ses.sql_hash_value
  AND  ses.sid         = acc.sid
  AND  ses.lockwait    IS NOT NULL;
```

If your database has many users logging on to the database using the same user ID, you can obtain the operating system process ID using the following script:

```
# lockproc.sql
SELECT ses.username||'('||sid||')'  users, acc.owner owner,
        acc.object object, ses.lockwait, prc.osuser os_process
  FROM  v$process prc, v$access acc, v$session ses
 WHERE prc.addr       = ses.paddr
   AND ses.sid        = acc.sid
   AND ses.lockwait   IS NOT NULL;
```

To observe the blocking user sessions and the waiting user sessions all in a single statement, you can run the following script.

```
# lockhldr.sql or blocker.sql
TTITLE 'User Blocking and Waiting for Other Users'
SELECT DISTINCT  o.object_name, sh.username||'('||sh.sid||')'  "Holder",
sw.username||'('||sw.sid||')'  "Waiter",
           DECODE(lh.lmode, 1, 'NULL', 2,
                  'row share', 3, 'row exclusive', 4,  'share',
                     5, 'share row exclusive' , 6, 'exclusive')  "Lock Type"
FROM all_objects o, v$session sw, v$lock lw, v$session sh, v$lock lh
 WHERE lh.id1  = o.object_id
  AND  lh.id1  = lw.id1
  AND  sh.sid  = lh.sid
  AND  sw.sid  = lw.sid
  AND  sh.lockwait is null
  AND  sw.lockwait is not null
  AND  lh.type = 'TM'
  AND  lw.type = 'TM'
/
```

To obtain more information on the type of lock being held, you can run the following script. The id1 column in the V$LOCK table is the OBJECT_ID of the object being locked. The OBJECT_ID can be used to search the DBA_OBJECTS table to determine the object and the object's owner.

```
# tranlock.sql or alllocks.sql
TTITLE 'Transactions Experiencing Lock Contention'
  SELECT DECODE(11.lmode,  2, 'Row-S(SS)', 3,'Row-X(SX)',
                    4, 'Share', 5, 'S/Row-X(SSX)',
```

```
                                6, 'Exclusive', 'Other') Mode_Held,
                DECODE(11.request,  2, 'Row-S(SS)', 3,'Row-X(SX)',
                                    4, 'Share', 5, 'S/Row-X(SSX)',
                                    6, 'Exclusive', 'Other') Lock_Requested,
                11.id1, 11.id2
    FROM v$lock 11
  WHERE type = 'TX'
     AND    (11.id1, 11.id2) in
                  (SELECT 12.id1, 12.id2
                      FROM v$lock 12
                      AND 11.id1 = 12.id1
                      AND 11.id2 = 12.id2
                      AND 12.request > 0);
```

To obtain all locks held by all users, you can run the following query:

```
SELECT s.username, 1.type, o.object_name,
          DECODE(11.1mode,  2, 'Row-S(SS)', 3,'Row-X(SX)',
                            4, 'Share', 5, 'S/Row-X(SSX)',
                            6, 'Exclusive', 'Other') Mode_Held
  FROM dba_objects o, v$session s, v$lock 1
  WHERE s.sid        = 1.sid
    AND o.object_id  = 1.id1;
```

Foreign key locking problems

The following output lists all foreign keys that do not have an index on the child table; for example, we have a foreign key on the EMP table to make sure that it has an existing valid DEPT row. The foreign key is placed on the EMP (deptno) column pointing to the DEPT (deptno) primary key. Obviously, the parent table DEPT requires an index on deptno for the foreign key to point to. There is one effect of the foreign key that is not widely known: Unless an index is placed on the child table on the columns that are used in the foreign key, a share lock occurs on the parent table for the duration of the insert, update, or delete on the child table.

What is a share lock? The effect of a share lock is that all query users hoping to access the table have to wait until a single update user on the table completes his or her update. Update users cannot perform their update until all query users complete their queries against the table. The bottom line is that if the parent table is a volatile table, the share lock can cause the most incredible performance degradation. At a recent benchmark, we had the entire benchmark grind to a halt because of this locking situation. If the parent table is a nonvolatile table, you may be able to get away without the index on the child table because the lock on the parent table is of no importance.

The negative factor of the index on the child table is that we have observed tables with as many as 20 indexes on them. Response times have been severely damaged because of maintaining the excessive number of indexes. Our advice to these sites has been to use only foreign key constraints on columns that have an index that can be used for other purposes (e.g., reporting) or that point to a nonvolatile reference table. Most tables have difficulty maintaining acceptable performance if they have more than 10 indexes on them.

You may wish to take the foreign keys offline during the day and put them online at night to report any errors into an exceptions table. You should do this when the parent table is not being accessed.

```
# fkeys.sql
TTITLE ' Foreign Constraints and Columns Without an Index on Child Table'
SELECT acc.owner||'-> '||acc.constraint_name||'('||acc.column_name
       ||'['||acc.position||'])'||' ***** Missing Index'
  FROM  all_cons_columns acc, all_constraints ac
 WHERE  ac.constraint_name = acc.constraint_name
   AND  ac.constraint_type = 'R'
   AND  (acc.owner, acc.table_name, acc.column_name, acc.position) IN
  (SELECT acc.owner, acc.table_name, acc.column_name, acc.position
     FROM   all_cons_columns acc, all_constraints ac
        WHERE  ac.constraint_name = acc.constraint_name
               and   ac.constraint_type = 'R'
    MINUS
     SELECT table_owner, table_name, column_name, column_position
       FROM all_ind_columns)
ORDER BY acc.owner, acc.constraint_name, acc.column_name, acc.position;
```

Contention right now

Oracle provides a means of performing a spot check on any contention currently occurring in your database. The information that you receive is a list of all contention happening "right now." It is not cumulative. The results will fluctuate from one run to the next.

```
# sesswait.sql
SELECT event, count(*)
  FROM v$session_wait
  GROUP BY event;
```

EVENT	COUNT(*)
Null event	4
buffer busy wait	4
client message	23
control file sequential read	1
db file sequential read	6
log file space/switch	37
pmon timer	1
rdbms ipc message	6
smon timer	1

The figures in the example are taken from a site that had 2,500 users running through a transaction processor. The figures were taken when a redo log file switch was taking place. This is the time when you would observe the most waits on your system. There is usually a response time pause of between 1 and 2 seconds for a log switch. If you have ongoing waits on the items listed below, you should investigate further:

- Free buffer waits: DBWR not writing frequently enough; increase checkpoints

- Latch free: any one of a number of latches is causing contention

- Buffer busy waits: contention for a data, index, or rollback buffer

- db file sequential reads: I/O contention caused by indexed lookups

- db file scattered read: I/O contention caused by full table scans

- db file parallel write: not checkpointing often enough

- undo segment extension: too much dynamic extension or shrinkage of roll-back segments

- undo segment tx slot: not enough rollback segments

To determine which users are experiencing contention, you can run the following script:

```
# userwait.sql
SELECT ses.username || '('||sw.sid||')' users, event
  FROM v$session ses, v$session_wait sw
 WHERE ses.sid = sw.sid;
```

To determine the objects that your users are accessing when they are forced to wait for disk I/O, you can run the following query. The objects that are listed are not always the cause of the wait; but if the object continually appears on the list, there is a good chance that the object is one of several causing a disk I/O bottle-neck on the disk that stores the object.

```
# objwait.sql
set heading off
set pagesize 999
set verify off
set feedback off
set echo off
column aa newline
spool ext2.sql
column nl newline
SELECT 'doc ' nl,
       'User '||v$session.username||'('||v$session_wait.sid||')' nl,
       v$sqltext.sql_text nl,
       '#' nl,
       'select segment_name, segment_type ' nl,
       'from dba_extents ' nl,
       'where file_id='||v$session_wait.p1 nl,
       '  and '||v$session_wait.p2||' between block_id and block_id
          +  blocks -1);'
```

```
  FROM v$session, v$sqlarea, v$session_wait
 WHERE (v$session_wait.event  like '%buffer%'
                     OR
        v$session_wait.event  like '%write%'
                     OR
        v$session_wait.event  like '%read%')
   AND v$session_wait.sid     = v$session.sid
   AND v$session.sql_address = v$sqlarea.address
   AND v$session.sql_hash_value = v$sqlarea.hash_value
/

spool off
@ext2.sql
```

12

Tuning Parallel Server

Oracle's parallel server option (PSO) is a relatively new product that offers sites the potential for improved scalability, price/performance, and recoverability. Oracle is committed to parallel server, and each new release has contained improvements, particularly in the performance area. Oracle7.3, in particular, greatly reduced inter-instance communication and also reduced both the number of locks held and the amount of time the locks are held. Before you start to use parallel server, you must plan how best to use it. If you're not careful, it can damage, rather than improve, your performance.

Introduction to Parallel Server

Parallel server allows multiple instances, each operating a separate node, to share a single database. Some platforms also allow multiple parallel server instances to run on a single machine. In this case, each instance has its own set of detached processes and redo logs. The data files and control files are shared by both instances.

Parallel server is designed to allow an instance to be brought down, either voluntarily or involuntarily, without affecting the transactions running on other instances. No committed data in the failed instance will be lost. There will, however, be a small amount of degradation in response time during recovery if blocks in the failed instance are being accessed by other instances.

The ability to spread instances across different machines provides you with scalability. Many hardware vendors offer machines that have upper limits on both memory and numbers of processors. With parallel server, though, if you have a machine with a 2-gigabyte upper limit on memory and your memory requirements grow beyond the 2 gigabytes, you can split your users across two machines. Each machine will have its own instance, but all users will share the same database.

If you are running parallel server on two different machines and you lose one of the machines, the product allows your key users to log on to the machine that is still running. Parallel server also tells the node that is still running to recover the instance that has crashed. To allow these functions, the disks that contain your database must have physical cables attached to both machines.

Many sites have both online transaction-processing (OLTP) users and batch users. Mixing the two types of users in one instance often has a devastating effect on response times. To address this problem, most sites set standards dictating that batch jobs that run for more than n minutes (usually 5) cannot run during prime production hours. However, this is not a satisfactory scenario at many sites that need to run management reports requiring timely information. With parallel server, System Global Areas (SGAs) can be specifically tuned to support OLTP users in the instance on one machine and batch users in the instance on the other machine. You can have disks hard-cabled to both machines and also use the second machine for other purposes, such as reporting from another database. If the machine that runs the main database (usually a substantially larger machine) goes down, an instance can be started on the second machine to bring the database up. Your users can log on to the second machine without the need to run parallel server.

Parallel server is an extra-cost Oracle option. In addition to buying parallel server itself, you will also need to purchase a distributed lock manager from your hardware vendor. Having lock management software running on many machines will often degrade your performance by more than 5% even if you aren't running parallel server. Our experience indicates that users running parallel server often experience up to 20% worse response times than users running on a single instance. (Note, though, that the difference is coming down with each new release of Oracle. The most important improvements involve having fewer locks and holding on to locks for less time.)

Given the possible performance problems, you are probably wondering why anybody would opt for parallel server. The answer is simple: cost savings, recoverability, and reduced administration of a single database. Parallel server is also the engine that most observers believe will support the emerging technology of massively parallel systems, which promises brilliant performance and excellent scalability. Purchasing many small machines is considerably cheaper than purchasing fewer large machines. In addition, an application designed to run using parallel server can provide very acceptable response times (assuming that your design is suitable for parallel server and you have tuned your instances and locking correctly). Reductions in hardware costs can provide your organization with huge cost savings.

NOTE   Oracle client-server, distributed database, and multithreaded server can often provide the same hardware cost savings as parallel server, with superior performance. Some sites opt for a combination of parallel server and client-server; in such cases, client-server users log on to a particular instance, which forms part of a parallel server shared database. It's a case of choosing the best option for your site.

Parallel server will run very well on certain types of applications and very poorly on others. Parallel server is best suited to the following types of applications:

- Query-intensive applications, such as decision support systems, in which data is usually loaded nightly and heavy query activity by lots of users takes place during the day

- Applications that need to run both batch and OLTP users, each accessing different sets of tables and indexes

- Applications that are CPU-intensive, rather than I/O-intensive

- Applications that update different tables, in which users of each application are able to use a different instance

- Applications that update the same tables but at different times

- Applications in which users access tables on a location basis; for example, New South Wales accounts users have no reason to see Victorian users' data, and vice versa

In general, parallel server is unsuited to the following:

- Applications that perform many inserts, updates, and deletes on tables, clusters, and indexes, in which it is difficult to split user access to different tables, clusters, and indexes

- I/O-intensive applications in which particular tables, indexes, and other database objects are hit heavily by all users

Parallel Server Architecture

Parallel server runs under two main configurations: a loosely coupled architecture and a massively parallel architecture. A third type of configuration, a tightly coupled architecture, can run parallel server as a node. Some platforms allow you to have multiple parallel instances on a single node; with others, you must have the second and subsequent instances located on other machines that are part of a loosely coupled or massively parallel configuration. There are potential performance bottlenecks associated with each type of configuration. Each configuration is described briefly below, but if you are running parallel server at your site, you need to learn as much as possible about the different types of hardware configurations, so you can purchase the most suitable hardware to support your parallel server applications.

Tightly Coupled Systems

Tightly coupled systems (symmetric multiprocessors, or SMPs) have multiple processors on a single box. Some platforms provide a distributed lock manager (DLM) that allows you to run separate parallel instances on a single machine. Other SMP platforms cannot run parallel server in their own right. They can, however, make up part of a parallel server configuration. Performance on these machine types is limited by the bandwidth of the common bus, as shown in Figure 12-1.

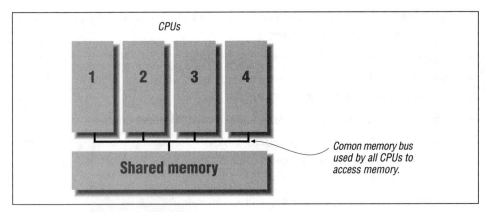

Figure 12-1. Tightly coupled architecture

Loosely Coupled Systems

Loosely coupled systems are stand-alone computers that have access to a shared set of disks (see Figure 12-2). Each computer has its own CPU(s) and its own memory. Communication between the machines takes place over a high-speed bus. The bandwidth of the high-speed bus places a very real limit on the number of nodes that are able to share your disks and hence your database. We have found that some loosely coupled system hardware does not scale much beyond two nodes. Despite rapid advancements in parallel server, you must be sure of scalability and must benchmark your applications to prove that your own hardware will work properly.

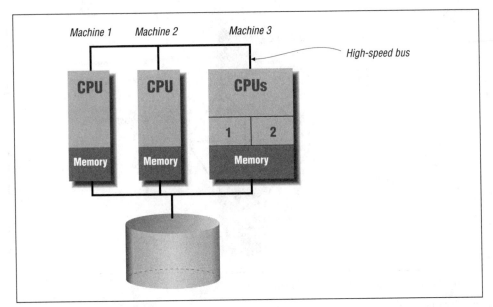

Figure 12-2. Loosely coupled architecture

Massively Parallel Architecture

The massively parallel architecture is similar to the loosely coupled architecture, but there is one important difference. There are multiple, high-speed links between the nodes, instead of the bus used by loosely coupled systems (see Figure 12-3). Because each node can simply be an inexpensive processor, this architecture can provide an organization with an incredible cost/performance benefit. Many of the latest small MPP machines are using the same chips as the most powerful MPP machines; each node has its own memory.

The MPP architecture is able to support thousands of nodes. This makes the architecture much more scalable than its loosely coupled counterpart. All nodes have high-speed access to the shared disks. MPP processing is a definite growth area in the marketplace, and its use in large, mission-critical applications is made possible through parallel server.

Parallel Server Locking

Thoroughly understanding parallel server locking mechanics is essential for tuning your system. The locks that are used most frequently and have the largest bearing on parallel server response time are the following:

- Parallel cache management (PCM) locks
- Table locks

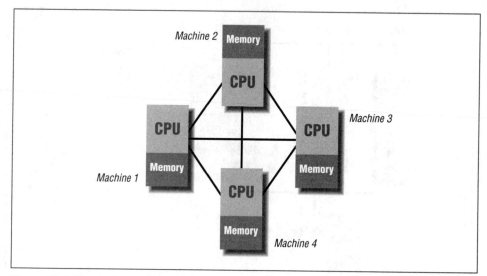

Figure 12-3. Massively parallel architecture

- Transaction locks
- System change number (SCN) locks

PCM locks are opened when the Oracle database is opened and are closed when the Oracle database is closed. SCN locks are opened as each process starts. Table locks and transaction locks are opened by a database transaction and are closed when the transaction terminates.

PCM Locks

PCM locks are managed by the distributed lock manager to maintain consistency of data blocks in the SGAs of the various instances. The distributed lock manager is a piece of software provided by your hardware vendor. The PCM locks work in addition to standard row-level locking. Each PCM lock controls one or more database blocks.

PCM locks are tunable by setting the following INIT.ORA parameter:

```
GC_FILES_TO_LOCKS
GC_DB_LOCKS
GC_TABLEPSACES
GC_SEGMENTS
GC_SAVE_ROLLBACK_LOCKS
GC_ROLLBACK_SEGMENTS
GC_ROLLBACK_LOCKS
```

See the section called "INIT.ORA Parameters" later in this chapter for details.

If a user on Instance B requires a database block that is currently in Instance A's SGA, Instance B must first acquire the PCM lock that controls the database block in shared mode for a read and exclusive mode for an update. In the case of an update, the DLM will send a message informing the first instance to do the following:

- Write out all dirty blocks covered by the PCM lock to disk

- Downgrade the lock on the first instance to indicate that there is no longer a conflict

Instance B will then read the block from disk.

NOTE   Some blocks may have been written because they happened to be controlled by the same PCM lock.

If the transaction on Instance A has not completed, a tug of war may occur between the two instances as they pass the buffers back and forth via the disk, driven by each instance's need to obtain blocks under the control of the same PCM lock.

By now, you are probably contemplating setting the number of PCM locks to a level that guarantees that there is one lock per block. Unfortunately, there are a few problems with doing that:

- Most DLMs have an upper limit on the number of PCM locks allowed. You must find out about any upper limits from your hardware vendor.

- Each DLM lock uses memory; and for OLTP applications with very large tables, this may limit you. Each DLM lock uses between 180 and 1,200 bytes, depending on your hardware. Assuming hardware that uses 1,200 bytes and a 4-kilobyte block size, a 1-gigabyte table will use approximately 250 megabytes of memory for DLM locks (assuming one DLM lock per block).

  Oracle7.3 introduced releasable lock elements called fine-grained locks (in contrast to hashed locks, which are nonreleasable locks). Before Oracle7.3, you had to use the memory-consuming hash locks. Because fine-grained lock elements can be reused, you do not need to specify as many lock elements as before Oracle7.3, so there is a large reduction in memory requirements. There is a tradeoff, though. Fine-grained locks save lots of memory, but they run more slowly because of the get and release lock requirements. They are not recommended for read-only tablespaces or for applications that perform many table scans.

You will still need to preallocate fine-grained releasable lock elements using the new GC_RELEASABLE_LOCKS parameter but will allocate them in the DLM only when you need them. Before Oracle7.3, the hashed lock elements were fixed and preallocated in the SGA and the DLM. The hash locks were specified by the GC_FILES_TO_LOCKS parameter.

You can have a combination of fine-grained and hashed locks in your parallel server environment. If you specify the following, file 1 will use 1,000 hashed locks and file 2 will have 10,000 fine-grained locks available to it. 2=0 implies that file 2 has no hashed locks.

```
GC_FILES_TO_LOCKS="1=1000:2=0EACH"
GC_RELEASABLE_LOCKS=10000
```

- The larger the block size (specified by the DB_BLOCK_SIZE parameter) used for your database, the fewer the PCM locks that are required, but the higher the chance of having clashes of instances between rows that are contained within a single block. Oracle7.3 and later uses between 70 and 150 bytes per block, which ends up being about 30 megabytes of memory for the 1-gigabyte table created in a 4-kilobyte database.

- The more PCM locks you have, the longer it will take to start your database and the longer it will take to recover your database (and we mean *long*—like 30 minutes plus!).

- Certain types of database objects do not require as many PCM locks as others. If your application is designed and your database constructed with this in mind, the need for PCM locks may be reduced significantly, as we describe later in this chapter.

SCN Locks

SCN locks are used to time stamp changes made to your database. On most platforms, the SCN locks are controlled by DLMs. Oracle informs us that a cheaper way of handling SCN locks is currently being worked on and will provide excellent performance improvements.

Table Locks

Table locks can cause substantial overheads. They are used mainly to ensure that the table structure remains consistent for the duration of your transaction. If you can avoid making schema changes, you can set the DML_LOCKS parameter to 0 to improve performance significantly.

Transaction Locks

Transaction locks can usually cause problems only in a large OLTP application in which many short updates are taking place. The contention can be worsened by the delay of the rollback segments, where the rollback segment header and rollback segment blocks are being pinged from one instance to the other. Consider using discrete transactions, which totally remove the potential for rollback segment bottleneck as well as eliminating transaction lock overhead in parallel server.

Parallel Server Design

We can't stress enough that your physical database design is the make-or-break element of parallel server performance. Brilliant hardware advances are being made in disk load sharing using such technologies as RAID and load sharing across multiple CPUs. Parallel server introduces a new dimension to tuning because now you are tuning cross-machine communication. The more you can avoid cross-machine communication in your design, the better. As you add each new application to your parallel server database, go through the same stringent steps to ensure that it can be tuned for your architecture.

We have noticed that some sites seem to be fixated on parallel server without carefully considering all of the other options. Yet some of these other options make a lot of sense. The most obvious alternative to parallel server is to run the application(s) on a single machine. Tightly coupled SMP computers provide excellent performance; if your application is scalable on a single machine, for absolute best performance it is usually best to remain on that machine. This may not be possible given your numbers of users, your transaction mix, and the scalability of your current machine. If not, there are other options you can consider.

If you need to support both decision support users and large numbers of OLTP users, you might consider having a second machine that has its own instance and database. The second machine will be tuned explicitly for decision support, and the first machine will be tuned for the large number of OLTP users. The decision support database may have data fed into it via snapshots from the OLTP machine.

The disks on the OLTP machine may be shared between the two machines. If the OLTP machine goes off the air for whatever reason, a database instance can be started on the second machine against the OLTP database, and the OLTP users can log on to the second machine to achieve a fast recovery. The decision support instance can remain running if you want it to. You can achieve all this without having to deal with the contention problems of parallel server. With such a setup, users can log on to the decision support machine and access the OLTP database using SQL*Net; very little performance degradation is associated with this scalable option to parallel server. The downside of this approach is that you will have to administer multiple databases.

Another multiple database option is to have databases separated by application or location. For example, the personnel application might be in one database and the accounting application in another. If data must be shared across instances, SQL*Net links can be used. The cost-based optimizer has made huge advances in improving the response times of cross-database queries with the later versions of Oracle. Snapshots can be used to transfer reference and other data. Distributed databases are also an option. You may also decide to partition separate databases by state, client, or some other characteristic. The alternatives are plentiful, and it is essential that you select the best for your own organization.

Table Categories

To choose the best configuration possible for your organization, your designer must be aware of which parts of your database are going to require cross-machine communication if you select parallel server. Each table should be categorized as either a read-only table or a table that data is inserted into or deleted from.

Read-only tables

Read-only tables and their indexes require very few (if any) PCM locks. They are usually loaded into at night from other sources and are read from during prime usage times.

Tables used for inserts and deletes

For these tables, you will have to do some further investigation. Ask these questions:

1. Can the table be broken into subordinate tables? For example, the ACCOUNTS table might be broken into the ACCOUNTS_NSW table and the ACCOUNTS_VIC table. Note that later releases of Oracle provide partitioned views (for example, ALL_ACCOUNTS, which is a UNION ALL of ACCOUNTS_NSW and ACCOUNTS_VIC), which considerably speed up access to joined tables using parallel query capabilities.

2. If the table cannot be broken into subordinate tables, can it be set up in such a way that users from one location can access only a certain part of the table? For example, the key might include the location and account number, rather than the next sequential account number.

3. Is the table extremely large (as it may be when the parallel server option is used), and is it likely that different users will rarely access the same blocks (and PCM locks)? With very large tables, many of the blocks will be written to disk by the DBWR because they have been aged out using LRU processing of the buffer cache. This overcomes the writing to disk problem created by pinging (described later) because the data have already been written. Large tables will often experience a memory problem if they have too many PCM locks.

4. Is the table inserted into heavily? This question is important to establish the degree of FREELIST GROUPS required. (See the section called "Tables, Indexes, and Clusters" later in this chapter.)

5. Are the tables small, and are they frequently accessed by different applications or different groups of users? The small tables can cause more damaging locking problems than larger tables, particularly if the tables are indexed. Certain tricks can be performed, such as limiting the rows per block by increasing the PCTFREE when the table is created, not having an index on the table, having one PCM lock per block, or breaking the table up into smaller tables.

Suitable Applications

The diagrams in this section illustrate the applications or combination of applications that are most suited to parallel server. There is no shortcut to determining whether parallel server is suitable for your site. You must perform detailed design on your site's data usage.

Batch and OTLP instances

One approach is to have separate instances for batch and OLTP (see Figure 12-4). In this case, your design would usually have to include a mechanism for transferring data from the OLTP set of tables to the batch set of tables. This would typically be done by using periodic snapshots, ideally overnight. If you decide to perform your snapshots during prime OLTP usage times, carefully test and perform ongoing monitoring of the effect on performance. The OLTP instance would be tuned for OLTP users, and the batch instance would be tuned for batch users. (See the section called "Tuning Instances" later in this chapter.)

The batch part of the database usually contains a combination of summary data and historical data. Triggers are often a good means of populating both types of table. Despite the fact that they are instance-independent, they can still cause locking problems by updating many rows (controlled by one PCM lock) that another instance might need to read or update. Be careful to include the triggers in your parallel server benchmarks if that is the approach you propose to use for your table population.

Historical tables often tend to be extremely large. It usually pays to break the tables into more manageable sizes, using different table names (e.g., ACCOUNTS_ 90, ACCOUNTS_91, etc.) with a partitioned view containing a UNION ALL to allow queries against all of the data. The trade-off is that your application programs will need the intelligence to know which table to insert into. The benefits are improved recoverability times, ease of purging (drop an old table off the view and add a new one), speed, and ease of index creation on the smaller tables and the ability to move the tables across disks to get the absolute best performance.

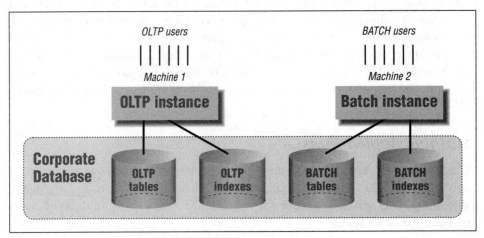

Figure 12-4. Separate instances for batch and OLTP

Database partitioned by application

Another approach is to partition your database by application. There will often be a need to share certain reference tables (for example, departments or error messages). This type of data tends to be quite static and is best placed into a read-only tablespace that is shared by Personnel and Accounts users (see Figure 12-5).

Some users may cross boundaries and perform work in both the Personnel and Accounts applications. Such users should have separate login sessions, one for the Personnel machine and one for the Accounts machine. Each login will go through the appropriate instance.

If your applications need to perform long-running batch processing during prime production hours, you might consider having the Personnel batch users and the Accounts batch users on a third instance. Ideally, you'd transfer data to the batch tables overnight. If the transfer of data takes place during prime hours, it will probably pay to have the batch and OLTP users for that application on the same machine and tune the machine to avoid contention.

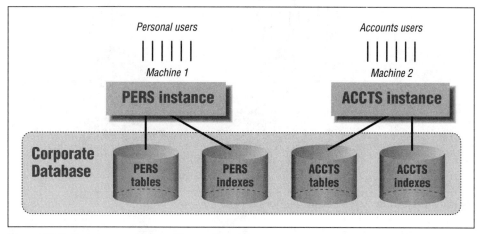

Figure 12-5. Database partitioned by application

Database partitioned by geographic location

A third approach is to partition your database by geographic location (see Figure 12-6). With this structure, you have the choice of using separate table names or different schema owners within your database. Having separate schema owners is usually better; this lets you use synonyms and have one set of source code that runs across all applications. Having different owners lets you perform tasks such as exports a little more easily, allowing you to export multiple schemas quite simply.

Once again, you can share reference data from a read-only tablespace. Batch users can use a third instance if tables used by batch users are not being changed heavily by OLTP users. If the batch users are accessing the same tables as those being modified by OLTP users, it is best to place them into the same instance but to ensure that their SQL is tuned and their resource usage is governed.

Database partitioned by client

A fourth approach is to partition your database by client (see Figure 12-7). This is helpful when your database has many clients, each with information specific to its own business. Usually, the only type of cross-client reporting is done by the company that is running the database. Some reference table, such as error messages that are not shared, can be placed into their own read-only tablespace.

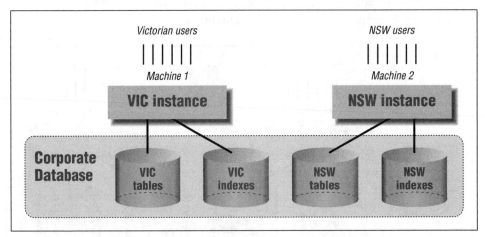

Figure 12-6. Database partitioned by geographic location

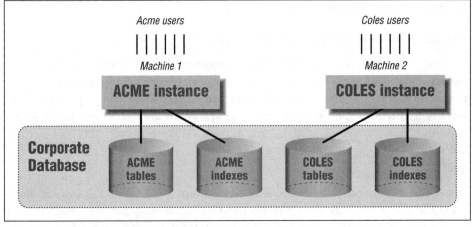

Figure 12-7. Database partitioned by client

Tables accessed by multiple instances

The final, and usually the least suitable, design may be appropriate when certain tables must be accessed by users on more than one instance and a single machine is not scalable enough to cope with the number of users. As we mentioned earlier, other architectures, such as client-server, distributed database, and transaction processors (including multithreaded servers) also offer scalability. Consider all of these in addition to parallel server.

If you plan to use parallel server, perform extensive benchmarks to prove that it can provide acceptable response times at your site. You should also provide ongoing tuning of the tables and their indexes from the parallel server perspective. Use a design similar to one of the four examples described above for as many tables and indexes as possible.

The table that is accessed by multiple instances shown in Figure 12-8 has been split into four parts by using the command

```
ALTER TABLE accounts ALLOCATE EXTENT
    (SIZE 500M DATAFILE '/oracle/raw/accts/datafile1.dbf'  INSTANCE 1);
```

Each instance inserts into the data file corresponding to its extent allocation. Unfortunately, processing of indexes is not so straightforward. Oracle's B-tree structure makes it difficult to separate entries, particularly at the root level of the index. To avoid index contention, you need to introduce a method of having users from separate instances access different parts of the index. One method of achieving this is to have the instance ID be part of the index key.

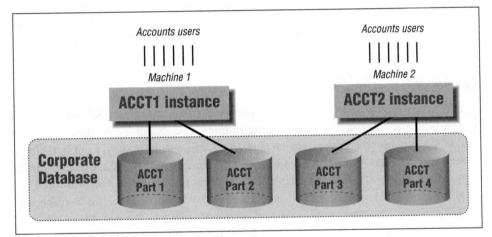

Figure 12-8. Database in which table uses multiples instances

Other Design Issues

This section summarizes a number of other design issues to consider when you are using parallel server.

Avoid pinging

We stress throughout this chapter that the key to good parallel server design is to avoid having one instance updating the same table blocks, index block, and even rollback segments that the other instances are updating. The absolute worst case is the one in which the two instances are inserting into the same indexed table using a sequence that continually hits the same index blocks. This may occur when the next value is a numeric sequence that comes from an application next value table.

If a user on instance PRODB requires a block that a user on instance PRODA has just updated, a physical write of the block to disk will take place, followed by a physical read by the user requesting the modified block. As we've discussed elsewhere, this process is known as a *ping* (as in ping-pong). If the modified row affects an index, one or more index blocks will also have to be written to the database and then physically read to the other instance. If the users on PRODA then need to read the block, we end up thrashing the disk; the same blocks are being pinged from one instance to the other via the database disk.

Dealing with the same table

When multiple instances insert into the same table, consider making the instance part of the unique key. Sequence ranges may also be cached on a per-instance basis; for example, the sequence on the PRODA instance may start with 1000 cache 1000, and the sequence on PRODB may start with 100000 cache 1000. This may not always be possible because you might need to maintain contiguous numbers for auditing purposes. If it is not possible, the only real option is to have separate tables.

Dealing with read consistency

You may encounter read consistency problems when using parallel server; these are particularly relevant for long-running queries. For example, suppose you have a SELECT statement commencing at 3:00 p.m. that requires data from a table or index that has had many changes made to it after 3:00 p.m. If the long-running job is on a different instance from the one making the changes, you will force not only the data and index blocks to be pinged and written to disk, but also the rollback segment headers and rollback segment blocks. These operations are essential for Oracle to maintain read consistency. We strongly recommend that you run the report and the updates against the same database instance.

Adding to an existing environment

If you are running your application using a single instance and expect to adapt the application to a parallel server environment, you must follow all of the steps that are required for a new application. Adding new applications to an existing tuned parallel server environment can potentially result in abysmal performance for the new applications and can also have a harmful effect on the performance of all the other applications that are using the existing parallel server environment. If you are dividing the processing of a single table by allocating extents to an instance, it will pay to sort your data before loading them into the table so that the users of different instances are likely to access different parts of the table.

Parallel Server Database

This section summarizes hints for tuning different components of your parallel server database.

Data Separation

Follow these rules for separating data:

- If at all possible, ensure that database instances are not accessing the same data.

- Place data that are accessed by different instances on different disks.

- If possible, store the data stored by different instances into different tables. For example, if your database runs the accounting systems for many different organizations, consider having a separate set of tables for each organization. Place each instance's tables into its own tablespace.

Data Files

Follow these rules for data files:

- Ideally, have each data file be accessed by only one instance.

- If you are using UNIX, use raw devices with parallel server. In fact, raw devices offer excellent performance advantages even if you are not using parallel server because these devices allow you to avoid the UNIX buffer cache for reads to and writes from the database. Use symbolic link capabilities to assign a meaningful name to the raw device. Keep your raw devices the same size wherever possible to allow them to move to other disks to assist with spreading the I/O load.

- As with nonparallel server data files, consider striping your rollback, table, and index data files using operating system striping, Oracle striping, or both.

- Ideally, place redo logs for each instance onto separate disks. If your machine has many inserts, update, and deletes, they will be hit very heavily. Having the redos on separate disks also allows you to monitor the redo activity of each of the instances by the operating system disk I/O monitoring commands. If your redos are hit heavily, consider striping them.

- Use Oracle parallel query if it works well with parallel server on your platform. To run parallel query well in a parallel server environment, you need low latency, high bandwidth, and reliable interconnect. There are plans to make all platforms able to support both options in the future. (See Chapter 13, *Tuning Parallel Query*.)

Tablespaces

Follow these rules for tablespaces:

- Try to separate tables and indexes that are accessed by a particular instance into their own tablespace(s) (e.g., INDEX_TSPACE, TABLE_TSPACE). In fact, you should do this whether you are using parallel server or not. Separating tables and indexes helps performance by allowing concurrent reads of indexes and their associated table data.

- Place read-only tables and indexes into tablespaces that are exclusively assigned for read-only objects. Read-only tablespaces may contain objects from multiple applications because there will be no lock contention for these objects. However, we usually recommend that you have one read-only tablespace per application to assist in recovery and to allow particular applications to be taken offline for whatever reason. Make use of read-only tablespaces if you are using Oracle7.1 or later.

- Keep rollback segments in their own tablespaces

- Place the set of rollback segments for each instance on a separate disk. Use the ROLLBACK_SEGMENTS parameter in the INIT.ORA file specific to each instance to specify the rollback segments relevant to that instance. Note that you must have rollback segment names that are unique across all instances.

- Keep temporary segments in their own tablespace. Assign the users of each instance their own temporary tablespace. Use the following command:

  ```
  ALTER USER gurry TEMPORARY TABLESPACE;
  ```

  The tablespace type TEMPORARY is available in Oracle7.3 and later; it helps to reduce inter-instance communication.

- Place tables and indexes that have potential for PCM locking problems into their own tablespaces (e.g., ACCOUNTS_TABLE_DATA). Doing this allows you to fine-tune the important parameter GC_FILES_TO_LOCKS and to more easily identify the objects that are experiencing lock contention.

- Put indexes in their own tablespaces. Indexes have a higher potential for locking problems than tables and usually require a larger number of PCM locks. Putting indexes in their own tablespaces allows you to assign PCM locks specific to data files in that tablespace (via the GC_FILES_TO_LOCKS parameter).

Tables, Indexes, and Clusters

If all instances perform queries only against tables, contention will not occur and data partitioning by instance will not be required. However, if one instance performs updates, or if both instances perform updates against the same tables, there is potential for severe lock contention. You can't control the placement of data into indexes, as a result of Oracle's B-tree structure, which causes indexes to have a higher potential for locking problems. You will usually need to set the PCM locks higher for the table's indexes than for the table itself.

Consider using hash clusters to eliminate the need for the index altogether. Hash clusters also give you some control over the placement of rows in the table, which will help to eliminate PCM lock contention.

Inserting into a table, index, or cluster from multiple instances can potentially cause contention for free lists. A free list is a list of extents into which rows can be inserted. You set the number of free lists when you create your table via the FREELIST parameter on the CREATE command. Note that this parameter refers to one instance only. To specify separate free lists per instance, you must set the FREELIST GROUP parameter, with the number of groups equaling the number of instances that are concurrently inserting into the same table. We strongly advise that you set FREELIST GROUPS for tables that have rows inserted into them from multiple instances.

The following commands guarantee that inserts for either of two instances will insert into different data files and avoid free list contention. Allocating extents specific to an instance can be used only for clusters and tables, not for indexes. Free lists and free list groups can be used for tables, clusters, and indexes.

```
CREATE TABLESPACE finance_tables
        DATAFILE '/dev/raw1' SIZE 4k REUSE;

ALTER TABLESPACE finance_tables
        ADD DATAFILE '/dev/raw2' size 1000M ,
                                '/dev/raw3' size 1000M;

CREATE TABLE account (account_no NUMBER(9),.........)
        STORAGE (INITIAL 4k NEXT 1000M
                    PCTINCREASE 0
                    FREELISTS 12
                    FREELIST GROUPS 2)
    TABLESPACE finance_tables;

ALTER TABLE account ALLOCATE EXTENT
    (SIZE 1000M DATAFILE '/dev/raw2'   INSTANCE 1');

ALTER TABLE account ALLOCATE EXTENT
    (SIZE 1000M DATAFILE '/dev/raw3'   INSTANCE 2 ');
```

In Oracle7.3 and later, you also have the ability to allocate an extent to an index. When you need a free block to insert a new entry, Oracle picks it up from the new extent.

Sites that use parallel server tend to have a number of very large tables, often tens of gigabytes in size. Oracle7.2 introduced big performance improvements in partitioned views that work nicely with parallel server. The parallel query option also provides you with a means of querying separate tables through a view containing UNION ALLs (as shown in the following example).

Partitioned views may help by lessening the amount of time it takes to create indexes, as well as speeding up recovery. They also provide you with a means of spreading tables and their indexes optimally across disks. From the parallel server perspective, you may be able to have the different tables accessed by users on different instances.

Partitioned views are created by putting CHECK CONSTRAINTS on a table, as shown below:

```
ALTER TABLE fin_transactions_94 ADD CONSTRAINT c_fin_yr_94
      CHECK (transaction_date between '01-jul-94' and '30-jun-95');
ALTER TABLE fin_transactions_95 ADD CONSTRAINT c_fin_yr_95
      CHECK (transaction_date between '01-jul-95' and '30-jun-96');
ALTER TABLE fin_transactions_96 ADD CONSTRAINT c_fin_yr_96
      CHECK (transaction_date between '01-jul-96' and '30-jun-97');
```

You can now create a view as follows:

```
CREATE_VIEW all_fin_transactions AS
      SELECT *
        FROM fin_transactions_94
      UNION ALL
      SELECT *
        FROM fin_transactions_95
      UNION ALL
      SELECT *
        FROM fin_transactions_96
  /
```

The query

```
SELECT SUM(transaction_amount)
  FROM all_fin_transactions
WHERE transaction_date BETWEEN '01-aug-95' AND '02-aug-96'
  /
```

will scan tables FIN_TRANSACTIONS_95 and FIN_TRANSACTIONS_96 (avoiding the much larger table scan that would have been necessary if the FIN_TRANSACTIONS_94 had been included in the same table).

Tuning Instances

One of the most significant advantages of using parallel server is that it allows you to tune the instance to suit the types of users using the node. If you have separated your OLTP users from the batch users, the batch instance will have a larger value for the DB_BLOCK_BUFFERS, SORT_AREA_SIZE, and LOG_BUFFER INIT.ORA parameters. The OLTP instance will most likely have a large SHARED_POOL_SIZE. The OLTP machine will probably be more powerful and have more processors. The batch machine is likely to make much larger use of parallel query, so you will have to set PARALLEL_MIN_SERVERS and the other parallel query parameters for this instance. (The next section summarizes parameters.)

Depending on the types and numbers of users on each of the instances, you may have a machine that is just the right size to suit your needs. The catch is that the machine must have adequate I/O slots to be able to share the disks with the other machines that share the database. The maximum number of I/O slots, and therefore the number of disks that the machine can handle is an essential piece of information. In some cases, the hardware vendor may advise you to use disk clusters (many disks on one channel) to overcome the lack of I/O slots, but this may turn out to be unsatisfactory because of the high potential for disk I/O bottlenecks.

Remember that if you have partitioned your application for parallel server, users must log on to the appropriate instance. If users have to log on to two applications, they may need to have two physical logins, one for each machine. Alternatively, there may be an operating system menu. With UNIX, use ORACLE_SID to point to the application on the current machine and TWO_TASK to direct users to the instance on the other machine.

INIT.ORA Parameters

Most tunable parallel server INIT.ORA parameters begin with the letters GC_. In setting these parameters, your aim is to eliminate as much lock contention as possible—in particular pinging and false pinging. You must be aware of the types of locks that parallel server uses and have a good understanding of pinging.

Pinging

As we mentioned earlier, a ping occurs when a database block of some kind (e.g., an index block, data block, segment header block, undo header block, undo block, or any other block) is switched ("pinged") from one database instance to another. A disk write occurs on one instance, and a disk read occurs on a second instance. This may happen when you are using parallel server and a user process using one instance modifies rows within the same table or index block. The block in the buffer cache is changed from an XCUR (exclusive current mode) to a CR (consistent read mode) in the instance that is writing the block to disk. The instance that is reading from disk will set the lock on the block to an XCUR. In using parallel server, the key is to reduce pinging as much as possible.

False Pinging

False pinging occurs when the GC_FILES_TO_LOCKS parameter is not set high enough for specific data files. The total number of PCM locks is specified by the parameter GC_DB_LOCKS. All instances must have the same value set for this parameter. If you do not set the GC_FILES_TO_LOCKS parameter, PCM locks are distributed evenly among all of the data files. For example, if you have 10 data-files and GC_DB_LOCKS is set to 1000, each data file will have 100 PCM locks. This may not always be appropriate because certain data files may require different PCM lock granularity.

One PCM lock may control multiple table or index blocks (perhaps blocks 1 to 10). If a second instance requires any one of the 10 blocks being managed by a PCM lock in the first instance to perform a DML operation (insert, update, or delete) and the first instance has dirtied any of the blocks in the group of 10, all of the dirty blocks controlled by the PCM lock will need to be written to disk. This is particularly damaging to performance. (Note, though, that Oracle7.3 has made huge strides in reducing false pinging in this case.)

The types of database components that experience pinging and false pinging are listed in Table 12-1.

Table 12-1. Database components and pinging

Type	Ping	False Ping
Data blocks (table, cluster, and index)	Yes	Yes
Sort blocks	No	No
Segment headers (table, cluster, and index)	Yes	Yes
Rollback header	Yes	No
Rollback blocks	Yes	Yes
Free lists	Yes	Yes

Parameter Summary

This section briefly describes the parallel server parameters.

GC_DB_LOCKS

Total number of PCM locks; used to control locks on table and index data blocks. All instances must have the same value set for this parameter. To obtain the best performance, it is almost always necessary for you to set the numbers of locks per data file using the GC_FILES_TO_LOCKS parameter. This parameter and GC_FILES_TO_LOCKS are the most critical parameters for the tuning of parallel server. GC_DB_LOCKS needs to be equal to or larger than the number of locks in GC_FILES_TO_LOCKS.

The advantage of setting the number of PCM locks high is that it lessens the chance of damaging PCM lock contention. The disadvantages are that it may take considerably longer to start and recover your database and that the locks may use a substantial amount of memory.

GC_FILES_TO_LOCKS

Assigns locks on a per-data-file basis, affecting table and index data blocks within the data file. If you add a data file to your tablespace, don't forget to add the GC_FILES_TO_LOCKS settings to the data file. GC_FILES_TO_LOCKS protects only data blocks, not rollback segment blocks. Don't assign locks to tablespaces that contain only rollback segments or tablespaces that are used exclusively for temporary segments. Group read-only tables/indexes together, and assign one lock only to that data file. Make the tablespace read-only (Oracle7.1 and later) to ensure that no updates occur to the tablespace. PCM locks are distributed evenly among all data files if you do not set the GC_FILES_TO_LOCKS parameter.

Set the parameter as follows:

```
GC_FILES_TO_LOCKS = "<file#> = <#locks> [!<Blocking factor>]
    [EACH]...."
```

where *file#* is the internal database file number. To obtain the appropriate file number from your database, use the command

```
SELECT * FROM DBA_DATA_FILES;
```

You can specify a number of files with the same definitions using the format 1,2,3, to represent file1, file2, and file3. Alternatively, you can specify 1-3.

#locks is the number of PCM locks to have against the data file.

Blocking factor is an optional parameter that dictates the mapping of PCM locks to data files. If it is not specified, it defaults to 1. As a simple example, imagine that you have a data file with 32 blocks, and you specify a locking factor of four blocks; the mapping will look like this:

PCM Lock	Database Blocks							
1	1	2	3	4	17	18	19	20
2	5	6	7	8	21	22	23	24
3	9	10	11	12	25	26	27	28
4	13	14	15	16	29	30	31	32

If the optional parameter *EACH* is specified, each of the data files specified will be allocated the specified locks and mapping.

GC_RELEASABLE_LOCKS

(Oracle7.3 and later) Number of fine-grained locks available to the instance. Fine-grained locks are releasable and reusable and can save a lot of memory in comparison to the hashed locks, which are specified by the GC_FILES_TO_LOCKS parameter. Fine-grained locks do have a slight performance hit. It is usually best to use a combination of fine-grained and hashed locks. Use hashed locks for applications that have many full table scans or read-only tablespaces. Most large OLTP applications will need to use fine-grained locks because of the massive memory requirements of using hashed locks. You must set this parameter to at least the size of the buffer cache (DB_BLOCK_BUFFERS).

GC_TABLESPACES

Affects locking on the header block for the deferred rollback segment. The deferred rollback segment is used when a rollback is requested on a tablespace that is offline. When the tablespace comes back online, the rollback is applied to the tablespace automatically. Unless you are taking a number of files offline concurrently, don't change the parameter from its default.

GC_SEGMENTS

Controls segment header blocks. A segment header block is the first block of a table or index. It contains the extents within the table or index as well as other information. Set the value of this parameter to a value that causes the least possible number of pings. The default parameter can cause a lot of false pings. The segment header blocks are usually accessed in shared mode for full table scans (SELECTs) and in exclusive mode for bumping up the high-water mark (INSERTs). The following query shows which objects hash the same segment PCM lock:

```
# samepcm.sql
SELECT MOD(header_block, lprime(r.value * 1.5) lock_no,
             segment_name,
             segment_type
   FROM dba_segments , v$parameter
  WHERE name = 'gc_segments'
    AND segment_type in ('TABLE', 'INDEX', 'CLUSTER')
  ORDER BY lock_no;
```

GC_SAVE_ROLLBACK_LOCKS

Affects locking on the header block for the deferred rollback segment. As for GC_TABLESPACES, unless you are taking a number of files offline concurrently, don't change the parameter from its default.

GC_ROLLBACK_SEGMENTS

Controls the locking on the rollback segment header block, sometimes referred to as the transaction table. Set this parameter to the total number of rollback segments in your database. If you add rollback segments to your database, don't forget to adjust this parameter.

GC_ROLLBACK_LOCKS

Controls the locks on rollback segment blocks. Increase the value of this parameter if you see a lot of pinging on undo blocks. Each rollback segment gets GC_ROLLBACK_LOCKS assigned to it, regardless of the rollback segment sizes. It is useful to have rollback segments equally sized.

DML_LOCKS

Setting this parameter may help to avoid the severe performance degradation that may occur as each transaction opens a table lock when it accesses the table and closes the table lock when it closes the transaction. If you are not going to modify your database schema, you may receive a pleasant performance boost by setting DML_LOCKS=0. Oracle7.2 and later offer a command that has the same affect as setting DML_LOCKS to zero, but rather than setting the locks at database level, you can set the locks at table level as follows:

```
ALTER TABLE accounts ENABLE/DISABLE TABLE LOCKS;
```

Ongoing Tuning

All of the tuning that you would perform on a single-instance database is also valid for parallel server. (See Chapter 9, *Tuning a New Database* and Chapter 11, *Monitoring and Tuning an Existing Database*, for full details.) When tuning parallel server, start up the database in a consistent instance order. Also, tune all of the individual instances that make up the parallel server environment.

To obtain the number of blocks written to the database to satisfy pings, run the following query. The output indicates the percentage of physical writes that are the result of pings. The nearer to zero the better. Figures as high as 10% usually indicate that you should redesign your table or index access:

```
# pingwrts.sql
SELECT(a.value / b.value) * 10
  FROM v$sysstat a, v$sysstat b
 WHERE a.name = 'DBWR cross instance writes'
     AND b.name  = 'physical writes';
```

CATPARR.sq and Its Views

Oracle provides a script, *catparr.sql*, that you must use to get the most out of parallel server. The directory in which the file is located depends on your operating system. On UNIX systems, it is found in the *$ORACLE_HOME/rdbms/admin* directory. It must be run as SYS or INTERNAL. The script creates a series of objects that can be viewed to obtain all kinds of useful parallel server tuning information. Running this script creates the full set of tables and views listed below.

EXT_TO_OBJ_VIEW

This view lists all extents used by various objects. If you select from the view, it takes several minutes to run; the amount depends on the number of objects and extents in your database. The view is not used in its own right, but only to populate a table called EXT_TO_OBJ, which is used by the V$PING and V$CACHE views (also created by *CATPARR.sql*).

EXT_TO_OBJ

This is the table created from the view EXT_TO_OBJ_VIEW. It is used to speed up subsequent access to the V$PING and V$CACHE views. You must recreate the table for future accesses to these views; this table is created at a particular point in time and will be outdated unless it is recreated each time V$PING and V$CACHE information is retrieved.

V$BH

This view shows the status of each buffer in the buffer cache. It does not point to a database object, but it is extremely useful in identifying potential bottlenecks. The following two statements provide you with valuable tuning information. The first example:

```
# blkpings.sql
SELECT  df.tablespace_name, df.file_name, SUM(NVL(buf.xnc,0)) "PINGS"
  FROM  dba_data_files df, v$bh buf
  WHERE df_file_id = buf.file#
  GROUP BY df.tablespace_name, df.file_name;
```

provides you with another way of getting information on how many times a block has been pinged out of the buffer cache on the instance you are investigating. The block is pinged when another instance requests the block that this instance is protecting in exclusive mode. Design your application to minimize the number of pings. The next example:

```
# pcmbydfl.sql
  SELECT df.tablespace_name, df.file_name,
           buf.lock_element_addr   COUNT(*)
    FROM dba_data_files df, v$bh buf
  WHERE df_file_id = buf.file#  v$bh
    GROUP BY df.tablespace_name, df.file_name, buf.lock_element_addr
      HAVING COUNT(*) > 1;
```

provides you with the count of PCM locks that are locking your buffers by data file. The ideal situation is to have no more than one PCM lock per buffer, but this may not always be practical. If you have two or more buffers covered by the one PCM lock, false collisions can occur, which can adversely affect performance. See GC_FILES_TO_LOCKS and the other INIT.ORA parameters mentioned earlier in this chapter to obtain more information on how to set PCM locks.

V$PING

This view provides you more information on the specific object that has been pinged to another instance. It is probably better to use the FILE_PING view (described later in this section) because it runs faster and is more accurate. Don't forget to recreate the EXT_TO_OBJ table by running *catparr.sql* again before accessing the output of this view.

The most common causes of file contention highlighted by this view are the following:

- Free list contention, which is occurs when you are inserting into a table. This can be recognized by a single block having multiple copies in the SGA. If the block is the second block in the table, it is fair to assume that free list contention is occurring. Increase the values of the FREELIST GROUPS and FREELISTS parameters, as described in the section called "Tables, Indexes, and Clusters" earlier in this chapter.

- Index contention, which is caused by inserts or deletes on an indexed table. You can query V$PING to see the number of data blocks in the first extent of the index that have multiple copies in the SGA and have a high number of pings. If the problem is substantial, it can usually can be solved only by partitioning the usage of the index perhaps by adding an instance specific column to the leading part of the index key, for example,

```
# indexcnt.sql
SELECT  usr.name, vp.name, vp.kind, SUM(vp.xnc),
   SUM  (vp.lock_element_addr)
  FROM  sys.user$ usr, v$ping vp
 WHERE  vp.owner# = usr.user#
 GROUP  BY usr.name, vp.name, vp.kind;
```

V$CACHE

This view shows the full contents of the buffer cache, whether the blocks have been pinged or not. You will find this view useful for tuning the buffer cache, as well as tuning parallel server. The purpose of the view is to ensure that the contents of the buffer cache are as you would expect them to be for optimal performance and to pinpoint the objects that are experiencing pinging. Objects that are pinging excessively may be tables, clusters, indexes, or rollback segments. If a particular object has excessive pings and is sharing a tablespace, you may consider placing it into its own tablespace and placing a high number of PCM locks against its data files using the INIT.ora parameter GC_FILES_TO_LOCKS.

V$LOCK_ELEMENT

This view contains one entry for each PCM lock that is used by the buffer cache. The total number of PCM locks is controlled by the GC_DB_LOCKS parameter. PCM locks are used to protect one or more database blocks. They are all maintained in the v$lock_element table. The following query shows the number of blocks allocated for each block class:

```
# classblk.sql
SELECT  class, count(*)
  FROM  v$lock_element
  GROUP BY class;
```

The following query shows the average number of blocks protected by each class:

```
# classavg.sql
SELECT  class, avg(block_count)
  FROM  v$lock_element
  GROUP BY class;
```

V$CACHE_LOCK

This view is useful if your operating system lock manager provides you with tools for monitoring PCM locks that are occurring. You must first identify the lock element by providing the index and class and join to the V$BH view using the lock_element_addr column.

V$LOCKS_WITH_COLLISIONS and V$FALSE_PING

These views provide you with information on false ping activity in your instance. Ideally, you should investigate all of your instances using these views. If false ping activity is high, increase GC_FILES_TO_LOCKS for the data files that are experiencing the highest numbers of false pings.

V$LOCKS_WITH_COLLISIONS

This view groups by the PCM lock (lock_element_addr) and lists all PCM locks that have at least two buffers assigned (where each buffer has been pinged at least 100 times). The assumption is made that false pings will occur because of the buffers being mapped to the same PCM lock. If the readings are substantial, once again you should increase your PCM locks. If that can't be done because of memory or DLM limitations, you should redesign your objects to make them partitioned.

V$FALSE_PING

This view shows each object and file that has buffers that have been pinged more than 100 times and that share a PCM lock with another buffer that has also been pinged 100 times. The assumption is that the likelihood of false pinging under this scenario is extremely high. Once again, increase your PCM locks using the GC_DB_LOCKS and GC_FILES_TO_LOCKS parameters.

V$LOCK_ACTIVITY

This view shows the DLM lock operations that are currently occurring. To determine if there is lock contention, use the following query. It tells you the number of lock operations that caused writes to the database and the number of blocks written:

```
# blkwrits.sql
SELECT value / (a.counter + b.counter + c.counter) "Ping Rate"
  FROM v$sysstat,
    v$lock_activity a,
    v$lock_activity b,
    v$lock_activity c
WHERE a.from_val      = 'X'
  AND a.to_val        = 'NULL'
  AND b.from_val      = 'X'
  AND b.to_val        = 'S'
  AND c.from_val      = 'X'
  AND c.to_val        = 'SSX'
  AND name            = 'DBWR cross instance writes';
```

If Ping Rate < 1, DBWR is writing fast enough: no writes to the database are occurring as a result of lock activity.

If Ping Rate = 1, each lock activity that has potential to cause a write to disk does cause a write to occur.

If Ping Rate > 1, false pings are definitely occurring. The percentage of false pings is (Ping Rate − 1) / Ping Rate * 100. Increase your PCM locks.

FILE_PING

This view provides you with the number of files pinged per data file. The frequency column in the view indicates the number of times that a block has been pinged. This will help you set GC_FILES_TO_LOCKS on a per data file basis and GC_DB_LOCKS to indicate the overall number of PCM locks available. This view provides you with similar information to V$PING and should be used in preference to it because it runs faster and is more accurate.

```
# filelock.sql
SELECT ts_name "Tablespace", file_name, frequency
  FROM file_ping;
```

FILE_LOCK

This view is essential background information in establishing the spread of locks across a data file, as set by the GC_FILES_TO_LOCKS parameter. For example,

```
# filelock.sql
SELECT ts_name "Tablespace", file_name, start_lk, nlocks, blocking
  FROM file_lock;
```

The start_lk column indicates the first lock corresponding to the data file; *nlocks* is the number of locks allocated to the data file; and *blocking* is the number of blocks that each PCM lock protects.

Using V$SYSSTAT

V$SYSSTAT has several other statistics that are useful in tuning parallel server. Run the following:

```
# globlcks.sql
SELECT substr(name, 1, 25), COUNT(*)
  FROM v$sysstat
 WHERE name LIKE 'global%'
    OR name LIKE 'nxt scns gotten%';

"global lock converts (async)"  are mostly PCM locks
"global lock converts (non sync)"  are mostly used for SCN locks
"global lock gets (non async)"  are mostly Table and Transaction
        locks opens
"global lock releases (async)"  are mostly Table and Transaction
        lock closes
"next scns gotten without going to DLM" are SCN locks
```

Continue to tune as long as tuning continues to decrease the number of locks shown in the output for a consistent level of workload. Reducing lock converts will also improve your scalability. This report does not show fine-grained locking which is an option in Oracle7.3 and later.

Here is another ratio from the V$SYSSTAT that demonstrates the scalability of your parallel server site:

```
# convert.sql
SELECT  ((a.value + c.value + d.value) - b.value) * 100
                   /
          (a.value + c.value + d.value)   "Lock Conversion Ratio"
    FROM v$sysstat a, v$sysstat b, v$sysstat c, v$sysstat d
   WHERE a.name = 'consistent gets'
     AND b.name = 'async lock converts';
     AND c.name = 'db block changes';
     AND d.name = 'consistent changes';
```

If you have fully tuned your parallel server site and your lock conversion ratio drops below 95%, there is a strong possibility that your site will not scale as new nodes are added. Once again, remember that this query does not take Oracle7.3 and later fine-grained locking into account.

13

Tuning Parallel Query

This chapter describes Oracle's parallel query option (PQO)—introduced with the release of Oracle7.1—and makes recommendations on how to use it most effectively. It also discusses other Oracle features you should use with PQO to get the best possible performance. Many of the INIT.ORA parameters that we describe in this chapter will improve your performance even if you are not using PQO.

We are always amazed at the number of people who believe that parallel server is the same as parallel query and at how few sites use parallel query—let alone use it effectively. How does parallel query differ from parallel server? Parallel server uses multiple instances and their associated System Global Areas (SGAs) against a single database and, by doing so, helps with your site's scalability and recoverability. Parallel query, on the other hand, uses multiple processes against a single database and has the primary purpose of improving your site's performance. To complicate matters, parallel server and parallel query can be used together—at least in theory. Using the two together is an option, not a necessity; and to the best of our knowledge, the two features are rarely used together. Our advice to sites that are not currently using PQO is to start using it. Oracle7.1.6 and later versions have made huge advances in PQO's ability to improve your site's performance.

Introduction to Parallel Query

The parallel query option can provide you with impressive performance improvements if it is used appropriately. Before reading any further, be aware that PQO will help only with database queries that perform at least one full table scan. Note, though, that PQO can be used even if only part of the query contains a full table scan. A typical example may be a join in which one table is accessed via a full table scan and the other via an index.

Users of tuned OLTP applications with large numbers of concurrent users rarely experience improved online performance when they use PQO. Nevertheless, OLTP applications still have their long-running overnight reports, data loads, and large tables and indexes to administer, which makes PQO a valuable option. PQO is most useful for long-running batch reporting, overnight data loads, and many of the long-running database administration tasks, such as rebuilding indexes, performing database reorganizations, and performing database recovery. It is also often useful for conversions and is a must for decision support applications. PQO provides you with the largest benefits when dealing with very large tables, especially when indexes on the tables are being sorted or created.

At present, the parallel query option is not free of charge. Oracle bills you for it, classifying it as a separate option to the Oracle7 Server. Is it worth purchasing? Before you make the decision on whether to purchase PQO, consider the characteristics described in the following sections.

System Architecture

PQO can usually optimize your processing only if you are using symmetric multiprocessors (SMPs), massively parallel systems (MPPs), or loosely coupled systems (clusters). Although PQO will run on other configurations, it will often make your processing run considerably more slowly on those systems. The exception is where a full table access without sorting and joining is I/O bound on a single-processor machine. In this case, you can often improve your performance by striping your table and using PQO. (Most single-processor machines that have a well laid out and properly tuned database and application are CPU-bound, not I/O-bound.) If your machine fits the configuration required and your application is suited to PQO, it may provide excellent performance improvements.

Oracle Features

Oracle is very committed to PQO. Each new release of Oracle7 improves an already proven performance-enhancing product. We have observed performance improvements of as much as a factor of five using Oracle7.2 compared with Oracle7.1. Oracle7.3 PQO is even faster. Oracle7.2 provided the statement CREATE TABLE *tname* AS SELECT * FROM *tname*, which has the ability to run in parallel mode both in selecting the data and in inserting it into the new table. The option enforces the NOT NULL and other *check constraints* as the rows are inserted. Oracle7.3 went one step further in significantly improving the parallel query optimization, which is now built into the access path selection. The optimizer is aware of the number of CPUs on the machine and the number of disks that store the table. It may choose a parallel table scan, which is cheaper than a sequential index scan. The EXPLAIN PLAN feature has been expanded to provide additional information to assist the tuning task prior to running your query.

Other new features that Oracle has provided with each major release include:

- Oracle7.1.3: parallel index creation
- Oracle7.1.5: direct reading (avoiding the buffer cache)
- Oracle7.2: the ability to create a table as SELECT in PARALLEL, sort direct write (avoiding having to write through the buffer cache), an index direct write (avoiding the buffer cache), and an UNRECOVERABLE option (which avoids writing to the redo logs) for index and table creation
- Oracle7.3: hash join, histograms, MPP device affinity, parallel anti-join to speed up NOT IN, Cartesian product, parallel UNION and UNION ALL, and async readahead

PQO Architecture and Operation

The parallel query architecture is shown in Figure 13-1.

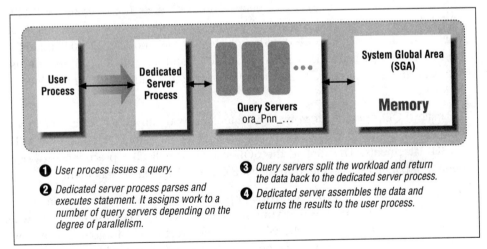

Figure 13-1. Parallel query architecture

The dedicated server process has the ability to partition some types of queries to assist with throughput. If a sort statement is written as follows:

```
SELECT /*+ PARALLEL(electoral_roll 2) */ *
  FROM electoral_roll
  ORDER BY surname;
```

PQO may assign two query servers to select the data from the electoral_roll table: one query server process to sort A to M and one query server to sort N to Z. What this means is that even though the degree of parallelism is 2, the actual number of server processes may be five: Two are used to retrieve rows from the database, two are used to sort the data retrieved, and the fifth process is the dedicated server process.

The operations that can take advantage of PQO include the following:

- Full table scans

- Sorts for GROUP BY, ORDER BY, DISTINCT, and JOINS as long as there is at least one full table scan in the query

- Sort merge and nested loop JOINS, as long as there is at least one full table scan in the query

- Aggregation including GROUP BY, MIN, MAX, and AVG, as long as a full table scan is performed

- Hash joins in Oracle7.3 and later

- CREATE TABLE *tname* AS SELECT * FROM *tname*; if you are using Oracle7.2 or later

You can use PQO for SELECT statements, and subqueries in UPDATE, DELETE, INSERT, and CREATE TABLE statements. The PQO does not operate for INSERT, UPDATE, and DELETE statements, except in subqueries. UNION, INTERSECT, and MINUS are also not parallelized, although the UNION and UNION ALL are able to be run in parallel using hash joins in Oracle7.3 and later. PQO can also be used for performing parallel loads into a table using SQL*Loader and parallel recovery of a database.

To make PQO operate for your SQL statement, you can either set a hint in your statement or set the degree of parallelism using the CREATE TABLE or ALTER TABLE statements. The hint in the SQL statement will take precedence over the degree of parallelism specified in the CREATE or ALTER table statement.

In special cases, we recommend the use of hints to make your statement self-documenting and to ensure that your statement uses PQO consistently even when the PARALLEL clause against the table is set incorrectly or is forgotten. The downside of using hints is that you cannot always guarantee that a hint will work—for example, when the hint refers to an index that does not exist. Another reason why you may reconsider using hints is if you perform a hardware upgrade.

```
SELECT /*+ PARALLEL(electoral_roll, 2) */ *
  FROM electoral_roll
  ORDER BY surname;
```

If you use a table alias, you must specify the alias in the hint as shown in the following example:

```
SELECT /*+ PARALLEL(er, 2) */ *
  FROM electoral_roll er
  ORDER BY surname;
```

If you do not wish to use PQO for the query, enter the following statement:

```
SELECT /*+ NOPARALLEL */ *
   FROM electoral_roll
   ORDER BY surname;
```

To specify the number of servers in the CREATE TABLE statement, structure the statement as follows:

```
CREATE TABLE electoral_roll
    (Electoral_No  NUMBER(10)   NOT NULL
     Surname       VARCHAR2(40) NOT NULL)
   STORAGE  (INITIAL 200M NEXT 200M)
   PARALLEL (DEGREE 2);
```

In the example shown, the degree of parallelism equals 2. If PARALLEL is specified without a degree of parallelism (2 in the example), Oracle obtains the degree of parallelism based on an estimate of the size of the table and the INIT.ORA parameter PARALLEL_DEFAULT_SCANSIZE. Oracle7.3 makes the parameter PARALLEL_DEFAULT_SCANSIZE obsolete and replaces it with a much more sensible default (the number of CPUs on your machine or the number of disk devices that the table is spread across, whichever is smaller).

NOTE   You have the option of specifying the PARALLEL 5 syntax or PARALLEL (DEGREE 5) syntax in your DDL statements. Both have the same meaning.

The following example alters the table's degree of parallelism:

```
ALTER TABLE electoral_roll
PARALLEL (DEGREE 2);
```

The next statement turns off PQO for full table scans against the table:

```
ALTER TABLE electoral_roll
NOPARALLEL;
```

We strongly recommend that you not rely on Oracle's estimate of the degree of parallelism for a table or index. Always specify the degree of parallelism if you use the PARALLEL in the CREATE or ALTER TABLE command (e.g., PARALLEL (DEGREE 4); not simply PARALLEL). As we've mentioned, you also have the option to specify the degree of parallelism using a hint in the SQL statement, which gives you total control over the degree of parallelism for each statement. If the SQL statement has a WHERE clause that will use an existing index, such as the statement shown below, the index will be used in preference to the parallel full table scan, despite the fact that the table has been created with the parallel option.

```
SELECT *
  FROM electoral_roll er
 WHERE state_code in ('VIC', 'NSW')
 ORDER BY surname;
```

If you wish to use the parallel query processing and force a full table scan, use the following query:

```
SELECT /*+ PARALLEL(er, 2)  FULL(er) */ *
  FROM electoral_roll er
 WHERE state_code in ('VIC', 'NSW')
 ORDER BY surname;
```

The PARALLEL hint does not force a full table scan all by itself. It simply provides Oracle with the degree of parallelism to use if a full table scan is required. To force a full table scan, you must use the PARALLEL and FULL hints together.

PQO Design Considerations

This section describes some of the design issues you'll have to face when considering the use of the parallel query option.

Denormalized Summary Tables and/or PQO

PQO provides the largest benefit to applications in which large tables need to be scanned, for example, a financial transaction table. In such an application, each account may have many thousands of financial transactions. All together, the table may contain hundreds of millions of transactions spread over five financial years of data. Usually, the design decision for an application of this kind will be made to create a denormalized summary table by financial year, with running financial totals. You might also consider having a summary table on a per-account, per-financial year basis, because financial year totals are commonly queried online and by batch reports. The denormalized tables would usually be maintained by application source code (or trigger) at the time the transaction is applied to the database.

PQO purists may argue that denormalized summary tables are unnecessary, because you can scan a huge table using PQO considerably faster than you could perform a serial table scan (not using PQO). Our experience has been that the summary tables will usually run considerably faster than PQO. PQO is of most benefit in cases in which the access rules to the table are not so obvious. For example, what if your users require all kinds of summary information and need to access the data in a multitude of groupings? You have to maintain many summary tables, and PQO is ideally suited to this scenario.

Our recommendation is to treat each case on its merits. There are no hard-and-fast rules about whether your application should use PQO. If the summary access path requirements are well-defined it is usually best for your application to maintain summary tables as the transactions are entered. If the access rules are not well-defined or if there are too many summary tables to maintain, use PQO. Having too many summary tables has an adverse effect on OLTP user response times if the application has to continually maintain them. If you do decide that it is more efficient to create summary tables using PQO, make use of the UNRECOVERABLE clause.

Deciding On an Index or PQO

Parallel query processing adds a new dimension to the question of whether it is better to retrieve data using an index or a full table scan. The parallel query option is able to scan the table significantly faster than a full table scan running serially if the table is striped across disks and if the query is running on a multi-CPU computer.

Gone is the old rule of thumb that you should perform a full table scan rather than use an index if more than 15% of the rows in a table are to be retrieved. The exact percentage depends on the length of the row and the total length of the columns in the index. With PQO, the correct figure may be nearer to 5% because while index search response times remain the same, now full table scans can be performed significantly faster using PQO.

However, if the entire set of columns being retrieved in the SELECT statement is being stored in the index, the figure may be closer to 30% or 40%. This is because all of the required data can be retrieved from the index without having to access the table. Obtaining data from the index often requires significantly fewer physical reads, depending on the length of the index columns compared to the length of the rows in the table. The index will be much more efficient if it includes an ORDER BY and if the index columns in the index are in the same sequence as those in the ORDER BY. The index can be used to retrieve the rows in the correct order without having to sort the rows in temporary segments. Under these circumstances, you should use the index in preference to using PQO.

Assume that a table named electoral_roll has an index ER_INDX1 on the columns (state_code, surname). The statement

```
SELECT state_code, surname
  FROM electoral_roll
 WHERE state_code in ('VIC', 'NSW')
 ORDER BY state_code, surname;
```

can be replaced by

```
SELECT  /*+ INDEX_ASC (electoral_roll er_indx1) */
           state_code, surname
   FROM electoral_roll
  WHERE state_code in ('VIC', 'NSW');
```

or you could use

```
SELECT  /*+ INDEX_ONLY (electoral_roll er_indx1) */
           state_code, surname
   FROM electoral_roll
  WHERE state_code in ('VIC', 'NSW');
```

Notice that the ORDER BY command has been removed from the statement, and we are now relying on the index to provide the rows in the desired sequence. No sorting is required, nor is any access to the table.

If you run the EXPLAIN PLAN and confirm that an index-only search is being performed, we recommend that you leave the ORDER BY in the statement. This will make your statement more understandable to people who have not read this chapter. It will also return the rows in the correct order, even if a new index is created that makes the original index specified in the hint redundant. You may have a new index on STATE_CODE, SURNAME, and a new column FIRST_INITIAL and decide to remove the original index. The latest Oracle (7.1.6 and later) optimizers are smart enough to realize that the index satisfies your sorting requirements without having to go to the table.

If the rows have to be retrieved in descending order, you can use the following hint:

```
SELECT  /*+ INDEX_DESC (electoral_roll er_indx1) */
           state_code, surname
   FROM electoral_roll
  WHERE state_code in ('VIC', 'NSW')
  ORDER BY state_code desc surname desc;
```

If you are after all of the rows, not just those in which the state_code is ('VIC', 'NSW'), simply remove the WHERE clause; the rows will still be retrieved in sequence.

The following statement will also retrieve the indexed rows in ascending sequence without having to access the table. It is probably better to use hints, however, unless you are still using Oracle Version 6.

```
SELECT  state_code, surname
    FROM electoral_roll
  WHERE  state_code > chr(1)
         AND surname   > chr(1);
```

We recommend that you use the INDEX_ASC hint and the ORDER BY clause (make ascending order explicit because Oracle continually warns us that ascending order for indexes may not be the default behavior in the future). A word of warning: Don't rely too heavily on hints. Oracle will ignore the hint if it is faulty in any way. Run your statements through EXPLAIN PLAN to ensure that the statement will be processed as you would expect it to be.

There is some concern among DBAs that creating indexes using PQO could potentially cause the index entries to be stored in ascending order. This is not true. The resulting index has all of the properties of a serially created index.

Purging Strategies

Purging strategies are often overlooked until an application enters production. At that point, sites begin to realize that their large tables are becoming difficult to manage because of the size of both the table and its associated indexes. Usually, a large percentage of the data in the tables is not required and can be purged. However, deleting rows from large tables is very inefficient. It takes a huge amount of time, and the tables' overall size is not reduced unless you rebuild the table and its indexes. PQO provides huge run-time reductions when combined with the UNRECOVERABLE option of the CREATE TABLE and CREATE INDEX and the COMPATIBLE and SORT_DIRECT_WRITES INIT.ORA parameters.

Another excellent feature that expedites the purging task is partition views, introduced with Oracle7.3. You simply recreate the view to remove the oldest table and to include a new table. You can then back up and drop the oldest table. All this can be done with little interruption to your users.

Partition views are created by putting CHECK constraints on a table:

```
ALTER TABLE fin_transactions_94 ADD CONSTRINT C_FIN_YR_94
        CHECK (transaction_date between '01-jul-94' and '30-jun-95');
ALTER TABLE fin_transactions_95 ADD CONSTRINT C_FIN_YR_95
        CHECK (transaction_date between '01-jul-95' and '30-jun-96');
ALTER TABLE fin_transactions_96 ADD CONSTRINT C_FIN_YR_96
        CHECK (transaction_date between '01-jul-96' and '30-jun-97');
```

You can now create a view as follows:

```
CREATE_VIEW all_fin_transactions AS
        SELECT *
          FROM fin_transactions_94
        UNION ALL
        SELECT *
```

```
        FROM fin_transactions_95
     UNION ALL
   SELECT *
     FROM fin_transactions_96;
```

If you enter the query

```
SELECT SUM(transaction_amount)
  FROM all_fin_transactions
WHERE transaction_date between '01-aug-1995' and '02-aug-1996';
```

the query will scan the tables FIN_TRANSACTIONS_95 and FIN_TRANSACTIONS_96, thus avoiding the much larger table scan that would have been needed if the FIN_TRANSACTIONS_94 table had been included in the same table.

Full Table Scans and Indexes

Another design consideration that is relevant to PQO is the situation in which a nested loop or merge join occurs where one of your tables is accessed by using a full table scan and PQO and the other table(s) are accessed by using an index. The indexed table will potentially cause a severe bottleneck if each row returned from the driving table using the PQO servers has to then have an index scan followed by a disk I/O to retrieve that data from the table. Attempt to store all of the columns required by the statement from the indexed table into the index to avoid the disk I/O to the table.

Skew and Striping

Another issue that you should consider is the skew of your data. If you are using Oracle's striping facility and are having your data entered via OLTP transactions, the OLTP query servers may have an unbalanced workload, particularly if a sort or table join is involved. If your table stores financial transactions and you are using PQO to retrieve all of the rows for the current financial year, one data file is likely to return all of the required dates that satisfies your WHERE clause. You should ideally use operating system striping under these circumstances.

When the tables are huge, some sites split their tables up by financial year, which improves manageability. It also provides the opportunity for you to use Oracle striping and achieve load sharing.

Constructing Your Database for PQO

When you construct your database, your major goal is to share the disk I/O load across disks to avoid I/O bottlenecks. Before you decide how to configure your database to use PQO effectively, realize that accessing data in memory is considerably faster than accessing data from disk. A single processor demanding data from a disk will invariably have to wait because the disk will not be able to provide data quickly enough to keep the processor occupied (unless the processor is performing resource-consuming tasks such as sorting or joining to other tables). Having multiple PQO query processes accessing the disk will worsen the disk bottleneck. You *must* stripe your tables to use PQO effectively.

This section lists a set of rules to follow, or at least consider, in creating a database for PQO. Some of the rules are obvious, such as the need to stripe; others are rules that we've learned only as a result of our many PQO benchmarks.

1. Stripe the table or index that is being accessed using PQO across multiple disks using either Oracle's striping facility or operating system striping. What is Oracle striping? Oracle stripes are created by using the CREATE TABLESPACE command, where the tablespace contains several data files, each located on a different disk. The table or index is created with INITIAL and NEXT sizing that fits nicely into each file and a MINEXTENTS clause equal to the number of files. Oracle7.2 and later PQO uses Oracle striping very effectively. It allocates extents (data files) to each query process in a round-robin fashion. Oracle striping is also standard Oracle and is generic across all machine types.

   Use operating system striping if your machine provides it and your tables or indexes are used by OLTP users as well as for PQO processing. Use Oracle striping if your machine does not offer operating system striping or if your table is used exclusively for PQO operations, Oracle striping usually provides better performance than operating system striping for PQO operations.

   Of course Oracle and operating system striping are not mutually exclusive. As we've mentioned, Oracle7.2 and later provides round-robin data file allocation of query servers; it may pay for your site to have multi dimensional striping using both Oracle and operating system striping for the best performance and flexibility.

2. Ensure that your disk controllers are not creating a bottleneck. Be aware of which disks are on which controllers, and stripe your tables/indexes across disks that are on different controllers

3. If you are using UNIX operating system striping, avoid using cooked files unless you are using asynchronous or direct I/Os. If you are not using asynchronous or direct I/Os, use raw devices. If you find raw devices difficult and are striping cooked files, monitor your disk I/Os to ensure that they are spread evenly across your disks. If they aren't, either use raw devices or consider Oracle striping.

   We have found that on certain UNIX machines, using cooked files for striping has resulted in the first disk's I/Os exceeding the remaining disks I/Os. This is caused by the inode having its modified date continually updated. If this is the case on your machine, you should use raw devices.

4. Stripe the indexes being created using PQO across multiple disks by using either Oracle's striping facility or operating system striping. Ideally, have the same number of stripes on the index as you have on the table from which it is created.

5. If you are creating a table by selecting from another using Oracle7.2 PQO, be sure that both tables are striped to avoid potential bottlenecks.

6. If you are performing a sort that requires writing to the temporary segments on disk (the entire sort cannot be performed in memory), make sure that you have your temporary segments striped across several disks. The number of disks that are striped across should equal the largest degree of parallelism that you use for the tables being sorted.

It is nice to make your extent sizes a multiple of the SORT_AREA_SIZE. This does not provide a huge performance benefit, however, because the sort data is often written from memory to disk in variable-sized chunks (particularly if you are using a large SORT_AREA_SIZE). The size of the chunks depends on many factors, including internal memory fragmentation. The extent size should be large enough—for example, 100 megabytes—to avoid contention for the ST00 lock. Prior to Oracle7.2, this lock can effectively make a parallel sort perform like a serial sort if your extents are too small.

If you have a mix of OLTP users and parallel query users, you should ideally have one temporary tablespace specifically set up for parallel query sort requirements and another with significantly smaller DEFAULT settings for the OLTP users. Use the ALTER USER TEMPORARY TABLESPACE *temp_large* to point the users to the appropriate temporary tablespace.

7. If you are using Oracle7.3, create a tablespace specifically for temporary segments, (CREATE TABLESPACE *temp* TEMPORARY). The temporary tablespace cannot contain permanent objects (tables, indexes, rollback segments, etc.). Oracle maintains a separate cache of extents that it allocates to temporary segments and hash joins. This effectively avoids contention on the ST00 lock mentioned above. Don't forget to set the COMPATIBLE parameter to whatever version of Oracle7 you are running (e.g., 7.1.5, 7.2.1, or 7.3.1). If you are using Oracle7.2 or later, set SORT_DIRECT_WRITES=TRUE to gain considerable performance gains by bypassing the buffer cache for sorting.

8. Consider placing into its own tablespace each large table being accessed by PQO and each index being created by PQO. This gives you greater flexibility in striping and moving the data file across disks. If you have multiple jobs performing many simultaneous operations, it also allows you to more easily

identify the I/O for a particular table or index (via SQL*DBA and V$FILESTAT table monitoring).

9. If you decide to use operating system striping, be aware that Oracle will read the DB_BLOCK_SIZE * DB_FILE_MULTIBLOCK_READ_COUNT and set your stripe size to that size or to a multiple of that size. For example, if you have a DB_BLOCK_SIZE of 4 kilobytes and a DB_FILE_MULTIBLOCK_READ_COUNT of 16, set the stripe size to 64 kilobytes. Note that the largest multi-block I/O that Oracle is able to read on most platforms is 64 kilobytes. You also need to consider the proposed usage of the object. For example, set the stripe size large (e.g., 64 kilobytes), for tables and temporary segments that are used exclusively for long-running batch work, including PQO processing. Indexes and tables used for OLTP processing can be given a smaller stripe size (e.g., 8 kilobytes).

10. Size the extent sizes in your table or index to minimize the number of extents, for example, CREATE TABLE... STORAGE (INITIAL 500M NEXT 500M PCTINCREASE 0 MINEXTENTS 10). This will provide improved performance because it keeps Oracle from having to continually modify the UET$ and FET$ that are tables used to record extent information. Oracle7.3 allows an unlimited number of extents per database object, but there is still a negative performance impact when a large number of extents are thrown.

11. When you load data into the table using SQL*Loader, the first extent of the table is not used. Set your INITIAL extent small in your CREATE TABLE statement, for example, STORAGE (INITIAL 1k NEXT 500M). If you are using Oracle striping, make sure that you size your initial data file accordingly, that is, (INITIAL extent size + 1 * NEXT extent size).

12. If you use massively parallel processors in conjunction with Oracle striping, each file in the tablespace should ideally be local to a different node in the MPP.

13. If your table is scanned multiple times and you have enough memory, consider storing your entire table in cache using the ALTER TABLE tname CACHE. Caching a table provides an alternative to PQO that you should consider when benchmarking. If your statement contains joins to other tables, caching the table may provide disappointing performance improvements. This is because the bottlenecks are in obtaining the joined rows, not in initially reading data from the driving table. If you are joining and using Oracle7.3 or later, it may pay to dedicate more memory to hash joins instead.

14. Oracle7.3 has a new command that we recommend you use to create an index from an existing index (ALTER INDEX index_name REBUILD), which can be built in parallel. It can also be built by using the UNRECOVERABLE clause, which avoids writing to the redo logs and speeds up the index build

considerably. Interestingly, UNRECOVERABLE is the default if your redo logs are not being archived.

15. Oracle7.3 also introduced bitmapped indexing, which speeds up the index creation and reduces storage requirements considerably. Bitmapped indexing is most effective for single-column low-cardinality data, for example, (YES, NO) or (ON, OFF) or (MALE, FEMALE). If your table has low cardinality, use bitmapped indexes.

16. If you are using the cost-based optimizer, it is essential to get a large enough sample to share the PQO sort load sharing. For PQO index creation and sorting, the base table is randomly sampled to find sort keys, which are then evenly divided and handed to sort processes. Poor sampling will lead to one of the sort processes causing a bottleneck. Prior to 7.1.6, Oracle recommends that you use the ANALYZE statement to sample around 20% of the rows or use the rule-based optimizer and hints. For Oracle7.1.6 and later, you should sample as many rows as possible using the compute option with the ANALYZE statement. Generally, analyzing 5% or more of the rows provides superior performance.

   Oracle7.3 introduces histograms that you should take advantage of for superior distribution of workload. An interesting characteristic of histograms is that to make them work effectively, you should pass constant values to them, rather than bind variables. This implies that each statement will be stored separately in the shared pool area. The performance gains that histograms provide heavily outweigh the disadvantage of storing multiple statements in the shared pool area.

17. Always set your PCTINCREASE to 0 for tables, indexes, and temporary segments used by PQO.

18. Ensure that you have enough space in your database to fit your tables, indexes, and temporary extents. Some parallel operations use the INITIAL extent size for all query servers; others use the NEXT extent size. To avoid confusion, make the INITIAL and NEXT extents the same size. Be aware that if you have 10 query servers and an extent size of 100 megabytes, you will need 1 gigabyte of disk space free, even though the eventual object size may be somewhat smaller after Oracle performs trimming.

INIT.ORA Parameters

You must set several INIT.ORA parameters correctly to use PQO to best advantage. The parameters that will have the largest effect on PQO performance are PARALLEL_MAX_SERVERS (maximum number of parallel query servers available on your instance) and COMPATIBLE and SORT_DIRECT_WRITES (avoid reading and writing through the buffer cache). Other recommended parameter settings are listed in this section. The Oracle buffer cache bottleneck has been a huge headache when running multiple large batch jobs simultaneously or when OLTP users run at the same time as large batch jobs. You can improve performance quite a bit by avoiding the buffer cache for sort data as well as for data being read by PQO. Take advantage of the use of COMPATIBLE and SORT_DIRECT_WRITES. The SORT_AREA_SIZE parameter can also have a significant effect on PQO performance.

Note that Oracle7.3 has attacked the major multiprocessor points of contention by providing multiple LRU lists and multiple SQL latches.

PARALLEL_MAX_SERVERS

Maximum number of servers that are allowed to exist concurrently. If you set your maximum servers to 20 and you have five SQL statements requesting a degree of parallelism of 5 each, the fifth statement will be forced to run a full table scan using a single server. Set the value to:

maximum number of PQO users * their maximum degree of parallelism * 2

PARALLEL_MIN_SERVERS

Number of servers that are created when an instance starts. Oracle will spawn more server processors as required, which does provide a small overhead on performance. The performance overhead is most noticeable when you are processing a small table. The number of servers can be reduced as queries complete and the server is idle for the amount of time specified in the PARALLEL_SERVER_IDLE_TIME parameter. The number of servers running never falls below the value specified in PARALLEL_MIN_SERVERS.

PARALLEL_SERVER_IDLE_TIME

Number of minutes that a server remains idle before Oracle can terminate it.

PARALLEL_DEFAULT_MAX_SCANS

Maximum degree of parallelism available for any full table scan.

PARALLEL_DEFAULT_SCANSIZE

Used to calculate the degree of parallelism for a table that has been created or altered using the PARALLEL option (without a degree of parallelism specified for it). We recommend that prior to Oracle7.3, you do not rely on Oracle's calculating the degree of parallelism. Specify the degree of parallelism using either a hint in the SQL statement or as a parameter in the CREATE TABLE or ALTER TABLE statement (PARALLEL 4). This parameter is made obsolete in Oracle7.3. The new setting for the default degree of parallelism is either the number of disks across which the table is spread or the number of CPUs on your machine, whichever is smaller.

PARALLEL_MIN_PERCENT

A new parameter introduced in Oracle7.3. If a query has a degree of parallelism requirement and is unable to obtain the percentage of query servers specified in this parameter, the query will terminate with an error. The default value for this parameter is 0, which allows your query to run with whatever resources are available. If you have long-running jobs that run considerably faster if they are able to use the full quota of query servers, it may pay to set this parameter to 50 or higher and restart the query when the required number of servers becomes available.

COMPATIBLE

Set to the release of the Oracle RDBMS that you are currently running; if you do this, you will be able to take full advantage of any new features that are provided. This inappropriately named parameter can provide you with huge performance improvements. Oracle7.1.5 introduced the ability to bypass the buffer cache (direct reads) for table scans and sorts (COMPATIBLE=7.1.5). Oracle7.3 introduced temporary tablespaces that improve the performance of sorts and hash joins (COMPATIBLE=7.3.1).

SORT_READ_FAC

Assists sort merges. The setting of this parameter influences a sort's internal memory allocation and optimizer decisions. We recommend that you set it to 25%, to 50%, or to the value set in the DB_BLOCK_MULTIBLOCK_READ_COUNT parameter.

SORT_DIRECT_WRITES

Introduced in Oracle7.2. It provides considerable performance improvements (often five times or more) through bypassing the buffer cache when writing sort data to the temporary tablespace. You must have adequate memory to take full advantage of this parameter. Each query process will have its own set of direct write buffers; the total memory requirements is (number of query servers * SORT_WRITE_BUFFERS * SORT_WRITE_BUFFER_SIZE). To enable sort direct writes, set SORT_DIRECT_WRITES=TRUE.

SORT_AREA_RETAINED_SIZE

Set to the same size as the SORT_AREA_SIZE when using PQO. The SORT_AREA_RETAINED_SIZE is the amount of memory that each query server process is assigned when sorting takes place. Given the larger size of the sorts that are normally performed when using PQO, sort memory usage will quickly increase to the SORT_AREA_SIZE. If PQO queries run at the same time as OLTP, it may pay to keep the SORT_AREA_RETAINED_SIZE at perhaps 64 kilobytes, because every single user will use the larger amount of memory. If you are running PQO out of OLTP hours, consider shutting down your database and adjusting the SORT_AREA_RETAINED_SIZE to the same size as the SORT_AREA_SIZE (1 or 2 megabytes). If your database is exclusively PQO, with few users and plenty of memory, set the SORT_AREA_ RETAINED_SIZE to 1 or 2 megabytes.

SORT_AREA_SIZE

Maximum amount of memory that each user process can use to perform sorting. If the SORT_AREA_RETAINED_SIZE is sufficient, it will not rise above it. With PQO, this parameter also represents the amount of memory assigned to sorting for each parallel query server. When the area is filled with sorted data, it is written to the temporary tablespace. Because the SORT_AREA_SIZE is assigned on a per-user basis or, in the case of PQO, on a per-parallel server basis, it can quickly consume all of your machine's memory, causing excessive paging and or swapping. OLTP users usually require between 64 and 256 kilobytes. PQO processes perform best when the SORT_AREA_SIZE is set to between 1 and 2 megabytes, although if the whole sort can be performed in memory without having to write to the temporary segments on disk, the best setting for the SORT_AREA_SIZE will be considerably larger. If PQO programs are run out of OLTP hours, consider shutting down and restarting your instance with the larger SORT_AREA_SIZE.

SHARED_POOL_SIZE

Set large enough to avoid a PQO performance bottleneck. Parallel query servers use an area within the shared pool for query server to query server communication, that is, where one process is performing a table scan and the second process is sorting the data received from the first process. One parallel query user with a high degree of parallelism tends to use more shared pool area than several parallel query users with a degree of parallelism totaling the same as the single user.

DB_BLOCK_BUFFERS

Set large enough to avoid a severe bottleneck. Generally, anything below 10 megabytes is inadequate. We recommend that you bypass the buffer cache as much as possible, particularly when PQO jobs are running at the same time as OLTP users. If you are using Oracle7.2 or later, set SORT_DIRECT_ WRITES=TRUE. Also, don't forget to set the COMPATIBLE parameter to the version of Oracle that you are currently running. If you are using 7.1.5 or later, setting COMPATIBLE correctly will cause direct reads (bypassing the buffer cache) for all full table scans and sorts. With SMP, you must set this parameter because of the added potential of performance degradation caused by latch contention in the buffer cache.

DB_BLOCK_SIZE

Set to a value such as 8 or 16 kilobytes if your database is used exclusively for long-running PQO-style jobs. Our benchmarks indicate that a minimum of

4 kilobytes should be used for an Oracle7.x database regardless of whether it is a mixed database (mixing OLTP users with batch reporting and updates), an exclusively OLTP database, or a decision support-style database with many long-running jobs and few OLTP users. Note that the default block size is 2 kilobytes on many UNIX machines.

HASH_JOIN_ENABLED

Introduced in Oracle7.3 to enable hash joins, a new innovation that provides an alternative to sort merge joins. Hash joins perform considerably faster when the number of rows being joined for the two sides of the join are significantly different. Specify HASH_JOIN_ENABLED=TRUE.

HASH_AREA_SIZE

Introduced in Oracle7.3 to provide memory for each process performing a hash join. Oracle says that this parameter can be still increased considerably in size and continue to provide excellent performance improvements. Remember that it is used on a per-process basis and that there is potential for damaging paging and swapping if it is set too high.

ALWAYS_ANTI_JOIN

Introduced in Oracle7.3. Setting it to HASH allows a parallel hash anti-join of that old resource hog, the NOT IN clause.

Setting the Degree of Parallelism

To set the optimal degree of parallelism, you must understand what it means to change its value. Increasing the value of the PARALLEL parameter by 1 creates an additional query server process (or two query server processes if the statement requires a sort; one query process reads from the table, and the other is passed the data so it can perform the sort).

Disks are always going to provide a bottleneck for today's high-speed processors. Note, however, that disk caching is advancing at a rapid rate. If multiple query processes are attacking one disk, the disk will be running red hot unless the process is required to perform a sort or join to other tables. Each query process is assigned to a CPU. If each process is performing resource-intensive tasks (CPU intensive), the CPU can become the bottleneck.

For a full table scan with no sorting or joins, we recommend that you set the degree of parallelism to the number of disks on which the table is spread. If a sort or join is involved, our benchmarks indicate that performance improvements often occur if you set the number of query processes to twice the number of CPUs available on your system. We have also found that if PQO statements hit the same tables/indexes/temporary segments, it is best to run these statements one after the next.

PQO provides the best performance improvements on SMP machines on which the data files, and hence the tables being scanned, are scattered across many disks. Our figures indicate that the number of disks across which a table is striped should be no greater than twice the number of CPUs. Ideally, the CPUs are underutilized, and there is adequate memory to dedicate to sorting. File striping can be done either automatically (using the operating system) or via the Oracle striping facility.

If you are performing a sort in your PQO processing, you must be sure that there is free memory on your system to accommodate the multiple sort areas as well as your SGA. One sort area is assigned in memory per query process. Thus if the degree of parallelism is 40 and the SORT_AREA_SIZE is 100 megabytes, you will need 4 gigabytes of sort area. If there is not adequate memory, your response times will degrade markedly as a result of damaging paging and/or swapping. It is usually best to set your sort area size to about 2 megabytes unless you can fit your whole table in memory.

Before you set the degree of parallelism, it's best to benchmark the query on the configuration and use the actual table it is intended to run against. This is not always possible, because the query may be one-time-only or the environment may not be usable for testing. Oracle provides the EXPLAIN PLAN feature (described in the section called "Using EXPLAIN PLAN to Tune PQO" later in this chapter) to help check how Oracle will use PQO. Always run it against your query to ensure that it will use PQO in the way you expect; you can use hints in your SQL statements to be sure.

You need to take the following information into account in selecting the most appropriate degree of parallelism for your SQL statement:

- The number of CPUs on your machine; generally, the degree of parallelism should never exceed twice the number of CPUs on your machine.

- Whether the tables are striped and how many disks they are striped across. Tables, indexes, and temporary segments *must* be striped to take advantage of PQO. The degree of parallelism usually should equal the number of disks for PQO with no sorting or joining.

- The sizes of the table (it's usually not worth using PQO on small tables) and whether your table can be cached into memory (if so, it may run faster than PQO).

- The limit on the number of processes on your machine (the number that will cause your PQO operation to fail).

- The speed of your CPUs and disks. These may change our parallelism recommendations, especially as disk caching improves.

- The amount of query processing on the system. It is often better to run the PQO jobs one after the next if they access the same tables or if you do not have many processors on your machine.

- The mix of database usage. For example, the same table may be used by OLTP users during the day and by PQO at night.

Ongoing Tuning of Query Servers

The ideal way to monitor and tune the query servers is to check the elapsed run time of the queries using PQO. The problem is that other factors may also be influencing response times, such as other jobs running at the same time as the PQO job. Oracle provides two tools to help with ongoing tuning: the V$PQ_SYSSTAT table and the EXPLAIN PLAN facility.

You should also be familiar with your operating system commands to monitor your disk I/Os, CPU usage, memory usage and paging, and swapping rates. You should also be able to identify your query server processes. For example, on Dynix, the query servers have the format ora_P*nnn*_DEV, where *nnn* represents the digits identifying the query server number and DEV is the database instance.

Using the V$PQ_SYSSTAT Table

The V$PQ_SYSSTAT virtual table helps with setting the INIT.ORA parameters PARALLEL_MIN_SERVERS (number of servers that are started for use when the instance is started) and PARALLEL_MAX_SERVERS (largest number of servers that may exist in your instance). When extra servers are required, they are allocated, but the total number of servers cannot exceed the value specified in PARALLEL_MAX_SERVERS.

After the query has completed, the query servers will remain active for the number of minutes specified in the PARALLEL_SERVER_IDLE_TIME. The number of servers will never fall below the PARALLEL_MIN_SERVERS setting.

To view the current status of the Oracle parallel query servers, run the following query during peak PQO usage:

```
# pqstatus.sql
SELECT statistic, value
  FROM v$pq_sysstat
/

STATISTIC                          VALUE
------------------------------  ----------
Servers Busy                          0
Servers Idle                          5
Servers Highwater                    11
```

```
Server Sessions                  33
Servers Started                   6
Servers Shutdown                  6
Servers Cleaned Up                0
Queries Initiated                 3
DFO Trees                         3
Local Msgs Sent                 304
Distr Msgs Sent                   0
Local Msgs Recv'd               288
Distr Msgs Recv'd                 0

13 rows selected.
```

Note the following about these statistics:

- If the number of servers busy is continually equal to the value assigned to PARALLEL_MAX_SERVERS, increase PARALLEL_MAX_SERVERS if you have sufficient CPU resources on your system. This prevents Oracle from having to continually start up new servers. It also means that some jobs may be missing out on the full set of servers that they require to run optimally.

- If the number of servers busy is continually higher than PARALLEL_MIN_SERVERS, consider increasing the PARALLEL_MIN_SERVERS parameter to the Servers Busy value. Starting up query servers can take time. We've noticed that starting up a database with a high number of PARALLEL_MIN_SERVERS lengthens the startup time considerably.

- If the number of servers started and shut down is occurring at a rapid rate, consider increasing the value assigned to PARALLEL_SERVER_IDLE_TIME.

We've noticed something interesting about Pro*C and the other Pro languages. Unless you explicitly specify HOLD_CURSOR=NO and RELEASE_CURSOR=YES, Oracle will keep the query servers assigned to your program. Make sure that you don't let this occur.

Other views that will be of interest to you are V$PQ_SESSTAT and V$PQ_SLAVE. V$PQ_SESSTAT gives you details on the PQO usage of your current session. V$PQ_SLAVE provides you with statistics on the amount of time that various PQO sessions have been running.

```
SQL> desc v$pq_sesstat
 Name                            Null?    Type
 ------------------------------- -------- ----
 STATISTIC                                VARCHAR2(30)
 LAST_QUERY                               NUMBER
 SESSION_TOTAL                            NUMBER
```

```
SQL> desc v$pq_slave
 Name                                   Null?    Type
 ------------------------------------   -------- ----
 SLAVE_NAME                                      VARCHAR2(4)
 STATUS                                          VARCHAR2(4)
 SESSIONS                                        NUMBER
 IDLE_TIME_CUR                                   NUMBER
 BUSY_TIME_CUR                                   NUMBER
 CPU_SECS_CUR                                    NUMBER
 MSGS_SENT_CUR                                   NUMBER
 MSGS_RCVD_CUR                                   NUMBER
 IDLE_TIME_TOTAL                                 NUMBER
 BUSY_TIME_TOTAL                                 NUMBER
 CPU_SECS_TOTAL                                  NUMBER
 MSGS_SENT_TOTAL                                 NUMBER
 MSGS_RCVD_TOTAL                                 NUMBER
```

Using EXPLAIN PLAN to Tune PQO

If you are using Oracle7.1 or Oracle7.2, examine the PLAN_TABLE using the following query:

```
# pqoplan1.sql
SELECT SUBSTR(LPAD(' ',2*level-1) ||
             DECODE(id, 0, statement_id, operation)   ||
             ' ' || options   || ' ' || object_node , 1, 79)
                         "Parallel Query Plan Step"
  FROM plan_table
  START WITH id = 0
CONNECT BY PRIOR id = parent_id
         AND PRIOR NVL(statement_id, 'X') = NVL(statement_id, 'X');
```

Pay particular attention to the OBJECT_NODE and OTHER columns. The OBJECT_NODE column shows you the order in which output from the operations is performed; the OTHER column shows you the SQL text or parallel operation that the query server is performing for each step. The problem with the other column is that it is defined as LONG. To get the SQL test, enter the following query. (Excuse the untidy layout of the query's output.)

```
# pqoplan2.sql
SELECT SUBSTR(LPAD(' ',2*level-1) ||
             DECODE(id, 0, statement_id, operation)   ||
             ' ' || options   || ' ' || object_node  , 1, 60)   , other
  FROM plan_table
START WITH id = 0
CONNECT BY PRIOR id = parent_id
         AND PRIOR NVL(statement_id, 'X') = NVL(statement_id, 'X');
```

The two parallel operations that we have observed in the OTHER column are as follows:

- Output consumed in parallel, indicating that data is being received serially and then sent to parallel query servers for parallel processing

- Operation combined with parent (child), which indicates that there is no inter-process communication between the operator and its parent or child

When analyzing the EXPLAIN PLAN, note the following:

- Correlated subqueries cannot be parallelized; convert them to joins.
- Sort/merges normally provide better performance than nested loops for PQO.
- Be aware that INDEX RANGE scans cannot be parallelized but indexes can be searched in parallel to satisfy a nested loop. Try to have all of the required columns in the INDEX if possible to avoid the read to the indexed table and an almost certain bottleneck.
- The ideal is to retrieve all of the data that you're going to need from a single table if possible. If the table is used exclusively for PQO, give serious consideration to adding some redundancy to avoid the need to join or, worse still, have subqueries.

Oracle7.3 introduced an additional column to assist with the PQO tuning task: OTHER_TAG informs you of how each PQO step is performed. Possible values are as follows:

null
> Table scan will be performed serially using a single process

serial_to_parallel
> Table is scanned using a single processor, but the data is passed to multiple processes running in parallel

parallel_to_parallel
> Full table scan is performed by a number of query processes running in parallel, and the data is passed to a second set of processes, which are also running in parallel

parallel_to_serial
> Table is scanned using multiple processes, but the data is passed to a single process

parallel_combined_with_parent
> The table is scanned in parallel, and the next step is handled by the same parallel process

parallel_combined_with_child
> Same as parallel combined with parent

Ideally, full table scans of substantial amounts of data should be performed by using parallel_to_parallel, parallel_to_serial, parallel_combined_with_parent, or parallel_combined_with_child. If you have a sort of large amounts of data and high cardinality (many distinct values), the ideal is likely to be parallel_to_parallel.

```
# pqoplan3.sql
SELECT SUBSTR(LPAD(' ',2*(level-1)) ||
           DECODE(id, 0, statement_id, operation)   ||
            ' ' || options   || ' ' || object_name   || other_tag, 1, 79)
                        "Plan Step with Parallel Path"
 FROM plan_table
 START WITH id = 0
CONNECT BY PRIOR id = parent_id
        AND PRIOR NVL(statement_id, 'X') = NVL(statement_id, 'X');
```

If you are using TKPROF with Oracle7.1 to retrieve parallel query information, you're going to be very disappointed, because parallel query usage information is totally missing. Oracle7.2 and later revisions of TKPROF provide the information that you'll need.

Creating Indexes in Parallel

PQO can significantly speed up the creation of indexes. The larger the table, the greater the performance improvement. PQO will also speed up the creation or enabling of PRIMARY KEY and UNIQUE KEY constraints when you use the USING INDEX clause of the ALTER TABLE command.

To tune index creation effectively, be aware that PQO performs these steps to create the index:

1. The base table is randomly sampled in parallel to find index keys that will evenly divide into N subranges, where N is the degree of parallelism.

2. Each producer process scans $1/N$ of the base table and sends (key, rowid) pairs to each of N consumer processes using dividing keys found in step 1.

3. Each of the N consumers sorts and builds its part of the index. The sort and the index are stored in temporary segments.

4. The N consumers pass the temporary segment database information to the coordinator, which assembles the B-tree index structure using the data passed to it from the other servers.

Your resulting index has all of the properties of a serially created index. Relying on the index to return rows in sequence works the same as it always has. Make sure that you use the INDEX_ASC or INDEX_ONLY hints.

The parallel index creates extents into one temporary extent per process. The extents are then merged into one final permanent segment. Each index *must* have at least N extents, preferably of the same size, with each stored on a separate disk.

To create an index in parallel mode, use the CREATE INDEX statement as shown in the following:

```
CREATE INDEX electoral_search_ndx1
    ON electoral_roll (electoral_zone, surname, initial)
```

```
          STORAGE (INITIAL 200m NEXT 100m)
      PARALLEL (DEGREE 6);
```

To create the index without using PQO, specify

```
CREATE INDEX electoral_search_ndx1
    ON electoral_roll (electoral_zone, surname, initial)
        STORAGE (INITIAL 200m NEXT 100m)
    NOPARALLEL;
```

If you do not specify a degree of parallelism in the CREATE INDEX command, the table's definition will be used.

Other factors that will significantly improve the performance of index creation are the UNRECOVERABLE option on the CREATE INDEX command and the Oracle7.3 option that allows you to create an index from a current index (rather than having to read from the table). Index creation requires sorting, so don't forget to tune your SORT_AREA_SIZE, and temporary tablespaces, as well as setting the COMPATIBLE (Oracle7.1.5 and later) and SORT_DIRECT_WRITE (Oracle7.2 and later) parameters.

Note that enabling a UNIQUE or PRIMARY KEY CONSTRAINT to create an index will not run in parallel. You must create the index first and then enable or add the constraint.

Using PQO to Speed Data Loads

SQL*Loader will speed up data loading if you specify DIRECT=TRUE to bypass the redo logs. PQO can further speed up data loading if it is used correctly and if your data load lends itself to parallel loading. PQO will benefit the loading of a large tables if the table is spread across a number of disk devices using either Oracle or operating system striping facilities. If the table is on a single disk drive, PQO will invariably lead to a disk I/O bottleneck.

To use PQO for data loading, issue the following SQL*Loader statements:

```
sqlload userid=gurrym/mark control=accload1.ctl direct=true parallel=true
sqlload userid=gurrym/mark control=accload2.ctl direct=true parallel=true
```

Notice that multiple SQL*Loader sessions are required to force the parallel processing. Each of the control files, *accload1.ctl* and *accload2.ctl*, will contain a FILE clause, which has a different file name assigned to it. The filename that is specified is the database file from which the temporary segments are allocated. The files specified in the FILE clause should be on different disk devices to maximize throughput.

```
LOAD DATA
INFILE   'accload.dat'
FILE  = '/tmp/acctemp1.dat'
INSERT INTO TABLE accounts ...
```

From the parallel data load, PQO uses temporary segments to load the data (as specified in the FILE parameter above). The temporary segments are merged and then inserted into the table directly above the high water mark.

Indexes do not get created during the parallel load. You must create them manually after the data load completes. You can speed up the creation of your index using the PARALLEL option. You will then have to enable your primary and unique key indexes, because there is no parallel option on the CREATE CONSTRAINT commands.

Note the use of the high-water mark, which is the farthest point to which the table has been expanded. If a high number of deletions have taken place, you may be wasting a significant amount of storage in your table. If you are deleting a lot of rows from your table, seriously consider rebuilding your table using the Oracle7.2 function UNRECOVERABLE. The ability to recreate indexes using UNRE-COVERABLE and create the indexes in PARALLEL will also help. Oracle7.3 also introduced the CREATE TABLE tname AS SELECT..., which can also be run in parallel.

Use the parallel clause as follows if you do *not* wish to use the parallel option:

```
sqlload userid=gurrym/mark control=accload1.ctl direct=true parallel=false
```

Performing Parallel Recovery

Parallel recovery can help to speed up the instance or media recovery of your database. Oracle provides an INIT.ORA parameter, RECOVERY_PARALLELISM, which specifies the number of recovery processes. The value of the parameter must be greater than 1 and must not exceed the value assigned to the PARALLEL_MAX_SERVERS parameter. The number of recovery processes can also be specified in the RECOVER command, as shown in the following examples. The RECOVER clause setting takes precedence over the RECOVERY_PARALLELISM setting.

The following command performs database recovery using 10 parallel recovery processes:

```
RECOVER DATABASE PARALLEL (DEGREE 10);
```

This command performs tablespace recovery using 10 parallel recovery processes:

```
RECOVER TABLESPACE tablespace name PARALLEL (DEGREE 10);
```

This command performs data file recovery using 10 parallel recovery processes:

```
RECOVER DATAFILE 'datafile name' PARALLEL (DEGREE 10);
```

You can also specify a RECOVER clause setting of PARALLEL (DEGREE DEFAULT) which sets the number of recovery processes to twice the number of data files being recovered, as follows:

```
RECOVER DATABASE PARALLEL (DEGREE DEFAULT);
```

To perform a recovery in serial mode (single-recovery process), do not set the RECOVERY_PARALLELISM parameter to TRUE in the INIT.ORA file and do not specify the PARALLEL option in the RECOVER clause. If the RECOVERY_PARAL-LELISM clause is set to TRUE, you can force the recovery to operate in serial mode using the command

```
RECOVER DATABASE NOPARALLEL;
```

In this case, data is read from the redo logs sequentially, and several recovery processes are started to perform the recovery to the various data files. To get the full benefits of parallel recovery, it is best to have your database spread across many disks and controllers. The benchmarks that we have run indicate that the databases that receive the greatest performance improvements are on machines that do not support asynchronous I/O. The greater the number of disks requiring recovery, the more significant the performance improvements.

14

*Tuning Database
Backup and Recovery*

Database recovery: Two words that strike fear into the heart of every DBA. Database backup and recovery are large and complex topics. This chapter does not cover the full range of backup and recovery products, techniques, and case studies. It focuses on the performance aspects of backup and recovery—how the database administrator can best prepare for and streamline the backup and recovery process.

Oracle database backup and recovery are extensively documented within the Oracle manuals and in books and papers by a number of third-party authors. We recommend that you read this chapter in parallel with the detailed recovery information found in those other sources. But regardless of how much research you do, there is no substitute for actual hands-on experience. Read all the books and papers you can, then put these principles into practice. We shudder at the number of times we've heard a DBA say, before beginning a critical recovery, "I've never actually tried this before. I hope it works."

The DBA's Responsibility

The single most important role of a DBA is to guarantee data integrity and availability. Remember the first lesson for DBAs: Data integrity comes before availability as a goal.

Too many DBAs take big risks and shortcuts simply to ensure that a database is sure to be available at 8:00 a.m. It's not worth it. If database recoverability is exposed in any way, assess the situation, measure the danger, and then act. If you know that last night's backup failed and that you have no secondary backup, you *must* shut down the database immediately. Performing a backup during core business hours may take some aggressive explaining to management. Losing a disk and then explaining that the database is unrecoverable because last night's backup failed is unthinkable. Yet the probability that two failures will occur on the same day is a lot higher than you may think. Why waste time, energy, and money capturing corporate data when you cannot guarantee that you'll be able to reproduce the data the next day?

Backing Up the Database

There are several ways to back up an Oracle database, each with its own advantages and disadvantages. You need to develop and document a clear, concise backup strategy before any application begins data entry. This philosophy is not only limited to production environments. Development and QA databases also need to be recoverable. In fact, because of the instability of the data in these environments, they are often more subject to recovery exercises than the production environment.

We believe that a database backup strategy, in its simplest form, can be summed up in a single word: redundancy. We have never heard a DBA complain that he or she has too many copies of an export to choose from. On the other hand, have you ever pondered why you always need the backup tapes from last month the very day after you've overwritten them?

The complexity and type of database backup strategy are governed by a number of factors, including the following:

- Backup window time frame
- Recoverability timeliness
- Data volatility
- Available disk space
- Available memory
- Available tape space
- Staff expertise
- Peripheral data transfer rates
- Machine architecture

The following sections briefly describe the most commonly used backup utilities.

EXP: the Export Utility

The EXP (export) utility is the simplest, and probably one of the safest, forms of database backup. You should export all databases on a regular basis. Exports can be used as the primary or secondary backup procedure at your site.

EXP utility advantages

There are a number of advantages to using EXP, including the following:

- Simplicity
- Safety
- Compatible data format (version and hardware)
- Data structure integrity checking
- Data defragmentation
- Single object recoverability

The following sections describe the most important of these advantages.

Compatible format. Export dump files are the only data format that is compatible across all Oracle operating system platforms. An export file can be moved from UNIX to VMS to DOS to OS/2 and still be readable. This is not possible with any of the other standard database backup utilities.

Structure validation. The export utility not only backs up the data, but also validates its internal structure. Oracle objects can be internally corrupted in one way or another.* Exporting data is the best way of detecting data structure problems before it is too late. Other backup utilities cannot identify object corruption; they simply duplicate the corruption in the backup file. If the problem is not picked up early, the data may not be recoverable at all.

Scan each export log for all occurrences of "ORA-" and "EXP-". Incorporate this log file scanning into your standard export routines. Make sure that the DBA is automatically notified if any errors are detected.

Data defragmentation. Data is always exported in contiguous fashion, regardless of how fragmented they may be within the database. If you specify COMPRESS = Y on the export, you can alter the physical table definition to allow all data to be compressed into a single initial extent.

The simplest and safest way to defragment an Oracle database is to perform a full database export, specifying COMPRESS = Y, and then drop all data objects and reimport the database. This will guarantee contiguous database objects, each contained in an efficient, single initial extent. If the tablespace already exists, remember to defragment the empty tablespace or to drop and recreate it (with the REUSE option) before importing the data.

---

* Though not very often; we personally have encountered a corrupted object only four times in nine years.

It is possible to drop a number of fragmented tables from a tablespace and not be able to reload them. When the objects are reloaded, the new INITIAL extent clause causes objects to be placed in new locations; fragmentation can result.

The crudest form of tablespace defragmentation is to simply create and then drop a single table that spans the entire tablespace. In the following example, assume that the EMP tablespace is 100 megabytes in size:

```
DROP ALL OBJECTS FROM TABLESPACE emp;
CREATE TABLE xx STORAGE (INITIAL 99 M);
DROP TABLE xx;
```

Single object recoverability. Creating export dump files allows us to recover or restore all or only some of the database. Individual tables can be restored without affecting other associated objects. This is not possible with most other conventional forms of backup. Any individual object, constraint, or grant can be extracted from a dump file.

Export utility disadvantages

There are also some disadvantages to using the export utility, including the following:

- Large output files
- Incompatibility among versions
- Restricted data defragmentation
- Inability to guarantee data integrity
- Slowness
- Single point-in-time recovery

The following sections describe the most important of these disadvantages.

Large output files. Because export files are operating system and Oracle version-independent, they are very verbose. Data compaction is kept to a minimum. It is often desirable to have a copy of the last export(s) of your database on disk. This can facilitate faster recovery turnaround and is safer than having to recover a dump file from tape. Unfortunately, many sites do not have the luxury of retaining exports on disk, and these sites must rely on tape storage. Export dump file compression via operating system utilities is an alternative worth considering. (See the section later in this chapter called "Exporting via compression.")

Incompatibility. Not all versions of the export utility work exactly the same. As the RDBMS has undergone major changes over the last few years, so have the export/import routines. The internal sequencing of exported objects can vary from version to version. What may appear to be a simple table export may in fact be quite complex.

When a table is exported, so is all of the following information about it:

- Table definition
- Storage requirements
- Data
- Triggers
- Grants
- Indexes
- Constraints

Over the years, items have been added and their export sequence has been modified. These changes have, in turn, affected the import routine. Oracle6 would always export (and thus import) index definitions *after* the table rows and the table grants. Early versions of Oracle7 slightly altered this approach. Primary key indexes were created before data were imported, as part of the CREATE TABLE clause. This can affect the size of an index (indexes are often larger when created before data is bulk loaded) and thus the duration of the import. Oracle7.1 (and later) has rectified this situation and now creates the primary key after data has been loaded, regardless of whether you set the INDEXES= parameter to YES or NO.

Differing versions of EXP and IMP may also behave differently. We used to export from our Oracle7.0.16 production database every night. When necessary, we would refresh our development database with a subset of the data. However, when we upgraded our development database to Oracle7.1, we began to mysteriously lose sequences when refreshing data. This problem turned out to be version and operating system dependent and was fixed when we moved our production database to Oracle7.1.

Always test *any* change to the database or its supporting environment. Just because a feature or function worked in one version does not guarantee that it will work in the next.

Restricted defragmentation. Although data defragmentation is a desirable characteristic of EXP, the defragmentation that is performed doesn't solve all of the space problems that arise with this utility.

Database object compression is not the most desirable form of export. Export allows only for object extents to be united into a single initial extent. The utility doesn't allow you to specify a multiplying factor for future growth. It would be much better to be able to specify an overall growth factor (of perhaps 25%) for objects to expand into.

Even when the EXP utility compresses object extents, it modifies only the INITIAL extent setting. The NEXT extent size remains as it was. (Expanding the NEXT extent size by the same factor as the INITIAL extent would be helpful.) Object fragmentation can also be caused by poorly calculated NEXT extent sizes. Unfortunately, not increasing the NEXT extent size and setting the INITIAL extent just big enough to hold the current object data virtually ensures that it won't be long before you'll have to repeat the whole defragmentation exercise.

Conversely, EXP cannot shrink oversized objects. The database can determine how big the table is and how much of this space is utilized. Applying a compression factor to decrease objects may sometimes be of value.

No guarantee of data integrity. An export can take many hours for large databases. If users are accessing the database or update reports are running, the data integrity of that database cannot be guaranteed. The EXP snapshot may not be a true point-in-time representation of the data. For example, a parent-child table combination may have inconsistent rows (orphaned children). A summary table could be incorrect. Database referential integrity constraints could be violated as the result of the EXP/IMP interaction. After importing the data, constraints may be invalid and not able to be enabled until the data is corrected.

Oracle7 has introduced a new EXP option, CONSISTENT = YES. This parameter instructs the export utility to take a read-consistent view of the data. This option alleviates the integrity problems mentioned above but presents its own set of issues. To guarantee read-consistency, all committed data changes must be sourced from the rollback segments. If these data is unavailable, the export will fail for that table with the error "SNAPSHOT TOO OLD." (See the discussion in Chapter 8, *Selecting a Locking Strategy.*) In a large volatile database, this would be the norm rather than the exception. Is an inconsistent export of the database better than no export at all?

Slowness. Another major drawback of the export utility is its speed. Very large databases may take more than 24 hours to export. This is not an acceptable form of backup. Rather than abandoning export or exporting only on weekends or at month's end, try to speed up the process. Enlarging the export buffer size can help to reduce the overall elapsed time by allowing EXP to read and write larger amounts of data at one time. For example,

```
EXP/ ROWS=Y BUFFER=1024000 FILE=exp.dmp
```

Breaking the export task up into many smaller processes is also possible on multi-processor machines. (See the section called "Exporting on SMP/MMP machines" later in this chapter.)

Point-in-time recovery. Some people think that a database that is restored from an export dump file can then be rolled forward by applying all archive logs that have been generated since the time of export. Unfortunately, EXP/IMP backup and recovery are point-in-time only and cannot be rolled forward.

Incremental exports

Incremental exports are an extension of the ordinary EXP utility. Such exports allow the database to keep track of which objects have changed since the last incremental backup and to export only those changed objects.

Three types of incremental backup are available:

Complete
    Takes a copy of the entire database

Cumulative
    Exports changed objects since the last complete backup

Incremental
    Exports changed objects since the last incremental, cumulative, or complete backup

There are a number of disadvantages to performing incremental exports:

- All types of incremental backups must be exported as user SYS or SYSTEM or have EXP_FULL_DATABASE privilege.

- An entire table will be marked as needing export even if only one row has been inserted, updated, or deleted in it. This is also the case if any grants have been altered, indexes modified, storage parameters altered, or even table comments added or edited.

- A complete export must be taken of the full database on a semiregular basis. This export, as we described previously, can take a very long time.

- Incremental exports can be executed only for the entire database. If the database is very large and volatile, an incremental export could also be very large (in the worst case, as large as a full export).

- With incremental backups, administration and complexity are greater and more subject to human error.

- Export read-consistency (requested by specifying CONSISTENT = YES) is not supported with incremental exports.

- The overall recovery time from a set of incremental exports will actually take longer than a normal full export. A full import from the complete incremental export needs to be applied, followed by the most up-to-date cumulative export, followed by all subsequent incremental exports.

- Single tables are not recoverable from incremental exports. To get one table, the whole database and all its objects must be restored.

Another downside of incremental exports is database object validation (discussed above). If the table has not been modified, it will not be read by the export program (and so it will not be validated).

Exporting on SMP/MMP machines

If you have the luxury of more than one CPU, you can achieve enormous improvements in your exports by breaking the database up into logical parts (by table, usercode, etc.) and performing the exports simultaneously. Experiment with which table groupings work best for you. Remember to balance disk I/O (which tablespaces are on which disks, which disks are the dump files being written to, etc.) and the number of CPUs you have. At one site that we tuned, by dividing the database up into 20 simultaneous exports, we were able to reduce an export backup from 27 hours to 3.5 hours on an eight-CPU machine.

WARNING   Dividing up the export does introduce the possibility of human error. You can easily miss some data in the exports. As the DBA, it is up to you to add another entry to the export script each time you add a new user, table, tablespace, to the database. If you don't do this, or the like, the object will not be included in any export.

When you do simultaneous exports in this way, it's a good idea to include a full export of the database (specifying ROWS = n) to ensure that you have a copy of the entire database schema. Unless you do this, public objects (synonyms, views, etc.) and all database user accounts that do not actually own data objects are normally not exported.

The following UNIX example illustrates this type of export:

```
#! /bin/sh
exp user1/pword file=user1.dmp buffer=64000 2> user1.log &
    exp user2/pword file=user2.dmp buffer=64000 2> user2.log &
    exp user3/pword file=user3.dmp buffer=64000 2> user3.log &
        wait
    exp user4/pword file=user4.dmp buffer=64000 2> user4.log &
    exp user5/pword file=user5.dmp buffer=64000 2> user5.log &
```

```
exp user6/pword file=user6.dmp buffer=64000 2> user6.log &
   wait
exp sys/pword file=system.dmp rows=n buffer=64000 2> sys.log &
```

Exporting via compression

It is often a good idea to compress your exports. Under UNIX, the *compress* and
uncompress utilities are handy and reliable. Other operating systems have their
own variants on compression utilities. We've found that compression provides a
space savings of as much as a factor of five (a compression ratio of 5:1) and sometimes even higher for common export dump files. This usually allows us to retain
at least last night's export dump file on disk. In fact, in many cases, using
compression may allow you to hold the exported copy of the database on disk,
rather than on tape. The trick to compression is to *never* hold the export dump
file in its raw state. By redirecting the export output directly to the compression
utility, it is compacted as it is generated and is thus never held in its uncompressed form.

Always remember to spread the export I/O whenever possible. The database data
files, the export dump file, and the compression pipe should all be on different
physical devices.

Exporting data directly through a compression utility may also help to speed up
the process. Even though we are increasing overheads via the extra compression
process, multiple CPUs will compensate for the additional overhead. You can still
save elapsed time by reducing the amount of overall disk I/O.

The following UNIX example shows an export via a UNIX pipe using compression:

```
# export.sh

#! /bin/sh
bin/rm /dsk1/usr1.pipe
bin/mknod /dsk1/usr1.pipe p
cat /dsk1/usr1.pipe | compress > /dsk9/usr1.dmp.Z &
exp / file=/dsk1/usr1.pipe buffer=64000 2>& usr1.log
```

The next example shows a corresponding import:

```
# import.sh

#!/bin/sh
bin/rm /dsk1/usr1.pipe
bin/mknod /dsk1/usr1.pipe  p
zcat /dsk9/usr1.dmp.Z > /dsk1/usr1.pipe &
imp usr1/pwd file=/dsk1/usr1.pipe buffer=64000 ...... 2>&usr1.log
```

As useful as export compression may be in alleviating an acute shortage of disk
space, it does not always solve the problem. We've been involved with very large

Oracle databases that had single tables in excess of 15 gigabytes (frightening, isn't it?). Exporting a single huge table was not possible because the export file exceeded the maximum file size on our UNIX platform (2 gigabytes). The immediate solution was to export the table via pipe compression. No good again! Even after the export dump file was compressed, it exceeded 2 megabytes. What could we do?

The first possibility was to export the database (and the large table) to a *null device*. Most platforms have a null device implementation of one kind or another. This option did at least allow us to retain the log file and validate database object integrity. Here is the UNIX example:

```
exp / full=y file=/dev/nul 2>& exp.log
```

Obviously, the option cannot be used as a secondary form of recovery. There is no dump file for recovery!

The second possibility was a little riskier. If you try this, test extensively before committing your database to its care. By using an operating system function that splits a file over multiple physical disks, we can break up the export dump file. The UNIX *split* command automatically breaks a file up and appends a nonmeaningful suffix to the file name. Again, by manipulating the UNIX pipe, we can redirect these files to separate physical disks. For example, under UNIX, specify

```
# exp_lrge.sh

#! /bin/sh
/bin/rm /dsk1/exp.pipe
/bin/rm /dsk1/disk.pipeaa   /dsk1/disk.pipeab   /dsk1/disk.pipeac

/bin/mknod /dsk1/exp.pipe p
/bin/mknod /dsk1/disk.pipeaa p
/bin/mknod /dsk1/disk.pipeab p
/bin/mknod /dsk1/disk.pipeac p

cat /dsk9/exp.pipe | compress | spilt -b 2000 /dsk1/disk.pipe &
cat /dsk1/disk.pipeaa > /dsk1/exp_aa.dmp.Z &
cat /dsk1/disk.pipeab > /dsk2/exp_ab.dmp.Z &
cat /dsk1/disk.pipeac > /dsk3/exp_ac.dmp.Z &

exp /  file=/dsk9/exp.pipe buffer=64000 2>& exp.log
```

To import a very large database under UNIX, specify

```
# imp_lrge.sh

#! /bin/sh
/bin/rm /dsk9/exp.pipe
/bin/mknod /dsk9/exp.pipe  p

zcat/dsk1/exp_aa.dmp.Z  \
```

```
/dsk2/exp_ab.dmp.Z   \
/dsk3/exp_ac.dmp.Z   >  /dsk9/exp.pipe  &

imp / file=/dsk9/exp.pipe buffers=64000   2>& exp.log
```

Single-task exports for UNIX

Oracle provides single-task processing on UNIX platforms. Such processing combines both foreground and background processes into a single executable. This approach elevates slower interprocess communication and can be very rewarding on some platform configurations.

To link a single-task EXP executable, specify the following under UNIX:

```
make -f oracle.mk expst
```

In general, neither we nor Oracle tends to recommend the use of single-task utilities (EXP. IMP, SQLDBA, SQL*Forms, etc.) Use this UNIX feature only in very special situations (e.g., one-time data loading), not as standard practice.

Faster export scanning

Verbosity is a very handy feature of an export dump file. Most DDL statements are held in full (uncompressed text) and within a continuous line (no line feeds). Rather than executing a long import, specifying the INDEXFILE = *x.x* option to extract a table definition, try performing a text search on the dump file. The results and speed of exports can be surprising.

For example, to find all tables owned by user SCOTT, you might specify the following under UNIX:

```
fgrep 'CREATE TABLE "SCOTT".' exp.dmp
```

grep returns

```
CREATE TABLE "SCOTT"."EMP" ( ......
```

If you combine the pattern-matching routines of *fgrep* and *egrep* with the string manipulation techniques of *sed* and *awk*, you'll find that anything is possible. The following illustrates the use of *fgrep* under UNIX:

```
fgrep 'CREATE SEQUENCE "' exp.dmp
CREATE SEQUENCE "EMP_NO" MINVALUE 1 ......
CREATE SEQUENCE "DEPT_NO" MINVALUE 1000 ......
CREATE SEQUENCE "CLASS_NO"  MINVALUE 1......
```

Many database objects are at the beginning of the export dump file. After the file was scanned for a few seconds, all the above sequences had been displayed. At this point, we were able to safely abort the *fgrep* command.

Image (Cold) Backups

Image or cold backup is just a fancy term for copying all the *important* files to another location. There are no secrets, no magic; if you think you may need a particular file, copy it. Image backups are one of the fastest and simplest types of database backup and are a good choice as a primary or secondary backup strategy.

Remember the following:

- The database must be shut down while you perform the image copy.
- Image backups provide only a single point-in-time recovery and must be coupled with archived redo logs to allow you to perform variable point-in-time (roll forward) recovery.

You *must* copy the following files:

- All database files
- At least one control file (preferably all control files)
- At least one online redo log duplex set (preferably both)

You *may* copy the following files to help in recovery:

- INIT.ORA file
- All special DBA scripts (both SQL and operating system scripts)
- All duplexed online redo logs
- A full descriptive trace file definition of your database. You can obtain this file by specifying the following SQL statement: ALTER DATABASE backup_control_file TO trace_file.

Image backup advantages

Image backups are a very popular way to back up an Oracle database. Their main advantages include the following:

- Simplicity
- Safety
- Fast recovery
- Restorable from tape with no recovery required
- Point-in-time recovery if archives are available
- Ability to source data files from multiple backup cycles if all archives are available

The following sections describe the most important of these advantages.

Safety and simplicity. Image backups are one of the safest ways to back up an Oracle database; they are considerably faster than hot backups (described in the next section). (We are actually of the opinion that this reputation of safety is mainly due to the fact that cold backups are easier than hot backups to understand and implement.) Whatever type of backup you perform, be sure to test carefully with actual physical recovery exercises. *Never* expect a procedure to simply work the first time.

Speed. Doing an image backup is more concise and usually faster than an export.

Multiple backup cycles. Database files can be sourced from different image backup cycles as long as all relevant archived redo files are available. This provides a form of redundant recovery. If a tape or file is unreadable, then the next oldest backup of the missing database file can be used. Under these circumstances, the database must be recovered (archived logs applied) before the database can be opened. If you intend to use this facility as a secondary form of recovery, do not place your only copy of the archive redo files on the same tape as the database image files. If the tape is corrupt and you are forced to go back to the previous tape, you will have no archived redo files to roll forward. Time to check the want ads!

Full or point-in-time recovery. If a database file or number of files need recovery (in the event of hardware failure, etc.), only those particular data files need to be recovered. Once the files have been restored, all applicable archives (archives generated from the time of the cold backup to the recovery point-in-time) will have to be applied. The rest of the database can remain online and will continue to be available to users.

Image backup disadvantages

There are also some disadvantages to using image backups, including the following:

- No standard backup utility or script
- The database must be down
- Must back up the entire database (without archives)
- Point-in-time recovery requires archives
- No internal data validation

- Must have a compatible control file
- The database must be shut down cleanly

The following sections describe the most important of these disadvantages.

No standard script. Oracle does not provide any standard backup routine or script file to use in copying database files to tape. Each DBA has to write his or her own script, and this requirement tends to be the weakest link in the recovery chain. These routines need to be tested, retested, and retested again.

The database must be down. There are two common reasons for image recovery procedures to fail: Either the database has not been shut down cleanly, or the database has been started up during the backup cycle. There is nothing to stop the database from being mounted during recovery. If the database is open, the image backup files are useless.

Point-in-time recovery requires archives. Image backups provide only a point-in-time copy of the database. Restoring from an image backup will only bring the database back to the exact moment it was shut down before beginning the backup. To bring the database up to date, you will need to apply all archived redo logs during recovery.

Full database backup only without archives. Image backups can be performed on the entire database only if the database is not in archive mode or if archives are not being retained. To successfully restore the database, all files must be from the same backup, including the control and online redo file(s). Very large databases cannot be broken up and backed up over several nights unless all archived redo files are available and database recovery is performed.

No data validation. Image backups do not validate database objects. If an object has been corrupted, image copies will copy the error over and over again to all of your backup tapes. The EXP utility is the only way of validating the physical database data.

No defragmentation. Image backups do not perform tablespace defragmentation. The copy of each data file includes all prior fragmentation. The EXP utility is the only way of defragmenting database objects.

Compatible control file needed. Image backups are useless unless a compatible control file is available. Back up your control files with every data file backup and every database schema modification. (This is done with the ALTER DATABASE CREATE TABLESPACE statement.)

If no control file is available, you can create one with the statement ALTER DATA-
BASE CREATE CONTROL FILE. Regenerating a control file is possible only if you
know the exact definition of the database (from the original CREATE DATABASE
statement) and all of the associated data files that have been added since.

Database shut down. The database must be closed cleanly before an image
backup is taken. This is a common mistake that many DBAs make. Oracle clearly
states (though the advice is hidden away in the manuals) that the database must
be shut down cleanly to guarantee that the database can be restored. This means
that you must specify the basic SHUTDOWN command, not SHUTDOWN IMME-
DIATE or SHUTDOWN ABORT. In the following example, active applications will
need to be closed, opened, and then closed again:

```
Oracle 6                       Oracle7

sqldba                         sqldba lmode=Y
>shutdown immediate            >connect internal
>startup exclusive             >shutdown immediate
>shutdown                      >startup restrict
                               >shutdown
```

Speeding up image backups

A downside to image backups is the total time it takes to copy the entire database. Because the database must be down, it is consequently unavailable to the
people who count—the users. But there are several ways to reduce this downtime.

One way to reduce downtime for image backups is to copy the database files to
another disk rather than directly to tape. The files can then be moved to tape at a
later date. As simple and attractive as this method may sound, its is also just as
impractical. Any site with the luxury of enough spare disk for an entire copy of its
database should have a serious talk with the capacity planning division.

Nevertheless, it may be possible to hold a *compressed* copy of your database on
disk. Using the UNIX *compress* utility, we have been able to compress a database
down far enough to hold on our spare disk(s). The amount of compression is
directly related to the amount and type of data stored in your database. We have
experienced compression factors from 4:1 all the way up to 500:1 (a brand new,
empty data file).

Today, most Oracle database files are placed on mirrored disk arrays. Some very
critical databases are on three-way mirrored disks. You can exploit this hardware
redundancy to help reduce backup downtime. Once the database has been shut
down, split the mirror and then start up the database. This can mean a total downtime of a few minutes. The second (mirrored) disk array is then mounted using
alternative volume identifiers, and the image backup is performed. Once the

image backup is complete, the mirrored disk array is then remounted and the disks are silvered (synchronized). The can all happen while the database is available and still active. This method does present certain risks for "two-way" mirrored arrays (the database is temporarily mounted on a single disk array), but it can be very effective for databases that have the luxury of three-way disk systems.

A second very effective way of speeding up image backups is to let someone else do it. Most backup routines use standard tape copy commands (e.g., UNIX *cpio*, *tar*, and other copy commands) without looking at the alternatives. But many hardware vendors and/or third party companies provide backup utilities that communicate directly with the Oracle database. One such product that we used a few years ago would simultaneously back up nine different data files to three separate tape devices. The utility would even attempt to logically balance disk I/O by grouping data files on the basis of the disk subsystem they were on. We were able to copy 15 gigabytes of database files directly to tape in less than 2 hours. We considered this backup utility to be very impressive at the time. But the newer utilities are even better. The latest backup utility that we've used backs up our 220-gigabyte database in 4 hours. You begin to wonder whether anything is actually getting written to the tape when the data is moving that fast! These tape backup utilities are becoming more and more prevalent. If something suitable for your site was not available last year, don't despair; it may well be available now.

If you do choose to use any of these tools, remember to test and retest all areas of the backup routine before committing your database to its protection. The more sophisticated the tool, the more sophisticated the problems and the greater the possibility that something will go wrong.

Hot Backups

Hot backups are very similar to cold (image) backups, except that the database can remain up during the backup and available to all users. Hot backups are generally considered to be rather complex and fragile, and they're traditionally fraught with danger. If anything is going to go wrong, it always seems to go wrong with the hot backups. Of course, this is not always true. People just seem to remember a down database for a lot longer than a simple SQL syntax error. Although there are some risks associated with hot backups, they can actually be a very secure and complete form of backup when they are carefully executed in a controlled environment.

When you run a hot backup, you must also back up the archived redo files, You must also notify each tablespace of the beginning and end of a hot tablespace backup via the following commands:

```
SQL>    ALTER TABLESPACE xxxx BEGIN Backup;
   ....  copy datafiles for tablespace xxxx to tape  ...
SQL>    ALTER TABLESPACE xxxx END Backup;
```

Always create a backup version of the control file to copy to tape. This control file is generated by the command

```
SQL>    ALTER DATABASE Backup Controlfile to 'control_file.dbf.backup;
```

You *must* copy these files during a hot backup:

- All database files
- A "backed up" control file
- All archived redo logs

You *may* also copy these files to help in recovery:

- INIT.ORA file
- All special DBA scripts (both SQL and operating system scripts)
- A full description TRACE file of your database; you create this by specifying the following from SQL:

```
ALTER DATABASE backup control file to TRACE; )
```

It may also be desirable to put the current online redo log file on tape. Simply force a log file switch before copying the archived redo logs to tape as follows:

```
SQL>    ALTER DATABASE SWITCH LOGFILE;
```

Hot backup advantages

There are a number of advantages to running hot backups:

- Database availability
- Fast recovery
- Point-in-time recovery roll-forward
- Database can be backed up over several nights
- Data files can be sourced from multiple backup cycles if all the archives are available

The following sections describe the most important of these advantages.

Database availability. The one big advantage of hot database backups is that the database remains available to the users. Applications that must be available all day, every day (7×24 applications) *must* use hot backups as their recovery strategy.

Backup over several nights. Hot backups can be performed over several nights. The entire database does not have to be copied every time the database is backed up. Many sites with very large databases split their database tablespaces up over several nights, performing back-to-back rolling hot backups.

Different hot backup cycles. Database files can be sourced from different hot backup cycles provided that all relevant archived redo files are available. This provides a form of redundant recovery. If a tape or file is unreadable, then the next oldest backup of the database file can be used. The database must be recovered (archived logs applied) before the database can be opened.

Point-in-time recovery. If a single database file or a number of files need recovery (as a result of hardware failure, etc.), only those particular data files need to be restored and recovered. Once the files have been restored, all applicable archives (archive logs generated from the time of the cold backup to the recovery point-in-time) will have to be applied. The rest of the database can actually remain on-line and available to users.

Hot Backup Disadvantages

Hot backups do have a number of disadvantages as well:

- No standard backup routine or script
- Backups are useless without all archived logs
- No internal data validation
- Must have a compatible control file
- Larger redo log files
- More complex backup and restore procedures
- Database needs recovery if database fails during a hot backup

The following sections describe the most important of these disadvantages.

No standard backup routine or script file. Oracle does not provide any standard backup routine or script file to copy database files to tape. Each DBA has to write his or her own scripts, and this usually tends to be the weakest link in the recovery chain. These routines need to be tested, retested, and tested again.

Mark beginning and end. You must execute the SQL command

```
ALTER TABLESPACE xxxx BEGIN BACKUP
```

before copying each tablespace data file(s). If this command is not issued correctly, the copy of the tablespace will still proceed but will be useless. You must also execute the SQL command

```
ALTER TABLESPACE xxxx END BACKUP
```

after copying each tablespace data file(s). If this command is not issued correctly, the tablespace remains in backup mode, preventing the database from being shut down cleanly. If the database is shut down (via a system crash or a SHUTDOWN ABORT command), the database requires recovery before it can be opened. Archived logs will need to be applied from the time the BEGIN BACKUP statement was issued. This could be several days ago!

No object validation. Hot backups do not validate database objects. If an object has been corrupted, the backup will copy the error over and over again to all of your backup tapes. The EXP utility is the only way of validating the physical database data.

No tablespace defragmentation. Hot backups do not perform tablespace defragmentation. The copy of each data file includes all prior fragmentation. The EXP utility is the only way of defragmenting database objects.

Incomplete copy. Hot backups by themselves provide an incomplete copy of the database. They are useless if any archived redo log is missing. Unlike image (cold) backups, they cannot be restored to the point in time when the database was shut down for the backup. The best you can do is to roll the database forward to a point immediately prior to the *lost* redo log and pray that the database is in a stable state (no incomplete transactions) at that point in time. A complete cold backup can always be restored to the backup point-in-time. A database that is two days old is probably better than no database at all—but you must be the judge of that.

Size of redo logs. Placing tablespaces in backup mode affects the size of the redo log files. Instead of only the modified data being written to the redo log for each change, the entire Oracle data block is written. This enables the recovery process to recover from a hot (open) data file. As clever as this may be, it can cause serious bottlenecks on the log buffers, redo logs, and archiving process. Try to limit the period of time a tablespace is in backup mode. Do not place the entire database in backup mode for the duration of the backup. Run hot backups at the correct time of day, that is, when the database has low updating activity. This may not always be at night. Overnight update processing will take longer than necessary if hot backups are running in parallel. Consider running the backups during normal working hours when the update activity may be less.

Compatible control file. Hot backups are useless if no compatible control file is available. Be sure to generate (and copy) a backup control file with every hot backup and every database schema modification (new tablespace, etc.). This is done via the SQL command

```
ALTER DATABASE BACKUP CONTROLFILE TO '/xxx/control.backup;"
```

If no control file is available, you can create one with the statement

```
ALTER DATABASE CREATE CONTROLFILE
```

Regenerating a control file is possible only if you know the exact definition of the database (from the original CREATE DATABASE statement) and all the associated data files that have been added since.

Unforgiving nature. A common complaint about hot backup recovery is the unforgiving nature of the process. If you do not execute the recovery correctly, it can make matters much worse. If the recovery process fails or is executed incorrectly (incompatible datafiles, control files etc.), you could end up losing everything. As true as this may be, it is usually caused by incorrect/untested backup procedures or mistakes made during the database restore/recovery. Again, we must stress the importance of testing and retesting both the backup routines and the various possible recovery scenarios.

Speeding up the hot backup process

The suggestions provided for image backups in the section called "Speeding up image backups," earlier in this chapter, are equally applicable to improving the efficiency of hot backups.

Note the following about hot backups: The physical size of your database is too large to copy in one go; break it up over several nights. Remember, though, that this does mean a longer recovery period (more archived logs to apply), and a greater exposure to the backup process. Instead of relying on one hot backup recovery cycle and one full day's worth of archive logs being recoverable from tape, you may now have to rely on two or three days' worth.

Oracle Database Backup Summary

This section summarizes the advantages and disadvantages of the types of backups we've examined.

For database exports using the EXP utility:

- Database is available to users.
- Performs internal database integrity checks while exporting.

- Easy to recover a single table.

- Backup dump file upward compatible across Oracle versions.

- Backup dump file compatible across hardware versions.

- Generally the slowest form of backup and recovery.

- No point-in-time roll forward of any kind is possible.

- Difficult to guarantee data referential integrity and/or consistency.

- Very difficult to mix and match data from varying export files.

For image (cold) backups:

- Generally regarded as the safest form of database backup.

- Database can be started up as at time of backup. Rolling forward archive logs is not mandatory.

- Data files can be restored and point-in-time recovery actioned. Database recovery will be necessary and all archives must be available.

- Data files can be mixed and matched from varying backups. Database recovery will be necessary, and all archives must be available.

- Database must be down (unavailable to users). The cold backup is useless if database is accidentally left running.

- Does not perform a database integrity check.

- Backup is not compatible across hardware platforms.

- Backup is not reliably compatible across Oracle versions.

- Difficult to recover a single table.

For hot backups:

- Database is available to users.

- Data files can be restored and point-in-time recovery actioned. Database recovery will be necessary, and all archives must be available.

- Data files can be mixed and matched from varying backups. Database recovery will be necessary, and all archives must be available.

- Database can be backed up in parts, over several nights, to reduce the size of the backup window.

- Database will need recovery if accidentally shut down (crashed) while a tablespace is in hot backup mode.

- Hot backup is useless without all relevant archive logs.

- More archive log files are generated while the database is in hot backup mode.

- Does not perform a database integrity check.

- Difficult to recovery a single table.

- Backup file not compatible across hardware platforms.

- Backup file not reliably compatible across Oracle Versions.

Preparing to Recover the Database

How do you prepare for a database recovery? With the same word we offered for backup: redundancy. You can never have too many control file backups. You can never have too many recovery options. Always prepare for the worst case.

This section describes what you need to do before recovery—how you can monitor your system and collect the information you'll need (badly) when you're actually in the throes of recovery.

Documenting the Database

Too many sites rely on knowledge that resides only in the heads of a select group of people. At some sites, that group consists of only one individual. Don't make this mistake. Prepare extensive documentation about the availability and recover-ability of the data at your site.

Ask these questions about *availability*:

- How long is acceptable downtime?

- Is one set of data more important than another?

- Which database/application should I restore first?

- Does one tablespace depend an another?

- Does one database depend on another?

As part of this exercise, compile a detailed list of data interdependencies. Imagine spending all night recovering a database data file, only to be told that the data is accessed only by quarterly reports, even worse, that the data is no longer required and the application has been replaced.

Does the database really need to be rolled forward from the last available backup? Was yesterday a public holiday in New York, so no data changes were possible? Is it acceptable to lose one hour of user processing time and have the database back online in two hours—or should you perform a full database recovery, which would take four hours?

Can a portion of the database be restored and operational while the remainder of the database is still being recovered?

Availability questions can be answered only by the user base. Ask them while you have time to discuss them. Rushed decisions at 3:00 a.m. are often poor ones.

Ask these questions about *recoverability*:

- Which applications perform image backups?
- Which applications perform hot backups?
- Are there any current export files available?
- Where are the archived log files kept?
- Where are the tapes kept?
- Do I have any free disk space on another machine?
- Are the database disks mirrored?
- What recovery tools are in place for each database?

DBAs are often in control of many databases on many varying machines. Compile a detailed list of each instance's backup routines. Draw up a list of procedures for all common disaster situations. Ask the following:

- Can the database be temporarily recovered to another node?
- Where can you quickly acquire a replacement disk?

Each database should have an alternative recovery area allocated. This area must be on another node (i.e., development machine). This one area could be reserved for all production instances. (We sincerely hope that you will never need to recover two databases at the same time.) This area must be large enough to hold the minimal data files necessary for a partial database recovery (system and roll-back) and the largest potentially recoverable tablespace. (See the discussion of point-in-time partial database later in this chapter.)

DBA Tools and Scripts

You can avoid the recovery ulcers that plague so many DBAs by using a rigorous set of database utilities. They'll provide the information necessary to help you through the darkest days of recovery. The following list is a set that we currently use. These scripts provide information that we've required at one time or another over the course of 10 years of database recoveries. But don't regard these scripts as complete. Every new version of Oracle provides more functions, better reporting, and safer recovery alternatives. You can never have too much information at recovery time.

Nightly reporting scripts

We run the set of scripts contained in this section every night against each data-base instance. They allow us to retain a rolling, weekly set of all information and tell us everything we might need to know about the database. Not all scripts are directly linked to the recovery procedure, but they all provide general database support information that may be necessary when the database is unavailable. All output is gathered on a separate host (a DBA command post), never on the source machine. If you put the database information on the source machine, it will be readily available when the database is up and running. But when the machine has crashed, where do you get this information? What do you do when the system administrator rings you at 3.00 a.m. to find out which files need to be recovered after the machine comes back up. It is very difficult to use this time to prepare for a recovery if you have no current details on the database or its phys-ical structure.

All the report output is prefixed with instance name and suffixed with "day", thus enabling us to retain the last seven days of output on a rolling basis. These reports can also help to track database discrepancies within the last seven days.

The following shell script is run from the DBA command post host:

```
#dba_post.sql

#! /bin/ksh
sqlplus user/pword@T:${1}:${2}  @objects.sql>  ${1}.objects.`date +%d`
sqlplus user/pword@T:${1}:${2}  @files.sql>  ${1}.files.`date +%d`
...      ...     ...     ...     ...
sqlplus user/pword@T:${1}:${2}  @io.sql>  ${1}.io.`date +%d`
```

Monitoring initiation script:

```
#! /bin/ksh
. ./DBA_monitor  thor  FIN
. ./DBA_monitor  zeus PER
... ... ... ...
. ./DBA_monitor  zeus  PAY
```

Monitoring output:

```
FIN_objects.Mon      FIN_files.Mon      FIN_io.Mon
FIN_objects.Tue      FIN_files.Tue      FIN_io.Tue
FIN_objects.Wed      FIN_files.Wed      FIN_io.Wed
FIN_objects.Thu      FIN_files.Thu      FIN_io.Thu
FIN_objects.Fri      FIN_files.Fri      FIN_io.Fri
FIN_objects.Sat      FIN_files.Sat      FIN_io.Sat
FIN_objects.Sun      FIN_files.Sun      FIN_io.Sun

PER_objects.Mon      PER_files.Mon      PER_io.Mon
PER_objects.Tue      PER_files.Tue      PER_io.Tue
PER_objects.Wed      PER_files.Wed      PER_io.Wed
```

```
PER_objects.Thu      PER_files.Thu      PER_io.Thu
PER_objects.Fri      PER_files.Fri      PER_io.Fri
PER_objects.Sat      PER_files.Sat      PER_io.Sat
PER_objects.Sun      PER_files.Sun      PER_io.Sun
```

The following sections detail our favorite nightly monitoring scripts.

files.sql. This script lists all database files. Its purpose is to readily display the location of all database files and help to track any new files that have been added during the past week. From this report, we can tell exactly what the database structure was at the time of recovery. These reports also help to identify potential database weaknesses, such as the fact that the online redo files are on the same disk as the duplexed redo files.

```
# files.sql
COL name  FORMAT a60 heading "Control Files"

SELECT name
FROM    sys.v_$controlfile
/

SELECT name, value
FROM    sys.v_$parameter
WHERE   name LIKE '%archive_dest%'
OR      name LIKE '%dump_dest%'
/

col Grp     format 9999
col member  format a50 heading "Online REDO Logs"
col File#   format 9999
col name    format a50 heading "Online REDO Logs"
break on Grp

select *
from    sys.v_$logfile
/

col sequence#     format 99999  heading "Seqn"
col archive_name  format a55     heading "Archived REDO Logs"
col time          format a17

select sequence#, archive_name, time
from    sys.v_$log_history
where   rownum < 10
/

col Tspace     format a15
col status     format a3  heading Sta
col Id         format 99
col Mbyte      format 9999
col name       format a50 heading "Database Data Files"
col Reads      format 99,999,999
col Writes     format 99,999,999
```

```
break on report
compute sum of Mbyte on report

select F.file_id Id,
       F.file_name name,
       F.bytes/(1024*1024) Mbyte,
       decode(F.status,'AVAILABLE','OK',F.status) status,
       F.tablespace_name Tspace
from   sys.dba_data_files F
/


Control Files
-------------------------------------------------------------------
/dsk4/PRD/db/admin/PRD_control1.dbf
/dsk0/PRD/db/admin/PRD_control2.dbf
/dsk5/archive/PRD/admin/PRD_control3.dbf


Control Files          VALUE
-------------------    -------------------------------------------------
control_files          /dsk4/PRD/db/admin/PRD_control1.dbf, /dsk0/PRD/db/
                       admin/PRD_control2.dbf, /dsk5/archive/PRD/admin/PR
                       D_control3.dbf
log_archive_dest       /dsk5/archive/PRD/arch
background_dump_dest   /dsk4/PRD/db/dump
user_dump_dest         /dsk4/PRD/db/dump
core_dump_dest         /dsk4/PRD/db/dump


  GROUP# STATUS   Online REDO Logs
-------- -------  -------------------------------------------------
       1          /dsk5/archive/PRD/redo/PRD_log1_A.dbf
       1          /dsk4/PRD/db/redo/PRD_log1_B.dbf
       2          /dsk5/archive/PRD/redo/PRD_log2_A.dbf
       2          /dsk4/PRD/db/redo/PRD_log2_B.dbf
       3          /dsk5/archive/PRD/redo/PRD_log3_A.dbf
       3          /dsk4/PRD/db/redo/PRD_log3_B.dbf


  Seqn Archived REDO Logs                              TIME
------ -------------------------------------------     -----------------
5049 /dsk5/archive/PRD/arch_PRD_1_5049.dbf             10/17/95 07:23:58
5048 /dsk5/archive/PRD/arch_PRD_1_5048.dbf             10/17/95 07:19:12
5047 /dsk5/archive/PRD/arch_PRD_1_5047.dbf             10/16/95 16:38:05
5046 /dsk5/archive/PRD/arch_PRD_1_5046.dbf             10/16/95 14:56:14
5045 /dsk5/archive/PRD/arch_PRD_1_5045.dbf             10/16/95 14:09:25
5044 /dsk5/archive/PRD/arch_PRD_1_5044.dbf             10/16/95 13:39:47
5043 /dsk5/archive/PRD/arch_PRD_1_5043.dbf             10/16/95 12:54:08
5042 /dsk5/archive/PRD/arch_PRD_1_5042.dbf             10/16/95 12:45:42
5041 /dsk5/archive/PRD/arch_PRD_1_5041.dbf             10/16/95 12:37:05
```

```
    ID Database Data Files                           MBYTE Sta TSPACE
    --- -------------------------------------------  ----- --- ---------
     1  /dsk0/PRD/db/PRD_system1.dbf                    100 OK  SYSTEM
     2  /dsk0/PRD/db/PRD_rbs1.dbf                       100 OK  RBS
     3  /dsk0/PRD/db/PRD_temp1.dbf                      500 OK  TEMP
     4  /dsk0/PRD/db/PRD_tools1.dbf                      25 OK  TOOLS
     5  /dsk0/PRD/db/PRD_users1.dbf                      25 OK  USERS
     6  /dsk1/PRD/db/PRD_supply_data1.dbf              1000 OK  SUPPLY_DATA
     7  /dsk2/PRD/db/PRD_supply_index1.dbf            1000 OK  SUPPLY_INDEX
     8  /dsk1/PRD/db/PRD_supply_data2.dbf              500 OK  SUPPLY_DATA
     9  /dsk2/PRD/db/PRD_supply_index2.dbf             500 OK  SUPPLY_INDEX
    10  /dsk0/PRD/db/PRD_rbs2.dbf                        50 OK  RBS
    11  /dsk3/PRD/db/PRD_stocktake1.dbf                 250 OK  STOCKTAKE
    14  /dsk1/PRD/db/PRD_supply_data3.dbf              300 OK  SUPPLY_DATA
                                                      ----
    sum                                               4350
```

ts_size.sql. This script monitors the free space within each database, tablespace, and data file. This gives us an early warning of any potential space problems and a detailed view of all object growth over the last seven days.

```
# ts_size.sql
col T_space   format a15
col fname     format a34
col Use_Pct   format 999.0 heading Used%
col Total     format 99999
col Used_Mg   format 9999.0
col Free_Mg   format 9999.0

define Blk_size=2048/* Set Oracle Block Size */

break on T_Space on report
compute sum of Total   on report
compute sum of Used_Mg on report
compute sum of Free_Mg on report

select decode(x.online$,1,x.name,
              substr(rpad(x.name,14),1,14)||' OFF')  T_Space,
       replace(replace(A.file_name,'/databases/',''),'.dbf','') Fname,
       round((f.blocks*&Blk_Size)/(1024*1024)) Total,
       round(sum(s.length*&Blk_Size)/(1024*1024),1) Used_Mg,
       round(((f.blocks*&Blk_Size)/(1024*1024))
         - nvl(sum(s.length*&Blk_Size)/(1024*1024),0), 1) Free_Mg,
       round( sum(s.length*&Blk_Size)/(1024*1024)
         / ((f.blocks*&Blk_Size)/(1024*1024)) * 100, 1) Use_Pct
from   sys.dba_data_files A, sys.uet$ s, sys.file$ f, sys.ts$ X
where  x.ts#    = f.ts#
and    x.online$ in (1,2)/* Online !! */
and    f.status$ = 2/* Online !! */
and    f.ts#    = s.ts# (+)
and    f.file#  = s.file# (+)
and    f.file#  = a.file_id
group  by x.name, x.online$, f.blocks, A.file_name
```

```
/

select decode(x.online$,1,x.name,
               substr(rpad(x.name,14),1,14)||' OFF') T_Space,
       'Total 'Fname,
       round(sum(distinct (f.blocks+(f.file#/1000))*&Blk_Size)
              / (1024*1024) ) Total,
       round(sum(s.length*&Blk_Size)/(1024*1024),1) Used_Mg,
       round(sum(distinct (f.blocks+(f.file#/1000))*&Blk_Size)
              / (1024*1024)
           - nvl(sum(s.length*&Blk_Size)/(1024*1024),0), 1) Free_Mg,
       round(((sum(s.length*&Blk_Size)/(1024*1024) )
          / (sum(distinct (f.blocks+(f.file#/1000))*&Blk_Size)
              / (1024*1024) )) * 100, 1) Use_Pct
from   sys.uet$ s, sys.file$ f, sys.ts$ x
where  x.ts#    = f.ts#
and    x.online$ in (1,2)/* Online !! */
and    f.status$ = 2/* Online !! */
and    f.ts#    = s.ts# (+)
and    f.file#  = s.file# (+)
group  by x.name, x.online$
order  by 1
/
clear breaks
tti off
set verify on
```

T_SPACE	FNAME	TOTAL	USED_MG	FREE_MG	Used%
RBS	/dsk4/PRD/db/PRD_rbs1	100	40.0	60.0	40.0
	/dsk4/PRD/db/PRD_rbs2	100		100.0	
STOCKTAKE	/dsk3/PRD/db/PRD_stocktake1	1000	948.2	51.8	94.8
SUPPLY_DATA	/dsk1/PRD/db/PRD_supply_data1	500	499.9	.1	100.0
	/dsk1/PRD/db/PRD_supply_data2	1000	932.6	67.4	93.3
SUPPLY_INDEX	/dsk2/PRD/db/PRD_supply_index1	500	221.2	278.8	44.2
	/dsk2/PRD/db/PRD_supply_index2	000	754.4	245.6	75.4
SYSTEM	/dsk4/PRD/db/PRD_system1	100	14.7	85.3	14.7
TEMP	/dsk4/PRD/db/PRD_temp1	200	200.0		
TOOLS	/dsk4/PRD/db/PRD_tools1	50	.0	50.0	.1
USERS	/dsk4/PRD/db/PRD_users1	50		50.0	
***************		------	-------	-------	
sum		4600	3411.0	1189.0	

T_SPACE	FNAME	TOTAL	USED_MG	FREE_MG	Used%
RBS	Total	200	40.0	160.0	20.0
STOCKTAKE	Total	1000	948.2	51.8	94.8
SUPPLY_DATA	Total	1500	1432.5	67.5	95.5
SUPPLY_INDEX	Total	1500	975.6	524.4	65.0
SYSTEM	Total	100	14.7	85.3	14.7
TEMP	Total	200		200.0	
TOOLS	Total	50	.0	50.0	.1

```
USERS            Total                          50           50.0
***************                             ------  -------  -------
sum                                         4600   3411.0   1189.0
```

objects.sql. This script builds a detailed profile of all database objects. It serves as a checklist for comparison after a database rebuild or recovery. There is nothing worse than losing a database, recovering it, and being blamed for the fact that 27 synonyms have mysteriously disappeared. It's always a nice feeling to know that you had 697 synonyms before the database crashed and the same 697 after you have finished the recovery. The output also serves as a quick review of who owns what objects.

```
# objects.sql
break on report

compute sum of Tab on report
compute sum of Ind on report
compute sum of Syn on report
compute sum of Vew on report
compute sum of Seq on report
compute sum of Trg on report
compute sum of Fun on report
compute sum of Pck on report
compute sum of Prc on report
compute sum of Dep on report

select  username,
        count(decode(O.type,  2,O.obj#,'')) Tab,
        count(decode(O.type,  1,O.obj#,'')) Ind,
        count(decode(O.type,  5,O.obj#,'')) Syn,
        count(decode(O.type,  4,O.obj#,'')) Vew,
        count(decode(O.type,  6,O.obj#,'')) Seq,
        count(decode(O.type,  7,O.obj#,'')) Prc,
        count(decode(O.type,  8,O.obj#,'')) Fun,
        count(decode(O.type,  9,O.obj#,'')) Pck,
        count(decode(O.type, 12,O.obj#,'')) Trg,
        count(decode(O.type, 10,O.obj#,'')) Dep
from    sys.obj$ O,
        sys.dba_users U
where   U.user_id = O.owner# (+)
group   by  username
order   by  username
/
```

USERNAME	TAB	IND	SYN	VEW	SEQ	PRC	FUN	PCK	TRG	DEP
USER1	0	0	164	0	0	0	0	0	0	0
USER2	0	0	164	0	0	0	0	0	0	0
USER3	0	0	164	0	0	0	0	0	0	0
USER3	0	0	165	0	0	0	0	0	0	0
STOCKTAKE	21	50	1	0	0	0	0	0	1	0

SUPPLY	147	151	6	4	11	0	0	3	7	1
SUPPLY_RDR	0	0	74	0	0	0	0	0	0	0
SYS	77	71	1	389	9	4	0	25	0	1
SYSTEM	60	1	59	41	5	0	0	0	0	0
****************	------	------	------	-----	-----	----	----	----	----	-----
sum	305	273	697	434	25	4	0	28	8	2

extents.sql. This scripts lists objects containing more than one extent. This provides valuable information for planning future defragmentation database reorganizations. All objects that exceed 75% of their MAXENTENTS values or have more than 20 extents are flagged for future investigation. This is information you will need to prevent objects from exceeding their space limits.

The following reports show that a number of indexes and tables have grown since their initial creation; one object in particular has exceeded 20% of its MAXEXTENTS threshold.

```
# extents.sql
set pages      50000
column owner              format a12     heading 'OWNER'
column segment_type       format a5      heading 'TYPE'
column tablespace_name    format a12     heading 'TABLESPACE'
column segment_name       format a28     heading 'NAME'
column max_extents        format 999     heading 'MAX'
column extents            format 999     heading 'EXTS'
column pct                format 999     heading '%'
column Error       format a4      heading 'FIX'

break on owner skip 1 on tablespace_name on segment_type

select   owner,
         tablespace_name,
         segment_type,
         segment_name,
         max_extents,
         extents,
         extents/max_extents*100 PCT,
         decode(sign(75 - (extents/max_extents*100)), -1, '***',
         decode(sign(20 - extents), -1, '****', '')) Error
  from   sys.dba_segments
 where   extents       > 1
   and   segment_type != 'ROLLBACK'
   and   segment_type != 'CACHE'
   and   owner         != 'SYS'
 order
     by owner.
        tablespace_name,
        segment_type
/
```

OWNER	TABLESPACE	TYPE	NAME	MAX	EXTS	%	FIX
STOCKTAKE	STOCKTAKE	TABLE	WAREHOUSE_SOH_HISTORY	99	2	2	
			CURRENT_COST	99	8	8	
			PRICE_LISTS	99	2	2	
			CR_DB_HEADER	99	2	2	
			ADJUSTMENT_TEMP	99	2	2	
			RECONCILIATION_DAILY	99	12	12	
SUPPLY	SUPPLY_DATA	TABLE	CATEGORY_TRANSACTIONS	99	6	6	
			INVOICE_ITEMS	99	3	3	
			SUPPLIERS_UPDATE	99	21	21	***
			SII_COLLECTION	99	5	5	
			ILISWEEK	99	5	5	
	SUPPLY_INDEX	INDEX	ISS_NSW_TEMP1_PK	99	3	3	
			CR_DB_ITEM_PK	99	11	11	
			CR_DB_HEADER_I1	99	7	7	
			WAREHOUSE_FIFO_STOCK_I3	99	2	2	

chk_nxt_ext.sql. This script lists free space within a tablespace, along with any objects that have NEXT extents larger than the largest free block in that tablespace. Objects that cannot generate another extent are marked as needing immediate attention (panic mode!), and objects that cannot generate two more extents are flagged with a warning. This information helps you to fix space allocation errors before they become a problem.

The following example tells us that there is one object in the STOCKTAKE tablespace that cannot throw another extent and two objects in the SUPPLY_DATA tablespace that cannot throw two extents.

```
# chk_nxt.sql
col name        format a20
col Biggest     format 999999 heading "Biggest"
col Smallest    format 999999 heading "Small"
col Average     format 999999 heading "Average"
col Tot_Blocks  format 9999   heading "Exts"
col Tot_Free    format 999999 Heading "Total"
col Max_Ext     format 999999 heading "Max Nxt"
col Panic       format a13    heading  Panic

define Blk_Kb=2048 /* Define Oracle Block Size */

Select T.name, Tot_Blocks, Tot_Free, Smallest, Average, Biggest,
       max(S.extsize*&Blk_Kb) Max_Ext,
       decode(T.name,'RBS','',
         decode(sum(greatest(sign(nvl((S.extsize*&Blk_Kb),0)-Biggest),0)),
           0,
           decode(sum(greatest(sign(nvl((S.extsize*2*&Blk_Kb),0)
             - Biggest),0)),  0, '',
```

```
                    'Warn    (x'  ||
                    to_char(sum(greatest(sign(nvl((S.extsize*2*&Blk_Kb),0)
                              - Biggest),0) ) )  || ')' ) ,
                    'PANIC (x'  ||
                    to_char(sum(greatest(sign(nvl((S.extsize*&Blk_Kb),0)
                       - Biggest),0)))
                    || ')' )  ) Panic
  from      sys.seg$ S,
            sys.ts$ T,
            sys.Free_Blocks F
  where     F.ts# = S.ts# (+)
  and       F.ts# = T.ts#
  group
     by     T.name, Biggest,Smallest,Average,Tot_Blocks,Tot_Free
  order
     by     T.name
  /
```

TABLEPSACE	Exts	Total	Small	Average	Biggest	Max Nxt	Panic
RBS	19	163796	90	8621	102398	5120	
STOCKTAKE	11	53068	100	4824	9858	10240	**Panic (x1)**
SUPPLY_DATA	14	69106	4	4936	28750	20480	**Warn (x2)**
SUPPLY_INDEX	2	536932	251444	268466	285488	15360	
SYSTEM	1	87352	87352	87352	87352	630	
TEMP	41	204798	1030	4995	5120		
TOOLS	2	51148	50	25574	51098	50	
USERS	1	51198	51198	51198	51198		

quotas.sql. This report provides a detailed summary of space usage. It shows both user by tablespace and tablespace by user. It also shows which data files contain what application data and in this way helps us to decide which tablespaces are more important to the recovery process. The report is also helpful in pinpointing who is using large amounts of space and who is using space in the wrong tablespace(s).

The following example shows that the SUPPLY user is using 50 kilobytes of the TOOLS tablespace. Because this doesn't make sense in terms of the way we set up the database, we know that the situation needs to be investigated.

```
# quotas.sql
set pagesize 65
set newpage 0

column  username format a25 heading 'Username'
column  tablespace_name format a25 heading 'Tablespace'
column  used format 9,999,999,999 heading 'Bytes Used'
compute sum of used on username
break on username skip 1 on report

select owner username, tablespace_name,
```

```
        sum(bytes) used
from    sys.dba_segments
group
    by owner, tablespace_name
order
    by 1, 3 desc
/

compute sum of used on tablespace_name
break on tablespace_name skip 1 on report

select tablespace_name, owner username,
       sum(bytes) used
from    sys.dba_segments
group
    by owner, tablespace_name
order
    by 1, 3 desc
/
```

Username	Tablespace	Bytes Used
STOCKTAKE	STOCKTAKE	994,232,320
************************		-------------
sum		994,232,320
SUPPLY	SUPPLY_DATA	1,502,044,160
	SUPPLY_INDEX	1,023,041,536
	TOOLS	51,200
************************		-------------
sum		2,525,136,896
SYS	RBS	41,984,000
	SYSTEM	12,519,424
************************		-------------
sum		54,503,424
SYSTEM	SYSTEM	2,887,680
************************		-------------
sum		2,887,680

Tablespace	Username	Bytes Used
RBS	SYS	41,984,000
************************		-------------
sum		41,984,000
STOCKTAKE	STOCKTAKE	994,232,320
************************		-------------
sum		994,232,320
SUPPLY_DATA	SUPPLY	1,502,044,160
************************		-------------
sum		1,502,044,160

SUPPLY_INDEX	SUPPLY	1,023,041,536
************************		--------------
sum		1,023,041,536
SYSTEM	SYS	12,519,424
	SYSTEM	2,887,680
************************		--------------
sum		15,407,104
TOOLS	SUPPLY	51,200
************************		--------------
sum		51,200

io.sql. This report contains a detailed breakdown of all database I/O per disk and per data file. You can use it as a tool in diagnosing disk I/O bottlenecks over the past week.

NOTE   Statistics generated from this procedure improve in accuracy the longer the database has been running. They will be misleading if they are taken too soon after starting an instance.

```
# io.sql
break   on Brk   skip 1 on report

column  brk     noprint
column  name    format a46
column  Reads   format 99999990
column  Writes  format 99999990
column  R_Perc  format 999.0
column  W_Perc  format 999.0

compute sum of Reads  on report
compute sum of Writes on report

select  substr(F.file_name,1,instr(F.file_name,'/',-1)) Brk,
        replace(F.file_name,'.dbf','') name,
        S.phyblkrd  Reads,  round((S.phyblkrd  / R.value) * 100,1) R_Perc,
        S.phyblkwrt Writes, round((S.phyblkwrt / W.value) * 100,1) W_Perc
from    sys.v_$filestat S,
        sys.v_$sysstat R,
        sys.v_$sysstat W,
        sys.dba_data_files F
where   F.file_id = S.file# (+)
and     R.name = 'physical reads'
and     W.name = 'physical writes'
order   by 1
/
select  substr(F.file_name,1,instr(F.file_name,'/',-1)) name,
        sum(S.phyblkrd)  Reads,
        round((sum(S.phyblkrd) / min(R.value) ) * 100,1) R_Perc,
```

```
          sum(S.phyblkwrt) Writes,
          round((sum(S.phyblkwrt) / min(W.value) ) * 100,1) W_Perc
from      sys.v_$filestat S,
          sys.v_$sysstat R,
          sys.v_$sysstat W,
          sys.dba_data_files F
where     F.file_id = S.file# (+)
and       R.name = 'physical reads'
and       W.name = 'physical writes'
group     by substr(F.file_name,1,instr(F.file_name,'/',-1))
order     by 1
/
select    F.tablespace_name name,
          sum(S.phyblkrd)  Reads,
          round((sum(S.phyblkrd) / min(R.value) ) * 100,1) R_Perc,
          sum(S.phyblkwrt) Writes,
          round((sum(S.phyblkwrt) / min(W.value) ) * 100,1) W_Perc
from      sys.v_$filestat S,
          sys.v_$sysstat R,
          sys.v_$sysstat W,
          sys.dba_data_files F
where     F.file_id = S.file# (+)
and       R.name = 'physical reads'
and       W.name = 'physical writes'
group     F.tablespace_name
order     by 1
/
```

Database Data Files	READS	R_PERC	WRITES	W_PERC
/dsk1/PRD/db/PRD_supply_data1	170172	41.7	7365	34.5
/dsk1/PRD/db/PRD_supply_data2	114435	28.0	105	.5
/dsk2/PRD/db/PRD_supply_index1	19368	4.7	4443	20.8
/dsk2/PRD/db/PRD_supply_index2	2426	.6	292	1.4
/dsk3/PRD/db/PRD_stocktake1	94012	23.0	0	.0
/dsk4/PRD/db/PRD_system1	7814	1.9	194	.9
/dsk4/PRD/db/PRD_rbs2	0	.0	0	.0
/dsk4/PRD/db/PRD_rbs1	17	.0	5518	25.9
/dsk4/PRD/db/PRD_temp1	0	.0	3437	16.1
/dsk4/PRD/db/PRD_tools1	0	.0	0	.0
/dsk4/PRD/db/PRD_users1	0	.0	0	.0
	---------		---------	
	408244		21354	

Database Data Files	READS	R_PERC	WRITES	W_PERC
/dsk1/PRD/db/	284607	69.7	7470	35.0
/dsk2/PRD/db/	21794	5.3	4735	22.2
/dsk3/PRD/db/	94012	23.0	0	.0

/dsk4/PRD/db/	7831	1.9	9149	42.9
	---------		---------	
sum	408244		21354	

Tablespace Name	READS	R_PERC	WRITES	W_PERC
RBS	17	.0	5518	25.9
SUPPLY_DATA	284607	69.7	7470	35.0
SUPPLY_INDEX	21794	5.3	4735	22.2
STOCKTAKE				
SYSTEM	94012	23.0	0	.0
TEMP	7814	1.9	194	.9
TOOLS	0		3437	16.1
USERS	0		0	
	---------		---------	
sum	408244		21354	

hit_ratio.sql. This report displays the database I/O "hit ratio" over the space of a week. This ratio is applicable only to the total uptime of the database.

NOTE   Statistics generated from this procedure improve in accuracy the longer the database has been running. They will be misleading if they are taken too soon after starting an instance.

```
# hitratio.sql
col log_reads  format 999,999,999,999
col phy_reads  format 999,999,999,999
col phy_writes format 999,999,999,999
col ratio      format 999.000000

select A.value + B.value Log_Reads,
       C.value           Phy_Reads,
       round(100*(A.value + B.value - C.value) / (A.value + B.value),6)
Ratio,
       D.value Phy_Writes
from   v$sysstat A, v$sysstat B, v$sysstat C, v$sysstat D
where  A.name = 'db block gets'
and    B.name = 'consistent gets'
and    C.name = 'physical reads'
and    D.name = 'physical writes'
/
```

LOG_READS	PHY_READS	RATIO	PHY_WRITES
16,096,302	2,055,946	87.227220	21,327

sysstats.sql. This report shows all database parameter settings for the last seven days. This information can be valuable in problem tracking and database tuning. For example, it helps you to identify any changes made to INIT.ORA parameters.

```
# sysstats.sql
sql>    select * from sys.v$sysstat;
sql>    select * from sys.v$parameter;
```

dc_cache.sql. This report contains a summary of all data cache parameters within the Oracle SGA. You can tune these parameters for Oracle6. For Oracle7, the information is helpful only as reference; it helps you to compute the proper size of the SHARED_POOL_SIZE parameter in Oracle7 databases.

```
# dc_cache.sql
set numw 8

select substr(parameter,1,20) parameter,
       gets,
       getmisses misses,
       decode(gets,0,100,round(100*getmisses/gets)) ratio,
       count,
       usage,
       decode(count,0, 100, round(100*usage/count)) capacity
from   sys.v_$rowcache
/
```

PARAMETER	GETS	MISSES	RATIO	COUNT	USAGE	CAPACITY
dc_free_extents	18570	104	1	41	31	76
dc_used_extents	95	49	52	24	2	8
dc_segments	646	255	39	232	229	99
dc_tablespaces	1469	5	0	14	5	36
dc_tablespaces	52	5	10	15	5	33
dc_tablespace_quotas	4	2	50	3	2	67
dc_files	0	0	100	1	0	0
dc_users	3667	29	1	42	29	69
dc_rollback_segments	9268	7	0	13	8	62
dc_objects	2888	550	19	614	610	99
dc_constraints	0	0	100	1	0	0
dc_object_ids	7	6	86	12	6	50
dc_tables	4977	354	7	380	376	99
dc_synonyms	456	108	24	116	108	93
dc_sequences	338	4	1	15	4	27
dc_usernames	6242	17	0	20	17	85
dc_database_links	0	0	100	1	0	0
dc_histogram_defs	0	0	100	1	0	0
dc_profiles	300	1	0	12	1	8
dc_users	0	0	100	1	0	0
dc_columns	28002	5228	19	5571	5563	100
dc_table_grants	5348	1638	31	1700	1638	96
dc_column_grants	0	0	100	1	0	0
dc_indexes	1948	237	12	281	258	92
dc_constraint_defs	258	119	46	159	119	75

dc_constraint_defs	7	4	57	5	4	80
dc_sequence_grants	16	7	44	8	7	88
dc_user_grants	2468	26	1	39	26	67

shared_pool.sql. This report shows statistics on both the shared pool and the block buffer areas of the SGA. The first SQL statement shows the total free space remaining in the shared pool. The second statement shows the number of times a SQL statement has to be (re)loaded and parsed within the shared pool. The last SQL statement shows the amount of free space currently in the SQL block buffer pool.

NOTE   Statistics generated from this procedure improve in accuracy the
              longer the database has been running. They will be misleading if
              they are taken too soon after starting an instance.

```
# sha_pool.sql
select S.name,
        S.bytes "Free Bytes",
       round((S.bytes/P.value)*100,2) Perc_Free,
       P.value / (1024*1024) SB_Pool_Mg
from   sys.v_$parameter P,
       sys.v_$sgastat S
where  S.name = 'free memory'
and    P.name = 'shared_pool_size'
/

select sum(loads),
       sum(EXECUTIONS),
       round((sum(loads) / sum(EXECUTIONS)) * 100, 4) Load_Perc
from   sys.v_$db_object_cache
/

select decode(STATUS,'FREE','Free','Used') Status,
       count(*)
from   v$bh
group  by decode(STATUS,'FREE','Free','Used')
/


NAME                          Free Bytes  PERC_FREE SB_POOL_MG
----------------------------- ----------  ---------- ----------
free memory                        66304        .32         20


SUM(LOADS) SUM(EXECUTIONS)  LOAD_PERC
---------- ---------------  ----------
       955           19195     4.9753
```

```
STATUS    COUNT(*)
------    ----------
Free           150
Used         15350
```

panic.sql. This script is our personal favorite—panic by name, panic by nature. In the unfortunate situation in which you have to rebuild the database from scratch (via the CREATE DATABASE command), this script provides you with a detailed breakdown of all the raw database components, scripted in SQL and ready to run. This one report has saved us from an embarrassing situation on more than one occasion.

The script automatically generates SQL to rebuild the following:

- Tablespaces (including multiple data files)
- User accounts (including tablespace quotas)
- Rollback segments
- Public synonyms
- Public grants
- Public database links
- Roles
- Profiles

You would never run the output from this script as is, but instead use it as a starting point to reconstruct your database. It's a good start simply to be able to replace your 20 gigabytes of data files back onto the same disks, each correctly sized, without having to think about "which files will fit where." While the data files are automatically being initialized by Oracle, you can get on with planning the next phase of the recovery. Prebuilding all user accounts before performing data imports also helps reduce the number of import errors and the number of views, triggers, and procedure compilation errors.

Having a detailed list of rollback segments, database links, tablespace quotas, and user accounts also helps to reduce those embarrassing oversights after you have completed the recovery. One very nice feature of this utility is the ability to reset all user passwords back to their settings in the lost database.

```
# panic.sql
set feedback off

Rem
Rem     Create All Tablespaces.
Rem

select 'create tablespace ' || T.tablespace_name || chr(10) ||
```

```
        'datafile ''' || F.file_name || ''' size ' || to_
char(F.bytes/1048576)
        || 'M' || chr(10) ||
        'default  storage (Initial ' || to_char(T.initial_extent) ||
        ' next ' || to_char(T.next_extent) || ' minextents ' ||
        to_char(T.min_extents) || chr(10) ||
        '         maxextents ' || to_char(T.max_extents) || ' pctincrease '
||
        to_char(T.pct_increase) || ') online;'
from
        sys.dba_data_files F,
        sys.dba_tablespaces  T
where
        T.tablespace_name  = F.tablespace_name
and     T.tablespace_name != 'SYSTEM'
and     F.file_id          = ( select min(file_id)
                                 from   sys.dba_data_files
                                 where  tablespace_name = T.tablespace_name )
/


Rem
Rem     Create All Tablespace Datafile Extents.
Rem

select 'alter tablespace ' || T.tablespace_name || chr(10) ||
        'add datafile ''' || F.file_name || ''' size ' ||
        to_char(F.bytes/1048576) || 'M;'
from
        sys.dba_data_files F,
        sys.dba_tablespaces  T
where
        T.tablespace_name = F.tablespace_name
and     F.file_id         != ( select min(file_id)
                                 from   sys.dba_data_files
                                 where  tablespace_name = T.tablespace_name )
/


Rem
Rem     Create System Roles
Rem

select 'create role '|| role ||
        decode(password_required,'N',' not identified;',
                                 ' identified externally;')
from    sys.dba_roles
/


Rem
Rem      Create System Profiles
Rem

select  distinct 'create profile ' || profile || ' limit ' || ';'
from    sys.dba_profiles
/
```

```
select  'alter role ' || profile || ' limit ' ||
        resource_name || ' ' || limit || ';'
from    sys.dba_profiles
where   limit   != 'DEFAULT'
and  (  profile != 'DEFAULT'
     or limit   != 'UNLIMITED' )
/


Rem
Rem     Create ALL User Connections
Rem

select 'create USER ' || username ||
        ' identified by XXXXX ' || chr(10) ||
        ' default tablespace ' || default_tablespace ||
        ' temporary tablespace '|| temporary_tablespace || chr(10) ||
        ' quota unlimited on ' || default_tablespace|| ' ' ||
        ' quota unlimited on ' || temporary_tablespace|| ';'
from    sys.dba_users
where   username not in ('SYSTEM','SYS','_NEXT_USER','PUBLIC')
/


Rem
Rem     Reset User Passwords
Rem

select 'alter USER ' || username || ' identified by values ''' ||
       password || ''';'
from    sys.dba_users
where   username not in ('SYSTEM','SYS','_NEXT_USER','PUBLIC')
and     password != 'EXTERNAL'
/
Rem
Rem     Create Tablespace Quotas
Rem

select 'alter USER ' || username || ' quota ' ||
       decode(max_bytes,-1,'unlimited',to_char(max_bytes/1024) ||' K') ||
       ' on tablespace '|| tablespace_name ||';'
from    sys.dba_ts_quotas
/


Rem
Rem     Grant System Privileges
Rem

select 'grant ' || S.name || ' to ' || U.username || ';'
from    system_privilege_map S,
        sys.sysauth$ P,
        sys.dba_users U
where   U.user_id   = P.grantee#
and     P.privilege# = S.privilege
and     P.privilege# < 0
/
```

```
Rem
Rem     Grant System Roles
Rem

Select 'grant ' || X.name || ' to ' || U.username || ';'
From    sys.user$ X,
        sys.dba_users U
where   X.user#  IN ( select  privilege#
                      From     sys.sysauth$
                      connect
                          by grantee#   = prior privilege#
                         and privilege# > 0
                        start
                          with grantee#  in (1, U.user_id )
                          and privilege# > 0
                    )
/


Rem
Rem     Create All PUBLIC Synonyms
Rem

select 'create public synonym ' || synonym_name || ' for ' ||
       decode(table_owner,'','',table_owner||'.') || table_name ||
       decode(db_link,'','','@'||db_link) || ';'
from   sys.dba_synonyms
where  owner = 'PUBLIC'
and    table_owner != 'SYS'
/


Rem
Rem     Create ALL Public Database Links
Rem

select 'create public database link ' || db_link || chr(10) ||
       'connect to ' || username || ' identified by XXXXXX using ''' ||
       host || ''';'
from   sys.dba_db_links
where  owner = 'PUBLIC'
/


Rem
Rem     Create Rollback Segments
Rem

select 'create rollback segment ' || segment_name ||
       ' tablespace ' || tablespace_name || chr(10) ||
       'storage (initial ' || to_char(initial_extent) ||
       ' next ' || to_char(next_extent) || ' minextents ' ||
       to_char(min_extents) || chr(10) ||
       ' maxextents ' || to_char(max_extents) || ') ' ||
       status || ';'
from   sys.dba_rollback_segs
where  segment_name != 'SYSTEM'
```

Output from the *panic.sql* script follows:

```
create tablespace RBS
datafile '/dsk4/PRD/db/PRD_rbs1.dbf' size 100M
default  storage (Initial 51200 next 51200 minextents 1
         maxextents 100 pctincrease 0) online;

create tablespace STOCKTAKE
datafile '/dsk3/PRD/db/PRD_stocktake1.dbf' size 1000M
default  storage (Initial 51200 next 51200 minextents 1
         maxextents 100 pctincrease 1) online;

create tablespace SUPPLY_DATA
datafile '/dsk1/PRD/db/PRD_supply_data1.dbf' size 1000M
default  storage (Initial 51200 next 51200 minextents 1
         maxextents 100 pctincrease 1) online;

create tablespace SUPPLY_INDEX
datafile '/dsk2/PRD/db/PRD_supply_index1.dbf' size 1000M
default  storage (Initial 51200 next 51200 minextents 1
         maxextents 100 pctincrease 1) online;

create tablespace TEMP
datafile '/dsk4/PRD/db/PRD_temp1.dbf' size 200M
default  storage (Initial 5242880 next 5242880 minextents 1
         maxextents 121 pctincrease 0) online;

create tablespace TOOLS
datafile '/dsk4/PRD/db/PRD_tools1.dbf' size 25M
default  storage (Initial 51200 next 51200 minextents 1
         maxextents 100 pctincrease 0) online;

create tablespace USERS
datafile '/dsk4/PRD/db/PRD_users1.dbf' size 25M
default  storage (Initial 51200 next 51200 minextents 1
         maxextents 100 pctincrease 0) online;

alter tablespace RBS
add datafile '/dsk4/PRD/db/PRD_rbs2.dbf' size 50M;

alter tablespace SUPPLY_DATA
add datafile '/dsk1/PRD/db/PRD_supply_data2.dbf' size 500M;

alter tablespace SUPPLY_DATA
add datafile '/dsk1/PRD/db/PRD_supply_data3.dbf' size 300M;

alter tablespace SUPPLY_INDEX
add datafile '/dsk2/PRD/db/PRD_supply_index2.dbf' size 500M;

create role BATCH identified externally;
create role SUPPLY_USER1 identified externally;
create role SUPPLY_READER identified externally;

create USER SUPPLY identified by XXXXX
```

```
default tablespace SUPPLY_DATA temporary tablespace TEMP
quota unlimited on SUPPLY_DATA  quota unlimited on TEMP;

create USER Oracle identified by XXXXX
default tablespace USERS temporary tablespace TEMP
quota unlimited on USERS  quota unlimited on TEMP;

create USER STOCKTAKE identified by XXXXX
default tablespace STOCKTAKE temporary tablespace TEMP
quota unlimited on STOCKTAKE  quota unlimited on TEMP;

alter USER SUPPLY identified by values '205DD262374D4A9D';
alter USER SUPPLY_RDR identified by values '4C8F240A18122986';
alter USER STOCKTAKE identified by values '0D2B39737E708D25';

alter USER SUPPLY quota unlimited on tablespace SUPPLY_DATA;
alter USER SUPPLY quota unlimited on tablespace SUPPLY_INDEX;
alter USER STOCKTAKE quota unlimited on tablespace STOCKTAKE;
grant UNLIMITED TABLESPACE to SYSTEM;

grant CREATE TRIGGER to SUPPLY;
grant GRANT ANY ROLE to SUPPLY;
grant CREATE ROLE to SUPPLY;
grant CREATE SEQUENCE to SUPPLY;
grant CREATE VIEW to SUPPLY;
grant CREATE PUBLIC SYNONYM to SUPPLY;
grant DROP ANY SYNONYM to SUPPLY;
grant CREATE ANY SYNONYM to SUPPLY;
grant CREATE SYNONYM to SUPPLY;
grant CREATE TABLE to SUPPLY;
grant ALTER USER to SUPPLY;
grant CREATE SESSION to SUPPLY;

create public synonym FORM_APP for SYSTEM.FORM_APP;
create public synonym FORM_AUTHUSER for SYSTEM.FORM_AUTHUSER;
create public synonym FORM_BLK for SYSTEM.FORM_BLK;
....................
create public synonym FORM_COMMENT for SYSTEM.FORM_COMMENT;
create public synonym SRW_TEXT_LONG for SYSTEM.SRW_TEXT_LONG;
create public synonym USER_PROFILE for SYSTEM.USER_PRIVS;

create rollback segment RBS1 tablespace RBS
storage (initial 10240 next 5242880 minextents 2
        maxextents 99) ONLINE;

create rollback segment RBS2 tablespace RBS
storage (initial 10240 next 5242880 minextents 2
        maxextents 99) ONLINE;

create rollback segment RBS3 tablespace RBS
storage (initial 10240 next 5242880 minextents 2
        maxextents 99) ONLINE;

create rollback segment RBS4 tablespace RBS
```

```
storage (initial 10240 next 5242880 minextents 2
       maxextents 99) ONLINE;
```

DBA_maint.sql

This script is a nightly maintenance check of the database. It can yield valuable database information and serve as an early warning of possible database problems. The most valuable feature of this routine is the nightly backup up of the control file, including a trace file copy of the control file structure. Having a copy of the control file over the last seven days is essential for database recovery protection.

You can never have too many copies of the control file. The control file structure must match the structure of the database you are trying to recover. For point-in-time recovery, this may be different from the current structure of the database (because new data files have been added, etc.).

We like to switch a new log file at the beginning of the day. This serves no real purpose other than starting each day with a fresh redo file and helping to verify that the archived log file directory has not been filled up by overnight processing.

```
# dba_maint.sql
sql>    alter database backup controlfile to 'FIN_cntrl_backup.&day' reuse;
sql>    alter database backup controlfile to TRACE noresetlogs;
sql>    alter system check datafiles;
sql>    alter system switch logfile;
```

```
Output :$Oracle_HOME/dbs :FIN_cntrl_backup.Mon        FIN_cntrl_backup.Tue
                          FIN_cntrl_backup.Mon        FIN_cntrl_backup.Tue
                          FIN_cntrl_backup.Wed        FIN_cntrl_backup.Thu
                          FIN_cntrl_backup.Fri        FIN_cntrl_backup.Sat
                          FIN_cntrl_backup.Sun
```

```
       user_dump_dest :18/09/95  00:15:05 ora_67492.trc   [Mon trace]
                        19/09/95  00:15:15 ora_345.trc     [Tue trace]
                        20/09/95  00:15:04 ora_34942.trc   [Wed trace]
                        21/09/95  00:15:47 ora_6934.trc    [Thu trace]
                        22/09/95  00:15:37 ora_12546.trc   [Fri trace]
                        23/09/95  00:15:06 ora_9035.trc    [Sat trace]
                        25/09/95  00:15:08 ora_9345.trc    [Sun trace]
```

The trace file output can also be very helpful in detailing exactly how the database was created. It provides the exact details of how the database was initially created and its current structure. This information is invaluable during recovery when you are trying to determine the format of the database at the point-in-time of the desired recovery.

```
    Dump file /oracle/PRD/dump/ora_21142.trc
Oracle7 Server Release 7.1.4.1.0 - Production Release
With the distributed and parallel query options
```

```
PL/SQL Release 2.1.4.0.0 - Production
Oracle_HOME = /oracle/v7.1.4
Oracle_SID = PRD
Oracle process number: 13 Unix process id: 21142
System name:HP-UP
Node name:thor
Release:A.09.04
Version:E
Machine:9000/887


Sun Sep 17 08:45:04 1995
Sun Sep 17 08:45:04 1995
*** SESSION ID:(13.451)
# The following commands will create a new control file and use it
# to open the database.
# No data other than log history will be lost. Additional logs may
# be required for media recovery of offline data files. Use this
# only if the current version of all online logs are available.
STARTUP NOMOUNT
CREATE CONTROLFILE REUSE DATABASE "XXXX" NORESETLOGS ARCHIVELOG
    MAXLOGFILES 16
    MAXLOGMEMBERS 2
    MAXDATAFILES 1000
    MAXINSTANCES 1
    MAXLOGHISTORY 100
LOGFILE
  GROUP 1 (
    '/dsk5/archive/PRD/redo/PRD_log1_A.dbf',
    '/dsk0/PRD/db/redo/PRD_log1_B.dbf'
  ) SIZE 10M,
  GROUP 2 (
    '/dsk5/archive/PRD/redo/PRD_log2_A.dbf',
    '/dsk0/PRD/db/redo/PRD_log2_B.dbf'
  ) SIZE 10M,
  GROUP 3 (
    '/dsk5/archive/PRD/redo/PRD_log3_A.dbf',
    '/dsk0/PRD/db/redo/PRD_log3_B.dbf'
  ) SIZE 10M
DATAFILE
  '/dsk4/PRD/db/PRD_system1.dbf' SIZE 100M,
  '/dsk4/PRD/db/PRD_rbs1.dbf' SIZE 100M,
  '/dsk4/PRD/db/PRD_temp1.dbf' SIZE 200M,
  '/dsk4/PRD/db/PRD_tools1.dbf' SIZE 25M,
  '/dsk4/PRD/db/PRD_users1.dbf' SIZE 25M,
  '/dsk1/PRD/db/PRD_supply_data1.dbf' SIZE 1000M,
  '/dsk2/PRD/db/PRD_supply_index1.dbf' SIZE 1000M,
  '/dsk1/PRD/db/PRD_supply_data2.dbf' SIZE 500M,
  '/dsk2/PRD/db/PRD_supply_index2.dbf' SIZE 500M,
  '/dsk4/PRD/db/PRD_rbs2.dbf' SIZE 50M,
  '/dsk3/PRD/db/PRD_stocktake1.dbf' SIZE 1000M
;
# Recovery is required if any of the datafiles are restored backups,
# or if the last shutdown was not normal or immediate.
RECOVER DATABASE
```

```
# All logs need archiving and a log switch is needed.
ALTER SYSTEM ARCHIVE LOG ALL;
# Database can now be opened normally.
ALTER DATABASE OPEN;
```

Some very busy systems with lots of diverse applications and limited memory will also need to regularly flush their shared buffer pool because this pool can become very fragmented. Large cursors and PL/SQL blocks insist on contiguous memory within the pool. Flushing the pool frees all shared pool blocks that are not currently in use. This temporarily degrades buffer performance, forcing all cursors to be reparsed as part of their next access. Databases that do not get shut down on a regular (usually nightly) basis and that are subject to shared buffer pool fragmentation should add the following statement to their nightly *DBA_maint.sql* routine:

```
sql>    alter system flush shared_pool;
```

If you do flush your shared pool, remember to repin all large, frequently accessed packages back into the shared pool. (See the discussion of pinning in Chapter 7, *Tuning PL/SQL.*)

```
sql>    execute PER.special_package.LoadMe;
sql>    execute dbms_shared_pool.keep ('PER.special_package);
sql>    execute FIN.special_package.LoadMe;
sql>    execute dbms_shared_pool.keep ('FIN.special_package);
```

Database maintenance scripts

The scripts in this section extend the reach of our database recovery tool box. As we've said before, we need a valid copy of the control file before we can attempt recovery. This means backing up a copy of the control file *every time* we alter the database structure. Rather than relying on ourselves or our team to remember to do this, we discipline the team to perform all database alterations via a number of script files. These script files ensure that the database will never be exposed in a recovery situation.

create_tablespace.sql. This script prompts the DBA for all of the information needed to create the new tablespace and automatically back up the control file. Remember that we need a control file that matches the structure of the database at all times.

```
# c_tspace.sql
create    tablespace &tspace
datafile '&file_spec' size &size_in_Mg M
default   storage ( initial     50K
                    next        50K
                    minextents  1
                    maxextents  100
                    pctincrease 0 )
```

```
/
alter database backup controlfile to '&tspace._control.bkp' reuse
/


sql>@create_tablespace.sql

    Enter value for tspace: GL
    Enter value for file_spec: /dsk2/PRD/db/PRD_gl1.dbf
    Enter value for size_in_mg: 200
```

alter_tablespace.sql

This script prompts the DBA for all of the information needed to alter an existing tablespace and automatically back up the control file.

```
# a_tspace.sql
alter    tablespace &tspace
add datafile '&file_spec' size &size_in_Mg M
/
alter database backup controlfile to '&tspace._control.bkp' reuse
/

sql>@alter_tablespace.sql

    Enter value for tspace: GL
    Enter value for file_spec: /dsk2/PRD/db/PRD_gl1.dbf
    Enter value for size_in_mg: 200
```

create_user.sql. This script prompts the DBA for all of the information needed to create a new user. This ensures that each user account will be set up with the correct default and temporary tablespace settings.

```
# c_user.sql
accept usr prompt 'New User          : '
accept pwd prompt 'Password [Externally] : '
accept ts  prompt 'Default Tspace [Users] : '
accept tmp prompt 'Temp Tspace      [Temp] : '
accept prf prompt 'User Profile       [] : '

set term off
set veri off

col pwd   new_value pwd
col ts    new_value ts
col tmp   new_value tmp
col prf   new_value prf

select decode('&pwd','','EXTERNALLY','BY &pwd') pwd,
       decode('&ts','','USERS','&ts') ts,
       decode('&tmp','','TEMP','&tmp') tmp,
       decode('&prf','',' ','profile &prf') prf
from   dual
```

```
/
set term on
set feed on

create user &usr
identified  &pwd
default tablespace &ts
quota unlimited on &ts
temporary tablespace &tmp
quota unlimited on &tmp &prf
/
grant connect to &usr
```

RI_disable.sql and RI_enable.sql. These scripts are used to disable and reenable referential integrity contraints on database tables. When data need to be reloaded into individual tables, deleting the old data can be prevented by referential integrity. Scripts to simply enable and disable integrity are often very handy.

```
RI_disable.sql

sql>select 'alter table '|| T.owner||'.'||T.table_name||
       ' disable constraint '||T.constraint_name||';'
from    USER_CONSTRAINTS T,
        USER_CONSTRAINTS F
where
        F.table_name     like upper('&Table_Name')
and     F.constraint_type  in ('P', 'U')
and
        T.R_CONSTRAINT_NAME = F.CONSTRAINT_NAME
/

sql>@RI_disable
    Enter value for table_name : DEPT

    alter table SCOTT.EMP disable constraint FK_EMP_DEPT;
    alter table SCOTT.SALES disable constraint FK_SALES_DEPT;


    RI_enable.sql

# tab_rl.sql
sql>select 'alter table '|| T.owner||'.'||T.table_name||
       ' enable constraint '||T.constraint_name||';'
from    USER_CONSTRAINTS T,
        USER_CONSTRAINTS F
where
        F.table_name     like upper('&Table_Name')
and     F.constraint_type  in ('P', 'U')
and
        T.R_CONSTRAINT_NAME = F.CONSTRAINT_NAME
/

sql>@RI_enable
    Enter value for table_name : SALES
```

```
alter table SCOTT.EMP enable constraint FK_EMP_DEPT;
alter table SCOTT.SALES enable constraint FK_SALES_DEPT;
```

DBA_connect.sql. This routine allows us to connect to a specific user account without knowing or initializing the password. This is helpful because changing passwords in the middle of the night during a recovery exercise can cause a real problem the next day. Obviously, you need DBA privilege to perform this action.

Certain applications, including Oracle Financials, have passwords encrypted into their application code. These passwords can be modified only by special routines. If you do not know the current password, you cannot change it from within the application.

```
# dba_conn.sql
sql>column password new_value _password_
    accept usercode char prompt 'Connect to Usercode : '

    select password
    from   sys.dba_users
    where  username = upper('&usercode')
    /

    alter user &usercode identified by _temp_password_
    /
    connect &usercode/_temp_password_

    alter user &usercode identified by value '&_password_'
    /
```

Recovering the Database

One of the most important tasks a DBA must perform before a database enters production is to set up a *recovery strategy* for the database. This is a very simple exercise that can yield valuable results. Strategies may differ for different organizations and databases. They may be very simple for noncritical databases, or they may be very complex for more business-critical applications.

NOTE   The commands SQLDBA and SVRMGR are interchangeable throughout this chapter. SQLDBA is not available after Oracle 7.2.

Hardware Failure Recovery

It's a sad fact that hardware failures happen, and always at the worst possible time. Don't bet the safety of your database against your hardware. You must practice hypothetical database recoveries over and over again so that you'll be ready when the real thing occurs. Draw up a report detailing what you will need to do to recover the database if you permanently lose a physical disk. You should also specify a number of alternatives in order of preference. For example:

```
/dsk1  Oracle binary software  a: Copy from development machine
                               b: Restore from "system" backup
                               c: Reload from original Oracle media

/dsk2  User home directories   a: Restore from "system" backup
          Online Redos "duplex A"  Copy from "duplex B" set

/dsk8  GL "table" data files   a: Recover from last backup, roll forward

/dsk9  GL "index" data files   a: Recover from last backup, roll forward
                               b: Recreate indexes manually
```

It isn't our intention to provide detailed recovery case studies in this book. Some good texts are available now that provide information beyond what is contained in the standard Oracle documentation. As a DBA, it's your responsibility to read everything you can find on database recovery. In this section, we provide information in an effort to make your recovery from hardware failure as smooth and timely as possible.

One spare disk on each production machine

Always have at least one spare (mounted) disk of a size that is as least as large as the largest database data file disk. There is nothing worse than losing a vital disk and having the means to recover your database but having no disk to place it on. The DBA at a site should have the privilege and knowledge to mount a disk or have 24-hour access to a system administrator who does. Never sacrifice the disk to other temporary uses. Temporary disk allocation ends up being permanent at most sites.

Spare disk capacity on each production machine

Be sure that each machine has immediate expansion potential. Spare disk bays, power supply, and disk controller capacity are all necessary. Database recoveries often take more physical disk space than the raw database. Multiple archive files will need to be recalled, and a duplicated recovery database may even need to be constructed.

On a number of occasions, we have found it quicker to back up the database directly to disk, rather than tape, before beginning a recovery. Spare disk capacity can give you an alternative recovery option.

Adequate hardware maintenance agreement with vendors

Does your current hardware maintenance contract meet your business needs? A 48-hour turnaround on a new CPU board may not be acceptable to your 500 users.

Compatible disaster recovery machine

Be sure that you always have an alternative, compatible machine available to you. This may be your development machine. The processing power and available memory do not have to be as large those of as your production machine, but they must be large enough to run your core business requirements in an emergency situation. Sufficient disk space is required to download the core application data from the database. Large history tables and the like can often be skipped.

Compatibility is the most important characteristic of your alternative hardware. It must have the *exact same*:

- Machine type/vendor

- Operating system version

- Oracle version

- Tape drive device(s)

- I/O connections (X25, TCP, etc.)

It must have *compatible*:

- Disk sizes

- Disk structure/layout

It is always good to establish some kind of *destruction priority* for your development machine. In the unlikely event that you have to quickly recover your production application to the development machine, which development databases/applications should you delete first? Your may even need to delete all of them. It is unlikely that you will have enough time to back up your development databases. Last night's backup may have to do.

Never compromise database standards

Compromising data file location standards to speed up a database recovery will invariably come back to haunt you at the worst possible time. Generally, data file layouts and physical disk structures have been well thought out and carefully designed before an application goes to production. It's a bad idea to compromise during the stress of a disaster.

Always mirror archived redo log disks. Never borrow that spare mirrored disk with the intention of replacing it when one finally becomes available. If the business requirements within your organization deemed it sufficient to mirror critical application data before the application went live, those same reasons still apply.

Always place database data files on dedicated data file disks. These disks are structured for I/O balance, application table grouping, database application recoverability, availability, and so on. If a tablespace fills up and needs to be extended, try to avoid temporarily placing a data file at a nonstandard data file location (such as root or user home disks). Losing a disk and not being sure what has been lost will only multiply the problem.

Publicize disk structure and layouts

You need to have an intimate knowledge of the disk layout on your machine. This isn't as easy as it sounds. With all of today's advances in virtual disk partitioning, disk striping, and RAID levels, the poor DBAs can make some very fundamental mistakes. Many alternatives are now available to build up and break down disk volumes. Both hardware- and software-level disk management utilities are beginning to flood the market. DBAs go to great lengths to reduce the odds of a disaster by painstakingly dividing conflicting database files up over all the available disks. *Never assume that a disk maps to a single physical device.*

You can use any of the following strategies on your machine:

Disk striping

> This means that multiple disks are all interlinked and that separate database data files may not be separated at all.

Disk partitioning

> This may mean that what looks like two 1-gigabyte disks is, in fact, a single 2-gigabyte disk—nice information to know before you begin laying out data files!

Virtual disk partitioning

> This is a different kind of headache. A logical volume can be built up from many smaller partitions on several physical disk devices. A problem can arise when an existing logical volume needs to be expanded. Rather than copy all the data to a larger volume, an extra partition is added to the current volume. Less work for the system administrator may mean a job loss for the unsuspecting DBA!

Disk mirroring

> This can present some surprises. We have consulted at sites that have absolutely guaranteed to us that our archived redo log volume was mirrored. On one occasion, we found that the disk was mirrored, but the mirror had unfortunately been automatically disabled by the operating system after detecting I/O errors. Nobody read the system log, so nobody noticed that the mirror was broken, for three months! On another occasion, we discovered that the two 1-gigabyte partitions that were being mirrored were actually on the same physical disk. This gave no redundant data protection and slowed down all I/O to that device.

Database Corruption Recovery

The other major cause of database recovery is database object corruption. Most often, application objects are corrupted and/or deleted by human error. Occasionally, application objects can be corrupted by the Oracle software itself.

Human error

This is the big one. For every recovery that is performed as a result of hardware failure, we estimate that at least four are caused by human error. Today's hardware is very reliable. Operating systems and application software are rigorously tested. Why can't someone invent the perfect DBA? Because we're human, that's why.

Those of you who have done any of the following, raise your hands:

- Dropped the wrong table
- Dropped the wrong user (via CASCADE)
- Deleted the wrong data file
- Truncated a table by mistake
- Dropped a sequence

To add extra complexity to the unfortunate DBA's lot, we also have users roaming around our precious databases running untested program!

A complicating issue with many of these disaster scenarios is that the database may still be functioning acceptably. Users of other applications in the same database are none the wiser. Even the affected application may still be operational, simply missing a single table or a handful of history tables.

Recovery from human error often takes several times longer than recovery from hardware failure. Hardware recovery means restoring the database to the current time. Object corruption means that the problem has happened in the past. A major problem of a point-in-time roll forward is that you must roll forward the whole database to the one point-in-time. You cannot roll forward a single data file, start up the database, extract the data, and then restart the roll forward to current time.

This is what you need to do to recover a single dropped table:

- Shut down the database cleanly
- Back up the entire database as it currently stands
- Restore the entire database from the last valid hot or cold backup

- Restore all archived redo logs from the time of the backup to past the time of corruption

- Recover (roll forward) the database to just prior to the time of corruption

- Open the database with the RESETLOGS options

- Export the lost information (EXP utility)

- Restore the entire database from the last (current) recovery

- Open the database in EXCLUSIVE mode

- Import the recovered tables (IMP utility)

- Shut down the database cleanly

- Back up the entire database again

- Open the database for normal user access

This action list makes hardware recovery seem simple!

One real danger of recovery from human error is that you are exposing a "healthy" database to many more dangers simply to recover a small group of objects. We have seen databases completely trashed because the DBA was just trying to recover a single 10-row table. He recovered the data files, performed the roll forward, opened the database, and recovered his one table. Everything was looking good. After restoring his original database, though, he discovered that he could not open it. He had corrupted his online redo log files by the RESETLOGS command from the point-in-time recovery. He went from losing a single 10-row table to missing the entire database. He was not happy.

Internal object corruption

Database objects can be accidentally corrupted by the database software itself. This corruption cannot be detected (or fixed) by either hot or cold database backups. The only way to identify a corrupted object is by reading the corrupted Oracle block. This can be done by an application program or by the EXP utility.

To recover from this type of corruption, you must restore the data from a noncorrupted backup and roll forward all changes (archive logs). Alternatively, you can recover the object(s) from a prior export dump file when no roll forward is possible. If you are fortunate enough to have corrupted only an index, it can be regenerated from the source table data.

Since object corruption cannot be detected by normal database backups, you must perform full database exports on a regular (nightly) basis.

With Oracle's support, it is possible to export data from a corrupted table by skipping the affected Oracle block(s). This does mean that whatever records are in the bad data block will be lost. This export facility is an undocumented feature and should be used only as a last resort under Oracle support guidance.

NOTE   Our only experiences with object corruption have been on Version
            6 databases. This does not mean that the problem will not occur
            with later Oracle versions, but it is encouraging that the problems
            appear to be less prevalent there.

Recovering Databases Onto a Secondary Machine

When we are confronted with a database recovery, our personal preference is to perform the recovery on another machine. Having already suffered the consequences of one human error, why place the database (and the DBA) at further risk by exposing it to a database recovery?

Database recoveries are a much easier and safer exercise when they are performed on another node. This way, the entire database does not need to be restored, only the section of the database from which you need to extract information. Using a secondary machine gives us multiple attempts at the recover and, more important, removes the possibility of corrupting "good" data files while attempting to recover a damaged one.

Most database recoveries that we've been involved with have required only partial database recovery. We usually have had to recover only one tablespace or one table. In many cases, we were fortunate enough to be able to keep the healthy part of the database online and available to the user base, while we recovered the corrupted portion on the backup (development) machine.

Point-in-time partial database recoveries are appropriate when any of the following have occurred:

- A table has been accidentally dropped.
- A rogue report has incorrectly updated 20,000 records.
- You need to reconstruct data as at the last month-end.

What is required?

This section describes what you need to perform a recovery on a secondary machine.

An alternative compatible machine. All partial database recoveries should be performed on a second node. The recovered database must be mounted with the same SID. Do not try to execute a partial database recovery on the production machine. Even though the machine *can* be down, it is a risk worth avoiding.

A modified copy of the INIT.ORA file. The INIT.ORA file should match the production version except for a few obvious modifications. Only one control file is actually necessary. Its location will need to be altered. You will have to alter all directory-dependent entries, such as archive and dump file directories. You do not need multiple database writers, parallel query processing and the like. The size of the shared buffer pool and block buffers can also be reduced to suit the smaller machine.

Here is an example of a production version of the INIT.ORA file (called *initPRD.ora*):

```
db_name                     = PRD
control_files               = ( /oracle/PRD/admin/PRD_control1.dbf,
                                /dsk1/PRD/admin/PRD_control2.dbf,
                                /dsk5/archive/PRD/admin/PRD_control3.dbf )

rollback_segments           = (rbs1, rbs2, rbs3, rbs4)

background_dump_dest        = /oracle/PRD/dump
core_dump_dest              = /oracle/PRD/dump
user_dump_dest              = /oracle/PRD/dump
log_archive_dest            = /dsk5/archive/PRD/arch
log_archive_format          = _PRD_%t_%s.dbf

db_writers                  = 4
sort_area_size              = 1048576
sort_area_retained_size     = 65536
db_block_buffers            = 35000
shared_pool_size            = 31457280
```

Here is the partial recovery *initPRD.ora* extract:

```
db_name                     = PRD
control_files               = /recover/PRD_control1.dbf

rollback_segments           = (rbs1, rbs2, rbs3, rbs4)

background_dump_dest        = /recover/dump
core_dump_dest              = /recover/dump
user_dump_dest              = /recover/dump
log_archive_dest            = /recover/archive/arch
log_archive_format          = _PRD_%t_%s.dbf

sort_area_size              = 65536
sort_area_retained_size     = 65536
db_block_buffers            = 2000
shared_pool_size            = 6000000
```

One valid control file. The control file must match the structure of the database being recovered. If the database is from two days ago, the control file must match the database structure as of two days ago. Only one control file is required. Although more can be used, they are of little use. This database is only a temporary being.

All relevant archived redo files. All archived redo files must be restored from tape. These files must cover the time from before the time of the backup from which the oldest data file was sourced to past the time of the required data recovery. All archives must be available. Missing the odd one here and there is not going to work.

Enough free disk space. The secondary machine requires enough spare disk to hold the SYSTEM, ROLLBACK, and corrupted tablespace(s). These tablespaces may be made up of several data files. Don't worry about trying to balance disk I/O. If all of the data files fit on a single disk, that's fine. In this case. we are concerned with recovering data, not the speed or contention of the temporary database.

Tablespace datafiles may be sourced from different backup cycles, even from different backup types (e.g., cold and hot).

Partial recovery steps

This section summarizes the most important steps you need to perform during recover. Remember that every system is different.

Restore all necessary files to the secondary machine. You must place copies of all of the files you will need during recovery on the secondary machine.

Build an abbreviated INIT.ORA file. This file contains only the parameters necessary during recovery. We described this in the section called "Internal object corruption" earlier in this chapter.

Mount the database. The following example shows sample commands:

```
SQLDBA> connect internal
SQLDBA> startup mount pfile=/xxx/xx/recover/initPRD.ora
```

Alter the location of all redo files. Remember to rename all online redo log files, including duplexed redo log files. You'll run commands such as these:

```
SQLDBA> alter database rename datafile '/.../.../redo/PRD_log1_A.dbf'
             to '/xx/xx/recover/PRD_log1_A.dbf';
SQLDBA> alter database rename datafile '/.../.../redo/PRD_log1_B.dbf'
             to '/xx/xx/recover/PRD_log1_B.dbf';
SQLDBA> alter database rename datafile '/.../.../redo/PRD_log2_A.dbf'
             to '/xx/xx/recover/PRD_log2_A.dbf';
SQLDBA> alter database rename datafile '/.../.../redo/PRD_log2_B.dbf'
```

```
                   to '/xx/xx/recover/PRD_log2_B.dbf';
SQLDBA> alter database rename datafile '/.../.../redo/PRD_log3_A.dbf'
                   to '/xx/xx/recover/PRD_log3_A.dbf';
SQLDBA> alter database rename datafile '/.../.../redo/PRD_log3_B.dbf'
                   to '/xx/xx/recover/PRD_log3_B.dbf';
```

Alter the location of all restorable data files. You'll run commands such as these to indicate the new locations of the data files being restored:

```
SQLDBA> alter database rename datafile '/.../.../system1.dbf'
                   to '/xx/xx/recover/system1.dbf';
SQLDBA> alter database rename datafile '/.../.../rback1.dbf'
                   to '/xx/xx/recover/rback1.dbf';
SQLDBA> alter database rename datafile '/.../.../rback2.dbf'
                   to '/xx/xx/recover/rback2.dbf';
SQLDBA> alter database rename datafile '/.../.../gl_dat1.dbf'
                   to '/xx/xx/recover/gl_dat1.dbf';
```

Move all nonrequired data files offline. All data files that are not involved in the restore (those that have not been restored to the development machine) need to be taken offline. During the database recovery, Oracle recognizes data files that are offline and simply skips all changes meant for those files.

```
SQLDBA> alter database datafile '/.../.../ap_tab1.dbf' offline;
SQLDBA> alter database datafile '/.../.../ap_tab2.dbf' offline;
SQLDBA> alter database datafile '/.../.../ap_idx1.dbf' offline;
        ...       ...      ...      ...
SQLDBA> alter database datafile '/.../.../gl_idx1.dbf' offline;
```

Recover database . Recover the database to immediately prior to the point of data loss or corruption. For example:

```
SQLDBA> recover until time 'yyyy:mm:yy:hh:mi:ss' using backup controlfile
       ... apply all archives ...
```

or

```
SQLDBA> recover until change nnnnnnnn using backup controlfile
       ... apply all archives ...
```

or

```
SQLDBA> recover until cancel using backup controlfile
          ... apply all archives ...
SQLDBA> cancel
```

After you've applied all archived log files requested by SQLDBA, you'll see the message "SQLDBA> Media recovery complete."

Open the database. The database can be opened only with the RESETLOGS option after a point-in-time recovery. This command initializes (overwrites) all online redo files and then checkpoints all online data files and control files. As a result, it may take some time.

```
SQLDBA>alter database open resetlogs;
```

At this point, you may be fortunate enough to have recovered your partial database to a stable point in time. If so, the database will open. If the database is not at a stable point (e.g., a data file requires further recovery), the following Oracle error (or something similar, depending on your operating system and Oracle version) will be issued from the DATABASE OPEN command.

```
ORA-1195 Online backup of file xxxx needs more recovery to be
consistent.
```

If this occurs, it means that a transaction was in an incomplete state at the exact time to which we recovered the database. All you need to do is continue with normal database recovery and roll the incomplete transaction back (hence the need to also recover the ROLLBACK tablespace). For example:

```
SQLDBA> recover database;
```

Apply all archived log files requested by SQLDBA (usually only one logfile). On completion of the normal recovery, you'll see the message, MEDIA RECOVERY COMPLETE. This time it is for real. Open the database again:

```
SQLDBA> alter database open resetlogs;
```

Immediately export the data you require. You now have successfully recovered a portion of your production database. By moving the recovery to another machine, we have eased the danger of a database restore/roll forward and moved the infamous RESETLOGS command away from our production data. More important, if things do not work out, you can delete everything and start again.

Partial database recovery does provide most sites with the ability to recover parts of their database on another node. It is unusual to have sufficient free space to rebuild your entire production database, but disk space for a portion of the database is possible. Anything is better than having to recover over the top of your existing database.

NOTE   A very annoying feature of the ALTER DATABASE RENAME datafile command is that the source (original) directory structure of the data file must exist. Even though you may be moving the file to a completely unrelated disk and disk structure, the old structure must be valid. When executing a partial database restore to your development machine, you will have to create the production directory structure for the database files that are involved. These directory structures do not have to be mount points as they probably are on the production node. We hope that this feature is a temporary oversight by Oracle and that it will be fixed in the near future.

Desperate Situations Require Desperate Measures

The following section covers some unorthodox alternatives to recovery situations. These suggestions are meant only to help you recover your database when nothing else works.

No current control file

If you can't find a control file, the first thing to do is to determine the exact structure of the database as of the time of recovery. Then try to locate an alternative control file from another backup cycle with the correct structure. Any backup cycle will do (cold or hot) as long the database structure is correct.

If you can't recover a control file, you can try to reconstruct a new control file from your daily trace output. This output should be generated as part of your normal daily database maintenance routines. (See the discussion of the *DBA_Maint.sql* script earlier in this chapter.)

As a last resort, try to source an old control file from the file system backup. It is possible to use an open (operational) control file to recover your database. Always make sure that at least one of your control files is also included in the file system backup. Oracle recommends that you do not try a database recovery via an open control file.

All of these forms of control file recovery need to use the recovery clauses:

```
SQLDBA>  recover database ...... using backup controlfile;
    ....     ....     ....
SQLDBA>  open database resetlogs;
```

Missing archive log(s)

Database recoveries are very difficult when a vital archive log is missing. Our first desperation move in this case is to try to figure out what time period the missing archive would have spanned. Then we would restore all online redo log files from the database backups immediately before and after that period. All databases should have at least three online redo logs. One of the redo logs, restored may actually be the one we want. It's a long shot, we know, but worth a try.

If you can't restore an archived log file, your only alternative is to roll forward the database to the last available log file prior to the missing one. Cancel the recovery, and open the database using RESETLOGS. An old database is usually better than no database.

NOTE   Always copy archived logfiles to a minimum of two tapes (not twice to the same tape) before they are removed from disk.

Missing online redo log file(s)

Corrupted or lost online redo log files should never lead to data loss for an Oracle7 (or better) database. Redo files should all be duplexed on different phys- ical disks. If one file is lost, simply copy the good (duplexed) online redo log file on top of the bad one.

One valuable feature of duplexed redo log files is that the database will continue to function as long as at least one copy of each online redo log file remains intact. This feature does have a downside. If an online redo log file is lost or corrupted, a simple warning message is recorded in the ALERT log file. This same warning is issued every time the database is started and shut down. Databases that appear normal and healthy can in fact be time bombs waiting to explode.

Loss of any redo log file while a database is closed down is not significant. Provided that the database was shut down cleanly, no information is required by the database from the latest redo log file. Simply open the database with the RESETLOGS clause. This action will cause the missing redo log file to be recreated.

Nevertheless, we have seen many databases exposed to redo log file loss. A common mistake is to place the duplexed redo log file sets on different logical disk partitions that actually prove to be on the same physical disk.

Another unforgivable mistake is to incorrectly duplex the redo log files onto the same disk. We have actually witnessed a case in which, rather than having two duplexed sets of three redo log files, there were three sets of two redo log files, with all three duplexes of the same logfile on the same disk. This gives zero protection and serves only to slow down the application by bottlenecking the redo disks. This is a bad mistake by the DBA at database creation time. The syntax for REDO LOGFILE GROUPS is a little confusing; always check it carefully. Two minutes spent looking up the correct syntax could save your database.

Missing data file(s)

A missing or unrecoverable data file should not mean the end of your recovery—or your career. The first task is to restore the missing data file(s) from the latest backup and roll forward the archived log files. If that tape is not restorable, don't give up. Provided that you have retained the archived log files for a period long enough to span several database backup cycles, the missing data file can be sourced from a prior database backup. You can even mix and match hot and cold backup data files from several backup cycles. Remember the following:

- Never purge archived log file tapes until you've achieved at least three full, successful database backups.

- Never place archived log files on the same tape as the database backup.

- Always copy archived log files to a minimum of two different tapes before deleting them from disk.

NOTE   Oracle recommends that you do not source data files for a single tablespace from different backup cycles. Although we have managed to recover a database with tablespace files mixed and matched from several sources in a test environment, we prefer not to do it if we can avoid it.

Lack of team experience

Oracle support must be sick to death of customers ringing up complaining that their database recovery is not working and asking what they should do. If you are unsure of what you are doing, ring support first, not after the damage is done. Companies pay large sums of money for support, so use it in the best way you can.

All members of the DBA team must practice database recoveries regularly. Doing so proves that your backup routines are solid and gives invaluable experience to your team members. We have had a number of debates with other DBAs who claim that particular functions or routines do or do not work. These opinions are often based on personal experiences from prior versions of Oracle or other operating systems. If you have a question or concern about database recovery, try it out in a controlled environment (one in which your career is not on the line).

Recovery scenarios described in books (this book included) always sound straightforward. Real life can be more complex. Never bet your database on something you have only read about in a book. Test, test, and retest as much and as often as you can.

Not enough disk space for an alternative recovery

Here's the situation: You want to do the safe thing and recover your database to an alternative host to extract some lost data. But recovering it to the production environment will open the database to unnecessary exposure and mean production downtime. Your development machine does not have sufficient disk space to restore the production database. What can you do?

First, try to perform a partial database recovery. This involves only the SYSTEM, ROLLBACK, and actual tablespace containing the lost data. Indexes, temporary tablespaces, referential integrity tables and the like need not be restored.

If the tablespace containing the lost data is too big to restore to the development machine, there may still be an alternative. If the tablespace is made up of several data files, restore only the single data file that contains the lost data segment. This is unconventional but possible. Details on which physical data file actually holds the segment(s) in question can be obtained from the table *sys.dba_extents.* If the SYSTEM, ROLLBACK, or tablespace data file(s) are still too large to be restored, you have a real problem.

As a safeguard to disk space problems, set a maximum database data file size to be less than or equal to the maximum disk size of your alternative restoration host. A 2-gigabyte data file will not fit on a 1.2-gigabyte disk drive, no matter how hard you try. We like to set an arbitrary maximum data file size of 1,000 megabytes. The 1,000-megabyte barrier gives us the necessary breathing space to compress whatever files are on those disks and then be able to restore our largest data file to it.

Ask Oracle

A number of undocumented INIT.ORA parameters and event settings are available. Many of these special functions are directly related to database recovery and associated recovery workarounds. However, even if you know what these undocumented features look like, never risk your database to an undocumented feature without first having talked to Oracle support. These features are operating system and hardware platform specific. What may have worked for your friend last week could trash your database. Ask Oracle.

Not Enough Time to Back Up Before and After Recovery

Always back up the entire database *before* beginning a production restoration in case you make it even worse. And always backup the entire database *after* a database recovery so that you have a stable point in time to recover from in case another problem occurs (problems always happen in threes). Convincing your organization that these backups are necessary can be difficult. Explaining that the recovery took only 30 minutes but that the database will be unavailable for another five hours can be downright dangerous. How can you speed up these database backups?

Is the database mirrored? In situations in which you are fortunate enough to have a mirrored database, simply split the mirror. Taking one full side of the mirror offline gives you your "before" database backup in a matter of minutes. If the recovery exercise is successful, silver the mirror again. If the database restore fails, copy the original mirrored data files over to the second set of mirrored disks and try the exercise again. The same principle can be used to back up the database after the recovery.

Do you have any spare disk space? Spare disk is always a valuable commodity. When we need to back up the database in a hurry, we compress the database to the spare disk. With SMP and MMP machines, several database data files can be copied and compressed in parallel. An average-sized UNIX database will compress down to only one-fifth its physical size. This means that a 10-gigabyte database can be held on a 2-gigabyte spare disk. (See the first example below.)

Once the database has been restored, users may not be prepared to wait for any type of backup. It is the DBA's responsibility to explain to his or her organization the risk it is taking by not backing up at this point and what the worst case scenario could be. If the organization still insists on making the database available to the user immediately, a hot backup is your only alternative. The hot backup could be either to tape or to a spare disk.

Parallel cold backup to disk

The following is a special cold backup script that we use to quickly copy a database to a spare disk. This script is best suited for SMP or MMP machines.

Multistreaming a cold backup directly to disk is often the only acceptable way of securing a backup before or after a database recovery. Tape backup can be unacceptably slow. Rather than relying on a single cold backup to tape before a critical database reorganization or software upgrade, we always take a simultaneous cold backup to our spare disk. The database is down while the normal tape backup is executing, so another copy to disk will not noticeably slow down the process by an additional amount. Restoring our database from disk rather than tape is also much quicker. If anything does go wrong, our backout window is a lot smaller.

```
# cold_dsk.sql

Script "cold_backup.sh" :
```

```
    #! /bin/sh
#
#  cold_backup.sh : This script compresses all database datafiles to a
number
#                  of spare disks
#

./cold_cp.sh 1 9 &
./cold_cp.sh 2 9 &
./cold_cp.sh 3 10 &
./cold_cp.sh 4 10 &

cp /dsk5/PRD/admin/control1.dbf /dsk9/spare/Cold_Bkup

for i in `ls /dsk5/PRD/redo/*`
do
    compress < ${i} > /dsk9/spare/Cold_Bkup/`basename ${i}`.Z
done


Script "cold_cp.sh" :

#! /bin/ksh
#
# cold_cp.sh : This script compress all datafiles on disk ${1} to
spare disk ${2}.
#

for i in `ls /dsk${1}/PRD/db/*`
do
    compress < ${i} > /dsk${2}/spare/Cold_Bkup/`basename ${i}`.Z
done
```

Hot backup to disk

DBAs should always have an arsenal of ad hoc database backup scripts. The following script allows us to execute a hot backup of our database at any time. Test all ad hoc backup scripts thoroughly before using them. Once you have a reliable backup script, keep it handy.

This UNIX script performs a hot backup of your database to a spare disk:

```
# hot_dsk.sql

! /bin/ksh

HOT=/CML/oracle/HOT/${Oracle_SID}
LOG=/dsk5/${Oracle_SID}/dump/alert_${Oracle_SID}.log

if [ -f $LOG ] ; then
    Bgn_Bkp=`egrep -ci '^alter tablespace .* begin backup' $LOG`
    End_Bkp=`egrep -ci '^alter tablespace .* end backup' $LOG`
    Diff_Bkp=`expr $Bgn_Bkp - $End_Bkp`
else
```

```
        mail oracle <<EOF
        ERROR - HOT BACKUP For "${Oracle_SID}" Has Failed
        Could not locate Alert Log - Please Investigate !
EOF
        exit 1
fi

sqlplus / <<EOF

    column tablespace_name noprint
    column seqn noprint
    set     pagesize        0
    set     linesize        132
    set     feedback        off
    set     sqlprompt       ""

    Whenever SQLERROR exit FAILURE

    select chr(1) tablespace_name, -9999 seqn,
           'alter system switch logfile;'
    from    dual
    UNION
    select chr(1) tablespace_name, -9998 seqn,
           'alter database backup controlfile to ''' ||
           '${HOT}/controlfile_${Oracle_SID}.HOT.full.before'' reuse;'
    from    dual
    UNION
    select tablespace_name, 0,
           'alter tablespace '||tablespace_name||' begin backup;'
    from    sys.dba_tablespaces
    where   status = 'ONLINE'
    UNION
    select tablespace_name, file_id,
           '!compress < '||file_name||'> ${HOT}/' ||
           substr(file_name,instr(file_name,'/',-1) + 1) || '.Z'
    from    sys.dba_data_files
    where   status = 'AVAILABLE'
    UNION
    select tablespace_name, 9999,
           'alter tablespace '||tablespace_name||' end backup;'
    from    sys.dba_tablespaces
    where   status = 'ONLINE'
    UNION
    select chr(255) tablespace_name, 9998 seqn,
           'alter database backup controlfile to ''' ||
           '${HOT}/controlfile_${Oracle_SID}.HOT.full.after'' reuse;'
    from    dual
    UNION
    select chr(255) tablespace_name, 9999 seqn,
           'alter system switch logfile;'
    from    dual
    ORDER
       BY  1, 2
```

```
        spool  /tmp/ora_HOT_backup.sql
        /
        spool  off
        start /tmp/ora_HOT_backup.sql
        exit
EOF

Bgn_Bkp=`egrep -ci '^alter tablespace .* begin backup' $LOG`
End_Bkp=`egrep -ci '^alter tablespace .* end backup' $LOG`

if [ $Bgn_Bkp != `expr $End_Bkp + $Diff_Bkp` ] ; then
        mail oracle <<EOF
        ERROR : HOT BACKUP For "${Oracle_SID}" Has Failed

        Number of "Begin Backup" stmts does not equal "End Backup"

        Please Investigate Immediately !
EOF
        exit 1
  if
```

We have several variants of this script, providing alternatives for somewhat
different kinds of situations. These variants include the following:

- Hot backup of a single tablespace. It is often good practice to take an extra
  backup of an important tablespace at the end of a large update routine.
  Rather than have to recover from the previous backup cycle and roll forward
  several hundred archived log files, we can establish an alternative recovery
  starting point.

- Hot backup of all data files on a single disk. When a disk begins to randomly
  report I/O errors, a hot backup of all data files on that disk is a valuable database safeguard. The disk may not be able to be replaced for a few days. A
  more up-to-date data file recovery point in the middle of the day can help to
  speed up the recovery process when that disk eventually self-destructs.

VI

Tuning for System Administrators

Part VI describes what Oracle system administrators need to know about tuning Oracle products. Because Oracle runs on so many hardware and software platforms, this discussion can't address them all. You'll have to work with your own operating system and vendor to get the most out of your overall system. This part does provide you with some system-specific performance guidelines. It also covers some of the main tuning jobs of the system administrator: dealing with long-running jobs, client-server tuning issues, and capacity planning.

15

Tuning Long-Running Jobs

In Chapter 3, *Planning and Managing the Tuning Process*, we introduced the special performance problems of long-running jobs—batch jobs that may run for many hours, usually overnight. Performance tuning so often focuses on short interactive jobs, ignoring these mammoth jobs that labor unnoticed overnight. This chapter describes special considerations for such jobs. The suggestions here supplement those in the rest of the book. Remember that most tuning—for example, tuning of SQL statements—is identical for batch and interactive jobs. Before you carry out any of these tuning suggestions, be sure that you have tuned your database and your SQL statements, as described in earlier chapters.

As the computer age moves forward, so do the power of our hardware, the capabilities of the software, and the size of the databases. We are now confronted with the real possibility of building *very large* databases. Some data warehousing environments are now doing data mining from Oracle databases that are many terabytes in size—hard to imagine, harder to tune.

The tuning of long-running jobs is one that the system administrator and the DBA will have to coordinate. Although many of the recommendations in this chapter involve DBA tuning operations, those requiring interaction with backup, recovery, and a number of other jobs will need to be coordinated with your system administrator.

Correctly Sizing Tables and Indexes

The accuracy with which you assign table and index sizes can contribute a great deal to the performance of long-running jobs. If a table or index fits in one large contiguous extent, Oracle could read the entire object with a single multiblock read. If the table or index consists of many small extents, scattered all over the disk (as the result of dynamic extension), the many disk accesses will slow down overall processing.

NOTE   OLTP applications generally don't see large performance degrada-
              tion when objects begin to fragment. Because small amounts of data
              is being randomly accessed by many simultaneous users, contigu-
              ous data won't make that much difference in such environments.

Example

The following example shows how poor table sizing damaged the performance of a typical long-running job. The following procedure was performed with a number of varying storage clauses.

We created a simple table:

```
ACCTS (acc_no    NUMBER(6),
       acc_desc  VARCHAR2(10) );
```

To populate the acc_desc column, we inserted 8,000 rows in the table, using the statements

```
INSERT INTO accts VALUES ( NULL, 'ACCT DESCR');
INSERT INTO accts SELECT * FROM accts;
```

We repeated the second INSERT statement until more than 8,000 rows were created. Next, we updated the table:

```
UPDATE ACCTS SET
acc_no = ROWNUM;
```

Then, on a UNIX machine with a single user, we dropped the table and recreated it, using various storage parameters.

Run 1

We first assigned the following STORAGE parameters to the ACCTS table:

```
(INITIAL 20K NEXT 20K PCTINCREASE 0 PCTFREE 70 PCTUSED 30)
```

Here is how long it took to insert, update, and drop:

Insert the last 4,000 rows:	3.62 seconds
Update the 8,000 rows:	27.42 seconds
Drop the table:	1 min, 31.17 seconds

In this case, there is no chaining because PCTFREE is adequate. The time needed to insert is relatively high because of the number of extents needed (because INITIAL and NEXT are not well sized). A large amount of time is needed to drop the table because of the high PCTFREE area left on all blocks and the large number of extents in the table.

Run 2

Now, suppose we assign the following STORAGE parameters to the ACCTS table:

```
(INITIAL 20K  NEXT 20K  PCTINCREASE 0  PCTFREE 10  PCTUSED 90)
```

Here is how long it took to insert, update, and drop:

Insert the last 4,000 rows:	0.92 second
Update the 8,000 rows:	52.82 seconds
Drop the table:	25.73 seconds

INSERT: Because we set a low value for PCTFREE, the time to insert the rows has been reduced because fewer extents are being created (fewer recursive database calls).

UPDATE: The time to perform the update is double the previous run because of extensive record chaining and/or migration. This resulted from the increase in the overall physical size of each record and lower free space allocated to the table.

DROP: The time to drop the table is less than the previous run because there are fewer extents to clean up.

Run 3

Now suppose we assign the following STORAGE parameters to the ACCTS table:

```
(INITIAL 500K  NEXT 500K  PCTINCREASE 0  PCTFREE 70  PCTUSED 30)
```

Here is how long it took to insert, update, and drop:

Insert the last 4,000 rows:	0.76 second
Update the 8,000 rows:	27.24 seconds
Drop the table:	5.29 seconds

This is the best result by far. There has been no row chaining, so the number of extents is minimized. The insert is five times faster than Run 1, the update is twice as fast as Run 2, and the table drop is 18 times faster than Run 1.

Run 4

Now suppose we assign the following STORAGE parameters to the ACCTS table:

```
(INITIAL 500K  NEXT 500K  PCTINCREASE 0  PCTFREE 10  PCTUSED 90)
```

Here is how long it took to insert, update, and drop:

Insert the last 4,000 rows:	0.47 second
Update the 8,000 rows:	46.47 seconds
Drop the table:	5.31 seconds

Inserts and drops are very fast because of the low value of PCTFREE (more records per block) and the minimizing of extents through larger INITIAL and NEXT settings. Updating, however, is slower because of the low PCTFREE value and the effect of record chaining.

Be sure you understand the negative effects of dynamic extension and row chaining, and the impact that different storage parameters will have on your performance. Single database updates do not *appear* to incur the performance overheads associated with poor object size. It is only when we execute an application module that has to perform several thousand operations that the accumulated overheads begin to show. As we have shown, proper sizing can have a major effect on how quickly your long-running jobs are able to operate.

Optimizing the PCTFREE and PCTUSED Parameters

Many DBAs fail to thoroughly investigate the optimal settings of the PCTFREE and PCTUSED parameters when creating database objects. Ignoring the problem and opting for the database defaults are all too common.

The PCTFREE parameter specifies the percentage of space in each segment's data block reserved for future record expansion. Records can be inserted into a data block only up until this threshold has been reached. After that point, no new rows can be inserted into that block until the free space percentage falls below the PCTUSED threshold. The default for PCTFREE is 10%.

The PCTUSED parameter defines the minimum percentage of data block used space that is necessary before the block is eligible for row insertion. A segment block is added to the free space list once its used space falls below this threshold. The default for PCTUSED is 40%.

You might set these parameters as follows:

```
CREATE TABLE emp (......) PCTFREE 5 PCTUSED 80
```

The combined sum of PCTFREE and PCTUSED must be less than 100. Correct choice of these parameters can be used to improve the efficiency of table and index segments. For example, tables that are insert-only (auditing tables, history tables, etc.) should have a PCTFREE setting of 1. This simple change to a table's storage definition can reduce its total disk space requirements by 10%. This means less object extension and less physical disk I/O when reading and writing: 10% more data can be read or written with a single data block read; 10% more data can be held in the database's SGA. This is a very simple way of increasing your block buffer cache without having to buy any more memory.

Exploiting Array Processing

This section describes a number of ways to improve the efficacy of array processing for long-running jobs.

ARRAYSIZE Parameter

You can specify the ARRAYSIZE parameter (through a number of different Oracle tools) to control the number of rows that can be returned from database by a single data transfer. If you set ARRAYSIZE correctly, multiple SELECT, INSERT, and UPDATE operations can be performed in a single access. This improves performance substantially, particularly for long-running jobs.

NOTE   Increasing the value of ARRAYSIZE has a major impact on client-server performance. Our benchmarks indicate that increasing ARRAYSIZE when you are running in a unitary environment has little or no effect on performance.

In Chapter 16, *Tuning in the Client-Server Environment*, the section called "Tuning ARRAYSIZE" describes how you can increase ARRAYSIZE, or its equivalent parameter in a number of Oracle tools, including SQL*Forms, SQL*Plus, and the precompilers.

Array SELECT Workarounds

A common problem in trying to exploit the virtues of array processing is not being able to access all data via a single array fetch database call. As we all know, data cannot always be sourced from a single table or even a single SQL statement. A multiple of individual database accesses may need to be performed to obtain all associated information. The following Pro*C code extract demonstrates this problem.

```
# arr_sel.sql
. . .
VARCHAR dept[100][5];
VARCHAR wk_dte[100][10];
DOUBLE  amt[100];
DOUBLE  discount[100];
. . .
EXEC SQL
SELECT dept_code, TO_DATE(:week_end_dte, 'ddmmyyyy'), retail_amount
INTO   :dept, :wk_dte, :amt
FROM   weekly_sales;

FOR (i = 0; i <= sqlca.sqlerrd[2]; i++)
{
  IF (amt[i] <= 10000)                 /* Get Associated Data */
  { EXEC SQL
    SELECT . . .
    INTO   :discount[i]
    FROM   discount_rates
    WHERE  TO_DATE(:wk_dte[i],'ddmmyyyy') <= sysdate
    AND    disc_amt <= :amt[i];
  }
  ELSE
  . . .
  . . .
  IF (amt[i] > 10000 && strcmp(dept[i],"1000") == 0) )
  { EXEC SQL
    SELECT . . .
    INTO   :discount[i]
    FROM   mgr_discount
    WHERE  disc_amt <= :amt[i];
  }
  ELSE discount[i] = 0;
}
```

As is demonstrated by this example, we can use array processing to access the initial data but then must individually calculate the discounted amount via a complex set of business rules that cannot be joined into the initial driving SELECT. Or can it?

By defining a stored database inline function to calculate the discounted amount (performing a number of different, database accesses), we can incorporate it into our SQL statement and continue to exploit array processing to the fullest.

```
# arr_upd.sql
. . .
VARCHAR dept[100][5];
VARCHAR wk_dte[100][10];
DOUBLE  amt[100];
DOUBLE  discount[100];
. . . .
EXEC SQL
SELECT dept_code, TO_DATE(:week_end_dte, 'ddmmyyyy'), retail_amount,
```

```
                calc_discount(dept_code, week_end_dte, retail_amount)
        INTO    :dept, :wk_dte, :amt, :discount
        FROM    weekly_sales;
        . . .
```

NOTE   Inline functions can also be used in INSERT, UPDATE, and DELETE statements to exploit array processing.

Array UPDATE Workarounds

Many updating batch routines need to perform complex business functionality. When they insert and/or update a large number of tables, they can't always use standard array-processing techniques. The following Pro*C code extract demonstrates a common real-world example:

```
. . .
VARCHAR dept[5];
VARCHAR wk_dte[10];
DOUBLE  amt;
. . .
WHILE ( read_next_record() != EOF )
{
   EXEC SQL
   UPDATE weekly_sales
   SET    retail_amount = retail_amount,0) + :amt
   WHERE  dept_code    = :dept
   AND    week_end_dte = TO_DATE(:wk_dte, 'ddmmyyyy');

   IF (sqlca.sqlerrd[2] == 0)  /* Update Failed so Must Do an Insert */
   { EXEC SQL
      INSERT INTO weekly_sales
      (:dept, to_date(:wk_dte, 'ddmmyyyy'), :amt);
   }
}
. . .
```

The difficulty with this simple example is that you do not know whether you will be performing an INSERT or an UPDATE to the table until after you have executed the UPDATE statement. When you execute an array update of 100 rows, some will work and some will fail. All you can deduce is how many failed; not which ones. Without executing the UPDATE and the INSERT one at a time, how can we exploit the array processing facility? Here is an example:

```
. . .
VARCHAR dept[100][5];
VARCHAR wk_dte[100][10];
DOUBLE  amt[100];
. . .
WHILE ( read_next_record() != EOF )
```

```
{
    EXEC SQL for 100
    UPDATE weekly_sales
    SET    retail_amount = retail_amount,0) + :amt
    WHERE  dept_code     = :dept
    AND    week_end_dte  = TO_DATE(:wk_dte, 'ddmmyyyy');

    IF (sqlca.sqlerrd[2] < 100)      /* Not ALL Updates Succeeded */
    {   EXEC SQL for 100
        INSERT INTO weekly_sales
        SELECT :dept, to_date(:wk_dte, 'ddmmyyyy'), :amt
        FROM   dual
        WHERE  NOT EXISTS
               ( SELECT 1
                 FROM   weekly_sales
                 WHERE  dept_code    = :dept
                 AND    week_end_dte = TO_DATE(:wk_dte,'ddmmyyyy') );
    }
}
. . .
```

At first glance, this approach may seem excessive and more expensive than processing the rows one at a time. The database does incur a greater amount of processing overhead; but when this is offset against the overheads that are incurred within a client-server environment, you'll realize total program savings.

Optimizing INIT.ORA Parameters

You'll typically run long-running jobs outside normal business hours, when fewer user processes are logged on to the system. At such times, valuable machine resources, such as real memory, can be put to better use. This memory that would normally be used to support a multitude of user connections to the database can be allocated to the database itself. The following INIT.ORA parameters detail a few of the more important parameters to consider resetting when you are running long-running jobs.

DB_BLOCK_BUFFERS

The buffer cache holds database data blocks for tables, indexes, rollback segments, and clusters. The larger the buffer cache, the more application data can be *cached* in memory, and the faster long-running jobs will execute. By holding more data in memory, you avoid expensive disk I/O that can adversely affect performance. Once data is read into the SGA, they become accessible to other processes, alleviating the need to read them again from disk.

During times of high application batch activity and low user connection numbers, DBAs should look at allocating up to two-thirds of their real memory to the database SGA. This would mean an SGA size of over 300 megabytes for a machine with 512 megabytes of memory. Assuming that the total number of different SQL statements will be less than during TPO operation (batch routines generally execute a small number of long-running statements), most of this memory can be directed to the buffer cache with no increase needed to the normal shared pool size.

DB_WRITERS, LIST_IO, and WRITE_ASYNC

Oracle uses a single database writer (DBWR) process to write all database changes to disk. By default, this process uses synchronous disk writes and can perform only one write at a time. During heavy batch updating periods, this single path to the disk(s) can cause a bottleneck, and you need to reduce it by increasing the output bandwidth of the database. Increasing the overall speed and total throughput of your database is important enough for normal day-to-day processing but absolutely paramount during batch processing and other periods of very high I/O. A few minutes spent investigating alternative I/O strategies can mean the difference between a high update program taking 1 hour and taking 4 hours to complete.

Oracle provides three different methods to help increase DBWR output. You can only use one, or sometimes two, of these features on any one platform, depending on your hardware, the version of Oracle, the operating system level, and the OS kernel patches you currently have loaded. Consult your *Hardware Installation Guide* for more details.

- *DB_WRITERS:* Instructs the database to spawn several DBWR processes to handle simultaneous disk updates. This option is supported only on SMP machines and should be set to a value of approximately twice the number of CPUs.

- *LIST_IO:* Causes the database to queue many I/O requests into a list and process it as a single I/O request. This provides nonblocking disk writes, allowing your program to continue executing after having queued the I/O. Most SVR4 UNIX releases support list I/O functionality.

- *WRITE_ASYNCH:* Permits a program to continue executing without having to wait for an I/O write to complete. The DBWR can continue writing modified database blocks out to disk without having to wait for each I/O operation to finish. You should use asynchronous I/O if it is available on your platform. Note that some older releases of Oracle use the INIT.ORA parameter IO_ASYNC_IO rather than WRITE_ASYNC.

DB_FILE_MULTIBLOCK_READ_COUNT

Long-running jobs tend to perform many times more database I/O than your normal OLTP activity. This I/O is often made up of full table scans, data aggregation, and data sorting. Increasing the DB_FILE_MULTIBLOCK_READ_ COUNT forces the database to read more data blocks when performing a sequential data scan (full table scan). Setting this parameter to a higher value for full table scans and long-running batch routines can help to reduce program times.

When altering this parameter, do not increase it beyond the physical I/O block size of your disk and/or controller. If you do, you will be performing several physical disk I/Os for every single logical database I/O and in this way may actually degrade overall performance.

SORT_AREA_SIZE and SORT_AREA_RETAINED_SIZE

In earlier chapters, we mentioned how important the tuning of memory and temporary segments are for OLTP performance. Because large batch jobs so often sort many thousands of records, the tuning of the sorting area is just as critical for such jobs. The section in Chapter 11, *Monitoring and Tuning an Existing Database*, called "Reducing Disk I/O by Increasing the Sort Area" describes in detail how to monitor the efficiency of sort operations and how to tune your system to improve sort performance. We summarize this information briefly here and tell you specifically what you can do to improve sort performance for long-running jobs.

By setting the INIT.ORA parameter SORT_AREA_SIZE, you specify the size of each process's sort area in memory. The Oracle RDBMS tries to perform the entire sort or sort/merge operation in this area of memory. If the area fills up, the system writes data out to temporary segments in the temporary tablespace. To prevent sorting from degrading performance, especially for long-running jobs, you need to set the sizes of SORT_AREA_SIZE and the temporary segments to the largest sizes you can. (The section called "Resizing Temporary Tables" later in this chapter describes how to change the size of the temporary tables for long-running jobs.)

If you are fortunate enough to be able to configure your database for batch-only periods, you should increase the SORT_AREA_RETAINED_SIZE parameter to equal SORT_AREA_SIZE. This parameter means that each process will be allocated its maximum sorting quota at connection time and will retain it for the duration of the session. If the SORT_AREA_RETAINED_SIZE parameter is lower than the SORT_AREA_SIZE parameter, Oracle will automatically release a process's memory if it believes that the sort area will not be referenced in the near future. This type of operation is beneficial only for OLTP applications that have many concurrent sessions spasmodically performing large transactions sorts.

If you suspect that sorting is slowing down processing in your system (a likely risk with long-running jobs), follow these tuning steps:

1. Before you incur any sort overhead, ask some basic questions: Is this sort really necessary? Has an index been inadvertently overlooked? Can a SQL statement be structured more efficiently?

2. Increase the value of the SORT_AREA_SIZE parameter. The maximum allowable value is system dependent.

3. Increase the value of the SORT_AREA_RETAINED_SIZE parameter to equal SORT_AREA_SIZE. This stops Oracle from automatically shrinking a user process's sorting memory back to an unacceptable level.

LOG_BUFFER

This parameter governs the amount of memory allocated to the redo log buffer within the SGA. All database changes are buffered to this area before being written to the redo logs. Increasing the size of the redo log buffers can produce surprisingly good performance benefits. This is even more so for large, long-running update tasks. If the log buffer is too small, contention will occur and updating tasks will have to wait while the buffer is continually flushed to disk. A log buffer of between 512 kilobytes and 1 megabytes is not unreasonable for batch-only processing periods.

LOG_CHECK_POINT_INTERVAL and LOG_CHECKPOINT_TIMEOUT

DBAs should try to reduce the number and frequency of database check-points, regardless of whether they are operations in OLTP or in batch mode. Checkpoints force all modified (uncommitted) database blocks to be written to disk, and also update all control and data file headers with the latest check-point number. Many large databases can have 50 or more data files, causing checkpoints to take several seconds (or even minutes).

Large, long-running updating jobs will obviously generate more changes, causing more checkpoints to fire. Setting the LOG_CHECKPOINT_TIMEOUT to zero (its default) and setting LOG_CHECKPOINT_INTERVAL to a very large number will result in checkpoints being generated only on a redo log switch.

LOG_ARCHIVE_BUFFERS and LOG_ARCHIVE_BUFFER_SIZE

Jobs that generate large numbers of database changes in a short period of time may experience some archive log contention. Simply put, changes are being written to the online redo logs faster than they can be copied to the archive disk. This can mean a "log writer unable to proceed" wait forcing your application job to also have to wait.

Increasing the values of both LOG_ARCHIVE_BUFFERS and LOG_ARCHIVE_BUFFER_SIZE will help to avoid this bottleneck and will contribute to the faster running of your application batch routines.

SMALL_TABLE_THRESHOLD

This parameter controls the number of blocks from one table that will be stored at the *most-recently-used* end of the buffer cache before the remainder of blocks are held at the *least-recently-used* end of the list. If your batch processing is repeatedly performing full table scans for the same table(s) over and over again and that table is of *moderate* size, increasing this parameter can mean that it will be retained within the Oracle buffer cache for a longer period of time.

PROCESSES

Reducing the number of processes (the PROCESSES parameter) in the INIT.ORA file limits the maximum number of concurrent database connections. This has very little effect on overall memory usage but helps to prevent mistakes. When the database is in batch mode, we may be allocating more physical memory to each process than usual. Maximizing the SORT_AREA_SIZE, increasing the DB_BLOCK_BUFFERS, and the like, all lead to higher physical memory usage. Lowering the PROCESSES parameter to just enough to handle the batch requirements prevents normal users from mistakenly logging on to the database and wasting large amounts of valuable memory resources. It also immediately highlights the fact that the database may still be mistakenly in batch mode before too many users are able to connect to the database and force the machine into uncontrollable swapping.

Disk Tuning

This section describes a number of approaches to increasing the efficiency of disk operations.

Resizing Temporary Tables

Long-running jobs often need to write data out to temporary segments on disk. For example, if you are sorting more data than can fit in your sort area in memory (specified in SORT_AREA_SIZE), Oracle will write data out to temporary segments. If you put your temporary segments in a separate tablespace, you can monitor disk and memory activity in this tablespace and determine whether its size needs to be increased.

The use of temporary segments is particularly important for long-running jobs because the job may fail if it cannot acquire a temporary segment. Such a failure might be the result of finding the tablespace (temporarily) full or having the process reach its maximum number of temporary (default) tablespace extents. The larger you make the INITIAL and NEXT allocations for the tablespace, the larger the temporary extents will be and the less likely the process will fail because the maximum allowable extents were exceeded.

By increasing the size of the temporary extents and thus reducing the number of temporary extents needed, you also reduce the CPU requirements of a long-running job. Segment expansion is very expensive in terms of CPU time. The internal overheads that are involved in searching the free list and allocating extents have a severe impact on long-running jobs.

Because the requirements of a long-running job are often very different from those of an interactive job, you may want to define two distinct sets of tablespace allocation information, one for daily processing and one for overnight processing. (This approach is similar to the one that we previously described for SORT_AREA_SIZE.) You assign much larger INITIAL and NEXT values for the tablespaces that are used overnight.

If you determine that temporary tablespace size is slowing down processing of your long-running job, follow these tuning steps:

1. Make sure that the temporary tablespace that is used by temporary segments is separate from the tablespaces that are used for application data, rollback data, and the system. For example:

```
ALTER USER scott DEFAULT TABLESPACE user_tspace
         TEMPORARY TABLESPACE temp_tspace;
```

2. Change the DEFAULT STORAGE parameter on the temporary tablespace:

```
ALTER TABLESPACE temp_tspace
        DEFAULT STORAGE (INITIAL      10M
                         NEXT         10M
                         PCTINCREASE 0);
```

One important feature to remember when modifying the temporary tablespace default storage clause is that it can be done without shutting down the database. DBAs can arrange to have one temporary tablespace setting during the day and another setting overnight.

Choosing Rollback Segments

Like tables and indexes, rollback segments may run out of space during processing and need to request additional extents. Dynamic extension can have a serious impact on performance, particularly on the performance of long-running jobs. RDBMS Version 6.0.33 introduced the ability to assign a transaction to an individual rollback segment. By assigning larger rollback segments to long-running update jobs, you can improve performance.

If your application rollback tablespace is not large enough to hold both the small and large rollbacks simultaneously, you can assign alternative rollback segments for daily and overnight processing. You will need to offline (or drop) all of the smaller OTLP rollback segments used for high-transaction daily usage and online a smaller number of larger rollback segments for overnight processing. When the overnight jobs are completed, you can then offline the larger rollback segments and reinstate the smaller segments. You assign a particular rollback segment to a transaction with the statement

```
SQL>   SET TRANSACTION USE ROLLBACK SEGMENT {segment_name}
```

To be effective, this statement must be the first DML statement (of any kind) after a successful connect, DDL, commit, or rollback statement. You must issue this statement after each subsequent commit or rollback. Figure 9-12 in Chapter 9, *Tuning a New Database*, illustrates how the alternative assignment of rollback segments works.

NOTE   Prior to Oracle7, we had to modify the ROLLBACK_SEGMENTS parameter in the INIT.ORA and bounce the database. This was not always convenient and often not possible. We now have the option of dynamically altering a rollback segments status, and even creating and dropping them, without having to shut down the database. Now there is no excuse for inappropriate rollback segment selection to slow down our long-running batch processing.

Avoiding Row Migration and Chaining

Row migration occurs when an existing record in a data block is updated so that its overall length increases and the block's free space is not sufficient to accommodate the extra data (i.e., the block is completely full). Provided that the total size of the updated record has not exceeded a data block, the entire record is migrated to another data block for that segment. The header (rowid reference) for that record still points to the initial data block but then has a second "pointer" to the Oracle block that actually holds the data. This means that a record can be migrated without having to modify any index references to the record. A single database I/O can, in fact, require multiple disk assesses.

On the other hand, if a single record cannot fit into an Oracle block, the record needs to be split up over multiple blocks. This usually occurs only for tables that contain a column of type LONG or LONG RAW. This is known as *row chaining*.

Any block may contain some whole rows, some partial rows from chained records, and record pointers to migrated records. How can you identify the migration and chaining of rows?

Record chaining

You can run a query against the V$SYSSTAT table to monitor the number of chained rows. In the output from the following query, the "table fetch continued row" shows the current number of rows chained since the last startup.

```
# row_chn.sql
SELECT SUBSTR(name,1,40),VALUE
    FROM    v$sysstat
    WHERE   name = 'table fetch continued row';
```

Now issue the following query to display the results:

```
SELECT COUNT(*) FROM table;
```

Now repeat the first query and compare the results. The variation indicates the number of chained rows.

Row migration

The following method identifies migrated rows. It shows the approximate total cumulative length of all rows within the block. Note that in this output, 1 byte is added for each column that is not null, 5 bytes are added for each row in the block, and approximately 100 bytes are added for each block header.

```
# row_mig.sql
SELECT SUBSTR(ROWID, 1, 8) blk
    FROM    __table_name__
    GROUP
        BY SUBSTR(ROWID, 1, 8)
    HAVING
        SUM(NVL(VSIZE(col1) + 1, 0)
            + NVL(VSIZE(col2) + 1, 0)
            + .....
            + NVL(VSIZE(col9) + 1, 0) + 5) > 'BLOCK_SIZE' - 100;
```

In Oracle7, you can use the ANALYZE command to identify chained rows. By issuing ANALYZE in the form

```
SQL> ANALYZE TABLE {BAD_TABLE} LIST CHAINED ROWS ;
```

you tell Oracle to record all chained and migrated row references into the system table CHAINED_ROWS, which is created via the SQL script *UTLCHAIN.sql*. You can also specify your own CHAINED_ROWS table by including an INTO clause in the ANALYZE command.

```
sql> ANALYZE TABLE {BAD_TABLE} LIST CHAINED ROWS INTO {MY_CHAINING_TABLE};
```

NOTE   Applications that suffer from extensive row chaining due to LONG and LONG RAW data columns should seriously look at increasing the DB_BLOCK_SIZE parameter to its maximum (8 kilobytes for most operating systems). A larger block size means that these long records will fit in to a smaller number of physical data blocks and help to reduce unnecessary disk I/O.

Running Jobs in Parallel

Overnight jobs are often run in single stream. That is, one unit of the overnight job stream must complete successfully before the next unit can begin. This approach may be necessary for certain parts of the overnight process. For example, you may need to run an extract of the database before you can do reporting, or you may need to run backups before you execute certain overnight reports. However, many of your processes may be able to be run in parallel. Doing so can considerably improve performance.

The number of jobs that can be submitted in parallel will vary from site to site. Although, in general, running jobs in parallel improves performance, if you submit too many jobs, the overall elapsed time may actually be greater than running jobs in a single stream. The CPU- and/or I/O-intensive nature of some jobs and the fact that they may be fighting for the same resources (software and hardware) determine their effectiveness when they are run in parallel.

We recommend that you never run more jobs in parallel than twice the number of CPUs. Carefully monitor the timings for these jobs to optimize overnight processing at your site. Try to run the jobs in a way that will spread resource demands (I/O, CPU, logical data) evenly across the system.

A very interesting and effective extension to parallel job scheduling is to parallelize the same job multiple times (that is *parallelize*, not *paralyze*!). We have often been faced with the task of tuning a long-running batch update program that simply takes too long. After having looked at the program source, pawing through the trace files, and reviewing all available indexes, we've had to report that it just doesn't go any faster. Data volumes will ultimately govern how long the program will take.

One program that we analyzed in this way was actually processing 2,500 sales transactions per minute, made up of three SELECTs, one INSERT, and two UPDATE statements—pretty impressive stuff when you think about it. An average of 750,000 transactions per week meant a total elapsed time of 300 minutes, or five hours! This was not as impressive when conveyed to the department management. What could be done?

If you are fortunate enough to be using a SMP machine, all is not lost. By carefully dividing your processing up into multiple streams, it is still possible to achieve approximately the same throughput per stream. Each stream must be configured to avoid resource contention. Continuing on with the prior example, we were able to achieve this by a very simple mechanism.

The original program source was

```
    . . .
    FOR X IN (SELECT * FROM weekly_sales) LOOP
        SELECT ...
        SELECT ...
        UPDATE ...
        SELECT ...
```

```
        UPDATE ...
        INSERT ...
    END LOOP;
    . . .
```

The program was amended to divide up the processing by even and odd store numbers. This ensured a fairly even split while keeping data contention to a minimum. Neither stream would ever be accessing the same record for reading or writing.

Stream 1: Even store numbers

```
    FOR X IN (SELECT * FROM weekly_sales WHERE mod(store_no,2)=0) LOOP
        ...
    END LOOP;
```

Stream 2: Odd store numbers

```
    FOR X IN (SELECT * FROM weekly_sales WHERE mod(store_no,2)=1) LOOP
        ...
    END LOOP;
```

The final result of this simple one-line change was an elapsed processing time of 175 minutes—a 42% improvement.

DBA Tuning for Long-Running Jobs

A number of DBA alternatives are available to help improve long-running job performance. The following sections detail some of the possibilities. Before rushing out and requesting these suggestions, be sure to weigh the costs. Nothing comes for free. Improving the performance of long-running jobs can often be at the expense of the OLTP operations.

Increasing Free Lists

Some long-running jobs can benefit from being split up into several smaller tasks, running in parallel. (We covered this in the previous section.) We can achieve best results only when parallelizing an INSERT task if we increase the number of table and index FREELSTS. This parameter governs how many free space chains will be allocated to an object. When two processes are simultaneously inserting rows into the same table, some contention can occur on the free list chain. When two batch tasks are inserting thousands of rows into the same table, contention will definitely occur.

Free lists can be set only at table or index creation. They cannot be modified by the ALTER command. DBAs must do their homework at schema creation time. Increasing the number of free lists has very little associated overhead other than the fact that the header block of each object requires a little more space to accommodate the extra list(s). This is a small price to pay for better performance.

Disabling Archiving

It is not uncommon to disable database archiving for the duration of a special long-running task. Disabling archives during day-to-day processing is not recommended but may be viable for special activities. For example, always disable the database archive during database reorganizations. Importing large amounts of data is very archive-intensive. If that you have already backed up the database (cold backup) and exported the data before truncating the table(s), being able to recover the database to the middle of a reorganization would seem pointless. Once the import has completed, you will need to enable archiving and back up the database again. You would be surprised at the number of DBAs who do not disable archiving before a major database reorganization.

Another situation in which we have regularly disabled archiving is during data "take-on." For example, in one case, an application was ramping up over time, and each week a new dealership was added to the system. This meant a sizable data load and the need to perform a conversion each weekend for *forty weeks*. We would back up the database at week's end, disable archiving, process the data load, reconcile the data, and then enable archiving at the end of the process. The final database backup was completed before Monday morning processing began.

The main purpose of disabling archiving in this case was not to speed up processing, but to allow the data take-on to proceed unattended. It generally took 24 hours of processing to load a dealership. With each archive enabled, this meant that the archiving disk would fill up regularly and would need to be copied to tape. Rather than having to staff the tape drives all weekend, by disabling archiving we could start the process Friday night and it would be completed by late Sunday afternoon. Other than the odd spot check to make sure that things were still moving, the whole process was self-contained, including final database backup.

Pinning Objects into the SGA

It is the DBA's responsibility to ensure that all large, critical procedures, packages, and triggers are pinned into the SGA. This process is covered in Chapter 7, *Tuning PL/SQL*. Pinning objects into memory yields best results for OLTP users. Because long-running jobs will load these packages into the SGA at the beginning of their job and hold them there for the duration of the task, performance improvements will be minimal (but every little bit helps).

Disabling Triggers, Constraints, and Referential Integrity

Substantial performance gains can be achieved for long-running jobs by disabling database triggers, constraints, and referential integrity. However, this is dangerous and should be done only with the full consent of all people concerned. We have been able to improve a SQL*Loader job three times over by simply removing three referential integrity foreign key constraints.

The best overall results are achieved in disabling table triggers. This is because we do we improve processing times, but also reenable the trigger with no overheads. Trigger activation is not retrospective and does not revalidate the data. If you are not careful, this may also mean that you can end up with database integrity problems in the longer term. When reenabling referential integrity and/or check constraints, the entire table is revalidated. Depending on what percentage of the table was affected (updated) by your long-running task, the overall overheads associated with disabling and enabling these constraints could outweigh the benefits.

Indexing All Relevant Columns

Indexing all columns referenced in a particular SQL statement can produce enormous performance gains for long-running jobs. Statements that join thousands and thousands of rows must first locate each record via the index and then physically fetch the record from disk. Skipping the overheads that are associated with the actual row read will substantially improve performance. The index will generally remained cached in memory, owing to its smaller size and intensive access. Records from a large table will be dispersed throughout the table and need to be read from disk (not found in the buffer cache).

The downside to expanding the index range is the fact that the index will become larger and will lose its uniqueness properties. For example, if the index over the dept_code column is used to guarantee unique department codes, adding the department description to the index will improve process efficiency but will lose the column uniqueness property associated with the index.

Table Caching

Oracle7.1 introduced the concept of table caching in the block buffer cache. Previous versions of the database relied on the SMALL_TABLE_THRESHOLD parameter to determine which tables would be cached during a full table scan. This parameter is no longer supported. DBAs can now include the CACHE option as part of a table's DDL definition.

As attractive as this may seem, table caching is not what you might expect. The entire table is not cached into the block buffer cache. As the table is accessed by a full table scan, data blocks are added to the most-recently-used end of the LRU list rather than the least-recently-used end. This causes the blocks to stay in the buffer cache for a longer period of time. For example:

```
create table EMP ( . . . )  CACHE
```

Don't specify CACHE for large tables. When that table is accessed by a full table scan, it will flush the entire buffer cache of all other data blocks, replacing them with the table being read. This action will mean that all frequently accessed information will be needlessly read from disk all over again.

Creating Overnight Extract Tables

Most sites run reports against fully normalized databases. However, as more and more overnight reports are scheduled, many involving complex multitable joins and full table scans, the system may become increasingly overburdened during this processing.

You'll frequently find that the reports that users produce tend to involve data from the same set of core tables and the same table joins. Rather than having to perform the same database access operations over and over again, you can create a single, highly denormalized extract table from the standard normalized database tables and let users run their reports against this extract table instead. (Most sites will need several such extract tables.) By doing this, you can realize enormous improvements in performance. Complex, multitable joins need to be performed only once, and performance can be improved still more by creating indexes against the extract tables. Make sure, though, to create these indexes *after* populating the extract table.

The most common method for producing extract tables is to populate the tables by running an automated process overnight, when performance needs might not be quite so pressing. Once the tables are created, programs that need these data can access the extract tables instead of the full database.

The performance gains from using extract tables can be significant. Some overnight reporting runs that we've tuned have saved several hours of processing. Queries of extract tables, rather than the database itself, are much faster as well.

Index Operations

This section describes a variety of index operations that may speed up your long-running jobs.

Creating Indexes After Inserts

When you are inserting large numbers of rows into a table, you'll find that dropping the indexes before you perform the insert is considerably faster than inserting into a table with all of its indexes intact. When you are running long-running jobs, this approach is particularly beneficial. As a rule of thumb, we recommend that if the insert will increase the number of rows by 20% or more, consider dropping the indexes temporarily. If the number of rows is significant, the performance gains can be major. However, if the insert will increase the number of rows in a table by less than 10%, it is better to leave the indexes in place. In this case, the amount of time taken to rebuild the index for all of the rows exceeds the amount of extra time to update the indexes as rows are inserted into the table.

Consider the following example. A table called TRANSACTION has zero rows in it. A conversion will insert 8192 rows into the table, which has one two-column index. With the index in place, inserting these rows takes 67.8 seconds elapsed time. Now try inserting rows into the table without the index, and then creating the index after the insertion has completed:

```
Insertion:           13.1   seconds
Index creation:      26     seconds
Net savings:         28.7   seconds
```

When you create indexes on large tables, make sure that you use the temporary tablespace for the sorting of rows. Make sure that the STORAGE allocation has been assigned correctly (via the DEFAULT STORAGE parameters) for the temporary tablespace. In addition, make sure that there is enough overall free space to fit the index into the temporary tablespace and the index's destination tablespace.

It is all very well to suggest that you drop your index(es) prior to a bulk data load, but physical table size can inhibit your ability to do so. Large tables with many millions of rows can take many hours to (re)build indexes. A number of new features have been introduced to speed up this process, as we describe in the following sections.

Parallel Index Creation

When Oracle7.1 introduced the parallel query option, it also brought the availability of parallel index creation. The table is broken up into several parts, with each partition sorted and written via a different database process. This functionality alone can speed up index creation several times over.

```
# para_idx.sql
CREATE INDEX weekly_sales_i1 ON weekly_sales (store_no, week_end_dte)
    TABLESPACE sales_idx
```

```
        STORAGE ( INITIAL 50M NEXT 100M PCTINCREASE 0)
        PARALLEL( DEGREE 8);
```

If you do decide to create indexes via the parallel facility, remember to adjust the storage clause sizings. Each parallel slave creates an index extent equal to the initial storage size. If the index was 200 megabytes in size and you choose to use a degree of eight, the initial extent size should be roughly one-eighth of that size. After having created the index, Oracle will automatically trim these extents back in size if it finds that the sizes are too big. This can make things even worse. Not only do you have an index with eight extents, but they may all have varying sizes.

Unrecoverable Index Creation

Oracle7.2 includes new features that permit us to build indexes in *unrecoverable* mode. This means that the index is created without generating redo information. This does not really change anything other than improve performance; not having to write redo information to the log files significantly reduces overall operation I/O.

```
    # unrc_idx.sql
    CREATE INDEX weekly_sales_i1 ON weekly_sales (store_no, week_end_dte)
        TABLESPACE sales_idx
        STORAGE ( INITIAL 50M NEXT 100M PCTINCREASE 0)
        PARALLEL( DEGREE 8)
        UNRECOVERABLE ;
```

Deferring Primary Key and Unique Constraints

When creating tables with primary keys or unique constraints, Oracle automatically creates a unique index to enforce the constraint. The downside to this is that when creating these constraints, Oracle cannot use the parallel or unrecoverable features that we've just described. The best thing to do is to manually create the unique index and then alter the table and add the constraint. If a valid index exists when a primary key or unique constraint is enabled, it will be attached to the constraint rather than building a duplicate index.

```
    CREATE TABLE weekly_sales
        ( store_no      NUMBER(6)   NOT NULL,
          week_end_dte  DATE        NOT NULL,
          ....
        );

    .... bulk data load ....

    ALTER TABLE weekly_sales add
        ( CONSTRAINT weekly_sales_i1
          PRIMARY KEY (store_no, week_end_dte)
          USING INDEX TABLESPACE sales_idx
                STORAGE (INITIAL 50M NEXT 100M PCTINCREASE 0)
        );
```

Should be coded as:

```
CREATE TABLE weekly_sales
     ( store_no         NUMBER(6)   NOT NULL,
       week_end_dte    DATE        NOT NULL,
       ....
     );

.... bulk data load ....

CREATE INDEX weekly_sales_i1 ON weekly_sales (store_no, week_end_dte)
     TABLESPACE sales_idx
     STORAGE ( INITIAL 50M NEXT 100M PCTINCREASE 0)
     PARALLEL( DEGREE 8)
     UNRECOVERABLE ;

ALTER TABLE weekly_sales add (constraint weekly_slaes_i1
                         primary key (store_no, week_end_dte) );
```

Earlier versions of Oracle7 insisted on validating the index when adding a new constraint. This means that instead of taking seconds to create a primary key constraint, it took approximately half the time that was required to build it in the first place. Even though this may seem a little extravagant, the combined elapsed time is still many times faster than creating the index as part of the primary key creation.

If it does take a long time for you to issue the "alter table ... add (... primary key ...)" constraint (i.e., the database is validating the index), consider skipping this step altogether. After all, adding the primary key constraint is just cosmetics once the unique index is in place. Finding a maintenance window large enough to rebuild the indexes can be difficult enough, but then adding another few hours to the process simply to add a table constraint definition is a little excessive. The table constraint definitions can be added the next day or even the next week when more time is available.

Using PL/SQL to Speed Up Updates

If you are performing a parent/child update (a common activity in long-running jobs), you can improve performance quite a bit by using PL/SQL, described in Chapter 7.

Consider the following example. A table called ACCOUNT_TOTALS is updated from various other systems to reflect the account's current expenditures against budget. Unfortunately, the system is not an integrated one, with data loaded into a transaction (child) table, and changes then made against the ACCOUNT_TOTALS table. There are about 10,000 rows in the ACCOUNT_TOTALS table and about 200 rows in the TRANSACTION table. Using SQL, you'd do the daily update as follows:

```
# pl_upd.sql
UPDATE account_totals  A
SET    current_exp = current_exp + ( SELECT daily_exp
                                     FROM   transaction T
                                     WHERE  T.acc_no = A.acc_no )
    WHERE   EXISTS      ( SELECT 'X'
                         FROM    TRANSACTION T
                         WHERE   T.ACC_NO = A.ACC_NO );
```

This type of update takes several minutes. Now suppose you use PL/SQL to achieve the same result:

```
DECLARE
     CURSOR read_tran  IS
     SELECT acc_no, daily_exp
     FROM TRANSACTION;
     --
     acc_no_store  NUMBER (6);
     daily_exp_store   NUMBER (9,2);
BEGIN
  OPEN read_tran;
  LOOP;
    FETCH read_tran INTO acc_no_store, daily_exp_store;
    EXIT WHEN READ_TRAN%NOTFOUND;
    --
    UPDATE account_totals A
    SET    current_exp = current_exp + daily_exp_store
    WHERE  acc_no      = acc_no_store ;
  END LOOP;
  CLOSE READ_TRAN;
END;
```

This form of the update takes seconds.

PL/SQL isn't always faster. Beware of daily transaction files that update more than 10% to 15% of the rows in the master table. With the PL/SQL method, more physical reads will be required against the ACCOUNT_TOTALS table using indexes than would be required with a full table scan using SQL.

Inline Functions

We have written at length about the advantages and tuning tricks that are available when exploiting inline SQL functions. This information is covered in Chapter 6, *Tuning SQL*, Chapter 7, and Chapter 16. Inline functions can also be used to improve the performance of long-running SQL queries and to cache data.

Speeding Up Queries

Consider the following example. The code extract shows a common query over a very large sales table, accumulating sales figures by processing department. The department description is reported for user convenience.

```
# inl_sel.sql
SELECT m.dept_code,
       NVL(d.description,'?'),
       SUM(m.retail_amount)
FROM   departments d,
       weekly_sales m
WHERE  sales_date between '01-JAN-96' and '31-JAN-96'
AND    m.dept_code = d.dept_code (+)
GROUP
    BY m.dept_code, d.description;
```

The trace file output generated from this simple database query is very interesting. It shows that a full table scan was performed on the weekly_sales table (2,477,175 rows) of which 576,742 records were for the time period in question. This means that over half a million table joins need to be performed with the department table, for the same department records, over and over again. The final result set was for only 384 distinct departments. This explains the very high number of logical database reads (2,319,688) compared to physical reads (12,736). The department table is very small and is cached into memory after the first access. Total elapsed time was over 11 minutes. The elapsed time is close to the total CPU time, indicating that the process is CPU-bound rather than I/O-dependent.

call	count	cpu	elapsed	disk	query	current	rows
Parse	1	0.35	0.38	2	4	7	0
Execute	1	0.03	0.05	1	0	2	0
Fetch	384	**616.35**	**681.17**	**12736**	**2319688**	3	**384**

```
Rows    Execution Plan
------- ---------------------------------------------------------
      0 SELECT STATEMENT    OPTIMIZER HINT: CHOOSE
 576742   SORT (GROUP BY)
 576741     NESTED LOOPS (OUTER)
2477175       TABLE ACCESS (FULL) OF 'WEEKLY_SALES'
 576741       TABLE ACCESS (BY ROWID) OF 'DESCRIPTION'
 576742         INDEX (UNIQUE SCAN) OF 'DEPT_PK' (UNIQUE)
```

So what happens when we modify this simple SQL statement to use an inline function call?

```
# inl_sel.sql
FUNCTION Lookup_Desc (Dept IN VARCHAR2) RETURN VARCHAR2 AS
  Dsc    VARCHAR2(30);
  CURSOR C IS
  SELECT description
```

```
      FROM    departments
      WHERE   dept_code = Dept;
   BEGIN
      OPEN  C;
      FETCH C in Dsc;
      CLOSE C;
      RETURN(NVL(Dsc,'?'));
   END;

   SELECT m.dept_code,
          Lookup_Desc(m.dept_code),
          SUM(m.retail_amount)
   FROM    weekly_sales m
   WHERE   sales_date between '01-JAN-96' and '31-JAN-96'
   GROUP
        BY m.dept_code;
```

The following EXPLAIN PLAN output tells a whole new story. The total number of records returned is still 384: a good start. The total elapsed and CPU times is almost half that of the original SQL statement. The combined number of physical reads (13102 + 386 + 20) is much the same as the original SQL, as you would expect; but the combined logical reads (14326 + 1605 + 1151) is a factor of 136 times less.

```
call        count      cpu elapsed      disk    query current    rows
-------    ------   ------- -------   ------- -------- -------- ------
Parse          1     0.45    1.45       362      435       13       0
Execute        1     0.02    0.13         1        0        2       0
Fetch        384   329.74  395.03     13102    14326        9     384


Rows       Execution Plan
-------    ----------------------------------------------------------
      0    SELECT STATEMENT   OPTIMIZER HINT: CHOOSE
 576742      SORT (GROUP BY)
2477175        TABLE ACCESS (FULL) OF 'WEEKLY_SALES'


begin :r:=Lookup_Desc(:a1);end;

call        count      cpu elapsed      disk    query current    rows
-------    ------   ------- -------   ------- -------- -------- ------
Parse          1     0.07    0.19         0        0        0       0
Execute      384     1.78    2.98       386     1605        6   73920
Fetch          0     0.00    0.00         0        0        0       0

call        count      cpu elapsed      disk    query current    rows
-------    ------   ------- -------   ------- -------- -------- ------
Parse          1     0.05    0.11         0        0        0       0
Execute      384     0.16    0.21         0        0        0       0
Fetch        384     0.29    1.13        20     1151        0     383


Rows       Execution Plan
-------    ----------------------------------------------------------
      0    SELECT STATEMENT   OPTIMIZER HINT: CHOOSE
     83      TABLE ACCESS (BY ROWID) OF 'DEPARTMENT'
    384        INDEX (UNIQUE SCAN) OF 'DEPT_PK' (UNIQUE)
```

How can we explain this? By looking at the number of times the inline function has been executed, we deduce that it is called after the WEEKLY_SALES table has been accumulated (grouped). Rather than needlessly joining to the department table 576,742 times, we join only 394 times. This explains the large difference in logical reads between the two statement executions.

The other less obvious point of interest is the difference in size of sort information written and sorted via the temporary tablespace. The sorted record size of the first example was approximately 29.7 megabytes (dept_code (4 bytes) + description (40 bytes) + retail_amount (10 bytes) * 576,741 rows). The data need to be written to the temporary tablespace, sorted, aggregated, and then read back into memory. The sorted record size of the second SQL statement was approximately 7.7 megabytes (4 bytes + 10 bytes * 576,741 rows). The vast difference in sorting overheads has also contributed to the saving processing statements.

Caching Data

A very nice feature of inline functions is the ability to exploit memory caching. Particularly with long-running jobs, data caching can yield enormous performance improvements. How does it work?

Using PL/SQL's dynamic table datatypes, we can preload data into memory or load as we go and not have to access the information from disk again. This is most beneficial when the function is a very complex and disk-intensive operation. The following example demonstrates this idea:

```
# inl_cach.sql
SELECT prod_code, locn_code, sales_date, sum(retail_amount)
FROM   weekly_sales
WHERE  sales_date BETWEEN '01-JAN-96' and '31-JAN-96'
AND    SALES.Chk_Range(locn_code) = 'TRUE';


Package Sales
AS
  FUNCTION Chk_Range(locn_code IN VARCHAR2) RETURN VARCHAR2;
  --
  PRAGMA restrict_referneces (Chk_Range, WNDS, WNPS);
END;

Package Body Sales
AS
Max_Locn    CONSTANT INTEGER := 400;
--
TYPE TAB_9  IS TABLE OF NUMBER(5)   INDEX BY binary_integer;
TYPE TAB_x  IS TABLE OF VARCHAR2(5) INDEX by binary_integer;
--
TAB_Loc     TAB_9;
TAB_Fnd     TAB_x;
--
--
```

```
FUNCTION Chk_Range (locn_code IN NUMBER  ) RETURN VARCHAR2 AS
CURSOR C1 IS
SELECT 'TRUE'
FROM   --table1--,
       --table2--.
       --table3--
WHERE  ......
AND    ...... ;
--
BEGIN
  IF (TAB_loc(locn_code) != locn_code) THEN
      TAB_loc(locn_code) := locn_code;
      --
      OPEN  C1;
      FETCH C1 INTO TAB_Fnd(locn_code);
      CLOSE C1;
  END IF;
  --
  RETURN (TAB_Fnd(locn_code));
END Chk_Range;
--
--
FOR i IN 1..Max_Loc Loop     -- Package Initialization Section
    TAB_loc(i) := 0;
    TAB_Fnd(i) := 'FALSE';
END LOOP;
END;
```

Note that the driving SQL statement will return thousands of rows in product sequence. The Chk_Range function validates that the location code in question is for the user's current state, security level, and so on. We know from our data that there is a maximum of 400 different locations. Unfortunately, these locations are fetched in a random order (product sequence), with the same locations being fetched time and time again. By holding the result for each location in a PL/SQL array, we can cut down on an enormous amount of repetitive processing. The location array is automatically initialized as part of the first reference to the package and will remain current until the database connection completes.

Two issues to remember when using array functions are the following:

- Data in the array can become *stale*. That is, the underlying database data may have been updated since you last evaluated that location. If this is a problem for you, don't use arrays.

- In the above example, we chose to initialize the array to a fixed size of 400 entries. This is an informed decision, based on knowledge of the maximum location number for our application. This may not always be possible. If you are dealing with a variable or large number of table entries, consider inserting array entries as they are encountered rather than preinitializing a set number. In such a case, you would need to change the array searching logic from a hashing key to a binary chop or even a full array scan. Each of these methods is acceptable because the data is already in memory and no disk accessing is required.

Minimizing the Number of Updates

One mistake that programmers make is to scan through entire tables to update one column. In long-running jobs, such processing can be particularly costly. Consider a table, called ACCOUNT, that has three columns:

```
acc_no    NUMBER(6)
acc_desc  CHAR(80)
category  CHAR(10)
```

You must update two columns, acc_desc and category.

Programmer A codes the following statements:

```
UPDATE account
SET acc_desc = 'CONSULTING SERVICES' ;

UPDATE account
SET category = 'INCOME' ;
```

Programmer B decides to place both updates in the same statement, which is much more efficient:

```
UPDATE account
SET acc_desc = 'CONSULTING SERVICES',
    category = 'INCOME';
```

You can realize similar savings when two columns are updated by selecting from another table. Some developers are not aware that they can update more than one column using a single SET clause. The following statement is very efficient:

```
# min_upd.sql
UPDATE account  A
SET  ( acc_desc,
     category ) = ( SELECT acc_desc, category
                           FROM   input_table I
                           WHERE  A.acc_no = I.acc_no
                    )
       WHERE   EXISTS    ( SELECT 'X'
                           FROM   input_table I
                           WHERE  A.acc_no = I.acc_no );
```

Tuning EXPORT and IMPORT Utilities

The Oracle utilities EXPORT and IMPORT are often used for backup and recovery. These functions are usually the last processes you think about when you are developing and tuning a new application. When we review tuning plans with clients, we usually don't even see EXPORT and IMPORT on the list of items to be reviewed. Yet these utilities can fail. A major job of the system administrator and the DBA is to prevent failures (e.g., media, software, incomplete application backup, or simply inadequate backup timing) and to minimize the damage that occurs if failures do occur.

For detailed information about using the EXPORT and IMPORT utilities for backup and recovery, see Chapter 14, *Tuning Database Backup and Recovery*.

Tuning EXPORT

The EXPORT utility, the most common tool for an Oracle database backup, produces a flat ASCII file that can be transported from one hardware platform to another. EXPORT backups are compatible for all Oracle platforms. There are a number of ways to tune EXPORT process.

By placing export dump file(s) on a different disk from the one used by the data that are being exported (database files), you can read and write faster, and you minimize disk contention. You can also improve performance by dividing large exports into several smaller exports that run in parallel. This can result in excellent performance if all of the individual exports are over tablespaces or user tables located on different physical disks.

If at all possible, export disk-to-disk rather than disk-to-tape. If your system does have enough spare disk capacity to hold the dump files, write them to disk and copy them to tape when the backup is complete.

EXPORT functions do allow you to perform incremental or cumulative exports, but we have not found these functions to be very useful. They seem to be a good idea in theory but not in practice. Unfortunately, the larger tables of a database tend to be the most volatile. If you're going to have to back up 90% of the database, you might just as well perform a full backup, which is likely to be more useful. Having a full backup provides the added benefit that recovery will require only a single file. Otherwise, you may find yourself having to deal with a whole week's worth of files.

Splitting the physical database into logical sections can help speed up exports. At one site where we worked, the application was for a financial lending institution, consisting of more than 30,000 active loans, and a loan history table of more than 4,000,000 records. Every action against a loan was written to the history file. Because the history table was added to every day, this ruled out the option of performing incremental or cumulative exports. Once the history was generated, it could never be modified or deleted. By splitting the history table into two pieces, one for the current month's history and one for the remainder of the time, it became possible to export only the active part of the database. For historic queries, a simple view could join the two tables. Splitting the table in this way reduced the length of the overnight export by two-thirds (from 200 megabytes to 70 megabytes). As part of this job, we developed a special monthly procedure that rolls the current month's history into the second, larger table. Then an EXPORT procedure exports the entire application. This procedure is shown in Figure 15-1.

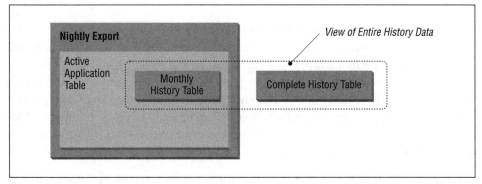

Figure 15-1. Monthly export

Set the EXPORT parameter BUFFER to as large a value as possible. A size of 64 kilobytes is usual; 10 megabytes is not uncommon. The maximum value of BUFFER is operating system dependent. Unfortunately, a large buffer size will not help when exporting (or importing) tables with LONG columns. The utility will read records from these tables *one record at a time.* This will significantly slow down the export operations for those particular tables. Always try to avoid LONG columns altogether or strip those columns off into their own table and export those tables as a separate exercise.

The physical timing of your database exports can be just as important as the backup itself. If an application backup is several days old, it may be as useless as the current damaged database. Individual application requirements usually determine how frequently you do your backups. Although your organization may allow exports to be done during business hours, this is often impractical. If interactive users are modifying data during the export, a consistent recovery point (snapshot) cannot be achieved. It is possible, and recommended, to export application data in "consistent mode," for example

```
EXP / ... CONSISTENT=Y ....
```

This means that all database objects are exported as at the time the backup began. This may seem to be the solution to our problems, but it does come at a cost. Rollback segments must be retained for the duration of the export, and this is not always possible. Export times will increase for active applications, because the data must be sourced from the rollback segments. Even worse, data can be skipped because a consistent snapshot cannot be reconstructed from the rollback segments.

Tuning IMPORT

The Oracle utility IMPORT restores all or part of a database from an EXPORT dump file. The success of a data import depends not only on its operation, but also on its timeliness. The more quickly you can restore database activity, the less application downtime your users will experience and the fewer complaints you'll hear.

The IMPORT utility is generally regarded as one of the slowest modes of database recovery. This is very true when recovering the entire database. An import will normally take three to six times as long as the export took. This is partly because it takes longer to write than it does to read and partly because imports have to recreate all database indexes. On the other hand, importing is one of the quickest ways to recover a single application object. Extracting a table or group of tables from an export dump file is a lot quicker and a lot easier than trying to recover them from a cold database backup.

To improve the performance of the import utility, place import files on a different disk from the one used for the database files. This allows you to read and write faster, and it minimizes disk contention. Divide large imports into several smaller imports that run in parallel. This can result in excellent performance if all of the individual imports are over tablespaces or user tables located on different physical disks. Parallel import processes can source their data from the same dump file. It is quite acceptable to have many processes simultaneously reading the same export dump file. Even though this may cause some file contention, importing processes spend most of their time writing to the database and very little time actually reading from the dump file.

Import only the information that is necessary for immediate system access. If an export file contains all of the essential information for recovery, plus a number of very large, noncritical tables, restore only the mandatory tables in your first pass. (For many applications, this may mean all tables.) It is normally very difficult to exclude a single table from an import. Tables can be skipped by creating dummy table definitions with incompatible column datatypes. These dummy tables should be created with very small INITIAL extents and in a nonapplication tablespace. When the import encounters such a table, it simply reports an Oracle error and continues on. The dummy table definitions are then dropped, and the individual tables can be imported, at a later time. For example:

```
CREATE TABLE emp_history (DUMMY VARCHAR2(1))
STORAGE (INITIAL 1K  NEXT 1K) TABLESPACE USERS;
```

Before you import any table, size and create all database datafiles first. Make sure that each table will fit into a single initial extent, and always factor future table growth into the INITIAL extent. Generate indexes after you restore tables and load data. The EXPORT utility allows you to nominally compress all object extents into a single initial extent. When these objects are then imported, all tables and indexes will be contained in a single extent.

```
EXP / ... COMPRESS=Y ...
```

If at all possible, import directly from disk, rather than tape-to-disk. It is preferable to keep the dump file on disk if your system has the capacity. Restoring from tape to disk and importing from tape are both time consuming. Remember that if you compress files, you can usually hold several dump files on disk. To allow Oracle dump files to be compatible across all platforms, Oracle makes them extremely verbose. Our tests show that simple, platform-specific compression utilities will reduce the size of exports to less than 25% of the original size. A simple compression could allow two or three export files to be retained on disk, rather than having to be copied to tape.

By default, IMPORT commits only after inserting all of the records of each table. This is usually possible only for smaller tables. Very large tables will not fit into the available rollback segments. To import large tables, set the COMMIT option within the IMPORT parameter file. This is the only way to import very large tables. For example, you can specify

```
IMP PARFILE = /usr/dump/import.par
```

where *import.par* contains

```
COMMIT   = Y
FROMUSER = OPS$SMITH
TOUSER   = OPS$JONES
```

Alternative Tuning of Exports and Imports

A number of unconventional alternatives are available to the DBA to help improve the EXPORT and IMPORT utilities. These tuning suggestions are not intended to be used in day-to-day business but may need to be used in times of desperation.

Single-task IMPORT and EXPORT

Oracle supports single-task IMPORT and EXPORT on all UNIX platforms. This means that the executable is operating in single-task mode (no shadow process) and has its own copy of the SGA. This mode can be up to twice as fast as normal (two-task) EXPORT and IMPORT modes. Single-task is not the Oracle default and must be explicitly linked by the DBA before it can be used. For example:

```
make -f $Oracle_HOME/rdbms/lib/oracle.mk expst
make -f $Oracle_HOME/rdbms/lib/oracle.mk impst
```

What is the problem with this approach? Single-task requires more real memory to operate. This is not really a problem because you would really run imports and/or exports simultaneously. The real issue is whether Oracle is prepared to support single-task operation. The answer to this depends on whom you talk to. The Oracle hot-line claims that this function is unsupported and should not be used; on the other hand, a number of Oracle's own tuning manuals hail its glory. Before committing your application and your future to single-task utilities, make sure that you can get full Oracle support.

Import with COMMIT = NO

This recommendation goes against everything we've said before, but in the right situation it can give better overall performance. When you need to load your database in a hurry, committing data at regular intervals will slow down overall processing. By deferring the COMMIT to the end of each table, we can achieve improvements up to twofold.

Why not do this always? To support such an import, you must have a rollback segment as large as your largest table. This allows loading a table in a single-transaction state. Most applications would not carry such large rollback segments for day-to-day usage. The disk requirements and backup overheads do not justify the need. You would also have to be prepared to tolerate the time required to roll back such a large table if something goes wrong during the import.

Huge SORT_AREA_SIZE size

One of the slowest parts of an application import is the process of recreating all indexes after the data has been loaded. This can be sped up by increasing the size of the SORT_AREA_SIZE to a very large value. If you are the only person on the system while recovering your database, a sort area size of one-third of your real memory would not be an unreasonable size.

Avoid primary keys and unique constraints

A real problem in creating primary key and unique constraint indexes is that the database cannot use parallel query facilities when building the indexes. This means that these indexes must be created in serial fashion. Replacing these constraints with common unique indexes has exactly the same effect as far as the database optimizer is concerned but means that we can build the indexes in parallel mode and save valuable recovery (import) time.

16

Tuning in the Client-Server Environment

The topic of client-server computing is the subject of many books, and we're not going to try to write another one here. The aim of this chapter is to summarize the specific ways in which client-server computing affects performance and how you can tune your client-server environment to get the best possible performance out of your applications.

Oracle has invested enormous resources to make client-server computing an effective and financially rewarding equipment choice. The trend in the industry is toward downsizing. Many large organizations that relied in the past on mainframe computing are now discovering how much money they can save by downsizing to a client-server configuration.

Advances in computing and networking have made client-server solutions, even for the largest systems, a reality. The advance in powerful, inexpensive microcomputers (even laptops) that deliver enormous processing power at a fraction of the cost of a mainframe, new networking facilities, and recent advances in chip technology and parallel processing all play a role in making client-server computing a viable solution to the most demanding application needs. When I was at university, my lecturer jokingly described the difference between a PC, a minicomputer, and a mainframe this way: "A PC is small enough to be transported by car, a mini can be transported in the back of a van, and a mainframe needs a semi-trailer, a large crane, and very careful movers." These words have finally rung true. Other than price, physical machine size rather than processing power may be the only way in which we distinguish types of computers in the future.

Despite the major benefits of client-server, we are not recommending that you rush, willy-nilly, out to buy a database server, file servers, and a truckload of PC workstations to replace your existing hardware—without a lot of planning, that is. If your existing applications have been developed with a mainframe mentality, downsizing the application, unchanged, is unlikely to achieve significant performance improvements. Client-server environments have just as many bad features as good ones. What you need to do, if you are serious about exploring the benefits of client-server configurations, is to learn how to exploit their good points while avoiding the bad ones. Tuning for client-server (the subject of this chapter) is vital if you are going to take advantage of this technology.

What Is Client-Server?

The term *client-server* can be defined with varying degrees of rigor and a multitude of interpretations. For purposes of this book, we define it as "two or more distinct computers working together. One computer (the server) performs the job of coordinating access to the Oracle database; the other computer (the client) serves the application users." In most environments, there are multiple client computers. To run applications in a client-server environment, a processor must be able to communicate between the server computer and the client computer(s), usually via a network.

Historically, Oracle has run in a unitary environment. In such an environment, user processes communicate with the database within the boundaries of the same physical computer. All processes (database and user) share the same memory, disk, and CPU resources. User terminals are typically dumb ones, incapable of functioning on their own. Each terminal is physically cabled to the central computer. A unitary environment is shown in Figure 16-1.

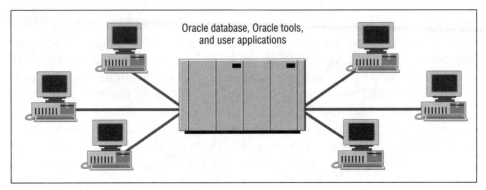

Figure 16-1. Running Oracle in a unitary environment

By contrast, Oracle client-server applications run on many CPUs, with the Oracle database and the application user process(es) communicating from different computers. Resources are not shared between the client and server. Instead, messages (usually called packets) are sent and received. Client processes act on their own, not as the result of concurrent operator requests. The typical mode of operation involves the database process looping idly on the database server, waiting to service client requests. Most application overhead is incurred at the client machine by the initiating client only and does not affect other clients.

There are many workable configurations of client-server networks. An organization's application needs, number of connected users, software requirements, and budget all play a part in dictating the right choice for a client-server implementation. Figure 16-2 shows one possible configuration. Each operator has a PC on his or her desk acting as a client machine. (In addition to running Oracle applications, these PCs can also be used to perform other, more traditional desktop functions, such as word processing.) The Oracle database (kernel and data files) resides on the database server, and all other components (Oracle tools, third-party software, and user files) reside on the file server. For this particular configuration, client PCs do not even need to have local hard disks. Network drivers and application objects, including Oracle tools, can be retrieved over the network from a common file server.

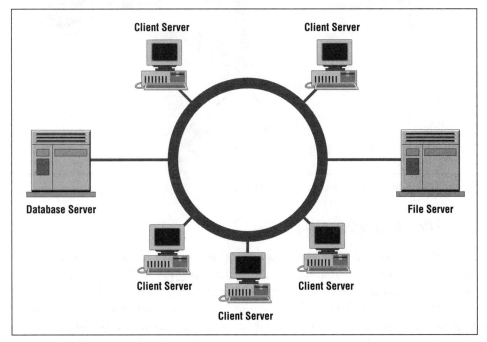

Figure 16-2. Client-server environment

Figure 16-3 demonstrates a different type of client-server configuration. In this example, a UNIX client-server application consisting of several client-servers is connected to a common database. Each server caters to a group of individual terminals (database connections), with each workstation reduced to a simple, dumb terminal emulator. No processing is performed for (or offloaded to) the user workstations.

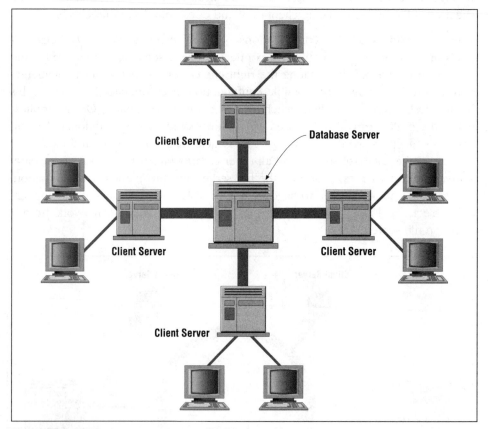

Figure 16-3. Client-server environment (UNIX network)

Network Topology

In a client-server environment, processes communicate with one another via a network. When you are tuning an Oracle database, you will need to provide for network communications. Remember that operators do not interact directly with the database server (backend processes), but rather with the client (frontend process). The physical arrangement of client and server nodes is called network topology. The choices of network arrangement, client and server node location, and overall network length can all affect application performance. Networks commonly make use of message routers and node bridges to build large environments that are often complicated but nevertheless efficient.

For the network demonstrated in Figure 16-2, the length of the physical network is likely to be a performance issue. The speed with which data packets are passed around a network is constant (typically 10 to 16 megabits). The larger the ring, the farther the packets will need to travel, and the longer they will take to reach their destination. If a great many terminals are added to the ring, obviously the ring becomes longer and each packet has to be inspected by a terminal (checking packet header destination information) many times before it can reach its ultimate destination.

On the other hand, the UNIX network identified in Figure 16-3 can support many varied topology arrangements. When you have a choice, make it carefully because application performance can be adversely affected by topology selection. Some of the more common network topologies are described briefly in the following sections.

Star Topology

In a star or radial topology, shown in Figure 16-4, all nodes are joined at a single point. These networks are common in situations in which all control is located at a central node and communication between nodes and remote stations is processed via that node. This relieves outlying nodes of control function overheads.

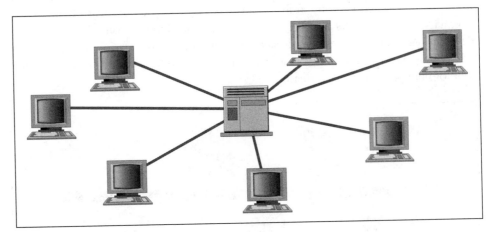

Figure 16-4. Star topology

Ring Topology

Ring networks are a very popular type of network topology. In a ring network, shown in Figure 16-5, all nodes are connected via point-to-point links, making up an unbroken loop. Network messages travel around the ring. Each node recognizes its own messages by looking for a specific message header and passes other messages further around the ring. Ring networks are less complex than star or hybrid networks because they do not require routers.

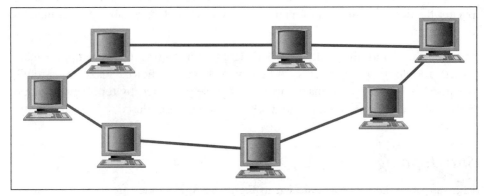

Figure 16-5. Ring topology

Bus Topology

Bus topologies, shown in Figure 16-6, function in a way that is similar to star and ring networks. All nodes are fully connected via a single physical channel and cable taps. Bus networks are frequently used for distributing control in local area networks. As with ring networks, each message must carry a node identifier. But unlike ring networks, messages do not have to be retransmitted, relieving each node of network control overheads.

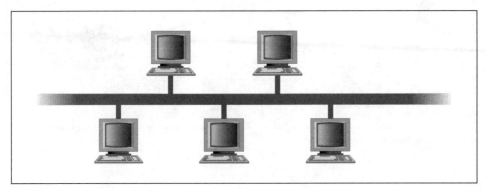

Figure 16-6. Bus topology

Hybrid Topologies

Unconstrained, hybrid network configurations, shown in Figure 16-7, are random in form. The number of connections is usually determined by budget. Because line costs are high, only physical connections that are actually needed are cabled in such networks.

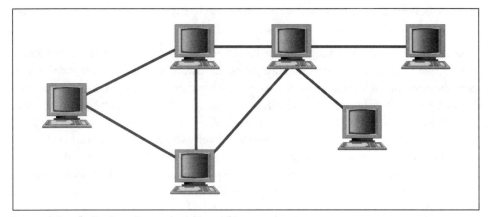

Figure 16-7. Hybrid topology

Where Should You Put the Network Hardware?

When you are considering where to locate your physical hardware in a client-server environment, make sure you are familiar with how Oracle will be interacting between the client and server processors. Oracle uses SQL*Net to communicate across the network. SQL calls are requested at the client machine and passed back and forth to the database processor. This program conversation can generate thousands of packets from a single application module of medium complexity.

If your company has its application client-server(s) and database server physically located at different sites, the distance this process-to-process communication has to travel could result in a response delay of as much as 20 seconds. You will find that a module that was performing adequately in a unitary environment (where all communication was within the single computer) may suddenly have its response times raised well above the required standards for your site.

The best way of improving client-server performance is to reduce the number of packets being transferred across the network. For applications that have been developed for a unitary environment, you'll have to do a substantial amount of programming. Before you undertake what might be a tedious rewrite, you can realize immediate performance improvements simply by locating the database and client-servers as physically close together as possible. This approach may sound simplistic, but it is remarkably effective because it allows you to put higher-speed lines between the processors.

Your ability to make this particular improvement obviously depends on your choice of network topology. The token ring topology shown in Figure 16-2 cannot benefit from this practice. Because each client server is actually a user workstation, it must be located on the user's desk.

The UNIX client-server configuration described in Figure 16-3, on the other hand, can achieve large performance gains from hardware location. Each workstation acts as a simple terminal emulator to each client processor. The communication between the workstation and the client is minimal. The communication between the client and the database server, however, is major. You can achieve huge savings by reducing the physical distance over which the database and client server(s) must communicate; at the expense of the few packets that move between the client server and the operators terminal. Figure 16-8 demonstrates how an Australia-wide network could be configured.

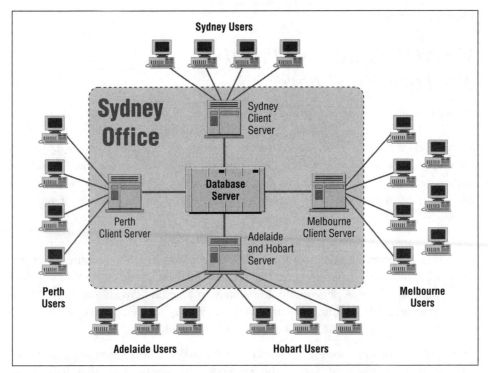

Figure 16-8. Wide-area network

Thin, Fat, and Three-Tier Client-Server Applications

You may have heard the terms *thin* and *fat* when talking about client-server applications. More recently, companies have been experimenting with *three-tier* environments. These terms simply indicate where the bulk of the application processing is being performed.

Thin client applications use the database for all application business rules. The client (frontend) presentation layer is very simple and relies entirely on the database for data integrity. These types of applications depend heavily on stored database procedures and functions, table triggers, schema-level referential integrity, and constraints. Thin clients tend to be more demanding of network resources, since they have to visit the database to validate even the simplest data entry. They tend to be more database vendor dependent, locking large amounts of development resources into the current proprietary database. Porting these applications to another database platform is difficult. On the other hand, thin client applications are much easier to port from one frontend vendor to the next. Only the presentation layer needs to be replaced, with all the business rule processing remaining hidden within the physical database itself.

Fat client applications are the exact opposite of thin ones. Fat clients are responsible for performing most of the application workload; they visit the database only when absolutely necessary. Fat clients are not responsible only for the presentation layer, but also for a large percentage of user input validation. Things like date range checking, code validation, and business rule processing are all executed at the client end. Fat clients tend to require considerably larger PCs (more memory, more disk, faster CPUs) but are lighter on network resources. They are less database vendor-dependent than the clients, with only the application schema itself held in the physical database. Porting fat client applications to another database platform is simpler than with a thin client application, but porting from one frontend vendor to the next is harder.

Three-tier client applications blend the advantages of fat and thin applications into one. Client PC requirements are reduced by having a very thin application presentation layer. The database server is built with a fat client-server mentality, acting purely as a data server with very limited business rule validation. Where is the work done? A third application server is situated between the client and the database servers. This server is responsible for performing as much code validation and business rule processing as possible. It is physically situated as close as possible to the host with which it will most communicate (usually the database server). Three-tier applications tend to be harder to build and more complex to write but more rewarding than fat or thin applications.

Before you decide on a fat or thin environment for your client-server applications, ask some fundamental questions:

- Do you have the network capacity to support thin client applications?

- Do you have the client-based hardware configurations to support fat client applications?

- Will you ever change your database and/or frontend vendors within the life span of this application?

- Is your environment (and budget) better suited to a combination of fat and thin programming strategies?

Distributed Databases

With distributed database processing, an organization's database can be strategically divided among multiple physical databases located on distinct database servers. From the user's point of view, however, there is a single logical database. For example, assume that a company's accounting department is in Melbourne and the manufacturing department is in Sydney, as illustrated in Figure 16-9. These two divisions have two distinct application modules, with very little data crossover. By intelligently placing the database servers in the two cities and adding a super-fast data communications link between the two, you can actually improve network and application performance.

With the two-phase commit feature, automatic and transparent updates guarantee that commits or rollbacks that are issued against a distributed database transaction are always performed as a single unit. Global database integrity is always maintained.

Client-Server Performance Issues

This section describes a variety of performance issues for client-server configurations.

Reducing Oracle Network Traffic

Reducing the number of packets transferred (trips) across the network is vital to making a client-server configuration run efficiently. The speed and efficiency of the network are the gating factors to a high-performance system. In a unitary environment, processes cross-communicate via a physical memory board. Messages do not need to be shuffled from one machine to the next. Many newer network configurations are yielding very impressive performance, but no matter how hard

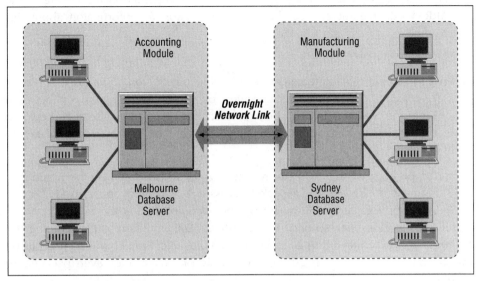

Figure 16-9. Distributed database processing

you try, you'll never be able to match the process-to-process performance of a unitary machine.

In numerous tests, we have concluded that the number of packets transmitted across a network is actually more important than the size of each packet. Both small and large packets take roughly the same amount of time passing between machines. Sending a large number of packets however, can wreak havoc on your system's response times.

Consider the following simple SQL query:

```
SELECT emp_no, emp_name
    FROM   emp
    WHERE  emp_dept = :emp_dept
```

This query generates a surprising number of network round-trips each time it is executed:

1. Open the cursor

2. Parse the statement (check its syntax)

3. Bind the variables

4. Describe (what are the fields numbers, characters, dates, etc.?)

5. Execute the statement (search the database)

6. Fetch the rows (the number of rows per fetch depends on the setting of the ARRAYSIZE parameter (see the following section for information about this parameter)

7. Close the cursor

When this sample SQL statement was executed directly on a database server, it took 0.34 seconds. When it was executed on a client-server network between Melbourne and Sydney, it took about 3.5 seconds. The only difference between these two trials was the physical distance between the client and the database servers.

Consider the huge savings you can realize if you can cut down on the number of transfers needed. Transferring a packet across a TCP/IP network from Melbourne to Sydney (approximately 550 miles) can be accomplished at the rate of approximately 120 packets per second. If the ARRAYSIZE you have specified is 1, 20 fetches are required to return 20 rows, and 26 blocks of data (packets) need to be transferred. If ARRAYSIZE is 20, however, only one fetch and seven packets are required.

It does not take long for the number of packets to build up to a point at which they have a significant impact on performance. Some SQL*Forms programs generate more than 1,000 packets. Not only do client stations need to wait for packets to be sent and received from the database server, the packets themselves begin to compete for a time slot on the network.

Tuning ARRAYSIZE

As we've mentioned, the ARRAYSIZE parameter controls the number of rows that can be returned from disk in a single network transfer. If you set ARRAYSIZE correctly, you can substantially reduce the number of network packets. An adequate value for this parameter allows multiple SELECT, INSERT, and UPDATE operations to be performed in a single database server access.

To figure out how many packets need to be transferred for a particular SQL statement or set of statements (for example, the series of network round-trips described in the previous section), divide the number of required fetches by the ARRAYSIZE in effect for your current database interface tool.

NOTE   Our benchmarks indicate that increasing ARRAYSIZE when you are running in a unitary environment has little or no effect on performance.

You can increase ARRAYSIZE, or its equivalent parameter, in a number of Oracle tools:

- *SQL*Forms*: Uses array processing by default.

- Precompiler 3GL languages (e.g., Pro*C): Support array processing implicitly. For example:

```
BEGIN DECLARE
FLOAT emp_no[100];
CHAR emp_name[30,100];
END   DECLARE

EXEC SQL
    INSERT INTO emp ( emp_no, emp_name )
             VALUES (:emp_no, :emp_name );
```

  If the values are part of an array of 200, 200 rows will be inserted with the one execution of the statement. Array selects, updates, and deletes are also supported.

- *Oracle Call Interface (OCI)*: Uses the OFEN parameter to specify the number of rows to be returned via each OEXN fetch. This is equivalent to ARRAYSIZE.

- *SQL*Plus*: You can set ARRAYSIZE in the SET command. The default is 20. If you set it to 200 or more, you will improve performance over the network. (MAXDATA must be large enough to contain that many rows.)

- *EXPORT and IMPORT*: Try to avoid executing these utilities across network nodes. If it is absolutely necessary, you can improve response time by setting the BUFFER parameter to an appropriate size. If the row length is 100 and BUFFER is 32,768, the effective array size is approximately 327. Most sites set their buffers on exports and imports to at least 32 kilobytes. Some UNIX sites set buffers as high as 1 megabyte. The maximum value is operating system dependent.

- *SQL*Loader*: Set the ROWS parameter to allocate a buffer or array size. The actual buffer size is set by multiplying the size of each row by the value you specify for the parameter. Set this value as high as possible for your site. The maximum is system dependent.

Tuning PL/SQL

PL/SQL's block structure makes its network performance very efficient. Each PL/SQL block can contain many individual SQL statements (SELECT, UPDATE, DELETE, and INSERT). Each block is passed to the kernel at the database server end in a single network transmission. The statements in the block are executed as a unit at the database end, and the results are returned on completion of the entire block. Overall network traffic can be reduced a thousandfold. Note that this functionality is applicable to all Oracle tools that use PL/SQL (except SQL*Forms, which has its own version of PL/SQL linked directly into its own executable). See Figure 16-10 for a comparison of SQL and PL/SQL operations.

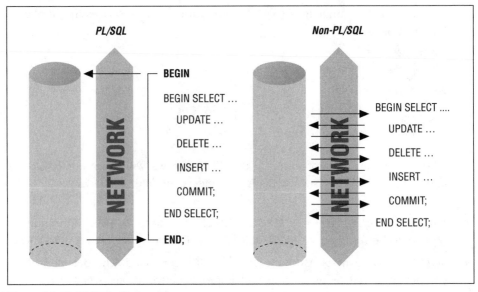

Figure 16-10. PL/SQL efficiencies

You can save additional network traffic by limiting the number of local field bindings within the PL/SQL block. Initialize each bind variable into a temporary PL/SQL-defined variable once, and reference that temporary variable for the remainder of the procedure. Alternatively, you could pass the bind variable as a procedure variable.

All of the Oracle tools support PL/SQL blocks and/or procedures and can use this functionality to improve their response times substantially.

Choosing Explicit SELECT Statements

You can reduce the number of network trips for SQL SELECT statements by using explicit, rather than implicit, cursors. Implicit cursors must perform a second fetch for every SELECT statement. If an application were to perform 100 implicit database selects within a single session, then the program would incur 100 extra database fetches and 100 extra network trips.

You can define an explicit cursor by specifying it in a DECLARE statement. You include this DECLARE in your PL/SQL code. Then, within the block, you may include OPEN, FETCH, and CLOSE statements. OPEN opens and parses the cursor and is required. FETCH fetches the cursor's current row and is also required.

CLOSE closes the cursor after all fetches have been completed and is optional. For example:

```
DECLARE
    CURSOR C IS
    SELECT  emp_name
    FROM    emp
    WHERE   emp_no = 1234;
BEGIN
    OPEN  C;
    FETCH C INTO . . . ;
    CLOSE C;
END;
```

If you do not specify an explicit cursor for a SELECT statement, PL/SQL will implicitly open a cursor to use when it processes each SQL statement, as shown below:

```
SELECT  emp_name
INTO    :emp_name
FROM    emp
WHERE   emp_no = 1234;
```

The savings associated with using explicit, rather than implicit, cursors can be significant in the client/server environment.

Combining SELECT Statements

Another simple way to reduce network traffic is to combine several unrelated SQL statements, as we suggested in Chapter 6, *Tuning SQL.*

The following statements were executed on a unitary Oracle database and then on a client-server database between Sydney and Melbourne. This simple exercise indicates that the time taken to traverse the network from client to database server is approximately 0.45 second. By simply combining both statements into one, we are able to improve the elapsed time on the client-server by more than 33%. In this first example, the following elapsed times result:

Unitary machine:

    0.54 second

Client-server configuration:

    1.45 seconds

```
DECLARE
    CURSOR C1 (E_no  number)  IS
    SELECT emp_name, salary, grade
    FROM    enp
    WHERE   emp_no = E_no;
BEGIN
    OPEN  C1 (342);
    FETCH C1 INTO  ..., ..., ...;
```

```
        CLOSE C1;

        OPEN  C1 (291);
        FETCH C1 INTO ..., ..., ...;
        CLOSE C1;
    END;
```

In this next example, the following elapsed times result:

Unitary machine:
   0.51 second

Client-server configuration:
   0.99 second

```
    SELECT A.emp_name, A.salary, A.grade,
           B.emp_name, B.salary, B.grade
    FROM   EMP A,
           EMP B
    WHERE  A.emp_no = 0342
    AND    B.emp_no = 0291 ;
```

SQL*Forms Base Table Views

When there is a substantial distance between the client and the database servers, you can improve performance by using *views* as module base (driver) tables.

SQL*Forms applications commonly perform two or three *post-change* triggers, as well as a *post-query* trigger, after every successful row fetch. These triggers are often used to look up foreign key descriptions and other such operations. Multirow modules may perform as many as 60 triggers (3 × 20 rows per screen) for every screen refresh. This, in turn, means 60 database calls, every one across the network.

If you have set the SQL*Forms SET parameter, ARRAYSIZE, to 20, then by creating a view over the base table and the three lookup tables, you can reduce the number of network calls from 61 to 1. If the form is a maintenance-type form, you'll have to incorporate special updating logic into the form to simulate base table updating.

Look again at the client-server application between Melbourne and Sydney. The creation of the view has reduced the elapsed time from more than 20 seconds to less than 2.5 seconds. The unitary elapsed times (1.74 and 1.61 second respectively) show that the overhead of the view is less than the combined overheads of opening, parsing, and executing the 60 individual triggers. The elapsed time of the client-server environment has actually been improved by tenfold. In this first example, the following elapsed times result:

Unitary machine:

   1.74 seconds

Client-server configuration:

   22.50 seconds

```
BASE TABLE        emp
DATABASE FIELDS   emp_no
                  emp_name
                  emp_dept    FK
                  mgr_emp_no  FK
                  emp_cat     FK


POST-CHANGE       LOOKUP dept description
                  LOOPUP manager name
                  LOOKUP category description
```

In this next example, the elapsed time for the client-server configuration has dropped dramatically:

Unitary machine:

   1.61 seconds

Client-server configuration:

   2.35 seconds

```
CREATE VIEW  EMP_VIEW
AS
SELECT E.emp_no, E.emp_name, E.emp_dept,
       E.mgr_emp_no, E.emp_cat,  D.dept_desc,
       M.emp_name mgr_name,
       C.cat_desc
FROM   category   C,
       department D,
       emp  M,
       emp  E
WHERE  E.emp_no     > 0
AND    E.emp_dept   = D.dept_code (+)
AND    E.mgr_emp_no = M.emp_no (+)
AND    E.emp_cat    = C.cat_code (+)

BASE TABLE  emp_view
DATABASE FIELDS  emp_no
                 emp_name
                 emp_dept
                 dept_desc
                 mgr_emp_no
                 mgr_name
                 emp_cat
                 cat_desc
```

Referential Integrity and Delete Cascade

The introduction of automatic database referential integrity was a major step forward for client-server technology. Developers can now build applications in which the majority of their integrity validation takes place without affecting the performance of the network. Each database modification can be instructed to cross-validate all associated references. When an integrity violation is detected. the database changes are rolled back, and an error is returned to the calling module.

The DELETE CASCADE clause is a valuable extension to referential integrity constraints. This facility not only guarantees data integrity, but also allows us to purge several tables with a single database call—all without affecting the performance of the network.

In the following example, the emp table includes an automatic referential integrity validation with the dept table. The emp_history table enforces referential integrity with the emp table and is automatically purged of all associated records when a row is deleted from the emp table.

```
Create Table emp
( emp_no      NUMBER(6),
  emp_name    VARCHAR2(50),
  . . .
  dept_no     NUMBER(4)  references dept(dept_no),
)

Create table emp_history
( emp_no      NUMBER(6)  references emp(emp_no) DELETE CASCADE,
  eff_date    DATE,
  . . .
)
```

For more information on database integrity, read the Oracle manuals in conjunction with *Chapter 8, Selecting a Locking Strategy*.

Automatic Table Replication/Snapshots

An automatic, asynchronous table replication feature allows read-only copies of an updatable master table. (Version 7.2 provides an update anyway capability at all replicated database nodes.) These replications can be refreshed at intervals defined by a user. A table snapshot can replicate a single table, a subset of a table, or a complex query join. You can refresh a table from either the entire master table data or a table subset (only the most recent changes).

To improve performance in a client-server configuration, make sure that you perform replication during off-peak network hours. Doing this will improve your performance, since users will not have to drag tables or table subsets across the network during high-peak hours. However, by doing replication during off hours, you do run the risk that a client may be using some obsolete data, so you may not want to do this for all of your tables. Carefully choose the tables to be replicated.

Stored Database Triggers

Stored database triggers are held within the database and are triggered automatically by the RDBMS kernel itself. Database triggers prior to Oracle7.3 are not stored in parsed (pcode) form and need to be (re)parsed on every reference. (See Chapter 7, *Tuning PL/SQL,* for further information on tuning database triggers.) Triggers can help to substantially reduce the overall amount of network traffic and improve client-server performance. Triggers can be attached to a single DML activity or to every row that is affected by the DML statement.

Programmers and developers can now perform numerous application validations and/or updates via a single application module call. No matter how complex or sizable the trigger may be, the total network traffic is limited to the initial database DML call.

A database trigger "warning" should also be included. Programmers, DBAs, and even application designers must be aware of all database triggers within an application. Something that appears to be a simple table insert may turn out to have triggered thousands of lines of unseen code, updating numerous other tables and even updating other distributed databases. This unseen behavior can lead to longer-than-anticipated response times and incorrect problem diagnosis. Most people's first reaction to spasmodic response times is to accuse the network.

Stored Database Functions, Procedures, and Packages

All database functions, procedures, and packages are held within the database and can be activated (called) by any client-server connection. (See Chapter 7 for further information on tuning database functions, procedures, and packages.) These features can substantially reduce the amount of network traffic and can improve overall client-server performance.

Entire application modules can be encapsulated into a single database procedure. These procedures may consist of many thousands of lines of PL/SQL code, may perform tens of database queries and updates, may trap and handle all error conditions, and may return results back to the calling module. All this power from a single database call! Here is an example:

```
Pro*C Program
    ....
```

```
EXEC SQL BEGIN DECLARE SECTION;
    VARCHAR prod[12];
    VARCHAR whse[5];
    DOUBLE  stk_on_hand;
EXEC SQL END DECLARE SECTION;
....
....
EXEC SQL EXECUTE
    BEGIN
        :stk_on_hand := Stk_On_Hand (:prod, :whse);
    end;
END-EXEC;
....
```

One downside of stored procedures, functions, and packages is the inability to batch the database calls. Most Oracle interface tools allow us to exploit array processing and perform hundreds of database selects, inserts, updates, and deletes via a single database call. How can we simulate these savings while still exploiting the power of the stored database objects?

One approach that we like to use is a little long-winded but can be most effective in a client-server environment. Assume that a batch routine will call a database procedure 100,000 times. Assume that the network overheads associated with this type of activity would be approximately 30% of the overall overheads. (The value of the overall network overheads would obviously depend on a number of outside influences, such as network speed, physical distance between client and server, and the amount of physical work that needs to be performed by the proce-dure.) If we can batch the procedure calls into two, we have immediately halved our network traffic. If we can batch the procedure calls into five, we have reduced the total network traffic be a staggering 80%. The following example demonstrates how the previous database call can simulate array batching via a second procedure. For example:

```
# sp_array.sql
Package  GL AS
      FUNCTION  stk_on_hand     (prod   IN VARCHAR2, whse   IN VARCHAR2)
         returns NUMBER;
      PROCEDURE stk_on_hand_X5 (i_cnt IN NUMBER,
                                prod1 IN VARCHAR2, whse1 IN VARCHAR2,
                                prod2 IN VARCHAR2, whse2 IN VARCHAR2,
                                prod3 IN VARCHAR2, whse3 IN VARCHAR2,
                                prod4 IN VARCHAR2, whse4 IN VARCHAR2,
                                prod5 IN VARCHAR2, whse5 IN VARCHAR2,
                                soh1 OUT NUMBER,    soh2 OUT NUMBER,
                                soh3 OUT NUMBER,    soh4 OUT NUMBER,
                                soh5 OUT NUMBER);
   END;

   PACKAGE BODY GL IS
      FUNCTION  stk_on_hand     (prod   IN VARCHAR2, whse IN VARCHAR2)
```

```
                           RETURNS NUMBER AS
    BEGIN
      ....
      ....
    END;


    PROCEDURE stk_on_hand_X5 (i_cnt IN NUMBER,
                              prod1 IN VARCHAR2, whse1 IN VARCHAR2,
                              prod2 IN VARCHAR2, whse2 IN VARCHAR2,
                              prod3 IN VARCHAR2, whse3 IN VARCHAR2,
                              prod4 IN VARCHAR2, whse4 IN VARCHAR2,
                              prod5 IN VARCHAR2, whse5 IN VARCHAR2,
                              soh1 OUT NUMBER,   soh2 OUT NUMBER,
                              soh3 OUT NUMBER,   soh4 OUT NUMBER,
                              soh5 OUT NUMBER ) AS
    BEGIN
    IF i_cnt >= 1 THEN
         soh1 := stk_on_hand (prod1, whse1);
        IF i_cnt >= 2 THEN
            soh2 := stk_on_hand (prod2, whse2);
           IF i_cnt >= 3 THEN
               soh3 := stk_on_hand (prod3, whse3);
              IF i_cnt >= 4 THEN
                  soh4 := stk_on_hand (prod4, whse4);
                 IF i_cnt = 5 THEN
                     soh5 := stk_on_hand (prod5, whse5);
                 END IF;
              END IF;
           END IF;
        END IF;
     END IF;
    END;



    Pro*C Program
    ....
    EXEC SQL BEGIN DECLARE SECTION;
       INTERGER i;
       VARCHAR  prod1[12];
       VARCHAR  whse1[5];
       DOUBLE   soh1;
       ....
       VARCHAR  prod5[12];
       VARCHAR  whse5[5];
       DOUBLE   soh5;
    EXEC SQL END DECLARE SECTION;
    ....
    ....
    FOR (i = 0; i <= 5; i++)
    {
      EXEC SQL EXECUTE
          BEGIN
             stk_on_hand_X5 (:i, :prod1, :whse1,
                             ....
```

```
                                      :prod5, :whse5);
        END;
    END-EXEC
    ....
```

A nice feature of this approach is the ability to support both calling methods. Programmers are able to code, test, and debug the single procedure (stk_on_ hand) call and then adopt the multiple procedure call (stl_on_hand_X5) with very little extra effort. Actual database activity is virtually identical. The single function call is still executed the same number of times. The extra overhead associated with the multiple procedure call is absorbed after the initial reference to the package; that is, all relevant procedures and functions are loaded into the shared pool and retained in parsed form for the remainder of the batch program.

Inline Database Functions

Inline database SQL functions are another feature of the RDBMS that you should exploit in the client-server world. (See Chapters 6 and 7 for further information on inline database functions). Using these functions can help to reduce the number of database calls and the amount of network traffic.

The most productive use of inline database functions for client-server applications is as a mode to reduce the number of database calls. Often, an application module will need to make several calls to different tables to extract related information. Inline functions permit us to combine these multiple database calls into a single database trip. The following example demonstrates this approach:

```
        TABLES : emp
               : sick_leave
               : holiday_leave

        SELECT E.emp_no, E.emp_name
        FROM   emp
        WHERE  E.emp_no = :emp_no

        SELECT SUM(S.days) sick_days
               sick_leave S,
        WHERE  S.emp_no = :emp_no

        SELECT sum(H.days) holidays
        FROM   holiday_leave H
        WHERE  H.emp_no = :emp_no
```

Rather than coding this SQL as multiple SQL statements, we can use the power of inline SQL functions:

```
        # inl_func.sql
          Function Sum_Sick_Leave (emp  IN number) RETURN NUMBER
        AS
```

```
        tot_days  NUMBER := 0;
        CURSOR C1 IS
        SELECT sum(days)
        FROM   sick_leave
        WHERE  emp_no = emp;
      BEGIN
        OPEN  C1;
        FETCH C1 INTO tot_days;
        CLOSE C1;
        RETURN (tot_days);
      END;

      FUNCTION Sum_Holiday_Leave (emp IN NUMBER) RETURN NUMBER
      AS
        tot_days  NUMBER := 0;
        CURSOR C1 IS
        SELECT sum(days)
        FROM   holiday_leave
        WHERE  emp_no = emp;
      BEGIN
        OPEN  C1;
        FETCH C1 INTO tot_days;
        CLOSE C1;
        RETURN (tot_days);
      END;

      SELECT E.emp_no, E.emp_name,
             sum_sick_leave(E.emp_no) sick_days,
             sum_holiday_leave(E.emp_no) holidays
      FROM   emp E
      WHERE  E.emp_no = :emp_no
```

Running Long-Running Jobs at the Server End

A common complaint of many sites is the fact that their batch processing is taking longer than their batch window. Running overnight reports, exports, imports, and other long-running batch jobs at the database server will improve overall response time in a client-server configuration. By eliminating the transfer of large amounts of data across the network and restricting the larger jobs to the database server(s), you can often improve performance by a factor of 10. In fact, you will get performance equal to what you would achieve by executing long-running procedures in a unitary environment.

Exploiting some of the ideas mentioned in the previous sections for long-running tasks can also dramatically improve long-running application modules. Very large array sizes (i.e., 100 plus) will improve performance times. Remember, though, that the larger the array size, the more real memory the process will require. Inline SQL functions, stored procedures, and packages will also reduce total network traffic and subsequent elapsed times for these jobs.

Tuning Precompilers for Client-Server

Sometimes, to get better performance out of critical areas of an application, developers may resort to developing these critical modules using a precompiler such as Pro*C or Pro*COBOL. We say "resort to" because using these precompilers is, for most programmers, more difficult than using the usual Oracle tools. For large, overnight processing jobs or complex and time-critical update routines (e.g., user exits), using the precompilers may prove necessary. They give you more detailed, low-level cursor and data control and, when used properly, can substantially improve performance.

You need to be aware of certain special considerations when you are using the precompilers in a client-server environment.

Arrays

Always use arrays if you are fetching, updating, deleting, or inserting more than one row in one operation for the same table. Pro*C allows the dynamic allocation and deallocation of memory to hold the array data. This allows the program to use and release memory resources as required. You might consider using a large array size; even one over 200 is not unreasonable.

Dynamic SQL

Use dynamic SQL features to limit the number of rows returned and to determine which indexes the optimizer will use. The precompilers support this facility. We were once asked to look at a Pro*C program that was performing very poorly. It turned out that the driving SELECT statement had no WHERE clause at all. There was no array processing. All rows had to be fetched from the database, one at a time; rows that were not needed were then pruned via a series of IF clauses. By incorporating the IF clauses into the driving SQL statement and introducing array processing, we were able to reduce the elapsed time of the routine from 4 hours to 25 minutes.

Parameters

If the same statements are used repeatedly within the program, set these parameters to minimize parsing:

```
HOLD_CURSOR        YES
RELEASE_CURSOR     NO
```

Do the reverse if cursors are referenced only once for the life of the program (in the initialization section). Set the following parameters to release unrequired cursor resources:

```
HOLD_CURSOR        NO
RELEASE_CURSOR     YES
```

PL/SQL cursors

Use PL/SQL explicit cursors whenever you need to perform multiple SELECTs, INSERTs, DELETEs, and UPDATEs.

Avoiding syntax checking

To speed up the precompiling of program source in the client-server environment, you can set the CHECK_SQL parameter to NO. No statement syntax checking will be performed against the database. (Setting this parameter should be a last resort; do it only if absolutely necessary to speed up program compilation times.) Note that you will have to set CHECK_SQL to NO if your precompiler program physically connects to more than one Oracle database.

NOTE   Precompiler programs that contain PL/SQL code cannot set CHECK_SQL to NO. The precompiler insists on performing semantic checking on the PL/SQL code (i.e., CHECK_SQL=SEMANTIC | FULL). This can be a real nuisance. Programs that do contain PL/SQL with a number of references to program bind variables can take a long time to compile. The only way to circumnavigate the syntax checking is to build the PL/SQL text into a program string variable and execute the code as dynamic SQL (known as precompiler methods 2 or 3).

Tuning the Network Itself

Several network equipment choices will have a major impact on client-server performance. There are a number of choices to consider when determining what network will best meet your organization's needs:

- Media bandwidth: For example, Ethernet is 10 megabits/second, and Async is only 0.0096 megabits/second.

- Communications protocol: Different protocols differ markedly in their performance. TCP/IP, DECnet, and APPC are known to be top performers; sync is known to lag behind.

- Physical protocol latency issues.

- Communication bus speeds at both the server and client ends.

Against these physical choices, you will have to balance the expected workload in your system—for example, the mix of work and whether the application will be performing mostly interactive jobs or many long-running jobs.

A communications protocol (common language) is required at both the client and server ends for the machines to communicate. The SQL*Net communications package (described in the next section) simply inherits all of the characteristics of its underlying network and communications protocol. If the network and communications protocol are built for speed, SQL*Net will perform accordingly.

Enlarging Packet Size

Most communication protocols allow you to adjust network packet sizes. Larger packet sizes require fewer overall packets and therefore less overall overhead. Oracle recommends that if the protocol allows you to choose, you select a minimum of at least 1,024 bytes.

Reducing Network Delays

In VTAM-based protocols, which have a built-in delay, you can improve performance by setting the DELAY parameter to 0.0. Doing this does require more of the CPU. You will have to assess your own system's CPU capacity and decide whether to set this parameter.

Tuning SQL*Net

SQL*Net is the Oracle communications *gateway* that allows users to access information residing on different databases, possibly stored on different machines. It runs across a variety of communications protocols (more than 20 at last count) and supports client-server applications as well as distributed database communication. SQL*Net can be used on a local Oracle database (shown in Figure 16-1) or in a client-server environment (shown in Figures 16-2 and 16-3). When the client is accessing a database on a remote computer, SQL*Net automatically handles all process communication connections.

Because many sites are still running SQL*Net Version 1, the following discussion mentions particular client-server performance issues for both Version 1 and Version 2. However, be aware that although Oracle is currently supporting both versions for all protocol types, official desupport of Version 1 is imminent.* For some Oracle features (e.g., multithreaded server, Oracle Name Server), you will need to be using SQL*Net Version 2, so we advise you to upgrade to Version 2 as soon as possible.

Tuning SQL*Net Version 1

The introduction of SQL*Net 1 was a breakthrough in database communication. It allowed us to build homogeneous networks that could communicate with Oracle

---

* See Support Bulletin 107883.96, June 30, 1996.

databases on more than 50 different hardware platforms. Later releases of SQL*Net 1 have proven to be very reliable and popular within the Oracle community.

To improve the performance of SQL*Net over your network, follow the suggestions for the particular product you are using:

SQL*Net Async

- Increase the packet size to the maximum allowable.

- Use raw mode instead of line mode.

- Reduce timeouts and increase retries in your connection scripts.

SQL*Net for DECnet

- Increase buffers to the maximum allowable.

SQL*Net for TCP/IP

- Use as large a buffer size as possible (by default, the TCP/IP buffer size is set to its maximum of 4,096).

- Use out-of-band breaks; this is not the default for Version 1. Out-of-band breaks can improve performance by as much as 50% when applied to TWO_ TASK; for example, in the following, the final "O" requests out-of-band breaks:

```
TWO_TASK=t:machine:dbase:,,,O )
```

This parameter reduces the regularity of interrupt checks by the RDBMS. In testing, we created a table with 30 rows called XX with a single column and performed the following query with out-of-band breaks turned on.

Before you can turn on out-of-band breaks, you must enable them. Start ORASRV as follows:

```
ORASRV 0
SELECT COUNT (*) FROM XX, XX, XX, XX; Response time = 8 seconds
```

We performed the same query with out-of-band breaks turned off:

```
SELECT COUNT (*) FROM XX, XX, XX, XX; Response time = 29 seconds
```

For SQL*Net ACCP/LU6.2

- Set PACING high to minimize APPC handshaking.

- Set RU size higher for better performance.

For SQL*Net for PC LANs

- Increase the Netware parameter MINIMUM PACKET RECEIVE BUFFERS from the default of 10 to a minimum of 100.

- Prespawn shadows processes to allow faster connections.

Tuning SQL*Net Version 2

SQL*Net Version 2 provides client-server applications with more functionality and greater flexibility. All of the Version 1 recommendations apply to Version 2 as well. In addition, there are several new features that affect client-server operations.

SQL*Net Version 2.0

SQL*Net Version 2.0 features that affect client-server performance are the following:

Multiprotocol interchange

> Through heterogeneous networking, Oracle can support communication across networks, using multiple protocols. Sites that have all their databases connect via a single protocol do not need to use this facility. In this way, SQL*Net Version 2 offers network transparency and protocol independence.

Diagnostics

> Improved diagnostics, including extensive logging and tracing facilities, have been built into Version 2.0.

Multithreaded server

> Version 2.0 introduced the multithreaded server. It provides a shared server environment allowing many user connections to communicate with the database via a single database connection. This facility is necessary only for databases that have large numbers of simultaneous database connections (several thousand) and need to reduce their total memory requirements. The multithreaded server should be used only where necessary.

Simultaneous version support

> Version 2 supports both SQL*Net Version 1 and SQL*Net Version 2 clients simultaneously. Note, however, that SQL*Net Version 1 cannot use the multiprotocol interchange, nor can it communicate outside the one community.

SQL*Net Version 2.1

SQL*Net Version 2.1 features include the following:

GUI-based configuration files

> Network configuration files can be generated automatically by the network manager utilities (i.e., netman). The files contain generic database connection descriptors (TNS connect descriptors) that are constant across all platforms and all protocols.

NOTE   A number of the earlier versions of the GUI *netman* utility were notorious for generating *listener.ora* files with mismatched closing parentheses. If you are having problems starting the listener utility, check this configuration file carefully.

Oracle Name Server

SQL*Net Version 2.1 (or better) is required to support the Oracle Name Server utility. This server provides a simple mode of centralizing networked database descriptors. (See later sections of this chapter for more details.)

Encrypted passwords

SQL*Net login passwords can be encrypted when transmitted across the network if both the client and server are running the same version of SQL*Net. Privileged database functions (starting and stopping databases, etc.) can also be performed by authorized staff via encrypted passwords within the network configuration files.

Dead connection detection

SQL*Net will automatically ping the client process at predetermined intervals, checking to see whether the client process is still operational. Orphaned database connections are terminated, and all object resources are released.

SQL*Net Version 2.3

SQL*Net Version 2.3 extensions include the following:

SQL*Net plug and play

The Oracle Name Server now supports network configuration automation. Complex client and server configuration files are a thing of the past. Features include dynamic client, database, and host registration; automatic network configuration replication of all Name Server details; and real-time client notification.

Network redundancy

SQL*Net 2.3 supports multiple connection routes from client to database server. The multithreaded server can now support multiple database listeners across different hosts, providing network fault tolerance. This facility can also act as an automatic network load balancer, which can choose the most efficient route to the database in question.

Enhanced SQL*Net Diagnostics

DBAs now have an improved insight into the operation of their database and client-server connections. Improved listener facilities allow the DBA to view each database connection by IP address, source machine, user name, and so on.

NOTE   One difference between SQL*Net Version 1 and Version 2 is particularly important to security. There is always a possibility that unauthorized users will gain access to a client-server network via remote logins (e.g., OPS\$ usercodes). Oracle recommends against your use of operating system logins to remote databases. This does not imply that you can't use OPS\$ usercodes within your database, but do avoid using them across the network, from one database to another. In RDBMS 6, proxy logins were enabled by default. In RDBMS Version 7, operating system logins are disabled by default (although Oracle does say security problems are much less likely to occur because of enhancements in OS login security).

Setting Up SQL*Net Version 2

SQL*Net Version 2 has always seemed to be a solution that's too hard for many people. When it first appeared in the early days of Oracle7.0, documentation was limited and sketchy. Many DBAs experimented with it and gave up in frustration. Why bother, they said; after all, SQL*Net 1 was working fine. We cannot put it off any longer however. Fortunately, current versions of Oracle include a network management utility (*netman*) that lets us graphically define our network configuration and generate all configuration files at the push of a button.

The downside to this network management tool is that it must be sophisticated enough to cater to the most complex of environments. Most Oracle environments are very simple, with two or possibly three database hosts; the *netman* tool itself, however, is rather overwhelming.

Remember these facts when setting up a SQL*Net 2 network:

- A *listener.ora* configuration file is required only on the database server(s) host.

- A *tnsnames.ora* configuration file is required only on client hosts that wish to communicate with remote Oracle databases.

- The configuration files *sqlnet.ora, tnsnav.ora, tnsnet.ora, protocol.ora*, etc. are all optional and are not usually required in a simple client-server environment.

- SQL*Net 2 default socket for TCP/IP UNIX networks is port 1521.

The following code extracts demonstrate the minimum SQL*Net 2 requirements for a simple client-server UNIX environment using TCP/IP protocol. Not all of the configuration options are mandatory, but they are recommended.

```
# listener.sql

#############
# listener.ora
```

```
#############
listener =
  (address_list =
     (address =
        (protocol = IPC)
        (key = FIN)
     )
     (address =
        (protocol = TCP)
        (host = 157.155.84.57)
        (port = 1521)
     )
  )
log_directory_listener = /opt/oracle/NET2/log
log_file_listener = listener.log
trace_level_listener = OFF
sid_list_listener =
  (sid_list =
     (sid_desc =
        (sid_name = FIN)
        (oracle_home = /opt/oracle/product/v7.1.6)
     )
  )


# tnsnames.sql

#############
# tnsnames.ora
#############
FIN =
  (description =
     (address_list =
        (address =
           (protocol = TCP)
           (host = 157.155.84.57)
           (port = 1521)
        )
     )
     (connect_date = (sid = FIN))
  )

# A SQL*Net1 alias can be optionally included as a migration interim
FIN_N1 = T:157.155.84.57/1525:FIN
```

Setting Up Oracle Name Server

The Oracle Name Server facility is a very powerful utility that many larger sites often overlook. The Oracle Name Server is completely separate from the host DNS (Domain Name Service) servers, although there are plans to eventually couple the two utilities. The Oracle Name Server does work on a similar principle, allowing the DBA to maintain instance characteristics without having to modify hundreds of client configuration files.

Imagine having a client-server environment with several thousand client workstations. Every time a new instance is created or an existing instance changes server, all client copies of the *tnsnames.ora* file need to be modified. Even environments that consolidate their configuration files onto LAN file servers still have a hard time trying to coordinate such changes. Wouldn't it be nice to roll out a single configuration file as part of the standard client software deployment and *never* have to change it again. Oracle Name server makes this possible.

Each client has a single *sqlnet.ora* configuration file that points to a number of Oracle Name Server hosts. The DBA only needs to (re)generate the Name Server network definition file (*/xxx/.*net) and deploy it to the Name Server hosts. Smaller environments would need only a single Oracle Name Server host (i.e., the database server itself), while large sites might have four or five of them, strategically located at the major client locations.

Remember these facts when setting up an Oracle Name Server network (version 1):

- SQL*Net 2.1 (or better) is required to run the Oracle Name Server.

- A *listener.ora* configuration file is required only on the database server(s) host.

- A *sqlnet.ora* configuration file is required only on the client machines.

- A *names.ora* and */xxx/.net* configuration file are only required on the Oracle name server(s) host.

- A *tnsnames.ora* configuration file is not required.

- The configuration files *tnsnav.ora, tnsnet.ora, protocol.ora,* etc., are all optional and not required in a simple client-server environment.

- SQL*Net 2 default socket for TCP/IP UNIX networks is *port 1521.*

- Oracle Name server *default socket* for TCP/IP UNIX networks is *port 1526.*

The following code extracts demonstrate the minimum Oracle Name Server requirements for a simple client-server UNIX environment using the TCP/IP protocol. A number of the configuration settings are specifically for the customer environment from which the files were *sourced.* Their values should be substituted for setting relevant to your environment.

Not all of the following configuration options are mandatory, but they are recommended.

Note that the *listener.ora* configuration file is the same as that shown for SQL*Net 2.

```
# sqlnet.sql
```

```
#############
# sqlnet.ora
#############
automatic_ipc = ON
sqlnet.expire_time = 10
trace_level_client = OFF
names.preferred_servers =
  (address_list =
     (address =
        (protocol = TCP)
        (host = 157.155.84.57)
        (port = 1526)
     )
     (address =
        (protocol = TCP)
        (host = 157.155.84.58)
        (port = 1526)
     )
  )


# names.sql

#############
# names.ora
#############
names.server_name = NameServer1.world
names.admin_region = (region =
                      (name = LOCAL_REGION.world)
                      (type = ROSFILE)
                      (file = /opt/oracle/NET/{xxx}.net)
                      (docname = PROTO)
                      (version = 34619392)
                      (retry = 600)
                     )
names.config_checkpoint_file = cfg00467
names.log_directory = /opt/oracle/NET
names.log_file = names.log
names.trace_level = OFF
names.trace_unique = FALSE
```

The above Oracle Name Server environment is configured to use a flat file network definition (i.e., *type = ROSFILE; file = /opt/oracle/{xxx}.net)*. It is possible to hold the network definition within an Oracle database itself and have the Name Server extract the information from the database. However, we prefer to use a flat file because this approach is easier to build, maintain, and understand. Storing the network definition in the database also requires the inclusion of a hard code database usercode and password within the *names.ora* configuration file—something that we like to avoid whenever possible.

Client-Server: Adapting It in the Real World

In this section, we describe a few real-world projects in which we have had to use unconventional approaches to overcome weaknesses in the client-server environment. They represent solutions to particular problems, not overall strategies, but they should give you some ideas on how you might get the best performance out of your own client-server configuration.

A Dedicated "Report" Server

On a number of occasions, we have had to look for alternatives to running large, database-intensive reports at the client workstation. A client-server environment focuses most of its processing power at the server and is at the mercy of its network bandwidth and client resource capacity.

When a user requests a medium-to-large report, not only do the data need to be brought across the network, but all associated processing overheads are also incurred at the client. Rather than suffering from this "normal" behavior, we can use some ingenuity to move the overhead associated with executing the report to a more powerful host machine. This machine may be the database server itself or may be a dedicated report server. Ideally, the report server would be more powerful than the normal client workstation and would have more memory and a faster network link to the database server. It would also be physically located as near as possible to the database server.

How does the report get started? The simplest way to do this is for the initiating client to do one of the following:

- Perform a *remote shell call* to the report server; passing report identifier, all associated parameter values and the destination printer. For example:

```
rsh -1 scott sydney "gl_balances / XXX YYY ZZZ lp034"
```

OR

- Write a *report request record* to the database, containing all associated parameter values and the destination printer. For example:

```
INSERT INTO report_queue
VALUES ('gl_balances', 'XXX', 'YYY', 'ZZZ', 'lp034');
```

A special report scheduler will need to be written and running on the report scheduler, waking up every few minutes, looking for report requests and spawning the subsequent tasks.

Deferred Transaction Processing

On a number of occasions, we would have liked to be able to defer a particular transaction and have it run in background mode, releasing the client workstation to continue with other activities. The transaction could conceivably take several minutes to execute. Rather than having the user wait for the transaction or having the transaction fail because a remote database and/or network is temporarily unavailable, the user could schedule the task to execute in the background, automatically retrying a predetermined number of times before eventually returning success or failure.

How do we schedule a database transaction? Beginning with Oracle7.1.3, we can use the database's own internal *job queuing*. This scheduling mechanism allows us to execute a predetermined stored procedure or package at a specific time (for a specified number of retries if necessary).

To execute the procedure Replicate_EMP interactively, we would code

```
BEGIN
  ...
  Replicate_EMP (:emp_no, action );
  ...
END;
```

To submit the procedure call in background mode, we would code

```
BEGIN
  ...
  dbms_job.submit (id, 'Replicate_EMP(' || TO_CHAR(:emp_no) ||
                   ',''' || action || ''');' );
  ...
END;
```

NOTE   When passing a procedure call to the *jobs* queue, remember to include the trailing semi-colon as part of the string text to execute.

Snapshot Replication Alternatives

An interesting feature of the Oracle database facility is to use it as an alternative to the normal snapshot replication. Often, snapshot replication leaves a lot to be desired. We must replicate the data exactly as held in the master database. Replicating a view does allow us to reformat the data but means that we can't perform fast refresh. Snapshot replication allows us to update only one table at a time (associated tables must be replicated as separate actions). A snapshot refresh is restricted to a single transaction state and therefore a single rollback segment. We can replicate to only one database at a time. Later versions of the Oracle RDBMS

do provide some answers to these problems but still fall a long way short for the
more complex replication requirements. Oracle allows us to overcome a lot of
these deficiencies.

Snapshot processing actually utilizes the jobs facility itself. When we use a normal
table snapshot, a trigger is created over the table to track record modifications.
With jobs, we can create our own trigger to simulate this functionality. This trigger
does not need to insert records into a snap$ log table, but rather, inserts jobs
requests. We can now program a replication procedure that can do virtually
anything: simultaneously update multiple tables, update different databases,
handle data integrity, set a particular rollback segment, and so on. The jobs utility
guarantees that each request will be processed in sequence and will retry a predetermined number of times.

The following example demonstrates how to create a table trigger that will submit
an entry in the jobs queue every time the table is modified:

```
# trg_job.sql
Create or Replace Trigger EMP_Jobs
After INSERT or UPDATE or DELETE on EMP
For each ROW

DECLARE
    id number;
    action VARCHAR2(1) := 'I';
BEGIN
    IF UPDATING THEN
        action := 'U';
    ELSIF
        DELETING THEN
        action := 'D';
    END IF;
    dbms_job.submit (id, 'Replicate_EMP(' ||
                        TO_CHAR (NVL (:NEW.emp_no,:OLD.emp_no)) ||
                        ',''' || action || ''');' );
END;
```

Local Cache

Every client has its own processor and memory. Oracle provides extensive
caching facilities on the server database itself (via the SGA, PGA, shared buffer
pool) but provides no caching facilities at the client workstation. However, at
several sites, we have used local memory on client machines to load static database data into a local cache that can be refreshed at regular intervals. Future
validation and reference of this data is performed via the client machine cache,
not the database. Client login time is obviously increased to initially load the local
data cache, but subsequent reads of the cache are hundreds of times quicker than
traversing the network and looking up the database.

At one particular site, we were able to compress more than 1,500 static code-table records into less than 30 kilobytes of memory via a SQL*Forms user exit (a very minor overhead for a major benefit). In one particular example, we were able to reduce the elapsed time for a single, multirecord SQL*Forms query from 14.7 seconds to 2.3 seconds using local cache.

This approach offers several advantages and disadvantages. Advantages include the following:

- It reads (static) data from the database only once.

- It loads data *selectively* into each user's cache, allowing implementation, for example, of complex security systems without suffering any of the ongoing overheads. Multiple table joins are performed once and loaded into the cache. Each user loads only his or her own view of the world.

- It avoids RDBMS overheads because it performs no subsequent SQL parsing or index searching. Oracle's SGA can be better used by other, more dynamic, core table data.

- It reduces network traffic. This is the biggest performance advantage. All data is held locally and do not have to be continually transmitted via the network.

- It allows local data to be stored more efficiently than in the database. We are able to use a smart compression algorithm (avoiding repetitive primary key and index overheads) and load only data that are relevant to the current user (i.e., location, security level dependent).

There are some disadvantages as well. The data must be static and unlikely to be changed or deleted. And when each user logs on to the system, the local cache must be initialized (loaded). This can take several seconds.

17

Capacity Planning

What does Oracle capacity planning have to do with performance tuning? Plenty! It doesn't matter how hard you tune: if your configuration is unable to cope with your workload, you will not be able to provide your users with acceptable performance and if you select a hardware configuration to suit an untuned application, you will end up buying more equipment than you need.

It's useful to have some idea of what your management budget is for hardware acquisition. You will usually find that "more of," "bigger," and "faster" will perform better. However, without having some idea of what your management expects to pay to upgrade your system, you may recommend too much hardware, only to find that your site can't afford the recommended configuration. Then you'll have to repeat the capacity planning exercise. Do it right the first time. Put in the effort necessary to purchase the most cost-effective hardware suiting your site's budget.

Before you begin capacity planning, be sure to choose an architecture that suits your situation. Become familiar with the architectural options that Oracle offers, and choose the one that best fits your needs. There's no point in performing a capacity planning study on a decision support database using a single process to retrieve and sort your data. Instead, use Oracle's parallel query option (described in Chapter 13, *Tuning Parallel Query*). Also, be aware of the impressive improvements that have been made with RAID technology, symmetric multiprocessing (SMP), and massively parallel processing (MPP) (described in Chapter 11, *Monitoring and Tuning an Existing Database*).

When you perform your capacity planning study, run the benchmarking just as you would run your production database. Set up similar table and index sizes, numbers of users, and, most importantly, the same architecture. If you are running (or plan to run) in archivelog mode in your production database, do the same in your benchmarking database. If you have 4,800 users in your production database, be sure to have the same number for your benchmarking. If you are using RAID5 for striping in production, be sure to have the same setup in your benchmarking database.

About Capacity Planning

Accurate capacity planning can save your organization a great deal of money. If you incorrectly evaluate your equipment needs and buy a machine that is too large, you will have spent more money than you need to on hardware. On the other hand, if you underestimate your workload requirements and buy a machine that is too small, you will not be able to satisfy the throughput and response times of your users. And if you don't plan for growth in the future, you may not end up with a machine that you'll be able to upgrade as you need more memory, disk devices, and processors.

It's easy to make a mistake. Some organizations buy equipment too early, before the applications that are going to run on the machines have been coded. The problem with this approach is that if more modern, cost-effective hardware appears on the market, you may not be able to take advantage of it. Many organizations play it too safe. They tend to overestimate their requirements because they fear cutting it too close, and they end up with more equipment than they need—and perhaps more than they can really afford. Other organizations don't plan ahead, and end up with too little processor, memory, or disk power a year or two down the road.

What's the right way to go about capacity planning? The following list contains our general advice. Later in this chapter are several checklists showing specifically how you gather the information you need to make an informed decision about your system resources.

- Take advantage of Oracle's portability. You can develop an application on a smaller and cheaper machine, and then use the same code to run on a larger machine once you've decided exactly which configuration you need.

- Forget about transaction rates and definitions, and concentrate on setting up a service agreement that will specify the required response times at your site. (See the discussion of tuning service agreements in Chapter 3, *Planning and Managing the Tuning Process.*)

- Put your effort into ensuring that every program will run within the required response times. You should buy a machine that is big enough for a tuned application, not an untuned one.

- Borrow a machine from your hardware vendor to use in your capacity planning. This is an excellent way to put the system you're considering buying through its paces. If your vendor won't agree, you may want to consider alternative sources.

- Ask for advice from other sites that have configurations similar to the one you're planning. Other sites' use of memory, disk, CPU, and workload mix can help you assess your own requirements.

- Plan your capacity planning exercise carefully. Follow the checklists we provide, and don't skimp on testing and documentation.

- Consider the use of client-server, parallel server, and multithreaded server computing. You can realize enormous financial savings and improved scalability, as we show in Chapter 16, *Tuning in the Client-Server Environment*. and Chapter 12, *Tuning Parallel Server*. However, before you race off and start using these features, read the chapters carefully to note pitfalls that the sales catalogues and Oracle documentation may not tell you about.

What Do You Need to Test?

To do an accurate capacity planning exercise, you basically tune your system, from start to finish, putting all of the components of the system through their paces, keeping track of what you've done, and assessing how well your results mesh with your present and future requirements.

What does it mean to have a well-tuned system? We explore this question in Chapter 2, *What Causes Performance Problems?* To summarize, a tuned system is one in which:

- As close as possible to 100% of your memory is used.

- Your disk load is spread evenly across devices, and all of your disks are operating marginally within their recommended maximum I/O rates.

- As close as possible to 100% of your CPU is used during peak periods, with no user programs waiting for the CPU.

- Network traffic is only marginally below the maximum recommended, with no collisions.

- There is an insignificant amount of paging and swapping going on.

- User throughput and response times meet the standards established for your organization.

See the illustrations of untuned and perfectly tuned systems (Figure 2-2 and Figure 2-3) in Chapter 2.

This section briefly summarizes some of the main performance goals of the different components of your system. Earlier chapters describe all of these components in much more detail.

Memory

In general, the more memory you have in your system, and the more memory you can devote to Oracle and its databases, the better your performance will be. Chapter 2 introduces the use of memory and its bottlenecks in the Oracle system. Chapter 9, *Tuning a New Database*, Chapter 11, and Chapter 13 describe in detail what the memory structures and requirements are.

Tune all of the Oracle areas of memory as best you can, and be prepared to shift memory assignments to meet changing needs. See the diagrams in Chapter 11 of overall memory, the System Global Area (SGA), the shared buffer pool, and other special areas. Make sure you don't use up all your memory. A good goal is 5% free memory at all times.

Be sure to find out what is the maximum amount of memory possible on your machine. We advise you to telephone some people at other, similar sites to confirm the upper memory limit and any restrictions on the use of the machine that occur if the full amount of memory is utilized.

Disk I/O

The main goal for disk use in your system is to spread the load evenly across the different disk devices so no disk is running at or exceeding its maximum recommended I/Os per second. Since the time we wrote the first edition of this book, disk I/O has been revolutionized by RAID technology (described in Chapter 9). Disk mirroring (RAID 0) has not only provided excellent recovery, but it has also improved query response times, because different user processes can read from both sides of the mirror. Striping with parity (RAID5) can also provide significant query improvements, but it can often markedly slow down updates, inserts, and deletes. Striping without parity (RAID1) can speed up queries, inserts, updates, and deletes, but it leaves you vulnerable to disk loss; use RAID1 only with mirroring. Become familiar with your RAID technology options, because it's essential that the person setting up the RAID technology have an understanding of the various database components and the effects that applying RAID may have on them. For example, it is usually foolish to stripe redo logs using RAID5 because they are rarely read from.

You should also be aware of the controllers and channels that control your disks. Find out the maximum numbers of disks possible on your machine and controller as well as the recommended maximum number of disks per controller. You will be surprised at how often the maximum and recommended numbers differ. You'll usually find that it is better to have many medium-sized disks (500 megabytes), rather than several large disks (one gigabyte), because the more disks you have, the more options you will have for sharing and balancing the load.

Remember, disk access is much slower than memory access. If you have not allocated enough memory for your shared pool, database blocks, and other objects to remain in memory, Oracle will have to go fetch them from disk, which slows down processing.

Make sure you define tables and other objects with the right sizes for both initial allocations and later expansion so you avoid problems of disk fragmentation, chaining and migration.

CPU

Since the time of the first edition, symmetric multiple processors (SMPs) and, to a lesser extent, massively parallel processors (MPPs) have become the norm, rather than the exception. Capacity planning now has a new dimension. You now need to take into account the number, as well as the speed, of the CPUs. Is it better to have two CPUs running at 66Mhz or one CPU running at 100Mhz? The answer to this question typically varies from one site to the next. You need to determine whether you can effectively use the additional CPUs. The ideal is to have more and faster CPUs, but your budget may not allow it.

It's essential to find out the maximum possible number of CPUs on your machine as well as what the effects of using those CPUs might be. There are machines on the market that will run 8 or 16 processors, but performance actually slows down when more than 4 are utilized. As with Oracle, new operating system releases can provide many performance improvements that may affect CPU effectiveness. Become familiar with future operating system capabilities so you can plan accordingly.

CPU is the most costly resource in your system, so make sure you size it correctly. Your main goal is to prevent CPU contention, a condition in which processes are waiting for the CPU. Often, CPU problems are actually caused by memory and disk problems. When there isn't enough room in memory for needed data and Oracle objects, like data dictionary items, the CPU is forced to page and swap processes. Poorly tuned SQL and ineffective placement of indexes is also a big CPU resource hog.

CPU MIPS (millions of instructions per second) can be a valuable guide in comparing machines and determining a machine's ability to meet your throughput needs. Although MIPS are not consistent across vendor boundaries, they usually are consistent within one vendor's product lines. Here is an example of how we use a MIPS rating to help in capacity planning. Figure 17-1 illustrates that as we add users to a machine, there is no decrease in the throughput per user until the sixth user is added; then, throughput degrades rapidly.

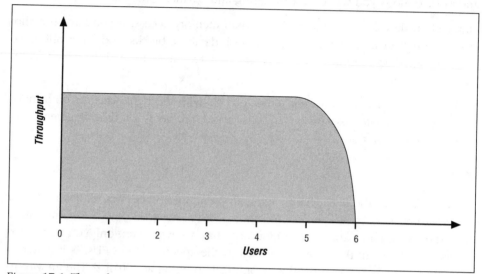

Figure 17-1. Throughput per user for one CPU MIP

Network

Client-server computing, rather than unitary processing, is now the most common architecture used for Oracle-based applications. Suddenly, all problems that other sites have had to worry about have become your problems as well. Make sure your network is fast enough to meet your needs, and that your equipment is positioned strategically. For example, if you are in San Francisco, and the bulk of your messages go to Los Angeles, your packets should not all be routed through New York. There are many special issues for client-server computing, described in Chapter 16.

Database

The way you tune your database will have an enormous impact on performance. An untuned database will unnecessarily eat up expensive hardware resources. Remember that your normalization (and sometimes denormalization) of data, your choice of indexes, your selection of primary and other types of keys, your use of parallel query and other such choices will have a lot to do with how much equipment you will need, and how little you can get by with. Chapter 5, *Designing for Performance* and Chapters 9, 11, and 13 discuss in detail the tuning issues for your database.

Capacity Planning Checklist

If you're going to end up with accurate information about your configuration needs, you must have a thorough and well-documented capacity plan. Without a thorough plan, you could easily overlook a critical part of the capacity planning exercise. The result will be that you will have to repeat the exercise or, far worse, your organization will buy equipment that is oversized or undersized for your configuration. For example, suppose you don't properly set your INIT.ORA parameters for the size of the configuration on which you're testing. Your testing results might lead you to conclude (erroneously) that the capacity of the machine is far less than it actually is.

This section summarizes the steps you need to follow to do a thorough capacity planning. Be sure to complete each step before moving on to the next one.

Step 1: Obtaining Background Information

Before you run anything on the computer, you need to collect some background information. Too often, system administrators are so eager to run transaction benchmarks that they don't correctly identify what they're benchmarking. Make sure you understand who your users are, how many there are, where they are located, and what they are doing. You also need to do some research into determining the most cost-effective hardware vendors. We have found that playing one vendor against another in a "Who is the fastest?" situation is rarely worth the time spent. Most vendors are reputable and the other vendors will soon pick out any faults with their hardware and operating system. Other sites running a system similar to the one that you propose to run will also provide valuable information. It is best to have decided on a vendor prior to performing your capacity planning and the associated benchmarking. If the vendor cannot provide the required response times given your budget, then try another vendor. Don't spend many months trying them all!

Finally, you need access to a machine that you can use to perform a thorough benchmark. If you are testing in a client-server environment, distributed database, or parallel server, make sure you have access to all of the machines you need to test. If you are running a capacity planning exercise for a decision support database, make sure that you have striping and multiple processors in place and are using Oracle's parallel query option.

Follow these steps:

1. Put one person in charge of controlling this capacity planning checklist, and assign every task to a particular, accountable person. Make sure every step is completed. As each step is completed, the person controlling the checklist

must place a checkmark against the item and place the information into a folder for future reference. Do not proceed past any point until all necessary information has been obtained.

2. Obtain the expected number of total users at all client sites.

3. Obtain the number of concurrent users at all client sites. If users will be allowed to log on to the system more than once, note this fact; treat each logon as a separate user for purposes of calculating memory requirements.

4. Categorize users of the application into roles, and specify their expected activities. For example:

```
Sydney:
     Management inquiries      2
     Account control          12
     Transaction entry        80
     Phone queries            30

Melbourne:
     Management inquiries      2
     Account control          10
     Transaction entry        60
     Phone queries            25
```

5. Determine the usage pattern of each of the programs; for example:

```
Financial Transaction Entry (AF100FR)      40%
Account Entry (AF120FR)                     25%
Account Balance Inquiry (AF110FR)           10%
Budget Inquiry (AF200FR)                    10%
Budget Maintenance (AF210FR)                10%
Other programs                               5%
```

This information will be used later to test the application realistically in a multiuser environment.

6. Obtain information on expected peaks and troughs of activity at your site, and remember that there might be month-to-month, and day of the month as well as hour-to-hour, variation. You can develop a graph like the one shown in Figure 17-2 for both daily and overnight processing. Remember when you are performing this capacity planning that you must be able to cope with the maximum load, not the average load. Most sites are running online transaction users during the day and long running batch updates and reports overnight. You must be able to cope with both.

7. Determine a workload that will give a true indication of the expected activity on your system. You must determine the maximum workload that you expect to have on your machine. (This is determined by the combination of the most resource-hungry programs and the maximum number of users.)

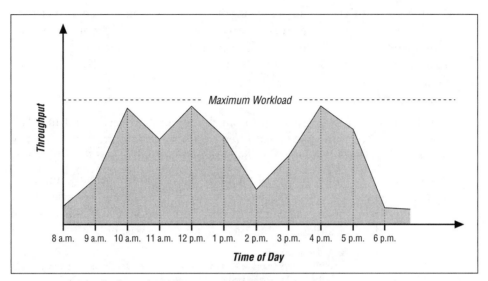

Figure 17-2. Sample throughput for capacity planning

8. Predict the future growth of your workload and users on your system. We recommend that you specify the anticipated figures for 3 months, 6 months, 9 months, 12 months, 18 months, 2 years, and 3 years in the future.

9. Obtain a full list of operating system parameters on your machine. (If you are running client-server, parallel server, or distributed database, get this list for both the application server and the database server.) These will differ from system to system. On Sun UNIX machines, the MAXUSERS configuration variable determines the sizes of many important parameters. There are also many parameters that you can set to determine the UNIX file buffer areas in memory; these allow you to specify the amount of memory available to different applications which will in turn dictate the amount of memory available to other applications. Under VMS, obtain the working set quotas. If these quotas are set too low, excessive paging and overuse of the CPU may result.

10. Document the version of every tool you are using; for example:

```
Oracle RDBMS 7.3.2
SQL*Plus 3.3
SQL*Net 2.3
SQL*Forms 3.0.18
Oracle*Forms 4.5
Oracle*Report 1.2
PRO*COBOL 2.0.16
PRO*C 2.0.12
SQL*Reportwriter
PL/SQL 2.4
SQL*Loader 2.1
Other products
Operating system
```

(Do this for both client and server if you are running in a client-server environment.) Because newer releases of some of these products provide performance improvements, you need to make sure you are using the most up-to-date software. For example, Oracle*Forms 4.5 offers significant improvements over previous versions by reducing both memory usage and the number of packets transferred in the client-server environment.

11. Obtain the size of swap space on both the application server and the database server. The swap space is an often-overlooked file on disk that must be kept contiguous and large enough to assist with performance.

12. Obtain the configuration details of the application, and the network and hardware configuration you are using for your capacity planning exercise. If you are benchmarking on an existing hardware configuration at your site, you will usually already have a diagram that you use for other reasons.

```
Machine name and IP address
Number of disks, the maximum allowable and the maximum recommended
Controllers and Channels, maximum allowable and recommended
Size and speed of disks in I/Os per second
Memory size, maximum allowable and maximum recommended
CPU MIPS rating, maximum allowable numbr of CPUs and maximum
    recommended CPUs
```

See the diagram in Figure 17-3 for a way to document these.

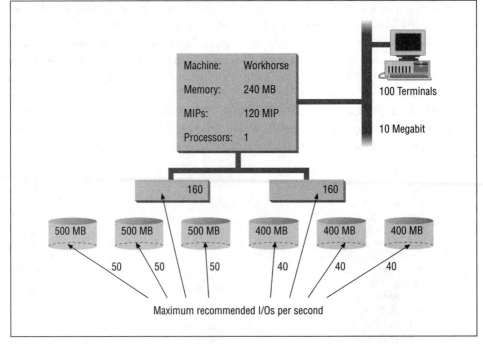

Figure 17-3. Typical configuration diagram

13. Obtain a network configuration diagram showing line speeds. This is particularly useful when you are running client-server.

14. Most applications have a test plan for the quality assurance of their systems. Obtain the plan for later use in the single-user application tuning exercise. This will assist in entering realistic values into the various programs and will ensure that you have performed a thorough response time test against all parts of the program.

15. Document the performance monitoring commands relevant to your operating system. These commands allow you to monitor disk I/O, CPU activity, memory usage, paging, swapping, and if applicable, the network activity. They are system-dependent. (See Chapter 18, *Tuning for Specific Systems*, for a summary of common commands used in VMS and UNIX systems.)

16. Get a complete list of operating system parameters from all machines used for the study.

17. Obtain a full list of disk partition layout used for the capacity planning exercise. Also document details of logical volume manager usage, raw devices, striping, and mirroring.

18. Include documentation on any components of the system that are used for backup and recovery, such as mirroring, and running in archivelog mode.

19. Provide details of the disks on which the following components reside. Indicate whether they are cooked files, raw devices, striped with parity, striped without parity, or mirrored. For striped files, indicate the stripe size.

    - Operating system
    - Swap and page files
    - Various Oracle tablespaces and data files
    - Redo logs
    - Archive logs
    - Any mirrored files

Step 2: Structuring the Database and SGA

The purpose of this step is to ensure that your database structure is tuned. Read Chapter 9 thoroughly for information about how to structure the original database and the SGA. Read Chapter 11 for how to change these values over time. Follow these steps:

1. If the application is to run on UNIX machines, ensure that raw devices are being used for all tablespaces and redo logs. If another system is being used,

make sure that the database files are contiguous on disk. This may require that you defragment the disk.

2. Consider striping, particularly if your architecture has the ability for a fine-grained strip size, for example, 8K or 16K. If you stripe without parity, ensure that your files are mirrored. Do not use RAID5 for files that have large numbers of inserts, updates, deletes, redo logs, or archive logs.

3. Make sure that your redo logs are on different disks from your data files and archive logs, and that your archive logs are on a different disk from your redo logs and data files.

4. Place heavily used tablespaces onto the same disk device used by lightly used tablespaces, or separate different tablespaces onto different disks. Keep in mind that no disk should be running at or exceeding its maximum recommended I/O-per-second rate.

5. Use many medium-sized disks rather than fewer large disks. In this context, a medium-sized disk is 500 megabytes, and a large disk is one gigabyte or greater. Choose medium-sized disks because the maximum I/O rates on both are usually the same, and the medium-sized disks allow better load sharing across disks.

6. If you have a decision support database or a database that performs a lot of batch processing, consider increasing your DB_BLOCK_SIZE parameter to 8K or 16K if your machine allows it. Online transaction processing systems should have their DB_BLOCK_SIZE set to 4K. Be sure to set the DB_BLOCK_SIZE parameter before you build your database.

7. Separate your tablespaces, as specified in Chapter 9. If you have a large amount of sorting, make sure that you have a separate temporary tablespace and that the INITIAL and NEXT extent sizes are larger than your SORT_AREA_SIZE. If you are using Oracle7.3 or later, create the tablespace as TEMPORARY.

8. Ensure that all tables and indexes have been presized to minimize the number of extents. You must rebuild any table or index consisting of more than three extents.

9. Make sure that you have set an adequate value for SHARED_POOL_SIZE. The value should be typically greater than 20 megabytes.

10. Set the DB_BLOCK_BUFFER parameter to fit as much of the tables, indexes, clusters, and rollback segments as possible in memory. A serious system should have its DB_BLOCK_BUFFER set to at least 20 megabytes.

11. Ensure that your LOG_BUFFER is sized adequately. It is unusual for a production system to run effectively with a LOG_BUFFER under 256K.

12. Make sure that you have placed as many terminals on the network as necessary to perform a realistic benchmark. Ideally, have the same number of terminals available as you will have users logged on to your system during peak usage times. If this cannot be organized, the second best scenario is to use a remote terminal emulator that will simulate the number of users.

13. Check that all of the objects, particularly indexes and constraints, that were in the development environment exist in your benchmark environment. To check this, you can produce an object difference listing. Run the following script in the benchmark environments; you must have created a database link called DEV to the development database from the benchmark database using the CREATE DATABASE LINK command.

```
SELECT owner, object_name, object_type
  FROM dba_objects@DEV
 MINUS
SELECT owner, object_name, object_type
  FROM dba_objects;
```

To ensure that there are no objects in the benchmark environment that should not be there, run the following query:

```
SELECT owner, object_name, object_type
  FROM dba_objects
 MINUS
SELECT owner, object_name, object_type
  FROM dba_objects@DEV;
```

14. Set a sufficient number of rollback segments, and size them appropriately for this system.

15. Set an appropriate value for FREELISTS before you create tables in which a number of transactions are being simultaneously inserted.

16. Make the INITRANS parameter large enough, especially if you have multiple transactions updating the same physical block of a table.

17. Make sure that the tables have been analyzed if you are using the cost-based optimizer. Ideally, analyze the tables with the COMPUTE option. If the tables are exceedingly large and you don't have time to compute the statistics, estimate at least 40% of your rows if you are using a version of Oracle earlier than Oracle7.3. For Oracle7.3 and later, estimate at least 20% of the rows.

18. If your tables have uneven skewness, and you are using Oracle7.3 or later, analyze your tables to produce a histogram. Uneven skewness means that one value for a column has a handful of rows, whereas other values may have many thousands of rows.

19. Set the following INIT.ORA parameters (and any others relevant to your situation) to the correct values for this system (see Chapter 9).

```
DB_WRITERS
LOG_BUFFER
LOG_CHECKPOINT_INTERVAL
DB_FILE_MULTIBLOCK_READ_BLOCK
_DB_BLOCK_WRITE_BATCH
CHECKPOINT_PROCESS
ENQUEUE_RESOURCES
COMPATIBLE
DB_BLOCK_LRU_LATCHES (Oracle7.3 and later)
DB_FILE_SIMULTANEOUS_WRITES
HASH_JOIN_ENABLED (Oracle7.3 and later)
HASH_AREA_SIZE (Oracle7.3 and later)
HASH_MULTIBLOCK_IO_COUNT (Oracle7.3 and later)
LOG_ARCHIVE_BUFFERS
LOG_ARCHIVE_BUFFER_SIZE
lOG_CHECKPOINT_INTERVAL
lOG_CHECKPOINT_TIMEOUT
LOG_SIMULTANEOUS_COPIES
LOG_SMALL_ENTRY_MAX_SIZE
LOG_ENTRY_PREBUILD_THRESHOLD (reappears in Oracle7.3 and later)
OPTIMZER_PERCENT_PARALLEL (if using parallel query option)
PARALLEL_MAX_SERVERS (if using parallel query option)
PARALLEL_MIN_SERVERS (if using parallel query option)
PARALLEL_SERVER_IDLE_TIME (if using parallel query option)
PARALLEL_MIN_PERCENT (if using parallel query option)
SEQUENCE_CACHE_ENTRIES
SESSION_CACHED_CURSORS (obsolete in Oracle7.3)
SORT_AREA_SIZE
SORT_AREA_RETAINED_SIZE
SORT_DIRECT_WRITES (Oracle7.2 and later)
SORT_DIRECT_BUFFERS (Oracle7.2 and later)
SORT_DIRECT_BUFFER_SIZE (Oracle7.2 and later)
SORT_READ_FAC (Oracle7.2 and later)
```

Step 3: Tuning the Application in Single-User Mode

Once your database has been tuned, the next step is tuning your application. The purpose of this tuning is to perform all transactions within the required response times for your site. If you don't do a thorough job of tuning the application, then your capacity planning will inevitably result in the purchase of an oversized and more expensive configuration in an attempt to provide better response and compensate for poor tuning. Remember, it takes only one inefficient program to cause poor performance in your entire system.

1. Set up your database with sufficient data volume to give a true indication of how the application will perform. Configure and structure that database according to the guidelines specified in Step 2:, "Structuring the Database and SGA," above. Your developers should have run EXPLAIN PLAN against their statements before they get to the benchmarking stage.

2. Turn the SQL trace facility on by setting the following INIT.ORA parameters:

```
SQL_TRACE                 TRUE
TIMED_STATISTICS    TRUE
USER_DUMP_DEST      desired destination
```

3. Check all programs individually using the QA test plan. Run all parts of the program to make testing as similar as it can be to production. For decision support systems where some of the reports are unknown, you can obtain sample report requests from your end users.

4. Prepare a document detailing all programs that are to be tested. If you skip even one program, a perverse law states that the very program you skip will bring your system to its knees.

5. Go through each program and record response times using a stop watch. The reason for using a stop watch is that the results must reflect the end user's perspective. Behind-the-scenes measurements often don't take into account problems like network collisions that seriously slow down end user response time. Remember, for most sites, response times must meet the standard specified. (Often, the maximum allowable response time is about 2.5 seconds for an online transaction processing system.)

6. Record the amount of memory, CPU, disk I/Os, and network activity against each program. If you are running client-server, you must get the readings from both the client and the server end. If you are running parallel-server, you must get the statistics from all machines used.

NOTE   If you are running a UNIX database server, the size of the process at the server end contains more than just the shadow process. It also contains the text of the Oracle executable, which must not be included in your memory sizing. Use the *ps* command with the appropriate option to determine the process size, and use the *size* command on the Oracle executable to determine the amount by which to reduce the shadow process.

---

7. After each program has been completed, run TKPROF against the trace file produced by the SQL trace facility. This file is located in the directory specified in the USER_DUMP_DEST parameter. See Chapter 10, *Diagnostic and Tuning Tools*, for information about interpreting this output. One particularly useful piece of output is "Full Table Scans." Another is the number of SQL statements that take longer than 0.4 seconds CPU, or that perform more than 125 disk reads. These values will help you determine if the correct index and driving tables are being used, and that the correctly optimizer decisions are being made.

8. Remove the trace file after it has been displayed. Rename the output file from the specified trace file name to *program_name.lis*, where *program_name* is

the name of the program being tested. You will need to log in again to the application to create a new trace file for the next program.

9. Document each program that is not performing up to the necessary response time standards. Use the format shown in Figure 17-4.

Program Response Time Report			
Menu Name	Program Name	Description / Function	Response
Accounts Account Maint	ACU100FR	Account Maintenance and Inquiry Screen Query List of Values on Acct Type List of Values on Cost Element Commit the New Account	1.2 seconds 0.5 second 3.5 seconds 1.8 seconds

This list of values requires attention because it exceeds 2.5 seconds.

Figure 17-4. Program response time report

10. Add indexes or adjust the offending statements as required, and retest the program. You may need to add a hint for the optimizer. We usually recommend that you persevere with the cost-based optimizer if you are using Oracle7.1 or later. Continue this process until you are satisfied that all response time problems have been remedied. If you have purchased the Oracle Performance Pack, use it! Oracle Expert provides some excellent input on new indexes that should be added or indexes that should be modified to reduce disk I/Os. Be sure to document any new index and program changes to make sure the changes are enforced when the application goes to production.

Here is an example of how you might proceed. In the previous example, one list of values program took 3.5 seconds to run. This slow performance is likely to be because indexes are missing or are not being used. The most common cause of Oracle's not using an index is finding an improper ORDER BY clause (one that does not include all of the key fields in the index). You can fix such problems by including a dummy WHERE clause in the statement or adding an appropriate index. See Chapter 7, *Tuning PL/SQL*, for information about SQL statement tuning.

11. If certain functions cause poor performance (for example, deleting hundreds of rows of data in an online transaction), you will need to find a smarter way to perform the function, or explain to the users at your site the tradeoffs between function and performance. (Actually, such problems should have been resolved at the time of application design.)

12. Adjust the response time columns in the Program Response Time Report after tuning.

13. To help with future tuning exercises, prepare a report on the outcome of the application tuning stage. Document the reasons why various changes were made to the application. This report will show all response times shown on the Program Response Time Report that exceed those specified in the service agreement.

14. If all participants in your site's capacity planning exercise are convinced that the application has been acceptably tuned, proceed to the multiuser application test.

Step 4: Tuning the Application in Multiuser Mode

The next stage of the capacity planning exercise requires you to test the application in a multiuser environment in which the transaction mix is as close to production as possible. There will probably be at least two iterations of this test, usually many more, with each new run making adjustments for performance. To rebuild your database back to the way it was, it's better to copy your data files to tape, rather than use EXPORT and IMPORT.

Remember that the database must be configured exactly the same way that it will be when the application enters production. If mirroring and striping are to be used in production, they must be used here as well. If the database is required to be run in archivelog mode in production, this database must also be run in archivelog mode. Typically you must have enough data to run your benchmark for 15 minutes or longer!

1. Run the *UTLBSTAT.sql* script to begin taking a snapshot of activity in your system. You will leave this script running for the duration of the test:

   SQLDBA> @UTLBSTAT

   (See Chapter 10 for a discussion of these tools.)

2. Organize your users so they perform realistic tasks that simulate real production conditions. Make sure they represent an accurate mix of user roles and programs. Plan ahead of time what each user's workload will be. Pay attention to the mix of queries and updates. If real production conditions include 90% queries and 10% updates, make sure that the benchmark contains a similar load. Your goal is to place your application under the maximum amount of stress it will suffer when it is running in production. Even if you use a remote terminal emulator (RTE), it is advisable to have at least a handful of users logged on and accessing the application as they will in the production database. They can compare their response times to those produced by the RTE. You will be surprised how often they are different. Believe your users!

3. Have your users log in and start work, according to the plan. Give them stop watches to use in their work. Tell them to document all functions that exceed the expected response times. If you are using an RTE, you must be able to capture response times that the end users will receive.

4. Every 2 minutes, run SQL*DBA MONITOR with the options shown below. (Make sure you don't use the same file name for each output!). The MON names below are for a VMS system; replace if necessary with your own Monitor function. As an alternative, you might decide to monitor using the V$ tables, as described in Chapters 10 and 11.

MON P

Monitor processes

MON ST

Monitor various statistics

MON I/O

Monitor the hit ratio of data in memory

MON F

Monitor the I/O distribution between database files

MON R

Monitor rollback segments

MON T

Monitor table usage

MON L

Monitor locks

5. Every two minutes, run the operating system commands available for your system to check the CPU, memory, and disk use at the database and server ends. Get 20 seconds worth of statistics each time. This information returns the average I/O per user, the average memory per user (at client and server ends, for client-server), and the average MIPS per user. For example, if you are running UNIX on a Sun, use the commands:

vmstat 5

CPU and memory usage

ps -aux

Individual process details

netstat -i

Network statistics

iostat -i

I/O statistics

For UTS, you would issue:

sar -m
> Memory usage

sar -C
> CPU usage

sar -d
> Disk usage

sar -y
> Terminal activity

Other machines have their own monitoring tools; for example, Glance on HPs offers sophisticated performance information. Use the tools that are most effective on your own machine, but be sure they don't affect your benchmark performance.

6. When the benchmark is complete, run the *UTLESTAT.sql* script. Stop the job and display the UTLBSTAT/UTLESTAT output. Chapter 10 provides details on how to interpret the output. If you have purchased the Oracle Performance Pack, use it! Oracle Expert will make recommendations on INIT.ORA parameters that need changing, as well as index problems and how to repair them.

7. Run the scripts on the floppy disk in the back of this book. Explanations on the next steps that you should take to improve performance are documented in the output.

8. Make any adjustments that will improve performance in your own particular system. (The next section provides some suggestions for doing this.) Now rebuild your database and rerun the benchmark.

Step 5: Fixing the Bottlenecks You Discover

Depending on the bottlenecks you discover in the system you are tuning, you may need to do some additional tuning. This step is very much a site-dependent one. For example, you may have a major problem with recursive calls to the database, whereas another site may have no problem at all. On the other hand, that site may be experiencing packet delays in its client-server environment, or locking problems in a parallel-server environment, while you may not have to worry about network performance because you're running in a unitary environment. Here are some guidelines for identifying bottlenecks and doing additional tuning. Chapter 11 describes all of these tuning operations in detail.

Memory. If your memory usage is 100%, and if paging and swapping are occurring at an excessive rate, you have a memory bottleneck. Decrease your memory usage by reducing the size of the SORT_AREA_RETAINED_SIZE, SORT_AREA_SIZE, DB_BLOCK_BUFFERS, LOG_BUFFER, or SHARED_POOL_SIZE parameters.

Decrease them in the order listed, reducing the SORT_AREA_RETAINED_SIZE first. Reduce SHARED_POOL_SIZE only as a last resort.

Disk I/O. If one or more disks are exceeding the recommended maximum I/Os per second, you have a disk bottleneck. Try to transfer tablespaces to alternative disks to reduce the load on the overworked disk. Combine heavily used tablespaces with those that are less frequently used. If you are using striping, use smaller stripe sizes and/or spread your striped files across more disks. Make sure that the controller is not bottlenecking and causing the disk bottlenecks.

CPU. If paging and swapping are causing excessive CPU activity, you have a CPU bottleneck. Most such bottlenecks are the result of memory or I/O bottlenecks. Untuned SQL, inappropriate indexes, or improper optimizer usage are the biggest causes of CPU bottlenecks. If your application, disk I/O, and memory are already tuned, you will need more CPUs and/or faster CPUs.

Network. If you are experiencing packet delays in a client-server environment, you have a network bottleneck. You may be able to change your application program code to eliminate this problem by reducing the number of required disk accesses. You may also be able to move your client and server machines closer together physically (ideally in the same building). Packages, procedures, functions, triggers, and constraints should be used heavily in this environment to reduce network bottlenecks.

Hit ratio. The hit ratio is the ratio of finding rollback, table, index, and cluster data in memory rather than having to perform I/Os from disk to retrieve the data. The hit ratio should be as high as possible. Anything above 95% is reasonable for online applications, although 99% is often achievable and anything above 85% for batch is reasonable. Batch applications are also often able to operate with a much higher hit ratio. You should consider the parallel query option, where practical, for batch applications.

Redo latch, library cache latch, and buffer cache latch contention. Reduce your latch contention. This contention usually occurs because a transaction has to wait for a latch to copy its data or code from disk into an area in memory. We have observed latch contention degrade benchmark performance by 30% plus.

Rollback extension and contention. Reduce your rollback extension and contention. Rollback extension occurs when a transaction making a lot of changes has to extend its size because the current rollback is not large enough to contain all of the rollback data. Rollback contention occurs when there aren't enough rollback segments, and some of the transactions requesting rollbacks are being forced to wait for a rollback segment to become available. Be very cautious when using the OPTIMAL clause. If you do use it, make sure that it is set reasonably to avoid excessive rollback segment shrinking and the associated waits.

Chaining, migration, and dynamic extension. Eliminate chaining, migration, and dynamic extension. Chaining occurs when a single row cannot physically fit into one Oracle block, as specified by the DB_BLOCK_SIZE parameter. You may need to consider enlarging DB_BLOCK_SIZE and rebuilding your database if chaining is too prevalent in your database. Also consider reducing your PCTFREE on the tables affected if the rows are not expanded in size.

Migration of rows occurs when a row is updated to include more data, and the row can no longer fit into the block that contains many other rows. The updated row is physically migrated (moved) to another block in the table. The index entries still point to the old block which then has a pointer to the migrated block. You are now required to read an additional block if you are using an index. To solve this problem, increase the PCTFREE on the table.

NOTE   Full table scans do not have their performance degraded by row migrations, because the scan simply reads the next block of rows regardless of whether the row has been migrated.

Dynamic extension occurs when tables, indexes, temporary segments, and rollback segments grow in size, and the current extents assigned are not large enough to store the extra information. They can degrade performance significantly.

Excessive I/O. Eliminate excessive I/O on particular data files. Excessive I/O will inevitably lead to a bottleneck on one of your disks. Consider both Oracle striping and operating system striping.

Locking problems. Locking problems can have a disastrous effect on your performance. You will often not see the problems until you put your system under the level of pressure that the benchmark imposes. Become familiar with all of the locking problems described in Chapter 8, *Selecting a Locking Strategy.* Foreign key locking, in which the child table in a parent- child relationship does not have its foreign key columns indexed, is a particularly dangerous problem.

When you are satisfied that you can't tune any more, and your system is still experiencing a memory, disk, CPU, or network bottleneck, start taking users off the machine, one at a time, until the bottleneck disappears. You will then know exactly how many users your machine can support with its current configuration. (Make sure before you remove users that your memory is being used to cache as much data as possible, and that the disk load is spread across disks as evenly as possible.)

If you are using less memory, disk, CPU, and/or networking than is available, try adding users until you deliberately cause a bottleneck. This way, you'll know how far you can push your system, and where its weak points might be. You must be aware of your machines scalability. Don't rely on simply moving to client-server, parallel-server, or distributed database to solve your problems. If your benchmark has been performed on a unitary machine, the application will usually run much slower on client-server and parallel-server.

Step 6: Reporting the Results of the Exercise

The final step is to report on the results of the capacity planning exercise. Don't sell your efforts short by failing to carry through by writing a thorough report to corporate management. Document your findings and recommendations in a professional report that can be distributed to the management at your site. The precise contents and format of this report will differ for different sites, but here are some general recommendations for what you need to include:

Management summary. This should not exceed three pages. It includes all your recommendations and associated costs. Include detailed information in appendices. Use graphical information wherever possible.

Aims. Major aims of the benchmark, including:

- Assure management that the hardware and architecture recommended will be able to provide sustained acceptable performance, and is cost effective, scalable, and falls within the flexibility and constraints of the organization's information technology strategy.

- Review and finalize the response time service agreement based on the best response times that can be achieved given the budget.

- Provide an indication of the costs of the hardware and software needed to run the application.

- Identify and repair bottlenecks.

- Fix any application programs not meeting required response times.

- Establish hardware/software configurations required for your sites.

- Fine-tune the Oracle RDBMS.

- Allow staff to see applications working under realistic conditions.

Tuning plan. Details of the tuning plan:

- Tuning of the application in single-user mode.

- Report indicating all programs and functions within programs with timings.

- Load test in the expected environment (e.g., client-server). Mention the number of users that participated and the throughput they generated or the RTE used. Highlight at what point response times and throughput began to degrade after all tuning was performed.

Exclusions. List any components of the application that were not benchmarked

- Any programs not run, including batch jobs
- Any hardware components missing (e.g., mirroring) which were proposed for the production database but were missing during the benchmark
- Any part of the architecture that was absent (e.g., the second instance in parallel-server)

Results. List the results of the benchmark:

- Average I/O generated per user (e.g., 500 I/Os per minute).
- Average memory per user (at both client and server ends for client-server configuration). Typical use is two megabytes per user.
- Average MIPS used per user (e.g., 0.3 MIPS per user). (MIPS ratings vary from one vendor to the next, but are normally consistent within vendors.)
- Network traffic generated by average user (e.g., 150 packets per minute).
- Any Oracle or operating system actions you must perform to make the application perform optimally; for example, in a UNIX system, you might need to use raw devices and decrease your UNIX file buffer cache from 20% to 5% of the machine's memory.

Using the sample figures above, and assuming that you have 150 concurrent users logging on to your application at the time of peak usage, typical Oracle hardware requirements for an online transaction processing system might look like this:

```
150 * 500 I/Os per minute = 7500 I/Os per minute or 125 I/Os per second
150 * 2 MB per user = 300 MB + SGA (typically 50 MB) = 350 MB memory
150 * 0.3 MIPS = 45 MIPS
```

Recommendations. List your recommendations:

- Size of the configuration that is required to run your application.
- Any adjustments that could be made to improve the performance. For example, try having more memory on the client (application server) and less on the database server.
- Any adjustments that were found to improve throughput (e.g., enlarging the swap space).
- Scalability recommendations to allow for future growth.

Supporting evidence. Detail what happens if the configuration varies from the one that you recommend.

Environment. Show full details of the environment in which you worked. Ideally this includes diagrams of your hardware configuration.

Programs. Show full details of all your programs and their subfunctions, including how they were tested to show they performed within the response time guidelines. Attach the Program Response Time Report (Figure 17-4).

Database. Show a list of the database configuration, rows per table, extents per object, and INIT.ORA parameters.

Adjustments. Show a list of all adjustments made and the reasons why they were made. For example, increasing the buffer cache from 4 megabytes to 40 megabytes improved response times by 33% with improvement in the hit rate of 10%.

18

Tuning for Specific Systems

The Oracle performance tuning information in this book applies, in virtually all cases, to all versions of Oracle, whether it's running on a variety of BSD, System V, or POSIX UNIX platform; an IBM mainframe; a Digital Equipment Corporation minicomputer; a Sun workstation; or an Apple Macintosh. Most of the advice is equally applicable to MVS, VMS, UNIX, and DOS. Nevertheless, there are system-specific performance issues related to your own particular configuration of hardware and software and the way that Oracle interacts with your system resources.

In general, the details of operating system tuning are beyond the scope of this book. You'll find some helpful information in the platform-specific *Oracle Installation and User's Guide* that comes with your version of the system. Your operating system documentation is the best source of information about the specifics of tuning general system resources. This chapter supplements those sources by providing hints for UNIX and VMS, two of the most popular operating system platforms for Oracle.

UNIX-Specific Tuning

This section contains hints for getting the best performance out of Oracle running on a UNIX platform. Where applicable, we distinguish between System V and BSD utilities command.

Shared Memory and Semaphore Requirements

Oracle uses shared memory and semaphores to communicate between user processes and the System Global Area (SGA). When Oracle databases start up, they insist on pre-allocating all SGA memory and semaphores equal to the maximum number of processes set in the INIT.ORA parameter file. If these resources are not available, the instance cannot start up. Unfortunately, if your database cannot initialize because of insufficient semaphores or because the maximum shared memory segment has been exceeded, it requires a UNIX kernel rebuild and a machine reboot. Oracle provides a list of recommended values for running a small-sized database; these are listed below. We suggest that you increase these parameters to meet your application needs. You will also need to also take into account the number of instances intended for a particular machine when setting these parameters.

Operating System	Shared Memory Parameters	Semaphore
Sun OS	SHMSIZE = 32768	SEMMNS = 200
	SHMMNI = 50	SEMMNI = 50
Solaris	SHMMAX = 8388608	SEMMNS = 200
	SHMSEG = 20	SEMMSL = 50
HP/UX	SHMMAX = 0x4000000	SEMMNS = 200
	SHMSEG = 15	QSEMMNI = 10
OSF/1	SHMMAX = 4194304	SEMMNS = 300
	SHMSEG = 32	
Ultrix	Use system defaults	SEMMNS = 60
		SEMMSL = 5
NCR	SHMMAX = 9mb	SEMMNS = 200
	SHMSEG = 15	
Dynix/PTX	SHMMAX = 11010048	SEMMNS = 200
	SHMSEG = 20	SEMMSLI = 85
DG/UX	SHMMAX = 4194304	SEMMNS = 200
	SHMSEG = 15	

Writing to Raw Devices

You can improve performance quite a bit by setting up your database files and redo logs as raw devices. By doing this, you avoid having to go through the UNIX buffer. Instead, Oracle writes directly from the SGA buffer area to disk. In this way, you reduce CPU activity substantially, avoiding memory paging between the UNIX buffer cache and the SGA. This approach also avoids the need to incur UNIX read ahead and UNIX file system overheads.

We have found that on systems that are dedicated to Oracle, the size of the UNIX buffer area can be reduced from approximately 15% to 5% of memory. With the memory you save, you can support more users, increase the sort area size, or perhaps even release the memory to another computer. By writing to raw devices in this way, we have seen overall performance increase as much as 50%.

To write to raw devices, you issue a CREATE DATABASE statement in the following form:

```
CREATE          DATABASE ACCOUNTS
CONTROLFILE     REUSE
DATAFILE        '/dev/raw1'   200M    REUSE,
LOGFILE         '/dev/raw2'   50M     REUSE,
                '/dev/raw3'   50M     REUSE,
                '/dev/raw4'   50M     REUSE;

CREATE          TABLESPACE ACCOUNT_DATA
DATAFILE        '/dev/raw5'   500M
DEFAULT         STORAGE   (   INITIAL      4K
                              NEXT         10K
                              MAXEXTENTS   110
                              PCTINCREASE  0   );
```

The UNIX buffer cache and the Oracle buffer cache can be independently tuned. Note that some machines do not allow the UNIX buffer cache to be tuned at all. For example, the SunOS dynamically adjusts the UNIX buffer cache. Some versions of UNIX, such as DYNIX on Sequents, provide an option to allow you to bypass the UNIX buffer cache and avoid the need for raw devices. It is important that you read your *Oracle Installation and User's Guide* for more information on how to best configure your own system.

You can generally figure out which UNIX parameters need tuning by looking for the letters "BUF". For example, on a Digital Equipment Corporation system running ULTRIX, the parameters that you need to tune are NBUF and BUFF-PAGES. NBUF is the number of buffer headers that controls the number of buffers that can exist, and BUFFPAGES sets the size of the buffer cache in 1-kilobyte pages.

Because raw devices can be a little tricky to set up and administer, we recommend that only sites with full-time experienced DBAs and system administrators use raw devices. You will also need to carry out a thorough capacity plan and data growth analysis before you lay out your raw device partitions. Raw devices provide little disk flexibility, and existing data files are difficult to move once the partitions are set up.

Latches

The Oracle RDBMS is composed of many source code modules. Approximately 100 of these are system-specific modules designed to handle operations such as memory allocation, process creation, and disk I/O. One important module of this kind is the one that acquires and handles latches. Latches are used to protect data structures inside the SGA (such as the hash table) and provide quick access to the database buffers.

A process that needs to access the hash table must first acquire and own the latch associated with the hash table. Under UNIX, the latch is associated with a byte of shared memory in the SGA. A process requiring the latch must first test the latch to determine whether it is available. If it is available, the process obtains it. If it is not available, the process establishes a method of queuing for the latch. UNIX has several methods of queuing, described in the following sections. The method you'll use depends on whether the version of UNIX being used is System V- or Berkeley-based and whether the system uses a single CPU or multiple CPUs.

Spin locks

The spin lock method of latching is used on multiple-CPU systems. Multiple processes operate simultaneously with one process per CPU. A latch is held for a brief moment (milliseconds). If a latch is required, chances are that a process running on any of a number of CPUs will soon be freed. By repeatedly retrying the latch (i.e., spinning on the latch), the waiting process is likely to be able to avoid using more costly operating system queuing facilities. The number of times the process will spin on the latch before relinquishing the CPU is determined by the INIT.ORA parameter SPIN_COUNT.

On single-CPU systems, spin locks are not applicable. If a process finds that a latch is busy, it must relinquish the CPU so that the process holding the latch can run. On Berkeley-based systems, the process will sleep for a predetermined timeout period before trying again.

Semaphore-based queues

System V UNIX systems use semaphore-based queues. If a process cannot acquire a latch, it joins a queue of processes waiting for the latch. This is done by updating a data structure in the SGA, indicating that it is waiting for a specific latch and then sleeping on its semaphore. The process relinquishes the CPU, allowing another process to run. When the running process has completed, the waiting process's semaphore is incremented, which causes it to awaken and attempt to retry the latch again. This method minimizes operating system overhead.

UNIX Commands to Monitor Performance

This section briefly looks at some of the commands that can be used to identify performance bottlenecks. Almost all machines that run UNIX have additional commands that can be used to monitor your system (for example, the *stats* command in the UTS environment). You must gather information on the commands that are relevant to your site.

Remember that you can issue the *man* command to display the syntax of the commands on your system; for example, *man vmstat*.

Identifying disk bottlenecks

As we have mentioned elsewhere in this book, you can improve performance by spreading the load across disk drives as evenly as possible. Each disk drive has recommended maximum I/Os per second. It is important that every disk drive operate within the recommended maximum.

iostat is a BSD UNIX command that allows you to identify the average number of transfers per second. In the simple example below, only one disk is being displayed, the system disk "dk0". The column to observe is the "tps" column, which is the average number of disk transfers per second since the last interval. The format of the *iostat* command is

iostat *drives interval count*

For example, this command produces the following output:

iostat 5 5

tty				dk0			id002			cpu	
tin	tout	bps	tps	msps	bps	tps	msps	us	ni	sy	id
2	125	4	1	0.0	4	0	18.5	1	0	2	97
0	0	0	0	0.0	0	0	0.0	2	0	0	98
0	0	0	0	0.0	0	0	0.0	0	0	0	100
0	0	0	0	0.0	3	0	43.3	0	0	0	99
0	0	0	0	0.0	0	0	0.0	0	0	01	00

System V machines use the *sar* -d command. The important column to observe is the "r+w/s" column, which show the reads and writes per second (on average) since the last interval, as follows.

sar -d

mel01	vic01 5.	1a-910507c	0419f	MIS-4/03		07/12/93	
17:53:53	device	%busy	avque	r+w/s	blks/s	avwait	avserv
17:53:58	sdisk04	5	3.1	3	12	43.5	20.8
	sdisk14	2	2.8	1	2	37.5	20.5
	sdisk24	9	1.5	4	25	12.2	23.0
17:54:03	sdisk04	4	1.2	1	8	6.1	29.0
	sdisk14	2	1.3	1	5	6.0	17.4
	sdisk24	1	1.1	1	2	1.0	18.7
17:54:18	sdisk14	1	1.0	0	2	1.5	31.5
	sdisk24	1	1.0	0	2	1.0	24.5
Average	sdisk04	2	2.3	1	4	30.4	23.7
	sdisk14	1	1.7	1	2	15.0	20.5
	sdisk24	2	1.4	1	6	10.0	22.6

It is always a good idea to try to preempt potential I/O bottlenecks during the application design phase. This is not a difficult task and can be very beneficial when trying to calculate the total number of disks your application will require. You need to first estimate the number of physical I/Os required per transaction. For example, a DBA could use TKPROF to break an application function down to its lowest I/O call. Summing the physical disk accesses gives the total number of disk I/Os required to perform the transaction.

For an OLTP system, assume that we require an average of six physical I/Os per transaction and that your application requirements will peak at 100 transactions per second, for a cumulative total of 600 disk I/Os per second. Each disk can conservatively perform 50 random I/Os per second. This means that we will require the data to be spread/balanced across at least 12 (600/50) disk drives. You will also need to consider the number and placement of disk controllers to sustain these peak disk throughputs.

Identifying memory bottlenecks

Memory bottlenecks occur when you are short on memory and excessive paging and swapping are occurring. Paging and swapping can dramatically degrade your system's response times. Paging occurs when part of a process is either shuffled within memory or paged to disk. Swapping occurs when an entire process is removed from memory and written to disk. Paging and swapping both use CPU, although swapping represents a bigger drain on your system if it becomes excessive. Swapping is of no concern if the process being swapped is a dormant process. Paging of the nonactive part of a process is also not a major concern; only a small portion of an active process is usually required in memory at any point in time to allow the process to proceed with its execution. But a major performance drain occurs when an active process is swapped out of memory or an active part of a process is paged from memory.

The usual cause of swapping and paging problems is insufficient memory to cope with the workload. To detect the amount of free memory on your computer, use the *vmstat* command under Berkeley UNIX or XENIX to look at overall system performance. The following example reports on five sets of statistics with 5-second intervals:

vmstat 5 5

procs			memory				page						disk				faults			cpu		
r	b	w	avm	fre	re	at	pi	po	fr	de	sr	d0	d1	i0	i1	in		sy	cs	us	sy	id
0	0	0	0	55340	0	3	11	0	1	0	0	0	0	2	0	52	162	75	1	2	97
0	0	0	0	55300	0	0	0	0	0	0	0	0	0	1	0	1096	248	104	2	1	97
1	0	0	0	55176	0	0	0	0	0	16	0	0	0	1	0	1234	389	210	2	2	95
1	0	0	0	54932	0	1	0	0	0	0	0	0	0	2	0	1241	384	211	3	1	95
0	0	0	0	54684	0	0	16	0	0	0	0	0	0	3	0	1236	421	215	3	3	94

The values that are of particular interest are "memory fre" (the free memory in kilobytes), "page po" (the number of 1-kilobyte pages that have been paged out), and "cpu sy" (the percentage of CPU being used by system activity such as swapping and paging). There is an abundance of free memory on our sample machine (53 megabytes is the minimum amount of free memory recorded). There is little chance of excessive paging and swapping under these circumstances.

For System V sites, you would issue the following:

sar -r

00:00:01	Freemem	Freeswp
02:00:00	12010	65636
04:00:00	10100	65636
06:00:00	14120	65636
08:00:00	16786	65636
10:00:00	12632	65636

The "Freemem" column in this example is the number of free memory pages on your system. In the example above, the minimum memory available (on our example system, a Pyramid with 2-kilobyte pages) is 20 megabytes. Excessive paging and swapping will not occur with this much free memory.

You can also observe the amount of swapping by using the *sar* -w command. Ensure that "swpot/s" (swap outs per second during the interval) and "bswot/s" (the number block swapped out per second) remain at 0.

sar -w

vic   vic   systemV 2.1.3   5995   07/12/93

16:57:50	cpu#	swpin/s	bswin/s	swpot/s	bswot/s	pswch/s
	rawch/s	canch/s	outch/s	rcvin/s	xmtin/s	mdmin/s
16:57:55	0	0.00	0.0	0.00	0.0	667
	2	0.00	0.0	0.00	0.0	398
16:58:00	0	0.00	0.0	0.00	0.0	613
	2	0.00	0.0	0.00	0.0	331
16:58:05	0	0.00	0.0	0.00	0.0	505
	2	0.00	0.0	0.00	0.0	295
16:58:10	0	0.00	0.0	0.00	0.0	567
	2	0.00	0.0	0.00	0.0	351
16:58:15	0	0.00	0.0	0.00	0.0	579
	2	0.00	0.0	0.00	0.0	324
Average	0	0.00	0.0	0.00	0.0	586
	2	0.00	0.0	0.00	0.0	340

Memory paging can be identified by the command *sar -p*. Paging is not as serious as memory swapping but should be monitored. Every system will experience some paging, but we must try to keep it to a minimum. Some of the platforms encourage higher levels of memory paging. Sun, IBM AIX, and DG-UX all consider high paging levels as normal. During low activity times, some platforms use free memory for read-ahead file buffering, distorting paging statistics.

sar -p

```
SunOS mecx05 5.3 Generic_101318-78 sun4m     06/24/96
              atch/s   pgin/s ppgin/s  pflt/s  vflt/s slock/s

08:00:01     0.13     0.64    1.84    28.01   49.09   0.00
08:15:01     0.38     0.30    0.70    35.88   72.35   0.00
08:30:00     0.98     0.26    0.52    32.68   57.70   0.00
08:45:00     0.08     0.13    0.22    32.31   56.54   0.00
09:00:01     0.90     0.63    1.12    29.89   50.82   0.00
09:15:00     1.96     1.37    8.78    79.23  154.68   0.00
09:30:00     1.06     0.37    2.03    80.60  147.61   0.00
09:45:00     1.35     0.32    0.59   107.54  192.61   0.00
10:00:00     0.08     0.05    0.08    65.43  115.33   0.00
10:15:01     0.08     0.22    0.52    82.30  154.51   0.00
10:30:01     4.02     1.70   13.99    65.95  109.22   0.00
10:45:00     5.10     3.00   29.69    67.56  115.41   0.00
11:00:01     4.64     3.86   24.11    51.09   89.97   0.00
11:15:00     0.95     9.51   23.49    72.71  133.46   0.00
11:30:00     0.21     0.42    0.83    73.13  119.29   0.00
11:45:00     0.12     2.61   24.07    78.70  129.57   0.00
12:00:01     1.88     1.83    4.73    88.46  143.22   0.00
Average      5.01     3.05   10.12    45.18   81.97   0.37
```

Identifying swapping bottlenecks

UNIX systems use disk swap space to temporarily hold portions of a process's memory. Swap space allows more processes to simultaneously run in a small amount of physical memory. Not all process memory is required at any one time. Dormant parts of a process's memory can be copied to disk until required at a later time.

A shortage of swap space can dramatically affect a system's performance. Your system can experience problems such as slow response times, failure to spawn subprocesses, or complete system hanging. Most UNIX systems should have total swap space between two and five times their physical memory size. Place swap space on your fastest disks, partitioned/spread across as many physical disks as possible.

The following example shows how to query swap space usage for BSD UNIX:

```
pstat -s
```

This example shows how to interrogate swap space utilization for System V UNIX:

swap -l

```
swapfile                   dev  swaplo blocks   free
/dev/dsk/c0t0d0s1         32,1       8 471736 444512
/CML/rts/spare1/swaptmp1    -        8 614392 588720
```

Identifying CPU bottlenecks

Under Berkeley UNIX, you can pinpoint CPU bottlenecks via the *vmstat* command (to observe overall system performance, similar to the *iostat* command described above) and *ps* -aux (to observe the percentage of CPU being consumed by each process).

vmstat 5 5

procs			memory		page						disk				faults			cpu		
r	b	w	avm	fre	re	at	pi	po	fr	de	sr	d0	d1	i0	i1	in	sy	cs	us	sy	id
0	0	0	0	55340	0	3	11	0	1	0	0	0	0	2	0	52	162	75	1	2	97
0	0	0	0	55300	0	0	0	0	0	0	0	0	0	1	0	1096	248	104	2	1	97
1	0	0	0	55176	0	0	0	0	0	16	0	0	0	1	0	1234	389	210	2	2	95
1	0	0	0	54932	0	1	0	0	0	0	0	0	0	2	0	1241	384	211	3	1	95
0	0	0	0	54684	0	0	16	0	0	0	0	0	0	3	0	1236	421	215	3	3	94

The three columns of particular interest are "us" (the percentage of CPU used by users), "sy" (the percentage of CPU used by system resources), which should be significantly less than the "us" reading, and "id" (the percentage of time that the CPU was idle).

ps -aux

USER	PID	%CPU	%MEM	SZ	RSS	TT	STAT	START	TIME	COMMAND
oracle	15343	0.0	0.9	304	1128	?	S	01:32	1:12	ora_smon_DEV6
oracle	15340	0.0	0.5	192	636	?	S	01:32	0:02	ora_pmon_DEV6
oraclev7	444	0.0	0.9	212	1084	?	S	Jul 11	0:11	ora_pmon_DEV7
oraclev7	445	0.0	1.2	208	1408	?	S	Jul 11	0:19	ora_dbwr_DEV7
oraclev7	446	0.0	1.0	208	1192	?	S	Jul 11	0:17	ora_lgwr_DEV7
oraclev7	447	0.0	0.0	344	0	?	IW	Jul 11	1:18	ora_smon_DEV7
oraclev7	448	0.0	0.0	228	0	?	IW	Jul 11	0:05	ora_reco_DEV7
peter	21810	0.0	0.0	1192	0	p4	IW	16:44	0:26	sqlforms30 -c vt100
peter	22346	0.0	0.0	444	0	p2	IW	17:43	0:02	runmenu50 PERS
oracle	15342	0.0	0.9	248	1096	?	S	01:32	0:11	ora_lgwr_DEV6
oracle	15341	0.0	3.2	328	3892	?	S	01:32	0:12	ora_dbwr_DEV6
mark	22757	0.0	0.4	288	536	p0	R	18:44	0:00	ps -aux
oracle	22347	0.0	0.0	528	0	?	IW	17:43	0:01	oracleS T:I,,5
root	8040	0.0	0.0	104	0	?	IW	Jul 12	0:12	orasrv
awanker	21032	0.0	0.0	272	0	q2	IW	15:12	0:04	sqlplus
oracle	21811	0.0	0.0	344	0	?	IW	16:44	0:31	oracleS T:I,,5

This display shows the Oracle processes only. The relevant column to observe in this case is the "%CPU". Any process using an unusually large "%CPU" should be checked. Notice also "%MEM" (the overall process's memory percentage displayed) and "SZ" (the virtual memory required for the data and stack segments).

Under System V, you can use the *sar* -u command to observe overall system activity.

sar -u

```
vic01     vic101 5.    1a-910507c      0419f      MIS-4/03            07/12/93

17:54:18      %usr      %sys      %wio      %idle
17:54:23       8         5         5         81
17:54:28       9         2         1         89
17:54:33      11         4         8         78
17:54:39       7         4         4         85
17:54:44       1         2         2         95

Average        7         4         4         86
```

The columns in this display are "%usr" (percentage of CPU allocated to user processes), "%sys" (system functions), "%wio" (waiting for I/O), and "%idle" (percentage idle).

You can use the *ps* -ef command to see a display of the amount of CPU time each process has used. The column to observe is the "TIME" column, which is the amount of CPU in minutes and seconds.

ps -ef

```
   UID      PID    PPID    C     STIME     TTY     TIME   COMMAND

oracle     189    1       0     Jul 11     ?       0:20   ora_db07_PERS
pers017    3049   8987    0     16:01:09   ttyp017 0:00   sqlplus
oracle     7680   1       0     Jul  7     ?       1:44   orasrv O opsoff
daemon     4858   7680    81    17:25:17   ?       5:53   oraclePERS T:I,,5
pers124    8069   8068    0     18:55:44   ?       0:00   oraclePERS P:4096,5,8,
pers172    8211   8210    0     18:56:54   ?       0:00   oraclePERS P:4096,4,7,
pers918    8092   8070    0     18:55:55   ?       0:00   sqlplus
oracle     171    1       0   · Jul 11     ?      22:51   ora_pmon_PERS
oracle     15793  15791   0     Jul 12     ?       0:00   oraclePERS P:4096,4,7,
daemon     1235   7680    0     06:01:08   ?       0:00   oraclePERS T:I,,5
oracle     186    1       0     Jul 11     ?       0:18   ora_db06_PERS
oracle     174    1       0     Jul 11     ?       2:52   ora_arch_PERS
pers118    15909  15905   0     Jul 12     ttyp048 0:00   sqlplus
```

Notice in the display that the PERS database instance has both client-server (oraclePERS T:I,5) users running TWO_TASK and users logged on in unitary fashion (oraclePERS P:4096,4,7,). The largest user of CPU is Oracle's detached process "ora_pmon_PERS". This usually indicates that the database instance has been up for a lengthy period. If one of the processes has an excessive amount of CPU (e.g., 10 minutes) and is increasing rapidly, it should be investigated.

Identifying network bottlenecks

As was mentioned in Chapter 16, *Tuning in the Client-Server Environment*, you must try to minimize the number of packets that your applications transfer across your networks. You must also be aware that bad packets can be passed across the network. Data corruption leads to performance problems because when an error is detected, your system requests the packet to be sent again. Corrupt packets are usually associated with an overloaded network. To discover whether your network is overloaded, use the *netstat* -i command. There will be several columns listed including "Ierrs" and "Oerrs," which represent the number of input errors, and number of output errors respectively. Ideally, both of these values should be zero. (Issue *man netstat* for a full explanation of *netstat* on your system.)

When you are running client-server, knowledgeable users will periodically ask you, "Is our network down?" Novice users will ask, "Why is the machine so slow?" There are several problems that may have occurred; the most common are the following:

- The database server machine is down

- The database instance is down

- SQL*Net (*orasrv*) is down

To test whether if the database machine or network is down, issue the command

ping {*machine_name*}

For example:

ping grumpy

```
Host is alive.
64 bytes from 157.125.98.6: icmp_seq=11. time=41. ms
64 bytes from 157.125.98.6: icmp_seq=12. time=44. ms
64 bytes from 157.125.98.6: icmp_seq=13. time=41. ms
64 bytes from 157.125.98.6: icmp_seq=14. time=41. ms
64 bytes from 157.125.98.6: icmp_seq=15. time=53. ms
64 bytes from 157.125.98.6: icmp_seq=16. time=41. ms
64 bytes from 157.125.98.6: icmp_seq=17. time=41. ms
64 bytes from 157.125.98.6: icmp_seq=18. time=41. ms
64 bytes from 157.125.98.6: icmp_seq=19. time=42. ms
64 bytes from 157.125.98.6: icmp_seq=20. time=59. ms

----grumpy PING Statistics----
10 packets transmitted, 10 packets received, 0% packet loss
round-trip (ms)  min/avg/max = 41/43/59
```

machine_name is the database server machine your users log on to. If the message "Host is alive" is returned instantly, you have no problem, with the machine being up, and your network is functioning correctly. If there is an irregular delay in the message being returned, you probably have an intermittent network problem that must be cured.

If the machine and network are running, you must now test whether the database instance is running. To do this, try logging on to your database server machine using SQL*Plus with your Oracle_SID set to your database instance ID. (Be sure that you do not have TWO_TASK set.) If this is not the problem, it must be the SQL*Net process *orasrv* that is causing the problem. Set TWO_TASK, and try logging on to the instance (on the database server machine) using SQL*Plus to confirm that *orasrv* is the problem. See your *Oracle Installation and User's Guide* for details on how to cure this problem.

Nonstandard UNIX Functionality

Many machines running UNIX have unique characteristics. You must be aware of what these characteristics are to get the most out of your machine. For example, extensive graphical performance monitoring tools are available on Sun computers and UTS (*stats* command). In the SunOS system, adjusting the MAXUSERS parameter affects the number of processes that are able to operate, the number of files that are allowed to be open simultaneously, and many other kernel table parameters. (See the Sun manuals for details.) Other machines offer dynamic tuning of operating system parameters; for example, DYNIX on Sequent machines offers a *vmtune* command. The list goes on. Check with your own system vendor for complete information.

Pinning SGA into memory

Oracle's SGA provides a data cache for database information. For this reason, having the SGA page or swap out to disk would defeat its purpose. In fact, doing so would require more system resources than reading the data directly from disk. Some platforms allow the SGA to be pinned into physical memory so that it cannot be paged or swapped. These platforms include the following:

- Sequent: *vmtune* parameter DIRTYHIGH frees memory for the SGA
- ATT GIS: *stune* parameter SHM_NAILED_GID1
- Data General: kernel parameter PERCENT LOCKABLE

Be careful when locking large SGAs into memory. Performance improvements made by Oracle will nearly always be at some other application's expense. If your machine is supporting several Oracle instances or other non-Oracle applications, you must be careful to balance machine resources evenly across all applications.

Smarter ways to export under UNIX

Space is at a premium on many machines. There are several ways in which you can save space. For example, under UNIX you can export directly to a compressed file by using named pipes, as follows:

```
$ mknod gl_export.pipe p
$ cat gl_export.pipe | compress > gl_export.dmp.Z &
$ exp gl/gl file=gl_export.pipe buffer=131072
```

You can also export to tape, which sometimes requires a symbolic link pointing to the tape device:

```
$ ln -s /dev/rst0 tape.dmp
$ exp gl/gl file=tape buffer=131072
```

You can take the idea of exporting via UNIX pipes one step further and use it to simultaneously export and import, even to another database. This saves the need to actually retain an entire dump file, even in compressed form.

```
$ mknod gl_export.pipe p
$ exp gl/gl file=gl_export.pipe buffer=131072 &

$ imp gl/gl file=gl_export.pipe commiy=Y buffer=131072
```

Single-task Oracle executables

Oracle executables default to TWO_TASK operation for the UNIX operating system. This means that each database connection consists of a foreground task (the user process) and a background task (the database process). This TWO_TASK configuration seems a little complicated but allows for better use of machine memory. The background task executes as the database user (via a *sticky* bit) and uses a shared copy of the SGA.

This interprocess communication does come at a cost. Oracle also supports SINGLE_TASK execution mode, which is substantially more efficient than the normal TWO_TASK mode, but does require more real memory. This mode is not the default, and there is some conjecture as to whether Oracle actually supports it. The official line seems to be that it does not, even though the mode is documented in Oracle's own tuning manuals.

Oracle tasks that can operate in SINGLE_TASK include SQLDBA, SRVMGR, IMP, EXP, SQLLOADER, and the like. For example, to compile the EXPORT executable, issue the following command:

```
$ make -f $Oracle_HOME/rdbms/lib/oracle.mk expst
```

DBAs should note that the resulting executable is suffixed by *"st"*:

```
$ expst gl/gl file=gl_export.pipe buffer=131072
```

UNIX-specific I/O parameters

Every UNIX operating system Oracle port has a number of I/O-specific parameters that are used to exploit features of that operating system. These parameters are specific to an Oracle version and/or operating system version and are set in the database INIT.ORA or the UNIX kernel itself. A number of these parameters are listed below; you will need to investigate whether they are applicable to your particular port.

Database writers

Can help to increase a database's writing bandwidth. This means that more database data can be written to disk at any one time. Oracle does not support database writers on all UNIX platforms. The parameter DB_WRITERS = nn must be included in the database's INIT.ORA file to activate extra database writer processes.

Raw partitions/devices

Another way to significantly increase I/O disk performance under UNIX specific operating systems. Raw partitions allow database processes to bypass the UNIX buffer cache, eliminating file system overheads altogether. This means that less buffer cache memory is required and that lower CPU overheads are necessary to perform an identical disk I/O request.

Raw partitions are generally considered to be harder to administer and more complex to implement, back up, and recover. Even though there is some truth in this argument, most of the mystery associated with raw devices is due to unfamiliarity rather than complexity.

Post/wait driver

An operating system kernel facility that provides an alternative to semaphores for interprocess communication. Semaphores are used to coordinate access to shared resources. One semaphore per process is allocated at database startup time. and semaphores are slow and expensive. The post/wait driver, on the other hand, provides a way to post a resource request and wait for its availability.

Asynchronous I/O

An operating system level utility that allows an application process to continue executing without having to wait for each disk write to complete. This minimizes the amount of dead time spent waiting for each I/O request to proceed and provides nonblocking disk writes.

Once the asynchronous I/O has been linked into your operating system kernel, you will need to enable it within the Oracle database. This is done by including the parameter ASYNC_WTRITE = TRUE in the database INIT.ORA file. (Some older versions of Oracle use the parameter USE_ASYNC_IO instead.) Some of the more common Oracle platforms that provide asynchronous I/O are the following:

- Solaris: Both raw and filesystem files
- SCO: Raw files only
- Pyramid: Raw files only
- Sequent: Raw files only

List I/O

A common feature of many SVR4 releases. List I/O allows several disk I/Os to be grouped into a list and performed as a single I/O request. Substantial performance gains can be achieved by list I/O and the way it allows nonblocking disk writes. Application programs can continue processing without having to wait for a disk write to complete. Always use list I/O before resorting to multiple database writers.

Direct I/O

A relatively new feature that is now available on a number of UNIX platforms. Direct I/O is similar to raw partitions in the way it allows I/O operations to bypass the UNIX cache and write directly to disk. What makes direct I/O attractive is the fact that it operates over normal file systems without any of the complexities or administration overheads associated with raw partitions.

KAIO (Kernelized Asynchronous I/O)

An option available on Solaris 2.4 that allows asynchronous I/O without using the *libaio* interface module.

pread(2)/pwrite(2)

A Solaris extension to the normal *read(2)/write(2)* that combines the normal *lseek(2)* system call with the default *read(2)/write(2)* call. This parameter can benefit heavily loaded OLTP systems.

_TRACE_FILES_PUBLIC and other undocumented parameters

A number of undocumented INIT.ORA parameters exist for each UNIX variant. Investigate these parameters for possible usefulness on your own system. The most popular of these parameters is _TRACE_FILES_PUBLIC. Setting this parameter to TRUE instructs the database to create all database trace files with public read access. These trace files are written to the UNIX directory specified in the INIT.ORA parameter, USER_DUMP_DEST. This removes a lot of annoying trace file *chmod* commands required by the DBA for developers who do not have read access to their own trace output.

As we've mentioned before, you can view all undocumented INIT.ORA parameters on your Oracle platform by executing the following SQL statement:

```
# undoc.sql
SQL>  SELECT ksppinm
      FROM   x$ksppi
      WHERE  substr(ksppinm, 1, 1) = '_';
```

Keeping all Oracle processes at the same priority

You must *never* adjust the priority of any of the Oracle processes, including optional processes such as additional database writers. Oracle itself is finely tuned and assumes that all of its processes will be able to communicate at the same priority.

Enlarging your System Global Area

We have visited sites where the DBA has claimed that they can't enlarge their SGA beyond a small size because their machine won't allow it. This may occasionally be the case, but very often this problem is caused because the SHMMAX parameter has not been set large enough. SHMMAX specifies the maximum single shared segment size. If it is not set large enough, starting Oracle with too large an SGA will fail.

Check the SHMMNI and SHMSEG parameters as well. All are documented in your *Oracle Installation and User's Guide*.

Public domain monitoring tools

As long as UNIX survives, so will a vast array of nonproprietary tools and utilities. Some smart university graduate is always posting a bigger, better, faster, smarter version of some neat utility on a public domain bulletin board somewhere. While we would never encourage a DBA or system administrator to jeopardize data by using an untested utility, be aware that a number of older, tried, and tested utilities are always handy.

The most common tools that immediately come to mind are *top* and *glance*. These utilities are both powerful weapons in your arsenal when you are trying to diagnose a hardware bottleneck.

top

```
last pid: 12884;   load averages:  0.34,  0.25,  0.27    13:42:18
185 processes: 183 sleeping, 1 zombie, 1 on cpu
Memory: 245M real, 18M free, 77M swap, 644M free swap
   PID USERNAME PRI NICE  SIZE   RES STATE   TIME   WCPU      CPU COMMAND
   239 root      34    0 1444K  668K sleep   7:39  0.00%    0.00% inetd
 11846 oracle    34    0   25M 1400K sleep   7:32  0.00%    0.00% oracle
   263 root      34    0 1288K  600K sleep   7:15  0.00%    0.00% syslogd
     1 root      34    0  748K  172K sleep   2:27  0.00%    0.00% init
   394 root      34    0 1792K  736K sleep   1:49  0.00%    0.00% opcle
   273 root      24    0 1424K  572K sleep   1:12  0.00%    0.00% cron
 11700 oracle    24    0   24M 1744K sleep   0:53  0.00%    0.00% oracle
 11977 oracle    34    0   25M 2092K sleep   0:39  0.00%    0.00% oracle
 12203 oracle    22    2 3032K 1136K sleep   0:24  0.00%    0.00% ivan
```

glance

```
B3692A GlancePlus    B.09.01  13:47:49 sylx20  9000/887 Current  Avg  High
--------------------------------------------------------------------------
Cpu  Util SSSSSSSSNNNNRUUUUUUUUUUUU                      |  48%    55%   69%
Disk Util FFFFVVVVVVVVVVVVVVVVVVVVVVVVVVVVVVVVVVVVVVVV   |  94%    93%   94%
Mem  Util SUUUUUUUUUUUUUUUUUUUUUUUUUUUUUB                |  54%    54%   54%
Swap Util RRRRRRRRRRRRRRRRRRRR                           |  37%    37%   37%
--------------------------------------------------------------------------
```

```
                            GLOBAL SUMMARY
Users=22
                        User   CPU Util  Cum    Disk              Block
Process  PID  PPID Pri Name   (200% max) CPU    IO Rate   RSS  VSS  On
-----------------------------------------------------------------------
PSMON    315   291 168 root    0.9/ 0.2  89M    0.0/ 0.0   340  3504 SLEEP
PSRUNFS 2592  2544 158 psoft   0.0/ 0.0  0ms    0.0/ 0.0  1308  5112 SLEEP
PSRUNFS 2544  2473 168 psoft   0.0/ 0.0  14s    0.0/ 0.0  1308  5112 SLEEP
dataser  639  6638 154 control 0.9/ 0.9  328M   0.0/ 0.3  7508 16824 SLEEP
glance  7215  6951 148 oracle  0.7/10.9  1010ms 1.3/20.1  1936  2772 IO
midaemo 2204  2203  50 root    3.3/ 2.4  864M   0.0/ 0.0  1372  1372 SYSTM
opcacta 2230  2225 168 root    0.0/ 0.0  503s   0.4/ 0.0   208  1724 SLEEP
ora_arch 961   958 156 oracle   .0/ 0.2  60s    0.0/ 4.5 110mb 115mb SEM
ora_arch 126  2123 148 oracle  3.5/ 0.2  158s  71.1/ 5.6 84968 94960 IO
ora_ckpt 128  2123 156 oracle  0.0/ 0.0  18s    0.0/ 0.1 84924 94824 SEM
ora_ckpt 963   958 156 oracle  0.0/ 0.0  8360ms 0.0/ 0.1 110mb 115mb SEM
ora_db01 131  2123 156 oracle  0.1/ 0.2  113s   2.4/ 2.4 84904 94804 SEM
                                                        Page 1 of 7
```

VMS-Specific Tuning

When Oracle first began to emerge as a relational database management system, the VAX operating system was one of the most popular platforms for Oracle systems. Loosely coupled VAX configurations were a common Oracle environment. Even though the VAX environment has been outpaced by the open-system UNIX environments, it is still a popular production platform. This section contains hints for getting the best performance out of Oracle running on a VMS platform.

VMS Tuning Parameters

Several VMS operating system parameters have an impact on Oracle's performance. The more important of these parameters are the following:

BALSETCNT

Maximum number of working sets in memory. If this is set too low, swapping can occur and will seriously degrade performance.

MAXPROCESSCNT

Maximum number of processes currently in memory.

SRP

Number of preallocated small request packets. In the SH MEM command, the free level should always be greater than 100. Use the SH MEM command to make sure the free level is at least 50.

IRP

Number of preallocated I/O large request packets. Use the SH MEM command to make sure the level is at least 25.

NPAGEDYN

Size of the nonpaged dynamic pool in bytes. Use the SH MEM POOLFULL command to make sure that NPAGEDYN is never less than 100,000 during peak times. If it is, increase the value.

PAGEDYN

Size of the paged dynamic pool in bytes. Use the SH MEM POOLFULL command to make sure that PAGEDYN is never less than 200,000.

MPW_HILIMIT

Upper limit of modified page list. This is a SYSGEN parameter that you must set to 15% of the total physical memory size. The default is 500 pages.

MPW_IOLIMIT

Lower limit of modified page list. This is a SYSGEN parameter that you must set to half MPW_HILIMIT.

MPW_WAITLIMIT

Number of pages of the modified page list that will cause a process to wait until the next time the modified page writer writes the modified page list. This parameter must be set to the same value as MPW_HILIMIT.

MPW_THRESH

Lower bound of pages that must exist on the modified page list before the swapper writes this list to the free page list.

VMS Tools to Identify Bottlenecks

We find the VAX/VMS operating system a pleasure to tune because of the vast array of tools that it offers and the comprehensive set of tuning manuals that Digital Equipment Corporation provides. This section simply introduces the basic commands that we would use to tune a VMS/Oracle site. We strongly recommend that you get more information from the VAX/VMS manuals and consider using such performance tools as the VAX Performance Advisor (VPA) and the VAX Software Performance Monitor (SPM).

A very good place to start when attempting to tune your VAX application is the MONITOR utility. This utility allows you to easily monitor and report almost every conceivable area of interest. A number of the more useful MONITOR alternatives are detailed over the next few pages. One of the best MONITOR parameters is SYSTEM. This gives a complete overview of how your machine and database are currently operating. For example:

MONITOR SYSTEM

```
Node: HOFF                  VAX/VMS Monitor Utility    1-JUL-1996 08:16:41
Statistic: CURRENT              SYSTEM STATISTICS
                                                        Process States
            + CPU Busy (200)        -+      LEF:  43      LEFO:   0
            |#####################|         HIB:  61      HIBO:   0
CPU    0 +-----------------------+ 200      COM:   7      COMO:   0
            |                     |         PFW:   1      Other:  2
            +-----------------------+       MWAIT:  0
            Cur Top:  (0)                             Total: 114
            + Page Fault Rate (190) -+      + Free List Size (82489)-+
            |##|###################|        |#########         |208K
MEMORY 0 +-----------------------+ 100 0 +-----------------------+
            |                     |        |####################  |10K
            +-----------------------+      + Mod List Size (10214) -+
            Cur Top:  (0)
            + Direct I/O Rate (80)  -+      + Buffered I/O Rate(174)-+
            |#####################|         |#####################|
I/O    0 +-----------------------+ 60  0 +-----------------------+150
            |                     |        |                     |
            +-----------------------+      +-----------------------+
            Cur Top: (0)                    Cur Top: (0)
```

Identifying disk I/O bottlenecks

As we have mentioned throughout this book, the primary goals of disk I/O tuning are to balance the load of I/O across devices, to have sufficient disks and controllers to allow load sharing, and to have disks that process data fast enough to satisfy your needs. To identify a disk I/O bottleneck, check first to determine whether there are any outstanding requests for I/O waiting in the disk queue. To determine this, use the command

MON DISK / ITEM = QUEUE

```
                        VAX/VMS Monitor Utility
                          DISK I/O STATISTICS
                          1-JUL-1996 08:19:15
```

I/O Request Queue Length		CUR	AVE	MIN	MAX
1DUA5:	(HSC0) HOFSLSPAK001	1.98	1.81	1.63	1.98
1DUA6:	(HSC0) HOFSYSPAK002	0.66	0.82	0.66	0.98
1DUA8:	(HSC0) HOFMISPAK003	0.00	0.00	0.00	0.00
1DUA14:	(HSC0) HOFSYSBCK552	0.00	0.00	0.00	0.00
1DUA15:	(HSC0) HOFADVPAK001	0.00	0.00	0.00	0.00
1DUA17:	(HSC0) HOFMISARC001	0.00	0.00	0.00	0.00
1DUA19:	(HSC0) HOFMISPAK002	0.00	0.00	0.00	0.00
1DUA43:	(HSC0) HOFMISPAK004	0.00	0.00	0.00	0.00
1DUA45:	(HSC0) HOFHOMPAK001	0.00	0.00	0.00	0.00
1DUA46:	(HSC0) HOFMISPAK001	0.00	0.00	0.00	0.00
1DUA218:	(HSC0) HOFSYSPAK552	1.65	1.48	1.31	1.65
1DUA219:	(HSC0) HOFMISPAK005	0.00	0.00	0.00	0.00

The average queue length should be no greater than 0.2. You can also use the MON DISK command to observe the I/O rates per second to determine if the I/O rates for each disk device are approaching the maximum number of I/Os per disk device. Use the command

MON DISK / ITEM = ALL

```
                        VAX/VMS Monitor Utility
                          DISK I/O STATISTICS
                          1-JUL-1996 08:24:55
```

I/O Operation Rate			CUR	AVE	MIN	MAX
1DUA5:	(HSC0)	HOFSLSPAK001	0.00	0.11	0.00	0.33
1DUA6:	(HSC0)	HOFSYSPAK002	9.96	13.17	9.96	18.60
1DUA8:	(HSC0)	HOFMISPAK003	7.30	5.31	0.00	8.63
1DUA14:	(HSC0)	HOFSYSBCK552	0.00	0.00	0.00	0.00
1DUA15:	(HSC0)	HOFADVPAK001	0.00	0.00	0.00	0.00
1DUA17:	(HSC0)	HOFMISARC001	0.00	0.00	0.00	0.00
1DUA19:	(HSC0)	HOFMISPAK002	0.66	0.44	0.33	0.66
1DUA43:	(HSC0)	HOFMISPAK004	0.00	1.32	0.00	2.32
1DUA45:	(HSC0)	HOFHOMPAK001	0.00	0.00	0.00	0.00
1DUA46:	(HSC0)	HOFMISPAK001	0.33	0.33	0.00	0.66
1DUA218:	(HSC0)	HOFSYSPAK552	1.32	1.88	0.66	3.65
1DUA219:	(HSC0)	HOFMISPAK005	0.00	0.00	0.00	0.00

If a disk is approaching its maximum load capacity, which is usually 40 I/Os per second, you should seriously consider spreading the load. Consult Chapter 13, *Tuning Parallel Query*, for advice.

You can also determine whether extraordinary activity is occurring by looking at the individual processes that are consuming most I/O activity. You might find out that last night's backups are still running! At several sites where we've worked, we've found that the root of performance problems is a developer investigating problems on the production machine.

To find out the heavy users of I/O and the ones succeeding in obtaining I/O, issue the command

MON PROC / TOPDIO

```
                        VAX/VMS Monitor Utility
                      TOP DIRECT I/O RATE PROCESSES
                          1-JUL-1996 08:22:19
                    0         5        10        15        20
                    + - - - + - - - + - - - + - - - + - - -+
                    |       |        |        |          |
  2023F3C6 PD_DETACHED_02  9  ##################
                    |       |        |        |          |
  2020439F BATCH_588       7  ##############
                    |       |        |        |          |
  20246551 BATCH_525       6  ############
                    |       |        |        |          |
                    |       |        |        |          |
                    |       |        |        |          |
                    |       |        |        |          |
                    |       |        |        |          |
                    + - - - + - - - + - - - + - - - + - - -+
```

To determine whether your system is suffering from excessive paging, you can query the paging statistics by specifying

MONITOR PAGE

```
                         VAX/VMS Monitor Utility
                       PAGE MANAGEMENT STATISTICS
                         28-JUN-1996 15:53:01
                              CUR        AVE        MIN        MAX
Page Fault Rate             120.33      96.41      49.66     122.25
Page Read Rate                0.00       3.08       0.00       7.33
Page Read I/O Rate            0.00       0.49       0.00       1.66
Page Write Rate               0.00       0.00       0.00       0.00
Page Write I/O Rate           0.00       0.00       0.00       0.00
Free List Fault Rate          0.00       4.32       0.00      11.66
Modified List Fault Rate      0.33       4.41       0.33      16.00
Demand Zero Fault Rate       28.66      50.79      28.66      95.68
Global Valid Fault Rate      91.33      36.30      13.66      91.33
Wrt In Progress Fault Rate    0.00       0.00       0.00       0.00
System Fault Rate             0.00       0.00       0.00       0.00
Free List Size            57616.00   57638.25   57573.00   57704.00
Modified List Size        10291.00   10303.25   10291.00   10335.00
```

If you discover that the disk containing your page and swap files is a problem and you suspect excessive paging and swapping, you can confirm this by using the MON IO command. Observe the "Page Read IO Rate" and the "Page Write IO Rate" in the output for paging and the "Inswap" rate for swapping. To help solve this problem, read the following section.

Identifying memory bottlenecks

Memory bottlenecks are almost always the result of excessive paging and swapping. The ideal situation is to have no paging and swapping activity at all; this option is usually too expensive because it requires the purchase of too much memory. VMS categorizes its paging into soft page faulting (within memory) or hard page faulting (to disk). Soft page faulting is preferable to hard page faulting because shuffling a process to memory is faster than moving it out to disk. Swapping occurs when an entire process is removed from memory and placed on disk. This is acceptable when a process is dormant but creates a performance problem when the process is active when swapped.

VMS differs from UNIX in that individual working sets (memory allocations) can be set on a per-user basis. We have found that categorizing your users into types and applying an appropriate working set quota for each user type can result in very efficient use of memory. For example, users who run complex forms will be assigned a larger working set quota than those who run simpler, smaller forms. You should have a large working set assigned to the user who runs overnight report so that you have the ability to assign a larger SORT_AREA_SIZE and avoid excessive working set increments and decrements and their associated CPU activity.

NOTE   VMS working set quotas are also assigned to the SYSTEM and Oracle user. Never reduce the working sets for these users unless you are absolutely certain that it is necessary. You must be in desperate need of memory and have reduced all other users' working sets before considering decreasing the working sets for these users.

The factor that determines whether either hard page faulting or soft page faulting occurs is the size of the page cache. (See the parameters MPW_LOLIMIT, MPW_THRESH, FREEGOAL, and FREELIM.) If hard page faulting is excessive, consider increasing these parameters as described in the previous section. If you have a lot of inactive users on your system, consider reducing the BALSETCNT parameter, which is the maximum number of working sets kept in memory. This will cause the swapping of dormant processes and provide more memory.

To determine which users are experiencing paging problems, run these commands:

MON PROC/TOPFAULT. Determines which processes are paging excessively. A well-managed site will be adjusting individual working sets frequently.

```
                              0           5          10          15          20
                              + - - - + - - - + - - - + - - - + - - - -+
   2024135F  _TNA2786:    16  |aaaaaaaaaaaaaaaaaaaaaaaaaaaaaaaaaaaaa      |
                              |         |          |          |          |
   2024093F  GVILLANI      6  |aaaaaaaaaaaa        |          |          |
                              |         |          |          |          |
                              |         |          |          |          |
                              |         |          |          |          |
                              |         |          |          |          |
                              |         |          |          |          |
                              |         |          |          |          |
                              + - - - + - - - + - - - + - - - + - - - -+
```

SHOW PROC/CONT. Determines how much memory each process is using and what it is doing. Make sure that a resource-consuming activity is not running during prime production time (not one of those developers again!).

```
                     Process _TNA2786:                     15:41:37
State                CUR              Working set              447
Cur/base priority    6/4              Virtual pages           3681
Current PC           7FFEE07E         CPU time      000:00:00:05.76
Current PSL          03C00000         Direct I/O               116
Current user SP      7FEB694C         Buffered I/O             419
PID                  2024135F         Page faults             2024
UIC                  [Oracle]         Event flags         E03D0007
                                                          80000000
$1$DUA218:[SYS2.SYSCOMMON.][SYSEXE]SHOW.EXE
```

SHOW SYS of MON PROC. Checks the memory being used by all processes.

```
Process Count:120       VAX/VMS Monitor Utility     Uptime:96 07:48:20
                             PROCESSES
   PID    STATE PRI   NAME            PAGES      DIOCNT   FAULTS  CPU TIME
2023C617  LEF    4  BATCH_238       153/443        178      613  00:00:15.9
20236D18  LEF    7  DROBERTS        10955/151     2379    22548  00:01:49.2
20237F19  LEF    4  FBELANTI_1      5335/7640     1411    11115  00:01:54.5
2023001A  LEF    5  ORA_SRVT004_FIN 837/2067       265     4996  00:00:14.7
2020011B  LEF   15  RDMS_MONITOR    0/95          1138    96136  00:02:22.9
2020011C  HIB   10  NETACP          0/988         1987     1571  01:59:48.3
2023341D  LEF    6  ORA_SRVT006_FIN 983/2177       290     5785  00:00:16.7
2020011E  HIB   10  LES$ACP         0/434           45      566  00:35:02.6
2020011F  HIB    9  REMACP          0/103            2       81  00:00:07.0
20232820  LEF    6  SERVER_00B2     114/373         63      737  00:00:01.5
20222F24  HIB    6  DCM_DISPLAY     105/2048     13766     6129  04:02:41.0
20239C26  HIB    6  Oracle          164/636        813    10597  00:00:34.3
2023F929  HIB    6  A2OPM_V1.5      304/1368       116     3740  00:10:40.7
2020012E  HIB   11  DCM_WATCH_DOG   105/490      56929     1278  09:04:06.4
2020082F  HIB    4  A4OPM_V1.5      321/1727       107     3757  00:06:01.3
```

Identifying CPU bottlenecks

CPU bottlenecks occur when there are processes waiting for CPU. CPU problems are commonly associated with memory and disk I/O problems. CPU bottlenecks can also occur when some user processes have been assigned higher priorities and are getting unfair use of the CPU. In addition to using the memory commands described in the previous section, use these commands:

MON STATES. The count returned should be as close to zero as possible and should never exceed 4. If any processes are experiencing CPU contention, they will appear with a state of COM or COMO.

```
                              VAX/VMS Monitor Utility
         +-----+                  PROCESS STATES
         | CUR |
         +-----+               28-JUN-1996 15:43:07
                              0         10        20        30        40
                              + - - - + - - - + - - - + - - - + - - - -+
Collided Page Wait            |
Mutex & Misc Resource Wait    |
Common Event Flag Wait        |
Page Fault Wait               |
Local Event Flag Wait      52 |aaaaaaaaaaaaaaaaaaaaaaaaaaaaaaaaaaaaaaaaaaaa
Local Evt Flg (Outswapped)    |
                              |
Hibernate                  65 |aaaaaaaaaaaaaaaaaaaaaaaaaaaaaaaaaaaaaaaaaaaa
Hibernate (Outswapped)        |
Suspended                     |
Suspended (Outswapped)        |
Free Page Wait                |
Compute                       |
Compute (Outswapped)          |
Current Process            1  |a
                              + - - - + - - - + - - - + - - - + - - - -+
```

MON PROC/TOPCPU. If MON STATES shows any processes waiting for CPU, this command allows you to perform further investigation:

```
                              VAX/VMS Monitor Utility
                              TOP CPU TIME PROCESSES
                              28-JUN-1996 15:43:42
                              0         25        50        75       100
                              + - - - + - - - + - - - + - - - + - - - -+
2023C244   BATCH_242      13 aaaaa
                              |         |         |         |         |
2022C9C0   ORA_SRVT009_FIN 3 a
                              |         |         |         |         |
202001AC   DECPS_DC        1
                              |         |         |         |         |
2024135F   _TNA2786:       1
                              |         |         |         |         |
2020011C   NETACP          1
                              |         |         |         |         |
2023E463   ORA_FINP_DBWR
                              |         |         |         |         |
20242B11   NBNS
                              |         |         |         |         |
                              + - - - + - - - + - - - + - - - + - - - -+
```

SHOW PROC/CONT. Views the current and base priorities.

NOTE   The higher the priority, the more CPU time slice a process will re-
              ceive. Do *not* adjust the priorities of any of the Oracle processes. Or-
              acle is finely tuned and depends on certain processes having
              identical priorities.

Other Tuning Hints

Here is an assortment of hints to make your Oracle system run more efficiently
under VMS:

Page and swap files

Make sure page and swap files are on a separate disk from the one that holds
the Oracle database. The page and swap files must be contiguous. The page
file is allocated dynamically, so it is important that the contiguous space on
disk is available to it. The swap file must be at least greater than or equal to
the value of (MAXPROCESSCNT * AVERAGE_WSQUOTA). To check whether
a file is contiguous under VMS, use the following command

```
dump / header / block (count : 0) file name
```

Types of transactions

Be aware of the types of transactions your users run. There may be a chance
that you can decrease the users' working set quotas, which will allow you to
free up memory for a larger SGA.

Contiguous disk space

Always defragment your disk before you create database files. This guarantees that the files will be contiguous on disk. In addition, you must make sure
that all programs are copied throughout the development life cycle (via the
COPY/CONTIG option) to ensure that programs are stored contiguously on
disk and to minimize the number of I/Os when the program is required to be
loaded into memory.

Shared executables

Ensure that all Oracle executables (e.g., SQL*Menu, SQL*Forms, SQL*Reportwriter, SQL*Plus) are stored as shared executables. The potential for memory
savings is enormous. Having SQL*Plus installed as a shared executable means
a saving of more than 1 megabyte per SQL*Plus user. Doing the same with
SQL*Forms saves nearly 2 megabytes per user. Sharing executables in this
way helps the whole system by freeing up memory that will allow the configuration to support more users or increase the size of the SGA. You will also
find that sharing executables reduces hard page faults.

SGAPAD

Ensure that the SGAPAD parameter is set large enough to store a large SGA. This parameter reserves contiguous shared memory. The larger the buffer cache, the faster Oracle runs. If you can increase DB_BLOCK_BUFFERS without having to relink this parameter, you'll have more flexibility in tuning.

VII

Appendixes

Part VII includes summary information. Appendix A is a summary of the features in recent Oracle releases, particularly those that have an impact on performance. Appendix B lists the common questions we hear about performance, their answers, and references to sections of the book where you can learn more. Appendix C contains a summary of how you can tune the Oracle Financials product. Appendix D describes the Oracle Performance Pack. Appendix E summarizes tuning suggestions for Oracle Forms. Appendix F provides two case studies that demonstrate common tuning issues. Appendix G, a list of Oracle's dynamic performance tables, is provided on the companion disk.

A

Summary of New Features

Oracle Corporation has introduced many new features over the years. It seems that every few months, a new version of Oracle hits our shelves with bigger and better functionality. In addition to describing these features in the relevant sections of this book, we have summarized them in this appendix so that you can refer to a single source when planning your migration path.

To keep your applications running efficiently and to take advantage of new performance features available in Oracle, you need to constantly review, test, and exploit every new feature that comes along.

Some versions offer more than others. When Oracle7.0 was first introduced, it was a whole new ball game for DBAs. It is hard to remember *anything* from Version 6 that did not get changed. The following sections track the introduction, growth, and maturity of Oracle since the early days of Oracle7.0. For further details on these features, refer to the appropriate chapters within the book.

Oracle7.0 Features

Performance enhancements

- Shared SQL pool
- Hashing clusters
- Optimal rollback segment size
- Multithreaded server
- Dedicated checkpoint process

SQL extensions

- Cost-based optimizer
  - ANALYZE command:
    Computed and estimated statistics,
    VALIDATE structure,
    LIST CHAINED ROWS
  - SQL hints
- TRUNCATE TABLE
- UNION ALL
- DELETE CASCADE
- Distributed option (two-phase commit)
  - Support for new datatypes:
    VARCHAR2
    LONG
    LONG RAW
    MLSLABEL
- Read-only snapshots
- RDBMS PL/SQL support
  - Stored procedures and functions
  - Stored packages: Persistent package variables
  - Table- and row-level triggers
  - Referential integrity constraints
  - Check constraints
  - Default values
- Enhanced view support
- CREATE VIEW WITH FORCE
- CREATE OR REPLACE VIEW
- SELECT * Support
- ALTER VIEW COMPILE
- Rollback segment enhancements
  - Online/offline run-time modification
  - Optimal size
  - PCTINCREASE parameter no longer supported

Backup and recovery improvements

- System change number (SCN) point-in-time recovery
- ALTER DATABASE backup control file (to trace)

- Multiplexed online redo logs
- Parallel server recovery improvements

Enhanced database security

- Roles
- Profiles
- System and object privileges
- Tablespace quotas
- Auditing enhancements
- ALTER SYSTEM command

Database structural changes

- New ROWID Format
- Maximum data file increased to 1,022
- MAXEXTENTS now data block size dependent
- SELECT access to tables while creating an index
- ALERT file name structure modified
- TRACE file name structure modified

Interactive menu interface for SQL*DBA

Parallel server support

Database alert support (DBMS_ALERT package)

Database session pipe support (DBMS_PIPE package)

SQL*Net 2.0

PL/SQL 2.0

- PL/SQL screen output (DBMS_OUTPUT package)
- Procedure and function overloading
- Dynamic user-defined tables
- User-defined records
- Local and/or stored procedures
- Local and/or stored functions
- Stored packages

Oracle7.1 Features

Performance enhancements

- Parallel query support
- Table cache extension

- Direct database reads for full table scans and sorts (Oracle7.1.5)
- Session cursor caching

SQL extensions

- Symmetric (multimaster) replication
- Inline SQL functions
- Unlimited number of triggers per table
- Remote sequence number support
- Dynamic SQL package
- Database job scheduling package (unsupported)

Backup and recovery improvements

- Parallel recovery
- Read-only tablespaces

Enhanced database security

- Remote database password encryption
- Remote_Login_PasswordFile support
- Snapshot groups

Introduction of GUI server manager (pending replacement of SQL*DBA)

SQL*Net 2.1

- GUI configuration support
- Oracle name server 1.0 support
- Encrypted passwords
- Dead connection detection

PL/SQL 2.1

- Inline stored SQL function support
- Dynamic SQL package
- PL/SQL shared pool package (DBMS_Shared_Pool Package)

Oracle7.2 Features

Performance enhancements

- Cost-based optimizer improvements
- Round-robin index and temporary tablespace extent allocation
- Virtual (V$) table indexing
- UNRECOVERABLE option
  - CREATE TABLE ... AS SELECT ...

— CREATE INDEX ...

- Parallel query extensions

  — CREATE TABLE ... AS SELECT ...

  — User-definable hash function cluster keys

- Parallel server improvements

  — Batch allocation of INSERT PCM locks

  — FREELIST GROUPS for indexes

  — FREELIST GROUP selection for INSERT operations

SQL extensions

- Cursor variables
- Dynamic data file resizing
- FROM clause "immediate view" query support
- Internal RDBMS job scheduling (supported)
- ALTER ROLLBACK SEGMENT *xxx* SHRINK TO *size*

Backup and recovery improvements

- Dynamically resizable data files
- Checksum computation and verification of data blocks and redo log blocks
- Internal RDBMS program registration
- Improve hot backup media recovery

Enhanced database security

- Wrapped PL/SQL
- Trusted stored procedures
- Network security improvements
- Enhanced space management facilities

SQL*Net 2.2

- Automatic client load balancing
- Secure network services security enhancements

PL/SQL 2.2

- Cursor variable support
- Server-side PL/SQL debugging
- Wrapped PL/SQL
- User-defined subtypes

Oracle7.3 Features

Performance enhancements

- Cost-based optimizer improvements

- Hash joins
- Parallel SQL execution of UNION and UNION ALL operations
- Faster index builds utilizing existing indexes
- Temporary specific tablespaces
- Direct database writes for sorting
- LRU latch scalability

SQL extensions

- Cost-based optimizer histograms
- Updatable "joined" views

Backup and recovery improvements

- Deferred transaction recovery at startup
- Standby database support
- Data file resilvering improvements
- Enhanced media recovery status reporting
- DBVERIFY utility to validate database data files
- Enhanced space management facilities
  — Unlimited extents
  — Tablespace COALESCE command
  — Object free space deallocation

Enhanced database security

- Parallel server security enhancements
  — Fine-grained locking
  — Instance registration
  — Parallel query resource awareness
  — Delayed-logging block cleanout

SQL*DBA discontinued

Faster export via direct path

Dynamic INIT.ORA system configuration

Improved multimedia support

Internet/World Wide Web support

SQL*Net 2.3

- Oracle name server 2.0 plug and play support
- Network route redundancy
- Enhanced diagnostics

PL/SQL 2.3

- Enhanced PL/SQL tables support
    - Multiple columns (PL/SQL records)
    - Call-by-reference support of PL/SQL tables
    - Record COUNT, FIRST, LAST, EXISTS, NEXT, PRIOR, and DELETE
    - Enhanced cursor variable support
- Stored (compiled) database triggers
- Direct flat file I/O support

OLAP support

- Bitmapped indexing

Oracle Trace support

Oracle Expert support

Oracle 8.0 Features

Performance enhancements

- Table partitions
- Index-only tablespaces
- LONG table-specific tablespaces (large data block size)
- Parallel INSERT, UPDATE, and DELETE support
- Support for up to 1,000 columns per table

SQL extensions

- Maximum fixed-column length increased to 2,000 bytes
- Maximum variable-column length increased to 4,000 bytes
- Object-oriented RDBMS support

Backup and recovery improvements

- No begin/end backup operation required for hot backups

Enhanced database security

- Database password lifetime expiration
- Minimum password length
- Password history
- Database password lifetime expiration

Full dynamic INIT.ORA system configuration

New ROWID format (increased from 6 to 10 bytes)

*UNRECOVERABLE SQL*Loader data loading*

B

Hot Tuning Tips

This appendix contains the performance questions that we are asked most frequently, along with brief answers and pointers to other sections in the book where you can get more information. (If no specific section reference is given, skim the whole chapter for information in this area.) The appendix is divided by role: planners and managers, designers and analysts, programmers; database administrators, and system administrators. In a few cases, the same question is asked from the perspective of several different roles because the advice for each role may be somewhat different.

Questions from Planners and Managers

Q: *Our organization's computer staff has asked for a larger computer. How can I be sure that there really is a need for a larger machine?*

This is a commonly asked question and a very sensible one. If you buy too large a configuration, it will cost your organization many millions of dollars. If you buy too small a configuration, it may severely disrupt your organization's day-to-day workload. Make sure your computer staff is able to answer these questions before you seriously consider buying a larger computer:

- Has your application been completely tuned? Is every response time within the standard specified in your service agreement? There can be no exceptions to the rule. Do not proceed past this point until your application is totally tuned!

- What is your average amount of memory per user, the expected disk I/Os per user, and the average CPU MIPS per user in the current configuration? You must know what you are using now before you can assess statistics for any new equipment or applications you'll be considering.

- What is the expected growth rate in users at your site? You'll usually need to plan for growth, but in some organizations, the number of users will actually be expected to drop over time. Make sure you have correct projections for your own organization.

- What resources are causing the most performance problems in your system? Is the machine short of memory? Is it experiencing CPU wait times? Is it I/O bound? Is it experiencing network bottlenecks? Make sure you get solid answers from your DBA and system administrator.

References:

Chapter 17, *Capacity Planning*

Q: *What size machine do I need?*

One of the advantages of Oracle is that applications can be developed on a small computer and run in production on a much larger computer. After you have cost-justified a computer purchase, seek information from other sites that are running similar sizes and types of applications. This is particularly necessary when you are buying a package written in Oracle. When you are ready to buy a computer for an application that you have developed in-house, you can get a more accurate idea of how big a configuration you need by running some of the programs on the type of computer you are thinking of buying. It is essential that individual programs be tuned prior to the test.

Ideally, collect statistics on the average I/O, CPU MIPS, memory usage, and network usage per user. Combine this information with the expected number of users and make some allowance for unanticipated activity on the system (perhaps 15%). This will give you a reasonably accurate formula for a realistic configuration.

References:

Chapter 17

Q: *My production users keep complaining that response times are poor. My computer staff denies it. Is there a way in Oracle to determine response times from an end-user perspective?*

Your computer staff will provide you with all types of performance figures, but these will probably be disjointed, for example, the time taken for the SQL statement against the database or the network response times for a predefined request. Production users are sometimes prone to overreact to response time problems, particularly when a system is slow. You need a means of having an independent function log put into the application and run as a production user would run.

Many application development tools (SQL*Forms included) provide functionality that allows the recording and replaying of keystrokes to simulate an interactive online user. Some sites use this facility effectively to record response time variations. It can also be used to provide proof that response times are within the requirements specified in your organization's tuning service agreement. It works like this: You record the time of day just before running (replaying) the recorded function(s) and/or inquiries using the recorded keystrokes; after exiting the routine, you again record the time of day. If your site is running a client-server configuration, make sure you run the same script from the various client machines. This is necessary because of the possible variable response times that may exist at the various client machines. The limitation of this approach is that only a subset (nonupdate) of the business functionality can be replayed.

Q: *How can I increase the chances that my application will perform well?*

Like any other construction, if sound foundations are not in place for Oracle applications, the construction is doomed to failure. Here is a summary list of key performance hints that will help you to plan and manage your Oracle system to get the best performance out of it.

- If possible, make sure your development staff consists of people who have worked on highly tuned Oracle applications in the past. There is no substitute for experience.

- Identify and correct potential problems early in the development life cycle. If poor decisions are made during analysis and design, fixing the problem later on will take a lot longer and cost a lot more money.

- Make sure you have solid standards (for software selection, version control, modular programming, system libraries, and other such topics) in place at all stages of the development life cycle.

- Put in place a tuning service agreement that includes strict response time requirements. If you are buying a canned package, make sure that package also meets your standards for response time.

- Do not allow developers and quality assurers to work on the same machine as production users.

- Remember that, like one bad apple in the barrel, one Oracle program, or even one SQL statement, that performs very poorly has the potential to degrade the performance of all of the functions in the system. Worse still, if you put an untuned application on a machine that was previously running tuned applications, the untuned application will degrade the performance of all of the applications on the machine.

- Make sure that programs are developed and maintained in a modular fashion. This will decrease development time and memory requirements, and it will make the application easier to maintain.

- Make sure to log inactive users off the system after a specified period of time. Also, monitor those users who repeatedly log on two or three times, making sure there is a genuine need for their behavior.

- Code applications to best suit the particular configuration you are running. For example, make sure that your staff members are aware of the additional coding considerations for tuning client-server.

- Do not allow users to submit untuned ad hoc queries that will compete with online transaction-processing users on your system. Set up a procedure to review and tune all such ad hoc queries before they are run.

- Don't size your configuration too small; this may cause organization-wide poor response if an unanticipated workload appears on your machine.

- Check with other sites for their experiences with configurations similar to the one your site intends to use.

References:
Chapter 1, *Introduction to Oracle Performance Tuning*
Chapter 2, *What Causes Performance Problems?*
Chapter 3, *Planning and Managing the Tuning Process*
Chapter 4, *Defining System Standards*
Chapter 16, *Tuning in the Client-Server Environment*
"What Is Client-Server?" in Chapter 16
"Client-Server Performance Issues" in Chapter 16

Q: *What hardware should I buy?*

This is always a tough question to answer and one that should not be answered solely by the application DBA.

Q: *What level of Oracle support should I have?*

This simple question, unfortunately, does not have a simple answer. The required level of Oracle support is usually a cost-justified decision. Oracle has recently introduced a new set of advanced support categories. These categories range from Gold through Silver to Bronze. Many businesses ask me whether they actually need this support. My answer is always the same: "If you cannot afford the downtime, you will have to be able to afford the advanced support." Each manager needs to weigh the cost of his or her application's downtime. For example, can you afford to be off the air for 7 days, or is 1 day the absolute maximum acceptable outage? The Oracle support that you finally choose will need to be carefully balanced against the cost of your application outage.

Q: *Why should I upgrade to the next release of Oracle?*

Many customers have been forced to upgrade their version of Oracle software. This exercise can be time consuming, expensive, and very frustrating. So why do you have to upgrade? The usual reason is a desupported version of an Oracle release or a bug in your current version of Oracle that is fixed only in the next release with no back ports. Both of these reasons seem to confuse management when you try to explain how long it will take to actually perform the upgrade, the amount of application testing that will be necessary, and the overall cost of the exercise in real dollars. There is no reason I can give that will ease your pain. Always remember that no Oracle upgrade is simple. You must treat upgrades with due respect, extensively test your application before upgrading your production environment, and prepare for the worse.

Q: *Do I have to upgrade to the next release of Oracle?*

Oracle does not insist that you continually upgrade to the current release but will not provide version support for releases that have been classified as desupported. Normally, a minimum of 18 months notice is given before a release is desupported. This still does not mean that Oracle can force you to upgrade your release. We support a number of customers who still have Version 6 databases. Their decision to remain on older versions is partly due to the expense and inconvenience of upgrading and partly due to circumstance, for example, key applications have not been certified (upgraded) against current Oracle releases.

Q: *Should I rewrite all my applications using GUI developments tools?*

Many managers are faced with the decision of whether to continue supporting/maintaining their existing applications or to replace them with a new GUI design. Even current developments are faced with the indecision of character mode or GUI user environments. Our answer is always the same: use the environment that suits your user needs. GUI applications made a huge push a few years ago; if it wasn't GUI, it wasn't good enough. Ideas have since changed. Project leaders are recognizing the importance of character-based applications and the advantages they present. Many users are becoming more and more frustrated with inconveniences of GUI applications and the time it takes to enter a large amount of data. In summary, do not feel pressured to develop GUI applications; develop what suits your user base. More important, do not feel pressured to replace existing character-based applications if they are still meeting your user requirements.

Questions from Analysts and Designers

Q: *I have problems making overnight jobs perform. Are there ways I can improve their responsiveness?*

From a design perspective, there are many ways to improve the responsiveness of overnight jobs. This book assumes that the design specification is detailed enough to determine the language used in development and a pseudo-English description of what each statement should do. The designer will also have a large say in the physical tables that the programs use. Overnight jobs normally include data loads to and from other applications as well as overnight reports. The following checklist summarizes special considerations for the design of overnight jobs:

- If you are transferring data from an application, make sure that each table that is to have data taken from it has a column that stores the date modified. This will make it more efficient to transfer the day's changes using an index on the date-modified column.

- If data load tables have to be created for any temporary tables, make sure the table and any indexes created on the table are correctly sized. Create the indexes after the rows have been placed into the tables. Following this advice causes your application to run significantly faster. It is also much faster to drop and recreate tables instead of deleting from a table.

- Be aware that PL/SQL offers advantages in performing updates.

- Make sure there aren't multiple UPDATE statements against the same table. There are ways of updating many columns with a single statement.

- Don't join tables or perform MINUS operations across the network. Distributed database transactions, both query and update, can have disastrous effects on both network and database performance.

- Look for alternatives to all "complex" SQL statements. Do not be afraid to experiment; for example, do not use NOT IN in your program, try NOT EXISTS instead.

- Create an extract file or a number of extract files for overnight reports. These extract files can then be used by all of the reports, instead of requiring each individual report to traverse through many tables in the database over and over again. Make sure that the extract tables are correctly sized.

- Be aware of the power and speed of the MINUS command when you are performing audit checks of tables that store running totals against tables storing individual transactions (e.g., financial year totals for a region against individual transactions for a region).

References:

Chapter 15, *Tuning Long-Running Jobs*

Q: *A request has been made for users at my site to be able to run reports during peak usage times. Benchmarks have shown that they will run too long and adversely affect the interactive users. What can be done?*

To achieve acceptable response times for reports that are run during prime production times, consider the following:

- You may need to provide data redundancy, particularly to store aggregated totals.

- If the users need to run several reports against the same set of data, create a temporary extract table for the users' selection criteria; this table can then be reused for subsequent reports. Doing this avoids the expensive task of traversing repeatedly through many database tables.

- If the data "as of last night" is satisfactory for any reports, produce a set of multi-indexed redundant tables and run the reports against them. Ideally, there should be no more than three extract files.

- Make sure that each report has been extensively tuned in the development and quality assurance environments before it is placed into production. An untuned report will have a very damaging effect on a site's response times.

- If any reports run for longer than 2 minutes, ask the question "Must this report be run during prime usage times?" Ideally, no online report should run for longer than 45 seconds. This goal often appears out of reach; but given sufficient effort, redundant storage of data can usually help you meet this goal.

References:

"Denormalizing a Database" in Chapter 5

"Creating Overnight Extract Tables" in Chapter 15

Q: *Our database is fully normalized, but response times are bad. How can this be?*

A fully normalized database is often not able to provide satisfactory performance for complex queries within a medium-to-large-sized application. You might need to consider denormalizing some of the data. Don't denormalize just for the sake of doing so. A good designer knows what the requirements of the data model are and what future user requirements will be. If you are considering denormalizing, first make sure your data model is fully normalized. Then check each step to determine whether the system resource to maintain the redundancy outweighs the improved query speed benefits achieved by storing the redundant data. Situations that are candidates for denormalization are the following:

- A fixed number of children, for example, 12 months of the year.

- Storing the most recent data in a parent, for example, the latest transaction date made against an account.

- Static data such as MALE or FEMALE. You can hard-code such data.

- Running totals, such as financial year totals for a given account.

- Reference (domain lookup) tables. You can combine these into one domain table.

Some relational theory dictates that surrogate keys must be created for all tables in case the natural key fields are required to be changed. If carried to its logical conclusion, this theory also dictates that the surrogate key will be transferred to all child tables. The problem is that most queries are made by using natural keys rather than surrogate keys. If the natural keys are not likely to change, or rarely change, the natural keys should be transferred to all child tables.

Keys should be stored below the immediate child of the owning table to the child of the child in any case; for example, the account ID may be transferred to the transaction and the transaction description table.

References:
  Chapter 5

Q: *I don't have experience with a relational database. The programmers, who are very experienced with Oracle, keep telling me my data model is not suited to a relational database and performance will suffer. How can I check this?*

If the data model that you have created is perfectly normalized, you might need to perform some denormalization to achieve acceptable performance. This is not unique to relational databases. Even high-speed hierarchical databases like IMS are full of redundancy.

It is important that the designer listens to the programmers for their reasoning on why response times may be affected by the data model. It is also important that the programmers are given the opportunity to provide feedback. The earlier these types of problems are determined, the better. If they are not found early, a lot of code may have to be reworked after the data model is changed.

Program reviews are essential to ensuring that the data model is adequate. They should be attended by the designer, the programmer who will write the program, and the DBA. Performance is one of the aspects that should be included in the review.

Here is one rule of thumb: If the programmer has to join more than five tables for any one query in an interactive program, there is a good chance that the data model is inadequate. This is often caused by the overuse of surrogate keys, while database searches are made by natural keys.

References:
  Chapter 5

Q: *When and what do I index? How many indexes should I have on each table, and how do I know when I have too many indexes?*

Some sites have rigid rules for the maximum number of indexes per table (usually five or six). Such a rule should be taken as a guideline, not as an absolute. If a table is not very volatile, there may need to be many more than six indexes simply to satisfy all search criteria.

The bottom line is that your response times must be within those specified within the tuning service agreement for your organization. If a seventh index is added to a table and causes a response time reduction from 45 seconds to 1 second and the modifications to the table have their response times increase from 2 seconds to 2.5 seconds, the users are likely to be happy to have the seventh index added.

Redundant extract tables are often created overnight for use by overnight reports and GUI users. These tables tend to contain many columns and are often accessed from many different angles. There is nothing wrong with having many indexes on these types of tables, because they will not be modified after their creation.

References:
  "Using Indexes to Improve Performance" in Chapter 6

Q: *When is it a good time not to index?*

In general, don't apply an index in the following circumstances:

- If all the columns of the required index already apply to another index over the same table with the same *leading* columns, in the same *order*

- When a table is better accessed using full table scans, because every time the table is queried more than 15% of the rows are returned

- When columns are very long. Indexes on very long columns are not recommended. Indexes on LONG and LONG RAW columns are not allowed and should not even be contemplated.

- When it may speed up one program at the expense of slowing down several other programs. It is a good idea not to index until this type of problem is fully resolved.

Q: *How far should I denormalize?*

You should not denormalize any more than is required to meet the response times specified by your site's service agreement. An astute designer will be aware of the parts of the data model that are likely to result in unsatisfactory performance. There are no hard-and-fast rules that can be followed. Judge each data model on its own merits.

Suppose that an inquiry screen is intended to display financial year running totals for an account from a financial transaction table. The maximum number of transactions that any account may have is 300. You'll need to perform 300 reads from the index plus an additional 300 from the table, totalling 600 physical reads. Assume that your site has a computer that can perform 50 I/Os per second; 600 physical reads will take 12 seconds. This is a case in which specifying a redundant table that stores an account's financial year totals could greatly improve performance. The type of calculation that we've done above does give an early warning that a redundant table might be required.

References:
    Chapter 5

Q: *Is it preferable to have a few large programs in an application or many smaller programs?*

The ideal way to develop an Oracle application is in a modular fashion. Code each function of the application (e.g., maintain account details) once in a separate form; do not repeat the same function many times. For example, don't include account detail updating functionality inside many application modules. Users may sometimes dictate that such specific modularization is not the way they would like to use the system, so you may have to balance different needs. There are ways to call modules to provide all combinations of functionality requirements.

Keep your online programs small and concise, and make sure that each performs a specific function. This approach will save development time because the same code will not have to be recoded over and over. It will also make the system more maintainable. From a performance perspective, smaller forms use less memory, thus making more memory available to add additional users or increase the size of tunable parameters such as the block buffer or the log buffer. This helps to improve the overall responsiveness of the system.

References:
    Chapter 4

Q: *Our managers are very keen on taking advantage of the GUI interfaces that are able to access the Oracle production database on an ad hoc basis. What design issues should I consider?*

The number of ad hoc GUI users accessing Oracle database is expected to grow significantly during the next few years. It is important that you design the data model to cope with growth in this area. Ad hoc GUI users tend to want to retrieve data from the data model as quickly as possible without having to understand the intricacies of a complex data model. The ideal way to present data to this type of user is usually in the form of a wide, denormalized table resembling a spreadsheet.

The best time to create this type of table is overnight. However, if this is unsuitable for the users at your site, you could create it in a fashion similar to the online reporting users described earlier. Consider the following:

- You may need additional redundancy, particularly to store running totals.

- If users will require several extracts against the same set of data, create a redundant spreadsheet table using the user's selection criteria and then reuse it for subsequent GUI downloads. This avoids the expensive task of traversing through many database tables.

- Tune each type of extract extensively in the development and quality assurance environments prior to being allowed into production. An untuned extract will have a very damaging effect on a site's response times.

- If any extract runs for longer than 2 minutes, ask the question "Must this extract be run during prime usage times?" Ideally, no online extract should run for longer than 45 seconds. This goal may seem out of reach, but if you try hard enough to implement redundant storage of data, you can usually achieve response times within this limit.

References:
 "Denormalizing a Database" in Chapter 5
 "Creating Overnight Extract Tables" in Chapter 15

Q: *How can I force Oracle passwords to expire after a preset time period?*

As DBAs, we are constantly asked this same question. Why don't Oracle passwords expire the same as operating system passwords? How can I force the users to change their passwords after initial account creation? The answer is never well received: "This is not possible at the moment." Oracle8 has finally committed to providing database password lifetime expiration.

Q: *Is there any way of performing flat file I/O from within the database?*

Oracle7.3 supports direct flat file I/O via a special database package extension. This package supports only server-side operations but goes a long way to curing a number of Oracle to non-Oracle communication problems.

Q: *Should I design for a single large package or several smaller packages?*

This is a very interesting question and one that needs thorough discussion before any decisions are made. We would never encourage an enormous, single application package; neither would we encourage hundreds of small, single-function packages. A happy medium needs to be reached. Grouping the application's procedures and functions into manageable packages is generally the best way to proceed. Each package contains related application modules that are closely related or interlinked. When the first module of the package is referenced, all other modules are also read and loaded, ready for further user access. Remember to pin larger packages into the shared pool at database startup time, moving some of the parsing overheads from the user process to the startup procedure.

Q: *Can we design and use our own SQL functions?*

Oracle7.1 was the first release to support user-defined inline functions. This facility is very powerful and should never be overlooked. Analysts and designers must have a thorough understanding of how inline functions work and the performance savings they can deliver. Inline functions are invaluable for client-server environments, large reporting programs, and even everyday OLTP querying.

Q: *Does Oracle provide any form of automatic job scheduling?*

A special RDBMS package is provided by Oracle to allow job scheduling. This package is called DBMS_JOB and was first officially supported with Oracle release 7.2. Designers must be aware that only Oracle's own stored packages and procedures can be scheduled. There is no support or communication with the outside world.

Q: *How can I hide the applications security module code from prying eyes while still making it generally available for public user?*

This is a very interesting question about a feature that any data-sensitive application requires. Some stored Oracle objects need to be protected from inquisitive users. You want users to execute the procedure without being able to actually read the code. You may need to issue special application gateway procedures to remote databases and/or clients. How can you do this without giving away all your trusted secrets? Oracle7.2 has introduced wrapped PL/SQL support. This allows us to encrypted (wrap) a PL/SQL module and issue it decoded form. Other Oracle databases can decipher the encrypted code while the human eye cannot.

After all, Oracle has been issuing many of its sensitive RDBMS procedures in wrapped form for many years.

Q: *Can my database communicate via the World Wide Web?*

Oracle7.3 has incorporated WWW access directly into the database kernel. By simply upgrading to this latest release and enabling the correct INIT.ORA parameters, it is all there, for free. Obviously, it is not as simple as this; a firewall will need to be established and restricted access will have to be set up and controlled. What is of importance is that access is now very plausible and quite possible.

Q: *Is a distributed Oracle database environment possible?*

Every Oracle textbook will tell you how to design and code a distributed database environment. We all know that it can be done in principle, but is it actually plausible? Distributed joins, two-phased commits, remote procedure calls and *N*-way snapshots are all supported by Oracle. So should you dive into a fully distributed environment? This question cannot be answered lightly. Other, outside influences need to be considered. Can your network support distributed traffic? Is it stable enough? Do you really need a distributed database? These and many other questions need to be answered before you even consider the task. Just because you can doesn't mean that you should.

Q: *Should we build referential integrity into our database?*

We have been involved with many databases—even those designed by Oracle's own staff—that have no referential integrity (RI) at all. RI is a logical concept that should be included in your database design. Incorporating it into your physical design should not be taken for granted. Similar to database normalization, RI is a good concept and works well most of the time. In areas in which performance may be tested, always reconsider database RI. Similar to normalization, we need to always consider denormalization for key areas that are essential to the application's performance.

Questions from Programmers

Q: *How do I structure a SQL statement for performance?*

There are many factors to consider in structuring a statement for performance. You must understand the Oracle optimizer, the benefit of indexes and how they are best used, the effect of positioning table names in the FROM clause, the availability and usage of SQL HINTS, and the order of the conditions in the WHERE clause. Pay attention to this checklist:

- Be sure to tune SQL statements thoroughly to return data in the least amount of time.

- Use a WHERE clause if at all possible to assist with index usage.

- Never do a calculation on an indexed column if you intend to use the index to assist with response times. For example, don't specify

  `WHERE SALARY * 12 > 50000`

- Never specify IS NULL or IS NOT NULL on index columns.

- If more than 25% of the rows in a table are going to be returned, consider a full table scan rather than an index.

- Avoid using NOT in any WHERE condition.

- Use UNION instead of OR.

- Avoid the use of HAVING; in general, use WHERE predicates instead.

- Minimize the number of times a table is queried and maximize the number of columns updated with a single SQL statement.

- Use table aliases to prefix all column names.

- Use DECODE to minimize the number of times a table has to be selected.

- Do not mix data types because it may prevent use of the index, for example, an index won't be used in the following:

  `WHERE EMP_NAME = 123`

- Use joins in preference to subqueries.

- The ordering of the table names in the FROM clause determines the driving table. If you are using the rule-based optimizer, if the clause is ordered correctly it can significantly reduce the number of physical reads required to satisfy the query. Oracle initially scans and sorts the table specified *last* in the FROM clause using any available indexes. Oracle then reads the second table, which is positioned *second to last* in the FROM clause and merges its data with the data returned from the table specified last. Therefore make sure that the table specified last in the FROM clause will return the fewest rows based on its WHERE conditions. This is not always the table that has the fewest rows in it.

- Consider breaking down complex, multitable join SQL statements into procedural PL/SQL blocks. This approach can be easier to code, easier to maintain, and more efficient overall.

- Learn to use the tuning utilities TKPROF and EXPLAIN PLAN. Both these tools have improved over the years and provide a wealth on insight into the internal workings of the database and the optimizer. A though understanding of both these tools is essential when beginning any large application tuning.

References:
  Chapter 6, *Tuning SQL*
  Chapter 7, *Tuning PL/SQL*

Q: *How do I tell how much elapsed time each statement uses in an overnight SQL procedure?*

It is good practice to run all long-running SQL procedures with the following settings:

SET TIMING ON

Shows the elapsed time needed for the SQL statement to complete, in the form `real: 1.2866`

SET TIME ON

Shows the time of day next to the SQL prompt; for example:

```
17:13:26 SQL>
```

DOC

Provides documentation entered by the programmer to indicate each step run in the procedure; for example:

```
17:15:32 DOC>
17:15:32 DOC> Running the load of the transaction table
17:15:32 DOC>
```

Q: *How do I investigate a problem with an application module?*

Developers are often overwhelmed by the size and complexity of an application module when trying to tune it. A single program may have hundreds and hundreds of individual SQL statements. Where do we start? The answer is really quite easy. By placing the program in trace mode and rerunning it, we are immediately able to identify those SQL statements that need to be tuned. This is nearly always less than 5% of the overall program statements. Once you have identified the poorer SQL statements, extract them as single entities, and tune them one at a time.

Programs can be placed in trace mode by:

- Placing the entire database in trace mode (i.e., INIT.ORA parameter SQL_TRACE=TRUE).

- Enabling trace within the program module. This will require a programming change to the module. For example, a Pro*C program would include the line

  ```
  EXEC SQL alter session set sql_trace = TRUE;
  ```

- Enabling trace mode once the program has began executing. This can be done via the ORADBX utility but will trace only SQL statements that are executed after the program have been activated.

References:

Chapter 10, *Diagnostic and Tuning Tools*

Q: *How do I investigate a problem with a SQL statement?*

Assuming that you have identified the particular SQL statement that is causing the problem, extract it from the program code and investigate it as a single item. SQL statements (nondynamic) will perform identically, whether they are executed as a single unit or contained within a complex routine.

You will need to isolate all bind variables and replace them within the statement with their corresponding constant values. SQL*Plus is the best utility to begin using for statement investigation. Set statement timing on, and repetitively execute the statement to check that it is actually slow. Many statements that you originally think are slow actually turn out to be part of slow programs or the result of slowness in other SQL statements.

Enable SQL_TRACE to identify which indexes (if any) are being used. Before you proceed, make sure you know all available indexes and have an idea of all desirable indexes. Use TKPROF to interpret the trace output.

The actual execution plan of a single SQL statement can be detailed via the EXPLAIN PLAN or TKPROF utilities. This utility not only indicates which indexes are being used, but also shows the sequence of the index execution and the internal data sorts and sort/merges that are performed.

Never be afraid to experiment. Every statement has many, many alternatives. Only one alternative can possibly be the most efficient. Try all the alternatives. Replace NOT IN clauses with NOT EXISTS clauses. Try using table joins rather than subqueries. Always break statements down to their lowest levels. Extract each subquery or UNION portion from the statement and test it on its own.

You should also identify data volumes via SQL*Plus. A statement may, in fact, be efficient, but may be acting over many thousands of records. If this is the case, you will need to revisit the application program and possibly redesign it. Try to break down the functionality into smaller actions. Use of array processing can improve SQL using large volumes of data.

Investigate any SQL statement using an ORDER BY, a GROUP BY, or a HAVING to make sure that the grouping or ordering is actually required. Many statements consume large amounts of system resources performing unnecessary table *sorting*, not realizing that the rows can be returned in the desired sequence via an index.

If your SQL statement contains a UNION clause, ask the question "can/should the UNION be replaced by a UNION ALL"? UNION statements need to pre-sort all selected rows and filter out and duplicates. This may be necessary in a small number of circumstances, but is often an unnecessary overhead that could have been avoided. UNION ALL statements return all records, duplicates included, so do not have to sort or filter either of the record data sets.

Be careful of type casting problems. Index paths will be used when testing SQL statements with constants, but may not be used when a bind variable is of an incorrect type.

After you have tuned an individual statement, replace the new SQL back into the originating routine and test for the problem again. Remember too that badly performing SQL can also be due to locking contention.

References:
    Chapter 6
    Chapter 7
    Chapter 8, *Selecting a Locking Strategy*
    Chapter 10, *Diagnostic and Tuning Tools*
    Chapter 16

Q: *Our site has decided to go with Oracle7. Can our SQL*Forms Version 3 application run under Oracle7? What changes are recommended to improve performance?*

In our experience, all applications that are developed by using SQL*Forms Version 3 for RDBMS Version 6 will execute as intended when run against RDBMS Oracle7. This includes user exits, SQL*Plus scripts, SQL*Reportwriter programs, and Pro*C programs. Existing applications do not need to be modified when the database is upgraded. A Version 6 database can also access an Oracle7 database via SQL*Net Version 1 without modification.

New versions of the tools have been released to support Oracle7 functionality. This allows SQL*Forms to access stored procedures and triggers, truncate tables, and so on. Existing SQL*Forms 3 applications will also function normally when these upgraded executables are used (but may need to be recompiled). This permits new functionality to be introduced gradually into an existing application as time permits.

Q: *Sometimes my SQL query runs fast; other times it runs slowly. How can this be?*

Many SQL statements appear to work efficiently. When you investigate them using TKPROF and EXPLAIN PLAN, you find that the statement is executing as intended. So why do statements sometimes run slowly?

The first place to begin is to check what other jobs are running at the time the SQL is performing badly. The problem could actually be some other process that is completely unrelated. When an Oracle task needs a resource, it simply takes it!

However, if the machine is not CPU- and/or I/O-bound, then this is not the problem.

Check the Monitor Locks display to determine whether another process has any resources locked that are required by the waiting SQL process.

The most common reason for this problem is the uneven data spread of the table. Indexes are worth their weight in gold if they limit the number of records that need to be searched. Suppose the EMP table has an EMP_STATUS field that records an employee's employment status (active or resigned). When querying all active employees, the SQL must process 25,000 rows. When querying resigned employees, the SQL has only 250 rows to process. This problem is magnified when the offending SQL also has an ORDER BY clause. Sorting 20 records can be performed in memory, but enormous sorts must write temporary segments to the temporary tablespace. If this situation begins to cause a real problem, try to make your indexes more precise.

References:
    Chapter 6
    Chapter 8

Q: *Is it possible to perform dynamic queries against the database?*

Dynamic SQL is a very powerful programming facility. Dynamic SQL statements can be individually shaped to suit individual situations. Each SQL statement can be formed to use the best possible indexes, removing repetitive AND/OR conditions that are not always required at all times.

All Pro* tools, Oracle Call Interface (OCI), and SQL*Plus facilities support dynamic SQL, some better than others. PL/SQL support of dynamic SQL was introduced with Oracle7.1 via the *dbmssql* package. This includes both client (local) and server-side (stored) PL/SQL. You can achieve enormous resource savings by using dynamic SQL. The WHERE clause can be altered. Even the ORDER BY clause can be added or altered. Dynamic SQL does increase the complexity of application development and maintenance.

References:
    Chapter 7

Q: *The form ran well in the test environment but is giving poor response in production. How is this happening?*

Many things can cause this situation, and you must investigate all of them. The most common problems are the following:

- Data volume variances between the two environments are always an area of concern. The development database has only a few hundred records per table. What was supposed to be a tuned, efficient program may turn out never to have been tuned. When applied against production data volumes, response times begin to reflect the inadequacy of the particular development environment.

- Indexes that are available within the development environment have not been generated or are different from the production environment. Extra indexes can even alter the performance of a SQL statement. The driving index is governed by the optimizer ranking but may not always be the best choice.

- Table and row locking contention always affect application performance. Most often during the development life cycle, programs are developed and tuned as standalone modules. When they are executed as part of the entire application, locking practices begin to conflict and damage response times.

- Poor response times can actually be due to a poorly tuned or configured production environment. The production machine may actually have memory shortages, disk I/O overloads, or abnormally high swapping. Before the migration of the last program, the machine was coping acceptably. One more program could actually have sent it over the limit.

- Different environment configurations can produce surprising results. Just because both environments are using Oracle does not mean that they will perform identically. If the target environment is a client-server environment, do not use a unitary development machine. If the physical distance between the two machines (client and server) is many hundreds of miles apart, allow for this during the development cycle.

References:
  Chapter 6
  Chapter 7
  Chapter 16
  Chapter 18, *Tuning for Specific Systems*

Q: *I am fine-tuning a program using TKPROF. I have noticed that the number of fetches on the tables is consistently twice the number of rows fetched. Why is this so?*

The reason for this problem is very straightforward. Every time the Oracle RDBMS performs a SELECT operation, it must execute a second database fetch to ascertain whether any more rows exist. If another row is located, an Oracle error is raised. The functionality is necessary to conform to ANSI standards.

It is easy to avoid this overhead. Use explicit cursors; you do this by specifying DECLARE, OPEN, FETCH, and CLOSE for all SELECT cursors. Do not use implicit, inline SELECT statements.

References:
"Using Explicit and Implicit Cursors in PL/SQL" in Chapter 7

Q: *How can I find out what indexes exist in a particular environment?*

Environment indexes are vital to the performance of an application. Be sure to document all indexes extensively and distribute them to your development staff. To review which indexes currently exist, use the Oracle views ALL_IND_ COLUMNS and ALL_INDEXES. See Chapter 17 for an example of the actual SELECT statement that you use to query (join) these tables.

References:
"Step 2: Structuring the Database and SGA" in Chapter 17

Q: *We are converting from a large non-Oracle application to an Oracle application. Loading the data into the new system takes four days. How can I reduce this time lag?*

Most data take-on tasks are performed via SQL*Loader. This utility is very fast and very effective. To speed up load times, increase the ROWS parameter to as large a value as possible. This parameter in effect increases the ARRAYSIZE or number of rows inserted per commit.

You can also achieve overall improvements by executing many simultaneous loads, provided that the loaded tables reside on different disks. Source data and the target database should also be positioned on different disks.

Do not load data into tables with prebuilt indexes, referential integrity, check constraints, or table triggers. Generate indexes after the table is fully populated. Do not perform data loads over the network. If you are using client-server architecture, perform all loads as a process on the database machine.

References:
"Tuning ARRAYSIZE" in Chapter 16

Q: *We have trouble getting our overnight reports completed within the required time frame. What can I do?*

Many areas of the overnight process can be improved, but programmers often neglect them. So much effort is put into refining online, interactive response times, but many fewer people seem to be concerned about whether the nightly routine takes 2 hours or 8 hours. However, when overnight processing cannot be completed during the overnight and encroaches onto the next day, all application users suffer. Chapter 15 describes the various areas of overnight processing that you can tune.

The first areas to address are SORT_AREA_SIZE, the Oracle buffer cache, temporary tablespace sizing, rollback segment allocation, rollback segment size, SQL array sizes, temporary extract tables, exploiting PL/SQL updating, breaking up the EXPORT, and tuning the EXPORT.

References:
   Chapter 15

Q: *My SQL is running very slowly. How can I tell whether it is using an index?*

The easiest way of identifying index usage is via the EXPLAIN PLAN facility. This utility can be run system-wide or as part of an individual connect session for a single SQL statement. You can use EXPLAIN PLAN standalone through SQL*Plus via the EXPLAIN PLAN verb or as a command line option of the TKPROF facility.

References:
   "SQL_TRACE: Writing a Trace File" in Chapter 10
   "TKPROF: Interpreting the Trace File" in Chapter 10
   "EXPLAIN PLAN: Explaining the Optimizer's Plan" in Chapter 10

Q: *I sometimes get errors when trying to recompile a very large database package. What is happening?*

Older versions of the RDBMS insisted on all cursors within the SGA's shared pool being held as a single contiguous block. This includes PL/SQL packages, procedures, and triggers. If your database has been operating for a while, the shared pool can become fragmented and not have a contiguous memory segment large enough to accommodate your package. This explains why your package will compile sometimes and not at other times. A short-term solution is to flush the shared pool. This clears out all nonrunning SQL statements. For example:

```
alter system flush shared_pool;
```

The other solution is to upgrade your database to Oracle7.3 or better, in which the requirement for a single, contiguous portion of memory has been lifted.

References:
   Chapter 7

Q: *Should I use stored procedures or packages?*

Both stored procedures and packages have their place in an application. Packages offer a little more flexibility and performance gains at the expense of taking a little longer to program. Because of the inherent flexibility advantages of packages (overloading, local package variables, multiple procedure loading, inline function support, etc.), we always recommend that programmers use stored packages rather than stored procedures.

References:
    Chapter 7

Q: *What can I do to speed up my database triggers?*

Row-level database triggers can be a very expensive way of applying business functionality. Programmers must investigate ways of reducing these overheads wherever possible. The following sections list some of the alternatives:

*   Avoid the trigger altogether. Many triggers can be replaced by table-level check constraints and/or column-level default values.

*   Reduce the size of the trigger text. Database triggers are not held in compiled form until Oracle7.3. If you are using RDBMS versions prior to this, move the trigger body text to a stored procedure and call the procedure from the trigger. This reduces the size of very large triggers down to a few lines.

*   Exploit the WHEN clause. Trigger WHEN clauses are held in compiled form and are part of the trigger definition. The WHEN clause is evaluated before any part of the trigger is executed. Properly formed WHEN clauses can reduce the run-time overheads dramatically.

References:
    Chapter 7

Q: *My database query is using indexes but is still slow. How can this be?*

Just because an index is being used does not always mean that the statement is efficient. Each index may be only one of many paths into the database. You must investigate whether any other (more efficient) index paths exist over the tables in question. What percentage of the table is being read? Would a full table scan be more efficient? Is the statement a multitable join? Are the tables and indexes in question fragmented with many extents? Is the overall application memory CPU or I/O bound? Does the index in question have a poor data spread? Is the correct index being used? Is the SQL driving table incorrect? If the SQL statement is a DML statement (UPDATE, INSERT, DELETE), are other processes locking resources that you require? Is your application running over a client-server environment and the statement clogging up network traffic? Is the SORT_AREA_SIZE too small?

One of the most common reasons for this problem is the use of an ORDER BY, HAVING, or GROUP BY clause. Even though the index is retrieving rows in the fastest possible manner, these types of clauses cause all rows fetched to be sorted before the first can be displayed. If more than 100 records are fetched, performance will be noticably affected. If more than 1,000 records are fetched, serious performance degradation will result.

In summary, you cannot assume that indexes will solve all your problems. Remember that SQL is the backbone of the database, not the indexes. Only by reading and applying all of the advice in this book can you completely answer the question.

References:
"The SQL Optimizer" in Chapter 6
"Selecting the most efficient table name sequence" in Chapter 6
"Efficient WHERE clause sequencing" in Chapter 6
"Which Is Faster: Indexed Retrieval or a Full Table Scan?" in Chapter 6
"Explicitly Disabling an Index" in Chapter 6
"Using WHERE Instead of an ORDER BY" in Chapter 6
"Optimizing INIT.ORA Parameters" in Chapter 15
"Exploiting Array Processing" in Chapter 15
"Creating Overnight Extract Tables" in Chapter 15
"Tuning ARRAYSIZE" in Chapter 16

Q: *I have developed a report that uses an index but still takes 45 minutes. An entire table is being reported upon. Can this be sped up?*

This problem is common and can take some investigation to solve. Other than addressing the underlying (driving) SQL statements (see the prior question), the most usual approach is to look at the amount of disk I/O and associated head movement that are needed as a result of the noncontiguous sequence in which the rows are read via the index. When large portions of a table are being read, it can be more efficient to perform a full table scan of the entire table.

Q: *We had a complex query that was very slow, and we replaced it with a view. The view is performing just as slowly. How can this be?*

Many programmers (and analysts) mistakenly believe that a view will cure the inadequacies of the underlying application design or of a poorly structured SQL statement. Views are simply shorthand representations of the underlying SQL. They can never be faster than their base SQL and, in fact, incur slightly more overheads. Views are not magical snapshots of complex multitable joins, nor are they automatically populated extract tables. Views of views will in fact cause even worse statement performance.

If your SQL statement is not performing the way it should, tune the statement; do not hide the poor performance in a database view.

Views can be used to speed up application performance over distant networks under certain circumstances. However, views do not solve general performance problems.

References:
   Chapter 6
   Chapter 16

Q: *I have a report that queries a large financial transaction table many times, totaling amounts for different types of transactions. This requires repeatedly reading through the table. Is there a better way?*

This problem is a common one and can be handled in a number of ways. Pay the most attention to your individual SQL statement(s). Assuming that the SQL has been tuned, what else can be done? A report should never have to traverse the same table more than once. Make use of the DECODE verb to satisfy varying selection criteria in a single table access. Depending on the reporting tool, you may also be able to use array processing (by setting ARRAYSIZE) to reduce network and database traffic.

Fetch only records of interest. Let the database do the work (via the various WHERE clauses), not the report logic! If the report is fetching a large percentage of the table rows, also investigate whether you might be able to disable table indexes altogether and use a full table scan. This will reduce I/O overheads and may improve overall performance.

References:
   "Using DECODE" in Chapter 6

Q: *A large table update is taking too long. How can I speed it up?*

Most programmers prefer to perform updates via one or more simple UPDATE statements. Even though this may be more attractive to code and clearer to read, the overall effect can be less efficient. If UPDATEs incorporate more than one subquery clause over the same table, they can often be combined into one subquery, reducing extensive I/O. This feature is commonly overlooked by many inexperienced programmers.

If you have larger updates, make use of array processing (ARRAYSIZE) whenever possible. This reduces overall network and database overheads.

PL/SQL is another powerful way to improve large UPDATE statement performance. Again, if the statement has a subquery clause, you can make improvements by setting up an outer driving loop (i.e., LOOP ... END LOOP) and performing the actual update multiple times inside the loop.

Large update routines should also consider locking strategies. These updates will prevent other processes from updating the same information. If you have processes that run for many minutes or more over core application tables during the day, you should consider batching the update into smaller, less restrictive units.

References:

"Using Pseudo-Code to Lock a Large Table" in Chapter 8
"ARRAYSIZE Parameter" in Chapter 15
"Using PL/SQL to Speed Up Updates" in Chapter 15
"Minimizing the Number of Updates" in Chapter 15

Q: *A large insert into a table is taking too long. How can I speed it up?*

All of the arguments for the previous question (large table updates) also apply to large table inserts. There are also several other ways to improve insert performance.

If possible, drop indexes over the table before inserting (importing) the new records and then recreate them afterward. This will give better overall insert performance.

For Oracle7 databases, disable all table integrity rules and stored triggers before loading the data and then reenable them on completion. All exception violations will be reported via an exception table.

If you are using a multiple-CPU machine, you might want to consider breaking your data into several smaller files and loading several streams simultaneously. With proper disk sharing and stream balancing, performance improvements can be linear (up to a point). Remember to increase a table's FREELISTS parameter to the maximum number of simultaneous streams to ease table contention during the data load.

References:

"Using Pseudo-Code to Lock a Large Table" in Chapter 8
"ARRAYSIZE Parameter" in Chapter 15
"Creating Indexes After Inserts" in Chapter 15
"Using PL/SQL to Speed Up Updates" in Chapter 15
"Minimizing the Number of Updates" in Chapter 15

Q: *How can I tell whether there are any indexes on my tables?*

You will need to execute the following query to identify all indexes for a table:

```
SELECT  INDEX_NAME, COLUMN_NAME
FROM    ALL_IND_COLUMNS
WHERE   TABLE_NAME = UPPER('__table_name__')
ORDER   BY COLUMN_POSITION
```

Q: *How can I tell whether there are any triggers on my tables?*

You will need to execute the following query to identify all triggers for a table:

```
SELECT DESCRIPTION, TRIGGER_BODY
FROM   ALL_TRIGGERS
WHERE  TRIGGER_NAME = UPPER('__trigger_name__')
```

Q: *How can I tell whether there are any referential integrity constraints on my tables?*

You will need to execute the following query to identify all referential integrity constraints for a table:

```
SELECT T.OWNER, T.TABLE_NAME, T.CONSTRAINT_NAME
FROM   ALL_CONSTRAINTS T,
       ALL_CONSTRAINTS F
WHERE  F.TABLE_NAME         = upper('__table_name__')
AND    F.CONSTRAINT_TYPE  in ('P', 'U')
AND    T.R_OWNER           = F.OWNER
AND    T.R_CONSTRAINT_NAME = F.CONSTRAINT_NAME
```

Q: *How can I tell whether there are any check constraints on my tables?*

You will need to execute the following query to identify all check constraints for a table:

```
SELECT CONSTRAINT_NAME, SEARCH_CONDITION
FROM   ALL_CONSTRAINTS
WHERE  TABLE_NAME        = upper('__table_name__')
AND    CONSTRAINT_TYPE   = 'C'
```

Q: *One table in our application takes much longer than other tables to query data, even though the index is very specific. What causes this and how can I speed it up?*

The most common reason for this problem is table and/or index fragmentation. If the table or the index is held in many extents, dispersed over the disk or a number of disks, performance will be affected. Ask your DBA to check your observations.

Other possible reasons for this problem may be row chaining and/or row migration within the table or poor index selectivity. If the indexed columns do not have an even spread over the table, the index can actually reduce performance.

Applications should never have both the table and its associated index(es) located on the same physical disk. This will cause the table to perform more slowly than other tables when reading via the index path.

You should also alert the system administrator to check the performance of the disk on which the table is located. Possibly, the disk is not as fast as other application disks (not all disks operate at the same speed), or the disk is exceeding its recommended I/O rates because of contention from other poorly tuned applications sharing the same disk.

Another possibility is a faulty disk. Normally, when devices encounter I/O errors, they perform a number of retries before giving up. This could also explain the problem.

References:
> "ANALYZE: Validating and Computing Statistics" in Chapter 10
> "Tuning I/O Spread" in Chapter 10
> "ONEIDXS.sql: Testing an Individual Index" in Chapter 10
> "Identifying Database Extents" in Chapter 10
> Chapter 18

Q: *I have the indexed column in the WHERE clause, but the index is not being used. Why?*

Indexes can be used only if at least the leading part of the index is referenced within the WHERE clause. Some indexes will actually be omitted from the execution path if other, more precise indexes exist over the same table (i.e., a UNIQUE index will override a nonunique index). If two indexes over a single table are both referenced via range predicates in the WHERE clause only one will be used; the other will be discarded.

The other more common reason is that the programmer has inadvertently incorporated the indexed columns within a SQL function. This could be via a complex DECODE or a simple date conversion macro.

Another possibility is that the cost-based optimizer has decided to deliberately ignore the index and use a full table scan. This decision is based on current database statistics and may not always be the best choice. Remember to refresh database statistics on a regular basis if you are using the cost-based optimizer.

References:
> "Explicitly Disabling an Index" in Chapter 6
> "Beware of the WHEREs" in Chapter 6

Q: *None of the SQL hints seem to be working. Why is this?*

SQL hints are a very powerful programming tool and should be exploited whenever possible. Unfortunately, hints are not as simple to code as they may first appear. Because hints are "intelligent" comments, they are simply ignored if they are incorrectly coded. No error or warning is given, no indication that the hint is being ignored. So when are hints ignored?

- Misspelled hints: Any misspelling of the hint type, table name, index name, and so on will result in the hint being ignored. Always remember to inspect the EXPLAIN PLAN output after every hint modification.

- Inappropriate hints: When a correctly structured hint is inappropriate within the context of the SQL statement, it is ignored. For example, if a hint references a table that is not included in the statement or an index that is not associated with the table, it is ignored.

- Conflicting hints: If a statement contains two valid hints that conflict with each other, they are both ignored.

- Invalid table identification: If tables in your SQL statement have aliases, then the alias must be referenced in the hint, not the actual table name.

- Invalid hint location: SQL hint can occur only immediately after the first SQL verb of the statement block. This means straight after the SELECT, DELETE or UPDATE verb. Positioning a hint anywhere else in the statement will cause it to be ignored.

- Older versions of PL/SQL: Prior to PL/SQL 2, all inline SQL hints are ignored.

Q: *Can I predict when a sort will take place?*

It is possible to preempt when a SQL statement will perform an internal record sort. This information can be used to determine what is the best access path to the database. The following SQL verbs will force a sort:

- GROUP BY
- ORDER BY
- DISTINCT
- HAVING
- UNION/MINUS/INTERSECT
- IN (... subquery ...)
- Merge joins

Questions from Database Administrators

Q: *I've just been appointed DBA at my site. I've been told that there are severe performance problems with production users. What do I do?*

We have observed that between 80% and 90% of all performance problems are caused by a poor database design or programs that are not coded efficiently. This leaves only 10% to 20% that can be gained by working on the database structure and parameters. If the application is correctly tuned, that 10% to 20% can be significant, however. The following steps will provide a structured path that you can follow to tune your site.

Gather information on any programs that are causing poor response times. Make *no* exceptions to this rule. You must thoroughly tune any poorly responding programs, then place them back into production with the response times rechecked. You must also repair locking problems.

Monitor the response times of users at all sites to establish whether the response problems are widespread or are confined to one site. Document information on each site's configuration, including the memory size, MIP rating of the CPU, recommended disk speeds, and network speeds. Also investigate usage patterns on a per-site basis. Do users log on to the system once or many times? What are the peak usage times? How many users are there? What are the typical memory, I/O, CPU, and network usage per user?

Next investigate the operating system monitor utilities.

If any disks are operating above their recommended I/O levels, is it possible to spread the disk load across other disks? If there is free memory remaining on the machine, disk I/O load can be transferred from the disks to memory. This can be achieved by enlarging the DB_BLOCK_BUFFER area, which will store tables, indexes, clusters, and rollback segments in memory. Disk writes can be reduced by increasing the amount of modified data buffered before writes are made to the redo log files. This is achieved by increasing the LOG_BUFFER parameter. Eliminating database fragmentation and chaining will also improve I/O problems. Increasing the size of the SHARED_BUFFER_POOL may also help to reduce disk activity. Savings will result only if the shared pool is currently too small and a lot of SQL statement reloading is occurring. If excessive disk writes to the temporary tablespace can be substantially reduced by increasing the SORT_AREA_SIZE parameter. A larger sort size reduces the number of database sorts that have to be buffered to disk because it is too large to fit into memory.

If there is a good deal of paging and swapping of processes caused by inadequate memory on the machine, Oracle's share of memory must be reduced by decreasing the size of the DB_BLOCK_BUFFER, the LOG_BUFFER, and the SHARED_POOL_SIZE parameters. It is possible at some sites that these changes can be made without adversely affecting Oracle's performance. Per-Oracle user memory usage can also be reduced by decreasing the SORT_AREA_SIZE parameter.

If there are regularly many processes waiting for the CPU, you can sometimes transfer the load from the CPU to disk by reducing the size of the DB_BLOCK_ BUFFER parameter. This should provide your site with better overall response.

However, it will reduce the likelihood of data being found in memory, and the reduced disk speed may slow down certain transactions.

If the network is causing the bottleneck, try to reduce the number of packets being passed across the network. This may require some recoding of programs. Locating the hardware appropriately (e.g., putting the client and server computers close together) can also improve responsiveness by sending the packets a lesser distance and making higher-speed lines a more cost-effective alternative. The number of packets transferred from the client machine to the user screen is minuscule compared to the large number of packets transferred from the server to the client processors.

References:
"Managing the Workload in Your System" in Chapter 3
Chapter 9, *Tuning a New Database*
Chapter 10
Chapter 11, *Monitoring and Tuning an Existing Database*
Chapter 16
Chapter 17
Chapter 18

Q: *How can I best use memory to improve response times? How can I monitor memory usage?*

Memory speed is at least several thousand times faster than disk access. If Oracle can be made to access more information from memory instead of disk, performance can be improved dramatically. Be careful not to use too much memory. If free memory is low, there is a high probability that paging and swapping will be excessive, which is much more damaging than the advantage of storing more information in memory. If many processes are waiting for CPU in certain situations, Oracle's use of memory can be transferred from memory to disk by decreasing the parameters that affect Oracle's memory usage. This is an unusual situation, however.

If there is spare memory on the computer, Oracle systems can normally be sped up by increasing the DB_BLOCK_BUFFER parameter. This will store more data from tables, indexes, clusters, and rollback segments in memory. These data is useful only if they are queried by many users. If many updates are occurring on a system, you can enlarge the LOG_BUFFER to write changed data to the redo logs less often but in larger chunks. This will result in reducing the number of I/Os. Individual Oracle users can obtain improved sort times by enlarging the SORT_AREA_SIZE parameter. This is particularly useful for overnight processing when sorted, long-running reports are produced.

If there is not enough memory on a machine, too much paging and swapping of processes occur as the operating system attempts to give all processes a fair share of memory. Oracle's share of memory must be reduced in these circumstances by reducing the DB_BLOCK_BUFFER, the LOG_BUFFER and the SHARED_POOL_SIZE parameters. At some sites, these changes can be made without adversely affecting Oracle's performance. Per-Oracle user memory usage can also be reduced, by decreasing the SORT_AREA_SIZE parameter.

To monitor memory usage, you must become familiar with the relevant operating system memory monitoring commands, including the total memory available, free memory, and the paging and swapping rates. Work closely with the system administrator to monitor any memory problems, especially on machines that also run non-Oracle systems. You and the system administrator must keep each other informed of any proposed changes to memory usage, including adjusting parameters or plans for changes in the expected number of users.

From the Oracle database perspective, you can monitor the number of SHARED_POOL_SIZE reloads, the number of recursive calls, or the BSTT/ESTAT output. The effectiveness of the buffer cache is detected by querying the database's hit ratio or the hit ratio in the BSTAT/ESTAT report. The closer the hit ratio is to 100, the more effective the use of buffer cache will be. Increase the cache until the hit ratio stops increasing, given that there is free memory and no consistent CPU waits. You can also set the DB_BLOCK_LRU_EXTENDED_STATISTICS parameter to monitor the effects of increasing the buffer, and can set DB_BLOCK_LRU_STATISTICS to monitor the effect of decreasing the cache. Observe the LOG_BUFFER effectiveness by the MON STAT SQL*DBA statistic "rdo spa wa" (redo space wait). This value should remain zero.

References:
    "Managing the Workload in Your System" in Chapter 3
    "UTLBSTAT.sql and UTLESTAT.sql: Taking Snapshots" in Chapter 10
    "Tuning Memory" in Chapter 11
    "Tuning the Buffer Cache" in Chapter 11
    "Sharing Executable Images" in Chapter 11
    "Reducing Disk I/O by Increasing the Sort Area" in Chapter 11
    "Monitoring and Tuning Redo Log Files" in Chapter 11
    Chapter 16
    Chapter 17
    Chapter 18

Q: *Creating an index on a large table takes hours and often crashes because of extent problems. Can I speed this up?*

Creating an index requires a sort, which can be sped up by using memory instead of disk. This can be achieved by enlarging the SORT_AREA_SIZE parameter. As each sort area size is filled in memory, the sorted entries will be written to disk and merged with the entries that have already been written. This sorting is done in temporary segments.

If you are using the parallel query option of the database, you can increase your index rebuilds many times over. The parallel query facility allows you to simultaneously use more than one machine CPU to read, sort, and write the index to disk.

Oracle7.2 introduced the UNRECOVERABLE option when building indexes. This allows the DBA to (re)build an index without having to write information to the online redo logs. This option can also help to improve your index build times many times over.

Always place temporary segments into their own tablespace so that the default temporary segment sizing can be altered. This is achieved by having users assigned a tablespace that contains no tables, indexes, or clusters as their default temporary tablespace. Temporary segments have initial and next extent allocation assigned using the default INITIAL and NEXT extent specifications of the temporary tablespace. A typical daily default setting is INITIAL extent 256 kilobytes and NEXT extent 256 kilobytes. Always set PCTINCREASE to 0 and PCTFREE to 0. To create a large index, the temporary segment will need its INITIAL and NEXT extents to allow large sorts to occur without exceeding the maximum number of extents. Ideally, the INITIAL extent should be large enough to fit the entire index into one extent. The NEXT extent must be large enough to ensure that even if you miscalculated in the index size, you still won't blow the MAXEXTENTS setting.

The index will eventually be stored on disk. If the space the index is going to use is scattered across the disk in a discontiguous fashion, its performance can only be reduced, both on creation and eventually when accessed. The size of the index must also be assigned, preferably with the entire index fitting into one extent. Always set PCTINCREASE to 0.

It is important to size an index correctly when it is created. Ensure that the index sizing is for the expected number of entries in 12 months' time, not the entries at the time of index creation.

References:
  "Creating the Tablespaces" in Chapter 9
  "Tuning Memory" in Chapter 11

Chapter 13, *Tuning Parallel Query*
"Resizing Temporary Tables" in Chapter 15

Q: *Even though a statement is using an index, it is still running too slowly. Is there a way of checking how well an index is structured?*

Index usage alone is not always sufficient to make a database query perform well. The index must also be specific enough to allow the values being checked to be found without reading too many rows from the index. Consider the following example. An index is placed on the ACCOUNT_ID column in the ACCOUNT transaction table. Each account can have as many as 10,000 transactions against it for a given financial year. If the query is made against the transaction table for a specific transaction date and ACCOUNT_ID, the whole 10,000 index rows may have to be searched. A more suitable concatenated index should be created on ACCOUNT_ID and TRANSACTION_DATE.

If multiple indexes exist, the question must be asked: "Is it the most specific index?" The ordering of the index columns can be important. The data must be retrieved from the index with as few physical reads to the database as possible. If all of the columns required by the SQL statement can be stored in the index, and the ORDER BY clause on the SQL statement is in the same order as the columns in the index, this will assist performance by avoiding the need to read the columns from the table.

If the rule-based optimizer is being used, the sequence of table names in the FROM clause can also have a significant effect on performance by indicating which table will be used as the driving table in the query. This is an issue when the rankings of the indexes available for both tables have the same ranking, for example, a single-column index that is nonunique.

Another area that may cause problems is if the index contains many extents and is scattered widely across the disk. This problem can be avoided by sizing the index correctly when it is created. Ideally, the entire index must be stored in the initial extent.

References:
"Selecting the most efficient table name sequence" in Chapter 6
"Efficient WHERE clause sequencing" in Chapter 6
"Using Indexes to Improve Performance" in Chapter 6
"Creating Indexes" in Chapter 9
"Creating Users" in Chapter 9

Q: *Dropping a table takes an excessive amount of time. What can I do to speed it up?*

If a table contains many extents, the used extents' dictionary table must flag each used extent as now being free. If the table contained several indexes that are also scattered across many extents, the extents that were being used will also have to be flagged as free. This drop function will be sped up if tables and indexes are sized correctly when they are created. This minimizes the number of extents that the table or index occupies.

References:

"Correctly Sizing Tables and Indexes" in Chapter 15

Q: *Deleting rows from a table takes forever. What can I do?*

Deleting all the rows from a table is usually significantly slower than dropping a table. This is because work has to be done to flag free space in every one of the blocks that contained a row. If the table has indexes, the entries in the index are marked for deletion. This is a very resource-consuming process. A trick that some sites perform is to update a row as deleted by setting a DELETED_DATE column to the date the row was deleted and to perform the actual deletions on a period-ical basis outside prime usage times.

Always remember to check whether you have any referential integrity and/or database triggers "enabled" when attempting large table deletes. These operations will slow down operation considerably. Rollback and redo log activity will add to the lengthy delays.

The TRUNCATE command deletes *all* rows from a table, and its performance is comparable to dropping and recreating the table and its indexes. This function does not cause rollback activity and does not write any detailed redo information.

References:

"Correctly Sizing Tables and Indexes" in Chapter 15

Q: *The import takes too long. What can I do?*

The import facility is normally used to perform a database reorganization or to recover part (a small number of tables) of a database. It is typically performed over a weekend. Any DBA who has worked at a medium- to large-sized site has felt the extra pressure over the reorganization weekend. What if the database is not rebuilt by Monday morning when the production users arrive for work? The faster the import can be made to run, the more time will be available to rerun the import if something goes wrong. Oracle imports take considerably longer than exports, mainly because indexes are created as part of the import, whereas only the INDEX statement, not the index entries, is exported. Typical time differences are 3 hours for the export and 12 hours for a full import.

To avoid the need for reruns, it is important that you realize the biggest causes of import failure. If a table or index has large initial or next extents, ensure that the appropriate sized extents are available before you run the import. Many DBAs reorganize one tablespace at a time. They will drop and then recreate the tablespace and then import the tables, indexes, and clusters that exist in that tablespace. If you overlook indexes that reside in other tablespaces placed on tables in the tablespace being reorganized, problems can occur. Make sure that these indexes are also catered for.

The buffer size that is chosen as part of the import can have an effect on the time taken by the import. With a larger buffer size, the system writes larger chunks of data less often than when there is a smaller buffer size. Another factor that may decrease the time taken is to drop all of the indexes and create them after the table has been imported into. This will speed up the import significantly. Enlarge the sort area size to ensure that much of the sorting required for the index is done in memory.

DBAs should investigate the possibility of using single-task imports for UNIX environments. This facility can improve importing times by up to 40%. Make sure your Oracle support team is willing to support single-task operations before committing your entire application to its care.

Another good practice to use is to precreate all tables that have PRIMARY KEY and/or UNIQUE constraints. These constraints are both part of the table definition and are created when the table is created. This means that you are importing data with indexes already in place. It is better to create the tables prior to the import, omitting the constraints and adding them after the database has been loaded.

Increasing the size of the import buffer (i.e., IMP BUFFER=102400) will also help to improve overall export times. This forces Oracle to read more information with each fetch. The import buffer must be held in real memory, so do not make it so large as to cause paging and/or swapping. A buffer size of 10 megabytes is not unreasonable for a one-time database reorganization.

References:
"Creating Tables" in Chapter 9
    "Creating Indexes" in Chapter 9
    "Reducing Dynamic Extension" in Chapter 11
    Chapter 14, *Tuning Database Backup and Recovery*
    "Creating Indexes After Inserts" in Chapter 15

"Tuning EXPORT and IMPORT Utilities" in Chapter 15
"Running Long-Running Jobs at the Server End" in Chapter 16

Q: *The export takes too long. What can I do?*

An export that takes too long will intrude into the window of time that is available to run other overnight jobs. Exports are an essential part of any backup strategy because they allow individual tables to be restored and also highlight any table corruption. There are several ways to speed up an export, including increasing the buffer size. Increasing the buffer size allows larger chunks of data to be written less often than when there is a smaller buffer size.

The export can also be broken up into several jobs, with each exporting different tables. The jobs can be run in parallel. Many DBAs export tables and indexes on a per-tablespace basis. Perhaps several tables require only weekly, rather than nightly, export. Some summary tables may not require exporting because they can be recreated from other tables. If you are running client-server, make sure that the export process is initiated and the export file written to the same machine as the one on which the database resides.

As with database importing, DBA should investigate single-task imports for UNIX environments. This facility can improve exporting times by up to 40%. Make sure your Oracle support team is willing to support single-task operations before you commit your entire application to its care.

Increasing the size of the export buffer (i.e., EXP BUFFER=102400) will also help to improve overall export times. This forces Oracle to read more information with each fetch. The export buffer must be held in real memory, so do not make it too large so as to cause paging and/or swapping. A buffer size of 10 megabytes is not unreasonable for a one-time database reorganization.

References:
   "Creating Tables" in Chapter 9
   "Creating Indexes" in Chapter 9
   "Reducing Dynamic Extension" in Chapter 11
   Chapter 14, *Tuning Database Backup and Recovery*
   "Tuning EXPORT and IMPORT Utilities" in Chapter 15
   "Running Long-Running Jobs at the Server End" in Chapter 16

Q: *Our overnight data loads from other applications are taking far too long. What can I do?*

Overnight data loads are a common occurrence at a lot of Oracle sites. Circumstances will vary from site to site, but regardless of the exact situation, you should attempt to minimize the amount of data being transferred from the other application. In every application, make sure that you include a DATE_LAST_CHANGED column against every table. Each night, transfer only the data that have changed across applications.

You must appropriately size any temporary load tables that are created and their associated indexes so that they fit within one extent. Ideally, place the temporary load tables onto different disks from those that contain the tables that are to be updated or added to. It is more efficient to TRUNCATE the temporary table than to delete from it. It is also faster to insert the data into the load tables and create the indexes afterward.

Choosing the appropriate columns to index on the temporary load tables is just as critical as for the application tables. These should also be sized to minimize extents. Attempt to store all temporary tables and indexes in one extent. You can do this by setting the INITIAL storage parameter large enough to store all of the data in the table. If fragmentation of the database doesn't allow the table or index to be stored in one extent, try to use as few extents as possible, making the NEXT storage parameter as large as the largest free extent.

Always try to minimize the number of updates against each table. You can use a single UPDATE statement to update many columns in a single table. Take advantage of PL/SQL for updates to minimize the number of rows read for update in the production tables.

If you are running client-server, perform all overnight processing at the database server end. If you are using SQL*Loader, make sure the ROWS parameter has been set large enough to reduce the number of array inserts into the database.

When you are running overnight jobs, there will be tend to be fewer users logged on to a machine and therefore more free memory than during prime usage times. This will allow you to enlarge the DB_BLOCK_BUFFER, LOG_BUFFER, and SORT_AREA_SIZE parameters. Increasing the parameters will usually improve performance, for the reasons described in the references below. Temporary tablespace default parameters may be increased to improve sort/merge operations, including index creation. Larger rollback segments may replace the smaller daily rollbacks at sites to improve the responsiveness of updates. Make sure that all of the changes you make for overnight processing are adjusted back to their daily sizes when you complete the overnight jobs.

References:
    "Creating Tables" in Chapter 9
    "Creating Indexes" in Chapter 9
    Chapter 14
    Chapter 15
    "Running Long-Running Jobs at the Server End" in Chapter 16

Q: *We've gone client-server. The system ran fine when it was running on one machine, but now it's slow. What can the problem be?*

Client-server adds a new dimension to tuning an application: the need for one processor to communicate with another across a network.

You must try to reduce the number of packets being transferred between processors. This is achieved by setting the relevant ARRAYSIZE parameter effectively in the product being used; tuning any relevant parameters in the communications protocol; taking advantage of DECODEs, UNIONs, and views in SQL*Forms; and applying features such as local cache.

The closer you can locate processors together, the less distance the packets will need to travel. The amount of processor-to-processor network traffic is significantly larger than the traffic from the application client (server) to the user's terminal. You can have an application server (client) that services Sydney users, for example, and an application server that services Melbourne users located in the same computer room. This will considerably reduce the distance the bulk of the network traffic has to travel. The network traffic from the application servers (clients) to the terminal is usually quite light in comparison.

If possible, you should attempt to run all long-running jobs at the database server end. These jobs will include overnight reports, overnight updates, and daily reporting functions. The daily reports requested can be placed into a table, with a job running continuously at the database (server) end, which will interrogate the table and use its contents to submit the appropriate program with any supplied parameters.

Oracle7 has many features that will improve client-server computing performance, including a multithreaded server (which increases the maximum number of possible user connections and performs automatic load balancing) and the storing of integrity constraints, stored procedures, functions, and packages (which will considerably reduce the number of packets transferred across the network).

SQL*Net Version 2 has an internal feature called *fastpath* that will minimize read and write times.

References:
   Chapter 7
   Chapter 16

Q: *The application ran fast in tests but grinds to a halt in production. What can the problem be?*

There are many possible causes for sudden increased response time in production. Are the indexes the same in both environments? Is the amount of data in production considerably larger? Is the distribution of data different in test and production? For example, a table in the test environment may have the same number of rows for all categories, whereas in production one category may have 95% of the entries, with the other 50 categories having only a handful of rows each.

You need to ask various questions about the operating system. How many users are logged on? Is there any free memory? Is excessive paging or swapping occurring? Is the disk I/O correctly balanced? Are there any network bottlenecks? Is the test environment running in the same type of configuration as the production environment?

It is not good practice to run the test environment in unitary (with the database users and the database on the one machine) and production in client-server or any other differing combination. Use the test environment as a response testing ground; be sure that it uses the same type of configuration as production.

There are also DBA issues to consider. Has the database been structured for an even I/O spread? Is memory being used effectively to store data, indexes, and rollbacks. Are the database segments fragmented or chaining and in need of repair?

Q: *Is it too late to start tuning an application after it has launched?*

It is never too late to begin the tuning phase. Granted, it is always better to start the application tuning right back at the very beginning during the design phases, but it is never too late. If you are unfortunate enough to be called in only at the end of a project when all the performance problems are beginning to float to the top, do not despair; improvements can still be achieved.

Q: *Should I be using the rule-based or the cost-based optimizer?*

This is always a difficult question to answer. Our general advice is not to consider the cost-based optimizer until at least Oracle7.1.6, and only for new developments. Converting existing applications that were originally written and tuned for the rule-based optimizer to the cost-based optimizer is often dangerous and disappointing. Existing applications that are best suited to the cost-based optimizer are those that are poorly written and/or untuned. The cost-based optimizer can achieve its best results with badly performing SQL statements. Remember that Oracle has warned us that the rule-based optimizer will be phased out in future releases.

References:
    Chapter 6

Q: *Are database triggers efficient?*

Like any well-written SQL statement, database triggers can be very efficient and productive. Conversely, poorly written database triggers can destroy an application. The DBA must be very careful with an application that contains many triggers. This is normally a sign of an inadequate database design, business rule changes during development, or inexperienced programmers. Efficient database triggers should be small and concise, exploiting stored packages and procedures. Additionally, database triggers should exploit the trigger definition WHEN clause.

NOTE   Oracle7.3 has introduced compiled database triggers. This further
             helps to increase the effectiveness of database triggers and ease
             some of their inherent overheads.

References:
   Chapter 7

Q: *Can creating views help to overcome performance problems?*

Some people have the misconception that views can provide better performance than running the query that created the view. Some DBMSes create duplicate data when a view is created. If this is the required effect, Oracle can achieve this by maintaining redundant tables.

In Oracle, a view will perform identically to the SQL statement that is used to create the view. There will be only a small overhead to parse the view. It is critical that you tune the statement that is used to define the view like any other SQL statement.

Views can provide certain performance benefits in a client-server environment. This is achieved by reducing the number of packets transferred across the network by reducing the total number of database calls. Another advantage of views is that they offer a means of applying security by showing specific users only the columns that they need to see, and they save programmers from having to recode complex SELECT statements.

Do not use views of views, except where they are absolutely necessary. Views of views are extremely hard to administer, maintain, and tune.

Q: *Is there a way of killing long-running jobs in Oracle?*

Version 6 of Oracle relies on the operating system to kill long-running jobs. SQL*DBA MON PROC can be used to determine the identifier of the offending process.

Oracle7 offers a large advantage in being able to prevent jobs from exceeding the amount of CPU used or exceeding disk I/Os. If jobs do exceed the limits specified, they are cancelled automatically. This is done by defining each user a database profile.

References:
  Chapter 10
  Appendix D, *Oracle Performance Pack*

Q: *I have a developer who can reference another user's table in a SELECT statement but not in a stored procedure. What is happening?*

This problem is very common and very annoying. The DBA has granted access on the table via a database role. This is all well and good for normal SQL references but not sufficient for referencing other tables in database objects (i.e., views, packages, procedures, functions, or triggers). The owning user must explicitly grant the necessary privilege to the user; privileges via a role is not sufficient. For example:

```
GRANT SELECT ON emp TO ops$peter WITH GRANT OPTION;
```

Q: *How can I see who is logged on to the database?*

Executing the following database query displays all current user processes:

```
SELECT nvl(S.OSUSER,S.type) OS_Usercode,
       S.USERNAME              Oracle_Usercode,
       S.sid                   Oracle_SID,
       S.process               F_Ground,
       P.spid                  B_Ground
FROM   sys.V_$SESSION S,
       sys.V_$PROCESS P
WHERE  s.paddr   = p.addr
ORDER  BY s.sid
```

OS_Usercode	Oracle_Usercode	Oracle_SID	F_Ground	B_Ground
BACKGROUND		1		8639
BACKGROUND		2		8640
BACKGROUND		3		8641
BACKGROUND		4		8642
BACKGROUND		5		8643
BACKGROUND		6		8644
BACKGROUND		7		8645
oracle	SYSTEM	13	28292	28294
s6	S6	16	3829:01	15829
oracle	SCOTT	18	28359	28360
s4	S4	28	7445:01	26605
oracle	SCOTT	31	28359	2366
oracle	SCOTT	32	28359	2367
oracle	SCOTT	34	28359	2368

Note that any sessions with a foreground process ID ending in ":01" are remote, client-server connections. When multiple sessions have the same foreground process ID, it is actually one user connection using multiple parallel query process slaves.

Q: *How can I tell whether a user is currently updating the database?*

Executing the following database query displays all user processes with rollback segment locks:

```
SELECT r.usn,      r.name,   s.osuser,
       s.username, s.sid,    x.extents,
       x.extends,  x.waits,  x.shrinks,
       x.wraps
FROM   sys.v_$rollstat X,
       sys.v_$rollname R,
       sys.v_$session S,
       sys.v_$transaction T
WHERE  t.addr       = s.taddr (+)
AND    x.usn (+)    = r.usn
AND    t.xidusn (+) = r.usn
ORDER  BY r.usn
```

ID	Name	OSuser	Username	SID	Extents	Extends	Waits	Shrinks	Wraps
	SYSTEM								
2	RBS1	oracle	SYSTEM	13	4	0	37	0	2
3	RBS2								
4	RBS3								
5	RBS4	s6	S6	16	4	3	418	1	3

Q: *How can I tell whether a user process is performing any disk I/O?*

Executing the following database query a number of times, a few seconds apart, will highlight the I/O activity of each user process:

```
SELECT S.SID, V.osuser, v.username,
       nvl(block_gets,0) + nvl(consistent_gets,0) Log_Reads,
       physical_reads Phy_Reads,
       decode(nvl(block_gets,0) + nvl(consistent_gets,0), 0, 0,
          round(100 * ( nvl(block_gets,0)
                        + nvl(consistent_gets,0)
                        - nvl(physical_reads, 0) )
                    / ( nvl(block_gets,0)
                        + nvl(consistent_gets,0) ), 2)) Ratio,
       block_changes Phy_Writes
FROM   sys.v_$sess_io S,
       sys.v_$session V
WHERE  S.sid = v.sid (+)
ORDER  BY s.sid
```

SID	OSuser	Username	Log_Reads	Phy_Reads	Ratio	Phy_Writes
2	oracle	SYSTEM	213	4	98.12	21

```
16 s6      S6              513       13   97.47          0
18 oracle  SCOTT         12213     3452   98.12       1203
28 s4      S4                3        3  100.00          0
31 oracle  SCOTT       1923213   235111   87.78          0
```

Q: *How can I tell what SQL a user process is currently executing?*

Executing the following database query displays the SQL statement that was last executed by a user process:

```
SELECT /*+ ORDERED */
       s.sid, s.osuser, s.username,
       nvl(s.machine,' ? ') machine,
       nvl(s.program,' ? ') program,
       s.process Fground, p.spid Bground, X.sql_text
FROM   sys.v_$session S,
       sys.v_$process P,
       sys.v_$sqlarea X
WHERE  s.sid = &SID
AND    s.paddr        = p.addr
AND    s.type        != 'BACKGROUND'
AND    s.sql_address  = x.address
AND    s.sql_hash_value = x.hash_value
ORDER  BY  s.sid

SID OSuser Username Machine  Program   Fground Bground Sql_Text
--- ------ -------- -------- --------- ------- ------- ------------
 16 s6     S6       thor     sqlplus   3829:01 15829
SELECT EMP, ENMP_NAME, E.DEPT, D.DESCRIPTION, CATEGORY FROM DEPT D,
EMP, E WHERE D.DEPT_NO = E.DEPT_NO
```

Note that the last SQL statement executed is available only if it has not been swapped out of the SGA shared pool.

Q: *How can I tell when one process is waiting on another?*

Executing the following database query displays when one process is waiting for a resource held by another user process:

```
SELECT substr(s1.username,1,12)     "WAITING User",
       substr(s1.osuser,1,8)           "OS User",
       substr(to_char(w.session_id),1,5)  "Sid",
       P1.spid                         "PID",
       substr(s2.username,1,12)     "HOLDING User",
       substr(s2.osuser,1,8)           "OS User",
       substr(to_char(h.session_id),1,5)  "Sid",
       P2.spid                         "PID"
FROM   sys.v_$process P1,   sys.v_$process P2,
       sys.v_$session S1,   sys.v_$session S2,
       sys.dba_locks w,     sys.dba_locks h
WHERE  h.mode_held       = 'None'
AND    h.mode_held       = 'Null'
AND    w.mode_requested != 'None'
AND    w.lock_type  (+)  = h.lock_type
AND    w.lock_id1   (+)  = h.lock_id1
```

```
AND      w.lock_id2   (+)      = h.lock_id2
AND      w.session_id          = S1.sid  (+)
AND      h.session_id          = S2.sid  (+)
AND      S1.paddr              = P1.addr (+)
AND      S2.paddr              = P2.addr (+)
```

WAITING User	OS User	Sid	PID	HOLDING User	OS User	Sid	PID
SYSTEM	oracle	13	28294	SCOTT	oracle	18	28360
SCOTT	oracle	18	28360	S6	s6	16	15829
S4	s4	28	26605	S6	s6	16	15829

Note that the *waiters* script references views from the Oracle supplied script *catblock.sql*. This script can be located in the directory *$ORACLE_HOME/rdbms/ admin* and must be loaded before *waiters* will work.

Q: *What performance advantages does SQL*Net Version 2 have over SQL*Net Version 1?*

SQL*Net Version 2 provides significant performance benefits over Version 1 by passing fewer packets across the network, using a feature called *fastpath*.

SQL*Net Version 2 offers UPIALL in all tools. This reduces the number of packets required to be passed across the network by having one pass open a statement and one close the statement, compared to SQL*Net Version 1, which requires many packets to be passed for each individual SQL statement.

Another major advantage of SQL*Net Version 2 is the multithreaded server, which significantly increases the maximum number of connections and performs load balancing automatically. The maximum number of users can be increased because a single dispatcher process controls many clients via a network-monitoring process that differs from SQL*Net Version 1 (in which each user process has the full SQL*Net overhead). SQL*Net Version 2 requires fewer system resources to handle the same number of users.

SQL*Net Version 2.1 is the minimum SQL*Net release to support Oracle Name Server functionality. This factor alone should be reason enough for large, distributed environments to upgrade to SQL*Net 2 as soon as possible.

References:
    "Tuning SQL*Net" in Chapter 16

Q: *The system response has been deteriorating over time. What are the possible causes?*

This is a common situation. There are a number of possible causes.

Indexes may be inappropriate or nonexistent. Indexes may not exist because the application designers did not envision the selection criteria that the users will use. With only a small amount of data, a full table scan might have been as fast as, or faster than, an indexed SELECT. As the number of rows in the database has grown, however, the missing index causes a dramatic degradation in response time.

Indexes may have been added to speed up a new program, which may cause existing programs to operate less efficiently. This may be the result of a new index ranking higher in the optimizer's ranking conditions than the index that provides the program with efficient performance or may result from the order of the WHERE clause causing the new index to be used.

Another common cause of performance degradation is database fragmentation, in which database segments span many extents. Chaining could also be a problem, but it is more likely to be picked up during the system test stage if the appropriate monitoring is performed.

External influences also affect many applications over time. New untuned or partially tuned applications often find their way onto a machine that is known for its good response times. This inevitably results in two systems performing badly rather than the one poorly tuned application.

Uncontrolled ad hoc queries against the production database by production users can also cause overall poor performance if the SQL queries are not optimally structured. Developers may also log in to a production database to check problems. It is essential for the DBA to be aware of all ad hoc activity either to ensure that it is done at times other than those of heavy usage or to be absolutely sure that the activity will not adversely affect performance if it must run during prime time.

There may also be many more users than there were in the past, causing memory on the machine to be fully utilized and paging and swapping to occur. Perhaps the degradation is caused by poor I/O distribution across disks. Other possibilities include inadequate use of memory to store database or dictionary information and contention in writing to the tables, rollback segments, or redo logs.

Additional database checks that should be made if there is sufficient free memory on your machine are the following:

- Ensure that the block buffer that stores table data, indexes, clusters, and rollback segments is large enough to provide a high hit rate. This guarantees that as much information can be found in memory (as opposed to disk) as possible.

- Make the shared pool large enough to ensure that Oracle database information is stored in memory and the number or SQL reloads is minimal.

- Enlarge the redo log buffer to reduce frequent I/Os to the redo logs if there is excessive I/O on the disk that contains the redo logs.

Contention problems that may be occurring and have to be investigated include the following:

- Redo log contention has a relatively small effect on database performance, but Oracle provides the tools to monitor it. Each minor improvement that can be made to the database may add up to a major improvement when combined with many other small improvements. Use the SQL*DBA MON ST screen to examine "rdo spa wa" (redo log space wait), the number of times a user is waiting for space in the redo log buffer.

- The redo log buffer latches can have multiple users trying to access them, and contention may occur. This problem is detected by viewing the SQL*DBA MON LA screen and inspecting the "redo allocation" and "redo copy latches" to ensure that the timeouts do not exceed 5% of the total willing to wait requests.

- Rollback segment contention can occur with contention for data buffers in the buffer cache area of the SGA or buffer contention due to rollback segment contention. Ensure that the block buffer section of the SGA is large enough to avoid contention. Also ensure that dynamic extension of rollbacks is not occurring for transactions that are modifying large amounts of data. If your application has many online transaction processing users, with only small amounts of data being modified, keep all of your rollback segments small to improve their chance of being kept in the buffer cache. If your site is performing many large updates, ensure that the large update transactions are assigned larger rollback segments.

- Table and row contention can also occur in which one user process is forced to wait for another user process to release the lock before proceeding. Code your application to minimize the chances of locking problems occurring.

References:
Chapter 3
Chapter 6
Chapter 11
"Correctly Sizing Tables and Indexes" in Chapter 15

Q: *Our system administrator has informed me that our system is I/O bound. What can I do?*

It is important to understand what "I/O bound" means. Simply put, it means that one or more disks are exceeding their recommend I/O usage, creating a bottleneck. Typical disks on a minicomputer have recommended maximum I/O rates between 30 to 60 I/Os per second. Excessive disk I/Os can dramatically degrade application response times.

When a database is initially created, there are steps that can be taken to ensure that the disk load spread is evenly balanced across disks and to ensure that the cause of the excessive disk I/O can be more accurately pinpointed. A summary of the rules follows:

- Locate redo log files on a disk other than the disk holding the database files.

- Split tables and indexes into separate tablespaces.

- Separate tables that are commonly used together onto separate disks. Try to combine infrequently used tables with frequently used tables.

- Have a separate temporary tablespace.

- Place users into their own tablespace.

- Store the Oracle products in a products tablespace.

- Store only the Oracle system tables in the system tablespace.

- Do not store any part of the Oracle database on the operating system disk; in particular, keep away from the operating system disk where paging and swapping takes place.

- Allocate many medium-sized tablespaces instead of fewer large tablespaces.

- Spread your disk I/O across as many disk drives and as many disk controllers as possible.

- Be aware of your machine-specific disk characteristics such as the advantages of raw devices on many UNIX systems.

Badly tuned application programs or a data model that is unable to provide adequate performance are the principal causes of systems becoming I/O bound. Make sure that programs are responding within the required site standard response times. If the response times are sufficiently tight (e.g., 95% of online responses within 2.5 seconds elapsed and no longer than 10 seconds elapsed for any online response), the likelihood of the application causing the system to be I/O bound is reduced significantly.

Many sites may require reporting of small batch updates during prime usage times. These jobs must also have their response times monitored closely. An appropriate maximum run time for such jobs at a typical site would be 95% of them running within 30 seconds elapsed with no job exceeding 2 minutes.

If the application has been tuned appropriately and the system is still I/O bound, you should investigate other sources of the problem. If one disk has become I/O bound, there will probably be a way of spreading the load by relocating tables and indexes into different tablespaces on alternative disks. A table and its indexes should be separated. Heavily used tables and lightly used tables should be placed on the same disks, with no one disk having too many heavily used tables on it.

Indexing problems can also cause excessive I/Os. Make sure that no indexes have been accidentally dropped or not recreated after a database reorganization. Ensure also that a new index that has been added to assist a new program is not adversely affecting other programs that may now be using the new index rather than a more optimally tuned index.

If free memory is available, you can increase the size of the block buffers, storing extra data, indexes, rollbacks, and clusters and/or enlarge the SHARED_POOL_SIZE. Doing this speeds up response times considerably for a tuned application. This is achieved by transferring the load from I/O to memory. If sorting is common in the application and there is sufficient memory, you can enlarge the SORT_AREA_SIZE parameter to force more sorting in memory rather than on disk. You can also enlarge the log buffer to reduce the number of writes to the redo logs.

References:
    "Managing the Workload in Your System" in Chapter 3
    Chapter 5
    "SQL Performance Tips and Hints" in Chapter 6
    "Using Indexes to Improve Performance" in Chapter 6
    "Creating the Database" in Chapter 9
    "Creating Tables" in Chapter 9
    "Creating Indexes" in Chapter 9
    "Creating Users" in Chapter 9
    "UTLBSTAT.sql and UTLESTAT.sql: Taking Snapshots" in Chapter 10
    "Tuning Disk I/O" in Chapter 11
    "Writing to Raw Devices" in Chapter 18

Q: *One disk is always on or above its maximum recommended I/Os per second. What can I do?*

Make sure that the application has been thoroughly tuned. Even a single badly tuned program that is not using indexes correctly or has an incorrect driving table can cause overall poor response times and an overworked disk. Do not run long-running batch jobs during prime production times, when the system contains many interactive users. Excessive I/Os may also occur when an index is missing. If the application is tuned correctly, there are certain measures that you can take to spread the disk load.

An inappropriate database structure can cause excessive I/Os across disks. Be sure to separate redo logs from database files onto separate disk drives. If possible, split tables from their indexes, and split commonly used tables onto different drives. Do not store any database files on the same disk as the operating system files. Even when you follow these basic rules, unbalanced disk loading can still occur.

The usual way to spread the disk load is to relocate tables and indexes into different tablespaces across disks. A database reorganization can help if there is more than one extent on table and index segments that exist on this disk. This will mean that more I/Os will be needed to access data than from a table or index that exists in one extent.

Excessive disk I/Os may also occur when there are many sorts taking place with an inadequate sort area size, and many users have their default temporary tablespace on a single disk. Enlarge the sort area size to alleviate the problem, or assign temporary tablespaces assigned for users to alternative tablespaces across several disks.

If the disk containing the redo logs is experiencing excessive I/Os, increase the log buffer size if sufficient memory is available. This will cause the redo logs to be written to less frequently.

If the operating system disk is experiencing excessive I/O, the usual cause is excessive paging and swapping. If this is the case, you will need to decrease Oracle's slice of memory, normally by reducing the DB_BLOCK_BUFFER size or in some cases the LOG_BUFFER or the SORT_AREA_SIZE.

If the disk containing the system tablespace that is experiencing problems has excessive I/Os, the probable cause is that you are storing more than just the system tablespaces in the tablespace. Other segments should be moved away from the system tablespace.

External influences also affect many applications. New untuned or partially tuned applications often find their way onto a machine that is known for its good response times. They may share the same disks as your application. You must be familiar with the operating system disk monitoring commands to detect this cause. Solving this problem may be a simple case of subtracting your application's disk I/Os from the overall system I/Os.

Uncontrolled ad hoc queries against the production database often attack individual large tables, and this can cause overall poor performance. It is essential that you be aware of all ad hoc activity to ensure that no part of the database is adversely affected.

Make sure you take advantage of any offerings the hardware vendor provides to enhance performance. For example, use raw devices if they are available, and take advantage of any disk caching ability your computer may have. You must work closely with the system administration staff to do this.

References:

"Managing the Workload in Your System" in Chapter 3
Chapter 5
"SQL Performance Tips and Hints" in Chapter 6
"Using Indexes to Improve Performance" in Chapter 6
"Disk I/O Checklist" in Chapter 9
"Creating the Database" in Chapter 9
"Creating Tables" in Chapter 9
"Creating Indexes" in Chapter 9
"Creating Users" in Chapter 9
"UTLBSTAT.sql and UTLESTAT.sql: Taking Snapshots" in Chapter 10
"Tuning Disk I/O" in Chapter 11
"Writing to Raw Devices" in Chapter 18

Q: *We keep running out of memory and swapping occurs. What can I do?*

Excessive swapping is probably the most damaging factor in a machine's performance. Simply put, swapping occurs when an entire process is moved from memory to disk. Excessive swapping is known as thrashing. This occurs when 100% of the CPU is spent continuously moving processes into and out of memory. Swapping of dormant processes is quite acceptable. Problems occur when memory is not large enough to store all active processes. It is essential that you work with the system administrator to ensure that there is always free memory. As a rule of thumb, at least 5% of memory must be free at all times, including peak activity times.

There are many ways to reduce memory usage, but as we have mentioned already, you must be careful not to squeeze free memory so tightly that overall performance begins to diminish. Memory prices are coming down considerably. This does not mean that memory usage should become reckless. The decreased memory usage will cause an increased I/O usage. Keep in mind that I/O is many, many thousand times slower than memory processing. After any changes are made to memory usage, the responsiveness of the system should be checked. Don't compare the response times to those when the system is in a swapping state. Compare them to the response times just prior to all of the memory being used.

One simple solution to the memory problem is to limit users to one login each. At some sites, users may be logged on three or four times. At others, users are logged on all day although they use the system only briefly. We have observed sites where people arrive at work, log on to the Oracle system, quickly check one inquiry screen, and do not use the application for the rest of the day. When a user is logged on, he or she uses memory. Consider logging users off the system after a period of inactivity. You might also investigate rotating shifts if these are possible at your site; for example, shift 1 works from 7:00 a.m. to 3:00 p.m. and shift 2 works from 3:00 p.m. to 11:00 p.m.

Some operating systems allow the sharing of executables in memory; for example, under VMS, executables can be stored once and shared by many users. If it is not installed as a shared executable, each user will have his or her own copy. This will quickly use all of the memory. Any executables that are not being used on a production machine can be removed from memory if they have been installed.

Another way to reduce memory usage is to reduce the size of the SGA. The areas that can be reduced are the SHARED_POOL_SIZE (reduce this only if it is over-sized), the log buffer (do not reduce it to the extent of causing contention for redo logs or excessive I/Os to the disks containing the redo logs), and the block buffer size (do not reduce it to a point at which excessive I/Os occur and the system response times rise above those set by the site's response time standard).

The amount of memory per Oracle user can also be adjusted by reducing the sort area size that sets the amount of memory per user for sorting. Although these parameters can be reduced, it is not advisable to decrease either of them by more than 50% of the default Oracle settings.

References:
   "Managing the Workload in Your System" in Chapter 3
   "UTLBSTAT.sql and UTLESTAT.sql: Taking Snapshots" in Chapter 10
   "Tuning Memory" in Chapter 11
   "VMS-Specific Tuning" in Chapter 18

Q: *How large a value should I set the DB_BLOCK_BUFFERS parameter to?*

The DB_BLOCK_BUFFERS parameter sets the amount of memory that Oracle will use to store tables, indexes, clusters, and rollbacks. This area is called the buffer cache, which is held in the SGA. Be careful that you do not enlarge the parameter to the point at which there is less than 5% free memory during peak usage time. If all the memory on the machine is used, the performance is likely to grind to a halt through excessive paging and swapping.

Our experience has shown that enlarging the parameter continuously to the point at which the hit rate of finding data in memory approaches 100% will improve the performance of Oracle at most sites. This is because memory access is many, many thousand times faster than disk access. If the hit rate of finding data, indexes, or rollbacks in memory improves even by only 5%, this may mean a significant reduction in I/Os during peak usage times of a system. If there is an abundance of free memory on a system, the dictionary cache and log buffer are tuned, and the hit ratios continue to increase when the parameter is increased, you should use the memory to enlarge the DB_BLOCK_BUFFERS. *However, it is critical that you leave free memory on your system at all times.*

There is an obvious exception to the rule. This occurs when the data is unlikely to be found in cache because large table scans are being performed on a continual basis from tables that are too large to fit into the buffer area. CPU will be consumed searching the cache, with little likelihood of the required data being found, and disk I/O will be required regardless.

Some sites take advantage of the fact that fewer users log on to the system at night, and consequently, more free memory is available at such times. Each night, they shut their instance down, increase the DB_BLOCK_BUFFERS parameter upward, run the long-running overnight jobs, and then shut the instance down again, adjust the parameter to its daily setting, and restart the instance.

References:

"Managing the Workload in Your System" in Chapter 3
"UTLBSTAT.sql and UTLESTAT.sql: Taking Snapshots" in Chapter 10
"Tuning Memory" in Chapter 11
"Optimizing INIT.ORA Parameters" in Chapter 15

Q: *We've had a user waiting for 30 minutes for a response. The user is not using an excessive amount of disk I/O or CPU. What can the problem be?*

The most likely cause is a locking problem. Often, a program performs well during testing as a single unit, but when many users operate many programs in a system test, locking problems occur. This system test is critical to detect any locking problems, as is a sound locking strategy for developers.

A common cause of locking problems is when users are updating information in an application and go to lunch, leaving the uncommitted transaction sitting on the screen. It is essential to train users not to leave uncommitted transactions for an excessive amount of time.

Another cause of this situation occurs when an overnight job locks a table, or rows in a table, that have failed to complete before the online users log on to the system and commence their day's work using online updates. A third cause occurs when an ad hoc update of the database is applied by a developer to the database during online usage times.

References:

Chapter 8

Q: *How do I know when my tables and indexes need to be reorganized? How is this best achieved?*

Ideally, tables and indexes should be sized to fit within a single extent. If a table or index has more than 10 extents, rebuild it to fit into one extent. The exception to the rule is when a table has been created by using the striping facility or the table and/or index has been created via parallel query tools.

You should also rebuild tables when chaining occurs on many of the rows within the table. This occurs when a row expands and can't fit within a single physical block. The problem is caused by too small a PCTFREE being specified for a table. Indexes are also subject to chaining if the columns in the index have increased in length.

Make sure that all tables and indexes are sized to allow for expected growth over the next 12 months. Never size an index or table for its current number of rows. When resizing tables, don't forget to recreate the indexes on the table.

Another situation in which tables and indexes may have to be rebuilt is the case in which the DBA requires free space in the database and the current tables or indexes are oversized. DBAs should ANALYZE their tables and indexes on a regular basis to monitor object growth and, conversely, object oversizing.

References:
   "Using Indexes to Improve Performance" in Chapter 6
   "Creating Tables" in Chapter 9
   "Creating Indexes" in Chapter 9
   "Correctly Sizing Tables and Indexes" in Chapter 15
   "Creating Indexes After Inserts" in Chapter 15

Q: *My site has a program that has been running for more than 30 minutes. How can I monitor the program to see which statements have caused the largest response delays? It appears the program may be stuck on one particular statement.*

Set the following parameters in the INIT.ORA file:

```
SQL_TRACE          TRUE
TIMED_STATISTICS   TRUE
```

Alternatively, include the statement ALTER SESSION SET SQL_TRACE TRUE at the start of the program. Then you will be able to run the TKPROF utility against the trace file created by the program to determine the timings for each statement. Some developers have the misconception that TKPROF has to run against a completed program's trace file and will take the same amount of time that the program took to run. This is not the case. The program can still be running when you run TKPROF, and the TKPROF output will take only a few moments.

Another method of monitoring a program that is via *oradbx*. The big advantage of *oradbx* is that you can monitor a program that is currently executing *oradbx* allows the DBA to alter a program's mode while it is still processing.

References:

> Chapter 6
> "SQL_TRACE: Writing a Trace File" in Chapter 10
> "TKPROF: Interpreting the Trace File" in Chapter 10
> "EXPLAIN PLAN: Explaining the Optimizer's Plan" in Chapter 10

Q: *When I use the SQL*DBA MONITOR screens, I see several hundred figures. Which are the important figures that can be used for tuning, and how do I interpret them?*

A summary of the parameters that are most relevant to the tuning process are listed below. Detailed information on how to repair the problems is given in this book.

    SQL*DBA> MON STAT 0 0 3

recursive calls

> Should be as close to zero as possible. If it is greater than zero, either the dictionary cache does not contain a required entry and a disk read has taken place on the system tables or dynamic extension is occurring. Either needs repairing.

dbw fre ne

> Indicates DBWR contention. This value should never exceed zero. If it does, this problem must be prepared.

buf bsy wa

> Compare with db blk get and consi get using (buf bsy wa / db blk get + consi get). If the result is greater than 10%, you have rollback contention.

rdo spa wa

> Should never rise above zero. If it does, a process cannot find space in the redo log buffer.

fre buf ins

> If excessive, the DBWR is not functioning well and too many buffers are being skipped to find a free buffer.

fre bf wai

> The number of times a free buffer was not available. The lower the value, the better.

    SQLDBA> MON IO

> Processes may be viewed to identify the biggest I/O user processes.

hit ratio

This parameter indicates the ratio of table, index, cluster, and rollback blocks found in memory. The closer to 1.00, the better the performance.

$$\text{Hit Ratio} = \frac{(\text{cumulative logical reads} - \text{physical reads})}{\text{cumulative logical reads}}$$

```
SQLDBA> MON LA
```

Make sure no latch has timeouts (more than 5% of total willing to wait).

```
SQLDBA>MON FILE
```

Make sure no file has excessive I/Os with disk exceeding maximum I/Os

```
SQLDBA>MON IO ALL
```

Make sure there are no waiters (lowercase) in the lock display screen

References:

Chapter 11

Appendix G, *Dynamic Performance Tables*

Q: *Our backups are taking too long. What can I do to speed them up?*

Every site has a certain fixed amount of time in which to perform such tasks as backups. Backups are critical; never give preference to running long-running batch jobs or reports. There is always a way of speeding up backups.

If archiving is turned on, you may shut your database down weekly to back up all database files and just back up the archive files nightly. Hot backups allow tablespaces to be backed up without having to shut down the database. This form of backup can be run with little effect on overnight processing.

If there is sufficient time overnight to perform a full image copy of your database with the database shut down, this will provide the fastest recovery. If possible, run disk-to-disk-image copies of all of the database files. As soon as this process has been completed, you can begin the overnight reporting and batch jobs with tape backups taken of the image copies of the database on disk.

Exports may be run at the same time that overnight reports are running because the tables are not being updated. To speed up these exports, they can be split up and run simultaneously on a per-tablespace basis. Multiple exports will run faster than one long export job. Some tables may not require exporting, such as redundant tables or historical tables.

References:

Chapter 14, *Tuning Database Backup and Recovery*

"Tuning EXPORT and IMPORT Utilities" in Chapter 15

Q: *We've achieved good response times for our application. What should I monitor to be sure that we can maintain these response times?*

Follow these guidelines:

- Make sure your machine has free memory at all times and is not experiencing excessive paging and swapping.

- Make sure that the I/O load is balanced across all disks and controllers.

- Make sure that the number of users waiting for CPU is never excessive

- Make sure that you consider performance when making all changes made to the network.

- Collect regular response time feedback from production users, and if the response times are unacceptable, investigate the cause.

- Be aware of the numbers of users being added to your system, and gauge what effect they will have on performance.

- If any part of the database is reorganized, always check to make sure that all expected indexes are resident.

- If any changes are made to the application, including table structure, program changes, or index changes, make sure they are thoroughly tested for performance to meet the levels specified in your site's tuning service agreement.

- Make sure you consider performance in making all changes to the database structure, for example, adding a tablespace.

- Make sure to monitor closely all ad hoc usage of the system.

- Be aware of any other applications running on your machine.

- Make sure that the hit rate of finding data, indexes, and rollbacks in memory is tuned as high as possible.

- Make sure that there is no segment in the database with excessive extents (dynamic extension). This includes tables (including temporary), indexes, and rollbacks.

- Make sure that the number of processes that are waiting for locks is minimized.

- Avoid all redo log and rollback contention in your database.

- Make sure that memory is being used adequately to assist sorting, especially of overnight jobs.

References:
"Managing the Workload in Your System" in Chapter 3
Chapter 5
"SQL Performance Tips and Hints" in Chapter 6

Q: *What is chaining and how can I tell whether it is having a negative impact on my users' response times?*

UPDATE statements cause chaining when a row expands beyond one physical database block. When each database block is created, it is given an area of free space; the size of this space is determined by the PCTFREE parameter in the STORAGE clause of the table or index that is being created. When a row in the block expands, Oracle attempts to store the row's information in the same physical block. If the PCTFREE is too low, however, the row's data will be spread across several blocks, and this can seriously degrade performance.

Chaining will definitely affect the performance of users. You must monitor for chaining by running programs to check chaining against tables on a regular basis, perhaps about twice a month.

References:

Q: *Is fragmentation on rollback segments bad?*

Having multiple extents for a rollback segment is not a bad thing because one rollback segment handles many transactions at a single time, each transaction requiring its separate extent within the rollback segment. One transaction may dynamically extend to many extents within the one rollback segment, however, and this can affect performance.

It pays to keep all extents the same size for a rollback segment, making the INITIAL and NEXT storage allocations the same size and setting the PCTINCREASE to zero. This will allow other transactions to reuse extents that were used by prior transactions.

Most sites have many online transaction processing users and a few longer-running update jobs. If your site has a mixed transaction size, you may have a couple of larger rollback segments and many small rollback segments. Make sure that the size of the small rollback segments is a multiple of the larger rollback segments.

Versions 6.0.33 and later provide the SET TRANSATION USE ROLLBACK SEGMENT *rollback_segment* command. You can issue this command for all long-running jobs to minimize dynamic extension of the rollback. Other users will have a good chance of being assigned one of many smaller rollbacks, which may be as small as 10 kilobytes in size, and this will increase the chance of the rollback being held in buffer cache.

Oracle7 offers a shrink-back facility to control the size of rollbacks. The rollbacks will automatically shrink back to the size specified in the OPTIMAL clause when the rollback was created. This facility is highly desirable and can be invaluable in limiting your rollback segments to a manageable size.

References:
  "Creating Rollback Segments" in Chapter 9
  "Tuning Rollback Segments" in Chapter 11
  "Choosing Rollback Segments" in Chapter 15

Q: *I've noticed that larger update jobs perform better if they are able to use larger rollback segments. Is there a way to force a job to use a larger rollback?*

In Version 6.0.33 and later, use the SET TRANSACTION USE ROLLBACK SEGMENT *rollback_segment* command mentioned above. Take advantage of this command by setting all larger transactions that will perform many data modifications to larger rollback segments. This will reduce dynamic extension and can speed up response times considerably.

References:
  "Choosing Rollback Segments" in Chapter 15

Q: *My site has a procedure that uses the SET TRANSACTION USE ROLLBACK SEGMENT rollback_segment statement to force the procedure to use a large rollback segment. The statement works well for some of the statements but uses other rollback segments for other statements. This has a harmful effect on our run time. What can the cause be?*

Your program must contain a COMMIT or ROLLBACK statement. As soon as a ROLLBACK or COMMIT statement is processed, a new transaction state is started and a new rollback segment is allotted. Ensure that each statement has the *SET TRANSACTION USE ROLLBACK SEGMENT rollback_segment* command in it, or remove the COMMIT and ROLLBACK statements from your script. Make sure auto-commit is not set on.

References:
"How Many Rollback Segments?" in Chapter 9

Q: *How do I know when the redo logs are correctly tuned?*

You can tune certain aspects of redo logs, as summarized below:

- There may be excessive I/Os being performed on the disks containing the redo logs. This problem is cured by enlarging the log buffer; this causes the system to write larger amounts of redo data less often. Our tests have indicated improvements of around 7% by enlarging the log buffer to 1 megabyte on medium-sized applications. You should also ensure that the LOG_CHECKPOINT_INTERVAL parameter is not set to a figure smaller than your redo logs. Each time a checkpoint occurs, a write is made to the database files. Set the LOG_CHECKPOINT_INTERVAL equal to or larger than the size of the redo logs. Make all redo logs the same size. Ensure that the redo logs are not too small, because this will also cause continual writes to redo log files. Redo log file sizes of 5 megabytes operate well at most sites.

- There may be contention of processes waiting to find free buffer space to place redo information into the redo log buffer. Once again, this can be cured by enlarging the log buffer.

- There may be contention occurring for the redo allocation latch, which allocates space in the redo log buffer. This problem is cured on multiprocessor systems by decreasing the parameter LOG_SMALL_ENTRY_MAX_SIZE to force the larger copy latch to be used. You should also increase LOG_SIMULTANEOUS_COPIES to twice as many as the number of CPUs. For multiprocessor systems, you can also increase the LOG_ENTRY_PREBUILD_THRESHOLD parameter to build more entries before writing them to the log buffer.

References:
"INIT.ORA Parameter Summary" in Chapter 9
"Creating the Database" in Chapter 9
"Avoiding Contention" in Chapter 11

Q: *Can I use my archive logs to roll forward from an export dump file?*

We are amazed at the number of times we are asked this question by inexperienced DBAs. You *cannot* roll forward a database that has been restored (imported) from an export dump file. If your only form of database back up is a regular export dump, you are wasting your time and machine resources having your database in archivelog mode.

References:
Chapter 14

Q: *Can I restore data files from different database backups?*

It is OK to mix and match database data files from two or more cold or hot database backups as long as you also have all relevant archive log files. The archive logs must span from the earliest restored data file up to the point in time you wish to recover to.

The ability to source database data files from different backup cycles gives us a form of backup redundancy. If one file cannot be read from last night's tape, restore the rest of the data files and retrieve the unreadable data file from the prior backup tape.

References:
    Chapter 14

Q: *Why do table locks remain after I kill the user process holding the locks?*

Database resource locks are never released instantly after a user process is terminated. Regardless of how the process finishes: network failure, process termination (i.e., kill *nnnn*), or user termination (i.e., Control-C). The RDBMS task PMON (process monitor) is responsible for detecting "dead" processes, releasing locked resources, and rolling back all uncommitted changes. The PMON task wakes up only every few minutes so a terminated process can appear to be still running after it has been killed.

Q: *Can I roll back after I have truncated a table?*

Table truncations have no rollback facility. When a table's data is truncated, all table (and index) extents are placed back on the free space list; no redo information is written to the rollback segments. This enables instant data deletion at the expense of data undo. Always ensure that you are doing the right thing before truncating a table. Your 30-second lapse in concentration could mean the end of a DBA career.

References:
    Chapter 8

Q: *Are there any alternatives to database snapshots?*

There are a number of alternatives to normal database snapshots. Often, snapshots are not sophisticated enough to cater to complex business requirements. They simply duplicate existing tables or views of tables, unable to make decisions. Some viable alternatives are the following:

- Two-phase commit: Rather than delay the remote update to a later point in time, you can always perform the distributed update at the same time as the local change. This is not always desirable because your local database update is at the mercy of your network and your remote database(s).

- RDBMS job queuing: Instead of writing a change log to a snapshot table, you can submit a database job to perform a predetermined procedure. Jobs allow us to pass parameters (i.e., the changed record's rowid) to existing stored procedures or functions. The database will automatically fire the job at the set time, performing any number of business requirements and distributed updates.

- Batch processing: Many DBAs are so overwhelmed with the desire to use database snapshots that they overlook the obvious. Normal nightly batch replication processing via PL/SQL, SQL*Plus, and even Pro*C can be just as efficient as and much less complicated than database replication.

References:

Chapter 6
Chapter 7
Chapter 8
Chapter 15

Q: *Why is my table larger in size after it is exported and imported?*

This is a common complaint of many DBAs. In trying to do the right thing, they schedule a full database reorganization to try to clean up fragmentation. The data is exported, the tables are dropped, tablespaces are defragmented and then all data is imported. So how can the size a table increase? What has happened is that all rows of the table have been inserted at the normal PCTFREE setting. If it is set at 20%, then 20% of the allocated space remains unused. When records are inserted under normal application operation, they are not at their full size. Some columns are inserted later; other columns are expanded in size as their values increase. This type of data expansion uses up the reserved free space. To prevent this problem from occurring, the DBA will need to set the PCTFREE table parameter lower (near to zero) during the data import and then back to the normal value for future application activity.

Q: *You mention an INIT.ORA parameter _OPTIMIZER_UNDO_CHANGES. This parameter is not documented and is not listed in my SQL*DBA SHOW PARAMETERS output. How do I get a list of all parameters?*

Run the following query to see the Oracle hidden parameters. These parameters will vary from one hardware platform to the next and from one Oracle release to the next.

```
SELECT KSPPINM
FROM   X$KSPPI
WHERE  SUBSTR (KSPPINM, 1, 1) = '_';
```

```
KSPPINM
-----------------------------------------------------------------
_trace_files_public
_latch_spin_count
_max_sleep_holding_latch
_max_exponential_sleep
_latch_wait_posting
_cpu_count
_debug_sga
_messages
_enqueue_locks
_enqueue_hash
_enqueue_debug_multi_instance
_trace_buffers_per_process
_trace_block_size
_trace_archive_start
_trace_flushing
_trace_enabled
_trace_events
_trace_archive_dest
_trace_file_size
_trace_write_batch_size
_controlfile_enqueue_timeout
_db_block_cache_protect
_db_block_compute_checksums
_db_block_hash_buckets
_db_block_multiple_hashchain_latches
_db_handles
_db_handles_cached
_wait_for_sync
_db_block_max_scan_cnt
_db_writer_scan_depth
_db_writer_scan_depth_increment
_db_writer_scan_depth_decrement
_db_large_dirty_queue
_db_block_write_batch
_db_block_cache_clone
_disable_blocking_waiters
_log_checkpoint_recovery_check
_switch_on_stuck_recovery
_log_io_size
_log_buffers_debug
_log_debug_multi_instance
_log_entry_prebuild_threshold
_disable_logging
_db_no_mount_lock
_log_blocks_during_backup
_allow_resetlogs_corruption
_corrupt_blocks_on_stuck_recovery
_rollback_segment_initial
_rollback_segment_count
_offline_rollback_segments
_corrupted_rollback_segments
_small_table_threshold
```

```
_reuse_index_loop
_row_cache_instance_locks
_row_cache_buffer_size
_kgl_multi_instance_lock
_kgl_multi_instance_pin
_kgl_multi_instance_invalidation
_passwordfile_enqueue_timeout
_mts_load_constants
_mts_fastpath
_mts_listener_retry
_init_sql_file
_optimizer_undo_changes
_sql_connect_capability_table
_sql_connect_capability_code
_sql_connect_capability_override
_parallel_server_sleep_time
_parallel_allocation
_use_fast_scn
_trace_instance_termination
```

References:

"INIT.ORA Parameter Summary" in Chapter 9

Q: *Is it possible to get a full list of all the available V$ performance monitoring tables?*

Run the following query to see the Oracle V$ tables. These tables may vary from one Oracle release to the next.

```
SELECT * FROM X$KQFVI;

ADDR        INDX   KQFVIOBJ   KQFVIVER KQFVINAM
--------  ---------- ---------- ---------- ----------------------------------
084DF51C       0 4294950915        1 V$WAITSTAT
084DF558       1 4294950916        1 V$ROWCACHE
084DF594       2 4294950917        1 V$PROCESS
084DF5D0       3 4294950918        1 V$BGPROCESS
084DF60C       4 4294950919        5 V$SESSION
084DF648       5 4294951097        1 V$SESSION_WAIT
084DF684       6 4294951103        2 V$SESSION_EVENT
084DF6C0       7 4294951101        2 V$SYSTEM_EVENT
084DF6FC       8 4294951083        1 V$LICENSE
084DF738       9 4294950920        2 V$TRANSACTION
084DF774      10 4294950921        4 V$LATCH
084DF7B0      11 4294950922        1 V$LATCHNAME
084DF7EC      12 4294950923        1 V$LATCHHOLDER
084DF828      13 4294950925        1 V$RESOURCE
084DF864      14 4294951065        1 V$_LOCK1
084DF8A0      15 4294950926        1 V$_LOCK
084DF8DC      16 4294950927        1 V$LOCK
084DF918      17 4294951068        1 V$TIMER
084DF954      18 4294950928        1 V$SESSTAT
084DF990      19 4294951107        1 V$MYSTAT
084DF9CC      20 4294951080        1 V$SESS_IO
```

084DFA08	21	4294950929	1 V$SYSSTAT
084DFA44	22	4294950930	1 V$STATNAME
084DFA80	23	4294950931	3 V$ACCESS
084DFABC	24	4294950932	1 V$DBFILE
084DFAF8	25	4294950933	1 V$ARCHIVE
084DFB34	26	4294950934	1 V$FILESTAT
084DFB70	27	4294950935	1 V$LOGFILE
084DFBAC	28	4294950937	1 V$ROLLSTAT
084DFBE8	29	4294950938	1 V$SGA
084DFC24	30	4294950939	1 V$SGASTAT
084DFC60	31	4294950940	3 V$PARAMETER
084DFC9C	32	4294950942	1 V$ENABLEDPRIVS
084DFCD8	33	4294950944	2 V$DISPATCHER
084DFD14	34	4294950945	1 V$SHARED_SERVER
084DFD50	35	4294950946	1 V$QUEUE
084DFD8C	36	4294950947	1 V$REQDIST
084DFDC8	37	4294950948	1 V$CIRCUIT
084DFE04	38	4294950949	1 V$LOADCSTAT
084DFE40	39	4294950950	1 V$LOADTSTAT
084DFE7C	40	4294950951	3 V$LIBRARYCACHE
084DFEB8	41	4294951028	6 V$SQLAREA
084DFEF4	42	4294951090	2 V$SQLTEXT
084DFF30	43	4294951092	1 V$OPEN_CURSOR
084DFF6C	44	4294951091	2 V$DB_OBJECT_CACHE
084DFFA8	45	4294951045	1 V$VERSION
084DFFE4	46	4294951111	1 V$CONTROLFILE
084E0020	47	4294951047	1 V$DATABASE
084E005C	48	4294951048	1 V$THREAD
084E0098	49	4294951049	2 V$LOG
084E00D4	50	4294951050	2 V$DATAFILE
084E0110	51	4294951051	1 V$LOGHIST
084E014C	52	4294951125	1 V$COMPATIBILITY
084E0188	53	4294951126	1 V$COMPATSEG
084E01C4	54	4294951066	1 V$INSTANCE
084E0200	55	4294951070	1 V$TYPE_SIZE
084E023C	56	4294951071	1 V$NLS_PARAMETERS
084E0278	57	4294951131	1 V$NLS_VALID_VALUES
084E02B4	58	4294951133	3 V$OPTION
084E02F0	59	4294951075	1 V$RECOVER_FILE
084E032C	60	4294951076	1 V$BACKUP
084E0368	61	4294951077	1 V$LOG_HISTORY
084E03A4	62	4294951078	1 V$RECOVERY_LOG
084E03E0	63	4294951084	1 V$FIXED_TABLE
084E041C	64	4294951088	1 V$SESSION_CURSOR_CACHE
084E0458	65	4294951089	1 V$SYSTEM_CURSOR_CACHE
084E0494	66	4294951093	1 V$MTS
084E04D0	67	4294951116	1 V$PWFILE_USERS
084E050C	68	4294951109	1 V$DBLINK
084E0548	69	4294951137	1 V$PQ_SLAVE
084E0584	70	4294951138	1 V$PQ_SESSTAT

Q: *Is it possible to get a full list of all the available X$ tables?*

Run the following query to see the Oracle X$ tables. These tables may vary from one Oracle release to the next.

```
SELECT  *
FROM    V$FIXED_TABLE
WHERE   NAME LIKE 'X$%'
```

NAME	OBJECT_ID	TYPE
X$KQFTA	4294950912	TABLE
X$KQFVI	4294950913	TABLE
X$KQFDT	4294950914	TABLE
X$KQFCO	4294951036	TABLE
X$KSPPI	4294950998	TABLE
X$KSLLT	4294950993	TABLE
X$KSLLD	4294950994	TABLE
X$KSLED	4294951094	TABLE
X$KSLES	4294951095	TABLE
X$KSLEI	4294951102	TABLE
X$KSUSE	4294951004	TABLE
X$KSUPR	4294951005	TABLE
X$KSUPRLAT	4294951006	TABLE
X$KSUSD	4294951007	TABLE
X$KSUSGSTA	4294951008	TABLE
X$KSUTM	4294951067	TABLE
X$KSUSESTA	4294951009	TABLE
X$KSUMYSTA	4294951106	TABLE
X$KSUSIO	4294951079	TABLE
X$KSUSECST	4294951096	TABLE
X$KSURU	4294951010	TABLE
X$KSUPL	4294951011	TABLE
X$KSUCF	4294951012	TABLE
X$KSUXSINST	4294951046	TABLE
X$KSULL	4294951082	TABLE
X$KSBDP	4294950990	TABLE
X$KSBDD	4294950991	TABLE
X$MESSAGES	4294950992	TABLE
X$KSMSD	4294950995	TABLE
X$KSMSS	4294950997	TABLE
X$KSMLRU	4294951099	TABLE
X$KGHLU	4294951105	TABLE
X$KSMSP	4294951100	TABLE
X$KSMCX	4294950996	TABLE
X$KSQRS	4294950999	TABLE
X$KSQEQ	4294951000	TABLE
X$KSQDN	4294951001	TABLE
X$KSQST	4294951085	TABLE
X$TRACE	4294951002	TABLE
X$TRACES	4294951003	TABLE
X$NLS_PARAMETERS	4294951043	TABLE
X$KSULV	4294951130	TABLE
X$KCCCF	4294951110	TABLE

```
X$KCCFN                    4294951037 TABLE
X$KCCDI                    4294951038 TABLE
X$KCCRT                    4294951041 TABLE
X$KCCLE                    4294951040 TABLE
X$KCCFE                    4294951039 TABLE
X$KCCLH                    4294951042 TABLE
X$KCBCBH                   4294950952 TABLE
X$KCBRBH                   4294950953 TABLE
X$BH                       4294950954 TABLE
X$KCBWAIT                  4294950955 TABLE
X$KCBFWAIT                 4294951081 TABLE
X$KCKCE                    4294951122 TABLE
X$KCKTY                    4294951123 TABLE
X$KCKFM                    4294951124 TABLE
X$KCFIO                    4294950957 TABLE
X$LE                       4294950958 TABLE
X$LE_STAT                  4294950959 TABLE
X$KCVFH                    4294951072 TABLE
X$KTADM                    4294951013 TABLE
X$KTCXB                    4294951014 TABLE
X$KTURD                    4294951022 TABLE
X$KTTVS                    4294951062 TABLE
X$KDNCE                    4294950962 TABLE
X$KDNST                    4294950963 TABLE
X$KDNSSC                   4294950964 TABLE
X$KDNSSF                   4294950965 TABLE
X$KDXST                    4294950966 TABLE
X$KDXHS                    4294950967 TABLE
X$KQRST                    4294950989 TABLE
X$KQRPD                    4294951141 TABLE
X$KQRSD                    4294951142 TABLE
X$KQDPG                    4294951098 TABLE
X$KGLOB                    4294950985 TABLE
X$KGLLK                    4294950986 TABLE
X$KGLPN                    4294950987 TABLE
X$KGLST                    4294950988 TABLE
X$KGLAU                    4294951104 TABLE
X$KGLTR                    4294951033 TABLE
X$KGLXS                    4294951034 TABLE
X$KGLDP                    4294951035 TABLE
X$KGLNA                    4294951064 TABLE
X$KKSBV                    4294951063 TABLE
X$KGICC                    4294951086 TABLE
X$KGICS                    4294951087 TABLE
X$KGLLC                    4294951108 TABLE
X$VERSION                  4294951029 TABLE
X$KQFSZ                    4294951069 TABLE
X$KZDOS                    4294951023 TABLE
X$KZSRO                    4294951024 TABLE
X$KZSPR                    4294951025 TABLE
X$KZSRT                    4294951115 TABLE
X$K2GTE2                   4294951052 TABLE
X$K2GTE                    4294951032 TABLE
X$KMMSI                    4294950972 TABLE
```

X$KMMDI	4294950973	TABLE
X$KMMSG	4294950974	TABLE
X$KMMDP	4294950975	TABLE
X$KMMRD	4294950976	TABLE
X$KMCQS	4294950970	TABLE
X$KMCVC	4294950971	TABLE
X$UGANCO	4294951109	TABLE
X$OPTION	4294951132	TABLE
X$KXFPCST	4294951113	TABLE
X$KXFPCMS	4294951117	TABLE
X$KXFPSMS	4294951118	TABLE
X$KXFPCDS	4294951119	TABLE
X$KXFPSDS	4294951120	TABLE
X$KXFPDP	4294951134	TABLE
X$KXFPSST	4294951114	TABLE
X$KXFPYS	4294951135	TABLE
X$KLLCNT	4294950968	TABLE
X$KLLTAB	4294950969	TABLE
X$KVII	4294951127	TABLE
X$KVIS	4294951128	TABLE
X$KVIT	4294951129	TABLE
X$KCVFHONL	4294951073	TABLE
X$KCVFHMRR	4294951074	TABLE
X$KGLTABLE	4294951056	TABLE
X$KGLBODY	4294951057	TABLE
X$KGLTRIGGER	4294951058	TABLE
X$KGLINDEX	4294951059	TABLE
X$KGLCLUSTER	4294951060	TABLE
X$KGLCURSOR	4294951061	TABLE

Q: *Is there a way I can structure a database particularly for performance?*

If you structure your database correctly from the outset, you will get excellent initial performance. You will also facilitate the close monitoring of the database to pinpoint which part of the database needs attention, and you will minimize the effects of any new requirements from the database, such as a new application being added to it. Follow these guidelines:

- Locate redo log files on a disk other than the disk holding the database files. Redo logs between 5 and 10 megabytes in size perform well at most sites.

- Split tables and indexes into separate tablespaces.

- Separate tables that are commonly used together onto separate disks. Try to combine infrequently used tables from frequently used tables.

- Have a separate temporary tablespace.

- Place users into their own tablespace.

- Store the Oracle products in a products tablespace.

- Store only the Oracle system tables in the system tablespace.

- Create tablespaces on a per-application basis. Tables and indexes that are shared by many applications are best placed into common tablespaces.

- Do not store any part of the Oracle database on the operating system disk; in particular, keep away from the operating system disk where paging and swapping take place.

- Allocate many medium-sized tablespaces instead of fewer large tablespaces.

- Spread your disk I/O across as many disk drives and as many disk controllers as possible.

- Be aware of your machine-specific disk characteristics such as the advantages of raw devices on many UNIX systems.

- Ensure that care is taken in sizing every part of the database to allow for growth. There should be enough free space in your database to rebuild the largest table in your application.

References:
    Chapter 9

Questions from System Administrators

Q: *The overnight backups are taking too long. What options are available to speed them up?*

Oracle offers you several ways to back up your system. If you are running with archiving enabled, you have the option of performing hot backups, that is, backing up to tape without shutting your database down. You must ensure that your archives are backed up to tape. If you don't have the time to perform a full image database copy nightly, hot backups may be a good alternative for you. If you use hot backups, we recommend that you take a full consistent database backup with the database shut down periodically—at least twice a month.

We recommend that all sites take an export of their database nightly. If you are running client-server, make sure that all exporting takes place at the database server end, not across the network. Consider having a larger BUFFER parameter for the export, having multiple exports running (with each exporting a different set of tables), and exporting from disk to disk, which is considerably faster than exporting to tape.

References:
    Chapter 14
    "Tuning EXPORT and IMPORT Utilities" in Chapter 15

Q: *Our CPU is overworked coping with the Oracle users. What can I do?*

One of the most common causes of an overworked CPU is a lack of memory on your machine. First, find out whether this is the case by issuing the appropriate command for your operating system. Oracle has several parameters that can be tuned to minimize the use of memory. The parameter that should be reduced first is the DB_BLOCK_BUFFER parameter, followed by the LOG_BUFFER and then the SHARED_POOL_SIZE. The SORT_AREA_SIZE (and SORT_AREA_RETAINED_SIZE), indicating the amount of memory reserved for each user process to sort in memory, is also an important parameter to tune.

If you have free memory, investigate which processes are using the most CPU resources. In our experience, these processes tend to be those from untuned programs or poor design of either the database or the program. They may also quite often be run by developers who shouldn't even be on the machine at the time.

References:
>   Chapter 2
>   Chapter 18

Q: *We have excessive paging and swapping. What can be done to Oracle to alleviate this problem?*

You must reduce your memory usage immediately by reducing Oracle's memory usage. Consider reducing DB_BLOCK_BUFFER, LOG_BUFFER, SORT_AREA_SIZE, and SHARED_POOL_SIZE in the order listed here.

There are many machine-specific ways of reducing memory usage. If you are running UNIX, consider reducing the UNIX buffer cache if you are using raw devices. If you are running VMS, make sure that all Oracle executables have been installed as shared.

References:
>   "Memory Problems and Tuning" in Chapter 2
>   "Tuning Memory" in Chapter 9
>   "Tuning Memory" in Chapter 11
>   Chapter 18

Q: *The Oracle application is I/O bound. What can be done?*

Your disk I/O must be spread evenly across disk devices and controllers. If one disk exceeds its maximum I/Os per second and if users requests are forced to wait in a queue for their reads or writes to occur, your users' response times will suffer accordingly. Follow this checklist to avoid excessive disk I/Os:

•   Keep developers and QA staff off your production machines.

•   Put redo log files and database files onto separate disk drives.

- Do not store any part of the database on the operating system disk.

- Split tables and indexes into separate tablespaces on different disks.

- Split tables that are commonly used into separate tablespaces on different disks.

- Avoid arbitrary site standards (we have found these at some sites), such as allowing only the system tablespace to reside on a specified disk.

- Size your tables, indexes, rollbacks, and temporary segments correctly to avoid dynamic extension and chaining.

- Make effective use of memory by storing as much data in memory buffers as possible, and allow sorting to take place in memory instead of disk wherever possible.

References:
    "Tuning Disk I/O" in Chapter 9
    "Tuning Disk I/O" in Chapter 11

Q: *We have a UNIX-based network that has many machines attached. Monitoring the network and Oracle database is giving me a real headache. Are there any tools on the market that provide online monitoring of distributed systems?*

We are aware of three excellent products that revolutionize the monitoring of distributed systems. Patrol, from Patrol Software, was developed under the guidance of Martin Picard, the former Director of Networking products at Oracle; Ecosphere was developed by Ecosystems; and DB-Vision, which has a very good reputation, was developed by Aston Brooke Software, Inc. All of these products allow system administrators to monitor and manage remote workstations and applications, including Oracle. All have attractive graphical frontends that make the job of administering a distributed network featuring an Oracle database a pleasure. These products are state-of-the-art; we are certain that as time goes on, more and more products will be developed in this area.

C

Tuning Oracle Financials

*Introduction to Financials Tuning**

Oracle Financials is an accounting package available from Oracle that includes modules for all accounting functions, including general ledger, accounts payable, accounts receivable, inventory, order entry, purchasing, payroll, and project accounting. At the time of writing, it is Oracle Corporation's fastest-growing business segment.

This chapter covers Release 10 of the main modules of Oracle Financials (General Ledger, Oracle Payables, Oracle Receivables, and Oracle Assets). It does not cover other Oracle Applications products, such as Oracle Manufacturing and Oracle Human Resources. The term *Oracle Applications* refers to the development environment used to write the products. (This was previously referred to as the *Application Foundation*). Smart-Client (GUI) issues are not covered. All menu paths shown refer to the system administrator's responsibility, unless otherwise stated. The path names and environment variables are specified as for UNIX.

---

* Many thanks to Stuart Worthington for writing this appendix. Stuart is a freelance Financials DBA, formerly with Oracle U.S. and Oracle Australia, currently working in Germany. He has worked with Release 10 since Release 10.2.2 and was the first DBA outside Oracle Corporation to install Release 10.

Financials is a cross between an online transaction processing (OLTP) application and a decision support system (DSS). Some Financials users will primarily enter data (e.g., invoice entry or journal entry); other users will run large background processes to produce Aged Trial Balances (ATBs) or to depreciate assets. This complicates some database decisions, since OLTP and DSS databases are typically configured differently. Do not compare Financials databases with OLTP-only databases. A hardware configuration that supports 250 users running a data-entry application, may support only 50 or fewer users running Financials.

Getting the most out of your hardware for a Financials database is very different from tuning an in-house application. Unless your site is writing a substantial amount of custom code, you will not be able to change any of the database design. Also, because you do not have access to most of the source code, you will not have many options to change the programs themselves. In addition, we recommend that you do not make too many changes to the indexing, since the Oracle developers have written their code with particular indexes in mind. By changing indexes, you might fall into the trap of making one particular program run faster, only to find that some other program (one you may never have heard of) that previously took an hour now needs to be killed after 12 hours!

Although there are a number of aspects of Oracle Financials that you can't tune, there are still many other areas in which your tuning can make a big difference in overall performance.

Financials is a big product by any standard. A typical installation has on the order of 1,000 tables, 450 sequences, 350 views, 300 forms, 400 reports, and 200 packages and procedures. Since most tables, views, and synonyms are used by more than one of the 20 or so database users, there are also thousands of grants and synonyms. These figures increase substantially if you have extra Financials modules, Regional Localizations, Translations, Oracle Manufacturing, or Oracle Human Resources. Several modules and database objects are very rarely used, and some aren't used at all by most sites, but this still leaves you with an unwieldy database. Fortunately, Oracle now provide tools to run almost all major Financials management functions, including creating all objects, checking for the existence of required files, and installing patches.

If you are running any version of Release 9 or earlier, our first recommendation is to upgrade to Release 10, which offers vastly improved documentation, quality control, management tools, and support. Release 10.4 and above also allow the use of Oracle kernel version 7.1.6, whereas earlier releases are supported only with versions 6 or 7.0 of the database.

As a general rule, you should plan to run the latest production version available. There were criticisms of product control with earlier releases, and some Financials controllers may have bad memories of going live with new releases, but these are largely historical. By the time you have finished testing and upgrading, there may well be a later version anyway. Releases 10.6 and later allow a new table structure for multiple sets of books, which is strongly recommended for future compatibility.

Note that is it not necessary, or even recommended, to upgrade via different versions. For example, it's possible to upgrade a Financials database from Release 9.3.7 to Release 10.6. It is not necessary to run Release 9.4.2 or Release 10.4.1 in between.

Installing Oracle Financials

If your Oracle Financials database has not yet been installed, you have a lot of decisions to make. If you are new to Financials, we recommend that you consider working with a DBA who already has experience in this area. You will probably learn much more by participating in a joint installation than by doing it yourself the hard way. With luck, you will have the luxury of being able to install the database and applications for a long testing and evaluation period, knowing that you will be able to completely rebuild your database before going live. Without careful planning, you might have to do this anyway.

The first thing you must do is to try an "RYM"—Read Your Manual(s). Although the Financials documentation set is dauntingly thick, it is thick for a reason. There is a lot you need to know. You won't normally be expected to know much about the applications themselves, but you will have to know a lot about how they fit together from a DBA's perspective. It is not unreasonable for a DBA who is experienced with Oracle but new to Financials to spend two weeks reading through the documentation before even creating the database.

While we're on the subject of documentation, you should make the effort to install and become familiar with Oracle Book. All Financials documentation now comes electronically, usually on CD-ROM. While Oracle Book isn't everyone's favorite browser, it does the job, and it will save you from having to guard all your manuals from users and developers.

Don't forget to check with Oracle support to be sure that your version of Financials is supported on the UNIX version and RDBMS version that you intend to run. Just because a given version of the kernel is supported on a certain version of UNIX and a given version of Financials normally runs against the same kernel version, it does not necessarily follow that you can run the combination together. Most combinations do work, but you may find odd problems with certain programs, and Oracle will probably refuse to support you. The Oracle Applications group maintains a list of certified combinations. Check the various combinations of operating system, RDBMS, and Financials as well before upgrading the version of UNIX and/or Oracle.

Sizing

Sizing a new database can be time-consuming. Financials is very disk-hungry, and many installations fail because unwary DBAs assume that Financials is just another application and that a 500-megabyte partition will be more than enough. It won't be. Most R10 installations of Financials require almost a gigabyte just to install the executables. If you are very short of disk space, you can delete directories later, including the install and upgrade directories for each module, but it is normally helpful to keep these for future reference.

Oracle Corporation supplies sizing questionnaires for each module, and you can use these to obtain a very precise estimate of how many rows in each table to expect and the average row lengths. In practice, it is generally very difficult to find the right people to answer your questions, and they often can't give exact answers. You will probably have to make some approximations, especially for smaller instances. Expect the numbers you are given to be different from those you actually see later on in production. Always aim to have more disk space than you initially need. Without enough disk space, administering a Financials database becomes exponentially more difficult, and you will find yourself spending more and more time shuffling files and tables around outside normal work hours and less time fixing real problems.

Financials has several tables with more than 100 or even 200 columns. Even though some of these columns are typically null, this results in very long row lengths. As a result, create your database with a DB_BLOCK_SIZE of at least 4,096 or 8,192 bytes. This will waste some space in small tables, but this is insignificant in comparison with the space you will save in the large tables with many columns. You will also be able to reduce your DB_BLOCK_BUFFERS, which will alleviate least-recently-used (lru) chain contention. It is not possible to change your DB_BLOCK_SIZE without recreating and reimporting your entire database.

Take the time to figure out how much space you'll need for executables, add at least an approximate database sizing, and then add a generous comfort factor. Don't forget that you'll need to upgrade one day, and you may need to keep two versions of Oracle and/or Financials online. Disk space really isn't that expensive these days, especially when you take into account how much of your time (and therefore your organization's money) you'll save. Our recommendation: Go for the extra gigabyte! Be similarly generous when choosing your sizing factor within *adaimgr.* Although any value from zero on up is possible, we would never recommend less than 25%, except for a throwaway development database. Note that sizing factors like 25%, 50%, 100%, 200%, 400%, and so on will result in less fragmentation.

When you are setting sizing factors in the Database Parameters screen within *adaimgr*, note that you can use short cuts if you want to set the temporary tablespace to be the same for all products. Instead of typing one of the standard options (e.g., S for sizing factor or T for temporary tablespace), which allow you to change the value for a single product, type "AT", which allows you to change the value for all of the products together. Similarly, you can use AM and AT to change the main tablespace and index tablespace for all products. This will allow you to save space and reduce system administration, but at a performance cost. Normally, we recommend separate tablespaces for the tables and indexes of all fully installed products. This will enable you to balance the I/O load between disks, although you will probably find that different disks are hot each day, depending on which concurrent jobs are running. Disk striping alleviates, but does not eliminate, this problem. Some sites may have data and index tablespaces for all shared products, but it is more usual to group the shared products together either in their own tablespaces (e.g., SHARED and SHARED_INDX) or to use the same tablespaces that are used by the Application Object Library. You have to create the tablespaces yourself; AutoInstall does not validate what you enter, nor does it create the tablespaces for you.

When you are deciding how many workers to run for your first AutoInstall, use one more than your number of processors, up to a maximum of 15. If you do not have disk striping, your maximum should be 8. If you notice excessive disk contention, you should reduce your number of workers for subsequent AutoInstall runs.

If you are an experienced DBA using Release 9 or later, and you want more flexibility than simply using the sizing factor, you might consider modifying the Object Description Files (ODFs). Under UNIX, these are stored under *$MOD_TOP/install/odf*, where *$MOD_TOP* represents the top module of any directory (e.g., $FND_TOP or $GL_TOP). The ODFs store the table definitions and sizings and provide a convenient method of presizing your tables and indexes. The tables are grouped together according to function.

Some ODFs that you might find of particular interest are the following:

```
$GL_TOP/install/odf/gljen.odf    GL journal entries tables
$GL_TOP/install/odf/glbal.odf    GL balances tables
$GL_TOP/install/odf/glflx.odf    GL code combinations
$GL_TOP/install/odf/gljim.odf    GL interface tables
$AR_TOP/install/odf/artrx.odf    AR payment schedules and transaction tables
$AR_TOP/install/odf/arati.odf    RA interface tables
$FA_TOP/install/odf/fadpr.odf    FA depreciation tables.
```

Editing these is particularly useful if you use scripts to change the NEXT extents of several objects on the basis of the space already allocated. This is because several Financials tables are, by default, created with a small INITIAL extent and a much larger NEXT extent. For example a 100% sizing factor for an installation of fixed assets will result in building the table FA_DEPRN_DETAIL with an INITIAL extent of 16 kilobytes and a NEXT extent of 1 megabyte. Some sites will not use this table at all, but the ones that do will need large sizing to avoid having to keep extending the table (eventually running into the MAXEXTENTS limit).

If you establish a basic building block for all your segments (perhaps 20 or 40 kilobytes), you can use the UNIX *sed* utility to edit all the *odf* files to ensure that all INITIAL and NEXT extents are multiples of this figure. This is useful for sites with a large DB_BLOCK_SIZE or with large numbers of objects that don't mind losing some disk space to reduce data dictionary fragmentation.

The *adodfgen* and *adodfcmp* utilities exist to check that what is in the data dictionary matches what should be there. You can use *adadmin* to do this for all products. Note that *adodfgen* and *adodfcmp* can also be used to compare two copies of a non-Financials application. They check only the data dictionary (e.g., the tables, indexes, and grants) but not the data. This is much more effective than checking manually or writing your own utility.

Character Set

You should probably consider which character set to use when creating a new Financials database. If you have any European customers or vendors, you may want to use WE8ISO8859P1, which allows for French accents, German umlauts, and other special characters. Note that with Oracle7, it is possible to change this at a later date, though the documentation says otherwise. What you have to do is update the SYS table PROPS$.

NOTE   Be careful in doing this update, or you will be unable to reopen your database without assistance from Oracle. (See Oracle note 105600.874.)

Online Backups

When you are live with an instance, you should almost always use online backups, at least during the week. Otherwise, you will run into problems shutting down the database when long-running concurrent jobs are active. This is quite apart from the fact that you can roll forward with online backups, and you don't lose any work if you need to recover.

Database-Level Tuning

The *adaimgr* utility looks for several parameters when starting up. These vary by version and are listed in *$APPL_TOP/install/applora.txt*. Note that it is possible to run *adaimgr* with values set to lower than these values, but you might run into errors and have to restart. Unless you are particularly short of memory, we recommend that you increase SORT_AREA_SIZE above the minimum, (e.g., to 1,048,576), since this will speed up your index builds. (Don't forget to reduce it later.) Note that there is a required parameter,_OPTIMIZER_UNDO_CHANGES, which is not checked. This is still required with Oracle7 and refers to an important change to the optimizer made in version 6.0.31.2 of the kernel.

The following information about this optimizer change is from the *$ORACLE_HOME/rdbms/doc/vms_readme.doc* file.

```
"For increased performance, additional subqueries are now transformed
into  joins by the optimizer. Queries with an IN subquery, such as:
    SELECT col_list FROM t1 WHERE col2 IN (SELECT col2 FROM t2)
are now transformed into the form:
    SELECT col_list FROM t1, t2 WHERE t1.col2 = t2.col2
when t2.col2 is known to be unique. The EXPLAIN command indicates the
new execution plan."
```

This change in the optimizer had the unforeseen effect of making some areas of Financials run more slowly. Although the new optimizer indeed resulted in increased performance for many queries and for most applications, it caused problems for certain long-running queries in Financials. These queries had been manually optimized by using subqueries to force a certain execution plan.

To allow an application to ignore this optimizer change and use the previous execution plan, you have to set this parameter to TRUE for all Financials databases. Don't forget your test and development instances, especially when your site is creating its own custom code. Otherwise, your developers and testers might be working with the wrong version of the optimizer. You should also check this parameter before making any changes to the indexes; your change might have unforeseen consequences.

Note that _OPTIMIZER_UNDO_CHANGES is a hidden parameter. It does not appear in V$PARAMETER, which is why *adaimgr* cannot check it. See the section in Chapter 9 called "INIT.ORA Parameter Summary" for a discussion of such parameters.

Financials still requires the OPTIMIZER_MODE parameter set to RULE. However, the cost-based optimizer is still used in some areas, since there are hints embedded in the SQL. Because of this, you should analyze all your tables. The *ADXANLYZ.sql* script in *$AD_TOP/sql* lets you do this. You should modify this script to analyze only tables, since this then automatically analyzes tables. There are also several other scripts under *$AD_TOP/sql* that you can use for database analysis and tuning, including *ADXLMCBC.sql*, *ADXRSQDP.sql*, and *ADXRSSIE.sql*.

Your SHARED_POOL_SIZE typically does not need to be set as high for normal use as for installation. For a single set of books, you might typically need only 10 or 15 megabytes. You can increase this value for multiple sets of books.

Most Financials instances running Release 10.5 or above should set the SHARED_POOL_RESERVED_SIZE parameter. This is new in Version 7.1.6 of the kernel, and helps reduce fragmentation of the shared pool. See the *readme* file under *$ORACLE_HOME/rdbms/doc* for a fuller discussion of this parameter. This parameter is particularly useful for Financials, since it has several large packages.

As a good starting point, set the following parameters in your INIT.ORA file:

```
shared_pool_reserved_size = 20% of shared_pool_size
shared_pool_reserved_min_alloc = 10000
```

You should monitor the V$SHARED_POOL_RESERVED table to determine whether these parameters need adjusting. See the *readme* file under *$ORACLE_HOME/rdbms/doc* for details.

Regardless of whether you are able to use the SHARED_POOL_RESERVED_SIZE feature, you should pin several packages. The *ADXGNPIN.sql* script in *$AD_TOP/sql* generates another script to pin all packages and functions. You generally don't need to pin all of these, but you can use *ADXCKPIN.sql* to modify the generated script to pin the packages and functions you need. You can then run this script every time you restart the database.

If you don't run this script, you may see error messages of the form

```
ORA-04031: unable to allocate 42948 bytes of shared memory ("FND_
REQUEST","PL/SQL MPCODE","BAMIMA: Bam Buffer")
```

You can record these error messages in the alert file by setting event 4031 in the INIT.ORA; for example:

```
event = "4031 trace name context forever level 4"
```

If you see such an error message, run the command

```
ALTER SYSTEM FLUSH SHARED_POOL
```

If you are lucky, you will be able to compile and pin the package without shutting down the database. Note that FND_REQUEST is normally the largest package in Financials and is used when submitting reports from the \ Navigate Reports Run screen.

Upgrading Oracle Financials

Applying patches to Financials is relatively straightforward. The patches are usually received in *tar* format (for UNIX) and are often compressed. Install them under *$APPL_TOP/patch* using the *uncompress* and *tar* commands. The *adpatch* utility then does most of the rest of the work for you. It will back up old versions, generate forms, and relink executables where required, and it always checks version number to avoid overwriting a more recent version. One step that it doesn't do is to regenerate report files. You will need to do this manually, using *r20conv* or *r20convm*, especially if you are running with translated code. Don't forget to read the supplied online documentation, since there may be extra steps that you have to run. You may want to update the *ADPATCH_README* file to record which Technical Assistance Request (TAR) number generated the patch or Product Change Request (PCR) that you received. Once you have tested the patch, this saves time if you wish to contact Oracle support to close or to update the TAR.

Don't underestimate the work involved when going from one release of Financials to another. Going from one major release to another (e.g., from Release 9 to Release 10) can take more than a week of downtime for large installations. This is after one or more trial runs. Even going from one minor release to another (e.g., from Release 10.4 to Release 10.5) is a major task.

As usual, you have to read the documentation. With Financials upgrades, this is even more important than it might otherwise be, since there are several gotchas out there waiting for you. Don't forget the preupgrade steps. For an upgrade from Release 9 to Release 10, these can take a day or longer and can involve several people. Note that you also have to run some preupgrade steps for shared products. If you miss preupgrade steps, your upgrade will fail. Most of the time, you'll be lucky, and you'll be able to correct the problem and restart the upgrade worker; but in certain circumstances, you may end up with corrupt data and have to go back to backups.

For sites running Revenue Accounting (RA) under Release 9, one of the biggest preupgrade steps is to transfer ownership of all the RA tables to Accounts Receivable (AR). This is because the RA module was merged with the AR module. The steps to do this described in the Oracle documentation will work, but there are quicker ways. The quickest way is to update the data dictionary directly, but Oracle will not support this approach, though they have used it internally.

For a test database, the approach we describe here is worth considering, but you should take great care and lots of backups. Briefly, you need to drop all synonyms and revoke all grants for the tables you wish to transfer. Then you must shut down the database, start it up, update the SYS tables TAB$ and TSQ$, then shut down the database again. Finally, you need to recreate synonyms and grants. This approach will work, but you shouldn't consider it for production databases, since Oracle will refuse to support you. We really tried hard!

For production databases, you can still save time by exporting all RA tables together, dropping all RA tables and AR synonyms pointing to RA tables, and then importing under AR and creating new synonyms pointing from RA to AR. It is possible to generate dynamic SQL scripts to drop the tables and synonyms and recreate the grants. Note that the import will report errors when AR attempts to grant to itself. This is not a problem. If you had separate tablespaces for AR and RA before, you can continue to use them, as long you remember to give the AR user a quota on the RA tablespaces.

When running postupgrade steps, it is generally wise to take an export of old tables that will be dropped, since these can be required at a later date. You can also leave these steps until a later date, but don't forget to run them later, since they drop several tables, thus cleaning up the data dictionary and releasing free space.

One step that you can run after completing your upgrade is to drop the RA user by specifying

```
drop user RA cascade;
```

This will take a few minutes to complete, since it drops all synonyms, grants, resources, and the like that refer to the RA user. Run this command only after all other postupgrade steps are complete. Take a full database backup and an export of the RA user just in case. If you are running multiple sets of books, be sure to export and drop the other RA users also.

Concurrent Request Processing

One of the most powerful features of the Application Object Library is its support of concurrent processing. This feature gives the system administrator many ways to fine-tune daily processing. Too many sites use default processing of a set number of concurrent managers that handle all programs for all users from the time when the database comes up to the time when it shuts down again. Some sites set up processing with enough managers so that nothing ever has to wait in the queue before being processed. However, this approach defeats one of the main purposes of having concurrent processing, which is to prevent long-running updates and reports from interfering with users' interactive processing.

At sites that have too many concurrent managers, the reasoning seems to be that they never want to have to wait for a quick job to hang around in the queue. For example, if someone is waiting for a rush check and all six concurrent managers are running FSGs, then the easy solution is to have 10 managers running so that no matter how many FSGs are running, checks can be printed any time. This approach solves one problem but creates another: You may end up with several large, nonurgent jobs running right in the middle of the morning when all of your data-entry clerks are working flat out getting processing ready for the end of the quarter.

Here is another possible reason for taking this approach. Consider the case in which a senior manager needs some reports in a hurry for the Board of Directors. She doesn't get them in time because the concurrent queue is too busy processing journal reversals and trial balances. After she has chewed out the system administrator (because the only concurrent request she cared about kept getting leapfrogged by everyone else's work), she insists that the number of concurrent managers be doubled to make absolutely sure this situation never happens again. Even though most of these extra managers will never be needed, they will still cause a small drain on the system because each requires at least one extra process and Oracle connection.

Some sites don't have enough concurrent managers. The system is so busy in the morning that the concurrent managers have been cut to a minimum. Unfortunately, this means that over lunch and in the evening, only a fraction of the CPU power, memory, and disk capacity that cost so much money are being used. The effect is that your finance department staff, for example, gets frustrated because the jobs they submit one day are still pending the next morning.

What's the solution? You could suggest a hardware upgrade, or you could take a more economical approach: Use the power of the concurrent managers to make your machine resources work more effectively. Be sure to read thoroughly the section on concurrent managers in your system administrator documentation to find out how the situations that we describe above should be handled. Here are some brief suggestions:

One good approach is to classify programs according to different request types, so that you might define one queue for the short, fast jobs that have to run right away and another queue for your long-running reports. Your long reports queue might not even get started up until late afternoon but will concurrently run enough large jobs to keep your machine fully used right through the night, when the clerks have gone home. Overnight response time isn't especially important. What you care about in this case is throughput. You might find that if you have three times as many jobs running, you'll get twice as much done overnight. This approach is a particularly important one for multi-CPU machines, in which you should aim for between one and three jobs running on each processor.

Are you still worried about that manager who chewed you out? Use the \ Navigate Profile Levels screen to set her "Concurrent:Request Priority" higher so that now she leapfrogs other people in the concurrent request queue. If she is your boss's boss, you might want to consider giving her her own personal queue!

Note that the request priorities affect only the order in which concurrent requests start. They do not affect the eventual runtime, so it doesn't make any sense to set all concurrent request priorities to 1, since this will have the same effect as setting them all to a number such as 50. In fact, having all concurrent request priorities set to 1 means that you cannot give any request a higher priority in the \ Navigate Concurrent Requests screen.

There are many different approaches to concurrent processing tuning. For instance, you could set default priorities at the application or responsibility level. You could grant a responsible user the system administrator responsibility so that he or she can change the priorities of jobs after they have been submitted. You could permit a different number of concurrent requests to run every hour of the day. You could educate users to put jobs on hold or request a start time in the afternoon. If you have a program that makes the lights go dim, you can use the \ Navigate Concurrent Programs screen to make it incompatible with itself, so that it can never be running more than once at a time. When required, you can reset the number of concurrent managers manually through the \ Navigate Concurrent Manager Define screen and then reset the managers using the \ Navigate Concurrent Manager Administer screen.

Most sites do not need this much flexibility in handling concurrent requests, but even for a small Financials instance (e.g., 10 concurrent users), you should, at a minimum, think about having separate queues for quick urgent jobs and long slow jobs, and you should set up work shifts so that more of the long jobs can run at night and more of the quick jobs can run during the day.

If you want to monitor your concurrent queues more closely, take a look at the wealth of information stored in the FND_CONCURRENT_REQUESTS table, normally owned by Oracle user APPLSYS. This table holds all the information in the \ Navigate Concurrent Requests screen and more. You can use this to answer questions such as the following.

How many jobs were in the queue at a given time and either running or scheduled to run? Run this query:

```
SELECT COUNT(*)
  FROM fnd_concurrent_requests
 WHERE request_date < TO_DATE
       ('&&WHEN','DD-MON-YY HH24:MI')
   AND requested_start_date < TO_DATE
       ('&&WHEN','DD-MON-YY HH24:MI')
   AND actual_completion_date > TO_DATE
       ('&&WHEN','DD-MON-YY HH24:MI');
```

How many jobs today had to wait 10 minutes or longer to run? Run this query:

```
SELECT COUNT(*)
  FROM fnd_concurrent_requests
 WHERE actual_start_date-greatest
       (request_date,requested_start_date) > 10/(24*60*60)
   AND request_date > TRUNC(SYSDATE);
```

How many jobs this week have taken longer than an hour to run? Run this query:

```
SELECT COUNT(*)
  FROM fnd_concurrent_requests
 WHERE NVL(actual_completion_date,SYSDATE) -
       actual_start_date > 1/24
   AND request_date > TRUNC(SYSDATE,'DAY');
```

There are several scripts in *$FND_TOP/sql* that you may also find useful--in particular, *afcmstat.sql, afimchk.sql, afrqrun.sql,* and *afcmrrq.sql.* It is worthwhile making a copy of the FND_CONCURRENT_REQUESTS table that will never get purged so that you can look back at how long a particular job normally takes when it is run with a certain set of parameters. This can be very useful in planning quarter-end. Don't be tempted not to purge at all, though. The Concurrent Requests screen will start to slow down. Because this is the screen that users use most and query most, you have to store the data you need somewhere else. If an open query in the Concurrent Requests screen takes too long, check to see how many records you have in there. If you have too many, then an open query will have to sort to disk, in which case you should either increase the SORT_AREA_ SIZE parameter or purge the concurrent requests table. See the section called "Archiving and Purging" to see how to reduce the number of rows. Make sure your users know that they can zoom to their most recent concurrent requests using \Help Requests.

Try to work with your accounting staff. They will be able to tell you about priorities and experiences: when they are running big jobs, which jobs can be killed and which are critical, which screens are slow, and which jobs seem to be taking longer and longer.

One problem you might encounter when using machines with 80386 processors is that memory "leaks" can cause the resident set size of the FNDLIBR processes to grow ever larger. You can reclaim some of this memory by reducing the number of concurrent managers, resetting them, setting the number of concurrent managers back to normal, and then resetting again.

Another problem you might run into on some platforms (e.g., ULTRIX) is that because the concurrent managers are started in the background, they are also run at a lower priority. Because Oracle performs best when all the user processes and all the background processes are running at the same priority, you can edit *$FND_*

TOP/bin/batchmgr so that the concurrrent managers are started up with the
normal priority using *nohup* and *nice -0.*

A final problem you might encounter is that when concurrent jobs are terminated
through the Concurrent Requests screen, there is a problem with some versions of
UNIX and some releases of the kernel; stray shadow processes may be left
running. When a process is running normally, there is a user process running
aiap (Financials) or *ar20rup* (the Oracle Applications version of Oracle Reports),
for example, and there is an Oracle shadow process. Both of these process IDs
can be found through the SQL*DBA Monitor Users screen or through UNIX using
the *ps -ef* command:

```
      UID    PID   PPID  C     STIME TTY       TIME COMD
sworthin    76     43  0 16:19:29 nty/018 0:06 aiap -s FNDPUB/PUB -c NCD101A
sworthin   116     76  0 16:19:38 ?        0:02 oraclefut1 P:4096, 3, 8,
   finmgr 21177  21074  0 02:02:32 ?        0:16 FNDLIBR FND Concurr_Processor
   finmgr 21180  21177  0 02:02:33 ?        0:31 oraclefut1 P:4096, 5, 8
   oracle   513    512 59 16:40:03 ?        0:22 oraclefut1 P:4096, 6, 9
   oracle   512    446  0  6:40:03 nty/01c 0:00 sqlplus  /
```

The shadow processes here are the *oraclefutl* processes. These can be owned
either by oracle or by the owner of the user process. Occasionally, the user
process is killed but the Oracle shadow process does not die. This problem seems
to happen more with CPU-intensive programs, especially custom code. The stray
process can cause problems for two reasons. First, it can hold locks, which often
cause problems for other users. Second, the process can run wild, using up as
much CPU as it can find. If you notice this happening, kill the Oracle shadow
process manually through UNIX. You will be able to see your action reflected in
the SQL*DBA Monitor Processes screen after a few seconds delay. It is possible to
create a job that automatically kills orphan Oracle shadow processes. Under
UNIX, specify *kill -15*, which will interrupt such processes and allow them to
clean themselves up, instead of *kill -9*, which kills them outright and requires
PMON to clean up. The process you are looking for will normally look like this:

```
   oracle   513    512 59 16:40:03 ?        0:22 oraclefut1 P:4096, 6, 9
```

Not that the parent SQL*Plus parent process has been killed, but the background
process continues to run. This process will eventually die, but not until it has
finished processing the statement it was running when the parent was killed. This
can take several minutes or even hours if a parent Aged Trial Balance report was
killed through the Concurrent Requests screen. Look for Oracle shadow processes
owned by *applmgr* that have a parent process ID of 1. Other processes you might
look for are stray FNDLIBR processes that were left behind when a database was
shut down before the internal concurrent manager was shut down. Unless you
kill them, these will run until the next machine reboot.

Archiving and Purging

Financials requires more housecleaning in the form of archiving and purging than most applications. In Release 10, there are several reports that do this for you. You can see them all by going to the \ Navigate Concurrent Program Define screen and querying for %Purge% in the Name field. The two you are likely to want to run most often are the following:

- Purge Concurrent Request and/or Manager Data (FNDCPPUR)

- Purge Signon Audit Data (FNDSCPRG)

FNDCPPUR purges the following tables:

```
FND_CONCURRENT_REQUESTS
FND_RUN_REQUESTS
FND_CONC_REQUEST_ARGUMENTS
FND_CONCURRENT_PROCESSES
FND_DUAL
```

You will probably want to run it daily. You can use the Resubmission interval in the "Run Options" zone. You can access this by quickpicking in the Report Options field of the first zone.

FNDSCPRG purges the sign-on auditing tables

```
FND_LOGINS
FND_LOGIN_RESPONSIBILITIES
FND_LOGIN_RESP_FORMS
```

Most sites that are running auditing will want to run this report at least every month. If you want to check or change your level of auditing, go to the \ Navigate Profile System screen, and query the site-level profile option "Sign-On:Audit Level". This can be set to NONE, USER, RESPONSIBILITY, or FORM so that you can store details of how often users log in or change responsibility or form. It is particularly useful to see who is logged in and what they're doing via the "Monitor Application Users" screen (\ Navigate Security User Monitor). However, it comes with a price. If you have Sign-On Auditing turned on at Form level, then a record is written to the database every time a user changes form, so you really need to trade off security and performance.

Sign-on Auditing is separate from auditing database row changes using the audit trail. You can see if you have the audit trail turned on by checking the site-level profile option "AuditTrail:Activate". Again, having this option turned off will give you better performance, but lower security.

The \ Row Who feature allows you to see who created a row and when, as well as who last updated a row and when. This is independent of Sign-on Auditing or the Audit Trail.

All accounting applications are disk-hungry, and Financials is no exception. You will come to know, if you don't already, the tables that just keep on eating into your database free space. Million-row tables are nothing unusual. We have seen all of the following tables contain more than a million rows:

```
GL_JE_LINES
GL_JE_HEADERS
GL_BALANCES
AP_EXPENSE_REPORT_LINES
AP_EXPENSE_REPORT_HEADERS
AP_PAYMENT_SCHEDULES
AR_PAYMENT_SCHEDULES
AR_CORRESPONDENCE_PAY_SCHED
AR_CUSTOMER_PROFILES
AR_CUSTOMER_PROFILE_AMOUNTS
AR_RECEIVABLE_APPLICATIONS
FA_DEPRN_SUMMARY
FA_DEPRN_DETAIL
RA_CUSTOMER_TRX
RA_CUSTOMER_TRX_LINES
RA_CUST_TRX_LINE_GL_DIST
RA_CUST_TRX_LINE_SALESREPS
RA_CUST_TRX_LINE_TAX_AUDIT
RA_CUST_TRX_SHIPMENTS
RA_SITE_USES
```

All of these tables can be archived and purged, though you may have to write the code yourself, get Oracle Professional Services to do it for you, or verify your code. Talk with your accounting staff about how many months of past data is really required. If, like most accountants, they never want to purge anything, then calculate how many extra disks they'll need to pay for per year, and let them work out a compromise. Don't expect sudden performance improvements after purging your large tables. You will save disk space, and therefore backup time, but you are unlikely to see any change in online or batch performance, since these tables are always accessed via indexes.

One table that is particularly difficult to plan for is GL_BALANCES. This table doesn't grow at a constant rate, but irregularly, particularly when budgets are being created or periods are being opened. Don't plan on taking any vacation for at least the first two months after going live. Remember that your users have deadlines too.

When you are archiving such large tables, you need to plan ahead. First remember that your bottleneck is likely to be the archiver, so either use "ping-ponging," so that your log files switch disks or (if you feel lucky) temporarily turn off archiving altogether.

Consider the following example. A medium-sized site running unattended overnight backups might move its Friday night backup to Sunday night. This allows the DBA to shut down the database, start it up in noarchivelog mode, run the purges, then start up the database in archivelog mode in time for the Sunday night backup. You should be able to recover users' work from a disk crash on Friday afternoon or Monday morning. Be careful, though. If Sunday night's backup isn't 100% reliable, you are vulnerable until your next backup. A safer alternative for sites that normally run archiving to disk is to archive to tape temporarily. That way, the archive runs faster and is less likely to run out of space.

While we're on the subject of backups, we would like to recommend that most production Financials sites run online or "hot" backups. Sites that run cold backups every night are not only risking losing a day's data entry if there is a disk crash before the next cold backup is complete, but they are also squandering machine resources. Although Financials will automatically restart any jobs in the concurrent queue after a database restart, long-running jobs will typically have to be killed when the data entry clerks start logging on. Properly managed, your hardware can do just as much work at 11:00 p.m. as at 11:00 a.m.

After a large purge, you should consider rebuilding your tables or at least your indexes. The same advice applies to tables that get purged much more regularly. You will often be surprised at just how much space you can save. We were able to save 120 megabytes by rebuilding the indexes alone on GL_INTERFACE at one size in Switzerland, and 13 megabytes just by rebuilding FND_DUAL at another.

Other tables that you should consider periodically rebuilding, especially after unusually large loads, are the following:

```
AR_INTERIM_CASH_RECEIPTS
AR_INTERIM_CASH_RECEIPT_LINES
RA_INTERFACE_LINES
RA_INTERFACE_DISTRIBUTIONS
RA_INTERFACE_ERRORS
RA_INTERFACE_SALESCREDITS
```

Do *not* delete rows in these tables. Normally, you should check that no users or concurrent jobs are accessing the table you want to build. Then lock the table in exclusive mode, export it, truncate it (reusing storage if you expect the tables to grow again to the same size), and reimport the rows, using ignore=y.

One table that sometimes can be purged from is AR_JOURNAL_INTERIM, which is written to by the Journal Entries Report (ARRGTA). If this program is interrupted, it can leave stray records in the table, sometimes several hundred thousand. These should be deleted. First, check which concurrent requests created the records with the statement

```
SELECT request_id, count(*)
FROM ar_journal_interim
GROUP BY request_id
/
```

Then delete all records that were created by requests that were interrupted. If there are no Journal Entries Reports running, you can truncate the table.

The GL Optimizer

The GL optimizer mimics a cost-based optimizer. It stores information about the selectivity of each of your segment values and creates indexes where appropriate. You should run the GL optimizer at least once a period or after creating a large number of segment values, defining a new chart of account, or changing the summary templates.

When your Accounting Key Flexfield is set up through the \ Navigate Setup Financials Flexfields Key Segments screen under the Application Developer responsibility, pay attention to the "Indexed" field in the segment zone. If this part of the implementation is being done in-house, we recommend that you index all segments that are likely to be queried on except for those with six or fewer values. For example, if you have duplicate cost center numbers in different departments and there is no connection between two cost centers with the same number, you shouldn't create an index on the cost center segment, although you should consider creating a concatenated index on the department and cost center segments. If you analyze the GL_CODE_COMBINATIONS table, you can measure how selective your indexes are by viewing USER_TAB_COLUMNS.

The GL optimizer is designed primarily to make FSGs run faster. We recommend that for validation of flexfields, you also create a nonunique concatenated index on the account segment, followed by all the other defined segments in flexfield order. Note that no indexes will be created when you define the Accounting Key Flexfield. You actually have to run the GL Optimizer through the \ Navigate Setup System Optimize screen from the "General Ledger Super User responsibility. In Release 10, this can now drop indexes that have been automatically created, but you should check in SQL*Plus to see if there are other manually created indexes that you no longer want.

To make FSGs run faster, avoid null values in your ranges when submitting. If you have a four-character numeric segment, enter 0000 and 9999 as the minimum and maximum values for the range.

Developer Utilities

Financials comes with some useful utilities that you can access through the menus. Try adding the DEVELOPER_UTILITIES menu to the OTHER menu with a prompt of "Utilities" using the \ Navigate Application Menu screen on a development database. Then when you follow the menu path \ Navigate Other Utilities, you have access to the following menu options:

Examine
> Allows you to check the field_name and block_name you are looking at. You can also use quickpick to view nondisplayed fields, global variables, and environment variables. It is also possible to change field values, which you should not allow on a production database. You can make this option more secure by setting the profile option "Utilities: Diagnostics" to "No" which requires the Oracle password when invoking the Examine option.

Zoom
> Defines zoom from the current field, zone, or form

HelpText
> Defines help text for the current field, zone, or form

UserExit
> Tests user exit

Debug
> Turns SQL*Forms debug mode on or off

Trace
> Turns SQL trace on or off

Memory
> Displays memory statistics

The Trace option is especially useful. If you have a particularly slow step in a screen, you can use this option to turn Trace on just before the step, and then you can turn it off again immediately after.

On the other hand, the Debug option is rarely useful, since there are so many triggers within Financials, owing to the nature of the development environment. (Try setting it to see what we mean!)

Financials Tips

This section summarizes additional tips for tuning Financials to best advantage.

* Financials passwords are *not* secure. Do not use Financials passwords that are the same as your operating system or Oracle passwords.

* If you need to copy databases, as is common with Financials, you can save time by copying and renaming the data files and log files, then creating a new control file. This is much quicker than using EXPORT and IMPORT, but also more dangerous, so you should take backups first. Once you have started up the new database, change the site level profile option "Site Name" to avoid confusion. This shows up on reports and also under \ Help Version. For the same reason, you should also change the name of the sets of books and the company name under Fixed Assets.

- Use \ Navigate Setup Financials Books from "General Ledger Super User", and \ Navigate Setup Options System from "Fixed Assets Manager, respectively. You should also turn off alerts that are not needed and review all repeating concurrent requests.

- If you experience disk contention in General Ledger, move the GL_CODE_COMBINATIONS and GL_JE_LINES tables to separate tablespaces on other disks.

- If you experience disk contention in Accounts Receivable, move the RA_CUSTOMER_TRX and RA_INTERFACE_LINES tables to separate tablespace on other disks.

- If you experience disk contention in Fixed Assets, move the FA_DEPRN_SUMMARY table to a separate tablespace on another disk.

- If AutoInvoice runs too slowly, check the indexes on RA_INTERFACE_LINES, RA_CUSTOMER_TRX, and RA_CUSTOMER_TRX_LINES. Query the "Line Transaction Flexfield" using \ Navigate Setup Financial Flexfields Descriptive Segments and see which segments are enabled for each context. You should have non-unique concatenated indexes for the corresponding interface_lines_attribute columns in RA_INTERFACE_LINES and RA_CUSTOMER_TRX_LINES and also for the corresponding interface_header_attribute columns in RA_CUSTOMER_TRX.

- If you are creating custom executables under UNIX, check the makefile you are using to make sure that it runs *mcs -d*; this feature shrinks executables by compressing the comment section.

- When defining your concurrent managers, set sleep to 10 or 20 seconds for interactive batch queues.

- Financials tends to generate lots of network traffic, even in character mode; this is inherent in SQL*Forms 2.3, on which the non-GUI versions of Application Object Library are based. If you experience network problems, consider using a tool such as EcoPad, which filters the traffic so that only real changes are sent when painting the screen.

- Check the scripts available in *$FND_TOP/sql*. You may want to have aliases set up for some of them; for example:

```
alias req='sqlplus / @$FND_TOP/sql/afcmrrq'
alias run='sqlplus / @$FND_TOP/sql/afrqrun'
```

  This requires an ops$ account and synonyms for the tables accessed.

- Dynamic creation of code combinations requires an exclusive lock on the GL_CODE_COMBINATIONS table. This might not be immediately possible if certain concurrent jobs are running. To check for this situation and other lock waits, run a script that calls *$ORACLE_HOME/rdbms/admin/utllockt.sql* and mails you if users are waiting for locks.

Resources for Financials Developers

This section lists a number of resources for Oracle Financials developers.

The Oracle Applications Users Group

The Oracle Applications Users Group (OAUG) was formed in the San Francisco Bay area at a kickoff meeting in May 1990. It now organizes two annual international conferences, one that is normally timed to be just before or just after the International Oracle User Group (IOUG) conference and one held in Europe. If you get the chance, you should try to attend at least one of these. It is also possible to receive CD-ROMs of the papers presented at the conferences. The OAUG also has a list of affiliated local user groups.

> Oracle Applications User Group (OAUG)
> 3121 E. Shadowlawn Ave., NE
> Atlanta, GA 30305-2405
> USA
> Phone: +1- (404) 240-0897
> Fax: +1- (404) 240-0998
> Email: 76263.1122@compuserve.com

The Oracle Applications List Server

There is an Oracle Applications list server run by Francois Gendron of Champagne, Parent & Associes in Montreal. (A list server is an electronic forum for people who share a common interest.) The Oracle Applications list server has more than 1,400 members, including some of the best in the business. To subscribe, send an email such as the following:

```
To: listproc@cpa.qc.ca
Subject: (Must be blank)

subscribe OraApps-L <your name>
```

If you are not familiar with list servers, be sure to read the first email you receive after subscribing. This will tell you the commands that you can use with the list server software. Please learn and respect the rules of the forum—in particular, those regarding headings and what you should or should not post. It's normally best to see how the server works for a few days before posting anything yourself. Don't confuse the server with Oracle support; no one gets paid for maintaining or contributing to the server. They do it out of a sense of electronic togetherness, so don't expect that you will always receive an answer to a question you post. Note that by default, you won't receive a copy of an email that you send to the server,

although you can request this by turning on the list server acknowledge feature
with:

```
set OraApps-L mail ack
```

Follow the same format when sending this command: email to *listproc@cpa.qc.ca*
with a blank subject line and no signature or footer, since the list server will
attempt to process these as appended commands.

Be careful when replying to email, since, by default, your reply will go to
everyone subscribed. If you wish to send a reply only to the sender, you should
forward email instead. Since the server generates so much email, if you try to read
it all, you may have the feeling you are drinking from a fire hose. In this case,
consider using the digest feature. With the digest, instead of receiving posts individually, you will receive one message per day containing a table of contents of
the posts of the day, followed by the text of these messages concatenated in
order. You can change your mail mode to digest by sending a message in the form

```
SET OraApps-L MAIL DIGEST
```

The two other most useful list server commands are

```
HELP
UNSUBSCRIBE OraApps-L
```

Software that automatically answers incoming email when you are away (e.g.,
with the UNIX *vacation* command will, of course, send an automatic reply to the
list server which can potentially go to all the users on the list. If one or more of
them are also on vacation and they also have automatic answering, they too may
reply to the list, setting up a looping situation. The list server software is designed
to filter out automatically generated reply messages, but it can do this only by
searching for standard strings such as "AUTO REPLY". If you use automatic
answering, check that your system will email any given user only once. This is
usually the default behavior. If you customize your reply (e.g., to give your date
of return, be sure to append to, rather than replace the standard canned response.
This will let list servers recognize that your reply has been automatically
generated.

Other Oracle-based list servers are:

> *oracle-l listserv@ccvm.kbs.net*
> *ocsig-l listserv@fatcity.com*
> *ocsig-board-l listserv@fatcity.com*
> *ocsig-warehouse-l listserv@fatcity.com*

There is a Usenet Group dedicated to Oracle:

> *comp.databases.oracle*

If you have Oracle support, then you can also access the Oracle Customer Information System (OCIS) web server on

http://www.oracle.co.uk/

This allows you to query bulletins and notes and the bug database and gives details of product availability and training courses. You need a username and password to gain access.

D

Oracle
Performance Pack

The Oracle Performance Pack is a set of performance tools that you can optionally purchase with Oracle Enterprise Manager (released with Oracle7.3). The
Performance Pack is a sophisticated replacement for SQL*DBA. It has impressive
capabilities, and we think it's worth the additional cost. This appendix highlights
many of the features of the products, as well a few gotchas that you should be
aware of before you start using them.

All of the Performance Pack products can be controlled from a central console
within Enterprise Manager. They provide you with a great deal of tuning diagnostic information, as well as recommendations on how to repair your performance problems.

NOTE   The Performance Pack is not a replacement for your DBA. It is a
toolset that your DBA can use to obtain tuning information and provide expert recommendations that would otherwise require special-
ist tuning knowledge. However, if the Performance Pack products
are used incorrectly, they can often make recommendations that
will actually make your performance worse.

The Oracle Performance Pack includes the following modules:

- Oracle Performance Manager
- Oracle Lock Manager
- Oracle Topsessions
- Oracle Tablespace Manager

- Oracle Expert
- Oracle Trace

Oracle Performance Manager

The Oracle Performance Manager provides all of the displays shown in Figure D-1.

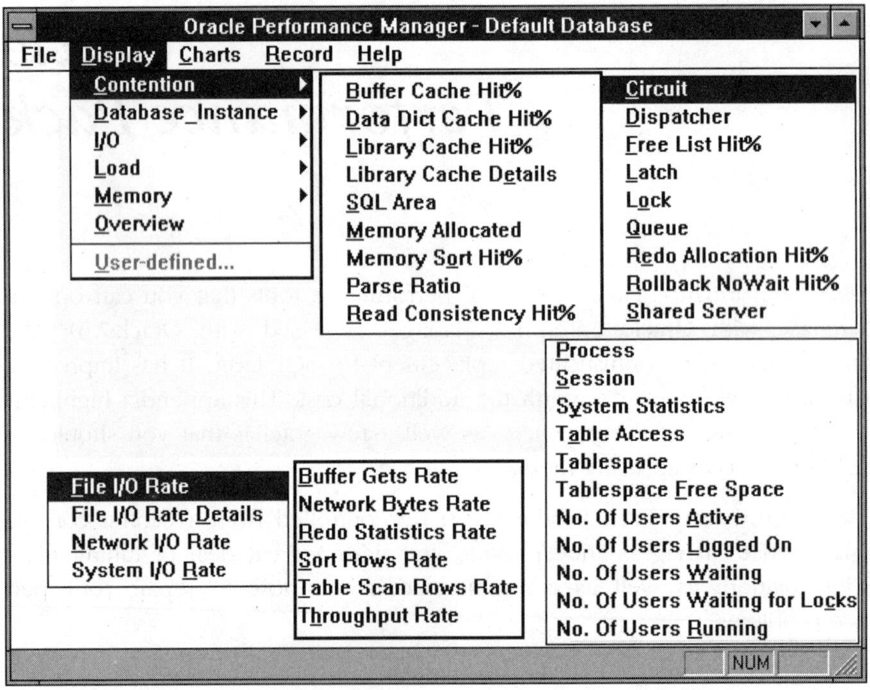

Figure D-1. Oracle Performance Manager

This product allows you to do the following:

- View the SQL statements behind the output that the product presents. You can modify the SQL and customize the appearance of charts to suit your own needs.

- Define your own charts with tailored SQL and chart specifications.

- Control the frequency of data collection. You can specify whether to gather data on request or automatically at given time intervals. The time intervals can be changed dynamically online.

- Record the readings and play back the readings for a selected time period. You can perform all kinds of analyses on the historical data.

- Define your own rules to enable you to list the top sessions that fit your selection criteria. For example, you can choose to select the 10 sessions that have the highest memory usage. The user sessions are returned to you with the largest memory user first.

- Get help with controlling disk usage, degree of fragmentation, and amount of free space.

Figure D-2 presents a graphical overview from the Performance Manager of how your database instance is performing.

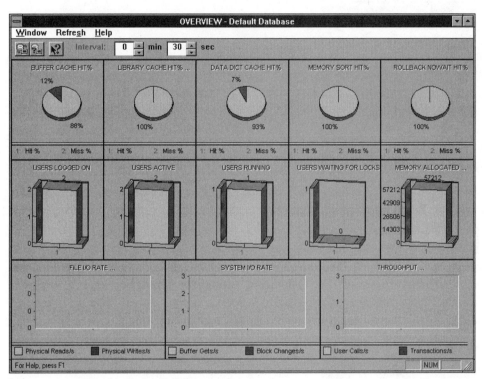

Figure D-2. How a database instance is performing

In Figure D-3, the current buffer cache hit percentage is 88%. This number should be 95%+ for an online transaction-processing application and 85%+ for batch processing. The most effective ways of improving your hit ratio are to tune your SQL statements, add indexes, or increase the DB_BLOCK_BUFFERS parameter.

Library cache hits represent the number of times a SQL statement, PL/SQL block, package, or procedure could be found in memory. In Figure D-4, the current reading is 100%, which is the best possible reading. If your reading is below 80%, consider increasing the SHARED_POOL_SIZE parameter.

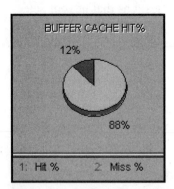

Figure D-3. Buffer cache hit ratio

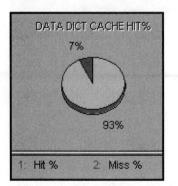

Figure D-4. Library cache hit ratio

In Figure D-5, the data dictionary cache hits is 93%. You get a miss for each dictionary item loaded from disk. The ideal reading is 99%+, but in this particular example. the database instance had not been running for very long and many of the dictionary items would have been loaded for the first time.

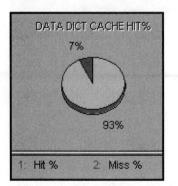

Figure D-5. Data dictionary cache hit ratio

The memory sort hit ratio (Figure D-6) is the number of times a user's entire sort could fit into memory and not have to use disk. Ideally, the hit ratio is 100%, but in very large batch applications, in which millions of rows are being sorted, this is not always possible. The most important information is whether the number of disk reads is very high during prime online usage times. If you have adequate free memory, consider increasing your SORT_AREA_SIZE parameter. Remember that SORT_AREA_SIZE is assigned on a per-user process basis and will quickly accumulate all of your memory if you have a large number of users performing large sorts on your machine.

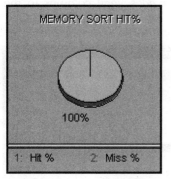

Figure D-6. Memory sort hit ratio

The rollback nowait ratio (Figure D-7) is the number of times a user has obtained a rollback segment without having to wait for another transaction to complete. The ideal ratio is 100%.

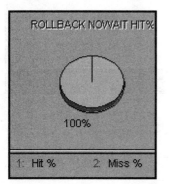

Figure D-7. Rollback nowait hit ratio

Oracle Lock Manager

The lock manager displays 10 columns across the screen—so many that the display is a little overwhelming. The information displayed is obtained from joining the DBA_OBJECTS, V$LOCK, and V$SESSION screen. The more important columns are the User Name, Session ID, Lock Type, Object Owner, Object ID, Object Type, Mode Held, and Mode Requested. If a user is blocking one or more users, the users are listed in a tree list, with each waiting user shown to the right of the User Name that is causing the locking problem.

In Figure D-8, the user MGURRY session 13 is waiting for MGURRY session 6 to release a lock on the TEST_LOCKING table. Notice that the type of lock is not shown on the screen. Our advice to Oracle: The screen is a great help, but please put the Mode Held and Mode Requested in place of Resource ID 1 and Resource ID 2. These very useful columns are currently displayed several columns to the right.

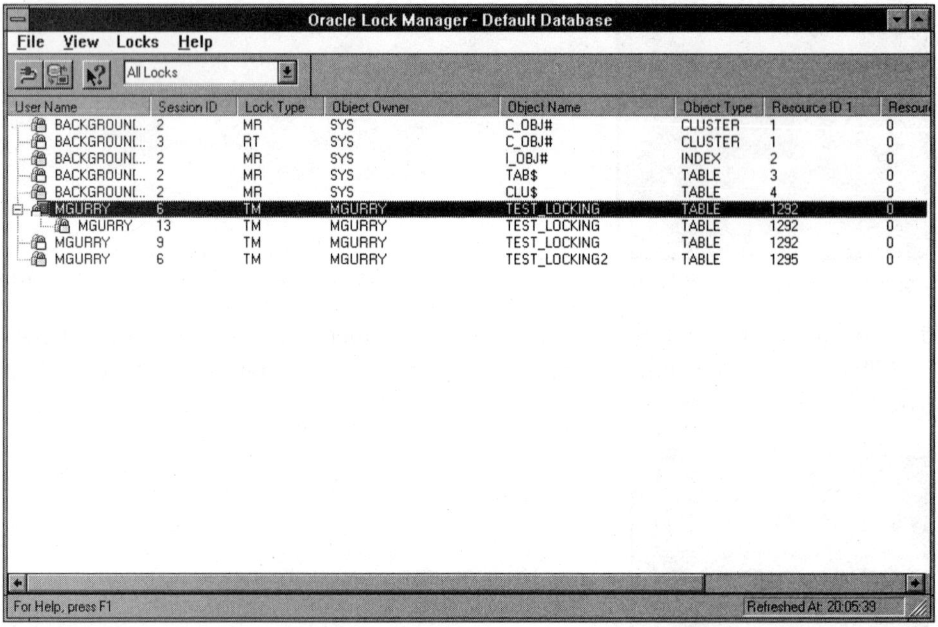

Figure D-8. Oracle lock screen

Oracle Topsessions (described in the next section) also allows you to view the same locking information for a given session.

Oracle Topsessions

Oracle Topsessions uses the following tables and views to extract its session information from the database:

```
V$SESSION
V$STATNAME
V$SESSTAT
```

```
ALL_TAB_COLUMNS
V$OPEN_CURSOR
V$SQLTEXT
V$LOCK
SYS.DBA_OBJECTS
SYS.DBA_WAITERS
PLAN_TABLE
```

Several of the screens return an error if you (or the user) do not have access to PLAN_TABLE and SYS.DBA_WAITERS. If you get the error, you must run *utlx-plan.sql* to create the PLAN_TABLE and *catblock.sql* to create the SYS.DBA_ WAITERS view.

Oracle Topsessions allows you to select the top *n* sessions, where *n* is a number that you can specify. The session details are displayed online, ordered in descending order by sort statistic. Possible sort statistics include CPU usage, memory usage, disk I/O usage, open cursors, and user transactions; you can specify the statistic that suits you. The next time you run Topsessions, the order that you selected last is presented as your default.

There are four major Oracle Topsessions display screens:

• The general screen shows you the 36 columns that now exist on the V$SES-SION table. You can drill down from this screen to obtain more detailed session performance information.

• The statistics screen lists the statistics for a given session from the V$SESSTAT table. You can filter your statistics by user, redo, enqueue, cache, operating system, parallel server, SQL, debug, other, and all.

• The locking details screen lists all of the locks held by the session and includes details on sessions that are blocked by this session. It also allows you to kill the session, as shown in Figure D-9. You should kill a session only if you know exactly what the user is performing. If the locking is caused by an application problem, fix the problem as soon as practical. For example, if the running sessions are those shown in Figure D-8, you might want to kill session ID 6, the session that is causing the waits. Don't kill a session without making sure that it will not cause a catastrophe.

• The cursor details screen allows you to list all of the cursors running for the session and their EXPLAIN PLAN details (which is brilliant), as well as the statement that is currently running. Make sure that the correct indexes are in place and are being used! Oracle Expert goes one step further by reviewing the execution plan and recommending the addition or modification of indexes. Figure D-10 displays the EXPLAIN PLAN screen.

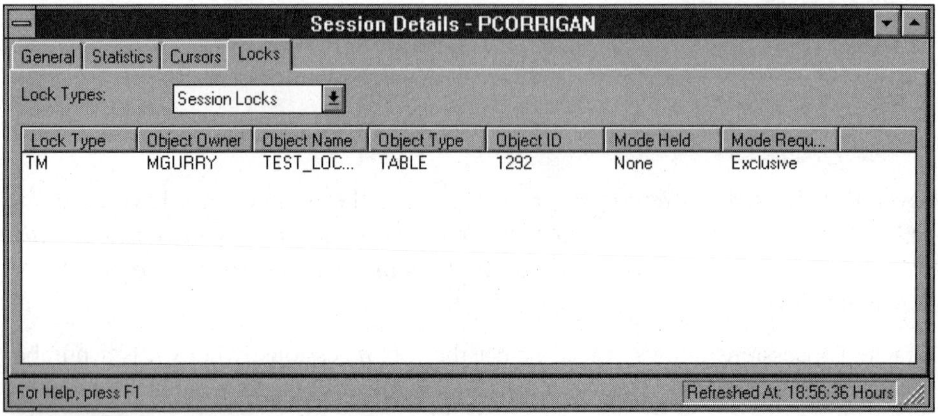

Figure D-9. Killing a session

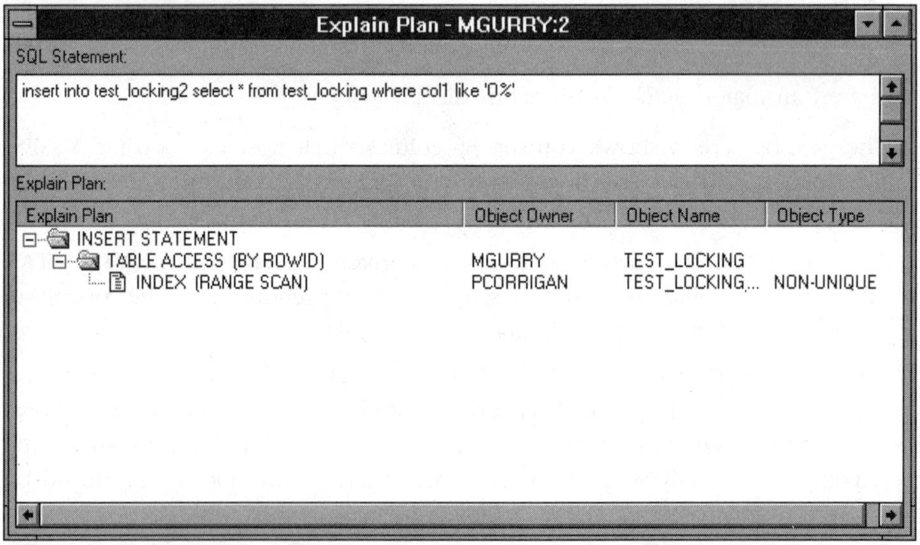

Figure D-10. Explain Plan screen

Oracle Tablespace Manager

The Tablespace Manager allows you to drill down and find out all kinds of details about a tablespace. The top level is the database instance, which drills down to the tablespaces within the database to which the instance is connected. Single clicking on a tablespace displays space usage for the tablespace; double clicking shows the data files within the tablespace. You can then drill down further to show the segments in the tablespace, space usage for each of the data files, and segments stored in each data file (see Figure D-11).

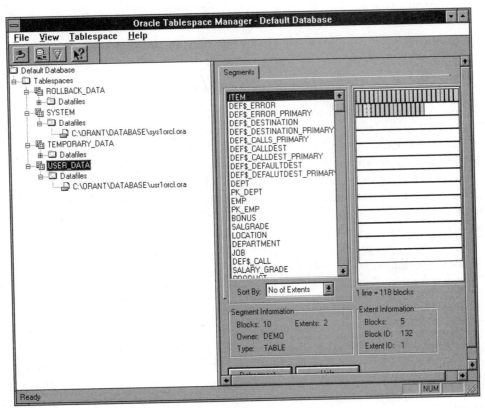

Figure D-11. Oracle Tablespace Manager screen

Two particular features that will help you to improve your performance are the ability to defragment a table and to coalesce adjoining extents (Oracle7.2 and later only).

The defragmentation option is a lot of fun, but it is not the kind of operation that you should run during peak online usage of your database. It creates an export file and a couple of supporting files used to rebuild the tables. Reliable sources have informed us that a future version of the Tablespace Manager will significantly improve the time taken to rebuild a table. It is essential that you have write permission to the directory from which the defragmentation job script is run; this is where the table rebuild files will be sent by default. You can override the default by specifying your own directory name if you wish. The name must not contain an environment variable. You also have the ability to retain default storage parameters, modify the parameters, or compress the segment into a single extent (the default).

Coalescing extents works effectively, and if you have a database that is deleting objects on a regular basis, the coalescing will assist performance. Oracle7.3 and later versions coalesce extents on a regular basis by default, so explicit coalescing should not be necessary. Ensure that your coalescing is not occurring so frequently that it is having a detrimental effect on your response times.

Oracle Expert and Oracle Trace

Anyone who has worked alongside an Rdb DBA knows that the Rdb system is renowned for its brilliant performance-monitoring tools. Now Oracle has the same tools, Oracle Expert and Oracle Trace. Oracle Expert lets you enter a new dimension of tuning by offering recommendations on how to set your site up to achieve the absolute best performance. The product also provides "what if" capabilities; for example, "What if I add 200 megabytes of memory? Will that solve our performance problems?" Oracle Expert creates scripts that implement its recommendations, as well as providing informative step-by-step descriptions of how it came up with its decisions. The product can recommend new indexes or modify existing indexes. This capability alone makes the product a mandatory part of your tuning strategy.

Oracle Trace is a general-purpose data collection product that can be used to collect detailed information on SQL events for Oracle Server Release 7.3. This SQL event data can be used as an optional source of database workload information by Oracle Expert. The standard source of workload data for Oracle Expert is a less sophisticated, but highly useful workload that can be automatically extracted by the tool from the SQL library cache (V$SQLAREA). If you are running many hundreds or even thousands of users and you have serious performance requirements, we advise you to use Oracle Trace to gather the workload data for Oracle Expert. Whether you are using Oracle Trace or the SQL cache workload, you will still get excellent benefits from using Oracle Expert.

Oracle Trace can also be used to provide details on all client-server transactions. The response times are broken down into client, network, and server response times to assist you with isolating any performance bottlenecks. Oracle has taken care of the server and SQL*Net instrumentation and will likely add Oracle Trace to the Oracle applications. You can also instrument your own applications with the Oracle Trace API for client-server event tracking. However, if you are running a small to medium site, you may not have the resources to set up Oracle Trace in your application programs. The same applies if you have purchased packaged software and don't have access to the source code.

Before you are presented with a list of Oracle Expert and Oracle Trace features, you should consider the way the products operate and how to use them most effectively. For example:

- You will need to spend some time on the products to make them work effectively. Oracle Trace, in particular, requires careful planning before it can be used to best advantage.

- Oracle Expert requires you to enter all kinds of environmental data, such as the amount of memory available on your machine and the percentage of memory being used. If you provide inaccurate information, Oracle Expert may spit incorrect recommendations right back at you.

- If you focus on a particular aspect of tuning (e.g., instance tuning) Oracle Expert will automatically select the data collection categories required to support that type of tuning. Be careful not to deselect these categories; if you do, Oracle Expert's analysis will be less than optimal. Fortunately, in this case the tools' Analysis Report will tell you that you didn't collect certain data that was required for a complete analysis.

- If your site has online transactions during the day and long-running batch jobs overnight, you should provide Oracle Expert with workload information on both. Otherwise, you may tune one at the expense of the other.

- Oracle Trace poses a 5% to 10% performance degradation if it is run continuously, so it's best to run the product when you have a real tuning need and limit the amount of data that you are gathering.

- The products require some disk storage in the database and some operating system files. Ensure that you allow enough storage and that your database objects are sized to avoid fragmentation and the exceeding of maximum extents.

- You must be using the cost-based optimizer to get meaningful recommendations from Oracle Expert. Ideally, analyze your tables with the compute statistics for the absolute best results. If your tables are too large to compute the statistics, estimate a sample of at least 40%.

- Having powerful tuning tools such as Oracle Expert and Oracle Trace in place does not mean that you have to put little effort into tuning your design. The products will not suggest how to normalize or denormalize your database to make it run more effectively.

Oracle Expert

Oracle Expert collects information from either Oracle Trace or the SQL library cache. The product will assist you with tuning your schema (sizing to avoid fragmentation), your instance (INIT.ORA) parameters, and your application (adding indexes or changing code). The product makes recommendations as well as producing the scripts to apply its recommendations. By showing you how to repair performance problems, Oracle Expert also serves an educational purpose.

As Figure D-12 shows, Oracle Expert accepts the following inputs:

- Database structure
- Instance information
- Schema information
- Environment
- Rule parameter values
- Workload
- Control parameters

And Oracle Expert produces the following outputs:

- Tuning recommendations
- Parameter files
- Reports
- Implementation scripts

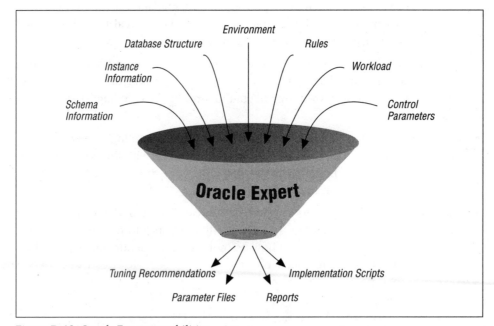

Figure D-12. Oracle Expert capabilities

We recommend that you create a separate tablespace and user to store all expert data in the database. The amount of data can get quite large if you load large amounts of Oracle Trace data. You should also set your storage parameters to ensure that Oracle Expert objects are not badly fragmented and can't exceed maximum extents.

Oracle Expert supports the following types of performance tuning:

- Instance tuning, including INIT.ORA parameters, I/O parameters, parallel query parameters, and sort parameters.

- Application tuning, including SQL tuning to eliminate duplicate statements with different case or spaces and access path analysis. Oracle Expert investigates SQL access paths to make sure that the most suitable index exists on the tables. If not, the product recommends new indexes or modification to indexes. One limitation of Oracle Expert is that it recommends index usage for the cost-based optimizer only, not the rule-based optimizer. Cardinality (how many distinct values a column has in a table) is taken into account, but skewness (how many rows exist for each of those values) is not. Until the skewness functionality is put into place, be careful not to drop an index that must be kept for best performance.

- Structure tuning, including the recommendation of default INITIAL and NEXT sizings on a tablespace. Oracle Expert will also recommend placement of your tables, indexes, and other database objects to ensure that different types of segments exist in the most appropriate tablespaces. It will also check to be sure that users have been defined with the most appropriate default and temporary tablespaces.

You can use Oracle Expert for either comprehensive tuning (all aspects of the database over time) or focused tuning (a particular area of tuning, such as access methods). You have the ability to tune the indexes on one table only if you wish.

Oracle Expert collects the following data:

Database name, version, users, tablespaces, and public synonyms
This information is captured automatically from the database at your request. Oracle Expert will adjust its recommendations depending on the version of Oracle you are running. This gives the product a distinct advantage over other products on the market. Oracle7.2 users will see SORT_DIRECT_WRITES as a recommendation, but Oracle7.1 users will not, because Oracle Expert realizes that the parameter is not available in that release.

Instance parameters and statistics
These are gathered from the V$ parameters and DBA views. The data is captured automatically from the database at your request. It is important that you obtain your tuning information from the database during peak usage times. If you enable or disable the parallel query option or the parallel server

option, or if you add more users to your database or install a new version of Oracle, you must refresh your instance information from the database.

Tables, constraints, indexes, and cluster information

These are gathered automatically by the product at your request. The data that are gathered include the storage used by tables, indexes and their columns, and the tablespace in which the objects reside. You may collect the schema information using an Oracle Expert scan, which executes a SELECT COUNT DISTINCT statement to gather cardinality details and other volumetric information. If you use the ANALYZE option, you should ideally compute the statistics by selecting a full table scan or, at the very least, obtain a sample of 40% or more rows if you use the Estimated/Limit option.

Logical device and other operating system and machine information

This is required for many of the recommendations. You must enter the details manually. If you enter incorrect details, Oracle Expert may provide incorrect recommendations. Enter the names of your logical disks, their physical location, their performance rating (enter 1 for fastest and higher values for slower disks), disk sizes in megabytes, percentage of free space on the disks, and whether the disk type is read-write or write-once. You will also need to provide the total memory on your machine, the average overall percent use of memory, the maximum percent use of memory at peak usage time, the average percent CPU utilization, the maximum percent CPU utilization, the number of CPUs, and the operating system page size expressed in bytes.

If you have more than one database on your machine or other applications, you will need to adjust the figures in Oracle Expert to allow for them. If you don't enter all of the details, Oracle Expert will use defaults, such as assuming that 80% of the memory is available for the use of this database. It also assumes that the database is the only database that runs on the machine and that no other applications are running that may affect the database performance.

Workload data

This is collected from either the SQL library cache (V$SQLAREA) or files created by Oracle Trace. Most sites will be able to use the SQL library cache method. Oracle Trace can be used to provide a more comprehensive workload profile if required, but there is more setup time than with the SQL cache method.

You request the workload data that you would like to process from the Oracle Expert selection screen. Information is obtained on the frequency, access paths, and importance of the transactions. You must be careful not to obtain a huge amount of information that is mostly useless. By specifying a schema and just a few tables, you can narrow your tuning and limit the amount of information that you have to wade through.

If you use the current SQL library cache to obtain your statistics, you must be careful to obtain your information at prime usage times. The cache will hold only the most commonly executed statements. If your cache is undersized or badly tuned, there is a possibility that even the most commonly used statements will not reside in it.

You also have a means of manually entering workload information. This option is normally used before completing your application programs. You manually extract your most vital and potentially damaging SQL statements and run them through Oracle Expert to observe its recommendations about indexes and other issues.

NOTE You can use Oracle Trace (described later in this appendix) to collect comprehensive tuning data from a specified database in real time. It includes details on all aspects of SQL performance, including that of triggers and constraints. You must load the Oracle Trace data into an Oracle database to allow Oracle Expert to perform analyses on it. Be careful to store the Oracle Trace data in a database other than the one you are tuning.

Rules

You can specify such rules as "the buffer cache hit ratio will not fall below 70%." You can change the rule values to affect the recommendations that Oracle Expert will make. You must have a sound knowledge of Oracle tuning considerations to adjust the various ratios and other rules. Chapter 9, *Tuning a New Database* and Chapter 11, *Monitoring and Tuning an Existing Database*, will assist you with most of the settings.

Control parameters

These affect the recommendations that Oracle Expert will make. One example is setting the workload class to DSS (decision support database). If DSS is set, Oracle Expert will make recommendations appropriate for a DSS database (e.g., use the parallel query option). Oracle Expert relies on you to enter the correct control parameter information.

Oracle Expert considers all its inputs and creates parameter files and implementation scripts that can be used to apply the recommendations. You can modify these scripts if you wish before applying them to your database. You must know your applications and database inside out before you apply the changes recommended by Oracle Expert. It is also best if you can test the changes before moving them into your production database.

Table D-1 shows the relative level of effort (low, medium, high) associated with different types of tuning.

Table D-1. Oracle Expert Considerations

Tuning Considerations	Instance Tuning	Application Tuning	Structure Tuning
Performance impact of collection on database	Low	Medium	Low to medium
Manual effort to collect or edit data	Low	Low to high	Low to high
Complexity of implementing recommendations	Low	Medium	High
Potential gain from implementing tuning recommendations	Medium	Medium to high	Medium

As was mentioned earlier, Oracle Expert allows you to modify a set of rules that will affect the recommendations provided by the product. A subset of the rules and our advice on how they should be set are as follows:

- Setting the maximum number of indexes per schema and table. Don't set the maximum number of indexes per schema because you may add objects and forget to reset the value. This will make Oracle Expert very hesitant about recommending required indexes. If you do set the maximum indexes per table, set it to 8 or more.

- Setting the minimum and maximum boundaries for each of the parameters. We suggest that you read about INIT.ORA parameters in Chapter 9, and don't set the values below or above the recommendations given.

- Multiplying INIT.ORA parameters. You can use a multiplier on many of the parameters, such as increasing the DB_BLOCK_BUFFERS parameter by the average number of concurrent users. You must be aware of the consequences of what you are setting, particularly on the parameters that increase memory usage. Don't leave yourself short of memory. You must also make sure that you gather your data during peak usage times so that you don't underestimate the effect of setting an overly large parameter for every person—for example, SORT_AREA_RETAINED_SIZE.

- Setting hit ratios to a low and a high value. The buffer cache hit ratio should not fall below 85% for batch and 95% for online users. Many other ratios that you can set in Oracle Expert are described in Chapter 11.

- The "Last Statistics Collection Importance" rule tells Oracle Expert how important the historical data is. If you are storing overnight batch job workload data and are adding the online workload data, it is best to include the old data in all of your recommendations. Tuning for batch jobs alone or online users alone will often provide you with recommendations that will have a harmful affect on the others performance.

- Looking at workload data. These data is broken into four elements: application, business unit, transaction, and SQL statement. Each element can be assigned an importance ranking, where 9999 is the highest and 0 is the lowest. You can also specify the frequency of each element, as well as the frequency cycle (e.g., hourly). The ranking, frequency, and cycle will all affect the recommendations that Oracle Expert will provide. If you want to test the effect of increasing the use of a particular transaction, increase the frequency figure; the product will recommend any adjustments to maintain ongoing good performance.

Now that you have collected and edited the data, you can instruct Oracle Expert to analyze the data. You have the ability to obtain a running summary of the product's recommendations. This is often useful; for example, one particular SQL statement may have required an index, and a SQL statement further along in the analysis may have required the index to be dropped. Oracle Expert provides information on its rationale; think of its very useful output as a mini-training session, set up especially for your site.

Oracle Expert considers interdependencies when it formulates its recommendations. For example, it looks at whether you are using the parallel query option when it considers the value of creating an index. In our opinion, this is another characteristic that sets this product head and shoulders above other tuning tools on the market.

You have the option to limit the amount of data analyzed by excluding particular categories and objects. If you are concerned about the performance provided on only two or three tables, for example, you can analyze your workload only for those few tables. In such cases, Oracle Expert may inform you that you are missing one or two indexes or that an existing index needs to have a column added to it to provide the best response times.

In some cases, you might want to override Oracle Expert's recommendations. One recommendation may say to decrease the LOG_BUFFER to 8 kilobytes. But you may have tried that modification before, and it only made things worse. Thankfully, we didn't see a single example of the product making poor recommendations during our testing.

Oracle Expert generates three types of output files:

- An INIT.ORA file, which you can use to replace your current INIT.ORA file

- A .SQL file, which contains the CREATE and DROP index statements

- A .TXT file, which contains the SQL statements to perform the structure rec-ommendations

The structure statements are used to alter default storage parameters on tablespaces as well as to ensure that users have access to the correct default and temporary tablespaces. The .TXT file includes the string <TBS>, which you will have to replace with the appropriate tablespace name.

Oracle Expert also performs "what if" analysis. Typical examples are "What if we increase the buffer cache to 100 megabytes?", "What if we add 256 megabytes of memory?", and "What if you have twice the number of users running an accounts transaction?" Oracle Expert gives advice on the changes you should make to your database to maintain or improve your performance.

Oracle Trace

Oracle Trace provides a means of capturing accurate and comprehensive perfor-mance data from the frontend client machines to the backend server machines, as well as the network in the middle. The data can be used to pinpoint the cause of performance problems, regardless of whether they are at the client application code end, in SQL*Net, or at the database server end. You will generally use Oracle Trace to collect data for products that already contain the Oracle Trace API calls, such as the Oracle Server 7.3 and SQL*Net 2.3. In this case, you do not have to get involved at all with the Oracle Trace API directly; you simply run a collec-tion and use the data in Oracle Expert or for some other analysis. However, should you choose to use Oracle Trace to collect performance data for your own applications as we encouraged earlier, then you will become very involved with the Oracle Trace API.

Your first impression of the product may be that it requires a lot of learning. The manuals are full of jargon that will be new to you, such as *instrumentation, events, facilities,* and many other terms. It also contains many application program-ming interface calls (APIs) that you can place into your code. Just to overwhelm you even more, there are hundreds of resource utilization components, such as CPU usage, that you can extract when your applications are running.

However, if you are patient, reading the manuals and trying the product will make you realize that the product is quite easy to implement. It will require some effort to place the API calls into your application code, but if you have a serious production application and you are setting a high standard for performance, the

Oracle Trace information is well worth the time invested. We suggest that you place the Oracle Trace calls into your programs as part of a site standard.

Oracle Trace is event-based, rather than time-based. This means that every time an event is performed (for example, every time the "accounts update transaction" is run), tuning information is stored for the "accounts update transaction event." Luckily, this doesn't mean that you will continuously record the tuning information every single time the event is run and eventually fill up your disk. You have the ability to turn the data capture on and off using the Oracle Trace screens. The events can be time-based (with a start and end), or they can be for a point in time (such as for an error or an exceedingly high reading).

You can collect tuning data from any product or program in which you place Oracle Trace API calls. If you do instrument your own applications, you will need to give some thought to the positioning of the API calls in your application programs to ensure that you get the most useful performance information. The more Oracle Trace API calls in your programs, the more specific information you will receive. Balance the usefulness of the data against the potential impact on your application's performance. At the very least, we suggest that your critical transactions include API calls so that they can track any potential performance problems that will have a serious impact on your business.

To tell Oracle Trace that you are recording performance information for your application, you must include epc_init as the first Oracle Trace API call. *Facility* is an Oracle Trace term for an application.* An *event* is similar to a transaction. Each event has an epc_start_event call at the start of the transaction and an epc_end_ event call at the end of the transaction. You can also run a point-in-time event by executing the API call, epc_event.

A fill list of Oracle Trace routines is listed in Table D-2.

Table D-2. Oracle Trace Routines

Oracle Trace Call	Description
epc_init	Must be called once at the start of you application before any other Oracle Trace calls take place
epc_add_reg_id	Adds a registration ID for this application
epc_remove_reg_id	Removes the application registration ID
epc_start_event	Start of a duration event
epc_end_event	End of a duration event

---

* "Facility" is an Oracle Trace term for an application that contains the Oracle Trace API. This is an archaic term that has carried forward from Oracle Trace's VAX VMS origins, and it will be replaced by the term "product" in the next release.

Table D-2. Oracle Trace Routines (continued)

Oracle Trace Call	Description
epc_set_cf_items	Passes cross-facility item values from a client process to a server process
epc_cf_value	Assigns values to cross-facility items
epc_get_cf_items	Retrieves all cross-facility items to a buffer
epc_context (Multi-threaded server)	Starts a new thread or restart an existing thread
epc_delete_context (Multi-threaded server)	End of a thread
epc_collect	Starts a collection within an application (facility)
epc_cancel	Stops a connection that was started by epc_collect
epc_bind	Binds a process to a collect that is currently running
epc_flush	All Oracle Trace data is placed into a memory cache before being written to collection files on disk. This facility will flush all of the memory entries from memory to disk.

To run Oracle Trace for an application that you have instrumented, you must create a facility definition file that contains information on the facility (application), event (transaction), items (tuning items such as physical reads), and classes (groupings of events and items), as shown in Figure D-13. For example, you might group SGA tuning items with the transaction Maintain Accounts into one class and might have a different grouping (calls) for the disk tuning with the same transaction and yet another class grouping debug events on the transaction.

Classes allow you to limit the amount of data that you are gathering on the basis of your need. When you create a new facility definition file, all of the events are included in a main class, referred to as the ALLCLASS. From there, you can create subclasses of events for specific purposes, such as auditing, performance monitoring, debugging, and so on. The Oracle Server currently has three predefined classes: ALLCLASS, DEFAULT (which collects substantially less data by excluding server "wait" events), and EXPERT (which is used to collect Oracle Expert workload data).

Oracle Trace lets you collect many types of tuning information, including the amount of CPU used in system mode and user mode, the number of file system inputs and outputs, the number of hard and soft page faults (paging to disk and paging within memory), and the maximum resident set size used (memory usage). The product can also select cross-facility information, which relates events across applications.

You use online screens to select the items that you would like to capture. When you capture items such as CPU, memory, and disk I/O, you should collect the same items at both start and end events. Oracle Trace then has the capability of

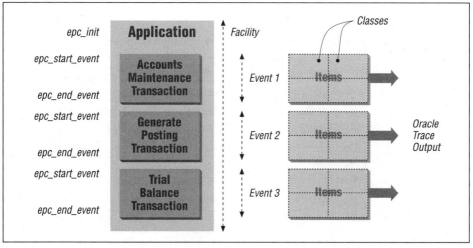

Figure D-13. Oracle Trace API calls, applications, and events

calculating the amount (delta usage) of the item by subtracting the start value from the end value.

The Oracle7.3.2 server and later has the ability to capture items without having any API calls placed into your programs. Recorded information includes the Oracle process ID, session ID, operating system username and terminal, wait time taken for an event, application module (if you have used the dbms_application_ info.set _module procedure in your programs), application action (if you have set the dbms_application_info.set_action procedure), number of cursors, SQL statement being run, number of rows processed, library cache misses, optimizer mode, UGA memory used, PGA memory used, DB block changes, DB block gets, consistent gets, redo entries, redo size, full table scan rows, number of memory sorts, number of disk sorts, rows sorted, CPU used by the session, elapsed session time, application ID, form ID, remote node connect ID, and transaction ID.

Each event has one or more of the mentioned items. The available events are listed in Table D-3:

Table D-3. Oracle 7.3.2 and Later Trace Events

Event	Description
Connect	Occurs every time a connection is made to the database
Disconnect	Occurs each time a disconnection is made from the database
Errorstak	Identifies a process that has an error
Migration	Logged each time a session migrates to a shared server process (disabled for Oracle7.3.2)
ApplReg	Registers where the application is at a point in time

Table D-3. Oracle 7.3.2 and Later Trace Events (continued)

Event	Description
Rowsource	Number of rows processed by an action in the execution plan
SQLSegment	SQL statement text
Wait	Time a wait occurred for disk I/O, a latch, enqueue log switch or any other wait; the time is recorded in one-hundredths of a second
Parse	Records the start and end of the parse of a SQL statement
Execute	Performs the execution of the parsed statement
Fetch	Data is returned; more than one fetch can be performed within the one SQL statement
LogicalTX	Start and end of a logical transaction
PhysicalTX	Start and end of a physical transaction that has caused the state of the database to change

Once you have worked out exactly what you need from Oracle Trace, you must analyze the information that the product collects for you. Be careful not to collect data unless you have a real need for that data. When you start your data collection, you will be asked to provide a filename and a maximum file size specified in kilobytes. The default filename on UNIX systems is *$ORACLE_HOME/otrace/ admin/.cdf/ name.cdf.* Make the name meaningful, and attach a date to the filename so that you can distinguish files at the operating system level. Don't place the file on the same disk as one of your heavily used database files or operating system files.

The data file that is produced by Oracle Trace can provide input for Oracle Expert so that Oracle Expert can made recommendations on your instance, schema, application, and environment tuning. You can interrogate the information if you wish to perform your own analysis by loading the data into Oracle tables, or you can obtain a report directly from the operating system file using the command

```
otrcrep [output path] [-pwl] [-P] [-h] {collection name}.cdf
```

where

output path

   is the output path of the report

-p

   allows you to specify a report for a specified process

-w

   sets the report width

-l

   number of lines per page

-P

lists all process Ids

-h

suppresses headers making the report shorter (highly recommended)

-s

SQL*Net data only

To load the data into the Oracle database, create the tables and indexes using the SQL script *$ORACLE_HOME/sysman/admin/otrcfmtc.sql*. You can now load your data into the tables using the command

```
otrcfmt [-f] [-c#] [collection name].cdf [user/password@database]
```

where

-f

formats the data file

-c#

specifies the commit interval; set this value to 200

Oracle provides a set of sample reports to gather various kinds of performance tuning information, including the frequency and duration of wait events, the number of connect events, library cache performance, number of fetches and rows per cursor execution, and much more. The reports are stored in the directory *$ORACLE_HOME/sysman/trace/sample*. To obtain the best run times for your reports you may need to add indexes to the trace tables. You can also add synonyms using *otrcsyn.sql*, can define the elapsed time function using *otrcfunc.sql*, and can create a summary table using *otrcdt.sql*.

E

Tuning Oracle Forms 4.0 and 4.5

This appendix summarizes a number of hints on tuning Oracle Forms 4.0 and 4.5 that we've been able to obtain from Oracle Worldwide Support. We suggest that you read these hints and combine them with the information we've presented in Chapter 16, *Tuning in the Client-Server Environment*. Before you turn your attention to Oracle Forms, be sure to tune your SQL and PL/SQL following the guidelines presented in Chapter 6, *Tuning SQL* and Chapter 7, *Tuning PL/SQL*.

The key to tuning Oracle Forms is to limit network traffic at every opportunity. You must make use of Oracle packages, procedures, functions, constraints, and triggers so that as much work as possible is performed at the server end.

GUI Tips

If you are using a Motif terminal, do the following:

- Set .mappedWhenManaged entries to False for relatively small applications. For example:

  ```
  Tk2Motif*field.mappedWhenManaged: False
  ```

- Set .blinkRate to 0 to reduce the traffic that items use for blinking effects. For example:

  ```
  Tk2Motif*field.blinkRate: 0
  ```

- See Tk2Motif files, Forms README files, and the installation guide for more information about other performance enhancements.

If you are running a windows session, use CDEINIT to shorten startup time.

General Tips

- Use explicit cursors to save a packet each time you issue a SELECT statement. Explicit cursors must exist in the DECLARE section of your PL/SQL module.

- Use the Performance Event Collection Services (PECS) facility to get performance details on all events within the form, including triggers, lists of values, displays or windows, canvases, procedures, and alerts. You can gather information on CPU and elapsed times and on how many times each event was executed. This tool is particularly useful for debugging as well as performance monitoring. To turn PECS on, use the syntax

  ```
  f45 module=accfrm userid=gurry/mark pecs=on
  ```

- Consider coding Oracle Trace API calls into your programs. (See Appendix D, *Oracle Performance Pack.*) The calls will enable you to obtain detailed runtime information at the client end, across the network, and within the database server. You will be able to pinpoint exactly where your performance problems are occurring.

- You can also call the procedures SET_MODULE and SET_ACTION in the DBMS_APPLICATION_INFO package to help the DBA determine which Forms4.5 program action is using which CPU, disk reads, and other tuning information. The information can be obtained from the VSQL, VSQLAREA, and V$SESSION tables.

- Use explicit cursors in your PL/SQL blocks for SELECTs. The explicit cursors are declared at the beginning of the PL/SQL routine. If you use implicit cursors, (i.e., place the SELECT between the BEGIN and END), an extra SELECT is issued against the table to check the TOO MANY ROWS exception. You will notice the negative effect of not using explicit cursors most on POST-QUERY and WHEN-VALIDATE-ITEM triggers.

- Use the deferred coordination option to not return all of the detail rows for a parent row unless the user moves to the details part of the screen. This will save a lot of unnecessary network traffic if the user has no intention of visiting the details.

- Each SQL statement is processed one at a time even if it is enclosed in a PL/SQL block. Consider calling a packaged procedure to issue a series of SELECT, INSERT, UPDATE, and DELETE statements to reduce network traffic.

- Perform validation using a single multipurpose stored procedure. This will save lots of individual cursors from being passed across the network. You should also consider using the WHEN-VALIDATE-RECORD trigger, which will validate many fields at once rather than one at a time.

- Use views to retrieve data from several tables when issuing a port-query. This is much more efficient than individual SELECTs in terms of number of packets transferred.

- Turn off the Auto-Refresh option of the LIST OF VALUES (LOV) function to avoid having to requery the database for the same reference data if the data have already been retrieved once. If your reference data table is less than 200 rows and will not be changed during prime online usage times, consider avoiding the requery to speed up response times.

- Set the Long-List property on the LOV option. If you do, your users have the option of adding an additional WHERE clause to refine the data returned. This will mean that far fewer rows may need to be returned, causing less network traffic and improved response times.

- Use *.plx* files to substantially reduce the load time.

- Make all forms modules modular to reduce the initial startup time. Rather than having one large form with several items, distribute the items into multiple forms if possible, and use CALL_FORM or OPEN_FORM calls.

- Use the Records Fetched block property can be useful when querying.

- Increase the number in the records-buffered block property to speed up processing if you have a lot of memory. We have found that setting it to 1.5 times the amount of rows that you wish to return is an optimal number. This produces some rows on the screen at the same time that the next buffer of rows is being queried.

F

Tuning Case Studies

We tune many sites each year. At most of these sites, we encounter the kinds of performance tuning problems described in the two case studies of actual databases included in this appendix. We include these representative cases in the hope that the discussion will prompt you to notice similar situations at your own site. All of the SQL scripts that were used to obtain the information shown in this appendix are described in Chapter 10, *Diagnostic and Tuning Tools,* and Chapter 11, *Monitoring and Tuning an Existing Database.* Descriptions of how to set your INIT.ORA parameters and structure your database are included in Chapter 9, *Tuning a New Database.*

Case Study Database 1

The PERS database that we look at in the first case study is actually performing quite well, although several areas can be improved. The list below summarizes our major findings; the following sections contain detailed explanations.

- There are not enough rollback segments, and this has caused some contention for the rollback segment header.

- There is an even I/O spread across disks.

- There are some locking problems at the transaction level; these are likely to be caused by tables having foreign keys and not having the associated indexes on the child table.

- There is a small number of statements that are providing inadequate response times.

- There is one statement in particular that appears to be a prime candidate for using bind variables.

- The shared pool area is badly fragmented, and critical packages have to be reloaded too often.

Observation 1

Oracle7.1.5 introduced a new method of splitting your shared pool into two distinct areas, one for large objects and one for smaller objects. The INIT.ORA parameter SHARED_POOL_RESERVED_MIN_ALLOC specifies the cutoff point. All packages, procedures, PL/SQL blocks, and SQL statements that are larger than or equal to the value of the parameter are placed into the area set up for larger objects. The rest are placed into the area for smaller objects. The large area is sized by the parameter SHARED_POOL_RESERVED_SIZE; the small area contains what is left in the shared pool area.

```
SHARED_POOL_SIZE - SHARED_POOL_RESERVED_SIZE
```

The current settings in the INIT.ORA file are

```
SHARED_POOL_SIZE                  50331648
SHARED_POOL_RESERVED_SIZE         0
SHARED_POOL_RESERVED_MIN_ALLOC    5000
```

The high number of misses on the library cache provide evidence of fragmentation. Misses are the second and fourth columns in the following output:

```
                            Gets    Misses
library cache            7518866    1258    248520         441
library cache pin       14471106   20324     14547         153
library cache load lock    23169       4         0           0
```

Recommendation:

Set the following:

```
SHARED_POOL_RESERVED_SIZE=25000000
SHARED_POOL_RESERVED_MIN_ALLOC=2500
```

Observation 2

Oracle offers a mechanism to pin objects into the shared pool area. The outputs below indicate that there has been a lot of reloading of critical objects. This may happen either because the shared pool area is undersized or because it is fragmented. The best approach to fixing this problem is to first eliminate the flushing and reloading of key objects by pinning them in memory. You should also avoid fragmentation in the shared pool by separating large objects (see Observation 1).

The output below provides details on the total number of reloads system-wide. The database instance had been restarted a few hours before the statistics were taken.

```
Tue May   7                                           page    1
                         Total Shared Pool Reload Stats

NAMESPACE              RELOADS
---------------- ----------
SQL AREA                13799
TABLE/PROCEDURE          9705
BODY                      137
TRIGGER                   687
INDEX                       0
CLUSTER                     0
OBJECT                      0
PIPE                        0
```

The following output provides you with an insight into the amount of memory that the larger packages and procedures are using. Oracle will often grab larger chunks of memory for an object than the amount the object actually needs. If you obtain the output on the same modules once they have been pinned, they are likely to use less memory.

```
                                                      page    1
Tue May  1
             Memory Usage of Shared Pool Order - Biggest First
       OWNER             NAME                                 SHARABLE_MEM
---------------- ------------------------------------ -----------
SYS              STANDARD - PACKAGE                          173,083
ADMFIN           SAS_PROCS - PACKAGE BODY                     95,431
ADMFIN           SAS_RULES - PACKAGE BODY                     77,383
ADMFIN           SAS_USER_FUNCTIONS - PACKAGE BODY            67,672
ADMFIN           SAS_RULES_FUNC - PACKAGE BODY                64,940
ADMFIN           SAS_RULES - PACKAGE                          53,279
ADMFIN           SAS_PROCS - PACKAGE                          52,911
SYS              STANDARD - PACKAGE BODY                       38,467
ADMFIN           SAS_RSHIP_DATA - PACKAGE BODY                27,892
SYS              DBMS_STANDARD - PACKAGE                       22,912
SYS              DBMS_UTILITY - PACKAGE BODY                   13,303
SYS              DBMS_DESCRIBE - PACKAGE BODY                  13,296
ADMCRP           PAR_PROCS - PACKAGE BODY                      10,103
```

You should aim for having no objects reloaded. The output below tells us that some packages that are critical to the Oracle kernel have been reloaded (STANDARD and DBMS_STANDARD). This is an absolute no-no! Pin these objects immediately!

```
Tue May  7
page     1
                  Loads into Shared Pool  - Most Loads First
OWNER             NAME
                                                    LOADS SHARABLE_MEM
----------------  ----------------------------------- ---------- ------
-
ADMFIN            SAS_GLOBALS - PACKAGE                  22        8,817
ADMCRP            PAR_PROCS - PACKAGE                     20        5,079
ADMFIN            SAS_RSHIP_DATA - PACKAGE                15        6,756
SYS               DBMS_STANDARD - PACKAGE                 12       22,912
ADMFIN            SAS_PROCS - PACKAGE                     11       52,911
ADMFIN            SAS_RULES - PACKAGE                     11       53,279
SYS               STANDARD - PACKAGE                      10      173,083
SYS               DBMS_DESCRIBE - PACKAGE                  7        4,368
```

The next output tells us how many times the various object have been executed. Notice STANDARD and DBMS_STANDARD. Now we have evidence as to why it is so critical that they remain in memory.

```
Tue May  7
page     1
Executions of Objects in the  Shared Pool  - Most Executions First
OWNER             NAME
                                                         EXECUTIONS
----------------  ----------------------------------- ------------
SYS               STANDARD - PACKAGE                       165,977
SYS               STANDARD - PACKAGE BODY                  165,977
SYS               DBMS_STANDARD - PACKAGE                   83,416
SYS               DBMS_STANDARD - PACKAGE BODY              83,416
SYS               DBMS_DESCRIBE - PACKAGE                    8,405
ADMFIN            SAS_PROCS - PACKAGE                        8,378
SYS               DBMS_UTILITY - PACKAGE                     8,106
SYS               DBMS_DESCRIBE - PACKAGE BODY               8,106
SYS               DBMS_UTILITY - PACKAGE BODY                8,106
ADMFIN            SAS_PROCS - PACKAGE BODY                   7,834
ADMFIN            SAS_RSHIP_DATA - PACKAGE                   2,012
ADMFIN            SAS_RULES - PACKAGE                        1,998
ADMFIN            SAS_USER_FUNCTIONS - PACKAGE               1,882
ADMFIN            SAS_RULES_FUNC - PACKAGE                   1,882
ADMCRP            PAR_PROCS - PACKAGE                        1,807
ADMFIN            SAS_RSHIP_DATA - PACKAGE BODY                238
ADMFIN            SAS_USER_FUNCTIONS - PACKAGE BODY            237
ADMFIN            SAS_RULES - PACKAGE BODY                     237
ADMFIN            SAS_RULES_FUNC - PACKAGE BODY                237
```

Recommendation:

Pin the following packages and procedures in memory. Perform ongoing monitoring, and pin others as necessary. You must run the SQL script *$ORACLE_HOME/rdbms/admin/dbmspool.sql* to create the packages that allow you to pin the objects. See the *create_p.sql* script in the *markg* directory on the accompanying disk.

```
execute dbms_shared_pool.keep('SYS.STANDARD');
execute dbms_shared_pool.keep('SYS.DBMS_STANDARD');
execute dbms_shared_pool.keep('SYS.DBMS_DESCRIBE');
execute dbms_shared_pool.keep('ADMFIN.SAS_PROCS');
execute dbms_shared_pool.keep('SYS.DBMS_UTILITY');
execute dbms_shared_pool.keep('ADMFIN.SAS_RSHIP_DATA');
execute dbms_shared_pool.keep('ADMFIN.SAS_RULES');
execute dbms_shared_pool.keep('ADMFIN.SAS_USER_FUNCTIONS');
execute dbms_shared_pool.keep('ADMFIN.SAS_RULES_FUNC');
execute dbms_shared_pool.keep('ADMCRP.PAR_PROCS');
execute dbms_shared_pool.keep('ADMFIN.SAS_GLOBALS');
execute dbms_shared_pool.keep('ADMBRK.BAS_AUTO_GENERIC');
execute dbms_shared_poolSAS.keep('ADMBRK.BAS_PI_SIGNOFF');
```

Observation 3

When indexes are missing, either by design or by mistake, severe performance problems often result. Even small tables can cause problems when they are joined with large tables. This is because the small table will become the driving table, and this has the potential for slowing response times down many times over. Tables without indexes are also not guaranteed to have uniqueness. The following list doesn't tell you that all of the tables must necessarily be indexed, but simply to provide a checklist.

```
Tue May  7                                                    page    1
                   Report on all Tables Without Indexes
ADMBRK            BRKT_ACCOUNTS_AUD
ADMBRK            BRKT_ACC_COUNT_DTL
ADMBRK            BRKT_ACC_C_DTL_AUD
ADMBRK            BRKT_ACC_TEST_AUD
ADMBRK            BRKT_ADD_HIST_AUD
ADMBRK            BRKT_ALLOC_EXM_AUD
ADMBRK            BRKT_ANUAL_RET_AUD
ADMBRK            BRKT_ASSET_LAB_AUD
ADMBRK            BRKT_BANK_HIST_AUD
   There were many many more...
```

Recommendation:

Give the list of tables without indexes to the developers to ensure that all tables that should be indexed have been indexed.

Observation 4

Tables that have many indexes on them will often have inserts, updates, and deletes that take a long time. On the other hand, to provide acceptable query performance, many indexes are often required on a table. The following table, for example, has a lot of indexes.

```
Tue May  7                                                    page    1
                    Tables which have > 6 Indexes
FINAN          FIN_SUBJ_GRP_INST                     9
```

Recommendation:

Check with the application development team to ensure that all of the indexes are required. Remove any indexes that are *not* required.

Observation 5

The following output presents information on the default settings on your tablespaces. The problems that stand out are the following:

• FINANCE01 has a PCTINCREASE of 50, which means there could be a huge amount of space wastage.

• The system tablespace has a PCTINCREASE of 0, changing Oracle's recommendation of 50%. This will make dictionary tables badly fragmented.

• The TEMP tablespace has an INITIAL and NEXT EXTENT smaller than the SORT_AREA_SIZE which is set to 64 kilobytes. This means that as soon as a sort on disk takes place, extents will be thrown at a rapid rate, and this is damaging to performance.

```
Tue May  7
page    1
                         Tablespace Information
BROKER01                 20480        8192             0
BROKER02                 20480        8192             0
CORP01                   20480       20480             0
CORP02                   20480       20480             0
LIFE01                   20480       20480             0
LIFE02                   20480       20480             0
LIFE03                   20480       20480             0
POLICY01                 20480        8192             0
RBS                      20480       20480            50
FINANCE01                20480       20480            50
FINANCE02                20480       20480             0
FINANCE03                20480       20480             0
FINANCE04                20480       20480             0
FINANCE05                20480       20480             0
FINANCE06                20480       20480             0
SYSTEM                   12288       12288             0
TEMP                     20480       20480            50
```

Recommendation:

Modify the PCTINCREASE on the tablespace FINANCE01 to 0; set the default storage PCTINCREASE on the system tablespace to 50; and change the INITIAL extent on the TEMP tablespace to 256 kilobytes. Consider setting the NEXT extent to 2 megabytes and the PCTINCREASE to 0.

Observation 6

Use of Oracle's foreign key constraints can cause severe locking problems on the parent table. If you are performing an insert, update, or delete on a child table (e.g., the EMP table that has a foreign key to the DEPT table) and an index is missing from the foreign key field on the CHILD table, a share lock is placed on the PARENT table.

What does all this mean? If you are missing an index on the foreign key column in EMP on DEPT_NO, nobody can perform any inserts, updates, or deletes on the DEPT until you have completed your change to EMP. It also means that if anybody is changing data in the DEPT table, you will have to wait for them before you can obtain your share lock.

The most likely situation in which you will experience locking problems is when multiple foreign keys are on an intersection table that has a large number of inserts. An example is the case in which an employee can be in many departments. You may have a table DEPT_EMP that has foreign keys to both the DEPT and EMP tables. You must also have an index on DEPT_NO and a separate index on EMP_NO to avoid the potential locking problem.

All of the foreign keys listed below have the potential to cause locking problems:

```
Tue May  7
page    1
            Foreign Constraints and Columns Without an Index on Child
Table
FAS-> FAS_DATA_FK2(USAGE_TYPE_ID[2]) ***** Missing Index
FAS-> FAS_DTA_TYPE_USE_FK2(DATA_TYPE_ID[1]) ***** Missing Index
FAS-> FAS_DTA_TYPE_XREF_FK2(DATA_TYPE2_CDE[1]) ***** Missing Index
FAS-> FAS_SGI_RELSHIP_FK2(ACTION_FAS_ID[6]) ***** Missing Index
FAS-> FAS_SGI_RELSHIP_FK2(ACTION_ROLE_CDE[4]) ***** Missing Index
FAS-> FAS_SGI_RELSHIP_FK2(OBJECT_FAS_ID[1]) ***** Missing Index
FAS-> FAS_SGI_RELSHIP_FK2(OBJECT_ROLE_CDE[2]) ***** Missing Index
FAS-> FAS_SUBJ_GRP_INST_FK1(SUBJECT_GRP_ID[1]) ***** Missing Index
FAS-> FAS_SUBJ_GRP_INST_FK1(USAGE_TYPE_ID[2]) ***** Missing Index
FAS-> FAS_SUBJ_GRP_INST_FK3(PARENT_SGI_ID[1]) ***** Missing Index
FAS-> FAS_USAGE_GROUP_FK2(USAGE_TYPE_ID[1]) ***** Missing Index
FAS-> FAS_VALIDN_AXPR_FK1(LEGIS_RULE_ID[1]) ***** Missing Index
FAS-> FAS_VALIDN_AXPR_FK2(BUS_STATUS_CDE[1]) ***** Missing Index
FAS-> FAS_VALIDN_RESULT_FK1(SUBJECT_GRP_ID[1]) ***** Missing Index
FAS-> FAS_VALIDN_RESULT_FK1(USAGE_TYPE_ID[2]) ***** Missing Index
FAS-> FAS_VALIDN_RESULT_FK1(VALIDN_AXPR_NUM[4]) ***** Missing Index
FAS-> FAS_VAL_STAT_TRNS_FK1(NEW_BUS_STATUS_CDE[3]) ***** Missing Index
FAS-> FAS_VAL_STAT_TRNS_FK1(NEW_PRC_STATUS_CDE[4]) ***** Missing Index
```

Recommendation:

Ask the application development teams to look at the parent tables to determine whether they are likely to have a high number of inserts. If so, either add an index on the child table or drop the foreign key.

Observation 7

There are too few rollback segments. Having too few rollback segments has caused many damaging locking problems. Notice the 305 waits on the Rollback Table 5, and notice the undo header and undo block waits in the following output.

Rollback Table	GETS	WAITS	Active Transactions
0	350	0	0
5	104779	1305	16

Tue May 7		page 1

CLASS	Get All Waits COUNT
data block	6569
sort block	0
save undo block	0
segment header	6
save undo header	0
free list	0
system undo header	0
system undo block	0
undo header	3615
undo block	1115

Recommendation:

This is an urgent fix, but one that is easy to perform. Add more rollback segments and remonitor the waits. Inform the development teams that long-running transactions must use the command

```
SET TRANSACTION USE ROLLBACK SEGMENT rname
```

where *rname* is a larger rollback segment.

Observation 8

At some stage in the future, the following table is going to cause a program crash because the database does not have an extent large enough to fit the table extension.

```
Tue May  7
page     1
        Database Objects that will have Trouble Throwing Extents
 FAS      FAS_RELSHIP       TABLE       FAS_DATA_03        209,715,200
```

Recommendation:

Issue the following command:

```
ALTER TABLE FAS_RELSHIP STORAGE (NEXT 50M);
```

Do this right away because you can't be certain when the table is going to blow. 50 megabytes is the largest contiguous extent in the tablespace where the table exists.

Observation 9

The cost-based optimizer has been enabled in this database (OPTIMIZER_MODE=CHOOSE). Analyzing some tables and not others can cause full table scans on the tables that are not analyzed. This is the case with the Oracle user PERSADM below.

```
Tue May  7                                              page    1
            Tables that Are Analyzed (Summary by Owner)
                    Analyzed         Not Analyzed
    FASADM              0                 98
    FASCNT              0                 49
    PERSADM            12                 10
```

Recommendation:

Analyze either all tables or no tables for a given owner. Don't mix and match, particularly where analyzed tables are joined to tables that are not analyzed.

Observation 10

There are many statements that could save memory and avoid fragmentation in the shared pool area, if they used bind variables. A few leading characters of the candidate statements are shown below.

```
    SQL Statements that are Similar in Shared Pool Area
    SELECT   S.BUS_STATUS_TSP,          3138
    SELECT DISTINCT  PO.               239
    SELECT DISTINCT  PO.ITS_ID, RT     234
```

Recommendation:

Approach the application development team to see if bind variables can be used.

Observation 11

The hit ratio is the percent of times that data (tables, indexes, rollback segments, sort data, and dictionary data) is found in memory (in the buffer cache) rather than having to be brought in from disk. Data that are brought in from disk use between five to eight times the amount of CPU that data that are found in memory use. The current hit ratio at this site is very good.

```
Tue May  7
page    1
                            The Hit Ratio
Consis Gets DB Blk Gets Phys Reads  Hit Ratio
----------- ----------- ---------- ----------
  372509497    4537948     6270214 98.3370225


Tue May  7
page    1
                              User Hit Ratios
User Session    Consis Gets DB Blk Gets Phys Reads Hit Ratio
--------------- ----------- ----------- ---------- ---------
BXRXCI(45)           541996          30     148242     72.65
EXBCSN(118)            6470         129       4586     30.50
XPSHAK(113)              15           0          1     93.33
XCPHAK(151)          204123        1610      68316     66.79
CFANIG(22)             4207          90       1547     64.00
SPAOOR(24)             6485          66       3635     44.51
```

Recommendation:

Leave DB_BLOCK_BUFFERS at its present size. Check on why some of the users are getting poor hit ratios and see whether the SQL that they are using can be tuned.

Observation 12

The I/O spread across disks is quite good. The only question that must be raised from the following output is "Why are there so many reads from the rollback segments?" This is usually caused by having a lot of users rolling back their changes or by having batch updates changing buffers that contain rows that other users are accessing.

```
Tue May  7
page    1
                         Disk I/Os by Datafile
NAME                        PHYRDS   READ_PCT  PHYWRTS   WRITE_PCT
------------------------    -------  --------  -------   ---------
/ORC05/PERS/corp01A.dbf     559,376    26.34    39,670     17.73
/ORC04/PERS/FINer03A.dbf    554,880    26.13    11,413      5.10
/ORC04/PERS/FINer05A.dbf    495,933    23.36    23,584     10.54
/ORC09/PERS/corp02A.dbf     170,615     8.04    38,941     17.40
/ORC07/PERS/FINer01A.dbf    147,566     6.95     6,562      2.93
```

/ORC05/PERS/FINer04A.dbf	60,416	2.85	31,211	13.95
/ORC06/PERS/broker01A.dbf	43,936	2.07	797	.36
/ORC04/PERS/life01A.dbf	30,999	1.46	24	.01
/ORC01/PERS/systemA.dbf	17,719	.83	2,003	.89
/ORC02/PERS/FINer02A.dbf	14,005	.66	11,859	5.30
/ORC06/PERS/FINer06A.dbf	9,791	.46	18,060	8.07
/ORC04/PERS/policy01A.dbf	7,811	.37	0	0.00
/ORC07/PERS/broker02A.dbf	5,361	.25	399	.18
/ORC03/PERS/rbsA.dbf	4,786	.23	36,194	16.17
/ORC04/PERS/life02A.dbf	222	.01	9	0.00
/ORC01/PERS/tempA.dbf	69	0.00	3,075	1.37
/ORC06/PERS/life03A.dbf	0	0.00	0	0.00

Recommendation:

Check that no batch jobs are running against the database updating data that online users will use. Also check that the work practices of the application users are as expected.

Observation 13

There are only two log files, which have been mirrored. It is best to have three or four or more redo log files, to allow the ARCH writer and DBWR to be able to keep up. Observe the messages in the alert file, and see whether they indicate problems in throwing new redo logs. Processing must halt until the ARCH and DBWR processes are able to catch up.

```
/home/dba/oracle/admin/PERS/dbfiles/log02.dbf
/dbback/PERS/mirror/log02.dbf
/home/dba/oracle/admin/PERS/dbfiles/log01.dbf
/dbback/PERS/mirror/log01.dbf
Sun May  5 16:50:52 1996
Thread 1 advanced to log sequence 2353
  Current log# 2 seq# 2353 mem# 0:
/home/dba/oracle/admin/PERS/dbfiles/log02.dbf
  Current log# 2 seq# 2353 mem# 1: /dbback/PERS/mirror/log02.dbf
Sun May  5 16:52:00 1996
Thread 1 cannot allocate new log, sequence 2354
Checkpoint not complete
  Current log# 2 seq# 2353 mem# 0:
/home/dba/oracle/admin/PERS/dbfiles/log02.dbf
  Current log# 2 seq# 2353 mem# 1: /dbback/PERS/mirror/log02.dbf
Thread 1 advanced to log sequence 2354
  Current log# 1 seq# 2354 mem# 0:
/home/dba/oracle/admin/PERS/dbfiles/log01.dbf
  Current log# 1 seq# 2354 mem# 1: /dbback/PERS/mirror/log01.dbf
Sun May  5 16:53:31 1996
Thread 1 cannot allocate new log, sequence 2355
```

Recommendation:

Add two new redo logs and mirror them. Also consider increasing DB_WRITERS to 4 to help the DBWR process, and LOG_ARCHIVE_BUFFER_SIZE to 64 kilobytes to help the ARCH process.

Observation 14

From a database recovery perspective, the spread of data files looks acceptable.

```
Tue May  7
                                                         page    1
                Breakup of files across Disks / Check Recovery
VALUE
-------------------------------------------------------------------
/dbback/PERS/archive/PERS.al
/ORCL01/PERS/systemA.dbf
/ORCL01/PERS/tempA.dbf
/ORCL02/PERS/FINer02A.dbf
/ORCL03/PERS/rbsA.dbf
/ORCL04/PERS/life01A.dbf
/ORCL04/PERS/life02A.dbf
/ORCL04/PERS/policy01A.dbf
/ORCL04/PERS/FINer03A.dbf
/ORCL04/PERS/FINer05A.dbf
/ORCL05/PERS/corp01A.dbf
/ORCL05/PERS/FINer04A.dbf
/ORCL06/PERS/broker01A.dbf
/ORCL06/PERS/life03A.dbf
/ORCL06/PERS/FINer06A.dbf
/ORCL07/PERS/broker02A.dbf
/ORCL07/PERS/FINer01A.dbf
/ORCL09/PERS/corp02A.dbf
```

Recommendation:

You must test all recovery scenarios to make sure they work. Check your support level with Oracle to determine the hours of support. Become familiar with which disks are on which controllers so that you'll know that the archive logs are always available.

Observation 15

The are a number of chained or migrated rows in the database. Run the command

```
ANALYZE TABLE tname COMPUTE STATISTICS
```

out of prime production hours, and look at CHAIN_CNT to see which tables are the culprits. You should then turn the Stats off for the rule-based optimizer using the following command:

```
ANALYZE TABLE tname DELETE STATISTICS;

Tue May  7
page    1
NAME                                          VALUE
------------------------------  ----------------
table fetch continued row                    55,672
```

Recommendation:

Locate the problem tables, and increase PCTFREE to allow for row expansion. This can be done by analyzing your tables and checking the CHAIN_CNT column in ALL_TABLES, USER_TABLES, or DBA_TABLES.

Observation 16

The following users have been performing lengthy full table scans, which can destroy your database performance:

```
Tue May  7                                            page    1
        Average Scan Length of Full Table Scans by User
User Process           Average Long Scan Length
------------------  -----------------------
GMSHAK(151)                      108,932
BXROBI(45)                       728,805
```

Recommendation:

Ask whether the users can run their jobs out of prime time, and determine whether the statements can be tuned.

Observation 17

There have been reasonable number of waits on the redo allocation latch in a short amount of time.

```
log_simultaneous_copies       0
log_small_entry_max_size 800
                                WAITS
redo allocation         1587748    12075      0         0
```

Recommendation:

Set the following:

```
LOG_SIMULTANEOUS_COPIES=2
LOG_SMALL_ENTRY_MAX_SIZE=150
```

The first parameter is the number of additional latches known as redo copy latches that can write to the log buffer simultaneously along with the default redo allocation latch. The second specifies that all changes with more than 150 bytes use the new latch.

Observation 18

The following SQL statements are causing unreasonable response delays:

```
SELECT lcoy.company_short_nme, fins.covered_last_nme,
       fins.covered_first_nme, fins.artant_last_nme,
       fins.artant_first_nme, fins.policy_id,
       fins.artdte, fins.policy_amt
FROM lums_life_company lcoy, lums_life_policy fins
WHERE lcoy.company_id = fins.company_id AND fins.art_dte between :1 and :2
ORDER BY lcoy.company_short_nme, fins.insured_last_nme,
       fins.covered_first_nme
```

```
  24031          11        2,184.64  Expected Response Time =     43.69
```

There were 20 pages of SQL that were running for longer than four seconds. The majority of the problems were caused by the indexes not being used by the cost based optimizer because it was unaware of the skewness of the data. See Chapter 6, *Tuning SQL*, for information about this situation.

Recommendation:

Make sure that all statements in the list are tuned to use the most appropriate indexes. Add indexes and change the driving table as necessary.

Case Study Database 2

The FINL database that we look at in this second case study is quite well tuned. Most of the areas for potential tuning are at the application end rather than at the DBA end. The following list summarizes our major findings; the following sections contain detailed explanations.

* A number of SQL statements are providing unsatisfactory performance.

* There is a small amount of locking in the application.

* A number of statements are candidates for bind variables. These save shared pool memory, as well as avoiding fragmentation of the library cache, which will improve performance. Use of bind variables will also avoid each new statement.

* A number of tables have an excessive number of indexes on them. There are also a number of indexes that are potentially superfluous and will confuse the cost-based optimizer.

Observation 1

The hit ratio is very good, indicating that the buffer cache is adequately sized.

```
Tue May   7                                      page     1
                       The Hit Ratio
    ConADMIN Gets       DB Blk    Gets Phys Reads    Hit Ratio
    -------------      --------   ---------------    ----------
       11044021        246492        334610         97.0363614
```

Recommendation:

The buffer cache is more than 100 megabytes for a relatively small application. It may be able to be decreased after the SQL statements have been tuned.

Observation 2

The I/O spread across disks is reasonable, considering that the database is sharing disks with the PERS production database. The reads are biased toward one disk with the writes fairly evenly spread.

```
Tue May   7                                      page     1
                     Disk I/Os by Datafile
NAME                        PHYRDS   READ_PCT    PHYWRTS   WRITE_PCT
------------------------   ---------  --------   -------   ---------
/oracle09/FINL/FIN01A.dbf    184,247    79.25     4,033       16.12
/oracle07/FINL/FIN02A.dbf     46,093    19.83    12,192       48.72
/oracle04/FINL/systemA.dbf     2,036      .88       338        1.35
/oracle03/FINL/rbsA.dbf          101      .04     2,823       11.28
/oracle04/FINL/temp01A.dbf        50      .02     5,640       22.54
```

Recommendation:

No action is needed.

Observation 3

The spread of files is adequate for recovery, with the archives being kept off disks that contain data files. The redos are also on a different disk from the data files and the archives, although mirrored redos are on the same disks as the archives.

```
Tue May   7                                      page     1
                Breakup of files across Disks / Check Recovery
VALUE
----------------------------------------------------------------------
/dbback/FINL/archive/FINL.al
/dbback/PERS/mirror/log02.dbf
/dbback/PERS/mirror/lo01.dbf
/oracle03/FINL/rbsA.dbf
/oracle04/FINL/systemA.dbf
/oracle04/FINL/temp01A.dbf
/oracle07/FINL/FIN02A.dbf
/oracle09/FINL/FIN01A.dbf
/home/dba/oracle/ADMIN/PERS/dbfiles/log02.dbf
/home/dba/oracle/admin/PERS/dbfiles/log01.dbf
```

Recommendation:

Make doubly sure that the directories */dbback* and */home* are on different physical disks from the database files. Also be aware of which controllers control the disks, and be sure that you have a plan to recover from controller error. If you have to bring files back from tape, ensure that you have enough disk space to copy all of the data files from the lost disk. There are only two redo logs, and this will cause contention in the future. Add more redo logs.

Observation 4

A small amount of chaining has been detected.

```
NAME                                    VALUE
------------------------------- ----------------
table fetch continued row                  86
```

Recommendation:

Determine which tables are causing the problem by issuing ANALYZE TABLE COMPUTE STATISTICS and observing the CHAIN_CNT column in the USER_TABLES view. Double the PCTFREE in the table(s) in question.

Observation 5

One user has performed a full table scan. Question the user to see what he or she was running.

```
Tue May  7                                           page    1
                   Table Access Activity By User
   User Process           Long Scans  Short Scans Rows Retrieved
-------------------- ------------ ------------ --------------
   KFGASI(37)                   1           21         72,583
```

Observation 6

There are a number of statements that are causing poor response times. The first three statements below have excessive disk reads. The remaining statements are finding data in memory, but are scanning far too many buffers. This is usually due to inadequate index usage.

```
Tue May  7                                           page    1
       List Statements in Shared Pool with the Most Disk Reads
SQL_TEXT
-------------------------------------------------------------------
DISK_READS EXECUTIONS Average 'EXPECTEDRESPONSETIME='       Response
---------- ---------- ------ ------------------------- ----------------
SELECT  A1.ui,title FROM  fas.TSR A0,fas.TSRE A1 WHERE  ( A0.rc
ordREC = A1.REC )  AND  ( (( rlUni 1679647  AND  loce = '0' ) AND
 rcREC = 7 ) )  ORDER BY   title ASC
```

```
     10512 3   3,504.00 Expected Response Time =        70.08

SELECT  A0.rli FROM  fas.TS0 WHERE  ( ( rlNa = 1679866
AND  loType = '0' ) )
     10814 2  5,407.00  Expected Response Time =        108.14
SELECT  A0.rlRe FROM  fas.TSLOCAT A0 WHERE  ( (eUft = 1683619
AND  locat = '0' ) )
     11148 2 5,574.00 Expected Response Time =        111.48
```

The following statements are finding data in the buffer cache but are still taking a long time to run because they are scanning a large number of buffers as well as merging buffer cache data. Having a larger buffer cache will not help these statements. Ask whether the most effective indexes being used.

```
SELECT  S.BUS_STATUS_TSP, Rfas( S.PERIOD_TYPE_CDE ), SUBSTR(SATION_ID,
        1, 4 ) || '/' || SUBSTR( R.ORGANISATION_ID, 5, 3 ) || '/' ||
        R.ORGANISATION_ID, 8, 2 ), Rfas( O.ORGANISATION_NME ), S.fas_ID
        DLNY_NUM, S.PRC_STATUS_CDE, S.BUS_STATUS_CDE, Rfas( L1.CODE ),
        Rfas( L2.CODE_DSC ), S.DISK_SEQ_NUM, S.SGI_ID, S.ENTERED
FROM  fasS_CODE_LOOKUP L1, E_LOOKUP L2, fasS_ORGANISATION O,
      fasS_PARTY_ROLE R, FINS_SUNST S
WHERE  L1.CODE = S.PRC_STATUS_
   5675243      5443        1,042.67  Expected Response Time = 5.21
SELECT SGI_ID FROM FINS_SUBJ_GRP_INST
WHERE N (SELECT ROWID FROM FINS_SUBJ_GRP_INST WHERE fas_ID = :1
        FORM_TYPE_CDE = 'AR_WUP' AND PERIOD_TYPE_CDE = :2
        UNION ROWID FROM FINS_SUBJ_GRP_INST WHERE fas_ID = :3
        AND FOCDE = 'AR' AND PERIOD_TYPE_CDE = :4)
   24579913     1487        16,529.87  AXPected Response Time = 82.65
```

There were 30 pages of statements with response times that exceeded 5 seconds, with most of the problems caused by the product being written to run across many databases and not specifically tuned for the Oracle optimizers.

Recommendation:

Tune all statements using the EXPLAIN PLAN, ORADBX, and TKPROF tools. One faulty statement not only provides poor response times to the user running the statement, but also affects the response times of all other users.

Observation 7

The following tables contain no indexes. This may not be the way the application is supposed to be set up. Tables without indexes can cause performance degradation when they are joined with other tables.

```
Tue May  7                                              page    1
              Report on all Tables Without Indexes
fas             fasACTDEF
fas             fasACTNAME
fas             fasACTSTEP
fas             fasADDRESS
fas             fasARCHIVEE
fas             fasAUDIfasOG
and many, many more......
```

Recommendation:

Verify with the application development teams that no indexes are missing.

Observation 8

Some of the tables have an unusually high number of indexes. This will adversely affect INSERT, UPDATE, and DELETE statement performance.

```
Tue May  7                                              page    1
              Tables which have > 6 Indexes
FAS             FASELECRECO                    7
FAS             FASNAME                        9
FAS             FASRECACFAST                  10
FAS             FASRECORD                     18
```

Recommendation:

Seriously question all indexes. It is very unusual for a table to have 18 indexes. (An exception may be a denormalized report table.)

Observation 9

Some tables have multiple indexes with the same leading column on a table. This situation often confuses the optimizers.

```
Tue May  7                                              page    1
              Indexes which may be Superfluous
FAS             FASCODES             CODETYPE
FAS             FASCONV              CVPROCID
FAS             FASFILEPLAN          OWNERFPREC
FAS             FASINDEXWOR          IXWORDTYPE
```

Recommendation:

Ask whether the indexes are required and whether they are confusing the optimizer.

Observation 10

No tables have been analyzed, although we were informed that the indexes have been analyzed on the FAS tables, following the advice of the software developers.

```
Tue May   7                                          page    1
                    Tables That Are Analyzed (Summary by Owner)
                         Analyzed              Not Analyzed
FAS                         17                     91
```

Recommendation:

If you plan to run the cost-based optimizer, run the ANALYZE TABLE tname COMPUTE STATISTICS command against all tables. If the indexes are analyzed and not the tables, unpredictable cost-based optimizer behavior frequently occurs.

Observation 11

The following statements are prime candidates for using bind variables. If you use bind variables, you will use less library cache memory, avoid reparsing the statements, avoid latch contention in the shared pool, and generally improve performance.

```
Tue May                                              page    1
              SQL Statements that are Similar in Shared Pool Area
SELECT * FROM FAS.FINARCHIVEE         135
SELECT * FROM FAS.FININDEXWOR         129
SELECT * FROM FAS.FINNAME WHER        275
SELECT * FROM FAS.FINRECLINK W        698
SELECT * FROM FAS.FINRECLOCAT         669
```

Recommendation:

Use bind variables wherever practical.

G

Dynamic Performance Tables

Dynamic performance tables are tables in which Oracle stores system statistics. Part V, *Tuning for Database Administrators*, describes how the DBA can access these tables to get information on system activity that may be helpful in tuning the database and other aspects of the system. When your database is first created, only SYS has access to the V$ tables. To allow other users to run products that require the V$ tables, such as SQL*DBA Monitor options and the Oracle Performance Pack products, you must run the script *UTLMONTR.sql* which is located in the *$ORACLE_HOME/rdbms/admin* on UNIX systems.

For a listing of the dynamic performance tables, see the disk that accompanies this book.

NOTE   The tables listed on the disk are from Oracle7.3.2; since the V$ tables change frequently, we will update these listings periodically in subsequent revisions of the disk. If you would like a full listing of all the V$ tables, you can access the V$FIXED_VIEW_DEFINITION view.

Index

About the Authors

Mark Gurry runs a consulting company, Mark Gurry and Associates, which provides both short-term and long-term consulting in Oracle tuning; database administration; development standards; application architecture and design; and general site audits and health checks. His short-term site audits and internal skills transfer are keenly sought after in Australia, and he plans to expand into the U.S. and Europe in early 1997. Mark's customers are in many areas, including the stock market; banking and finance; telecommunications; emergency services; local, state, and federal governments; computer hardware manufacturers; and many others. Many of the sites he consults at have as many as 5,000 concurrent users and databases that are several hundred gigabytes in size.

Peter Corrigan is a director of CPT Open Systems, a division of CPT Consulting, an Australian-based consulting company that is internationally recognized for its depth of performance tuning experience and quality service. It focuses on performance tuning of client-server systems, primarily Oracle and UNIX. Clients include major Oracle sites throughout Australasia, spanning numerous industry groups in both the government and private sectors. The company plans expansion into other countries in the near future. Peter's major roles include consulting in areas of environment performance audits; capacity planning; database administration; standards development; and application design and tuning of data warehousing and client-server systems. Peter is also the codeveloper of numerous Oracle software developments, including performance tuning tools, application development tools, and the internationally acclaimed Rainbow Financial package.

In addition to writing books, Mark and Peter are frequent speakers on the topic of tuning and programming at the Oracle Asia Pacific user group conferences and the local Victorian Oracle user group. They have also presented their own tuning course material for Oracle Australia throughout the Australian states.

Colophon

Our look is the result of reader comments, our own experimentation, and feedback from distribution channels. Distinctive covers complement our distinctive approach to technical topics, breathing personality and life into potentially dry subjects. UNIX and its attendant programs can be unruly beasts. Nutshell Handbooks help you tame them.

The animal featured on the cover of *Oracle Performance Tuning* is the honeybee, appreciated worldwide as a pollinator of crops and producer of honey. Honeybees are highly social creatures. A single hive or colony usually contains one queen (the only fertile female), fifty- to sixty-thousand workers (all sterile females), and a few hundred drones (the only males). Workers are responsible for locating and collecting the pollen, nectar, water, and resin necessary to the hive. When a worker locates such a source, she returns to the hive and performs a beedance. This dance communicates precise instructions—both distance and direction—enabling other workers to make a beeline to the booty. It takes about ten million such worker-trips to gather enough nectar to make one pound of honey. Workers also build and maintain the hive, and feed the colony.

There is no biological difference among female bees at birth. Queens are simply given larger cells in which to develop, and are allowed to continue their privileged diet of "royal jelly" long after the other developing bees are cut off from the delicacy. Royal jelly is a secretion generated from the glands of young workers. Worker larvae are nourished by it during their first six days of existence, drones receive it for eight days, while the queen gets it until she is fully grown. The first thing a new queen will do upon emerging from her cell is deliver a death sting to all the other larval queens. (The previous queen will have vacated the hive with a small entourage a few days before.) After a week or two, the new queen will mate with a few drones (who die immediately after copulation). The rest of the drones are then put out of the hive to starve. The queen returns to the hive and begins her job of laying over a thousand eggs a day.

Honeybees are native to Europe, Africa, and the Middle East. In Ancient Greece, honeybees were associated with a famous oracle. The regular god of prophecy was Apollo, who presided over the greatest of Greek oracles, at Delphi. Apollo gave his tricky brother, Hermes, a piece of the action on a smaller shrine farther down the slopes of the same mountain, Mt. Parnassus, where the prophecy was given by three honeybee-maidens, all sisters. Apollo gave them the ability to speak the truth, which they willingly did if they were fed honey and honeycombs; if not, they buzzed and buzzed and told only lies.

Edie Freedman designed this cover and the entire UNIX bestiary that appears on the Nutshell Handbooks. The beasts themselves are adapted from 19th-century engravings from the Dover Pictorial Archive. The cover layout was produced with Quark XPress 3.3 using the ITC Garamond font. Whenever possible, our books use RepKover™, a durable and flexible lay-flat binding. If the page count exceeds RepKover's limit, perfect binding is used.

The inside layout was formatted in FrameMaker 5.0 by Mike Sierra using ITC Garamond Light and ITC Garamond Book fonts, and was designed by Nancy Priest and Edie Freedman. The figures were created in Macromedia Freehand 5.5 by Chris Reilley. This colophon was written by Michael Kalantarian and Lenny Muellner.

More Titles from O'Reilly

Database

Oracle Performance Tuning, 2nd Edition

By Peter Corrigan & Mark Gurry
2nd Edition November 1996
964 pages, plus diskette ISBN 1-56592-237-9

The Oracle relational database management system is the most popular database system in use today. This book shows you the many things you can do to increase the performance of your existing Oracle system, whether you are running Oracle6, 7, or 8. You may find that this book can save you the cost of a new machine; at the very least, it will save you a lot of headaches.

"There's no substitute for in-depth know-how when it comes to tuning an Oracle database, and that's what you get in Oracle Performance Tuning. This book is required reading for every Oracle DBA..."—Ken Morse, Senior Product Manager, System Management Products, Oracle New England Development Center.

Mastering Oracle Power Objects

By Rick Greenwald & Robert Hoskin
1st Edition March 1997
508 pages, plus diskette ISBN 1-56592-239-5

Oracle's new Power Objects is a cross-platform development tool that greatly simplifies the development of client-server database applications. With Power Objects, you can develop applications for Windows, Windows 95, Windows NT, and the Macintosh in a remarkably short amount of time. For example, you can build a master-detail application that can add, update, and select records via a user interface—all in 30 seconds, with no coding!

Oracle's new Power Objects product is a cross-platform development tool that greatly simplifies the development of client/server database applications. With Oracle Power Objects (OPO) you can develop applications for Windows, Windows95, Windows NT, and the Macintosh in a remarkably short amount of time.

This is the first book that covers OPO Version 2. It's an in-depth work, aimed at developers, that provides detailed information on getting the most from the product. It looks thoroughly at the most advanced features of Power Objects, including lists, reports (using both the native report writer and the Crystal Reports product), built-in methods, moving data, and implementing drag-and-drop. It also discusses object-oriented principles, global functions and messaging, OCSx, debugging, and cross-platform issues. It even covers the use of PL/SQL with OPO and ways of integrating it with the World Wide Web.

Oracle PL/SQL Programming

By Steven Feuerstein, 1st Edition Sept. 1995
916 pages, plus diskette ISBN 1-56592-142-9

PL/SQL is a procedural language that is being used more and more with Oracle, particularly in client-server applications. This book fills a huge gap in the Oracle market by providing developers with a single, comprehensive guide to building applications with PL/SQL—and building them the right way. It's packed with strategies, code architectures, tips, techniques, and fully realized code. Includes a disk containing many examples of PL/SQL programs.

Advanced Oracle PL/SQL Programming with Packages

By Steven Feuerstein, 1st Edition Oct.1996
690 pages, plus diskette ISBN 1-56592-238-7

This book expands on the techniques provided in *Oracle PL/SQL Programming*, taking you deep into the world of PL/SQL packages. Packages give you the ability to do object-oriented design and development in PL/SQL right away—there's no need to wait for PL/SQL Release 3. With this book, you not only learn how to construct packages, you learn how to build them properly. The chapter on "Best Practices" could transform the way you write PL/SQL packages.

Oracle Design

By Dave Ensor & Ian Stevenson
1st Edition March 1997
546 pages, 1-56592-268-9

Oracle Design looks thoroughly at Oracle relational database design, an often-neglected area of Oracle, but one that has an enormous impact on the ultimate power and performance of a system. Even the most powerful hardware, the most sophisticated software tools, and the most highly tuned data and programs won't make your system run smoothly without an effective design strategy. Indeed, applications that have been designed poorly will never be able to perform well, regardless of the tuning and retrofitting performed later on. This book examines all aspects of database and code design including client/server, distributed database, parallel processing, and data warehouses. This book delves deeply into design issues and gives advice that will have a major impact on your database and system performance.

How to stay in touch with O'Reilly

1. Visit Our Award-Winning Web Site
http://www.oreilly.com/

★ "Top 100 Sites on the Web" —*PC Magazine*
★ "Top 5% Web sites" —*Point Communications*
★ "3-Star site" —*The McKinley Group*

Our web site contains a library of comprehensive product information (including book excerpts and tables of contents), downloadable software, background articles, interviews with technology leaders, links to relevant sites, book cover art, and more. File us in your Bookmarks or Hotlist!

2. Join Our Email Mailing Lists
New Product Releases
To receive automatic email with brief descriptions of all new O'Reilly products as they are released, send email to: **listproc@online.oreilly.com**
Put the following information in the first line of your message (*not* in the Subject field):
subscribe oreilly-news "Your Name" of "Your Organization" (for example: subscribe oreilly-news Kris Webber of Fine Enterprises)

O'Reilly Events
If you'd also like us to send information about trade show events, special promotions, and other O'Reilly events, send email to: **listproc@online.oreilly.com**
Put the following information in the first line of your message (*not* in the Subject field):
subscribe oreilly-events "Your Name" of "Your Organization"

3. Get Examples from Our Books via FTP
There are two ways to access an archive of example files from our books:

Regular FTP
- ftp to:
  ftp.oreilly.com
  (login: anonymous
  password: your email address)
- Point your web browser to:
  ftp://ftp.oreilly.com/

FTPMAIL
- Send an email message to:
  ftpmail@online.oreilly.com
  (Write "help" in the message body)

4. Visit Our Gopher Site
- Connect your gopher to:
  gopher.oreilly.com

- Point your web browser to:
  gopher://gopher.oreilly.com/

- Telnet to:
  gopher.oreilly.com
  login: gopher

5. Contact Us via Email
order@oreilly.com
To place a book or software order online. Good for North American and international customers.

subscriptions@oreilly.com
To place an order for any of our newsletters or periodicals.

books@oreilly.com
General questions about any of our books.

software@oreilly.com
For general questions and product information about our software. Check out O'Reilly Software Online at **http://software.oreilly.com/** for software and technical support information. Registered O'Reilly software users send your questions to: **website-support@oreilly.com**

cs@oreilly.com
For answers to problems regarding your order or our products.

booktech@oreilly.com
For book content technical questions or corrections.

proposals@oreilly.com
To submit new book or software proposals to our editors and product managers.

international@oreilly.com
For information about our international distributors or translation queries. For a list of our distributors outside of North America check out:
http://www.oreilly.com/www/order/country.html

O'Reilly & Associates, Inc.
101 Morris Street, Sebastopol, CA 95472 USA
TEL 707-829-0515 or 800-998-9938
     (6am to 5pm PST)
FAX 707-829-0104

Titles from O'Reilly

Please note that upcoming titles are displayed in italic.

WEB PROGRAMMING

Apache: The Definitive Guide
Building Your Own Web
  Conferences
Building Your Own Website
CGI Programming for the World
  Wide Web
Designing for the Web
HTML: The Definitive Guide,
  2nd Ed.
JavaScript: The Definitive Guide,
  2nd Ed.
Learning Perl
Programming Perl, 2nd Ed.
Mastering Regular Expressions
WebMaster in a Nutshell
Web Security & Commerce
Web Client Programming with
  Perl
World Wide Web Journal

USING THE INTERNET

Smileys
The Future Does Not Compute
The Whole Internet User's Guide
  & Catalog
The Whole Internet for Win 95
Using Email Effectively
Bandits on the Information
  Superhighway

JAVA SERIES

Exploring Java
Java AWT Reference
Java Fundamental Classes
  Reference
Java in a Nutshell
*Java Language Reference, 2nd
  Edition*
Java Network Programming
Java Threads
Java Virtual Machine

SOFTWARE

WebSite™ 1.1
WebSite Professional™
Building Your Own Web
  Conferences
WebBoard™
PolyForm™
Statisphere™

SONGLINE GUIDES

NetActivism   NetResearch
Net Law   NetSuccess
NetLearning   NetTravel
Net Lessons

SYSTEM ADMINISTRATION

Building Internet Firewalls
Computer Crime: A
  Crimefighter's Handbook
Computer Security Basics
DNS and BIND, 2nd Ed.
Essential System Administration,
  2nd Ed.
Getting Connected: The Internet
  at 56K and Up
Linux Network Administrator's
  Guide
Managing Internet Information
  Services
Managing NFS and NIS
Networking Personal Computers
  with TCP/IP
Practical UNIX & Internet
  Security, 2nd Ed.
PGP: Pretty Good Privacy
sendmail, 2nd Ed.
sendmail Desktop Reference
System Performance Tuning
TCP/IP Network Administration
termcap & terminfo
Using & Managing UUCP
Volume 8: X Window System
  Administrator's Guide
Web Security & Commerce

UNIX

Exploring Expect
Learning VBScript
Learning GNU Emacs, 2nd Ed.
Learning the bash Shell
Learning the Korn Shell
Learning the UNIX Operating
  System
Learning the vi Editor
Linux in a Nutshell
Making TeX Work
Linux Multimedia Guide
Running Linux, 2nd Ed.
SCO UNIX in a Nutshell
sed & awk, 2nd Edition
Tcl/Tk Tools
UNIX in a Nutshell: System V
  Edition
UNIX Power Tools
Using csh & tsch
When You Can't Find Your UNIX
  System Administrator
Writing GNU Emacs Extensions

WEB REVIEW STUDIO SERIES

Gif Animation Studio
Shockwave Studio

WINDOWS

Dictionary of PC Hardware and
  Data Communications Terms
Inside the Windows 95 Registry
Inside the Windows 95 File
  System
Windows Annoyances
*Windows NT File System
  Internals*
Windows NT in a Nutshell

PROGRAMMING

Advanced Oracle PL/SQL
  Programming
Applying RCS and SCCS
C++: The Core Language
Checking C Programs with lint
DCE Security Programming
Distributing Applications Across
  DCE & Windows NT
Encyclopedia of Graphics File
  Formats, 2nd Ed.
Guide to Writing DCE
  Applications
lex & yacc
Managing Projects with make
Mastering Oracle Power Objects
Oracle Design: The Definitive
  Guide
Oracle Performance Tuning, 2nd
  Ed.
Oracle PL/SQL Programming
Porting UNIX Software
POSIX Programmer's Guide
POSIX.4: Programming for the
  Real World
Power Programming with RPC
Practical C Programming
Practical C++ Programming
Programming Python
Programming with curses
Programming with GNU Software
Pthreads Programming
Software Portability with imake,
  2nd Ed.
Understanding DCE
Understanding Japanese
  Information Processing
UNIX Systems Programming for
  SVR4

BERKELEY 4.4 SOFTWARE DISTRIBUTION

4.4BSD System Manager's
  Manual
4.4BSD User's Reference Manual
4.4BSD User's Supplementary
  Documents
4.4BSD Programmer's Reference
  Manual
4.4BSD Programmer's
  Supplementary Documents
X Programming
Vol. 0: X Protocol Reference
  Manual
Vol. 1: Xlib Programming Manual
Vol. 2: Xlib Reference Manual
Vol. 3M: X Window System User's
  Guide, Motif Edition
Vol. 4M: X Toolkit Intrinsics
  Programming Manual, Motif
  Edition
Vol. 5: X Toolkit Intrinsics
  Reference Manual
Vol. 6A: Motif Programming
  Manual
Vol. 6B: Motif Reference Manual
Vol. 6C: Motif Tools
Vol. 8 : X Window System
  Administrator's Guide
Programmer's Supplement for
  Release 6
X User Tools
The X Window System in a
  Nutshell

CAREER & BUSINESS

Building a Successful Software
  Business
The Computer User's Survival
  Guide
Love Your Job!
Electronic Publishing on CD-
  ROM

TRAVEL

Travelers' Tales: Brazil
Travelers' Tales: Food
Travelers' Tales: France
Travelers' Tales: Gutsy Women
Travelers' Tales: India
Travelers' Tales: Mexico
Travelers' Tales: Paris
Travelers' Tales: San Francisco
Travelers' Tales: Spain
Travelers' Tales: Thailand
Travelers' Tales: A Woman's
  World

International Distributors

UK, Europe, Middle East and Northern Africa (except France, Germany, Switzerland, & Austria)

INQUIRIES
International Thomson Publishing Europe
Berkshire House
168-173 High Holborn
London WC1V 7AA, United Kingdom
Telephone: 44-171-497-1422
Fax: 44-171-497-1426
Email: itpint@itps.co.uk

ORDERS
International Thomson Publishing Services, Ltd.
Cheriton House, North Way
Andover, Hampshire SP10 5BE,
United Kingdom
Telephone: 44-264-342-832
  (UK orders)
Telephone: 44-264-342-806
  (outside UK)
Fax: 44-264-364418 (UK orders)
Fax: 44-264-342761 (outside UK)
UK & Eire orders: itpuk@itps.co.uk
International orders: itpint@itps.co.uk

France

Editions Eyrolles
61 bd Saint-Germain
75240 Paris Cedex 05
France
Fax: 33-01-44-41-11-44

FRENCH LANGUAGE BOOKS
All countries except Canada
Phone: 33-01-44-41-46-16
Email: geodif@eyrolles.com

ENGLISH LANGUAGE BOOKS
Phone: 33-01-44-41-11-87
Email: distribution@eyrolles.com

Australia

WoodsLane Pty. Ltd.
7/5 Vuko Place, Warriewood NSW 2102
P.O. Box 935, Mona Vale NSW 2103
Australia
Telephone: 61-2-9970-5111
Fax: 61-2-9970-5002
Email: info@woodslane.com.au

Germany, Switzerland, and Austria

INQUIRIES
O'Reilly Verlag
Balthasarstr. 81
D-50670 Köln
Germany
Telephone: 49-221-97-31-60-0
Fax: 49-221-97-31-60-8
Email: anfragen@oreilly.de

ORDERS
International Thomson Publishing
Königswinterer Straße 418
53227 Bonn, Germany
Telephone: 49-228-97024 0
Fax: 49-228-441342
Email: order@oreilly.de

Asia (except Japan & India)

INQUIRIES
International Thomson Publishing Asia
60 Albert Street #15-01
Albert Complex
Singapore 189969
Telephone: 65-336-6411
Fax: 65-336-7411

ORDERS
Telephone: 65-336-6411
Fax: 65-334-1617
thomson@signet.com.sg

New Zealand

WoodsLane New Zealand Ltd.
21 Cooks Street (P.O. Box 575)
Wanganui, New Zealand
Telephone: 64-6-347-6543
Fax: 64-6-345-4840
Email: info@woodslane.com.au

Japan

O'Reilly Japan, Inc.
Kiyoshige Building 2F
12-Banchi, Sanei-cho
Shinjuku-ku
Tokyo 160 Japan
Telephone: 81-3-3356-5227
Fax: 81-3-3356-5261
Email: kenji@oreilly.com

India

Computer Bookshop (India) PVT. LTD.
190 Dr. D.N. Road, Fort
Bombay 400 001
India
Telephone: 91-22-207-0989
Fax: 91-22-262-3551
Email: cbsbom@giasbm01.vsnl.net.in

The Americas

O'Reilly & Associates, Inc.
101 Morris Street
Sebastopol, CA 95472 U.S.A.
Telephone: 707-829-0515
Telephone: 800-998-9938 (U.S. & Canada)
Fax: 707-829-0104
Email: order@oreilly.com

Southern Africa

International Thomson Publishing
Southern Africa
Building 18, Constantia Park
138 Sixteenth Road
P.O. Box 2459
Halfway House, 1685 South Africa
Telephone: 27-11-805-4819
Fax: 27-11-805-3648

O'Reilly & Associates, Inc.
101 Morris Street
Sebastopol, CA 95472-9902
1-800-998-9938

Visit us online at:
http://www.ora.com/
orders@ora.com

O'REILLY WOULD LIKE TO HEAR FROM YOU

Which book did this card come from?

_____

Where did you buy this book?
- ❏ Bookstore
- ❏ Direct from O'Reilly
- ❏ Bundled with hardware/software
- ❏ Computer Store
- ❏ Class/seminar
- ❏ Other _____

What operating system do you use?
- ❏ UNIX
- ❏ Windows NT
- ❏ Macintosh
- ❏ PC(Windows/DOS)
- ❏ Other _____

What is your job description?
- ❏ System Administrator
- ❏ Network Administrator
- ❏ Web Developer
- ❏ Programmer
- ❏ Educator/Teacher
- ❏ Other _____

❏ Please send me O'Reilly's catalog, containing a complete listing of O'Reilly books and software.

Name _____ Company/Organization _____

Address _____

City _____ State _____ Zip/Postal Code _____ Country _____

Telephone _____ Internet or other email address (specify network)

Nineteenth century wood engraving
of a bear from the O'Reilly &
Associates Nutshell Handbook®
Using & Managing UUCP.

POST CARD

NO POSTAGE
NECESSARY IF
MAILED IN THE
UNITED STATES

BUSINESS REPLY MAIL
FIRST CLASS MAIL   PERMIT NO. 80   SEBASTOPOL, CA

Postage will be paid by addressee

O'Reilly & Associates, Inc.
101 Morris Street
Sebastopol, CA 95472-9902